D1519090

The Cambridge History of
Literary Criticism

VOLUME 7

Modernism and the New Criticism

This volume of *The Cambridge History of Literary Criticism* provides a thorough account of the critical tradition emerging with the modernist and avant-garde writers of the early twentieth century (Eliot, Pound, Stein, Yeats), continuing with the New Critics (Richards, Empson, Burke, Winters), and feeding into the influential work of Leavis, Trilling and others who helped form the modern institutions of literary culture. The core period covered is 1910–1960, but explicit connections are made with nineteenth-century traditions and there is discussion of the implications of modernism and the New Criticism for our own time, with its inherited formalism, anti-sentimentalism, and astringency of tone. The book provides a companion to the other twentieth-century volumes of *The Cambridge History of Literary Criticism*, and offers a systematic and stimulating coverage of the development of the key literary-critical movements, with chapters on groups and genres as well as on individual critics.

A. WALTON LITZ is Professor Emeritus of English at Princeton University. He is the author of numerous books on modernist literature, including *The Art of James Joyce* (1961) and *Introspective Voyager: The Poetic Achievement of Wallace Stevens* (1972), the editor of *Eliot in His Time* (1973), and the co-editor of *Ezra Pound's Poetry and Prose* (1991).

LOUIS MENAND is Professor of English at the Graduate Center of the City University of New York. He is the author of *Discovering Modernism: T. S. Eliot and His Context* (1987), co-editor of *America in Theory* (1988), and editor of both *The Future of Academic Freedom* (1996) and *Pragmatism: A Reader* (1997). Since 1994 he has been contributing editor of *The New York Review of Books*.

LAWRENCE RAINEY is Professor of English at the University of York. He is the author of *Ezra Pound and the Monument of Culture* (1991) and *Institutions of Modernism: Literary Elites and Public Culture* (1999), the editor of *A Poem Containing History: Textual Studies in Pound's Cantos* (1997), and co-editor of *Futurism: A Literary and Visual Repertory* (2000). Lawrence Rainey is founder and co-editor of the journal *Modernism/Modernity*, and writes reviews and essays for the *Times Literary Supplement* and *The London Review of Books*.

The Cambridge History of
Literary Criticism

GENERAL EDITORS
Professor H. B. Nisbet
University of Cambridge
Professor Claude Rawson
Yale University

The Cambridge History of Literary Criticism will provide a comprehensive historical account of Western literary criticism from classical antiquity to the present day, dealing with both literary theory and critical practice. The *History* is intended as an authoritative work of reference and exposition, but more than a mere chronicle of facts. While remaining broadly non-partisan it addresses, where appropriate, controversial issues of current critical debate without evasion or false pretences of neutrality. Each volume is a self-contained unit designed to be used independently as well as in conjunction with the others in the series. Substantial bibliographic material in each volume provides the foundation for further study of the subjects in question.

VOLUMES PUBLISHED
Volume 1: *Classical Criticism*, edited by George A. Kennedy
Volume 3: *The Renaissance*, edited by Glyn P. Norton
Volume 4: *The Eighteenth Century*, edited by H. B. Nisbet and Claude Rawson
Volume 5: *Romanticism*, edited by Marshall Brown
Volume 7: *Modernism and the New Criticism*, edited by A. Walton Litz, Louis Menand, and Lawrence Rainey
Volume 8: *From Formalism to Poststructuralism*, edited by Raman Selden

OTHER VOLUMES IN PREPARATION
Volume 2: *The Middle Ages*, edited by Alastair Minnis
Volume 6: *The Nineteenth Century*
Volume 9: *Twentieth-Century Historical, Philosophical, and Psychological Approaches*, edited by Christa Knellwolf and Christopher Norris

The Cambridge History of
Literary Criticism

VOLUME 7
Modernism and the New Criticism

Edited by

A. WALTON LITZ, LOUIS MENAND,
AND
LAWRENCE RAINEY

CAMBRIDGE
UNIVERSITY PRESS

PUBLISHED BY THE PRESS SYNDICATE OF THE UNIVERSITY OF CAMBRIDGE
The Pitt Building, Trumpington Street, Cambridge, United Kingdom

CAMBRIDGE UNIVERSITY PRESS
The Edinburgh Building, Cambridge CB2 2RU, UK   http://www.cup.cam.ac.uk
40 West 20th Street, New York NY 10011-4211, USA   http://www.cup.org
10 Stamford Road, Oakleigh, Melbourne 3166, Australia

© Cambridge University Press 2000

First published 2000

Printed in the United Kingdom at the University Press, Cambridge

Typeset in 10/12pt Sabon [VN]

A catalogue record for this book is available from the British Library

ISBN 0 521 30012 6 hardback

Contents

Notes on contributors   *page*   vii

Introduction   1
LOUIS MENAND AND LAWRENCE RAINEY

THE MODERNISTS

1   T. S. Eliot   17
    LOUIS MENAND

2   Ezra Pound   57
    A. WALTON LITZ AND LAWRENCE RAINEY

3   Gertrude Stein   93
    STEVEN MEYER

4   Virginia Woolf   122
    MARIA DiBATTISTA

5   Wyndham Lewis   138
    VINCENT SHERRY

6   W. B. Yeats   151
    LUCY McDIARMID

7   The Harlem Renaissance   167
    MICHAEL NORTH

THE NEW CRITICS

8   I. A. Richards   181
    PAUL H. FRY

9   The Southern New Critics   200
    MARK JANCOVICH

10 William Empson   219
    MICHAEL WOOD

11 R. P. Blackmur   235
    MICHAEL WOOD

12 Kenneth Burke   248
    EUGENE GOODHEART

13 Yvor Winters   260
    DONALD DAVIE

    THE CRITIC AND THE INSTITUTIONS OF CULTURE

14 Criticism and the academy   269
    WALLACE MARTIN

15 The critic and society, 1900–1950   322
    MORRIS DICKSTEIN

16 The British 'man of letters' and the rise of the professional   377
    JOSEPHINE M. GUY AND IAN SMALL

17 F. R. Leavis   389
    MICHAEL BELL

18 Lionel Trilling   423
    HARVEY TERES

19 Poet-critics   439
    LAWRENCE LIPKING

20 Criticism of fiction   468
    MICHAEL LEVENSON

    Bibliography   499
    Index   547

Notes on contributors

Maria DiBattista is Professor of English at Princeton University. Her publications include *First Love: The Affections of Modern Fiction* (1991); *Virginia Woolf's Major Novels: The Fables of Anon* (1980); and *Fast-Talking Dames* (2000). She has edited (with Lucy McDiarmid) *High and Low Moderns: Literature and Culture, 1889–1939* (1996).

Michael Bell is Professor of English at the University of Warwick. His publications include *Literature, Modernity and Myth: Belief and Responsibility in the Twentieth Century* (1997); *Gabriel Garcia Márquez: Solitude and Solidarity* (1993); *D. H. Lawrence: Language and Being* (1991); *F. R. Leavis* (1988); *The Sentiment of Reality: Truth of Feeling in the European Novel* (1983); and *Primitivism* (1972).

The late Donald Davie (1922–95) was Andrew W. Mellon Professor of Humanities at Vanderbilt University. He published numerous books of poetry and criticism. His classic critical studies include *Under Briggflatts: A History of Poetry in Great Britain, 1960–1968* (1989); *Czeslaw Milosz and the Insufficiency of Lyric* (1986); *Ezra Pound* (1976); *Ezra Pound: Poet as Sculptor* and *The Poet in the Imaginary Museum: Essays of Two Decades* (1977); *Thomas Hardy and British Poetry* (1972); *Articulate Energy: An Enquiry into the Syntax of English Poetry* (1958); and *Purity of Diction in English Verse* (1953).

Morris Dickstein is Distinguished Professor of English at Queens College and at the Graduate Center of the City University of New York, where he directs the Center for the Humanities. His books include *Gates of Eden: American Culture in the Sixties* (1977, 1997), and *Double Agent: The Critic and Society* (1992). His study of postwar American fiction appears in volume seven of *The Cambridge History of American Literature* (1999).

Paul H. Fry is the William Lampson Professor of English at Yale University. His publications include 'Classical Standards in the Romantic Period', in *The Cambridge History of Literary Criticism Volume 5* (2000); *A Defense of Poetry: Reflections on Occasional Writing* (1995); *William*

Empson: Prophet Against Sacrifice (1991); *The Reach of Criticism: Method and Perception in Literary Theory* (1983); and *The Poet's Calling in the English Ode* (1980). He has published widely on Romanticism and the Eighteenth Century, including essays on Wordsworth, the Sublime, Rousseau, and Dryden.

Eugene Goodheart is Edytha Macy Gross Professor of the Humanities at Brandeis University. His publications include *Does Literary Studies Have a Future?* (1999); *The Reign of Ideology* (1996); *Desire and its Discontents* (1991); *Pieces of Resistance* (1987); *The Skeptic Disposition in Contemporary Criticism* (1984); *Culture and the Radical Conscience* (1973); *The Failure of Criticism* (1978); *The Cult of the Ego* (1968); and *The Utopian Vision of D. H. Lawrence* (1963).

Josephine M. Guy is Senior Lecturer in the School of English Studies at the University of Nottingham. She has edited *The Victorian Age: An Anthology of Sources and Documents* (1998), and is the author of *The Victorian Social-Problem Novel: the Market, the Individual, and Communal Life* (1996); (with Ian Small) *Politics and Value in English Studies* (1993); and *The British Avant-Garde* (1991). She has also published essays on Oscar Wilde and Victorian cultural theory.

Mark Jancovich is Director and Senior Lecturer of the Institute of Film Studies at the University of Nottingham. He has written *Rational Fears: American Horror in the 1950s* (1996); *Approaches to Popular Film* (1995); *American Horror From 1951 to the Present* (1994); and *The Cultural Politics of the New Criticism* (1993). He has also contributed reviews and essays to *The Southern Literary Journal*, *Modern Fiction Studies*, *Journal of American Studies*, *The Modern Language Review*, and *American Literature*.

Lawrence Lipking is Professor of English at Northwestern University. He has written *Samuel Johnson: the Life of an Author* (1998); *Abandoned Women and Poetic Tradition* (1988); and *The Life of the Poet: Beginning and Ending Poetic Careers* (1981). He has also edited *High Romantic Argument: Essays for M. H. Abrams: Essays* (1981), and co-edited (with A. Walton Litz) the anthology *Modern Literary Criticism, 1900–1970* (1972).

Michael Levenson is Professor of English at the University of Virginia. He has co-authored *Spectacles of Intimacy* (2000) and edited *The Cambridge Companion to Modernism* (1988). He has written *Modernism and the Fate of Individuality: Character and Novelistic Form from Conrad to Woolf* (1991), and *A Genealogy of Modernism: A Study of English*

Literary Doctrine, 1908–1922 (1984), and numerous essays on James Joyce, T. S. Eliot, Joseph Conrad, Wyndham Lewis, and E. M. Forster.

A. Walton Litz is Professor Emeritus of English at Princeton University. He is the author of numerous books on modernist literature, including *The Art of James Joyce* (1961) and *Introspective Voyager: The Poetic Achievement of Wallace Stevens* (1972), the editor of *Eliot in His Time* (1973), and the co-editor of *Ezra Pound's Poetry and Prose* (1991).

Wallace Martin is Professor of English at the University of Toledo. He has written *Recent Theories of Narrative* (1986) and *The 'New Age' Under Orage: Chapters in English Cultural History* (1967). He has also edited *Orage as Critic* (1974); *The Yale Critics: Deconstruction in America* (with Jonathan Arac and Wlad Godzich, 1983): and *A Catalogue of the Imagist Poets* (1966, 1981).

Lucy McDiarmid is President of the American Conference for Irish Studies and Professor of English at Villanova University. She is the author of *Auden's Apologies For Poetry* (1990) and *Saving Civilization: Yeats, Eliot, and Auden Between the Wars* (1984). She edited (with Maria DiBattista) *High and Low Moderns: Literature and Culture, 1889–1939* (1996) and *Lady Gregory: Selected Writings* (1995). She received a Guggenheim Fellowship for her book *The Irish Art of Controversy* (2000).

Louis Menand is Professor of English at the Graduate Center of the City University of New York. He is the author of *Discovering Modernism: T. S. Eliot and His Context* (1987); co-editor of *America in Theory* (1988); and editor of both *The Future of Academic Freedom* (1996) and *Pragmatism: A Reader* (1997). Since 1994 he has been contributing editor of *The New York Review of Books*.

Steven Meyer is Associate Professor of English and Director of The Writing Program at Washington University in St. Louis. His publications include *Irresistible Dictation: Gertrude Stein and the Correlations of Writing and Science* and *Adventures with an Audience: The Complete Lectures of Gertrude Stein* (2000), as well as editions of Stein's *The Making of Americans* (1997) and *A Novel of Thank You* (1994).

Michael North is Professor of English at the University of California, Los Angeles. His publications include *The Dialect of Modernism: Race, Language, and Twentieth-Century Literature* (1994); *The Political Aesthetic of Yeats, Eliot and Pound* (1991); *The Final Sculpture: Public Monuments and Modern Poets* (1985); and *Henry Green and the Writing of his Generation* (1984).

Lawrence Rainey is Professor of English at the University of York. He is the author of *Ezra Pound and the Monument of Culture* (1991) and *Institutions of Modernism: Literary Elites and Public Culture* (1999); the editor of *A Poem Containing History: Textual Studies in Pound's Cantos* (1997); and co-editor of *Futurism: A Literary and Visual Repertory* (2000). Lawrence Rainey is founder and co-editor of the journal *Modernism/Modernity*, and writes reviews and essays for the *Times Literary Supplement* and *The London Review of Books*.

Vincent Sherry is Professor of English at Villanova University. He has written *James Joyce Ulysses* (1995); *Ezra Pound, Wyndham Lewis, and Radical Modernism* (1993); and *The Uncommon Tongue: The Poetry and Criticism of Geoffrey Hill* (1987). He is currently completing a book-length study of Anglo-American modernism and the Great War.

Ian Small is Senior Lecturer in English Literature at the University of Birmingham. He has written *Oscar Wilde Revalued: an Essay on New Materials and Methods of Research* (1993) and *Conditions For Criticism: Authority, Knowledge, and Literature in the Late Nineteenth Century* (1991). He has also edited *The Theory and Practice of Text-Editing* (1991) and *Studies in Anglo-French Cultural Relations: Imaging France* (1988).

Harvey Teres is Professor of English at Syracuse University. He has written *Renewing the Left: Politics, Imagination, and the New York Intellectuals* (1996) and numerous essays, including 'Remaking Marxist Criticism: Partisan Review's Eliotic Leftism', in *High and Low Moderns: Literature and Culture 1889–1939* (1996). He has written extensively on Marxist criticism and Wallace Stevens, contributing reviews and essays to *Modern Philology*, *American Literature*, and *The Wallace Stevens Journal*.

Michael Wood is Charles Barnwell Straut Class of 1923 Professor of English at Princeton University. He has written many books, most recently *Children of Silence: on Contemporary Fiction* (1998); *The Magician's Doubts: Nabokov and the Risks of Fiction* (1995); *Gabriel Garcia Márquez: One Hundred Years of Solitude* (1990); and *Stendhal* (1971). He has also written numerous essays and reviews for *The London Review of Books* and *The New York Review of Books*.

Introduction

Louis Menand and Lawrence Rainey

For readers over the age of fifty, modernism and the New Criticism are not just terms that refer to a remote and distant past, not just names that stretch across a map of venerable but vanished empires in the history of literary criticism. They evoke places where we have conversed with colleagues, or hours spent with books that still rest upon the shelves, only slightly discoloured with age. New Criticism has perhaps slipped more irretrievably into the past of professional literary studies than modernism, which continues to play a pivotal role in contemporary cultural debate as the governing term in discussions about the notion of 'the postmodern'. But for a history of literary criticism that is devoted to modernism and the New Criticism, the personal associations of both terms can easily undermine a dispassionate account. The subject extends into the present and lacks the corrective of a tranquil and healing hindsight. Moreover, situated at that troublesome crossroad where professional literary studies (New Criticism) meet with the broader cultural and social transformations of the twentieth century (modernism), it is a subject that engages some of our most passionate views about art and society, intellectuals and public culture.

The ongoing contemporaneity of these subjects inevitably affects the kinds of narration that one might offer, for several reasons. One has to do with the logic of historical insight, its foundations in differing temporal indices. Descriptions of the past are grounded in temporal perspectives derived from the future, or as Jürgen Habermas has expressed it: 'The historian does not observe from the perspective of the actor but describes events and actions out of the experimental horizon of a history that goes beyond the actor's horizons of expectations.'[1] Yet insofar as we ourselves are still actors whose horizons of expectations include much that was encompassed in the New Criticism and modernism, it is not immediately self-evident which interpretive framework, which new set of horizons, might best furnish a meaningful historical account of those subjects.

It is true that the New Criticism can be integrated into an essentially

[1] Jürgen Habermas, 'A Review of Gadamer's *Truth and Method*', in Fred R. Dallmayr and Thomas A. McCarthy, eds., *Understanding and Social Inquiry* (Notre Dame, 1977), p. 339.

whiggish and necessarily schematic account of the development of 'theory', an account that often underlies our everyday sense of professional literary studies' development during the last decades. In this view the New Criticism constitutes an initial stage which, along with its reshaping of 'practical' criticism and pedagogical practice, eliminates authorial intention and context as reference points for discussions about the meaning of literary works; that stage is followed by structuralism, with promise of more positive insights into the logic by which textual artifacts function; and structuralism, in turn, is followed by deconstruction, in which the radical instabilities of language, formally acknowledged but effectively suppressed in the structuralist account, are brought to the fore and elevated into a paradigm for all textual operations. Finally, as deconstruction is assimilated to various currents of feminist, psychoanalytic, and Marxist criticism, the New Historicism absorbs and supersedes all its predecessors, so providing a comprehensive framework in which to situate a narrative of New Criticism's rise and fall. Yet such an account would slight the sheer velocity that has marked these developments and the unforeseen consequences which have followed. (One can measure the speed of change by Jonathan Culler's books: his classic presentation of *Structuralist Poetics* appeared in 1975; his subsequent book, *On Deconstruction*, was published in 1982; yet it was in the same year that Stephen Greenblatt was coining the term New Historicism.)[2] The increasing rapidity with which one critical mode has yielded to another has tended to delegitimise the developmental narrative of ideas as an adequate way of accounting for critical change; unfolding intellectual debate is replaced by a chronicle that merely registers a succession of discrete and ultimately incommensurable events. 'The history of criticism', both as an intellectual concept and as a genre, gives way to the interim report that increasingly reads like a chronicle of *haute couture*, in which a catalogue of vertiginous changes reveals only the benumbing uniformity of factitious novelty. We are no longer confident that changes in criticism or literary theory exhibit the kind of developmental coherence once postulated in the notion of a history of literary criticism; such a purely internalist account of literary theory, while giving due attention to the philosophical background that has informed the evolution of theoretical protocols, risks losing sight of why such protocols have been deemed necessary at all.

To recognise that accounts of twentieth-century literary criticism must also consider the social and institutional pressures that have affected the formation of professional literary studies is not, however, to find a definitive solution to the difficulties that face a contemporary 'history of literary criticism'. Instead, it merely transposes the dilemma of contemporaneity

[2] The coining of the term is detailed by H. Aram Veeser in the 'Introduction' to his anthology *The New Historicism* (New York, 1989), p. xiii.

from one field to another, from the cooler heights of intellectual history to the more concrete but no less contested terrain of social history. Professors of literature today, after all, are part of the same institution in which the New Critics once worked, and, despite the many changes that have recently affected universities, a continuum of experience seems to bind us to our predecessors. But younger scholars especially are aware that a profound change has already begun to alter the terms of discussion: the incessant expansion of higher education that characterised the entire arc of the twentieth century, and particularly the period following World War II, is possibly at an end. To the extent that professional literary studies have adopted theoretical approaches that are increasingly hermetic or animated by political ambitions at odds with the sympathies of even the liberal and well-educated public, they risk a crisis of significant proportions, an unprecedented erosion of public support. That prospective crisis casts a fresh though colder light over the formative moments of modern literary criticism, the early development of the New Criticism. The rise of professional literary studies can no longer be traced solely in the coherent evolution of a theoretical corpus progressively purified of its connections with social reality and increasingly committed to linguisticality.

Although it is a commonplace to assimilate modernism and the New Criticism to one another, sometimes treating the latter as if it were merely a more systematic, more philosophical, or more academic articulation of formalist undercurrents within modernism, much is lost in assigning to either term the kind of monolithic coherence such a claim presumes. This is especially true for modernism, a term which has been the subject of intense discussion during the last two decades as the spread of debate about 'postmodernism' has put increasing pressure on the prior term to which it remains tethered, whether chronologically or conceptually. Much of the debate has centred less on modernism than on its relations with the avant-garde and with postmodernism, a function in part of the influence of Peter Bürger's widely discussed *Theory of the Avant-Garde*. For Bürger, the avant-garde project 'can be defined as an attack on the status of art in bourgeois society', or, as he further clarifies it, an assault aginst 'art as an institution that is unassociated with the life praxis of men'.[3] This attack takes place not at the level of contents or thematics in any particular work, but rather in how avant-garde works as a whole function, how they are produced, and how they are received. Insofar as they reintegrate art and life practices, insofar as they negate 'the category of individual creation' by, for example, using arbitrarily chosen mass products (e.g., the urinal of Marcel Duchamp's *Fountain* (1917)), and

---

[3] Peter Bürger, *The Institution of the Avant-Garde* (1974), tr. Michael Shaw (Minneapolis, 1984), p. 49.

insofar as they require or suggest participatory responses on the part of audiences, avant-garde art works reject the basic constituents of autonomous and bourgeois art.

Though Bürger's thesis explicitly concerns the historical avant-garde, it has furnished the impetus for subsequent arguments that postulate a rigorous distinction between the avant-garde and modernism, most notably those of Andreas Huyssen. According to Huyssen, '[i]n modernism art and literature retained their traditional 19th-century autonomy from every day life; ... the traditional way in which art and literature were produced, disseminated, and received, is never challenged by modernism but maintained intact'. In sharp contrast, '[t]he avant-garde ... attempted to subvert art's autonomy, its artificial separation from life, and its institutionalization as "high art"'.[4] For Huyssen, though, the force of this distinction derives less from questions about the notion of aesthetic autonomy than from the pressing reality of mass culture. 'Mass culture has always been the hidden subtext of the modernist project.'[5] Within that project, Huyssen argues, popular culture is gendered as female, construed as a threat of encroaching formlessness, and held at bay by reaffirming and refortifying the boundaries between art and inauthentic mass culture. Huyssen does not contend that avant-gardists were less sexist than their modernist contemporaries, but that the avant-garde's 'urge to validate other, formerly neglected or ostracized forms of cultural expression created an aesthetic climate in which the political aesthetic of feminism could thrive'.[6] Since feminism is a crucial component of recent developments in postmodernism, and since postmodernism is plainly an effort 'to negotiate forms of high art with certain forms and genres of mass culture and the culture of everyday life', it follows that postmodernism is the legitimate heir of the avant-garde.[7] The avant-garde and postmodernism share a genuine historical and ideological continuity, which turns upon the question of popular culture and firmly distinguishes them from a modernism that consequently seems little more than a reactionary or elitist fear of popular culture.

Bürger's and Huyssen's arguments offer welcome recontextualisations of modernism and the avant-garde. Bürger's thesis, for example, is useful in reestablishing a continuity of concerns between fin-de-siècle aestheticism and the historical avant-garde in debates about 'art and life'; Huyssen calls attention to a thematics that was plainly of concern to any number of modernist writers. Yet in tying his arguments about the 'institution of art' to a purely conceptual category, Bürger may lose much in the way of historical specificity, ignoring, for example, the development of a particular set of institutions which were essential to modernist production

---

[4] Andreas Huyssen, *After the Great Divide: Modernism, Mass Culture, Postmodernism* (Bloomington, 1986), p. 163.   [5] *Ibid.*, p. 47.   [6] *Ibid.*, p. 61.   [7] *Ibid.*, p. 59.

– the little reviews, the deluxe editions, a corpus of patron-collectors and investors, and specific groups of smaller publishers such as Alfred Knopf, Horace Liveright, and Ben Huebsch (to use the United States as an example). Similar, Huyssen's effort to distinguish modernism from the avant-garde achieves its schematic clarity at a cost to historical complexity. When he cautions that 'there are areas of overlap' between the avant-garde and modernist traditions, instancing first 'vorticism and Ezra Pound' and then 'radical language experimentation and James Joyce', scholars of Anglo-American literary modernism are likely to feel uneasy, having found that two of its three major figures (assuming that Eliot is the third) are now exceptions to the rule. Huyssen is doubtless correct to urge that 'it makes little sense to lump Thomas Mann together with Dada', but his dilemma might be more easily solved by declaring that Mann, whose lifelong ambition was to forge a style that would replicate the prose of the later Goethe, may not be a modernist at all, rather than by erecting a brittle distinction that misses as much as it includes.

Still, the most questionable aspect of the arguments of Bürger and Huyssen is their appeal to an oppositional paradigm, the presupposition that modernist or avant-garde art can be genuinely such only if it stands in an inimical relation to the ensemble of values found at large in the dominant culture, the culture of capitalism and the bourgeoisie. The paradigm's effects are especially apparent in their selection of subjects. Thus, Bürger's account of the historical avant-garde treats Dada and Surrealism but neglects the preceding development of Futurism – even though Marinetti had explicitly argued for the necessity of destroying the concept of art as early as 1912.[8] Dada and Surrealism, needless to say, nurtured political commitments more in tune with those of the historical left. Likewise, although the response to popular culture is Huyssen's touchstone for distinguishing modernism from the avant-garde, he offers no discussion of Marinetti's famous attempt to transform the music hall into a resource for the production of a new anti-art, nor does he treat the ambivalent outcome of the project, discernible already in 1914, when Marinetti performed at what was then the largest music hall in the world, only to be roundly jeered.[9]

In conformity with the opposition paradigm that informs the work of Bürger and Huyssen is a narrative that increasingly structures current accounts of modernism, reappearing especially in accounts of its relation to postmodernism. One sees its spell at work when Huyssen discusses

[8] See, for example, 'The Technical Manifesto of Futurism', originally published in May 1912, in R. W. Flint, ed., *Let's Murder the Moonshine: Selected Writings of F. T. Marinetti* (1971; rpt. Los Angeles, 1993), pp. 92–7.
[9] See Lawrence Rainey, 'The Creation of the Avant-Garde: F. T. Marinetti and Ezra Pound', *Modernism/Modernity*, 1 (September 1994), pp. 195–219.

modernism's decline in prestige and remarks that 'the administered culture of late capitalism' has 'finally succeeded in imposing the phony spell of commodity fetishism even on that art which more than any other had challenged the values and traditions of bourgeois culture'.[10] In a similar vein, it is urged that the twentieth century has witnessed two distinct revolutions in the field of culture, the first, a 'real' revolution, in which artistic activity was urgently politicised and innovation swept through all the arts, the second an equally important if less noted revolution in which universities and other institutions appropriated modernism's formal repertory, canonised its works and artists, and sapped its political energies.[11] Such accounts rehearse a fall narrative, in which an Edenic state of subversive energy imperceptibly yields to appropriation, assimilation, and containment by 'late capitalism' or its cultural instrument, academic criticism. In doing so, they merely re-articulate a variant of the concept of aesthetic autonomy which the modernists or avant-gardists are held to have destroyed, reinscribing the divorce between art and social reality that was already presupposed in the notion of aesthetic disinterestedness – but reinscribing it in the moralistic assumption that aesthetic virtue and commerce are antithetical. That assumption, in turn, rests upon a conception of the arts that has been distilled of material complexity and bears no relation to the realities of cultural production within complex, modern societies. The case of 'The Waste Land' should warn us against oversimplifications of this sort. During the course of discussions in 1922 about where to publish the poem, Eliot gave equal consideration to expressions of interest from three different journals: *The Little Review* (often deemed 'avant-garde', circulation 2,500), *The Dial* (usually considered 'modernist', circulation 9,000), and *Vanity Fair* (generally considered a 'commercial' publication, circulation 92,000). During the same period, all three journals were not only competing for 'The Waste Land', but were publishing new works by the same artists, among them Brancusi, Wyndham Lewis, and Ossip Zadkine.[12] Such competition suggests that there is little ground for sustaining a programmatic distinction between the avant-garde and modernism. The avant-garde was not located outside of or against the institution of modernism, but was firmly situated within it – just as the institution of modernism was not poised wholly outside or against the changing economy of the new consumerist and professionalist society which surrounded it, but was engaged in a more complex and ambiguous dialogue with it.

---

[10] Huyssen, *After the Great Divide*, p. 160.

[11] See, for example, Charles Newman, *The Post-Modern Aura* (Evanston, Ill., 1985), pp. 27–35.

[12] Lawrence Rainey, 'The Price of Modernism: Publishing *The Waste Land*', in Ronald Bush, ed., *T. S. Eliot: The Modernist in History* (Cambridge, 1990), pp. 90–133.

In this volume, therefore, modernism and the avant-garde are not treated as antithetical projects, but as interchangeable terms for overlapping institutions located firmly within the changing society of which they form a part. Without minimising modernism's radical reformulation of the formal repertory of the arts, and while acknowledging that many modernist writers repeatedly focused on common themes – the interaction of 'art' and 'life', the spread of mass culture, or issues such as gender, nationality, primitivism, technology, or the boundaries of subjectivity – we have tended to view modernism less in strictly formal or ideological terms and more as a social reality which was in continuous transformation, a complex reality which is effectively erased by ascribing to it a monolithic nature or essence that works to conceal, rather than analyse, the contradictions that stood at the heart of the modernist project. Modernism is not a subject which can be adequately treated by listing its loyalties, rehearsing its dogmas, or cataloging its formal devices. It is the outcome of a complex situation from which it can scarcely be disengaged; it is above all an overlapping set of institutions, a confirmation of agents and practices that coalesced in the production, marketing, and publicisation of an idiom, an identifiable language that was both shared and shareable, a serviceable tongue within the family of twentieth-century languages.

The key figure in the conventional assimilation of modernism and the New Criticism is T. S. Eliot, and the viability of this assimilation is a function of the complex of roles associated with him: the parts that Eliot himself wished to assume, the roles his contemporaries assigned him, and the roles in which he has been cast by subsequent critics. All these were, in reality, extremely fluid, and changed a great deal over the course of several decades. There was the inventive body of criticism that Eliot wrote between 1917 and 1924; the ways in which it was worked up into a corpus of acceptable interpretive techniques by I. A. Richards, among others, in the years immediately following; the brilliant exercise of those techniques by Richards's student William Empson; the renegade variant of Cambridge English established by F. R. Leavis and the group surrounding *Scrutiny* in the 1930s and 1940s; the way these various influences fed into the work of the American New Critics, such as Cleanth Brooks, John Crowe Ransom, Allen Tate, and Robert Penn Warren, a group with its own distinctive intellectual roots in the American South; and the gradual establishment of the New Criticism as a powerful critical orthodoxy within American universities, a development epitomised by Brooks's move from Louisiana State University to Yale in 1947. The rest, as they say, is history: the dominance and the increasingly ossified formalism of the Yale school as represented by W. K. Wimsatt (*The Verbal Icon* was published in 1954), and the assimilation of New Criticism to Continental structuralism, Saussurean linguistics, and phenomenology in the work of René Wellek, whose multi-volume *History of Modern Criticism* began appearing in 1955. The figure of Eliot as tutelary spirit hovered over the work of nearly all these figures, invoked to support any and (nearly) every viewpoint.

Yet in many ways the cultural prominence Eliot acquired, his peculiar role as a totemic figure whose prestige could be invoked to justify any number of views, may have skewed our understanding of modernism and its relations to the New Criticism. As a poet, Eliot represented an extremely limited segment of the spectrum of literary practices encompassed by modernism: his style adhered more closely to the aesthetics of symbolism than that of almost any other modernist, including Pound, Joyce, Stein, Lewis, and Moore. And his neoclassicism stemmed from a commitment to tradition and traditionalism far deeper, and far more radical, than anything adopted by most of his contemporaries. Pound's reckless embrace of fascism, Joyce's heady descent into the night-world of language, Stein's insistent pursuit of pure sound – these were alien to Eliot's temperament. They also, for the most part, stood outside the circle of his admirers' interests. One can read the entire corpus of major works by the principal New Critics and find not a single extended discussion of James Joyce. When Joyce became an object of interest for Anglo-American scholars, it was through the advocacy of critics firmly outside or opposed to the New Criticism – such as Harry Levin and Hugh Kenner, to cite only the most prominent examples. As for Gertrude Stein or Wyndham Lewis, a reading of the principal New Critics might leave one in doubt that they had ever lived.

But the New Criticism was, in America, the movement that successfully introduced literary criticism – the interpretation and evaluation of literary texts – into the university; and for all the limitations of its scope and ultimate influence as a doctrine of poetry, it established a pattern of institutional adjustment and legitimation which has been imitated by every critical movement since. This means that a history of modernism and the New Criticism is inevitably a history of the rise of the modern university as well.

The comparative history of the university reveals how intimately its morphology is bound up with the different histories of different nation-states. Generalisations useful for understanding German academic practice are not transferable to British universities or French universities. The American university is instructive in our context, though, because its roots are shallower, and its transformation, from the smaller liberal arts college to the large research institution, is consequently chronologically and philosophically stark. Understanding how literary criticism adapted itself to the new scholarly system in America – or the new scholarly system adapted itself to an activity such as criticism – is a way of understanding many of the changes internal to the history of literary criticism that are traced in the separate chapters in this volume.

The American research university was a creation of the late nineteenth century. It accompanied, and was itself a product of, the social phenomenon of the professionalisation of occupation. The modern professions – medicine, engineering, architecture, the law, and many others – first took the form they have today in the second half of the nineteenth century, when 'qualifying associations' and other accrediting agencies came into being to help distinguish certified practitioners from amateurs, dilettantes, and other unqualified types. The rise of professionalism was a response to the increasing complexity of advanced capitalist economies and the increasing volume of available knowledge in an age of science – developments that created a need for a range of workers expert in a range of specialised fields. The university constituted a response to this development in two senses. First, it operated as one kind of certifying institution, by training and conferring degrees upon future members of the professions. And secondly, it professionalised knowledge, organising its specialists by discipline – that is, by academic department – and assuming a virtual monopoly over the business of producing scholars.[13]

A field of knowledge in this new university system faced two requirements: it must constitute an independent area of study, with a clearly delineated subject matter and methodology; and it must be able to present itself as a sufficiently 'hard' discipline – that is, as an area of study in which measurable advances, on the model of the natural sciences, could be made, since the research university is specifically designed to facilitate and reward the production of new knowledge. Literary criticism, defined as the evaluation and appreciation of works of literature, has a hard time qualifying as an academic discipline under these criteria, and the campaign in the American university to establish criticism as a legitimate academic activity (as distinct from literary history, textual studies, and other clearly scholarly pursuits) was a long one, not fully successful until the 1940s.[14] So that a university-based person with a critical interest in literature during the first half of this century confronted a challenge that has no precedent in the history of talk about writing: he or she needed to conceive of the criticism of literature as an autonomous discipline with

---

[13] See Burton J. Bledstein, *The Culture of Professionalism: The Middle Class and the Development of Higher Education in America:* (New York, 1976), Bruce A. Kimball, *The 'True Professional Ideal' in America: A History* (Cambridge, Mass., 1992), Magali Sarfatti Larson, *The Rise of Professionalism: A Sociological Analysis* (Berkeley, 1977), and Laurence Veysey, *The Emergence of the American University* (Chicago, 1965).

[14] The story is told by Wallace Martin, in this volume; see also Gerald Graff, *Professing Literature: An Institutional History* (Chicago, 1987).

some claim to contributing to the accumulation and progress of knowledge.

It is easy enough to see, therefore, why Eliot's literary criticism, suitably interpreted, held a particular appeal for young academics, such as Richards, Empson, Leavis, and F. O. Matthiessen, and to young critics who would eventually be drawn into the academy, such as R. P. Blackmur and the American New Critics. For Eliot's criticism was ostensibly formalist, insisting on the recognition of literature as an object of study on its own terms; it was anti-impressionistic and almost scientific-sounding; it had the look of being theoretical rather than journalistic or belletristic. 'Image' connotes impression; 'objective correlative', though it is, at root, the same concept, sounds theoretical and analytical. Eliot's criticism seemed a deliberate departure from the sort of appreciatory criticism the turn-of-the-century man and woman of letters produced, and thus an ideal model for an academic literary criticism. It had rigour.

But although a professionalising economy and an intellectual culture obsessed with the promise of pure science pushed the university toward a research mission and a vocational mission in the decades around the turn of the century, there was also, thanks to the growing numbers of college students, a non-utilitarian demand on the academy. Introduced to the world of the arts, greater and greater numbers of people began to look to experts to help them discriminate among the products available. Consider the title of a book published in 1871 by Noah Porter: *Books and Reading: Or, What Books Shall I Read and How Shall I Read Them?* The title may strike us as the literary equivalent of a blunt instrument; but the year the book appeared, its author was made president of Yale. Charles William Eliot's 'Five-Foot Book-Shelf', the Harvard Classics, was addressed to the same need. Having created a new intellectual class of accredited scholarly experts, the American university was in a position to provide cultural guidance. The obvious question was, Why not integrate the introduction to an appreciation of culture into the vocational training provided by the modern college? And there occurred, in the first decade of the twentieth century, a reaction in America on behalf of 'liberal culture' against the professionalisation of scholarship and the utilitarian approach to education that characterised the early research universities – a reaction that led, among other things, to Charles William Eliot's replacement as president of Harvard in 1910 by A. Lawrence Lowell.

The modern university thus has a dual function: it trains, but it also liberalises. And the liberalising function provided an obvious point of entry for literary criticism into the academic world – as Leavis, for instance, would argue persistently in England (often to visiting American ears), and as Richards would argue throughout his career, first at Cambridge and later at Harvard, where he helped to write the famous 'Red

Book', the 1945 Harvard report stressing the importance of general (or liberal, non-specialist) education in democratic societies. The role played by the man or woman of letters – the role of guide to literature and the arts – might be played by the college teacher. So long, that is, as the practice of ntroducing people to the appreciation of literature could be adapted to the new institutional requirements. And here, too, Eliot proved to be a useful figure.

As the first real winners in the battle to achieve institutional standing for literary criticism in the United States, the New Critics got to write the history. This they accomplished in two landmark works in the 1950s, Wellek's multi-volume *History of Modern Criticism* (beginning in 1955) and Cleanth Brooks and William Wimsatt's two-volume *Literary Criticism: A Short History* (1957). These were not the first histories of criticism. George Saintsbury had published his four-volume History of Criticism and Literary Taste in Europe in 1900–4 – noting, in the final volume, that friends had questioned the premise that literature was indeed something that could be talked about in isolation. Wellek, in the preface to his first volume, was careful to draw a distinction between Saintsbury's project and his own. Saintsbury's *History of Criticism*, he wrote, is 'admirable in its sweep and still readable because of the liveliness of the author's exposition and style; . . . but [it] seems to me seriously vitiated by its professed lack of interest in questions of theory and aesthetics'.[15]

One purpose of Wellek's and Brooks and Wimsatt's histories was to establish an intellectual tradition for the modern university-based critic. The continuity of shared theoretical concerns was therefore important: the twentieth-century academic critic wanted to be seen in a line of critics reaching back to Aristotle – even though the kind of work the academic critic does is determined by pressures exerted by an institution which was, in America particularly, not designed with the production of literary criticism in mind. Thus Brooks and Wimsatt mention the emergence of the modern university only to disparage historical scholarship: they note with asperity that it was not until 1950 that the Modern Language Association voted to add the word 'criticism' to its constitutional statement of purpose. Criticism proper tends to float free, in their work, of the institutions in which it is produced. And in the standard academic history or anthology of literary criticism today, the academic critic is still placed in a sequence of poet-critics – Coleridge and Dryden and Horace – and of philosophers of aesthetics – Nietzsche and Kant and Aristotle. The figure to whom the academic critic is never tied is the guide to culture, the turn-of-the-century journalistic man or woman of letters – the figure who

---

[15] René Wellek, *A History of Modern Criticism: 1750–1950, Volume One: The Later Eighteenth Century* (New Haven, 1955), p. vi.

is, in many respects, the functional precursor of the academic professor of literature himself.

Eliot stands historically between twentieth-century academic criticism, with its tendency toward specialisation and theory, and nineteenth-century journalistic and generalist criticism. He is, to put it another way, the first non-academic critic who sounds like an academic critic. In the American university-based critics' effort to situate themselves within a history of criticism, to construct a tradition that reaches back before the formation of the modern university, Eliot is, in effect, the link. The Eliot who emerges from a history like Wellek's is, therefore, a theorist; the Eliot who is submerged is the practising poet and literary journalist – the man of letters.

For his part, in fact, Eliot insisted that his criticism was *ad hoc*, that it was formulated principally as a support to the kind of writing he and his friends were doing, or else that it reflected what he called, in 'To Criticize the Critic' (1961), his 'emotional preferences'.[16] 'I have no general theory of my own', he wrote in the last of the lectures collected in *The Use of Poetry and the Use of Criticism* (1933); 'but on the other hand I would not appear to dismiss the views of others with the indifference which the practitioner may be supposed to feel towards those who theorise about his craft. It is reasonable, I feel, to be on guard against views which claim too much for poetry, as well as to protest against those which claim too little; to recognize a number of uses for poetry, without admitting that poetry must always and everywhere be subservient to any one of them.'[17] Eliot was sceptical of the value of teaching literature in any form, historical or appreciatory. His dismissal of Arnold's belief that poetry might serve a socially redemptive function included a dismissal of Arnold's argument that an introduction to literature should constitute the core of a modern education. Of the various false Eliots that have emerged from his academic reception, the Eliot who believed in the socially exalting power of high culture is probably the falsest. And although, since the demise of the New Criticism in the 1960s, Eliot's authority has faded almost completely within the university, he continues to hold his place as a linking figure between the world of literature and criticism before its massive academic instantiation and the world of the twentieth-century English department.

Eliot was an avant-gardist who became a paragon of the academic literary establishment, a journalist who was credited with establishing the distinctive modernist poetic, a highbrow poet whose work provided half-a-

---

[16] T. S. Eliot, 'To Criticize the Critic', in *To Criticize the Critic: Eight Essays on Literature and Education* (New York, 1965), p. 19.
[17] T. S. Eliot, *The Use of Poetry and the Use of Criticism: Studies in the Relation of Criticism to Poetry in England* (London, 1933), p. 143.

dozen catch-phrases – 'In the room the women come and go', 'April is the cruellest month', 'Not with a bang but a whimper' – to middlebrow culture. He is therefore, in his many aspects, paradigmatic of the period, in *its* many aspects, covered in this volume. Our division of this history into three sections – 'The Modernists', 'The New Critics', 'The Critic and the Institutions of Culture' – is a division of convenience, meant to suggest not three distinct endeavours, but three ways of looking at a single period. Contexts are endless, of course: twentieth-century developments in philosophy, aesthetics, hermeneutics, linguistics, critical theory, Marxism, feminism, and psychoanalysis – all of which bear, directly and indirectly, on the work discussed here – are dealt with in two separate volumes in this series.

But suppose that we do not assume Eliot's centrality to the writing covered by this volume? Suppose we imagine this period of Anglo-American criticism with no Eliot in it, or with an Eliot definitionally marginalised – not Eliot the modernist literary theoretician, but Eliot the Anglican monarchist and would-be revivifier of English verse drama instead? This is effectively the way in which many literary historians, over the last two or three decades, have been imagining, or re-imagining, the modernist period – as a period of many modernisms.

When modernism is multiplied, the literary criticism associated with modernist writings is multiplied as well. There is, so to speak, a 'mainstream' modernism associated with the academic incarnation of the New Criticism – a modernism defined by its concentration on the distinctive character of poetic language and form. But there is also a modernist literature of identity, whose critics include Alain Locke, Virginia Woolf, and Gertrude Stein. There is a modernism of counter-modernity – in the work of Eliot, Pound, and Lewis, and in the early writings of the New Critics in the United States and in the writings of members of the *Scrutiny* circle in England. But there is also a 'liberal' reading of modernism, in the criticism of Edmund Wilson and Lionel Trilling, for example, which takes modernist writing as a bracing and, on the whole, constructive critique of modern liberal values. And there are a variety of politically radical modernisms, articulated in the literary manifestos of the various intense and short-lived movements of the period, from futurism onwards.

An account of modernism and the New Criticism, then, must acknowledge that modernist literary criticism took up themes and issues often broader and more wide-ranging than our standard historiography might suggest, questions addressed only in passing or implicitly by the New Critics, even as it must also acknowledge that our received account of modernism and the New Criticism continues to exert enormous pressure on recent reconsiderations, often when it is least acknowledged. Modernism, poised between the era of journalism that had been and the age of the university that was about to be, between an elite bourgeois culture that was passing and a middlebrow ethos and aesthetics that were already arriving, between a world of timeless verities and a cosmos of endless, perhaps factitious fashion, was an enterprise that was perennially on the brink, always ambiguous – ambiguity that may itself account for modernism's uncertainty regarding the nature of representation in art, its unremitting stress on the means by which illusions and likenesses are made. Looking back at modernism and the New Criticism, as one might look at an antique mirror from which the mercury has seeped and faded, we seem to scrutinise a perplexing, even haunted image of ourselves, uncertain how much of that resemblance is due to likeness, and how much to illusion.

The modernists

T. S. Eliot

Louis Menand

T. S. Eliot became a figure in the tradition he made himself famous by attacking. He was a critic of modern society and modern culture who ended up an icon within the institution that is one of modernity's moments, the twentieth-century university. This is a fate that may have disappointed him, but it would probably not have surprised him. His sense of historical perversity was pretty complete.

Eliot was a modern partly by temperament. He made a show, in his criticism, of depreciating writers to whom he owed a good deal of his voice as a poet and his principles as a critic. But he was a modern by circumstance, as well. For he could hardly have hoped to make himself the exception to the conditions he analysed with such mordant disapproval. When he criticised modern culture for its lack of a coherent moral ground, and for the idiosyncratic and makeshift value systems it produced to compensate for that lack, he did so in the name of doctrines – 'royalism', to take a notorious example – whose idiosyncracy is, to say the least, fairly pronounced. Eliot built his castle out of the stones he found lying around the yard of modernity, just as Wordsworth, Emerson, Arnold, and Pater had built theirs.

Most people are accustomed to drawing a distinction between modern art and literature on the one hand and modern life – the political, social, and economic conditions of modernity – on the other. They think of the first as the antagonist of the second: modern life runs along its track of disenchantment and demystification, and modern art and literature assess the damage. But this is a distinction Eliot always refused to recognise, and that refusal is the defining characteristic of his thought. It is what separates him in the end from the nineteenth-century critics with whom he otherwise shares so much; and it constitutes the proper grounds for calling him a reactionary. Eliot considered modern life and modern art and literature to be aspects of the same condition. A few writers seemed to him to have achieved a critical position within the culture of modernity – Flaubert, Baudelaire, Henry James. But Eliot identified the main stream of modern culture as romanticism, and he regarded romanticism as the secret friend and abetter of all the tendencies of modern life he most deplored: liberalism, secularism, laisser-faire.

Eliot began his career by isolating for criticism the domain of literary values – a strategy that was itself intended as an act of criticism, since he thought that one of the deplorable aspects of modern culture after the age of Johnson was the adulteration of poetry and the criticism of poetry by the intrusion of extraliterary interests. His earliest essays and reviews; his first volume of criticism, *The Sacred Wood* (1920); and the three essays on seventeenth-century poetry published in 1921 – 'John Dryden', 'Andrew Marvell', and 'The Metaphysical Poets' – are guided by the principle, as Eliot later expressed it, that 'when we are considering poetry we must consider it primarily as poetry and not another thing'.[1]

By 1924, though, when the essays on seventeenth-century poetry were reprinted as *Homage to John Dryden*, Eliot had come to regard formalist literary criticism as inadequate to the sorts of judgements he had it most at heart to make. 'I have long felt that the poetry of the seventeenth and eighteenth centuries, even much of that of inferior inspiration, possesses an elegance and a dignity absent from the popular and pretentious verse of the Romantic Poets and their successors', he wrote in the introduction to *Homage to John Dryden*, explaining his unhappiness with the essays he had written three years earlier. 'To have argued this claim persuasively would have led me indirectly into considerations of politics, education, and theology which I no longer care to approach in this way.' And in 1928, in the preface to the second edition of *The Sacred Wood*, he announced that 'poetry ... certainly has something to do with morals, and with religion, and even with politics perhaps', and that the consideration of 'poetry as poetry' constituted merely 'a point from which to start'. So that after *Homage to John Dryden*, Eliot's literary criticism – the principal books are *For Lancelot Andrewes* (1928), *Dante* (1929), *The Use of Poetry and the Use of Criticism* (1933), *Elizabethan Essays* (1934), *Essays Ancient and Modern* (1936), *On Poetry and Poets* (1957), and *To Criticize the Critic* (1965) – is complemented by the much broader sociological criticism of modernity mounted in *After Strange Gods* (1934), *The Idea of a Christian Society* (1939), and *Notes towards the Definition of Culture* (1948).

The issues that occupied Eliot as a critic are incompletely represented in his most widely read critical book – possibly the most widely read critical book in English in the middle third of the twentieth century – the *Selected Essays*, first published in 1932 and reprinted, with four additional essays, in 1950. More than thirty years after his death, in 1965, most of Eliot's criticism remains uncollected and unreprinted. In his early years in London, Eliot contributed to a range of magazines fronting a range of literary

---

[1] T. S. Eliot, *The Sacred Wood: Essays on Poetry and Criticism* (London, 1920; 2nd edn., 1928), p. viii.

and political positions, from the Fabian *New Statesman*, whose literary
editor was the arch-antimodernist J. C. Squire, to Wyndham Lewis's
Tyro. The reviews and essays written for the *Egoist*, where Eliot served as
assistant editor from 1917 to 1919, and for the *Athenaeum*, during the
editorship of John Middleton Murry in 1919–20, take up a greater variety
of subject matter – notably American literature and contemporary poetry
– than the reader of the *Selected Essays* alone might suspect. Between
1919 and 1937, Eliot reviewed frequently for the *Times Literary Supplement*. From 1922 to 1939, he edited the *Criterion*, for most of its existence
a quarterly, to which he contributed, along with essays, reviews, and
translations, a regular column. And he produced, in the 1930s and 1940s,
a considerable amount of political and religious commentary, published
in *Time and Tide*, the *New English Weekly*, the *Christian News-Letter*,
and other journals. Many of these pieces show Eliot responding (or
making an elaborate point of declining to respond) to issues of the day, a
topicality that contrasts with the high level of generality on display in *The
Idea of a Christian Society* and *Notes towards the Definition of Culture*.

For Eliot was – and the fact is sometimes lost sight of in the shadow cast
by the *Selected Essays* – a controversialist. He had a journalistic nose for
opportunity. He sensed, usually before his contemporaries did, when
reputations that seemed established had become moribund, and when
systems of value that seemed intact had lost their cogency. He brought to
these occasions 'solutions' that were not really original, except in the sense
that they sometimes represented a fresh synthesis, or an unexpected
application, of ideas already current. His strongest suit as a critic was not
originality or argumentative power, but scepticism. He could sustain –
like Joyce, whose work he admired but with whom he otherwise had little
in common – an attitude of seeing through everything. This is far too
corrosive an attitude to inform an effective social criticism; and Eliot's
social criticism, though it was once regarded with pious respect, did not
produce many disciples. But the scepticism underwrote a notably successful literary criticism.

Why was the success notable? How did Eliot become a major figure in a
culture whose leading tendencies he had devoted his career to disparaging? He might have done so as a critic honoured for his isolation, as the
representative of an adversarial position, a countermodern. But he became instead (after struggles for acceptance now a little underrated) a
paragon of the establishment – a paradox made even more complete by
the fact that his strongest influence was felt in, and transmitted through,
the university. Eliot never courted the academy; he went out of his way, on
various occasions, to insult it. But the modern academy, at a crucial
moment in its history, made a representative figure of Eliot. And this
suggests that the answer to the question of Eliot's success is likely to be

found not simply in what Eliot had to say, but in the institutional needs his writing was able to serve.

There are four terms with which Eliot the critic is commonly associated: 'objective correlative', 'dissociation of sensibility', 'impersonality', and 'tradition'. The phrase 'objective correlative' appears only once in Eliot's criticism. There is nothing original about the concept apart from Eliot's application of it, and it collapses very quickly under analysis. But everyone seems to understand almost intuitively what Eliot meant, and the term has entered the common vocabulary of criticism. 'The dissociation of sensibility' names a historical crisis the evidence for which is entirely speculative. The phrase itself appears perhaps two or three times in Eliot's own writing (though the general idea turns up fairly often), and most of the positive judgements it was originally designed to support – of Donne and Laforgue in particular – Eliot soon afterwards retracted. But the notion of a dissociation of sensibility informed a wholesale rewriting of literary history (by among others F. R. Leavis in *Revaluation* (1936) and Cleanth Brooks in *Modern Poetry and the Tradition* (1939)); it altered the commonly accepted estimation of a number of poets; and it even inspired several attempts to pin the blame for the putative crisis on one or another system of values, including Baconian science, Cartesian philosophy, and the rise of capitalism. 'Impersonality' and 'tradition' appear together in a single early essay of Eliot's, 'Tradition and the Individual Talent' (1919). Eliot withdrew the most startling implications of the argument of that essay in 'The Function of Criticism' (1923); and in *After Strange Gods*, he announced a devaluation of the term 'tradition' in favour of one with (as he proceeded unintentionally to prove) very little usefulness for literary criticism, 'orthodoxy'. Still, 'Tradition and the Individual Talent' remains the most frequently analysed and anthologised of Eliot's essays, and it is generally understood to contain the essentials of Eliot's aesthetic theory.

But did Eliot have an aesthetic theory? It might be said that the temptation to discover in Eliot's criticism some sort of theoretical system is the great danger in Eliot scholarship – except that it has been done many times, beginning most notably with F. O. Matthiessen's *The Achievement of T. S. Eliot* (1935), and the discovery has given such satisfaction. More to the point, the suggestion that a coherent theoretical system lies behind their particular judgements is one of the things that has given Eliot's essays their continuing appeal: Eliot, it has seemed, was in possession of an interlocking and consciously developed set of aesthetic criteria, and these could be brought to bear on the evaluation of poems and poets with consistent and (since taste can hardly help being a determinant of most theories) desirable results. When it began to appear, as Eliot gradually repudiated much of his early criticism, that his criteria were not truly literary at all, or that they were being applied principally with a view to facilitating a favourable reception of Eliot's own poetry and the work of his friends, Eliot's admirers and exegetes did not pay much attention.

Were those admirers simply projecting a spurious coherence onto a body of criticism that was largely *ad hoc*? Not entirely; Eliot's literary criticism does hang together. But they did mistake a little the nature and the agent of the coherence. The criticism hangs together because it reflects a generally diffused body of assumptions about literature and criticism that Eliot shared with his contemporaries. Eliot's distinction lies not in the provenance of the assumptions, but in the ingenuity with which Eliot put them to work. As Eliot used them, they can be reduced to a general theoretical description of literary production and reception, even if that description is not, in the end, especially helpful as a means of understanding literature, and even if the production of a systematic theory – of literature or of anything else – was never one of Eliot's ambitions.

Most commentators eager to attribute theoretical substance to Eliot's criticism begin with the work that Eliot did as a philosophy student. It is a natural starting point, for when Eliot arrived in London in late August 1914, after a hasty and disorganised departure from Germany, he was on his way to Merton College, Oxford, for a year's study on a Sheldon Travelling Fellowship from Harvard, where he was a doctoral candidate in the philosophy department. His famous first meeting with Ezra Pound took place in late September, about the time of Eliot's twenty-sixth birthday; a week or two later, Eliot also renewed an acquaintance with Bertrand Russell, whose course on symbolic logic he had attended the previous spring. During the next two years, these men served as the mentors of an ostensibly divided ambition; for Eliot engaged them as intercessors with his parents, who had expected that he would return to America, take his degree, and eventually join the Harvard faculty. Russell's assignment was evidently to assure Eliot's family that an academic career remained an unforeclosed possibility, Pound's to explain (as he did with considerable reference to his own case) how it was that a career as a poet and literary journalist in London was not financial lunacy.

In fact, Eliot seems to have made up his mind to abandon his academic career for the life of literature well before the end of his first year in England – probably before his marriage to Vivien Haigh-Wood, which took place on 26 June 1915. But he was not precipitate about making the switch; and he agreed, at his parents' insistance, to write his dissertation. It was completed in 1916, and called 'Experience and the Objects of Knowledge in the Philosophy of F. H. Bradley'. Apart from some reviewing, the dissertation marks the end of Eliot's career as a philosopher. It was mailed to the Harvard department, where it was admired by, among others, Josiah Royce, who was reported to have called it 'the work of an expert'.[2] But although the chairman of the department was still trying to induce Eliot to return to America and accept an academic appointment as late as 1919, the dissertation was never defended, and it remained unpublished until 1964, when it appeared under a slightly different title, and without the final page, which has been lost.

The dissertation is neither a defence of Bradley's philosophy nor a critique of it – though it adopts certain points in Bradley's theory and rejects others. The dissertation is an attack on, first, epistemology and psychology, and, second, philosophy itself. Its argument is purely destructive. Eliot does not attempt to replace epistemology and psychology with a better vocabulary for understanding the relations between the mind and the world, and he does not suggest some ways in which philosophy might take a more useful turn.

'Experience and the Objects of Knowledge in the Philosophy of F. H. Bradley' is a highly involuted piece of academic prose, studded, in the customary fashion of graduate theses, with references to thinkers whose work is now almost forgotten, and parts of it have given even professional philosophers trouble. But the main argument is not hard to summarise. In *Appearance and Reality* (1893), Bradley proposed a three-tiered structure of knowledge. The bottom layer he called 'immediate experience', which means, he says, 'first, the general condition before distinctions and relations have been developed, and where as yet neither any subject nor object exists. And it means, in the second place, anything which is present at any stage of mental life, in so far as that is only present and simply is.' The break-up of this felt unity gives us the world of relations – what Bradley calls the world of appearance – in which we recognise, perforce, a distinction between subject and object, percept and memory image, real and ideal, and so forth. This middle stage is transcended in turn, and subject and object are again fused and taken up into the highest unity, which Bradley called 'the Absolute'.

In the dissertation, and in an article on Bradley and Leibniz published in *The Monist* in 1916, Eliot endorsed Bradley's theory, but with two reservations. He refused to accept, or even to speculate about, the notion of an Absolute; and he rejected the propostion, put forward by Bradley in 'On Our Knowledge of Immediate Experience' (1909),[3] that immediate experience is a stage that actually occurs in the life of either the individual or the species. His grounds for requiring these reservations were simple: immediate experience (like its counterpart, the Absolute) cannot be an actual experiential condition, since that would mean making it an object of knowledge, thus violating the very premise of 'immediate experience',

[2] T. S. Eliot, *The Letters of T. S. Eliot, Volume 1: 1898–1922*, ed. Valerie Eliot (London, 1988), p. 142.
[3] In Francis Herbert Bradley, *Essays on Truth and Reality* (Oxford, 1914), pp. 159–91.

which does not recognise any distinction between a knower and a thing known; and, in any case, we cannot know what it would mean for subject and object to be fused, since such a state would be the ontological equivalent of death. 'Immediate experience', as Eliot remarks in his dissertation, 'at either the beginning or the end of our journey, is annihilation and utter night.'

But so long as it is used as a weapon and not a tool, immediate experience makes a potent analytic instrument. For it exposes the factitiousness of every metaphysical problem that depends on maintaining an essential distinction between subject and object, or on any of the other terms of relation that define Bradley's world of appearance. Immediate experience subverts the effort of the epistemologist to understand the relation between the mind and the objects it contemplates because it refuses to recognise the existence of an object separate from the mind that perceives it; and it subverts the effort of the psychologist to understand mental states because, as Eliot puts it, 'there is no such thing as consciousness if consciousness is to be an object or something independent of the objects which it has'. More than this, it makes a mockery of the efforts of metaphysicians to produce a theoretical account of experience, since those accounts must begin with some given, some isolable atom of experience, and the concept of immediate experience decrees that any such isolation must be a philosophically arbitrary, or ungroundable, decision. 'Knowledge is invariably a matter of degree', Eliot explains: 'you cannot put your finger upon even the simplest datum and say "this we know". In the growth and construction of the world we live in, there is no one stage, and no one aspect, which you can take as the foundation.' Terms of relation cannot be defended on philosophical grounds, only on practical ones: 'There is no absolute point of view from which real and ideal can be finally separated and labelled. All of our terms turn out to be unreal abstractions; but we can defend them, and give them a kind of reality and validity (the only validity which they can possess or can need) by showing that they express the theory of knowledge which is implicit in all our practical activity.'

The consequence of this position is to render theory-making in any systematic sense pointless, since after every brick has been turned to straw, it is futile to dream about walls. 'You start,' as Eliot puts it,

or pretend to start, from experience – from any experience – and build your theory. You begin with truths which everyone will accept, perhaps, and you find connections which no one else has discovered. In the process, reality has changed ... for the world of your theory is certainly a very different world from the world from which you began ... There occurs, in short, just what is sure to occur in a world in which subject and predicate are not one. Metaphysical systems are condemned to go up like a rocket and come down like a stick.

The dissertation is, in other words, a philosophical argument against philosophy.

Is the temperature of Eliot's argument warm or cool? Though one of his biographers has asserted that the dissertation 'resounds with confessions of suffering',[4] it is hard to see that Eliot had in mind anything more than a clever dismantling of philosophical pretension, intellectually continuous with, if scarcely in the muscular spirit of, the pragmatist assault on philosophical truth-claims for which William James had made the Harvard department famous. Eliot's own account of his intentions supports such a reading. In a letter written in 1915 to Norbert Wiener, who was spending a year at Cambridge while Eliot was at Oxford and who had sent Eliot a copy of a paper he had recently published on 'Relativism', Eliot observed that relativism can be 'worked out, under different hands, with an infinite variety of detail', leading to either a relative idealism or a relative realism. His own sympathies, Eliot explained, lay in 'a relative materialism'; and he went on to say:

I am quite ready to admit that the lesson of relativism is: to avoid philosophy and devote oneself to either *real* art or *real* science. (For philosophy is an unloved guest in either company.) Still, this would be to draw a sharp line, and relativism preaches compromise. For *me*, as for Santayana, philosophy is chiefly literary criticism and conversation about life; and you have the logic, which seems to me of great value. The only reason why relativism does not do away with philosophy altogether, after all, is that there is no such thing left to abolish! There is art, and there is science. And there are works of art, and perhaps of science, which would never have occurred had not many people been under the impression that there was philosophy.

However, I took a piece of fairly technical philosophy for my thesis, and my relativism made me see so many sides to questions that I became hopelessly involved, and wrote a thesis perfectly unintelligible to anyone but myself; and so I wished to rewrite it. It's about Bradley's theory of judgment, and I think the second version will be entirely destructive. I shall attack first 'Reality', second 'Idea' or ideal content, and then try to show sufficient reason for attempting to get along without any theory of judgment whatsoever. In other words, there are many objects in the world (I say many, as if one could draw a sharp line, though in point of fact it is degree everywhere) which can be handled as things sufficiently for ordinary purposes, but not *exactly* enough to be subject matter for science – no definition of judgment, that is, is formally either right or wrong; and it simply is a waste of time to define judgment at all.

No pathos is detectable in these remarks, and if there is pathos in the dissertation, it remains invisibly between the lines.

On the other hand, there is the poetry, which, unless we take the whole of Eliot's production to be an elaborate literary performance (or *only* an

---

[4] Lyndall Gordon, *Eliot's Early Years* (New York, 1977), p. 53.

elaborate literary performance), certainly does resound with confessions of suffering, and which is distinctly not content with the worldview of 'a relative materialism'. How could a writer who would not accept the notion of an absolute, even as a heuristic device, take for the theme of most of his poetry the agonies and enervations of failed transcendence? Eliot's own version of the relation between his scepticism and his spiritualism is that it was a refusal to resist the most extreme implications of the first that led him inexorably to the second; but by embracing faith, he emphasised, he was not repudiating the disposition to doubt. 'My own beliefs', he explained at the time of his formal entrance into the Anglican church in 1927, 'are held with a scepticism which I never hope to be rid of.'[5] In this journey toward belief, Bradley had played a role. '[W]isdom consists largely of scepticism and uncynical disillusion', Eliot wrote, elsewhere, in 1927; 'and of these Bradley had a large share. And scepticism and disillusion are a useful equipment for religious understanding.'[6] Indeed, he was willing to argue that faith is the inevitable refuge of the modern sceptic: 'The Church offers today the last asylum for one type of mind which the Middle Ages would hardly have expected to find among the faithful: that of the sceptic', he wrote in a column for *Time and Tide* in 1935. And in a sermon preached in the chapel of Magdalene College, Cambridge, in 1948, in which he speaks of Montaigne and Bertrand Russell (though not of Bradley), he announced, clearly in reference to his own history, that 'One may become a Christian partly by pursuing scepticism to the utmost limit.'

Of course philosophical, or anti-philosophical, scepticism need not lead inevitably to faith in the supernatural; it might lead, by an equally plausible intellectual route, to liberalism. Yet Eliot's antagonism to liberalism was already fully developed by 1916. He regarded liberalism – as he regarded pragmatism and later humanism – as an attempt to evade the implications of scepticism by devising a cheery anthropocentric system of values. The antiliberal animus is less explicit in Eliot's earlier criticism than it would become after 1924, in part because he had a polemical purpose in adhering to a formalist critical method, in part because his own religious commitment had not yet been made. When that commitment was made, the criticism assumed a different tone and emphasis, and one finds oneself in a new, more or less eschatological climate. Eliot once explained this shift as a historical development: the importance of Proust, he wrote in 1926, is that he stands 'as a point of demarcation between a generation for whom the dissolution of value had in itself a positive value, and the generation for which the recognition of value is of utmost import-

[5] Quoted in Peter Ackroyd, *T. S. Eliot: A Life* (New York, 1984), p. 163.
[6] T. S. Eliot, *Selected Essays*, new edn. (New York, 1950), p. 399.

ance'.[7] But it was more significantly the consequence of his own spiritual development. Stephen Spender once recounted an appearance by Eliot before an undergraduate club at University College, Oxford, in 1928:

> The question was raised whether there was any ultimate criterion for judging a work of art. How can we be certain that *Antony and Cleopatra* and the Acropolis continue always to be beautiful? T., an undergraduate, ... said that surely it was impossible to believe in aesthetic values being permanent, unless one believed in God in whose mind beauty existed. Eliot bowed his head in that almost praying attitude which I came to know well, and murmured words to the effect of: 'That is what I have come to believe.'

When Eliot had completed his dissertation, in 1916, and with it that part of his obligation to his family, he turned to the matter of establishing himself as a poet and literary journalist – a business in which he achieved a rapid and astonishing success. He confronted a literary scene in which the main lines of opposition had already been drawn, between a modernistic 'new' writing and a more conventional (though by its own lights innovative) 'Georgianism'. '[L]ike a sand-eel'[8] is the way an exasperated acquaintance described Eliot after meeting him in London in 1914, and there is indeed something eel-like about the manner in which Eliot negotiated the literary currents of the day. His earliest essays, 'Reflections on *vers libre*' and 'The Borderline of Prose' (both 1917), published in the Fabian *New Statesman*, were unsympathetic appraisals of some of the main tenets of British imagism; in the same year, he joined the staff of the *Egoist*, which Pound and then Richard Aldington had turned into the flagship of the Imagist movement, and contributed (among other pieces) two series of essays, under the titles 'Reflections on Contemporary Poetry' (1917–19) and 'Studies in Contemporary Criticism' (1918), criticising Georgianism. By 1919 he was appearing alongside Clive Bell, E. M. Forster, Lytton Strachey, and the Woolfs in Murry's *Athenaeum* and writing for the *Times Literary Supplement*, which had been Virginia Woolf's own principal critical outlet since 1905. But he had also published a pamphlet promoting Pound – *Ezra Pound: His Metric and Poetry* (1917) – and had contributed poetry to Lewis's vorticist *Blast* and criticism to Lewis's *Tyro*, thus allying himself with writers with whom Bloomsbury had no patience. 'I think my position in English letters is all the stronger', Eliot wrote to his Harvard chairman in 1919, explaining why he had recently turned down a position on the staff of the *Athenaeum*, 'for my not being associated with any periodical as an employee... In writing for a paper one is writing for a public, and the best work, the only work that in the end counts, is written for oneself.'

---

[7] T. S. Eliot, 'Mr. Read and Mr. Fernandez', *Criterion*, 4 (1926), pp. 752–3.
[8] Martin D. Armstrong to Conrad Aiken, 11 October 1914, Aiken Collection, Huntington Library.

The well-known essay on 'Hamlet and His Problems' (1919) is a good specimen of Eliot's early critical technique. This is the essay in which Eliot pronounces Shakespeare's play 'most certainly an artistic failure', a judgement that has sometimes been regarded as a piece of bravura iconoclasm. But Eliot was simply following the judgement of the book that was the occasion for his essay, J. M. Robertson's *The Problem of 'Hamlet'*, in which the play is called 'an aesthetic miscarriage'. As Eliot later acknowledged, in 'To Criticize the Critic' (1961), his general understanding of Shakespeare during this period owed much to Robertson's work – and he must have had in mind not only *The Problem of 'Hamlet'*, but also the essays in *Montaigne and Shakespeare* (1897; rev. edn. 1909). (The slighting remarks about romantic interpretations of *Hamlet* at the opening of Eliot's essay echo E. E. Stoll's *'Hamlet': A Historical and Comparative Study* (1919), the other work Eliot mentions in the essay.)

But Eliot's way of formulating *Hamlet*'s problem is his own. The difficulty, he argues, lies in Shakespeare's inadequate grasp of the principle of the 'objective correlative', which states that:

The only way of expressing emotion in the form of art is by finding an 'objective correlative'; in other words, a set of objects, a situation, a chain of events which shall be the formula of that *particular* emotion; such that when the external facts, which must terminate in sensory experience, are given, the emotion is immediately evoked.

The essay is a little fuzzy on the question of whether the trouble with *Hamlet* therefore has to do with an incongruity between the emotion Hamlet feels and his actual dramatic situation or with an incongruity between some emotion *Shakespeare* felt and the dramatic vehicle he selected in order to relieve himself of it. Evidently, Eliot considered that *Hamlet* suffered from both deficiencies, and Eliot even took them to be somehow related. There is no logical reason why this should be so, of course; for why should emotions Shakespeare might or might not have felt have any bearing on his failure to supply his character with an adequate objective correlative – or to construct in any other respect an artistically sound play?

In any event, the 'object correlative', as Eliot defines it, is a tautology: it cannot be read as saying anything more specific than 'The emotion expressed by a work of art is a product of the elements of that work.' (This is the consequence of Eliot's preferring the word 'only' to some forensically safer locution – 'The most effective way of expressing emotion in the form of art', for example.) This might still provide the basis for an unfavourable judgement of *Hamlet* if it could be shown that Shakespeare was unable to express the emotion Hamlet is supposed to be feeling, that we simply don't know what it is. But Eliot claims to know exactly what the emotion is, and not because Hamlet tells him, but because of an 'unmistakable tone' in the play. The emotion Hamlet feels is, precisely, the emotion that cannot be made proportionate to the occasions the world provides: it is '[t]he intense feeling, ecstatic or terrible, without an object or exceeding its object' – an emotion, Eliot goes on to say, 'which every person of sensibility has known'. The conclusion appears to be not that *Hamlet*, the play, fails to express a particular emotion, but that the emotion it expresses is not a proper emotion for 'the form of art', since it is not communicable by the means Eliot's formula requires.

In spite of these difficulties, the 'objective correlative' enjoyed a great success, and commentators have unearthed various antecedents: in the writings of Pater, Coleridge, and Schiller, and in the *Lectures on Art* (1850) of the American painter Washington Allston, where the phrase 'objective correlative' actually appears. But the formula lay much closer to Eliot's hand. Ford Madox Ford, in a review of Pound's *Cathay* (1915), had invoked 'a theory and practice of poetry that is already old – the theory that poetry consists in so rendering concrete objects that the emotions produced by the objects shall arise in the reader', and the passage is quoted by Eliot in *Ezra Pound: His Metric and Poetry*. One can find half a dozen other contemporaneous instances of the general notion; for the 'objective correlative' is simply the formula for an image, and it bears the same relation to those nineteenth-century antecedents that Imagism does to romantic poetics generally: it is a kind of minimalist, or demystified, version of a symbol.

The imagist aesthetic belongs to a general epistemological ideology that colours everything in late-nineteenth- and early-twentieth-century talk about art: the ideology of sensationalism. The conviction that art, and poetry in particular, ought to reflect the 'feel' of experience rather than some idea about experience has a long history, and the term 'image' is part of the vocabulary of this view as far back as the seventeenth century. But the deliberate divorce of sensation, as the basis for art, from anything to do with intellect is really the achievement of Walter Pater; and Pater's aesthetic lies behind nearly everything that Ford and Pound tried to do in their early years as polemical poeticists. Late-nineteenth-century aestheticism, though, associated as it was with the Wilde scandal, was not a movement modernists wished to be identified with, and Pater's name is virtually absent from modernist criticism except where his influence is deplored. The writer whose name does turn up in some of the places where Pater's might have is Henri Bergson, whose *Essai sur les données immédiates de la conscience* (1889; English trans. 1910), in particular, enjoyed an enormous influence in France and England in the first decades of the century. Bergson's argument that real inner experience – what he calls the *durée réele* – cannot be grasped by intellectual analysis, but only by intuition, held an obvious appeal to aestheticians; and his suggestion in the 'Introduction à la métaphysique' (1903; English trans. 1913) that it is the image, rather than the concept, that brings us closest to the object in its true nature seemed to T. E Hulme (who translated the 'Introduction') an argument for the superiority of poetic language. 'No image can replace the intuition of duration', wrote Bergson in the 'Introduction', 'but many diverse images, borrowed from very different orders of things, may, by the convergence of their action, direct consciousness to the precise point where there is a certain intuition to be seized.' Poetry, wrote Hulme in 1909, 'is not a counter language, but a visual concrete one. It is a compromise for a language of intuition which would hand over sensations bodily.'[9]

The path this principle took through British poetry over the next decade is such hotly contested ground that it's not worth attempting a genealogy of Imagist ideals. Pound called Bergson 'crap',[10] and though he read Hulme's pieces on philosophy and poetry in *The New Age* and listened to him lecture, he credited his own version of imagism to Ford. By 1912, the year Pound announced the existence of an imagist school, Hulme had in any case begun to reject Bergson, and to move, under the influence of Wilhelm Worringer's *Abstraktion und Einfühlung* (1908), in the direction of an antihumanist aesthetic that is nearly the polar opposite of Bergsonism. Two years later, Pound himself abandoned the movement he claimed to have started, and took up with the futurist-influenced vorticism of Wyndham Lewis. But the Imagist aesthetic had by this time become widely diffused, and it gave, in effect, another boost to the general prejudice in favour of sensation – the prejudice that informs, for instance, Virginia Woolf's Paterian defence of modernist fiction, and her attack on Edwardian materialism, in 'Modern Fiction' (1919) and 'Mr. Bennett and Mrs. Brown' (1924).

'Hamlet and His Problems' does not read as an Imagist-flavoured piece of criticism (the essay first appeared in the *Athenaeum*), for no Imagist would have thought to apply the standard of the objective correlative to an entire Elizabethan play. And the objective correlative is not readily recognisable as a stripped-down model of the romantic aesthetic, for the formula is made up to look like a hard-headed, Aristotelean deduction from the literary evidence, and the whole essay is clearly a displaced attack on romantic 'excess'. Yet 'Hamlet and His Problems' has surely appealed to so many readers because the fulcrum of its argument is an assumption about art that has been taken from a familiar tradition. Eliot succeeded in making a contemporary prejudice about art sound like a return to classical principles.

[9] T. E. Hulme, *Further Speculations*, ed. Sam Hynes (Minneapolis, 1955), p. 10.
[10] Ezra Pound, 'This Hulme Business', *Townsman*, 2 (1939), p. 15.

This reinscription of nineteenth-century literary values in the name of a debunking of nineteenth-century literary values is one of the striking features of Eliot's early criticism. The opening essay in *The Sacred Wood*, 'The Perfect Critic' (1920), is presented as an assault on 'impressionistic' criticism, with Arthur Symons standing in for Pater (Eliot calls him 'the critical successor of Pater'); yet when Eliot gets around to explaining what criticism ought to be, his prescription is not easily distinguished from Pater's own ('An impression needs to be constantly refreshed by new impressions in order that it may persist at all; it needs to take its place in a system of impressions', and so forth). And the aesthetic standard used in 'The Metaphysical Poets' (1921) to praise Donne and the other metaphysicals at the expense of nineteenth-century poetry – the standard of the unified sensibility, or 'felt thought' – was in common use in the nineteenth century to describe the poetry of Keats and Tennyson: it was essentially what Arthur Hallam had said of Tennyson in his famous essay of 1831. (The term was in common enough use in Eliot's own time, in fact, to describe the poetry of Donne: '[Donne] belonged to an age when men were not afraid to mate their intellects with their emotions', wrote Rupert Brooke in 1913.)[11]

The most arresting of these cases is the so-called doctrine of impersonality – an apparent attack on the values of originality and individuality which seems to have buried within it a conventionally romantic conception of poetic production. The argument appears in 'Tradition and the Individual Talent' (1919), the first part of which was published in the *Egoist* in the same month that 'Hamlet and His Problems' appeared in the *Athenaeum*, and it provides the solution to the riddle about the role of Shakespeare's emotions in the composition of *Hamlet*. (The arguments of the two essays, apart from the application of the objective correlative to *Hamlet*, are essentially combined in 'Modern Tendencies in Poetry', a talk which Eliot delivered under the auspices of the London Arts League of Service in 1919, and which was published in the Indian journal *Shama'a* in 1920.) Shakespeare must have undergone some sort of psychic distress, 'Tradition and the Individual Talent' suggests, for it is precisely to relieve such a distress that poems are written. The wrinkle in Eliot's version of this common view is that if the poem is successful – artistically successful – the personal distress disappears (temporarily, presumably, since there are more poems to be written). The poem does not express the personality of the poet; but without the spur of personal feeling, the poem would not have been written at all. 'Poetry is not a turning loose of emotion', as the celebrated sentences have it, 'but an escape from emotion; it is not the expression of personality, but an escape from personality. But, of course,

11 Rupert Brooke, 'John Donne, The Elizabethan', *Nation*, 12 (1913), p. 825.

only those who have personality and emotions know what it means to want to escape from these things.' Hence '[t]he emotion of art is impersonal' – not because a work of art is a piece of self-conscious intellectual craftsmanship, but because (to adopt a vocabulary Eliot carefully avoids) the refining fire of the imagination fuses the materials that have collected in the poet's mind, and the product that emerges transcends the merely personal.

This is so parallel to the account of poetic composition laid out by Wordsworth in the preface to *Lyrical Ballads* that Eliot actually takes a moment in the last pages of the essay to disparage 'emotion recollected in tranquillity' as 'an inexact formula'. For 'impersonality' was, of course, a nineteenth-century literary value in high standing. Arnold (in the preface to the first edition of his *Poems* (1853)) and Pater (in the essay on 'Style' (1888)) both gave the concept the same importance Eliot does. Only in the most greeting-card kind of romanticism does one find the simple equation between inner feeling and poetic expression that Eliot is attacking.

What sets Eliot's argument apart is the concept of tradition. Arnold and Pater, too, set great store by the kind of literary homework Eliot prescribes in 'Tradition and the Individual Talent' ('the historical sense compels a man to write not merely with his own generation in his bones, but with a feeling that the whole of the literature of Europe from Homer and within it the whole of the literature of his own country has a simultaneous existence and composes a simultaneous order'). But for Pater, scholarship (his term) was simply a requirement for mastering the medium: it helped the poet fine-tune his language to match more precisely the lineaments of what he called 'the vision within'. Eliot had a much grander ambition in view. In his account, the poet is the medium; and the 'medium' – the tradition as it passes through the poet's time – is what gets expressed.

At the centre of the argument in 'Tradition and the Individual Talent' are two propositions which do have theoretical force, and are calculated to unbalance traditional assumptions. The first is an attack on what the essay calls 'the metaphysical theory of the substantial unity of the soul' – that is, on the integrity and autonomy of the self. The poet doesn't express his or her personality not because it is healthy self-discipline not to, but because there is nothing so coherent as a personality to express. 'The poet's mind is in fact a receptacle for seizing and storing up numberless feelings, phrases, images, which remain there until all the particles which can unite to form a new compound are present together.' The new compound is the poem; but '[i]mpressions and experiences which are important for the man may take no place in the poetry, and those which become important in the poetry may play quite a negligible part in the man, the personality'.

The second theoretical proposition has to do with the relation between new and existing art:

No poet, no artist of any art, has his complete meaning alone. His significance, his appreciation is the appreciation of his relation to the dead poets and artists. You cannot value him alone; you must set him, for contrast and comparison, among the dead... The necessity that he shall conform, that he shall cohere, is not onesided; what happens when a new work of art is created is something that happens simultaneously to all the works of art which preceded it. The existing monuments form an ideal order among themselves, which is modified by the introduction of the new (the really new) work of art among them. The existing order is complete before the new work arrives; for order to persist after the supervention of novelty, the *whole* existing order must be, if ever so slightly, altered; and so the relations, proportions, values of each work of art toward the whole are readjusted.

Eliot is so automatically associated with the defence of a traditional canon that it has become difficult for some readers to see exactly what he is saying here. The term 'ideal order' is the crux of the misreading: it is clearly intended philosophically, not prescriptively. Our perception of the new work of art depends on our perception of the history of art, which takes a certain shape – is 'idealised' – in our minds. But once we have encountered the new work, that idea of the tradition is modified in turn. Value – by implication, significance of any sort – is a function of relation. Hence, the tradition cannot be monolithic.

The essay apparently strives to remind poets, and critics of poetry, of two facts of life that loose talk about creativity and originality encourage them to ignore. One is that few things are more likely to produce conventionality than the self-conscious effort to find something original to say, for the reason that there is nothing 'inside' which has not already come from outside. What you see when you look into your heart before composing is what you have been taught by the tradition to find there. The second reminder is that if the new work of art cannot be perceived in the context of everying that is already perceived as art, it will be not merely unappreciated, but unintelligible. This is not a stricture against innovation, since the work that only conforms will make no difference to us.

In which direction is 'Tradition and the Individual Talent' pointed? It takes its philosophical materials from late-nineteenth-century historicist hermeneutics, from ideas associated with Wilhelm Dilthey and Friedrich Meinecke (and renovated in our time by Hans-Georg Gadamer: 'Tradition is not merely a precondition into which we come, but we produce it ourselves and hence further determine it ourselves.'). The most striking use of this line of thought in English criticism before Eliot was made by a writer for whom Eliot expressed unaffected distaste, Oscar Wilde – particularly in 'The Critic as Artist' (1891). But Eliot's mind was probably more focused on local circumstances than it was on the history of ideas. The essay serves, for instance, as a kind of reply to Arthur Waugh, whose *Tradition and Change: Studies in Contemporary Literature* was published in the same year as Eliot's essay. Eliot would certainly have known Waugh's book, since it includes the famous review of *The Catholic Anthology* in which the poems by Eliot and Pound are likened to the antics of 'drunken helots' produced for the amusement of the court – a comparison that seems to have especially irritated Eliot. Waugh's comment in his introduction that 'even the rebel himself is most persuasive when he catches the voice of authority' is Eliotic enough; but the volume as a whole is a defence of the Georgian poets against the modernists, and the challenge it must have presented to Eliot was its appropriation of 'tradition' on behalf of the enemy. It can be said fairly decisively that Eliot succeeded in appropriating it back again, and in doing so established a modernist position that was as distinct from the hyperbolic avant-gardism of the futurists, who issued manifestoes about burning down the libraries, as it was from the tepid literary progressivism of the Georgians, whose 'traditionalism' Eliot was now able to recast as simple conventionality. Because they accepted tradition so uncritically the Georgians were unable to produce 'the really new' – a point Eliot makes over and over in his early periodical pieces: '[B]ecause we have never learned to criticize Keats, Shelley, and Wordsworth (poets of assured though modest merit), Keats, Shelley, and Wordsworth punish us from their graves with the annual scourge of the Georgian anthology';[12] 'Culture is traditional, and loves novelty; the General Reading Public knows no tradition, and loves staleness';[13] 'Simplicity was not hard won by the Georgians, it was given them by the fairy.'[14]

Eliot quickly began to slide away, though, from the relativism implicit in his account of the way the new and the old attain their perceptual 'fit'. At the outset of 'The Function of Criticism' (1923), published in his new journal *The Criterion*, he quotes, ostensibly by way of endorsement, the paragraph from 'Tradition and the Individual Talent' containing the phrase 'ideal order', and then proceeds to devote another, longer paragraph to telling us what he meant – a pretty clear signal that he has changed his mind. It turns out that what he meant was that 'there is something outside the artist to which he owes allegiance ... A common inheritance and a common cause unite artists consciously or unconsciously.' This not only loads up with the language of literary patriotism an idea that the earlier essay presents as a simple statement of fact – that art can only take its significance from its relation to previous art. It also teeters on

[12] T. S. Eliot, 'Observations', *Egoist*, 5 (1918), p. 69.
[13] T. S. Eliot, 'London Letter', *Dial*, 70 (1921), p. 453.
[14] T. S. Eliot, 'The Post-Georgians', *Athenaeum*, 11 April 1919, p. 171.

the brink of denying the other principal assertion of 'Tradition and the Individual Talent': that the poem happens by means of an interior mechanics whose operation remains a mystery (the 'shred of platinum' analogy). Two sentences later, we are, in fact, over the brink: 'And, as our instincts of tidiness imperatively command us not to leave to the haphazard of unconsciousness what we can attempt to do consciously, we are forced to conclude that what happens unconsciously we could bring about, and form into a purpose, if we made a conscious attempt' – which, among other things, explains how the author of *The Waste Land* turned into the self-conscious resuscitator of English verse drama. The intention of 'The Function of Criticism' is to apply the argument of 'Tradition and the Individual Talent' to criticism; but the result of the application, which logically ought to lead in the direction of Wilde's conception of interpretation as a new creation, is a conclusion remote from historicism. The goal of criticism turns out to be 'putting the reader in possession of facts which he would otherwise have missed' – 'with the further possibility of arriving at something outside ourselves, which may provisionally be called truth'.

The bulk of 'The Function of Criticism' is taken up with a polemical definition of the opposition between romanticism and classicism in terms which, although they become less crude in Eliot's later writings, never become more convincing. The romantic heeds the 'inner voice', which in 'Tradition and the Individual Talent' was simply a nonentity but which is now coherent enough to have a 'message': 'The inner voice ... sounds remarkably like an old principle which has been formulated by an elder critic in the now-familiar phrase of "doing as one likes" ... [It] breathes the eternal message of vanity, fear, and lust.' The classical writer (Eliot is following John Middleton Murry, though he is coming out, of course, on the opposite side of the issue) obeys 'Outside Authority'. The opposition is plainly one between the Protestant and the Catholic relation to scripture, and 'tradition' is evidently meant to play the part of the church.

This is such a departure from the way 'tradition' is used in the earlier essay, and such a bootstrap effort to lift the term out of the realm of cultural anthropology, to which it really belongs, that it was inevitable that Eliot would realise the need for another category entirely. In 1933, he delivered the lectures collected in *After Strange Gods* (1934), in which he explains that 'tradition' will no longer suffice as a name for the 'something outside ourselves'. For to exalt the cultural inheritance as the baseline of all value is to fall into the same error as humanism and pragmatism, and the error Eliot accuses nineteenth-century critics of in 'Arnold and Pater' (1930): setting up 'Culture in the place of Religion'. The twelve authors of the neo-Agrarian manifesto *I'll Take My Stand* (1930), with whose purposes Eliot expresses interest and sympathy at the outset of the lectures, rely, he says, too exclusively on 'tradition' in their prescriptions for the

re-establishment of what they take to have been the native culture of the
American south. 'Tradition itself is not enough', Eliot warns them; 'it
must be perpetually criticized and brought up to date under the supervision of what I call orthodoxy'.

This has the great advantage of making the final arbiter of critical
judgement a standard which is, in human terms, by definition unknowable
(the tradition is what we know); and Eliot proceeds in *After Strange Gods*
to use his new criterion to talk about modern literature with a kind of
otherworldly irrelevance that is still a little puzzling – hailing Joyce as 'the
most ethically orthodox of the more eminent writers of my time' and
damning Hardy and Lawrence for their heresy. The performance must, in
retrospect, have puzzled Eliot as well. His refusal to allow the book ever to
be reprinted is commonly assumed to have stemmed from second
thoughts about the comment concerning the undesirability of 'free-thinking Jews' in the ideal community. But Eliot never offered that as the reason
himself: in 1940 he was still defending the statement in private correspondence ('my view does not imply any prejudice on the ground of race, but
merely a recognition of what seems to be an historical social situation').[15]
No doubt he came to regret the attention the remark attracted; but one
suspects that he was also a little ashamed of the book's eccentricity as a
work of criticism. For he must have recognised that he had presumed to
collapse his categories in the very way he was accustomed to attacking
nineteenth-century critics for doing. Though he had announced in the
opening of the book that he did not regard it as a work of literary
criticism, it was, after all, works of literature that he was criticising. He
had, in effect, rewritten Arnold's *Literature and Dogma* as *Dogma and
Literature*. That he took literary criticism up into theology, instead of
reducing theology to literary criticism, hardly makes a difference. And
after 1934, Eliot's essays on individual writers, though heavily flavoured
with speculation about their relation to the religious issues he considered
important, suggest a self-conscious effort to return to *The Sacred Wood*'s
brand of formalism, and tend to concentrate on literary merits and de-
merits with some degree of sympathetic attention. *Contemptus mundi* is
not an appropriate intellectual condition for a critic of literature, and
Eliot, particularly in the 1920s and 1930s, suffered from a fairly advanced
case of it.

Eliot consistently attempted to adhere to the separation which 'Tradition and the Individual Talent' mandates between 'the man who suffers
and the mind which creates'. The formulation is fresher than the general
conception. The essay's account of artistic production echoes Bloomsbury
theorising about 'significant form': the distinction between the personal

[15] Eliot to J. V. Healy, 10 May 1940; quoted in Christopher Ricks, *T. S. Eliot and Prejudice*
(London, 1988), p. 44.

emotion with which the artist begins and the 'aesthetic emotion' the
spectator experiences can be found, for instance, in Clive Bell's *Art*
(1913). But Eliot's sense of this process, strikingly, insists that the man
must suffer – a requirement one doesn't find, for example, in Hulme's later
aesthetic theory, or even in Pound's, and one that has given many commentators a key to unlocking Eliot's relations as a poet with his nineteenth-century predecessors.

For Eliot's interest in other poets was often ignited by his identification
with what he understood to be their agonies of creation. Coleridge is one
example; but there are unlikelier ones, as well. In 1933 Eliot wrote a
critical note that served as part of the preface to the collected poems of
Harold Monro. Monro was hardly a modernist; as the proprietor of the
Poetry Bookshop, he had been the publisher of the Georgian anthologies.
But these categories don't interest Eliot, for he senses in Monro's poetry
the essential agon at work: 'It is a poet's business to be original', he says,
'in all that is comprehended by "technique", only so far as is absolutely
necessary for saying what he has to say; only so far as is dictated, not by
the idea – for there is no idea – but by the nature of that dark embryo
within him which gradually takes on the form and speech of a poem.' The
same view is given a more sustained exposition in the conclusion to *The
Use of Poetry and the Use of Criticism*, published in the same year. And
the embryo itself reappears in 'The Three Voices of Poetry' (1953), where,
expanding on some of the views of Gottfried Benn, Eliot speaks of the
'inert embryo' that is the germ of creation:

In a poem which is neither didactic nor narrative, and not animated by any other
social purpose, the poet must be concerned solely with expressing in verse . . . this
obscure impulse . . . He is oppressed by a burden which he must bring to birth in
order to obtain relief. Or, to change the figure of speech, he is haunted by a demon,
a demon against which he feels powerless, because in its first manifestation it has
no face, no name, nothing; and the words, the poem he makes, are a kind of form
of exorcism of this demon.

He goes on to say (still following the line laid down by 'Tradition and
the Individual Talent'): 'I don't believe that the relation of a poem to its
origins is capable of being more clearly traced.' No doubt he means this as
far as it goes, but it goes only half way; for though the poet can make no
more sense of how the poem came to be, the critic can. Eliot's view seems
to be this: the materials from which the poem is made are given to the poet
by the culture; and if his digestion of them follows the proper physiological course, the poem which is ultimately disgorged will be an emblem of its
historical moment (a transcendent emblem, if you like, since its appeal
will be transhistorical). Whether or not the cultural materials are judged
inferior from an ideological point of view has no bearing on the success of

the poem from a literary point of view (or, presumably, from a therapeutic point of view). The poet has no recourse to materials outside his moment – or to put it more precisely, he has no recourse to materials unconditioned by his relation to the worldview of his own moment. The worth of his poems can therefore only be a function of the fineness of his equipment. 'Had Massinger had a nervous system as refined as that of Middleton, Tourneur, Webster, or Ford, his style would be a triumph.'[16]

This is as determinist, and as sensationalist, as anything in Pater. And it creates the same sort of difficulty one encounters in Pater: if so much is conceded to forces over which the poet has no control, what ground remains on which to consruct a critical judgement? In a very general sense, this is a dilemma that plagues all modern criticism that theorises some relation between art and society – Marxist criticism as well as modernist. In Eliot's work, the issue is usually expressed as the problem of poetry and belief, and from the 'turn' in his thinking around 1923 on, this problem – the proper place of ideology, or belief, in literary appreciation and critical judgement – becomes the great riddle of his criticism.

It remains a riddle, too. For Eliot was as baffled by the problem as everyone else. In his case, the difficulty arose at the point of contact between his desire to maintain the autonomy of literature and literary criticism and his desire to inform, or to supplement, literary judgements by reference to ethical, religious, and other realms of value. The polemical purpose of *The Sacred Wood* had been to isolate the discussion of literature from extraliterary interests, a hygenic manoeuvre Arnold and Coleridge were reproached for failing to perform, and Aristotle and Remy de Gourmont were praised for understanding the need for. When Eliot reprinted the book in 1928, he did not relinquish his formalist principles, but he did indicate his belief that poetry 'certainly has something to do with' morals, religion, and politics. He went even further, though without being more specific, in the preface to *For Lancelot Andrewes*, also published in 1928, where he announced his wish 'to dissociate myself from certain conclusions which have been drawn from ... *The Sacred Wood*'. *After Strange Gods*, of course, is an adventure in ideological criticism; and in 'Religion and Literature' (1935) it is flatly stated that: 'Literary criticism should be completed by criticism from a definite ethical and theological standpoint.' But this dictum is then elaborated as follows: 'The "greatness" of literature cannot be determined solely by literary standards; though we must remember that whether it is literature or not can be determined only by literary standards.'

Critical inquiry, it seems, should begin with an examination of the literary accomplishment of the writer in question, thus affording the

---

[16] Eliot, *The Sacred Wood*, p. 131.

opportunity for some disinterested aesthetic appreciation before bringing him or her up to the supreme seat of ideological judgement – where unless the writer happens to be Dante, all thumbs are likely to be pointed down. The strategy works most effectively in Eliot's essays on those Renaissance writers in whom he took, throughout his career, such an intense personal and scholarly interest: Marlowe (1919), Massinger (1920), Donne and Marvell (1921), Davies (1926), Middleton (1927), Tourneur (1930), Heywood (1931), Ford (1932), Marston (1934). These are writers who belong to the world before the 'dissociation of sensibility', and yet that world is already (in Eliot's view) post-Christian, for the disintegration of European Catholicism is well underway. The spectacle of the poetic sensibility struggling to digest the scraps of the original faith, mixed together with various secular worldviews rushing in to fill the vacuum, is something that gives Eliot excitement as a critic, since it arises from a condition with which he seems to have identified as a poet.

The strategy yields a somewhat less persuasive criticism in the case of nineteenth-century writers – for instance, Blake (1920), Baudelaire (1930), Wordsworth and Coleridge (1933), Byron (1937), Yeats (1940), Goethe (1955). For (as Eliot tends to see it) by the nineteenth century, the triumph of secularism is essentially complete, the equipment of literary sensibility has largely broken down, the adulteration of poetry and criticism by extraliterary interests has begun. It becomes more difficult for the critic to isolate the poetic for appreciation because, paradoxically, the poetic has already been isolated, made into a frill on a package heavy with ideological dross. And yet the path of Eliot's criticism of the romantics and their successors opens out rather than closes up over the course of his career; he finds more to take an interest in each time he renews his acquaintance with those poets, and his willingness to renew the acquaintance strengthens.

His attitude toward Tennyson is illustrative. It is never more than condescending, but the condescending gesture is made with increasingly respectful flourishes. Tennyson was a prime object of modernist ridicule in the early years, and Eliot took a hand in the general phrase-making: 'I am inclined to believe that Tennyson's verse is a "cry from the heart" – only it is the heart of Tennyson, Latitudinarian, Whig, Laureate';[17] 'Tennyson was careful in his syntax; and, moreover, his adjectives usually have a definite meaning; perhaps often an uninteresting meaning; still, each word is treated with proper respect. And Tennyson had a brain (a large dull brain like a farmhouse clock) which saved him from triviality' (1918).[18] A. C. Bradley, lecturing on 'The Reaction Against Tennyson' in 1914, suggested that Tennyson's reputation could hardly sink much lower, but the

---

[17] T. S. Eliot, 'Reflections on Contemporary Poetry', *Egoist*, 4 (1917), p. 151.
[18] T. S. Eliot, 'Verse Pleasant and Unpleasant', *Egoist*, 5 (1918), p. 43.

diagnosis turned out to be optimistic; it was in 1923 that Harold Nicolson's *Tennyson: Aspects of His Life, Character, and Poetry* and Hugh I'Anson Fausset's *Tennyson: A Modern Portrait* fixed the twentieth-century conception of Tennyson as (in Auden's phrase) the 'stupidest' of the English poets.

So that when Eliot came to write again about Tennyson, in an essay on *In Memoriam* in 1936, he was able to imply that Tennyson had been rather underappreciated, and he turned the Victorian infection of poetry by 'ideas' to Tennyson's advantage:

The surface of Tennyson stirred about with his time; and he had nothing to which to hold fast except his unique and unerring feeling for the sounds of words. But in this he had something that no one else had. Tennyson's surface, his technical accomplishment, is intimate with his depths: what we most quickly see about Tennyson is that which moves between the surface and the depths, that which is of slight importance. By looking innocently at the surface we are most likely to come to the depths, to the abyss of sorrow. Tennyson is ... the saddest of all English poets, among the Great in Limbo, the most instinctive rebel against the society in which he was the most perfect conformist.

In 'The Voice of His Time', a BBC radio talk six years later, Tennyson benefits from the same style of praise: Tennyson 'felt and expressed, before it had come to other men, what was to be the emotional attitude towards evolution in his and the next generation. It is an attitude of vague hopefulness which I believe to be mistaken. But that does not matter: what matters is that Tennyson felt it and gave it expression.' *In Memoriam* thus constitutes a 'complex and comprehensive expression of an historic phase of thought and feeling, of the grandeur and tragedy of the Victorian age'. Though the materials are shabby, the poet has at least done with them what poets can. If it is objected that this method of judgement turns poetry into a symptom, it can be replied that in Eliot's view of the matter, the poetry of Dante is symptomatic, too; only Dante had the good fortune to symptomise health, and Tennyson the bad luck to symptomise febricity.

It is hard to miss the personal identification here with a writer who makes his mark as the author of a long elegiac poem constructed of scraps of lyric patched together to form a kind of diary of the soul – the whole enterprise invested with pathos because once the poem has been taken to the public's heart, it is no longer understood. 'It happens now and then', Eliot says in the 1936 essay on *In Memoriam*, 'that a poet by some strange accident expresses the mood of his generation, at the same time as he is expressing a mood of his own which is quite remote from that of his generation' – which is simply an echo of his own complaint five years earlier in 'Thoughts After Lambeth': 'when I wrote a poem called *The Waste Land* some of the more approving critics said that I had expressed the "disillusionment of a generation", which is nonsense. I may have expressed for them their own illusion of being disillusioned, but that did not form part of my intention.'

The chief approving critic Eliot had in mind was I. A. Richards – one of many writers (Herbert Read was another) who must often have thought they were following Eliot's lead only to find their work later adduced as a cautionary example of critical error by Eliot himself. In an article in *The Criterion* which became a chapter of *Science and Poetry* (1926), Richards cited the author of *The Waste Land* as a poet who had succeeded in 'effecting a complete separation between his poetry and *all* beliefs'. He intended this as praise; but Eliot understood it a little differently, and in 'A Note on Poetry and Belief' (1927), in *The Enemy*, he took exception to the implication that his poem was a testimony to the complete triumph of the scientific view over the religious in modern life. 'I cannot see that poetry can ever be separated from something which I should call belief, and to which I cannot see any reason for refusing the name of belief, unless we are to reshuffle names altogether.' But it takes only a little reshuffling to see the corner Richards had backed Eliot into; for if we call a 'belief' an 'idea' – that is, a consciously held view about the nature or meaning of experience – we run straight into the tangle of ideology in poetry that Eliot's own criticism had been designed to avoid.

The advantage of sensationalism is that an idea is given no greater standing in the materials of a poem than an image or a feeling – the basis, of course, of Eliot's famous praise of the metaphysical poets in 1921 ('A thought to Donne was an experience; it modified his sensibility'). The poet is the receptor rather than the originator of thought, and by virtue of this faculty becomes (though Eliot naturally avoids the expression) a true critic of life. The principle appears very early in Eliot's criticism, in his appreciation of Henry James. 'James's critical genius comes out most tellingly in his mastery over, his baffling escape from, Ideas', Eliot wrote in 1918. 'He had a mind so fine that no idea could violate it.'[19] In a review a year later of *The Education of Henry Adams*, in which Adams's sensibility is contrasted unfavourably with James's, this mastery is explicitly attributed to the sensuous capacity of James's mind ('certainly many men will admit that their keenest ideas have come to them with the quality of a sense-perception; and that their keenest sensuous experience has been "as if the body thought"').[20]

This standard makes it easy to disapprove of the kind of 'rumination' which Tennyson and Browning are accused of in 'The Metaphysical Poets'; but it runs two dangers. The first is that it makes the poet into a magpie, a mere basker in sensation for its own sake, and this is essentially

[19] T. S. Eliot, 'In Memory of Henry James', *Egoist*, 5 (1918), p. 2.
[20] T. S. Eliot, 'A Sceptical Patrician', *Athenaeum*, 23 May 1919, p. 362.

what Eliot accused Donne and Laforgue of, recanting his earlier judgements, when he delivered the Clark lectures at Cambridge University in 1926. The second is the danger Eliot kept having to confront as he backed away from the formalist principles of *The Sacred Wood*: that the critic will have no grounds for rating a poem that 'expresses' attractive ideas above a poem that 'expresses' inferior ones. Perfect allegiance to the worldview which informs the poem is obviously too strict a requirement; it is, in fact, counterinstinctual, since every reader of literature appreciates works which express a range of views much wider than his or her own particular beliefs. On the other hand, there must be an opening left for the critic to reject a poem solely because its views are simply unacceptable (as Eliot rejected Shelley, for instance); for, again, it is the common experience that in some cases the reader's beliefs do conflict with the writer's to a degree which makes appreciation impossible.

The line that separates the legitimate from the illegitimate introduction of belief into the terms of aesthetic judgement continually reappears in Eliot's comparisons between Dante and Shakespeare. An essay on Dante closes *The Sacred Wood*. It follows the essay on Blake, and the point of the juxtaposition – between a poet for whom philosophy was part of the ambience of his time and a poet who had to contrive a homemade mythological system (who, in the Arnoldian phrase, 'did not know enough') – is obvious. 'Dante, more than any other poet, has succeeded in dealing with his philosophy, not as a theory ... or as his own comment or reflection, but in terms of something *perceived*.' But it is the essay on *Hamlet*, earlier in the volume, that is the proper companion to 'Dante'; for Eliot's judgement there seems to be that Shakespeare was influenced by ideas which he picked up from Montaigne but which he did not have a sufficiently sensuous relation with to turn into art.

Still, Eliot was quite clear that Shakespeare's error could not have been helped by more thinking on his part. For Shakespeare's 'business', Eliot wrote in an essay on 'Shakespeare and Montaigne' in 1925, 'was to write plays, not to think'. It was Shakespeare's bad luck, Eliot continued two years later in 'Shakespeare and the Stoicism of Seneca', to live in 'a period of dissolution and chaos'. In such a time, 'any emotional attitude which seems to give a man something firm ... is eagerly taken up'; so that Shakespeare breathed an air that mixed 'the Senecan attitude of Pride, the Montaigne attitude of Skepticism, and the Machiavellian attitude of Cynicism' – all combining to produce 'the Elizabethan individualism'. This will not do as a worldview; but that cannot, Eliot insists, be counted against Shakespeare's poetry. And he proceeds to draw the comparison with Dante:

The difference between Shakespeare and Dante is that Dante had one coherent system of thought behind him; but that was just his luck, and from the point of view of the poetry is an irrelevant accident. It happened that at Dante's time thought was orderly and strong and beautiful ... Dante's poetry receives a boost which in a sense it does not merit, from the fact that the thought behind it is the thought of a man as great and lovely as Dante himself, St. Thomas. The thought behind Shakespeare is of men far inferior to Shakespeare himself... It does not make Dante a greater poet, or mean that we can learn more from Dante than from Shakespeare.

This looks as though it might be a promising way around the problem of poetry and belief, but there are several new difficulties, beginning with the question of whether Dante was not so great and lovely in the first place because, in fact, he had read Aquinas. There is, as well, the implication that Shakespeare's greatness is in some way connected to his having demonstrated the inadequacy of the worldview of 'Elizabethan individualism' – which, unless incoherent systems naturally criticise themselves, surely counts as praise for what Shakespeare 'thought'.

Eliot repeats his argument in 'Second Thoughts about Humanism' (1928): 'if you depreciate Shakespeare for his lower view of life, then you have issued out of literary criticism into social criticism ... I prefer the culture which produced Dante to the culture which produced Shakespeare; but I would not say that Dante was the greater poet, or even that he had the profounder mind.' That readers are being asked to draw a hard distinction between Dante the man and Dante the poet is stated explicitly in the little book on Dante Eliot published a year later. 'If you can read poetry as poetry', he goes on to say there, 'you will "believe" in Dante's theology exactly as you believe in the physical reality of his journey; that is, you suspend both belief and disbelief.' But when Eliot reaches the question of how we are to weigh the poetic value of Dante's beliefs, he makes an appeal that his own principles would seem to have ruled out of court: 'Goethe always arouses in me a strong sentiment of disbelief in what he believes: Dante does not.' 'Dante the man', in short, returns.

There are, then, belief systems to which even a formalist may object, and the problem is to define the threshold of acceptability in a sufficiently general and neutral way. Eliot attempted to do this in his Norton lectures, published in 1933 as *The Use of Poetry and the Use of Criticism*, by offering this guideline (in the lecture on Keats and Shelley):

When the doctrine, theory, belief, or 'view of life' presented in a poem is one which the mind of the reader can accept as coherent, mature, and founded on the facts of experience, it interposes no obstacle to the reader's enjoyment, whether it be one that he accept or deny, approve or deprecate. When it is one which the reader rejects as childish or feeble [as in Shelley's case], it may, for a reader of well-developed mind, set an almost complete check.

This calls for a standard of disinterestedness that might have given even Arnold some pause, since it assumes that it is possible to separate our notion of 'the facts of experience' from our particular 'view of life'.

When Eliot listed the worldview he considered intellectually legitimate, it turned out that he could name only two. 'Either everything in man can be traced as a development from below, or something must come from above', he asserts in 'Second Thoughts about Humanism'; 'you must be either a naturalist or a supernaturalist'. And in 'Modern Education and the Classics' (1932): 'There are two and only two finally tenable hypotheses about life: the Catholic and the materialistic.' Intellectually, this is a perfectly respectable position. The trouble with it is that neither the worldview of pure supernaturalism nor the worldview of pure materialism has any place in it for literature.

The weakness in Eliot's analysis of the problem of poetry and belief is its refusal to recognise that poetry itself has often been taken to constitute a belief system. Modern literature has always been read as embodying a set of values – not simply formal or aesthetic values – that occupy a middle ground between Eliot's two intellectually acceptable extremisms. Those values are not any more consistent than the values of, say, all of modern religion taken together, or all of modern philosophy. But they are not imported from philosophy or religion: they are values expressed through a certain strain of literature – through 'the tradition' as it was understood, and as Arnold, for instance, tried to interpret it, in the nineteenth century. This is the real significance of Eliot's formalism, and it takes us to the centre of his thought: the isolation of 'poetry as poetry' as the proper object of criticism was itself a judgement against the values of modern literature. As the first step in an antimodern reaction, though, formalism removed the grounds for further ideological critique. Having ruled 'extraliterary' motives out of the court of critical judgement, Eliot was compelled in effect to build another courtroom.

Eliot's thought is the sum of three kinds of writing: his literary criticism, his social and political criticism, and his poetry. The kinds complement each other but do not repeat each other, and each must be seen discretely before the full picture can emerge. The literary criticism, though it engages intermittently in theoretical inquiry, is largely practical, chiefly concerned with what a poet needs to know and think about the literature of the past. The social and political writing certainly does seek to intervene in the affairs of the day, but its stance is theoretical and interrogative: philosophical detachment, a disinterested examination of the intellectual merits of a given political position is what the times allegedly require – which is why, for example, the editor of *The Criterion*, unlike virtually every other intellectual in England, declined to take sides during the Spanish Civil

War. And the poetry gives us, so to speak, the prejudices – the 'feel' of modernity for a man of Eliot's principles and temperament. It is not entirely uncensored, but it operates with relative freedom in a realm generally kept out of bounds to the critical prose. One has only to reflect on how thoroughly Pound mixed his genres, and the effect the mixture produced, to appreciate Eliot's tact in keeping them separate.

Thus the difficulty of 'proving' the existence of views – for instance, antisemitism – that are not explicitly spelled out by Eliot himself. The remark about the undesirability of 'free-thinking Jews' in *After Strange Gods* belongs to a piece of theoretical speculation about the ideal community; the line 'The jew is underneath the lot' in 'Burbank with a Baedeker: Bleistein with a Cigar' (1919) (the lower-case 'j' is Eliot's original spelling) belongs to a poem constructed from literary references to Venice, and is thus among other things an allusion to Shakespeare's play. Each of these references to Jews is arguably a symptom of antisemitism, but the two sentences stand for quite different sets of prejudices. They are possibly defensible within the contexts in which they appear; and they do not add up to 'Eliot's view on the Jews'. But Eliot's writings all have a place, of course, within the larger story of Eliot's times, and it is the larger story that gives us some of the materials we need to begin to see how his thought hangs together.

By the time Eliot arrived in England, in 1914, the crucial turn in modernist thinking had already taken place. This was, to reduce it to a single episode, the reaction against Bergsonism. No aesthetic doctrine is more widely associated with literary modernism than the doctrine of the image, and no technique is more commonly cited in definitions of the modernist novel than 'stream of consciousness'. Both derived to a significant degree from Bergson's revision of empiricist epistemology, particular in the *Essai sur les données immédiates de la conscience* (1889), *Matière et mémoire* (1896), and *L'Évolution créatrice* (1907). But by 1912, the year Pound announced the existence of an imagist school of poetry, Bergson's chief literary disciple in England, T. E. Hulme, had already begun to turn against the master.[21]

Hulme was influenced by a book that had already received a good deal of attention in France, Pierre Lasserre's *Le romantisme français* (1907), an attack on cultural decadence. Lasserre argued that French culture was corrupted by a romanticism that had originated with Rousseau – 'le romantisme intégral', as Lasserre called him. Romanticism, on Lasserre's definition, was a cult of individuality, sentimentality, and perfectibilism; and against romanticism's 'generalisations monstrueuses de l'idée de volupté passive', he argued for a return to classicism. Much of *Le romanti-*

---

[21] See Michael Levenson, *A Genealogy of Modernism: A Study of English Literary Doctrine 1909–1922* (Cambridge, 1984), pp. 80–102.

sme français had first appeared in the *Revue de l'Action Française*, which Lasserre edited; for the attack on a romanticism conceived in those terms complemented the views of the leader of the Action Française, Charles Maurras, who had made classicism in art part of his nationalist and 'counter-revolutionary' political programme. Maurras's political views had, in fact, grown out of his own literary criticism: the Action Française began as a philosophical movement translating the principles of aesthetic order into principles of social and political order – and of the guarantors of political order, hierarchy and authority. 'We had seen the ruins in the realm of thought and taste before noticing the social, military, economic, and diplomatic damage that generally results from democracy,' Maurras wrote in 1920.[22]

In 1908 Lasserre became literary critic of the movement's new newspaper, *L'Action Française* (he would eventually break with Maurras and the Action Française, in 1914); and in 1911 he published there 'La Philosophie de Bergson', identifying Bergsonism with romanticism and condemning its emphasis on individuality, sensation, and irrationalism, and attacking Bergson for his Jewishness. The public celebration of the bicentennial of Rousseau's birth in June 1912 was aggressively protested by the Action Française, and by its youthful corps of activists, the 'camelots du roi', in particular; for it provided the movement with the opportunity to demonstrate a complicity between the ideals of romantic culture and the liberal politics of the Third Republic – together held responsible for a national decline that had begun with the defeat of 1870 and whose full extent had been made apparent in the Dreyfus affair. It was at about this time, in 1911 and 1912, that Hulme, who had been an admirer of the Action Française even during the period of his enthusiasm for Bergson, began producing his own articles promoting a return to classicism. 'Romanticism and Classicism' (ca. 1911) explicitly identifies the imagist preference for the 'hard' and precise against the vague and emotional in poetry as 'classical', though the Bergsonian faculty of 'intuition' continues to play a key role in the general aesthetic. In 'A Tory Philosophy' (1912), Hulme – following, he says, Lasserre and Maurras – contrasts a Rousseauistic romantic view, defined as 'the conception that anything that increases man's freedom will be to his benefit', with 'its exact opposite', the classical view, which holds that '[m]an is an extraordinarily fixed and limited animal whose nature is absolutely constant. It is only by tradition and organisation that anything decent can be got out of him.' By 1912, in other words, Hulme was already working toward the extreme position he would take in 'Humanism and the Religious Attitude' (first published as 'A Notebook by T. E. H.' in *The New Age* in 1915–16),

---

[22] Quoted in Eugen Weber, *Action Française: Royalism and Reaction in Twentieth-Century France* (Stanford, 1962), p. 9.

in which the doctrine of original sin becomes one component of a thorough-going antihumanist programme. 'Romanticism and Classicism' had spoken of 'a hundred years of romanticism'; in 'Humanism and the Religious Attiutude', romanticism essentially begins with the Renaissance.

Eliot's course did not exactly follow Hulme's, but it was propelled by the same currents. Eliot spent the academic year 1910–11 in Paris, where he attended Bergson's lectures at the Collège de France. He underwent, as he described it many years later, a 'temporary conversion'[23] to Bergsonism, and the influence of Bergson is palpable in his earliest modernist poems – particularly in the four 'Preludes' and 'The Love Song of J. Alfred Prufrock', all written around this time. Bergson is not the only influence on those poems, of course; for Eliot was also deeply affected by the nineteenth-century French poets whose work he had encountered in Arthur Symons's *The Symbolist Movement in Literature* (1899), which offers a transparently Paterian account of French symbolist practice, and which Eliot read (presumably in its second, expanded edition) at Harvard late in 1908. Eliot was, in short, very much formed as a poet by *le romantisme français* as it existed around the turn of the century.

So that when, during his first years in London, he was introduced by Pound to the criticism of Remy de Gourmont, he found Gourmont's conception of poetic style as the reflex of an entirely inner condition congenial; and Gourmont (who had himself been a minor symbolist poet) became one of the acknowledged sources of Eliot's brand of sensationalist aesthetics. Style, Gourmont explained in *Le problème du style* (1902), 'is a physiological product, and one of the most constant' – and this is the view that informs many of Eliot's early essays, notably those on Massinger (1920) and the metaphysical poets (1921). The phrase 'dissociation of sensibility' itself echoes language used by Gourmont in his essay on 'La Sensibilité de Jules Laforgue', printed in the first of the *Promenades littéraires* (1904). Eliot made Gourmont one of the heroes of 'The Perfect Critic' in *The Sacred Wood*, and the epigraph to that essay, from Gourmont's *Lettres à l'Amazone* (1914), indicates the extent to which, for Eliot, critical principles have their basis not in reason, but in sensation: 'Ériger en lois ses impressions personnelles, c'est le grand effort d'un homme s'il est sincère.' The existence of an objective correlative is known by the feeling the poem evokes: analysis of the sensation yields the critical principle. This is empirical enough for Eliot to be able to hint broadly in 'The Perfect Critic' that his own criticism is Aristotelean; but Pater's criticism is empirical in exactly the same sense, and Symons's fails only because it takes Paterianism to be a doctrine rather than a method.

[23] T. S. Eliot, *A Sermon Preached in Magdalen College Chapel* (Cambridge, 1948), p. 5.

Cutting against this whole conception of literary practices is Eliot's 'classicism', and this is where fitting the pieces together becomes problematic. 'I believe', Eliot writes in 'The Idea of a Literary Review', published as a kind of manifesto in *The Criterion* in 1926, 'that the modern tendency is toward something which, for want of a better name, we may call classicism... There is a tendency – discernible even in art – toward a higher and clearer conception of Reason, and a more severe and serene control of the emotions by Reason.' And he goes on to name six books that seem to him to exemplify this tendency (which his journal endorses): Charles Maurras's *L'Avenir de l'intelligence* (1905); Georges Sorel's *Réflexions sur la violence* (1907); Julian Benda's *Belphégor* (1918); Hulme's *Speculations* (1924); Jacques Maritain's *Réflexions sur l'intelligence* (1924); and Irving Babbitt's *Democracy and Leadership* (1925).

It is not easy to extract a common doctrine from these books. *Speculations*, to take the most obvious example, collects writings from Hulme's entire career, printing essays written under the influence of Bergson ('Bergson's Theory of Art', 'The Philosophy of Intensive Manifolds') alongside essays written under the influence of Worringer, and in reaction against Bergsonism ('Modern Art and Its Philosophy', 'Humanism and the Religious Attitude'). But there is nonetheless a kind of clubbiness about Eliot's list: Sorel's book had been translated into English by Hulme in 1916, and his introduction to the translation appears in an appendix in *Speculations*, the posthumous collection edited by Herbert Read, one of Eliot's assistants at *The Criterion*; Maritain, a *Criterion* contributor, was associated with Maurras and the Action Française as one of the founders and editors of the movement's *Revue universelle*, begun in 1920; when Benda's book was translated into English, a few years after Eliot's article appeared, the introduction was written by Babbitt, who had been one of Eliot's teachers at Harvard; and it was Babbitt who had first interested Eliot in *L'Avenir de l'intelligence*, which Eliot bought and read in 1910 or 1911, during his year in Paris. Eliot's list of works of 'classical' tendency in 1926 was not, in other words, an index of recent enthusiasms ('je peux témoigner de l'importante influence qu'ont eu sur mon développement intellectuel *L'Avenir de l'intelligence* et *Belphégor* (non que je veuille classer ensemble Maurras et Benda), et de même, sans doute, à une certaine époque, *Matière et mémoire*', he wrote in 1923 in the *Nouvelle revue française*). And although the publication of the list coincides with the general reconsideration of principles Eliot undertook after the publication of *The Waste Land* in 1922, he was already familiar with the complex of values the books represent.

Familiar enough, in fact, to have given a course on the subject. The 'Syllabus of a Course of Six Lectures on Modern French Literature by T.

Stearns Eliot, M. A.',[24] offered as part of the Oxford Extension programme in 1916, begins by noting that '[c]ontemporary intellectual movements in France must be understood as in large measure a reaction against the "romanticist" attitude of the nineteenth century'. According to the précis of the first lecture in the series, '[r]omanticism stands for *excess* in any direction. It splits up into two directions: escape from the world of fact, and devotion to brute fact. The two great currents of the nineteenth century – vague emotionality and the apotheosis of science (realism) alike spring from Rousseau', whose 'main tendencies' are enumerated as follows: 'Exaltation of the *personal* and *individual*'; 'Emphasis upon *feeling* rather than *thought*'; 'Humanitarianism: belief in the fundamental goodness of human nature'; and 'Depreciation of *form* in art, glorification of *spontaneity*'. The précis for Eliot's second lecture, 'The Reaction against Romanticism', opens: 'The beginning of the twentieth century has witnessed a return to the ideals of classicism. These may roughly be characterised as *form* and *restraint* in art, *discipline* and *authority* in religion, *centralization* in government (either as socialism or monarchy). The classicist point of view has been defined as essentially a belief in Original Sin – the necessity for austere discipline.' The rest of the course takes up the topics of nationalism, neo-Catholicism, and the movement 'away from both realism and purely personal expression of emotion' in literature; the writings of Maurice Barrès, Maurras, Lasserre, Charles Péguy, Sorel, Francis Jammes, and Paul Claudel; and the influence of Bergson, whose philosophy is summarised under the headings '(1) The use of science against science. (2) Mysticism. (3) Optimism.'

The sources of Eliot's conception of the antimodern movement are various, and not only French. The notion of the two nineteenth-century currents, naturalism and sentimentalism, flowing from Rousseau may have been taken from Paul Elmer More's *Aristocracy and Justice* (1915), which Eliot had reviewed appreciatively in *The New Statesman*. The identification of classicism with the doctrine of original sin is very likely from Hulme (whom Eliot never, in fact, met); and although none of Hulme's essays (then uncollected) is on the reading list for the course, his translations of Sorel and Bergson are – along with *L'Avenir de l'intelligence*, *Le romantisme français*, and Babbitt's *Masters of Modern French Criticism* (1912). The triumvirate of antimodern positions – classicism, monarchism, and Catholicism – which Eliot was to make famous when he declared his own allegiance to them many years later in the preface for *For Lancelot Andrewes* (1928) were explicitly Maurrasian: an article by Albert Thibaudet on 'L'Esthétique des trois traditions' in the *Nouvelle revue française* in 1913 describes Maurras's 'aesthetic' as 'classique,

---

[24] Reproduced in A. D. Moody, *Thomas Stearns Eliot, Poet* (Cambridge, 1979), pp. 41–9.

catholique, monarchique'. (Eliot's identification of Maurrasian royalism
with centralisation, though, is incorrect: Maurras was a monarchist, but
he favoured a decentralised political system. Bureaucracy is one of the
features of the liberal state Maurras inveighed against; it is opposed by
Sorelian syndicalist socialism, as well.) But Hulme had already presented
a similar package in 'A Tory Philosophy' (1912), which begins: 'It is my
aim to explain in this article why I believe in original sin, why I can't stand
romanticism, and why I am a certain kind of Tory.'

'Classicism', as Eliot uses the word when he is referring to this group of
writers, is simply a name for the reaction against liberalism and its culture.
That reactionary spirit is almost the only common denominator of Maurras's fascism, Sorel's socialism, Maritain's Thomism, Babbitt's humanism, and Hulme's antihumanism; and it makes 'classicism' an essentially
negative concept. The 'classicist' is in favour of any of those things the
liberal is supposed to imagine society can get along without: hierarchy,
faith, the higher (as opposed to utilitarian) rationality, the authority of
tradition, the sentiment of place. It follows that 'classicism' opposes
whatever is understood to threaten those virtues, and this is where the
position has its real bite. One example from Eliot's list of 1926 will
suggest how the classical critique works. Benda's *Belphégor: Essai sur
l'esthétique de la présente société française* was written mostly before
1914, but it was published in 1918. 'Some of us recognized [it]', Eliot later
recalled, 'as an almost final statement of the attitude of contemporary
society to art and the artist.'[25] Benda's book opens with a familiar,
Lasserrean attack on *le romantisme français*: 'Contemporary French Society demands that all works of art shall arouse emotion and sensation: it
insists that art shall cease to provide any form of intellectual pleasure.'
Immediacy, intuition, the 'romantic cult of originality' are named as the
characteristics of this art, and Bergson and William James are singled out
by Benda (as they are by Babbitt in *Masters of Modern French Criticism*)
as the philosophers of this aesthetic. The account is familiar; the question
Benda wants to address is how this had happened to French culture:
'Whence arises this frantic effort of present French society to force intellectual work into the realm of emotion?' One cause is 'the presence of the
Jews'. It is an explanation, he feels, that a racial analysis supports:
'Certain races seem to have an inherent rage for sensation which in other
races develops only in the course of years, just as certain species of animals
have by nature a certain virus which others have to acquire.' And this
helps to account for Bergson; for there are, it seems, two types of Jews:
'the severe, moralistic Jew, and the Jew who is always greedy for sensation
– speaking symbolically, the Hebrew and the Carthaginian, Jehovah and

---

[25] T. S. Eliot, 'The Idealism of Julien Benda', p. 105.

Belphegor [one of the Biblical names for Baal], Spinoza and Bergson'.

But this doesn't explain enough: 'I am willing to admit that present-day French society may have been precipitated into Alexandrianism by the influence of the Jews . . . But society was already Alexandrian.' There must be anterior causes, and Benda lists a few: the natural aging process of societies; 'the lowered standard of culture', which 'may be due to the entrance into French society of people of a different class, whose minds are in a state of nature (parvenus of trade, industry and finance, etc.)'; the disappearance of the leisure class; 'the enormous development of luxury in modern life'; and so forth. But one cause seems to him preeminent: 'one of the crucial reasons . . . why present French society's aesthetic is as we describe it, lies in the fact *that it is entirely created by women*'.

[A]ll the literary attributes exalted by contemporary aesthetics are those with which women are most highly endowed, and which form a kind of monopoly of their sex: absence of general ideas, cult of the concrete and circumstantiated, swift and entirely intuitive perception, receptiveness to sentiment alone, interest cen- tered on the self, the deepest, most intimate and most incommunicable self, etc. . . . The modern aesthetic is entirely made for women. Men struggle. Many try to imitate the literature of their rivals. Alas! They must succumb; there is a degree of unintellectuality and shamelessness to which they will never attain.

Women 'openly despise the mental structure of man and have set up a violent cult of the feminine soul . . . [T]hey alone of their class are now leading an easy, leisured existence; man is killing himself with work – and for them.' The same argument – that French culture has been poisoned by the influence of outsiders and women – is the burden of one of the four sections of *L'Avenir de l'intelligence*, 'Le romantisme féminin'. Romanti- cism, Maurras argues, is the literature of 'métèques indisciplinées'; it was introduced into France by foreigners, and its influence has been per- petuated by women.

Eliot shows the influence of the 'classical' line of thought most overtly not, as most commentators seem to assume, in his critical prose, but in his poetry. The poems through *The Waste Land* are saturated with images of social and cultural decadence, and the imagery is sometimes built on references to women and to Jews. It has been argued that the lines 'In the room the women come and go / Talking of Michelangelo' in 'The Love Song of J. Alfred Prufrock' (finished in 1911, shortly after Eliot's visit to Paris and his first reading of *L'Avenir de l'intelligence*) make no judge- ment about the quality of the talking the women engage in – that it is *their* prejudice, not Eliot's that has led readers to assume that the talk must be trivialising.[26] But if historical scholarship has any use at all, it surely gives us grounds for supposing that Eliot intended the lines to evoke an image of

---

[26] See Ricks, *T. S. Eliot and Prejudice*, pp. 12–24.

cultural debility, and precisely for the reason that they refer to women and not to men.

'Classical' thought also, of course, influenced Eliot's own social criticism, though here the differences are important. The theoretical community described in *The Idea of a Christian Society* (1939) was devised explicitly in reaction against the liberal society. And the emphasis on regionalism that characterises the arguments of *After Strange Gods* (1934) and the much more temperate *Notes towards the Definition of Culture* is designed as one way to make 'tradition' meaningful in a pluralistic age. On the other hand, Eliot was not, fundamentally, a nationalist. He took the position that culture is local, and that what is appropriate to Italy – as he speculated, in 'The Literature of Fascism' (1928) and elsewhere,[27] Mussolini's fascism might be – is probably for just that reason (and without inquiring much further into the matter) inappropriate to England. But he was not averse to transnational literary influences; the poetry makes that apparent. And his great crusade as an editor was on behalf of a pan-European culture, diversified according to language and regional tradition, though united as part of the civilisation of Western Christendom. Following the demise of *The Criterion* in January 1939 – the end of a decade in which, as Eliot put it in his final commentary, 'Last Words', '[t]he "European mind", which one had mistakenly thought might be renewed and fortified, disappeared from view' – Eliot's writing loses most of the stridency his campaign on behalf of 'classicism' had leant it, and takes up continually the subject of 'provincialism', which is a name for the inhibitions inflicted on the poet by his circumstances. This is the theme not only of *Notes towards the Definition of Culture*, but of much of the prose of the 1940s and 1950s. The lecture 'What Is a Classic?' (1944), for instance, which affirms the centrality of Virgil in European culture, is notable for its concessions to the difficulty English poets in particular have had in aspiring to the classical ideal of 'universality'. The most nearly classical period in English poetry is not, Eliot concedes, also the greatest period in English poetry.

Furthermore, Eliot's social views are more deeply informed by Christian faith than are those of, for instance, Maurras, who, though vociferously supportive of the Catholic church in France, was himself an atheist. Eliot may have wanted a religious state for some of the reasons Maurras wanted one – because it is conducive to moral order and to a mature acceptance of one's condition, for instance. But he also seems to have trusted in the redemptive power of Christianity as a spiritual force. This gives the antisemitism of *After Strange Gods* a different tilt from the antisemitism of the Action Française. Maurras's antisemitism (like

[27] See T. S. Eliot, 'A Commentary', *Criterion*, 7 (1928), p. 98.

Sorel's) derived from his reaction to the Dreyfus affair, which epitomised
for him the destructive consequences of the liberal concern for the individual at the expense of the group; Maurras first came to prominence as a
political figure, in fact, when he published an article in the *Gazette de
France* declaring Hubert Henry, the admitted forger of the evidence
against Dreyfus, a patriot. But the antisemitism of the Action Française
was an aspect of its extreme nationalism, and Maurras maintained it
(campaigning against Bergson's admission to the French Academy, for
instance) partly in hopes of attracting adherents among the masses by
exploiting what he took to be their inherent dislike of foreigners in general
and Jews in particular.[28] Eliot, though, was not a demagogue, or in any
sense a party man (he later felt that if Maurras had not made himself the
leader of a political movement, his ideas would have had greater effect).[29]
For Eliot, the exclusion of 'free-thinking Jews' from the ideal community
is a function first of his requirement that the members of the community
share a homogenous cultural and religious tradition, and secondly of his
desire that that tradition be Christian. Eliot did not, on the evidence of his
writings, dislike Jews (though there are a few disparaging remarks about
individual Jews in his correspondence); and he did not regard them as a
corrupting social element specifically because of their Jewishness. He
simply did not care about them. When the Pope condemned the Action
Française in 1926, and placed *L'Avenir de l'intelligence*, among other
writings, on the Index (making public an act that had been performed
secretly in 1914), Maritain, as a Catholic, broke with the movement. But
Eliot (rather slyly) took advantage of his Anglicanism to defend Maurras
at length in *The Criterion* in 1928, naming Maurras's influence on his own
religious development as one argument against the presumption that 'the
influence of Maurras . . . is to pervert his disciples and students away from
Christianity'.[30] And in 1948, three years after Maurras had been sen-
tenced to life imprisonment by a French court for collaboration with the
enemy – 'C'est la revanche de Dreyfus!' he cried when the sentence was
read'[31] – Eliot published a tribute to him, 'Hommage à Charles Maurras',
in the French paper *Aspects de la France et du monde*. If the situation of
Jews in Europe was not clear in 1928, it had certainly become clear by
1948; but that seems to have made no difference to Eliot's intellectualised
politics.

    When we reach the area of Eliot's literary criticism, we find that this
whole complex of social and political views, which constitutes his primary
intellectual base of reference from his earliest modernist poems up to the

---

[28] See Weber, *Action Française*, p. 199.
[29] See T. S. Eliot, *To Criticize the Critic and Other Writings* (London, 1965), pp. 142–3.
[30] T. S. Eliot, 'The *Action Française*, M. Maurras, and Mr. Ward', *Criterion*, 7 (1928),
       p. 202.   [31] Weber, *Action Française*, p. 475.

time of *Four Quartets*, fades into the woodwork. Eliot's judgements of particular writers, and to some extent his general scheme of literary history, coincide with the 'classicist' view of modernity; but the connection is almost never made explicitly, and Eliot generally discourages readers from drawing larger cultural lessons from his critical opinions (one of the reasons he sometimes seems to have gone out of his way to confound his followers by reversing his positions on some writers).

Although Eliot dedicated his 1929 volume on Dante to Maurras, and although it is evident that his admiration for Dante reflects a social and religious preference as well as a literary one, Eliot is always careful to make his standards of appreciation for Dante literary ones. The disparagement of Milton, in 'The Metaphysical Poets' and 'A Note on the Verse of John Milton' (1936), presumably has a political motivation, but the argument is always directed to poetic technique – formalist neutral ground. So that when Eliot blames Miltonic diction and versification for the aggravation of the dissociation of sensibility in English poetry, he is partly echoing the analysis of John Middleton Murry, no enemy of 'romanticism', who had argued in an essay that appeared six months before 'The Metaphysical Poets' that 'English blank verse has never recovered from Milton's drastic surgery; he abruptly snapped the true tradition, so that no one, not even Keats, much less Shelley or Swinburne or Browning, has ever been able to pick up the threads again.' (It is characteristic of his relations with Murry that when Eliot undertook to resurrect Milton in 1947, Murry was the critic he attacked for taking too severe a view of Milton's influence.)

The theory of the 'dissociation of sensibility' used to depreciate nineteenth-century British poetry can be seen to belong (as Eliot himself acknowledged in the second Milton essay) to a larger view of English political and religious history involving the consequences of the English Civil War. But Eliot himself never names a particular cause for the dissociation. The quotations from Chapman and Browning that Eliot uses to illustrate his argument express explicitly opposed worldviews; but so little attention is drawn to this fact by the rest of the essay that most readers assume that the quotations illustrate a stylistic development rather than an ideological one, and take the argument to be about changes in the nature of the figurative language of poetry. Given the identification between physiology and style upon which the whole notion of the dissociation of sensibility rests, Eliot could hardly have pointed out what his own quotations showed, since that would have meant attributing, in violation of sensationalist principles, significance to what writers consciously thought rather than to their style of symptomising. And, finally, although the doctrine of impersonality and the valorisation of tradition take on an extraliterary significance in the context of the 'classical' view, extraliter-

ary values are not made part of the discussion in 'Tradition and the
Individual Talent'. The 'classicism' in Eliot's literary criticism, in short, is
generally no more classical than the 'classicism' of Matthew Arnold, and
his whole conception of poetic sensibility and poetic practice is clearly
rooted in the nineteenth century. He often managed to recast nineteenth-
century literary values in a neoclassical-sounding language of decorum, as
in the case of the objective correlative; but there is nothing even spuriously
neoclassical about Eliot's view of poetry. Even the discontent with modernity is a modern literary attitude.

Where Eliot departed from most nineteenth-century critics, and particularly and explicitly from Arnold, was the issue of the social function of
literature. He agreed with Arnold that the progress of modernity entailed
the collapse of traditional institutions of moral authority (the church and
the hereditary aristocracy) but he did not believe that literature could
supply the missing element, that 'poetry will save us'. '[I]t is like saying
that the wall-paper will save us when the walls have crumbled'[32] was
Eliot's response when Richards echoed Arnold's line in *Science and Poetry*
(1926). The notion that literature could be successfully endowed with a
social or religious function was misconceived, he thought, and it led to
what he regarded as the central failing of modern thought, the confusion
of genres: poetry tried to be philosophy, literary criticism tried to be moral
or political criticism, the aesthetic experience proposed itself as a substitute for the religious experience (and conversely: philosophy became
literary or transcendentalist, religion became aestheticised or reform-
minded, and so forth).

'By showing where moral truth and the genuine supernatural are situate', writes Maritain in *Art et scholastique* (1920), 'religion saves poetry
from the absurdity of believing itself destined to transform ethics and life:
saves it from overweening arrogance.' Eliot quotes the sentence in the
chapter on 'The Modern Mind' in *The Use of Poetry and the Use of
Criticism*, and adds: 'This seems to me to be putting the finger on the great
weakness of much poetry and criticism of the nineteenth and twentieth
centuries.' He is a little shy, in 'The Modern Mind', about identifying this
confusion as 'romantic' (the essay is one of the places in which the
usefulness of the terms 'romantic' and 'classical' is questioned) but the
idea that romanticism blurs distinctions is an essential item in the 'classical' complaint.

Thus Eliot's insistence on treating poetry 'as poetry' by developing a
critical vocabulary that does not borrow from nonliterary genres. Even
after he had embarked, in the mid-1920s, on the task of finding an ethical
supplement to his criticism, Eliot persisted in citing this fundamental

[32] T. S. Eliot, 'Literature, Science, and Dogma', *Dial*, 82 (1927), p. 243.

principle, and Samuel Johnson, quoted as an exemplary critic in the introduction to *The Sacred Wood*, remained the touchstone. Neoclassical criticism, Eliot writes in 'Experiment in Criticism' (1929),

> recognized literature as literature, and not another thing ... [I]f you compare the criticism of those two centuries [the seventeenth and eighteenth] with that of the nineteenth, you will see that the latter does not take this simple truth wholly for granted. Literature is often treated by the critic rather as a means for eliciting truth or acquiring knowledge ... If you read carefully the famous epilogue in Pater's *Studies in the Renaissance* you will see that 'art for art's sake' means nothing less than art as a substitute for everything else, and as a purveyor of emotions and sensations which belong to life rather than to art ... I think we should return again and again to the critical writings of the seventeenth and eighteenth centuries, to remind ourselves of that simple truth that literature is primarily literature, a means of refined and intellectual pleasure.

'The Frontiers of Criticism' (1956), one of Eliot's last major essays, virtually repeats sections of 'Experiment in Criticism'; and the appeal, this time in an argument against the excessive use of scholarship in criticism, is to the same standard: 'We can ... ask about any writing which is offered to us as literary criticism, is it aimed towards understanding and enjoyment? If it is not, it may still be a legitimate and useful activity; but it is to be judged as a contribution to psychology, or sociology, or logic, or pedagogy, or some other pursuit – and is to be judged by specialists, not by men of letters.'

This divorce of literary criticism from other kinds of intellectual activity is one of the central reasons for the social and institutional success of Eliot's criticism. Most obviously, it enabled critics who held antagonistic political or religious principles to make use of Eliot's critical terms without the need for ideological disclaimers. Anyone can speak of an 'objective correlative'; it is not necessary also to believe that modern scepticism is insufficient as a worldview, and the formula doesn't require it, since Eliot never made the connection between the technical formula and counter-modernity explicit in his essay. But Eliot's criticism was also successful because it answered a specifically modern need to make literary criticism an autonomous discipline. This need was the consequence of the emergence of the modern university, with its formally defined disciplines and its scientist organisation of knowledge production. Eliot was not an academic critic. He had, as a young man in London, deliberately chosen a different path. But in reacting against what he took to be one of the principal errors of modern thought, Eliot produced a criticism that could be understood as presenting a highly disciplined theory of poetry and critical method. The specialisation and professionalisation Eliot's criticism seemed to represent were perfectly compatible with the division of labour in a modernised society, and in particular with the division of the business of inquiry within the research university. It was by 'curing' the modern error of mixing literature and criticism with nonliterary discourses that Eliot, contrary to anything he might have intended, ended up making a significant contribution to the culture of modernity.

2

Ezra Pound

A. Walton Litz and Lawrence Rainey

More than a quarter-century after his death, Ezra Pound remains the most controversial poet of the twentieth century. For some, his poetry lacks intellectual depth and emotional resonance. Its notoriety is the result of unconventional posing rather than a genuine contribution to the poetic tradition, and the many poets who have been beguiled by his example, chiefly Americans, have been misled into a sterile bypath. For others, his poetry retains a freshness, concreteness, and rhythmic power unmatched by any poet of the twentieth century. His irreverent posturing offers a salutary fillip toward reconsidering the task of poetry in advancing modernity, and his many imitators are a testimony to the enduring power of his achievement. Such conflicting evaluations are further complicated by the ongoing debate about Pound's politics – his interest in Mussolini, which began in 1923 and 1924 (not long after Mussolini's arrival in power in late October 1922), and his later anti-semitism, which swells into a consuming passion during the later 1930s. Pound's position within the canon will always be precarious, if only because his art and his life were equally reckless; and while some deplore the ongoing debate about Pound, viewing it as a slight to his achievement, many welcome it as a sign of the urgency that attaches to the questions posed by his career, questions so central to the intersection of ethics and aesthetics in late modernity that it would be unwise to muffle them with the reverential silence that can attend canonical status. 'He was one of us only, pure prose', Robert Lowell once wrote of Mussolini, and much the same might be said of Pound.

Although many would dispute Pound's poetic achievement and all will disagree with his political choices, at least by this point in time, few would deny the impact that his critical writings have had on the history of modern poetry and letters. For better or worse, they electrified the atmosphere of Anglo-American letters for decades, and even today they have a cheeky brusqueness that is alternately gladdening and annoying. Strangely, it is only recently that critics have attempted to assess Pound's critical writings in a more systematic fashion.[1] The task is formidable. In the

---

[1] See K. K. Ruthven, *Ezra Pound as Literary Critic* (London, 1990) and Ghan Shyam Sing, *Ezra Pound as Critic* (Basingstoke, 1994). The latter is a piece of uncritical hero-worship; the former a masterful tour of Pound's entire career.

course of his career, Pound wrote thousands of essays, reviews, squibs, and opinion pieces of various kinds. 'One work of art is worthy forty prefaces and as many apologiae', he once opined.[2] But his own output of critical writing was nothing less than prodigious.

Pound's criticism falls neatly into two phases, divided – as his whole poetic life was divided – by the decision to settle in Italy in 1924, a decision that led to an increasing concentration on social and political issues. The criticism of 1910–24, instead, was written during a period when Pound was deeply involved in the making of modernist literature, and when his discerning judgement led him to identify and promote the genius of Joyce, Frost, Eliot, Williams, Moore, H. D., Loy, and many others. It begins with his early investigations into medieval literature in *The Spirit of Romance* (1910), a youthful work which today is of interest chiefly to scholars, and his extensive essay, 'I Gather the Limbs of Osiris' (1911–12). Then follows the heyday of Imagism (1912–13) and Vorticism (1914–15), as well as his early speculations on the ideogram. The sheer velocity of Pound's development in these years can prove confusing.

Not only are the bulk and pace of his publications daunting, but their raw contemporaneity – the way they respond to a multiplicity of contexts – can make it difficult for the later reader, who now approaches the essays more than eighty years after they were first published, to assay their significance. Often they read like battle reports from the front lines of some vast polemical struggle; but the logic of individual skirmishes when glimpsed through the smoke and haze of battle, that notorious 'fog of war', can seem strangely hard to grasp. Later literary history has often cast Pound in the role of master strategist, carefully planning and conducting his campaigns. The truth is that he was much more like a field commander, responding *ad hoc* to changing contingencies whose significance would become clear only much later, when the battle was over. Pound was a skilful literary tactician, and his tactical talents were sharpened by his astute insight into the array of institutions that constitute literature as a field of cultural production, his keen capacity to see how the conflicting imperatives that guided authors, publishers, patrons, editors, readers, book-dealers, and collectors could overlap or converge in ways that might permit the construction of alternative institutional structures, fragile and yet functional, in which the work of modernism could get done. As a result, Pound's critical writings differ from those of many of his contemporaries. He offers not the tranquil meditations of Henry James or the alert responsiveness of Virginia Woolf, but an edgy polemicism that can be by turns provocative, cheering, irritating, or exasperating. The enduring value of his critical writing does not reside in its closure or complete-

---

[2] Ezra Pound, 'The Serious Artist', in *Literary Essays of Ezra Pound*, ed. T. S. Eliot (New York, 1968), p. 41.

ness, or in the considered and definitive statement, but in its fragmentary openness, its often flawed and yet always challenging response to new developments at once literary, cultural, and institutional, its imperfect and yet persistent attempt to ponder the status of poetry and literary art in a world that was changing with remarkable speed.

When Pound moved to London in late 1908, he entered into a metropolitan vortex that housed a great many different, often competing and conflicting worlds, a vortex to which he brought his own limited, though equally heterogenous, experience. His conservative and middle-class background was more than counterbalanced by bohemian postures derived from his literary reading, while his educational experiences at Hamilton College and the University of Pennsylvania had widened his horizons to include the emerging world of academic culture. After a brief but frustrating tenure as an academic at Wabash College in Crawfordsville, Indiana, Pound had set out for Venice, then London. A course of lectures that he gave at the London Polytechnic, devoted to the Provençal poets, soon brought him to the attention of Olivia Shakespear, a gifted though minor novelist who was married to a successful solicitor. Through her Pound gained access to a literary world that included the poet he admired more than any other, W. B. Yeats, and it was not long before he published his first poem in *The English Review*, a prominent literary journal then under the editorship of Ford Madox Ford. Yet for Pound the most significant event of his first year abroad took place not in London, but in Paris, where he stopped briefly in March 1910 while en route for a projected holiday in Italy. There he met Margaret Cravens, a thirty-year-old American who was studying music while tasting the pleasures of wealthy bohemia. Almost instantly she offered to become his patron, and for a period that lasted a little over two years (until her suicide in June 1912), Cravens furnished Pound with £200 (or $1000) per year.[3] It was Pound's principal source of income, and without it he might not have survived. Patronage had several effects on Pound. It freed him from the demands of the contemporary market for poetry, allowing him to pursue his own development. But it also encouraged that part of his thinking which owed much to his long study of the culture of Provence, a view that poetry flourished best in an aristocratic world that was essentially premodern, untouched by the coarse exigencies of capitalism.

After a return to the United States that was protracted by illness (June 1910 to July 1911), Pound moved back to London. His return prompted him to take up critical writing in earnest. He did so partly to earn money – Craven's subsidy furnished a reasonable income, but it required supplements – and partly to intervene more actively in contemporary literary

[3] See Omar Pound and Robert Spoo, eds., *Ezra Pound and Margaret Cravens: A Tragic Friendship, 1910–1912* (Durham, 1988).

debate, especially concerning poetry. To be sure, there was scarcely any debate in London in which to intervene. The audience for poetry was exiguous, and the 300–400 volumes of it that were published annually lay largely unread. Publishers such as Elkin Mathews, whose sign above his shop in Vigo Street identified him as a 'Vendor of Choice and Rare Editions in Belles Lettres', responded to this decline in sales by reducing print runs to ever smaller levels, adding finer paper, better printing and choicer bindings to give each book the air of genteel rarity that might appeal to collectors, if not readers. Pound published his first three books in London with Mathews (*Personae* (1909), *Exultations* (1909), and *Canzoni* (1910)), and they were all of this sort. Mathews had the printing done at the Chiswick Press, a 'fine' or deluxe printer; he kept the print runs down to 1,000 copies, and of those he bound only 250. Yet Mathews's sense of the market for poetry was fairly sound, as other evidence shows.

In February 1909, Galloway Kyle had founded the Poetry Recital Society, which was first intended to initiate modest reforms in elocution, but which soon expanded its range of interests and changed its name to the Poetry Society. The Society published a *Journal* (June 1909) which soon changed its name to *The Poetical* (October 1909) and then to *The Poetical Gazette* (February 1910), essentially a newsletter which recorded Society readings and soirees. The occasions were largely 'an excuse for pleasant social exchanges' and 'irrelevant snobbery', according to one historian.[4] But in late 1911 the Society unexpectedly accepted the proposal put forth by one of its members, Harold Monro, that it publish a monthly *Poetry Review*. (All expenses would be defrayed by Monro, while any profits at year's end would accrue to the Society.) Monro would edit it, while the Society would guarantee a purchase of 1,000 copies – exactly the same figure that Mathews adopted for his press runs.

Monro (1879–1932), who had been educated at Radney public school and Caius College, Cambridge, was the son of a prosperous civil engineer and had inherited a modest independence. After a year he quarrelled with the conservative Society and in 1913 went on to found a new journal, *Poetry and Drama*, which lasted for two years (1913–14). The new journal was complemented by Monro's shop, The Poetry Bookshop, a more enduring venture that lasted until 1935. Yet neither of these ventures was self-sustaining: as Monro's wife recalled, the shop 'always depended for its survival on the ... financial help that we were able to give it', and the same had been true of *Poetry and Drama*.[5] Poetry, to survive in the twentieth century, needed patronage. But that, in turn, posed other prob-

---

[4] Joy Grant, *Harold Monro and the Poetry Bookshop* (London, 1976), p. 36. My view of Monro is indebted to Grant's account throughout.
[5] Alida Monro, circular letter to patrons of The Poetry Bookshop, June 1935, quoted in Grant, *Harold Monro*, p. 165.

lems. For patronage is an essentially pre-modern form of social exchange, and its seemingly arbitary, and capricious character – by what criteria is someone tapped to be a recipient of patronage? is it merely dumb luck? the result of personal friendship? – is at odds with the meritocratic ethos and impersonal norms of assessment which characterise modern professional and expert systems. It also posed practical problems. Monro, for example, could provide only enough to support his journal and store, but not enough to help poets themselves. The only alternative seemed to be the strategy of Elkin Mathews, which replaced active readers with prosperous collectors of 'Choice and Rare Editions'; but whatever profit there was accrued to Mathews, not the poets. Such were the conflicting imperatives that governed poetry as an institution, at least as Pound experienced them in early 1912.

His divided response can be traced in his contemporary criticism. Beginning in late November 1911, Pound began to write regularly for *The New Age*. The weekly journal, financed with money by dissident members of the Fabian Society, was edited by Alfred Richard Orage and dedicated to the promotion of Guild Socialism, an uneasy amalgam of ideas which urged that workers could restore the dignity of work by returning to a guild structure (rather than a union). The journal's cultural coverage was more eclectic, hosting a variety of viewpoints, and Pound received a guinea (or £1 1s) for each contribution. It was not a mean sum, though it was also far from princely. On the eve of the Great War, the average industrial adult male worker earned £75 per annum, or roughly £1 5s per week, whereas the average annual income of the salaried class was about £340.[6] Such distinctions were not lost on Pound. He was courting Olivia Shakespear's daughter, and her family had resolutely forbidden them from marrying until Pound could show that he had an income of £500 per year.

Apart from the weekly *New Age*, where he appeared eighteen times in 1912, Pound also wrote *gratis* contributions for the monthly *Poetry Review* edited by Monro. In 1912 he made four appearances in the February, March, and October numbers: a group of eight poems, a critical essay that prefaced them ('Prolegomena'), a book review, and an introductory note to a group of poems by another author which Pound had selected. In addition to these two periodicals, only one other received sustained attention from Pound in 1912, and then not until much later in the year – *Poetry*, a new monthly which was published from Chicago and which issued its first number in October. Pound published three times in *Poetry* in 1912: two poems in its first number (October 1912); a book review in its second (November 1912); and an introductory note to

---

[6] Arthur Marwick, *The Deluge* (Boston, 1965), p. 23, citing Arthur Lyon Bowley, *The Division of the Product of Industry* (Oxford, 1919), p. 18.

accompany some poems by Rabindranath Tagore in its third (December 1912). *Poetry* was financed by a group of one hundred donors whose support had been solicited by the indefatigable Harriet Monroe, and unlike *The Poetry Review* it could afford modest payments. Its arrival on the scene meant that Pound could dispense with contributing to Monro's journal, if he so chose. When Monro went on to found and edit his successor to *The Poetry Review*, *Poetry and Drama* (1913–14), Pound gave it only three contributions in a two-year span.

'I Gather the Limbs of Osiris', which appeared in *The New Age* in twelve parts from November 1911 through February 1912, is Pound's most important essay in the period prior to the invention of Imagism.[7] True, it is not a typical essay: sections in prose alternate with sections in verse, the verse being Pound's translations from Provençal poets such as Arnaut Daniel or Italian poets such as Guido Cavalcanti and Dante. While this structure implicitly asserts the interdependence of critical and creative activities, it also introduces a disparity into the essay's tone, an uneasy oscillation between the etiolated ornateness of the poems and the modern informality of the prose. The essay is addressed to an educated readership that has 'advanced' political and cultural tastes, readers potentially receptive to its arguments, and to ensure its appeal to them Pound adopts two of the period's most dominant idioms.

One idiom derives from the long and recently renewed debate on art and life, a vast discussion whose origins go back almost two centuries, receding into the very foundation of modern aesthetics by Shaftesbury, Baumgarten, and Kant. By 1836 the French poet Théophile Gautier had written the 'Preface' to his novel *Mademoiselle du Maupin* (1836), in which he formulated the classic expression of one extreme pole in the debate, declaring the categorical independence of *l'art pour l'art*, art for art's sake. Art, in Gautier's view, was wholly opposed to utility and life. Gautier's discussion would prompt the more probing reflections of Baudelaire in his celebrated essays on 'The Poetic Principle' (1850) and 'New Notes on Edgar Poe' (1859), and the work of both authors would migrate across the English Channel to reappear in complex ways in the works of Ruskin, Pater, Swinburne, and Wilde.[8] But by the 1890s there was a perceptible shift in the balance of opinion. Oscar Wilde's trial and

---

[7] Ezra Pound, 'I Gather the Limbs of Osiris', in *Ezra Pound's Poetry and Prose*, ed. Leah Baechler, James Longenbach, and A. Walton Litz (New York, 1991), vol. 1. All further references are given within the text; to help readers locate quotations, 'a' or 'b' are used to designate which of the two columns a quotation appears in. The other key essay from this period is 'Prolegomena', which first appeared in *Poetry Review*, 1.2 (February 1912), pp. 72–6; it is now reprinted in *Ezra Pound's Poetry and Prose*, vol. 1, pp. 59–63. All further references are given within the text; citations from this essay are not followed by references to columns, as the text was originally printed across the entire page.

[8] On this vast debate, see Gene H. Bella-Villada, *Art for Art's Sake* (Lincoln, Nebr., 1996).

conviction in 1895 cast discredit on the notion of art for art's sake, while the same period witnessed the rise of Henri Bergson and his philosophical outlook postulating the existence of an *élan vital* ('life force') which was opposed to, and transcended, the mechanism and fatalism of advancing science. In Edwardian Britain, more specifically, there was also an upsurge of interest in the work of Samuel Butler, whose emphasis on 'life' and 'will' became the focus of renewed discussion when his novel *The Way of All Flesh*, was published posthumously in 1903 and his ideas were popularised by George Bernard Shaw in *Man and Superman* (1904). By 1912, as T. E. Hulme complained, 'All the best people take off their hats and lower their voices when they speak of Life.'[9]

Pound, in 'I Gather the Limbs of Osiris', appeals to the increasingly widespread reaction against the late Victorian cults of art and decadence, and the correspondingly enthusiastic embrace of that ambiguous notion, 'Life'. 'I am more interested in life', Pound proclaims early in his essay, 'than in any part of it' (45b). The Provençal poet Arnaut Daniel, notwithstanding his notoriously difficult style, is praised because he portrays 'medieval life as it was' (50a). Poetry must once more aspire 'to be a vital part of contemporary life' (69a), while only perdition awaits the 'writer that thinks from books, convention, and *cliché*, and not from life', Pound writes in a contemporaneous essay, 'Prolegomena' (63). However variously, Pound plants himself unequivocally on the side of 'life' over 'art'. Though he has often been charged with fostering a mandarin formalism, it is not an accusation that will bear scrutiny. Indeed, Pound's later interests in social criticism and politics have their origins in this early and consistent critical bias.

There is a second idiom that also appears throughout 'I Gather the Limbs of Osiris' – the vocabulary of efficiency. 'Efficiency', one historian has noted, 'was one of the great shibboleths of the Edwardian period', a favourite byword that was invoked by everyone from reformers of the army and navy to social workers and scientific researchers.[10] And the epitome of efficiency was the engineer, the technocrat whose only criteria were the impersonal standards of utility and efficiency, whose decisions were outside, beyond, or even above the mundane realm of ideology. The rhetoric of efficiency is pervasive in 'I Sing the Limbs of Osiris'. The humanities, Pound urges right at the start, should follow the proceedings of 'technical and practical education' (44b), where the goal is to 'make a man more efficiently useful to the community'. Likewise, 'when it comes to presenting matters to the public, there are certain forms of … effi-

---

[9] Quoted in Jonathan Rose, *The Edwardian Temperament, 1895–1919* (Athens, Ohio, 1986), p. 74. See Rose's entire discussion on 'The Meanings of Life', pp. 74–116.
[10] Rose, *The Edwardian Temperament*, p. 117; see his entire discussion in chapter 4, 'The Efficiency Men', pp. 117–61.

ciency to be considered' (44b). What characterises the engineer, of course, is precision – and so also the poet. The poet Guido Cavalcanti is praised because he renders emotions 'precisely' (47a). The poet Arnaut Daniel has felt a hunger to unite sense, sound, and rhythm, but felt it 'more precisely than his fellows' (49b). What Dante learns from Arnaut Daniel is that same 'precision of observation and reference' (49b). The special quality of both Cavalcanti and Daniel, not surprisingly, is 'a virtue of precision'. If it is not 'precision' that Pound prizes, then it is its variant, accuracy. 'Obviously we must know accurately a great many facts' (44b). 'Accuracy of sentiment here will make more accurate the sentiment of the growth of literature as a whole' (45a). Arnaut Daniel, once again, is 'accurate in his observation of nature' (49b). The problem with many people is that they don't 'have any exact, effable concept' of what they mean (57a). Technique in the arts is 'the means of conveying an exact impression of exactly what one means' (57b). Likewise, 'three or four words in exact juxtaposition' suffice to achieve an aesthetic miracle, but their juxtaposition really 'must be exact' (58a), and their form must be 'exactly adjusted' (69a).

'I Gather' also abounds in metaphors from the world of recent engineering. Important facts 'govern knowledge as the switchboard governs an electric circuit' (44b). The reader who encounters unfamiliar poems is like the layman who has entered 'into the engineering laboratory' and sees 'successively an electric engine, a steam-engine, a gas-engine, etc.' The power of these machines is entrusted 'to the engineer in control', who by now is obviously a figure for the poet (48b). Words 'are like great hollow cones of steel', and we must 'imagine them charged with a force like electricity'. Above all, the engineer's aesthetic demands that the cones be made 'to act without waste ' (58a). Instead, the engineer-poet must ensure that 'the force' of his words is 'multiplied' (58a). Other verbal counterparts to 'force' are 'intensity' and 'energy'. What distinguishes every individual is 'some peculiar and intense way' of perceiving the world. What great classics of art possess is beauty, but beauty of 'greater intensity' (53b). And just as the poet-engineer controls 'this peculiar energy which fills the cones' (58a), so the critic or scholar who acts like him will present 'the energetic part of his knowledge' (69a). The 'force' or 'intensity' or 'energy which fills the cones', Pound eventually informs us, is 'the power of tradition', and what regulates that power is what Pound calls 'the gauge' of technique. Here, in a nutshell, is Pound's earliest model for understanding literary creation. The 'force' or 'energy' of tradition is regulated by 'the gauge' of technique, which is under the control of the poet-engineer, who in turn has constructed 'engines' of words ('an electric engine, a steam-engine, a gas-engine, etc.' (48b)). Sometimes, as here, Pound seems to distinguish carefully between 'the engineer' and the machine that he controls; but other times, as in his discussion of the 'intensity' which characterises the individual, his rhetoric works to conflate the two, blurring together the engineer, the machine, and the forces which they produce. It matters very little, however. In one sense, Pound is doing little more than reproducing a Romantic notion of the artist as an expressive individuality, but draping it under the period's techno-language. Yet in another sense, Pound is doing something quite different, for at certain key points his notion of expressive individuality gives way. What really drives the 'cones' that are like words is 'the power of tradition'. Likewise, Pound evinces only scorn for 'critics who think I should be more interested in the poetry which I write myself than in "fine poetry as a whole"'. After all, he urges, 'the *corpus poetarum*' (or the whole body of poets) is 'of more importance than any cell or phalange' (45b). This conflict, between an impulse toward anonymity or collectivity (tradition, the *corpus poetarum*, fine poetry as a whole) and an equally insistent impulse toward individuation, toward an emphasis on the 'intensity' of the individual poet ('the truth is the individual' (57b)), is one that is never resolved in Pound's critical writings. Nor need it be, for in Pound's hands it becomes a productive contradiction that accounts for so much of what is distinctive about his aesthetics and poetics, which can be viewed as neo-romantic or seen as neo-classical with equal validity, precisely because Pound nowhere resolves this central question. For this same reason, critics of equal good will can find that Pound's emphasis on impersonality results in an open poetics that corrodes or subverts the autonomy of the traditional bourgeois subject, or that his emphasis on the particular 'intensity' of each poet reinforces a late romantic cult of genius and an individualistic subjectivity which, to critics from the left, is a pernicious illusion.

Four more points need to be made about this early and crucial essay. One is the way in which Pound's rhetoric of technical expertise sometimes shades over into a slightly different register, one that leaves the cool gleam of the engineering aesthetic for the warmer glow of aristocratic refinement. One can see this elision take place from one sentence to the next, as the term 'precision' gives way to 'fineness'. 'In each case their virtue is a virtue of precision. In Arnaut, as I have said before, this fineness...' (54a). Again, what characterises Arnaut Daniel is a sense of 'fineness' (as in the word, refinement), a 'fastidious' distaste for redundancy or crudeness (49b). 'We advance by discriminations' (48a), Pound tells us, and in particular 'the artist discriminates' or draws still finer distinctions between 'one kind of indefinability and another' (57b), always striving for 'an entanglement of words so subtle, so crafty' (58b). Fineness, fastidiousness, subtlety, discrimination – this register will rise and fall in importance in Pound's work, but it will remain a persistent undertow. In part it represents a temperamental bias of Pound's; in part it reflects the social setting in which poetry was situated in the years just before the Great War, its location within a genteel world of elite bourgeois culture.

A second point about 'The Limbs of Osiris' and its contemporary companion, 'Prolegomena', concerns a further ambiguity within the figure of the poet-engineer. At one point in 'Osiris', Pound sets forth an elementary anthropology of craftsmanship. 'Every man who does his own job really well has a latent respect for every other man who does *his* own job really well', respect which creates a common and 'lasting bond' among all people. As a consequence, intimate familiarity with a specific craft is immediately recognisable, for any statement made by someone possessing such intimacy instantly 'proves him the expert' (57b). The term 'expert' here seems to reinforce the more general note of professionalism that we have already discerned in 'Osiris'. After all, one common synonym for 'expert' is 'specialist', which is exactly the term that Pound uses to characterise the engineer, whom he calls 'a specialist, a man thoroughly trained in some ... branch of knowledge' (48b; my ellipsis). In such an account of the 'expert', emphasis falls on the concept of 'training', on the impersonal system which produces professionals. But in 'Prolegomena', instead, Pound gives a very different sense to the word, drawing a sharp distinction between the professional and the expert. Taking up the question of who should assess poetry, amateurs or professionals, Pound writes:

> I should not discriminate between the 'amateur' and the 'professional', or rather I should discriminate quite often in favour of the amateur, but I should discriminate between the amateur and the expert. It is certain that the present chaos will endure until the Art of poetry has been preached down the amateur gullet ... [and] the amateurs will cease to try to drown out the masters.   (61)

Pound's usage of 'expert' in this passage does not reinforce a rhetoric of professionalism; instead, it undermines it. Whereas 'the specialist' and the 'professional' are those whose position derives from impersonal systems of training and practice, 'the expert' is one whose authority derives from unusual ability or mastery which is the result of experience, something in addition to mere training and practice. Among specialists, in other words, 'experts' are the aristocrats, individuals endowed with unusual talents which lift them above the prevailing ethos of impersonality which otherwise typifies the modern professional system. Just as Pound often uses 'fineness' and related words to introduce an aristocratic element within his otherwise impersonal vocabulary of 'precision' and 'accuracy', so he uses the term 'expert' to introduce a similarly alien note within the otherwise neutral register of professionalism.

A third point needs to be made: though Pound is often credited with having invented the avant-garde in English poetry, the author of 'Osiris' adamantly insists that his activities be disassociated from all contemporary movements. The one cultural event that was on the lips of nearly everyone at this time was the 'Post-Impressionist Exhibition' of December 1910, which had shown an English audience the new developments taking place in the visual arts across the Channel and aroused unprecedented debate. ('On or about December 1910', Virginia Woolf said famously, 'human character changed.') Yet Pound firmly divorces himself from such matters. 'I have no desire to set up a babel of "post-impressionists in rhythm"' (67b), he writes at one point. 'I do not in the least wish ... to start a movement' (69b), he reiterates, while in the contemporary essay 'Prolegomena' (February 1912) he again dismisses the idea of 'there being a "movement" or my being of it' (62). These denials complement the rhetoric of aristocratic fineness and tasteful distinction. They bespeak a fastidious disdain of the noise and clamour that characterises the public sphere of journalism, debate, and disagreement.

Finally, it is worth calling attention to the conclusion to 'Prolegomena', for it introduces yet another rhetorical register which will recur throughout Pound's career:

As to Twentieth century poetry, and the poetry which I expect to see written during the next decade or so, it will, I think, move against poppycock, it will be harder and saner, it will be ... 'nearer the bone'. It will be as much like granite as it can be ... We will have fewer painted adjectives impeding the shock and stroke of it. At least for myself, I want it so, austere, direct, free from slither.   (63)

These terms require little comment. They announce a predilection which Pound will never abandon, a bias toward ascetic sobriety, toward restraint and austerity, often figured as 'hardness'. Indeed, the only modification that will occur to this schematic preference will be its gradual gendering, with the 'hard' turned into a vehicle of masculinity, and 'the soft' turned into a vessel of femininity. Feminist critics have highlighted this distinction and its reverberations in Pound's thinking – and with good reason. In his voluminous writings on social and topical questions, including contemporary suffragism, Pound rarely evinces a sympathetic understanding of the dilemmas and social constraints that modern women faced.

Not all of Pound's criticism stemmed directly from journalism. Some of it arose from a quite different venue, the private lecture series. Pound gave the first such series of his career in early 1912, only weeks after completing 'I Gather the Limbs of Osiris'. The series comprised three lectures (14, 19, and 21 March), each on a different theme – Guido Cavalcanti, Arnaut Daniel, and Anglo-Saxon verse. The location in which they were held – 'the private gallery' within the home of Lord and Lady Glenconner at 34, Queen Anne's Street – tells us much about the aristocatic world of elite bourgeois culture in which Pound's early career unfolded. A sedate residential oasis in perhaps the choicest location in London, overlooking St James's Park, Queen Anne's Street was virtually a museum of eighteenth-century architecture, with most of its houses built in 1704. No. 34, built just a bit later, had recently been refurbished by its new inhabitants, Lord and Lady Glenconner, who had lavished their attention on the 'private gallery' that occupied the first floor, the site for their remarkable collection of thirty-seven masterpieces by Watteau, Fragonard, Turner, Reynolds, Raeburn, Romney, Gainsborough, Hogarth, and others. Lord and Lady Glenconner were in-laws of the Prime Minister, Herbert Asquith, and Lady Glenconner took a special interest in the Poetry Society, whose *conversazioni* she sometimes hosted. Her own book of verse, *Windlestraw*, had been privately printed at the same Chiswick Press which Mathews had used for Pound's books.[11]

Pound's lectures were plainly conceived as a device to make money. With the site furnished gratis by the condescension of Lady Glenconner, and with ticket prices inflated far above those which prevailed at public events, even a limited audience would result in significant earnings. Yet everything about the lecture was presented in such a way as to disguise that fact. The audience was limited indeed, restricted to fifty persons only (as notices of the event carefully underscored). It was not, in other words, a public performance open to whoever would pay. Tickets, the same notice stated, were not commodities to be purchased, but favours that might be bestowed 'on application' to Lady Low.[12] Here, in short, was a private retreat from the realm of public life, a closed circle insulated from the grim imperatives of a commodity economy, a space in which literary culture served as a medium of exchange for a restricted aristocracy of sensibility.

Pound's second lecture treated Arnaut Daniel, and we can reconstruct its contents from an essay, doubtless drawn partly from this very lecture, which he published on the same subject only a few weeks later, 'Psychology and the Troubadours'.[13] To compare its verbal texture with that of 'I

[11] On Queen Anne's Gate, see Dan Cruickshank, 'Queen Anne's Gate', *Georgian Group Journal*, 2 (1992), pp. 56–67. On number 34, see Department of the Environment, *List of Buildings of Special Architectural or Historic Interest: City of Westminster, Greater London*, part 5 *Streets Q-S* (London, 1987), pp. 1333–7. For contemporary photographs of the building, see Lawrence Rainey, *Institutions of Modernism: Literary Elites and Public Culture* (New Haven, 1999), pp. 22–5. On the property's owners, see Simon Blow, *Broken Blood: The Rise and Fall of the Tennant Family* (London, 1987); Anonymous, 'In the Great World: Lord and Lady Glenconner', *Sketch*, 10 December 1913, p. 298. See also Caroline Dakers, *Clouds: The Biography of a Country House* (New Haven, 1993), pp. 160–76.
[12] The programme is reproduced in Rainey, *Institutions of Modernism*, p. 27.
[13] Ezra Pound, 'Psychology and the Troubadours', in *Ezra Pound's Poetry and Prose*, vol. 1, pp. 83–99; page references are given in the text in parentheses.

Gather the Limbs of Osiris' can be instructive. As before, Pound deplores 'that condition which we see about us, and which is cried out upon as "the divorce of art and life"' (84). Similarly, many of the keywords from the earlier essay also reappear. Pound praises 'the *accurate* artist', the one who exhibits 'a sort of hyper-scientific precision' and 'exactness of presentation' (84). And once again he lauds 'that precision through which alone' a great many subjects can be treated (84). He even brings up 'the common electric machine' and 'the telegraph' (91–2), though his invocation of mechanical devices is briefer and more muted. More pronounced, instead, are his evocations of aristocratic values. Exactness is now defined simply as 'an accumulation of fine discriminations' (84). And Arnaut Daniel is no longer the broad Chaucerian realist who rendered 'medieval life as it was'. He has become the hermetic poet whose lyrics resist intelligibility, though not for those who truly understand art:

They are good art as the high mass is good art . . . [His] sort of canzoni is a ritual. It must be conceived and approached as a ritual. It has its purpose and its effect. These are different from those of simple song. They are perhaps subtler. They make their revelations to those who are already expert.   (86)

Indeed, the troubadours and their audience were an 'aristocracy of emotion' (88). Pound is moving as far as possible from the public sphere of transparency and democratic norms. His ideal, at least in this essay, is shaped by the ethos of a courtly culture, its cultural economy of patronage, and its rhetorical economy of obscurity.

The great irony of this event is that it transpired on the very day that Filippo Tommaso Marinetti, the founder and promoter of Futurism, gave his first public lecture in London, at Bechstein Hall (now Wigmore Hall), a lecture intended to publicise the contemporaneous exhibition of Futurist pictures at the Sackville Gallery. There can be no doubt that Pound knew of Marinetti's lecture, since his fiancée sent him a note advising him that she planned to attend. The two lectures differed radically in subject, style, and tone. Whereas Pound lectured about the medieval past, Marinetti talked about modernity; and whereas Pound flattered his audience, Marinetti berated it, castigating the English as a 'nation of sycophants' who adhered to 'worm-eaten traditions'. The English had created modernity, he charged, and then betrayed it. The reception of the two lectures also differed sharply. Pound's went entirely unnoticed by the contemporary press. Marinetti's was promptly made the subject of the lead editorial in the next day's *Times*, and thereafter in other prominent newspapers. The Futurist exhibition turned into a smash success, garnering more press coverage than even the Post-Impressionist Exhibition. Within the month of March alone, articles and reviews on Futurism appeared in the *Times*, the *Daily Telegraph*, the *Pall Mall Gazette*, the *Illustrated London News*, the *Daily Graphic*, the *Evening News*, the *Glasgow Herald*, the *Morning Leader*, the *Observer*, the *American Register and Anglo-Colonial World*, the *Daily Chronicle*, the *Daily Express*, the *World*, the *Sketch*, the *Art News*, the *Athenaeum*, the *Nation*, the *Bystander*, the *Daily Mirror*, the *Academy*, the *Spectator*, the *Tripod*, the *Manchester Guardian*, and the *English Review*.[14] What Marinetti had revealed was the way in which a certain kind of discursive formation – let us call it 'the avant-garde', for lack of a better term – could be harnessed to the novel power of the emerging mass media, an institution that could bridge the 'divorce between art and life' in ways unimaginable under the protocols of the private lecture series, the genteel salon, or the polite review.

Pound's response was Imagism, though it is important to note that it took him nearly five months to formulate it. There were several reasons for the delay. From May through July 1912 he was away from London, chiefly in Paris and southern France. When he returned, two events occurred which only reinforced his nascent sense that contemporary poetry would have to be presented to the public as a concerted polemical onslaught in the style of Marinetti. One was the publication of F. S. Flint's article on French poetry in the August number of *The Poetry Review*, a fifty-nine-page essay which divided recent French poetry into movements and schools along lines made familiar by Marinetti's publicisation of Futurism, and culminating with a substantial account of Marinetti and Futurism itself. The essay proved so popular that the August number was sold out immediately, sparking still further debate. The other occurred in mid-August when Pound received an invitation from Harriet Monroe to contribute to a new journal that she was founding in Chicago, *Poetry: A Magazine of Verse*. On 18 August Pound wrote back not only to confirm his collaboration, but to offer himself as a talent scout or foreign correspondent. More important, he was enclosing a new poem, 'a sort of post-Browning Imagiste affair'.[15] It is the first reference to Imagism in all his extant writing, and it makes clear that it was the occasion offered by Monroe which precipitated his plans to launch Imagism. Now he had a vehicle in which to launch a movement of his own – if he so wished. Yet his attitude toward such a project was more divided than our received accounts would suggest.

A few days later Pound added a brief 'Prefatory Note' to the second and final set of proofs for a new volume of poetry, *Ripostes*, which was

---

[14] 'A nation of sycophants' and 'worm-eaten conventions' are from the *Daily Chronicle*, 20 March 1912, p. 2, col. 6. For references to all the newspapers cited here, see Patrizia Ardizzone, 'Il futurismo in inghilterra: Bibliografia (1910–1915)', *Quaderno*, 9 (1979, special issue on *futurismo/vorticismo*), pp. 91–115; and Valioer Gioè, 'Il futurismo in inghilterra: Bibliografia (1910–1915)–Supplemento', *Quaderno*, 16 (1982), pp. 76–83.

[15] Ezra Pound, *Selected Letters of Ezra Pound, 1907–1941*, ed. D. D. Paige (New York, 1971; 1st edn, 1950), p. 9.

scheduled to appear in October. The note prefaced not Pound's own poems, but a group of five poems by T. E. Hulme which were humorously labelled 'The Complete Poetical Works of T. E. Hulme' and appended to the volume. They were included for 'good fellowship' and 'good custom', Pound's note explained, but especially for the good memory of 'certain evenings and meetings of two years gone'. That obscure allusion was followed by another, still more obscure:

As for the 'School of Image', which may or may not have existed, its principles were not so interesting as those of the 'inherent dynamists' or of *Les Unanimistes*, yet they were probably sounder than those of a certain French school which attempted to dispense with verbs altogether; or of the Impressionists who brought forth:
'Pink pigs blossoming upon the hillside'; or of the Post-Impressionists who beseech their ladies to let down slate-blue hair over their raspberry-coloured flanks.
'As for the future, *Les Imagistes* ... have that in their keeping.'[16]

What were readers supposed to make of these cryptic comments? Within a single sentence Pound had packed in references to six different schools or movements:

1. the School of Images, which may or may not have existed
2. the 'inherent dynamists'
3. *Les Unanimistes*
4. a certain French school which attempted to dispense with verbs altogether
5. the Impressionists
6. the Post-Impressionists

The School of Images (1) was Pound's cryptic name for an informal discussion group about poetry which had occasionally met in 1910. *Les Unanimistes* (3) were a circle of French poets centred around Jules Romains, who urged that the modern city endowed all its residents with a common metropolitan world-view, making them *unanime* (literally, in French, of one *anima*). 'Impressionists' (5) was a term that some contemporaries used to characterise the writing of Ford Madox Ford and Joseph Conrad, because of their concentration on rendering a character's impressions, rather than 'objective' description. (Neither, of course, ever wrote a sentence of the sort that Pound furnishes.) 'Post-Impressionists' (6) was a term derived from Roger Fry's recent exhibition of contemporary painting, but by 1912 journalists were facetiously applying it to anything vaguely fashionable or *au courant*, and Pound's use of the term is patently

[16] The 'Predatory Note' is reproduced in Ezra Pound, *Personae*, revised edn. by A. Walton Litz (New York, 1990), p. 266.

in the same spirit. (The example of 'post-impressionist' literature that he furnishes is entirely his own concoction.) But the references to '"the inherent Dynamists"' (2) and 'a certain French school which attempted to dispense with verbs altogether' were less playful allusions. They plainly referred to Futurism. The Futurist painters had stressed the importance of rendering the dynamic force-lines of objects in motion, while Marinetti, in the famous 'Technical Manifesto of Futurist Literature' (May 1912), had urged that writers use verbs only in the infinitive in order to destroy the verb's subjection to the 'I' of the writer. And while we today tend to think of Futurism as an Italian phenomenon, not a 'French school', contemporary Britons tended to regard it as French – in part because all the manifestos were first published in French, in part because Marinetti himself gave all his lectures in French, in part because press coverage frequently quoted in French or simply treated it as French. (Frank Flint's successful essay on recent French poetry had culminated with Futurism.)

Yet the passage's obscure allusions are less important than its rhetorical strategies. To say that the School of Images is 'not so interesting' as the 'inherent Dynamists' is of course to dismiss 'the inherent dynamists' as most uninteresting indeed. More importantly, it dismisses them in a certain way – with a fastidious yawn and a hint of aristocratic hauteur. Equally revealing is the way in which the School of Images is praised. The play or irony so apparent in the succession of negations establishes an affirmation that is fragile and specular, a mimicry of real affirmation. The School of Images, or its successor the new group of Imagistes, are not a movement, but the mimesis of a movement. And when read in biographical terms, it suggests how reluctant Pound was about the project of launching Imagism.

By October 1912, when the cryptic 'Prefatory Note' appeared at the end of *Ripostes*, Pound's personal circumstances had suffered three further changes. Back in June, when Pound had gone to southern France for a walking tour, he had learnt that Margaret Cravens had committed suicide, leaving him without the patronage which nourished his courtly ideal of cultural production. In late October, moreover, the publishing firm Swift and Company went bankrupt; they had signed an exclusive publishing contract with Pound which had guaranteed him £100 per year. These reverses in Pound's personal finances were complemented by a literary setback as well. In mid-September, Harold Monro had announced that he would be issuing an anthology of *Georgian Poetry* which was to be edited and financed by Edward Marsh, assistant to the Undersecretary for the Navy, Winston Churchill. But because the volume was meant to include only work published within the last two years, and because Pound chose not to extract a poem from the forthcoming *Ripostes*, nothing by him was

included. The volume appeared shortly before Christmas 1912 and was
an immediate success; within a year it had sold over 9,000 copies, a
remarkable figure that far exceeded the 250–500 copies which had
marked the sales of Pound's books.[17] A small but perceptible rift was
growing between Pound and Monro, and during the course of 1913 it
would be further compounded by the vexing question of Futurism.

These developments prompted Pound to new efforts to publicise
Imagism. On 10 December 1912 he wrote 'Status Rerum', an essay that
reported on 'the state of affairs' in literary London (*Poetry*, January
1913). After ten paragraphs discussing various authors, Pound took up
the subject of Imagism:

> The youngest school here that has the nerve to call itself a school is that of the
> *Imagistes*. To belong to a school does not in the least mean that one writes poetry
> to a theory. One writes poetry when, where, because, and as one feels like writing
> it. A school exists when two or three young men agree, more or less, to call certain
> things good; when they prefer such of their verses as have certain qualities to such
> of their verses as do not have them.
>
> Space forbids me to set forth the program of the *Imagistes* at length, but one
> of their watchwords is Precision, and they are in opposition to the numerous
> and unassembled writers who busy themselves with dull and interminable
> effusions...[18]

The rhetorical contrasts contained within the first paragraph are astounding. It begins with tough-guy posturing ('The young school here that has
the nerve to call itself a school'), then swerves into a tart repudiation of
'theory'. Pound, in these remarks, was echoing the complaint of contemporary reviewers of the Futurist exhibition, who had found that the
paintings too closely adhered to a theory, and therefore were insufficiently
individual. Pound, in other words, was presenting Imagism as a kind of
anti-Futurism. Whereas Futurism dabbled in theory, offered vast claims
about art and modernity, and produced paintings that looked alike or
anonymous, Imagism was something casual, informal, individualistic,
perhaps even a bit English. 'One writes poetry when, where, because, and
as one feels like writing it.' Imagism, in short, did not issue theoretical
proclamations or manifestos. It was the outcome of 'two or three young
men agreeing, more or less' (and note the studied informality of 'more or
less') 'to call certain things good'. And whereas Futurism urged the
destruction of Venice, demanded the demolition of museums, or called for
the abolition of libraries, Imagism opposed only 'interminable effusions'.

All this should make clear the remarkable extent to which critics have

---

[17] On *Georgian Poetry*, see Grant, *Harold Monro*, pp. 92–9, with sales figures on p. 96.
[18] Ezra Pound, 'Status Rerum' (10 December 1912), in *Ezra Pound's Poetry and Prose*, vol.
1, pp. 111–13; all quotations are from p. 112.

falsified Pound's position in literary history, presenting Imagism as the first avant-garde movement in English literature. In reality it was something quite different. It was the first anti-avant-garde. Still more astounding, it is Pound himself who achieved the rhetorical transformation whereby Imagism was transformed from a rearguard into an avant-garde movement. But to appreciate that, we need to trace the public articulation of Imagism and Pound's critical writings a bit further.

Four weeks after writing 'Status Rerum', Pound returned to Imagism again, dictating to Frank Flint an article which would ostensibly provide readers with inside reportage:

> Some curiosity has been aroused concerning *Imagisme*, and as I was unable to find anything definite about it in print, I sought out an *imagiste*, with intent to discover whether the group itself knew anything about the 'movement'. I gleaned these facts.
>
> The *imagistes* admitted that they were contemporaries of the Post Impressionists and the Futurists; but they had nothing in common with these schools. They had not published a manifesto. They were not a revolutionary school; their only endeavor was to write in accordance with the best tradition, as they found it in the best writers of all time, – in Sappho, Catullus, Villon.

Flint compliantly accepted Pound's dictation, signed his own name to it, and so enabled Pound to post if off to *Poetry*, together with Pound's 'A Few Don'ts by an Imagiste'.[19] Pound thereby became not just a participant in Imagism, but also its chronicler. Yet the tones in which he chronicled Imagism are highly revealing. Once again Pound presents Imagism as a movement that is not merely different, but different *in kind* from the movements which have dominated debate in the last three years, Post-Impressionism and Futurism. Imagism is their antithesis. Far from being disturbing or 'revolutionary', Imagism is reassuring, even Arnoldian in its 'endeavour to write in acordance with the best tradition' as it was found in 'the best writers of all time'. And we can hear, in the repetition of 'the best', a translation of the ancient Greek *aristos* (meaning 'the best'), which makes up part of the word *aristocracy*. If Imagism is in fact a movement, then it is the aristocrat of movements. Whereas Marinetti's manifestos are peppered with rules and prescriptions for writing, painting, or composition, the Imagists have merely 'a few rules, drawn up for their satisfaction only, and they had not published them'. The Imagists are not noisily seeking attention from the press or approval from the public. They are not like those foreigners from France or the Continent; they are people who can circulate in good society, act with good form, and shun the noisy world of publicity and theatricality.

[19] [Ezra Pound and] F. S. Flint, 'Imagisme', in *Ezra Pound's Poetry and Prose*, vol. 1, p. 119; Ezra Pound, 'A Few Don'ts by an Imagiste', *ibid.*, p. 120–2.

The famous 'few rules', of course, were these:

1. Direct treatment of the 'thing', whether subjective or objective.
2. To use absolutely no word that [does] not contribute to presentation.
3. As regarding rhythm: to compose in sequence of the musical phrase, not in sequence of a metronome.

What to make of these has long been a matter of debate. With hindsight, Pound's prescriptions appear to be no more than common sense, essential principles proper to all good writing. Yet it is equally true, as Daryl Hine has noted, that 'No one can read the magazine verse of the time ... without feeling how much the corrective was need.' Viewed as a response to the challenges posed by Futurism, however, it seems a timid and unimaginative address to the questions about art and modernity, the avant-garde and mass culture which Marinetti had raised.

In April of 1913 Gino Severini had a solo show of paintings and sculptures at the Marlborough gallery, an exhibition which was followed in May by yet another exhibition devoted to Futurist sculpture. The debate about Futurism was renewed. In September of 1913 Harold Monro devoted an entire issue of his new journal, *Poetry and Drama*, to the subject of Futurism. Accompanied by translations of more than thirty poems and a generous editorial overview, it was notable for how sharply it contrasted with the discussion of Imagism in the previous number, to which it had given only two paragraphs. It included a translation of Marinetti's latest manifesto, the famous 'Destruction of Syntax – Wireless Imagination – Words-in-Freedom'. Monro had long been interested in seeing poetry break out of its aristocratic confines in the Poetry Society. The surging sales of his *Georgian Poetry* and the popular interest in Futurism were, he thought, signs that his hopes were being fulfilled. In his editorial preface to the number, he hailed Marinetti for auguring a dissolution of the distinction between poetry and popular culture, art and life. Rhapsodising about the sheer size of Futurism's audience – in Italy it had 'gained the support of no less than 22,000 adherents' – Monro was overjoyed to report that Marinetti's anthology of *The Futurist Poets* had sold thirty-five thousand copies in its French and Italian editions. This fact in itself, he said, constituted 'Marinetti's most interesting attitude'. Here was poetry 'no longer ... withheld from the people' by 'educationalists', 'intellectuals', or the commercial press. Here was poetry 'intended for immediate and wide circulation' and 'regaining some of its popular appeal'. Marinetti was restoring poetry to the status it had occupied in an earlier era, when 'the minstrel and the ballad-monger then represented our modern Northcliffe'.[20] Marinetti, in other words, was bridging the gulf that modernity had interposed between art and life, putting poetry back into the place it had occupied within an organic and pre-modern community, the world of the minstrel and ballad-singer. But Monro's most telling remark was the reference to 'our modern Northcliffe'. In 1896 Northcliffe had founded the *Daily Mail*, a new kind of newspaper that stressed concise writing, attractive competitions, and alluring advertisements, developing a format that blurred the traditional distinction between news and entertainment. By 1902 its circulation topped one million, then the largest in the world, and Northcliffe had become the personification of early mass culture. Conflating Marinetti with Northcliffe, poems with newspapers, Monro inadvertently signalled the risks inherent in the collapse of life and art for which he longed. Was there no distinction at all between poetry and the most ephemeral of literary commodities, the daily newspaper?

It was at this point that Marinetti himself arrived for another visit to London. Press coverage was more intense than ever as Marinetti gave daily lectures and readings that were copiously reported in the capital's dailies and weeklies. One reading he gave was at the Poetry Bookshop owned and managed by Monro. Another, we know, was witnessed by Wyndham Lewis, and still another by Pound's fellow-Imagiste, Richard Aldington. It was in these readings and lectures that Marinetti hammered home a point which he had been steadily developing since mid-1912, his belief that the concept of aesthetic autonomy was a destructive force to be utterly rejected. 'Art is not a religion', he declaimed on 17 November at the Poets Club, 'not something to be worshipped with joined hands.' Instead, it 'should express all the intensity of life – its beauty ... its sordidness', and 'the very complexity of our life to-day'.[21] Four days later the *Daily Mail* – and what venue could have been more revealing than Northcliffe's mass newspaper? – published Marinetti's latest manifesto, 'The Variety Theatre' or 'Le Music-Hall', a work which set forth an intransigent defence of that enormously popular but critically despised form. The music hall, Marinetti urged, was the quintessentially modern cultural form, all the more 'significant by reason of the unforeseen nature of all its fumbling efforts and the coarse simplicity of its resources... [It] destroys all that is solemn, sacred, earnest, and pure in Art – with a big A.'[22] It was a far cry from the elitist complacency in which Pound had been able to indulge as late as mid-June 1912.

But Pound, too, had changed much in the course of 1913, though in ways quite different from Marinetti. First, in July 1913 he began his long association with *The New Freewoman*, a dissident feminist journal that

[20] Harold Monro, 'Varia', *Poetry and Drama* 1.3 (September 1913), pp. 263–5.
[21] *Times*, 18 November 1913, p. 5, cols. 5–6.
[22] Filippo Tommaso Marinetti, 'The Meaning of the Music Hall', *Daily Mail* (London) 21 November 1913, p. 6, col. 4.

was being rapidly transformed into an organ of philosophical individualism, soon to be renamed *The Egoist*. It quickly became the gathering-place
for Imagist poetry when its editor, Dora Marsden, discerned a similarity
between her own philosophy of aristocratic individualism, complete with
a theory of language, and the poetry of the Imagists. Second, and more
important, was his meeting with the widow of the late Ernest Fenollosa,
who had read some of Pound's early poetry and by December had entrusted her husband's unpublished paper to Pound. Over the ensuing months,
Pound began to explore the nature of the Chinese written character which,
he believed, resisted Western tendencies toward abstraction (i.e., art)
because it was composed of signs drawn from physical reality (i.e., life).
Years later, in *ABC of Reading* (1934), he summed up what he had
learned from Fenollosa:

In Europe, if you ask a man to define anything, his definition always moves away
from the simple things that he knows perfectly well, it recedes into an unknown
region, that is a region of remoter and progressively remoter abstraction.
    Thus if you ask him what red is, he says it is a 'colour'.
    If you ask him what a colour is, he tells you it is a vibration or a refraction of
light, or a division of the spectrum.
    And if you ask him what vibration is, he tells you it is a mode of energy, or
something of that sort, until you arrive at a modality of being, or non-being, or at
any rate you get in beyond your depth, and beyond his depth...
    But when the Chinaman wanted to make a picture of something more compli-
cated, or of a general idea, how did he go about it?
    He is to define red. How can he do it in a picture that isn't painted in red paint?
    He puts (or his ancestors put) together the abbreviated pictures of
    ROSE   CHERRY
    IRON RUST   FLAMINGO
That, you see, is very much the kind of thing a biologist does (in a very much
more complicated way) when he gets together a few hundred or thousand slides,
and picks out what is necessary for his general statement. Something that fits the
case, that applies in all the cases.
    The Chinese 'word' or ideogram for red is based on something everyone
KNOWS.[23]

The 'ideogrammic method' – the building up of general notions from
concrete particulars that are juxtaposed but not necessarily linked by
syntax – appealed to Pound's deep-rooted preference of life over art and
became a major technique in his later criticism and poetry. *Guide to
Kulchur* (1938), for example, has to be read in the same way as *The
Cantos*, and in it Pound gives the best definition of his aim: 'The ideogrammic method consists of presenting one facet and then another until at
some point one gets off the dead and desensitized surface of the reader's

[23] Ezra Pound, *ABC of Reading* (New York, 1960; 1st edn., 1934), pp. 19–22.

mind, onto a part that will register.'[24] It is a dynamic method, and when it succeeds the eye and mind jump from one word or image to another like an electrical charge. The reader actively joins with the poet in constructing meaning. Ultimately, this would become the method of Pound's *Cantos*.

Pound's view of the image, in other words, was profoundly altered by his reading of Fenollosa. One need only compare one account of Imagism that he wrote in 1913 with another that he wrote in September 1914. The earlier one, called 'How I Began' (June 1913), explains how and why he wrote the famous 'demonstration' poem, 'In a Station of the Metro'.

For well over a year I have been trying to make a poem of a very beautiful thing that befell me in the Paris Underground. I got out of a train at, I think, La Concorde and in the jostle I saw a beautiful face, and then, turning suddenly, another and another, and then a beautiful child's face, and then another beautiful face. All that day I tried to find words for what this made me feel. That night as I went home along the rue Raynouard I was still trying. I could get nothing but spots of colour. I remember thinking that if I had been a painter I might have started a wholly new school of painting. I tried to write the poem weeks afterwards in Italy, but found it useless. Then only the other night, wondering how I should tell the adventure, it struck me that in Japan, where a work of art is not estimated by its acreage and where sixteen syllables are counted enough for a poem if you arrange and punctuate them properly, one might make a very little poem which would be translated about as follows:

'The apparition of these faces in the crowd:
Petals on a wet, black bough.'

And there, or in some other very old, very quiet civilization, some one else might understand the significance.[25]

It is fascinating to compare this early account with the much fuller treatment of the poem in Pound's essay 'Vorticism' (September 1914).[26] What has intervened is his developing theory about the simultaneity of the image. The account in 'Vorticism' describes art as an 'equation' for emotions (279), a precursor of Eliot's 'objective correlative'; poetry as a possible vehicle for the 'language of form and colour' (279); Chinese poetry as a model of concision and 'simultaneity'; the '"one-image poem"' as 'a form of super-position, that is to say it is one idea set on top of another' (281); the successful poem as a record of the 'precise instant when a thing outward and objective transforms itself, or darts into a thing inward and subjective' (281).

At its deepest reaches the 'Image' appealed to the mystical, neo-Platonic

---

[24] Ezra Pound, *Guide to Kulchur* (New York, 1970; 1st edn., 1938), p. 51.
[25] Ezra Pound, 'How I Began', originally in *T. P.'s Weekly* (London) 71.552 (6 June 1913), p. 707; now in *Ezra Pound's Poetry and Prose*, vol. 1, p. 147.
[26] Ezra Pound, 'Vorticism', originally in the *Fortnightly Review* (New Series), no. 573 (1 September 1914), pp. 461–71; now in *Ezra Pound's Poetry and Prose*, vol. 1, pp. 275–85; references to specific pages are given in parentheses within the text.

strain in Pound's thought, which is evident from the earliest poems to the last cantos. Such a spiritual belief lies behind his statement, in an excited footnote to the 1914 'Vorticism' essay, that the Japanese Noh drama – where the 'unity consists in one image, enforced by movement and music' – might provide a model for the 'long imagist or vorticist poem' (285). Like most of his contemporaries, Pound was engaged in a lifelong project to write a long poem (the traditional hallmark of the great poet) that would preserve the compressed, nervous, 'instantaneous' qualities achieved in the new poetry.

Finally, the Image was almost an object of worship, an icon that could draw the mind from the material to the spiritual.

It is in art the highest business to create the beautiful image; to create order and profusion of images that we may furnish the life of our minds with a noble surrounding ... [we should] put forth the images of beauty, that going out into tenantless spaces we have with us all that is needful – an abundance of sounds and patterns to entertain us in that long dreaming; to strew our path to Valhalla; to give rich gifts by the way.[27]

Here the new emphasis on technique and conscious precision is subsumed under a dream of nobility that is common to much great art, and that Pound singled out for special praise in his 1914 review of Yeats's *Responsibilities*.

By the time that Pound's anthology *Des Imagistes* was finally published (March 1914 in New York and in April in London), Pound was already moving on. The time for a confrontation with Marinetti had finally come, for by then it was well known that Marinetti was going to return to London in late May and June, where he was scheduled to launch a series of Futurist concerts from the stage of the largest music-hall in the world, the Coliseum in London. As if preparing the new tone that would mark his work, Pound wrote in the *Egoist* of February 1914: 'The modern artist must live by craft and violence. His gods are violent gods... Those artists, so called, whose work does not show this strife, are uninteresting.'[28] It was a far cry from the intricate prose which had signalled the birth of Imagism only eighteen months earlier, in August 1912. Vorticism lay just around the corner.

With funding provided by Wyndham Lewis's mother and Kate Lechmere, Pound and Wyndham Lewis planned a periodical that would be the verbal counterpart to the kind of music-hall performance which Marinetti had postulated as the new form of cultural modernity. As a consequence,

[27] Ezra Pound, 'Ikon', originally in *The Cerebralist* (London, 1 (December 1913), p. 43; now in *Ezra Pound's Poetry and Prose*, vol. 1, p. 203.
[28] Ezra Pound, 'The New Sculpture', originally in *The Egoist*, 1.4 (16 February 1914), pp. 67–8; now in *Ezra Pound's Poetry and Prose*, vol. 1, pp. 221–2, here p. 222.

it combined the light inconsequentiality of music hall with threatening declarations. Its typography so plainly stemmed from Futurist practice that it was recognised as derivative by every contemporary reviewer, and even the famous lists of 'Blasts' and 'Blesses' (or curses and praises) was lifted from Apollinaire's 'merde à' and 'rose à' which had appeared in Marinetti's magazine, *Lacerba*. Yet the journal was not entirely inconsequential: buried among the many names to be blasted was that of 'Lord Glenconner of Glen'. It was a sign that Pound had finally renounced his dream of poetry nestled among aristocratic patron-*saloniers*, that he had finally moved forward to the world of public engagement that was typified by Marinetti. Yet tellingly, the performances of Marinetti at the Coliseum and of *Blast* in the reviewer's columns would be poorly received.

When Marinetti stepped forward on the stage to introduce the concert with a brief lecture on the Art of Noises, things turned ugly. As the *Times* described it:

Signor Marinetti rather mistook his audience yesterday afternoon, when he tried to deliver an academic exposition of Futurist principles at the Coliseum, and he had, in consequence to put up with a rude reception from a gallery which seemed fully qualified to give him a lesson in his own 'Art of Noises'.[29]

What the *Times* reviewer termed 'an academic exposition of Futurist principles' was precisely the kind of serious and self-reflective discourse that the Coliseum sought to exclude. And so it did. After a few minutes the curtain was unceremoniously lowered. There was a danger, the stage manager later claimed, 'that people would start throwing things'. For subsequent performances the Coliseum's owner and manager, Oswald Stoll, obliged Marinetti to include a gramophone playing records by Edward Elgar, just 'to bring a little melody into the act'.[30] The engagement was a fiasco.

Why didn't Marinetti's performance succeed, when it was he himself who had envisaged the music-hall as the ideal medium of modern cultural production? The answer is that Marinetti's idea of modernity wasn't modern enough. The Coliseum, which had been constructed only ten years earlier, in 1904, was a music hall of a new kind. It had been constructed so that its site was directly visible from the exit of Charing Cross station, intended to address the crowds of respectable, prosperous people who poured into the metropolis for a day's shopping excursion, 'middle class people for whom a visit to a serious play might seem too

---

[29] 'Art and Practice of Noise. Hostile Reception of Signor Marinetti', *Times*, 16 June 1914, p. 5, col. 4.

[30] Stage manager quoted in Felix Barker, *The House that Stoll Built: The Story of the Coliseum Theatre* (London, 1957), p. 83, who also recounts Stoll's decision to include the gramophone, pp. 83–6.

ambitious and a visit to a music-hall far too racy', as the owner put it.[31] Seeking to please this audience, he presented them with a sanitised version of music hall, one far removed from the institution's origins in the working and lower-middle classes. Marie Lloyd, the greatest of all the music hall stars whose death in 1922 T. S. Eliot would construe as the demise of genuine English culture, was never allowed to perform at the Coliseum: her racy lyrics and double entrendres were too vulgar. The new music hall, instead, was addressed to a middle class increasingly defined by consumerism. Marinetti's dreams of the music hall were based on his experience in Italy, where it was still a vital, turbulent genre of urban popular culture, a hybrid form addressing a public still making the transition from a largely agrarian to a wholly urban way of life, speaking to their hybridised experience by mingling motifs of the village carnival with more modern genres to treat the dislocations of urban experience.

Blast failed for a slightly different reason. Every biographer of Pound has quoted G. W. Prothero, the staid editor of the *Quarterly Review* where Pound had once published an essay on troubadours, who wrote to Pound saying he couldn't publish anything by a contributor to 'such a publication as *Blast*. It stamps a man too disadvantageously'.[32] The implication is that *Blast* aroused a furore, provoked scandal and outrage, and was typical of the avant-garde experience. But a glance at contemporary reviews reveals a different story:

Almost all the pictures reproduced are (like the typesetting of the first pages) Futurist in origin, and nothing else. And as for the productions of the literary Vortices, these are not even so fresh as that . . . All it really is is a feeble attempt at being clever. *Blast* is a flat affair. We haven't a movement here, not even a mistaken one.[33]

A week later another reviewer wrote:

One can forgive a new movement for anything except being tedious. *Blast* is as tedious as an imitation of George Robey [a great music-hall comedian] by a curate without a sense of humour . . . to make up of the pages of *Blast* a winding sheet in which to wrap up Futurism for burial is to do an indignity to a genuine and living aristic movement. But, after all, what is Vorticism but Futurism in an English disguise – Futurism, we might call it, bottled in England, and bottled badly? . . . the two groups differ from each other not in their aims, but in their degrees of competence.[34]

[31] Quoted in Barker, *The House that Stoll Built*, p. 11.
[32] For examples, see Humphrey Carpenter, *A Serious Character: The Life of Ezra Pound* (Boston, 1988), p. 250; Noel Stock, *The Life of Ezra Pound* (Harmondsworth, 1974; 1st edn., 1970), p. 203. The letter, it goes almost without saying, was published by Pound himself.
[33] Solomon Eagle [John Collings Squire], 'Current Literature: Books in General', *New Statesman*, 3, no. 65 (4 July 1914), p. 406.
[34] Anonymous, 'The Futurists', *New Statesman*, 3, no. 66 (11 July 1914), p. 426.

Their responses were representative. *Blast* gave Pound and Lewis a certain degree of notoriety, but little more. 'As a result of these sociable activities', Lewis later recalled, 'I did not sell a single picture, it is superfluous to say.'[35] If *Blast* was an attempt to assimilate the concept of art to that of the commodity along the lines proposed by Marinetti, it was a failure. Another commodity already occupied that space. For Pound, as also for Marinetti, the commodity economy was moving so fast that it was difficult to forestall its power to devour anything that stood in its path.

Pound now turned elsewhere. On the one hand, he cast off Imagism with a vengeance, leaving its remnants to Amy Lowell, who turned up in London a few weeks after the publication of *Blast* with plans to publish a new series of Imagist anthologies, only to find Pound utterly uninterested. His thoughts were already turning elsewhere, in directions suggested by his comments on what had recently happened to the sculptor Jacob Epstein, comments which he published in January 1915:

I beg you may pardon digressions, but is it or is it not ludicrous that 'The Sun-God' [a major statue by Epstein] (and two other pieces which I have not seen) should be pawned, the whole lot, for some £60? And that six of the other works are still on the sculptor's hands? And this is not due to the war. It was so before this war was heard of.

One looks out upon American collectors buying autograph MSS. Of William Morris, faked Rembrandts and faked Vandykes. One looks out on a plutocracy and upon the remains of an aristocracy who ought to know by this time that keeping up the arts means keeping up living artists; that no age can be a great age which does not find its own genius.[36]

It was in response to these words that Pound received a letter from John Quinn, the New York lawyer and cultural patron whom he had met briefly while in New York in 1910. Quinn had correctly detected a reference to himself in Pound's mention of 'American collectors buying autograph MSS. Of William Morris.' Born in 1870, the son of Irish immigrants, Quinn was a classic variant of the Horatio Alger story. Armed with law degrees from Georgetown and then Harvard, he had descended on New York at the age of twenty-five. Within five years he had graduated to a junior partnership in the firm of Alexander and Colby, and within another six he had struck out on his own. His field of expertise was financial law, but he was also possessed by a resolve to make himself an educated man. He read voraciously – everything modern, everything Irish. In 1902 he had gone on his first trip abroad to Dublin and London, where he met W. B. Yeats's father, then Yeats's brother, Jack, then Yeats himself, and then everyone involved in the Irish literary scene. From Jack Yeats he

[35] Wyndham Lewis, *Blasting and Bombardiering* (1937; rpt. New York, 1982), p. 47.
[36] Ezra Pound, 'Affirmations. III', originally in *The New Age*, 16.12 (21 January 1915), pp. 311–12, now in *Ezra Pound's Poetry and Prose*, vol. 2, pp. 6–8, here p. 8a.

bought nearly a dozen paintings; from the father he bought one and commissioned four more. It was the beginning of a lifelong passion that would grow and last until his death in 1924. Quinn became the greatest collector of contemporary art in America in his time, buying works from nearly every major artist of the period. But his interest in literature was no less lively. By 1911 he was already buying manuscripts from Joseph Conrad, and through his collaboration with Pound, his role in the formation of literary modernism would become critical. It is telling that Quinn would eventually own the most important manuscripts to both *The Waste Land* and *Ulysses*, the greatest works of English-language modernism in verse and prose.[37]

Beginning in 1915, Quinn began to seek Pound's counsels on the purchase of paintings by Wyndham Lewis and sculptures by Henri Gaudier-Brzeska and Jacob Epstein, also giving Pound small commissions or fees for his interventions. Meanwhile, the two began to look around for a literary magazine that could house the authors favoured by Pound. In early 1916 Pound made a proposal to the *Little Review*, a small magazine (2,500 subscribers plus 600 in street sales) which had just moved from Chicago to New York. Pound would become the journal's 'Foreign Editor', furnishing it with a subvention that would cover the cost of all the pages which he would edit. The choice of materials to include would be his, and Quinn would furnish Pound with another subvention with which he could pay small sums to contributors and a modest salary (£60 per year) to himself. In the years between 1917 and 1919, Pound published Wyndham Lewis's *Tarr*, the serial version of Joyce's *Ulysses*, poems and critical essays by T. S. Eliot, and a mélange of Pound's own poetry and critical prose. Pound's criticism was transformed into editorial practice, evident in his astute awareness that embracing the most significant writing of his time in a single venue would create a suggestive sense of coherence. The power of that suggestiveness is still apparent today in ongoing debate about modernism and its significance.

There is also a perceptible change that takes place in Pound's rhetoric during this period, one that occurs less in his critical writings than in his correspondence. One can see it at work already in 1917, when Pound answers a query from Margaret Anderson about how best to announce his collaboration with the *Little Review*: 'If it is any use for adv[ertising] purposes, you may state that a single copy of my first book has just fetched £8 (forty dollars).' Or again, when William Bird asked him how best to advertise *A Draft of XVI. Cantos*, Pound would urge the same argument in 1924: 'Your best ad is the quiet statement that at auction recently a

---

[37] On Quinn, see B. L. Reid's classic biography, *The Man From New York* (New York, 1968). For a selection of his correspondence with Pound, see *The Selected Letters of Ezra Pound to John Quinn, 1915–1924*, ed. Timothy Materer (Durham, 1991).

copy of Mr. Pound's [first book] 'A Lume Spento published in 1908 at
$1.00 (one dollar) was sold for $52.50.'[38] Again, in 1921 when Pound
briefly took up with the *Little Review*, he argued that Anderson and Heap
should publish twenty-two photos on these grounds:

> It is worth while publishing them all, not as an expense but as an investment, this
> number should be a permanent property for you … I think it is a perfectly solid
> investment for anybody's money.[39]

In these justifications to potential consumers, whether readers or editors, Pound no longer advanced claims about the intrinsic aesthetic value
of art-works. Instead he offered claims about performance records and
'investment'. Significantly, when writing to John Quinn in 1922 about
magazines which might require his support, he told him: 'I shall only "so
advise you" after I feel sure you'll get your money's worth.'[40] Such
remarks may betray the influence which the patronage of Quinn had on
Pound. As a lawyer involved in Wall Street transactions, and as a patron
whose means were limited in comparison with the period's wealthier
collectors, Quinn was inevitably concerned about whether one could 'get
your money's worth' from particular purchases or acts of patronage. To
collect successfully it is also necessary that one sell some of one's hold-
ings from time to time, and hence that one watch the market with care.
Quinn was no different from any other collector in this regard. But such
care made his patronage necessarily different from the kind of patronage
which Lady Glenconner had once bestowed on Pound or poets such as
John Drinkwater, for in the rough world of high finance in which Quinn
worked, appeals to sentiment and beauty were not permitted. And
Quinn's own personality, which was marked by a deep distrust of sentimentalism, only accentuated this vein of his thought. Now the justification for buying a work was no longer an appeal to art, but an
appeal to the notion of investment. Modernism, like Marinetti a
few years before, could no longer sustain its faith in the independent
integrity and coherence of the aesthetic. Art was giving way to life,
but by this point in time life was inseparable from the world of an
expanding commodity economy. To preserve itself, modernism turned
elsewhere: to the shadowy world of collecting and dealing in rarities, a
world which it now modernised by assimilating art to the world of

---

[38] Ezra Pound to Margaret Anderson, 10 May 1917, in Thomas L. Scott and Melvin J.
Friedman, eds., *Pound/Little Review: The Letters of Ezra Pound to Margaret Anderson*
(New York, 1988), p. 46. Ezra Pound to William Bird, May 1924, Bird Papers, Bloom-
ington, Indiana University Library.

[39] Ezra Pound to Margaret Anderson [29 April–4 May 1912], in Scott and Friedman, eds.,
Pound/Little Review, p. 271.

[40] Ezra Pound to John Quinn, 4–5 July 1922, *The Selected Letters of Ezra Pound to John
Quinn*, p. 212.

investment. Patron-*saloniers* gave way to a new breed, patron-investors.

Pound, meanwhile, undertook the task of putting his engagement with Imagism into an account of recent literary history. In April 1917 he published an essay titled 'Status Rerum – The Second', glancing backward to the essay with which he had first announced the creation of Imagism four years earlier in 1913.[41] Imagism, he now declared, had gone 'off into froth'. Its defects were 'sloppiness, lack of cohesion, lack of organic centre in individual poems, rhetoric, a conventional form of language'. Imagism, in short, had become Amygism, Pound's dismissive moniker for the works which had been published by Amy Lowell acting as editor and patron of Imagism after 1915. Now, in collaboration with T. S. Eliot, Pound went on to champion more formal verses as an antidote to the excesses of *vers libre*, a decision that he later recalled in these terms:

at a particular date in a particular room, two authors, neither engaged in picking the other's pocket, decided that the dilutation of *vers libre*, Amygism, Lee Master-ism, general floppiness had gone too far and that some counter-current must be set going. Parallel situation centuries ago in China. Remedy prescribed 'Emaux et Camees' (or the Bay State Hymn Book). Rhyme and regular strophes.[42]

The result of this calculated decision was the quatrain poems in Eliot's second volume and the taut stanzas of *Hugh Selwyn Mauberley*. Imagism would forever after be presented as a temporary cleansing of the palette, a reformation in poetic diction, a necessary step prior to the development of more significant and enduring achievements.

But the rewriting of Imagism's history was scarcely the full extent of Pound's activities. From 1917 to 1920 he produced a torrent of critical writings. The period witnessed some of his most important essays, includ-ing two series on 'Elizabethan Classicists' (in *The Egoist*) and 'Early Translators of Homer' (also in *The Egoist*) – these two would be Pound's most important considerations of translation; another series derived from his longstanding project to organise the notes of Ernest Fenollosa, 'The Chinese Written Character as a Medium for Poetry' (*Little Review*); two more series of essays in social criticism; a defence of individualism and a critique of socialism called 'Provincialism the Enemy' (*The New Age*, 1917); and a survey of contemporary periodicals in England and the US, 'Studies in Contemporary Mentality' (*The New Age*). He also wrote numerous book reviews, publicising new volumes by Eliot, Joyce, Will-iams, Marianne Moore, Mina Loy, as well as posthumous publications by Henry James. And if all that were not enough, he continued to publish

---

[41] Ezra Pound 'Status Rerum – The Second', originally in *Poetry*, 8.1 (April 1916), pp. 38–43; now in *Ezra Pound's Poetry and Prose*, vol. 2, pp. 151–3; all quotations from p. 151.

[42] Ezra Pound, 'Harold Monro', originally in *The Criterion*, 11, no. 45 (July 1932), pp. 581–92; now in *Ezra Pound's Poetry and Prose*, vol. 5, pp. 357–64, here p. 363.

almost weekly reviews of art exhibitions and musical concerts for *The New Age*. The writings were occasional in nature, often hastily written and repetitive, frequently digressive and meandering, and just as often outrageously entertaining. Some critics have charged that Pound wrote too much and too swiftly, and consequently that he never formulated a grand vision of art or definitive meditations about a single author. But as K. K. Ruthven has noted: 'We should be grateful that Pound responded so engagingly and energetically to new writing in the literary journalism he professed to despise.'[43]

Why Pound wrote so much is not hard to discern. The essays which Pound published in *The New Age* were by now an essential source of income; wartime inflation was boosting prices to unprecedented levels, and at war's end it was estimated that they had risen 350 per cent. The increase in Pound's output of periodical contributions in these years is nothing short of remarkable. In 1915 and 1916 his contributions to periodicals had totalled fifty and thirty-two items respectively, both prose and poetry; but in the four years running from 1917 to 1920, they jumped to seventy-four, one hundred and twenty-six, ninety-three, and ninety-seven publications – almost one piece every three to four days. The effect of writing at this pace becomes apparent already in 1918, when Pound abruptly concludes his translation of an essay by Jules Romains with a startling address to the reader: 'It is of course wholly ridiculous that I should leave off my work to make translations.'[44] Already Pound was growing tired. In late 1920 he would leave London for good, and by the time that he moved to Paris in early 1921, he was determined to spend more time writing poetry. As he told Margaret Anderson:

Point I never can seem to get you to take is that I have done more log rolling and attending to other people's affairs Joyce, Lewis, Gaudier, etc. (don't regret it). But I am in my own small way, a writer myself, and as before stated. I shd. like (and wont in any case get) the chance of being considered as the author of my own poems rather than as a literary politician and a very active stage manager of rising talent.[45]

Just as tellingly, in a contemporary essay he announced for the first time a renunciation of art: 'the symbolist position, artistic aloofness from world affairs, is no good *now*'.[46]

After his move to Paris, a marked change took place in the pace of Pound's critical writings. The man who had annually written ninety-seven contributions to periodicals (1917 to 1920) now produced barely fifteen

43 Ruthven, *Ezra Pound as Literary Critic*, p. 155.
44 Ezra Pound, 'Unanimism', originally in *The Little Review*, 4.12 (April 1918), pp. 26–32; now in *Ezra Pound's Poetry and Prose*, vol. 3, pp. 81–4, here p. 84.
45 Ezra Pound to Margaret Anderson, [22? April 1921], in Scott and Friedman, eds., *Pound/ Little Review*, p. 266.
46 Ezra Pound, '[A Review of] *Credit Power and Democracy*, by Maj. C. H. Douglas and A. R. Orage', originally in *Contact* (New York), 4 ([Summer 1921]), p. 1; now in *Ezra Pound's Poetry and Prose*, vol. 4, p. 156.

per year (from 1921 through 1926). Moreover, of the ninety contributions which he produced in that six-year span, twenty-one were letters-to-the-editor. The change in publication patterns was accompanied by two others. One was a perceptible estrangement between Pound and John Quinn, partly due to the legal imbroglio surrounding the seizure and trial of *Ulysses* in late 1920 and early 1921, and partly due to Quinn's reservations about the way in which Pound set about publicising the Bel Esprit project to aid T. S. Eliot financially in early 1922. The other change was Pound's growing interest in Italian Fascism, interest that began to crystallise in 1923. By early 1924 Pound was writing letters to Mussolini through a mutual acquaintance, proposing that the new dictator take Pound on as an advisor who would direct a programme of Italian cultural renovation. In December 1924 Pound left Paris for Italy. As he later recalled, 'I bet on Italian fascism ... and came here to live in the middle of it.'[47]

As a result of his deepening interest in fascism, Pound once more took up his pen. Every year from 1927 on is marked by a staggering increase in periodical contributions. But the subjects that attracted him now were politics and economics. He was no longer interested, he told one correspondent in 1935, in 'Yawpin' 'bout licherchoor'. When T. S. Eliot put together a collection of his *Literary Essays* in 1954, he dismissed its 'narsty title'.[48] In the long struggle which the competing claims of art and life had waged for Pound's allegiance, life had finally won its definitive victory. Yet life, when stripped of an aesthetic sphere whose integrity and coherence could pose an alternative to the use-values of the market place, became nothing but the marketplace itself. That was unacceptable for Pound, and instead he turned to Fascism.

In one of his later writings, 'Date Line' (1934), Pound attempted to summarise the aims of criticism as he conceived it.

1. Theoretically it tries to forerun composition, to serve as gun-sight, though there is, I believe, no recorded instance of this foresight having EVER been of the slightest use save to actual composers...

2. Excernment. The general ordering and weeding out of what has actually been performed. The elimination of repetitions. The work analogous to that which a good hanging committee or a curator would perform in a National Gallery or in a biological museum; the ordering of knowledge so that the next man (or generation) can most readily find the live part of it, and waste the least possible time among obsolete issues.[49]

The interesting thing here is that Pound's second category, which he

---

[47] Ezra Pound, unpublished essay, 'Fascism or the Direction of the Will' (revised version), ts. p. 2; in Beinecke Rare Book and Manuscript Library (Yale University), YCAL Mss. 43, Box 89, Folder 3360.

[48] Both letters quoted in Carpenter, *A Serious Character*, pp. 117, 816,

[49] Ezra Pound, 'Date Line', originally in Ezra Pound, *Make It New* (London); now in *Literary Essays of Ezra Pound*, 1934, pp. 74–87.

clearly thinks of as vital but less important than the first, covers the entire range of what is conventionally called 'criticism'. The primary aim of Pound's ideal critic is 'demonstration'; he must not only 'excern' the best and reorder the literary tradition but embody these discoveries in his imaginative writing. This was Pound's method from the beginning.

In 'Date Line' Pound also describes the various 'kinds' of criticism, ranking them in an ascending order of importance, and his categories provide a neat overview of his critical life.

1   Criticism by discussion

The range of this category is immense. Pound wrote literally thousands of essays, but he considered these writings the least important part of his 'criticism'. Under this heading would fall his many reviews, generously written in the service of contemporary letters (one thinks of his role as the tireless promoter of Frost, Joyce, Eliot, and a host of other important figures), as well as his more general essays on critical procedure and poetic language. All these writings reveal Pound as a critic of the 'moment', alive to the immediate needs of English and American poetry.

Most of Pound's conventional criticism – such as his essays on Imagism and Vorticism – was part of a campaign to revitalise and redirect the language of poetry. Therefore it must be read against the background of a particular literary scene, and in the context of a desire to reshape literature according to his notion of 'tradition'. But in spite of the occasional nature of Pound's criticism, it never seems dated, since it remains a vital part of the literature it helped to create. Pound's essays live because they still embody the excitement and sense of discovery of the modernist enterprise.

2   Criticism by translation

Under this heading would come Pound's evocative rendering of the Anglo-Saxon 'Seafarer', his adaptations from the Chinese in *Cathay*, his translations and adaptations from the Latin and Provençal languages, his versions of Greek tragedy. Appearing at crucial turns in his poetic life, these 'translations' from one culture to another are just as much a part of his literary criticism as his conventional essays, and have had at least an equal impact on the development of modern literature. Robert Frost once said that poetry is what is lost in translation. Pound took the opposite view; he believed that the essential 'virtue' of a poem could be preserved and even enhanced in translation. In an early essay called 'How I Began', he said that he wished to know by the age of thirty 'what part poetry was "indestructible", what part could *not be lost* by translation, and – scarcely less important – what effects were obtainable in *one* language only and were utterly incapable of being translated'.[50] Borrowing Pater's words (from a passage in his preface to *The Renaissance*), one can say that Pound wished to preserve 'the virtue by which a picture, a landscape, a fair personality in life or in a book, produces this special impression of beauty or pleasure, to indicate what the source of that impression is, and under what conditions it is experienced'.[51]

3 Criticism by exercise in the style of the given period

According to Pound, the final test of the poet is his ability to recognise and recreate various traditional 'styles', since this is an essential device for bringing past and present into alignment. *Hugh Selwyn Mauberley* (1920), for example, is a museum of imitated styles, each playing a crucial role in Pound's criticism of the immediate foreground and background of English poetry. Ranging from echoes of the poets of the 'nineties and the Pre-Raphaelites to a marvellous pastiche of Elizabethan songs in 'Envoi', *Mauberley* gives us Pound's view of the 'tradition' in a form more subtle than his discursive criticism. Poem VI ('Yeux Glauques') distils a considered overview of the Pre-Raphaelites into a few tight stanzas, while Poem VII ('Siena Mi Fe; Disfecemi Maremma') lays bare the poets of the 'nineties with a concision suggested by its title, in which Dante's La Pia tells her tragic sory in one line.

4 Criticism via music

Whatever one may think of Pound's musical theories and his excursions into composition (he wrote two operas), these activities were part of his emphasis on the musical aspect of language (*melopoeia*) 'wherein the words are charged, over and above their plain meaning, with some musical property, which directs the bearing or trend of the meaning'.[52] Since *melopoeia* cannot be 'translated' in any usual sense of that word, Pound felt that the only way to convey this aspect of earlier poetry is through music.

[50] See note 25.
[51] Walter Pater, *The Renaissance: Studies in Art and Poetry (The 1893 Text)*, ed. Donald L. Hill (Berkeley, 1980), pp. xx–xxi.
[52] Ezra Pound, 'How to Read', originally published in 1931, now in *Literary Essays*, pp. 15–40, here p. 25.

5   Criticism in new composition

The most important of Pound's work would fall under this category of
ultimate criticism. One example is Canto I, which provides a masterly
synthesis of 'Criticism by translation', and 'Criticism in the style of a given
period'. Here the account of Odysseus' descent into the underworld (from
Book XI of the *Odyssey*) is retold in a compressed form inherited from a
Renaissance translator and styled in imitated Anglo-Saxon metre (since
Pound felt the Old English epics had many of the qualities of the *Odyssey*).
The result is a series of 'overlays' that gives us a critical perspective on the
quest of the modern artist and actually recreates a tradition.

Turning from the kinds of his criticism to the particular mode of attack
found in his essays, the first thing to note is the 'comparative' nature of
Pound's writings. Partly because he was trained as a student of the middle
ages, when Europe was a single culture, Pound's interests were always
international. Like T. S. Eliot, he felt that the America of the early
twentieth century had a culture too thin to nourish a modern poet, and he
spent most of his adult life abroad. But always his aim was to revitalise
American poetry and American culture by purging it of insularity. As he
said in a little poem of 1912 ('Epilogue') dedicated to his 'five books
containing mediaeval studies, experiments and translations':

> I bring you the spoils, my nation,
> I, who went out in exile,
>   Am returned to thee with gifts.

In pursuing his methods of comparison and 'translation' Pound was
always pragmatic: he thought of himself as a worker in a laboratory,
trying out new combinations and looking for evidence of unsuspected
possibilities.

As for the critical judgements that flow from Pound's comparative
studies, they depend in large measure on his hierarchy of the arts.

(a) *The inventors*, discoverers of a particular process or of more than one mode
and process...

(b) *The masters*. This is a very small class, and there are very few real ones. The
term is properly applied to inventors who, apart from their own inventions, are
able to assimilate and co-ordinate a large number of preceding inventions...

(c) *The diluters*...

(d) ...The men who do more or less good work in the more or less good style of
a period...

(e) *Belles Lettres*... [Those] who are not exactly 'great masters', who can
hardly be said to have originated a form, but who have nevertheless brought some
mode to a very high development.

(f) ...the starters of crazes.[53]

It is a sign of Pound's obsessive desire to instigate new movements, to redirect the course of literature, that he ranks the inventors first. Eliot must have had this in mind when he said that 'Chinese poetry, as we know it today, is something invented by Ezra Pound.'[54]

A brief catalogue of the major figures in Pound's tradition, and of his glaring omissions, will give a clear sense of the values he wanted to raise from the dead. In the classical world Pound's first admiration is for Homer, whose narrative drive and masterful psychology he always praised; after Homer come the Latin poets (Catullus, Ovid, Propertius) whose wit, precision, and lack of sentimentality seemed proper antidotes to the diffuseness of much contemporary verse. In the Middle Ages it is the troubadours, masters of intricate verse-forms and the musical phrase, that Pound most cherishes, along with Dante's ability to make the spiritual visible in concrete imagery. After Dante comes Villon, with his total honesty and realism, and the Renaissance translators of Greek and Latin, who in their own time strove to 'Make It New'. Next would be the sixteenth- and seventeenth-century masters of song and musical statement: Waller, Campion, Dowland. In the nineteenth century Pound's focus is on those French poets who were exponents of the iron turn of phrase (Laforgue) and precise presentation of emotion (Gautier), and on the masters of ninetenth-century prose fiction – Stendhal, Flaubert, James – who led him to his dictum, 'Poetry should be at least as well written as prose', by which he meant that most contemporary verse was loose and vague compared to the density of Flaubert or Joyce.[55] Among his own contemporaries, Pound's unerring taste led him to single out those figures we still associate with the heroic early age of Anglo-American modernism. As the eye moves through this catalogue one thing is obvious: Pound was determined to create a tradition that would satisfy his own deepest needs and those of his age, without regard for any judicious sense of 'the canon'. Hence his persistent attacks on Milton, which – like Eliot's – were done with an eye toward Milton's influence on the language of poetry, but which – unlike Eliot's – were never modified after the revolution in modern poetry had been won.

Equally revealing are the obvious omissions from Pound's tradition: Shakespeare and the Elizabethan dramatists (so crucial to Eliot), the entire eighteenth century, Romanticism, many of the great Victorians. In the task of making a new start and scrubbing clean the palette of English poetry, a great deal of the best in older literature had to be ignored or

[53] Pound, 'How to Read', pp. 23–4.
[54] T. S. Eliot, 'Introduction (1928)' to Eliot, ed., *Ezra Pound. Selected Poems* (London, 1928), p. 14.
[55] Ezra Pound, 'Mr. Hueffer and the Prose Tradition in Verse' (1914), *Ezra Pound's Poetry and Prose*, vol. 1, p. 245.

actively denigrated. Pound was conscious of the risks involved in his pillaging of the past, but he felt they were well worth taking.

It is easy to see how Pound's critical methods and his idea of tradition determined the major techniques of his poetry (or did the early poetic successes determine the course of his criticism?). The method of bringing past and present together through literary or mythical allusions; the technique of *personae*, which enables the modern poet to speak with the voices of other ages or other personalities; the artistic use of various imitated or 'period' styles – these signatures of Pound's poetry are consonant with his firmest critical aims. His prose and poetry should be read together, and in chronological order, to give a full perspective on his extraordinary achievement.

In the second issue of Eliot's *The Criterion* (January 1923) Pound published an essay 'On Criticism in General' that has never been collected. It is a summing-up, and suggests in its abrupt form that Pound (writing from Paris) is putting his early criticism behind him, just as he had already left behind London and would soon depart from Paris. After 1923 much of Pound's criticism takes a more openly pedagogic aim, and is addressed more to *les jeunes* and American educators than to his literary contemporaries. Some of the lists and precepts in 'On Criticism in General' became the foundation for *How to Read* (1929–31) and its successor, *ABC of Reading* (1934), where Pound is simplifying his earlier ideas in textbook form. At the same time, his growing obsession with political and economic theories began to coarsen both his prose and his judgements, and his last 'critical' book – *Guide to Kulchur* (1938) – is marked by wild swings between subtlety and bombast: in fact, in content and form it is a paradigm for some of the later Cantos. The political, economic, and philosophical parts of *Guide to Kulchur* reveal a mind not only out of touch with contemporary reality but one out of touch with its earlier ideals of style and precision. On the other hand, the book is shot through with luminous memories and brilliant perceptions. One is constantly reminded of the critic Pound once had been – the man who did as much as any other to shape the literary assumptions of Anglo-American modernism.

3

Gertrude Stein

Steven Meyer

'It is necessary that there is stock taking. If there is such necessity, can we critically abandon individualism. One cannot critically abandon individualism. One cannot critically realise men and women.'[1]

Though all literary criticism may be read as implicit commentary on the writer's own practice, Gertrude Stein's is especially self-regarding, always explicitly about her compositional practices. Even the pleasure she takes in viewing paintings, the subject of the least ostensibly literary of her *Lectures in America* (1935), proves inseparable from her writing. Paradoxically, this is because the two complementary forms of experience do *not* overlap; everyone, Stein declares at once grandly and tentatively, 'is almost sure to really like something outside of their real occupation', and in her case 'looking at pictures' is 'the only thing', apart from her 'real' occupation, writing, which she 'never get[s] tired of doing'.[2] Such self-reflexivity, typical of modernist poetry and fiction yet fairly exceptional in twentieth-century criticism, should not be dismissed as a sign of self-indulgence. Instead, Stein's multiple accounts of herself writing, and of her writing self, form a trenchant critique of the idealist assumptions which continued to operate in the critical writing of her modernist contemporaries, despite being called into question by their creative work.

---

[1] Gertrude Stein, 'As Fine as Melanctha', *As Fine as Melanctha* (New Haven, 1954), p. 256. Stein tells us that the title of this 1922 work was suggested by a request from Harold Loeb for 'something of hers that would be as fine as Melanctha' for the avant-garde journal *Broom*; see Stein, *The Autobiography of Alice B. Toklas* (hereafter *Autobiography*) (1933; rpt. New York, 1990, p. 206. In fact, it doesn't seem to have been Loeb but *Broom*'s co-editor Alfred Kreymborg who prompted Stein's quite stunning meditation on the implications of such a request. Among the letters from Kreymborg to Stein in the Yale Collection of American Literature is one dated 21 September 1921 in which Kreymborg writes: 'We have decided "against" the two books Mr. Loeb brought back with him, but not against using something of yours serially if we can find anything which is anywhere nearly as fine as Melanctha.' Within a month they had decided *for* 'If You Had Three Husbands', which was published in three instalments in the January, April, and June 1922 issues of *Broom*; see Kreymborg's letter to Stein dated 10 October 1921 and letters from Loeb to Stein, also in the Yale Collection, of 5 June and 7 July 1922. As for 'As Fine as Melanctha', it remained unpublished until nearly a decade after Stein's death.

[2] Gertrude Stein, 'Pictures', *Lectures in America* (1935; rpt. Boston, 1985), p. 59.

Hence, when her concerns become expressly literary near the end of 'Pictures', the contrast she makes between the 'literary ideas' of painters and those of writers directly leads to a dismissal of that staple of literary criticism, 'the writer's idea': 'Of course the best writers that is the writers who feel writing the most as well as the best painters that is the painters who feel painting the most do not have literary ideas.' Accordingly, such writing cannot properly be understood in terms of the writer's – or indeed any – organising idea, any 'central thing which has to move' even if 'everything else can be quiet'.[3] Arguments against the abstraction of thought from feeling are, of course, commonplace among modernists, yet unlike Eliot or Joyce or Woolf – whose criticism is dissociated from the 'sensuous thought' of their creative work and to that extent remains unself-critical – Stein's literary criticism is premised on a recognition that her ideas are ultimately incommensurate with the literature they are designed to address. Her considerable authority as a critic derives from her ability to keep her reader alert to this incommensurability even as one grants the usefulness of her ideas and the precision of her formulations.

The distinctive formal qualities of Stein's criticism derive from her revision of several key arguments of William James's concerning knowledge and consciousness.[4] James's psychology-based epistemology is translated by Stein, his student between 1893 and 1897, into an analysis of the extraordinary degree of self-consciousness and immediacy of awareness that writing permits. In the pages just preceding the famous chapter on 'The Stream of Thought' in his *Principles of Psychology* (1890), James distinguished two forms of knowledge which he labelled 'knowledge of acquaintance' and 'knowledge-about'. 'I am acquainted with many people and things', he observed, 'which I know very little about, except their presence in the places where I have met them ... I cannot impart acquaintance with them to anyone who has not already made it himself. I cannot *describe* them ... At most, I can say to my friends, Go to certain places and act in certain ways, and these objects will probably come.' All 'elementary natures', he added, 'together with the kinds of relation that subsist between them, must either not be known at all, or known in this dumb way of acquaintance without *knowledge-about*'. Generally speaking, 'the words *feelings* and *thought* give voice to the antithesis. Through

---

[3] *Ibid.*, pp. 89–90.
[4] For interpretations of James's influence on Stein which stress other features of James's pragmatism and psychology than those discussed here, see Lisa Ruddick, *Reading Gertrude Stein: Body, Text, Gnosis* (Ithaca, 1990), passim, Richard Poirier, *Poetry and Pragmatism* (Cambridge, Mass., 1992), passim, and Judith Ryan, *The Vanishing Subject: Early Psychology and Literary Modernism* (Chicago, 1991), pp. 89–99, as well as my 'Writing Psychology Over: Gertrude Stein and William James', *The Yale Journal of Criticism*, 8.1 (Spring 1995), pp. 133–64.

feelings we become acquainted with things, but only by our thoughts do
we know about them.'[5]

Stein's characterisation of her work 'Melanctha' (1905–6) in her 1926
lecture, 'Composition as Explanation', follows the general outlines of
James's distinction. Because 'the composition forming around [her] was a
prolonged present', and therefore involved 'a marked direction of being in
the present', she created in her narrative of American wandering a similarly 'prolonged' present. 'Naturally I knew nothing of a continuous present
but it came naturally to me to make one.' Knowing nothing *about* such a
present Stein was nonetheless acquainted with it, since, as she notes, it
characterised the 'natural composition in the world as it has been these
thirty years'.[6] Still, in arguing for the prolonged or continuous present as a
compositional feature in her writing, and not just of the world around her,
Stein challenged James's claim that one 'cannot impart acquaintance . . .
to anyone who has not already made it himself'. Starting with 'Melanctha'
she endeavoured to communicate acquaintance with 'people and things'
by obliging herself and her readers to attend to the 'continuous present'
formed in the process of writing (and reading) her words and sentences.
Despite agreeing with James that 'all the elementary natures' and 'the
kinds of relations that subsist between them' are known exclusively by
'way of acquaintance', she refused to make the further concession that
such acquaintance was necessarily 'dumb' or incommunicable. In order to
convey present experience in words without losing the quality of 'being *in*
the present', however, one would have to regard feelings of acquaintance,
and in particular the experience of 'feeling writing', as more than just 'the
germ and starting point of cognition', with 'thoughts the developed tree',
as James phrased it in 1890.[7]

By 1904 James was criticising his earlier, too restrictive conception of
feeling in print (as 'for seven or eight years past' he had been doing in the
classroom) by means of the notion of 'experience' advanced in *Essays in
Radical Empiricism*. The dualist distinction between 'the subject or bearer
of . . . knowledge' and 'the object known' did not correspond to what he
called 'realities of experience'; instead of 'the "I think" which Kant said
must be able to accompany all my objects', an 'I breathe' – the awareness,
however indistinct, that one is breathing – accompanies the objects of
one's thought. Furthermore, James proposed that 'philosophers ha[d]
constructed the entity known to them as consciousness' on the basis of this
sense of breathing, perhaps combined with 'other internal facts' such as

[5] William James, *The Principles of Psychology* (Cambridge, Mass., 1983), pp. 216–18
(emphasis in original).
[6] Gertrude Stein, 'Composition as Explanation', *What Are Masterpieces* (Los Angeles,
1940), p. 31.   [7] James, *The Principles of Psychology*, p. 218.

the sensation of 'muscular adjustments' in one's head.[8] 'Thoughts in the concrete are fully real', he acknowledged; yet he took this to mean that they are 'made of the same stuff as things are' rather than out of an alternative 'mind-stuff'.[9] Even when thoughts take the form of 'knowledge-about' they remain embodied and inseparable from feeling.[10]

With her emphasis on 'composition as explanation' and 'acquaintance with description' – the latter phrase having served as the title of a remarkable meditation composed shortly after she delivered 'Composition as Explanation' in 1926 – Stein situated herself with respect to James's 'radical empiricism' much as Eliot, with his 'dissociation of sensibility', stood in relation to the 'logical atomism' of Bertrand Russell's *Our Knowledge of the External World* (1914). Russell set himself flatly against James's radical empiricism in this work, which was based on the Lowell lectures he delivered while Eliot was studying with him at Harvard. Determined 'to preserve the dualism of subject and object in my terminology, because this dualism seems to me a fundamental fact concerning cognition', Russell acknowledged in the earlier 'Knowledge by Acquaintance and Knowledge by Description' (1910–11) that his principal interest was with 'the nature of our knowledge concerning objects in cases where we know that there is an object answering to a definite description, though we are not acquainted with any such object'.[11] Here he readily dissociates thought from feeling as both James and Stein did not, and as Eliot, at least in the 1921 essay on the Metaphysical poets in which he coined the phrase 'dissociation of sensibility', did only with great reluctance and on an

8 William James, 'Does "Consciousness" Exist?', *Essays in Radical Empiricism* (1912; rpt. Cambridge, Mass., 1976), pp. 4–5, 19. James observes that in the 'larger *Psychology*' he had already 'said a word' concerning the 'internal facts besides breathing (intracephalic muscular adjustments, etc.)' in relation to self-consciousness; see James, *The Principles of Psychology*, p. 288, for his discussion of the 'peculiar motions in the head or between the head and the throat' which comprise 'the portions of my innermost activity of which I am most distinctly aware'.

9 James, 'Does "Consciousness" Exist?', p. 19. 'I mean only to deny that the word ["consciousness"] stands for an entity, but to insist most emphatically that it does stand for a function', James explains. 'There is ... no aboriginal stuff or quality of being, contrasted with that of which material objects are made, out of which our thoughts of them are made; but there is a function of experience which thoughts perform, and for the performance of which this quality of being is invoked. That function is *knowing*; (p. 4, emphasis in original).

10 James's insistence on the physiological basis of thought in feeling stands behind the 'philosophy of organism' of Alfred North Whitehead and the 'neural Darwinism' of the contemporary neuroscientist Gerald Edelman, in addition to Stein's experimental writing; see Alfred North Whitehead, *Science and the Modern World* (1925; rpt. New York, 1967), p. 143 and Gerald Edelman, *Bright Air, Brilliant Fire: On the Matter of the Mind* (New York, 1992), p. 37. I examine the relations between these figures in *Irresistible Dictation: Gertrude Stein and the Correlations of Writing and Science* (forthcoming).

11 Bertrand Russell, 'Knowledge by Acquaintance and Knowledge by Description', *Mysticism and Logic and Other Essays* (1917; rpt., London, 1951), pp. 210, 214.

apparently historical and contingent basis, rather than as logically incontrovertible.

The reverberations from this dispute concerning feeling's reach in matters of cognition, together with post-Romantic considerations of the constitutive role of feeling in poetry, account for the embrace of Stein's perspective in 'Composition as Explanation' by poets as different as William Carlos Williams, Laura Riding, and William Empson. 'The whole of writing', Williams asserted in the 1929 essay 'The Work of Gertrude Stein' (written with the assistance of Louis Zukofsky), 'is an alertness not to let go of a possibility of movement in our fearful bedazzlement with some concrete and fixed present.'[12] As for Empson, his early 'Poem about a Ball in the Nineteenth Century', which may have been written in response to Stein's visit to Cambridge to present 'Composition as Explanation' – Empson was a student there at the time – was 'meant to be direct description' and to 'disregard meaning'. It begins, in obvious imitation of the irregularities of Stein's hesitating, waltz-like syntax: 'Feather, feather, if it was a feather, feathers for fair, or to be fair, aroused'.[13] As Riding suggested in the 1927 *Survey of Modernist Poetry*, Stein 'creates duration but makes it absolute by preventing anything from happening in the duration'; consequently she is able to convey acquaintance through verbal means without falling back on fixed description or any historicised form of knowledge-about.[14]

Structured around a narrative account of Stein's career, 'Composition as Explanation' might seem ill-equipped to convey an equivalent acquaintance with her writing. Nonetheless, Stein manages to navigate between the Scylla and Charybdis of literary history and the 'literary idea', thereby resisting the idealist norms of most literary criticism. By contrast, Williams and Riding convey the impression in their essays on Stein that it is the ideas expressed which count, rather than the medium in which they are expressed: this, despite arguing firmly against such norms. Before I describe several developments which led to Stein's readiness, however great her misgivings, to produce her own version of literary criticism, I need to explain why I have chosen to consider only the lectures that she delivered between 1926 and 1936 under this heading. There are actually four distinct modes of composition in which Stein reflects on her writing practices: autobiographical, meditative, exemplificatory, and literary

---

[12] William Carlos Williams, 'The Work of Gertrude Stein', *Selected Essays* (New York, 1969), pp. 117–18; Peter Quartermain discusses Zukofsky's contribution to the essay in *Disjunctive Poetics: From Gertrude Stein and Louis Zukofsky to Susan Howe* (Cambridge, 1992), pp. 213–14.

[13] William Empson, *Collected Poems* (San Diego, 1949), pp. 10, 95.

[14] Laura Riding and Robert Graves, *A Survey of Modernist Poetry* (1927; rpt. St. Clair Shores, Mich., 1972), p. 285.

critical. The more conventionally autobiographical writing, such as *The Autobiography of Alice B. Toklas* (1932) and *Everybody's Autobiography* (1936), includes the expression of any number of literary ideas (remarks, for instance, concerning the guiding principles and significance of writing by Stein and others). But these often forcefully expressed ideas are provisional and conversational. This is, to be sure, what makes them remarks.[15] On the other hand, much of Stein's writing after 'Melanctha' is meditative and self-reflexive, involving a persistent commentary on the act of composition as it is occurring. In some of this meditative writing, extending from the 1923 'An Elucidation' through the 1935 *Geographical History of America*, a more general inquiry into the nature of writing takes centre stage, and Stein offers examples of what it is like to 'feel writing' as distinct from just having 'literary ideas'. Later works of this sort, such as *Four in America* (1932–3) and *The Geographical History of America*, undoubtedly traffic in literary ideas, yet these ideas remain incidental to the overall shape of inquiry.[16] In a final category of writing, however, Stein takes her experience as a writer – the actual experience of writing as well as the internal dynamic of her writing over time – and expresses it in the form of literary ideas. The corpus of this uncompromising literary criticism consists of the fourteen lectures she delivered in the decade between 1926 and 1936: 'Composition as Explanation', the six *Lectures in America*, the four lectures collected in *Narration*, 'How Writing Is Written', 'An American and France', and 'What Are Masterpieces'.[17] The earliest of these, 'Composition as Explanation', stems, like

[15] 'Remarks', Stein cites herself not once but twice in the *Autobiography* as having remarked to Hemingway, 'are not literature.' First, Toklas recalls a story in which Hemingway wrote 'that Gertrude Stein always knew what was good in a Cezanne'; Stein 'looked at him and said, Hemingway, remarks are not literature'. (In light of the literary and extraliterary concerns Stein expresses in her lecture 'Pictures', one may note that this account immediately follows the twin observations that 'it is a good thing to have no sense of how it is done in the things that amuse you' and 'one can only have one metier as one can only have one language'.) Later in the *Autobiography* Toklas corrects herself: 'Hemingway was preparing his volume of short stories to submit to publishers in America . . . He had added to his stories a little story of meditations and in these he said that The Enormous Room was the greatest book he had ever read. It was then that Gertrude Stein said, Hemingway, remarks are not literature'; see Stein, *Autobiography*, pp. 76–7, 219. Remarks are thus only to be used if they are not taken too seriously, not frozen in the form of 'literary ideas' – as quasi-statements of fact – but instead remain sufficiently fluid that they can be rearranged, re-marked, as Stein demonstrates here. She is neither the first nor the last writer to observe that literary values don't necessarily coincide with values of fact.

[16] Although *Four in America* contains some extraordinary criticism of Shakespeare, the work as a whole falls under the category of Stein's more systematic investigations of writing. To be sure, one could always extract the Shakespeare criticism from its immediate context (as one could also do with similar passages in *The Geographical History of America*), but that would be to treat it simply as a set of intriguing literary ideas. In neither form – as part of a systematic investigation or as a set of ideas – is it criticism of the distinct variety Stein carves out for herself elsewhere.

[17] Three book reviews, of Sherwood Anderson's *A Story-teller's Story* (1925), Alfred Kreymborg's *Troubadour* (1925), and *Oscar Wilde Discovers America*, by Lloyd Lewis and Henry Austin Smith (1936), are included in *Reflections on the Atomic Bomb*, ed.

its distant cousin, 'An Elucidation', from jacket copy which Stein prepared
for her 1922 collection *Geography and Plays*. The story of that work's
publication warrants telling here, as it sets the stage for Stein's subsequent
attempts to 'realise ... just what her writing meant and why it was as it
was' through strategies, alternately, of exemplification, autobiography,
and literary criticism.[18]

As early as August 1920 Stein proposed to John Lane, then reprinting
Three Lives in England, that he publish a collection of her writing to be
called *Geography and Plays*.[19] Although this suggestion never got off the
ground, by the end of 1921 Stein had signed a contract for the book with
the Four Seas Company of Boston, a 'prestige' vanity press whose roster
included Williams's *Kora in Hell*.[20] The president of the firm, Edmund
Brown, desired some reassurance for the prospective reader: a 'good part'
of the manuscript, he observed in correspondence with Stein, 'is Greek to
me'. He asked Stein for 'a statement of your method of work and your
aims ... your own expression as how best for the ordinary reader to read
the more cryptic examples of your work'.[21] In response Stein proposed
that Sherwood Anderson, whom she had recently met and who had
expressed a desire to write about her, might supply an 'explanatory
preface'.[22] Brown, delighted with this unexpected windfall, still pressed
for 'a short biographical sketch ... which we can use to great advantage in
our preliminary publicity'.[23] The resulting 'Autobiographical Note' included a number of explanatory statements that at Stein's own suggestion

Robert Bartlett Haas (Los Angeles, 1973). Stein also reviewed Hemingway's *Three Stories
and Ten Poems* for the Paris edition of *The Herald Tribune* in 1923 and Anderson's
Puzzled America for *The Chicago Daily Tribune* in 1935. In addition, during World War
II she wrote two brief essays, 'Realism in Novels' and 'American Language and Literature'.
Although the latter appeared in French translation in 1944, neither essay was published in
English until 1988 when Shirley Neuman provided carefully edited versions in *Gertrude
Stein and the Making of Literature*, ed. Shirley Neuman and Ira B. Nadel (Boston, 1988).

[18] Stein, *Autobiography*, p. 209.
[19] In a letter dated 12 August 1920 Lane observed that '[w]ith regard to "Geography and
Plays"', I cannot undertake to publish this until I see how "Three Lives" is going to sell'.
The letter is in the Yale Collection of American Literature.
[20] Stein was directed to Four Seas by Kate Buss, a New England journalist and acquaintance
of Ezra Pound's whose *Studies in the Chinese Drama* was being published by the firm.
Earlier publications by Four Seas included Conrad Aiken's *The Jig of Forslin* in 1916 and
Williams's *Al Que Quiere!* in 1917 and *Sour Grapes* in 1921. In 1924 the firm would
publish Faulkner's first book, his collection of verse *The Marble Faun*, and in 1927
Mourning Dove's *Co-ge-we-a: The Half Blood: A Depiction of the Great Montana Cattle
Range*, possibly the first novel by a Native American woman; see Mary Dearbon,
Pocahontas's Daughters: Gender and Ethnicity in American Culture (New York, 1986),
p. 18.
[21] Letter from Brown to Stein, dated 7 December 1921, in the Yale Collection of American
Literature.
[22] The phrase is Brown's, in a letter to Stein dated 5 January 1922, in the Yale Collection of
American Literature.
[23] Letter from Brown to Stein, dated 5 January 1922, in the Yale Collection of American
Literature.

were later collected on the back cover of the volume.[24] These remarks comprise Stein's first public statement of method and aims; yet, phrased in the most general terms ('using every form that she can invent to translate the repeated story of everybody doing what, what they are being', 'a book of her examples in which she gives some of each of her experiences', 'her realization of people's, people and things, ways of revealing something'), they seem deliberately detached from any consideration of 'how best . . . to read the more cryptic examples' of her work. A draft of the concluding lines makes the rationale behind her reluctance to explain herself clearer. 'She continues', she had written, 'to experiment and renew her realizations of people and objects, ways of revealment.'[25] The final word, 'revealment', although no neologism – its pedigree stretches at least as far back as the sixteenth-century *A Mirror for Magistrates* – combines 'revelation' and its antithesis, 'concealment'. It was in the twists and turns of this admixture, in her ability to subject the received language to her alembic, that Stein located the method and aims of her writing; but she could only tell this by not saying so.

'Composition as Explanation': winter / spring 1926

Because her compositional practices had developed directly against the intentional, purposive use of writing as a means of talking *about* anything, Stein could not write about her 'way' with words in a conversational mode. Discursive explanation went against the grain of her writing; instead of conveying her own experience, it distanced the reader from the 'feeling' of the writing. As the post-War decade progressed, however, and Stein became more and more a Paris institution, she was increasingly surrounded by younger writers. Among them, Sherwood Anderson was probably the most distinguished. Already famous when he met Stein in 1921, two years after the appearance of *Winesburg, Ohio*, he nonetheless

---

[24] Letter from Brown to Stein, dated 23 September 1922, in the Yale Collection of American Literature. 'I have arranged a paper jacket very much in accordance with your suggestions', Brown wrote. 'I have nothing on the front except the title, author, and a reference to the preface by Mr. Anderson, which I think is a good selling point – and your own suggestion for the back of the jacket; but on the flap, in addition to a list of your other books, I have put in a resume of our "Literary Note" material.' A copy of the 'Autobiographical Note' is included in the Yale Collection of American Literature. Brown made the request for a 'biographical sketch' in the letter dated 5 January 1922 and had already received the sketch a month later when he observed in a letter tentatively dated 7 February 1922: 'The material you have sent to help us with the advance circular is just the thing that I was anxious to have. It is not only good material for a circular, but it makes interesting reading, which is more than one can say for most book circulars.'

[25] This is from one of a number of drafts of the 'Autobiographical Note', which along with several proof sheets are to be found in the Yale Collection of American Literature.

presented himself to her in the guise of a disciple.[26] He seemed genuinely to grasp the way she 'work[ed] with words' – her attentiveness to what he would call, in his introduction to *Geography and Plays*, 'the little house-keeping words, the swaggering bullying street corner words, the honest working, money saving words' – and he was the first major writer willing to sing her praises in public, to propose that her writing was 'the most important pioneer work done in the field of letters in my time'.[27] When Anderson agreed to introduce her book of 'samples of me', of 'xperiments of all kinds', she exulted: 'I have never had more genuine emotion than when you came and understood me and it is a great delight to me to know that it is you who is to present me. *Presentez moi* as they say in French.'[28] She was happy to be introduced by him, as she was not yet prepared to introduce herself.

Four years later, when she delivered 'Composition as Explanation' at Oxford and Cambridge, this had changed, in no small part owing to the publication the previous fall of *The Making of Americans*. Stein always insisted that *Making* was central not only to her own development as a writer but also to the development of twentieth-century writing, that is, of recognisably twentieth-century writing from the writing which preceded it. That is a grand claim, and on the surface of it quite unlikely, since the work wasn't even published until 1925. While doubtless one can document occasions of direct influence, as in Ernest Hemingway proofreading a hundred pages of the text for publication in the *Transatlantic Review* in 1924, the real substantiation must rest on other grounds.[29] Indeed, one might question whether even in Stein's own career *Making* led directly to the writing which followed it, starting with *Tender Buttons* in 1912. (The

---

[26] As Sylvia Beach commented, when she asked Stein whether she might bring Anderson 'around' to 27 rue de Fleurus to meet her: 'he is so anxious to know you for he says you have influenced him ever so much & that you stand as such a great master of words'; see Donald Gallup, ed., *Flowers of Friendship: Letters Written to Gertrude Stein* (New York, 1979), p. 138. 'For some reason or other', Toklas says in the account of the meeting in the *Autobiography*, 'I was not present on this occasion, some domestic complication in all probability, at any rate when I did come home Gertrude Stein was moved and pleased as she has very rarely been. Gertrude Stein was in those days a little bitter, all her unpublished manuscripts, and no hope of publication or serious recognition. Sherwood Anderson came and quite simply and directly as is his way told her what he thought of her work and what it had meant to him in his development. He told it to her then and what was even rarer he told it in print immediately after'; see Stein, *Autobiography*, p. 185.

[27] Sherwood Anderson, 'Introduction' to *Geography and Plays* by Gertrude Stein (1922; rpt. Madison, 1993), pp. 6, 8.

[28] Ray Lewis White, ed., *Sherwood Anderson/Gertrude Stein: Correspondence and Personal Essays* (Chapel Hill, 1972), pp. 11–12.

[29] Concerning Hemingway's experience Toklas comments in the *Autobiography* that in 'correcting proofs . . . you learn the values of the thing as no reading suffices to teach it to you', and adds that 'it was at this time' that Hemingway 'wrote to Gertrude Stein saying that it was she who had done the work in writing The Making of Americans and he and all his had but to devote their lives to seeing that it was published'; see Stein, *Autobiography*, p. 217.

compositional values of the pieces collected in *Tender Buttons* are about as different from those of *Making* as it is possible to imagine.) If *Making* truly epitomises epochal changes in compositional practice, then one should be able to show not only that, like Edith Wharton's *The Custom of the Country*, it takes the transition from the nineteenth to the twentieth century as its subject, but also that the transition actually occurs on its pages, that in the context of the typically nineteenth-century 'history of a family's progress' which frames the work, the narrator's slowly developing sense of the 'reality' of writing effectively captures the first unmistakable stirrings of the twentieth century.[30] It is in this respect, rather than through mechanisms of direct cause and effect, that 'all modern writing' may be said, as Stein announced in the jacket copy of *Geography and Plays*, to have 'sprung' from her 'early experiments'. In 'Composition as Explanation' she links both claims when she observes of her writing up to the World War that 'so far then the progress of my conceptions was the natural progress entirely in accordance with my epoch'.

Although Stein describes her development as a writer here in terms of changing 'conceptions' of writing, the expression of these 'literary ideas' is sufficiently obscure as to render them quite unhelpful as critical categories. All the same, two of the categories in 'Composition as Explanation' – 'beginning again and again' and 'the continuous present' – have become mainstays of commentary on Stein's writing. Their relative clarity is due not to any conceptual precision which they may be said to possess in themselves but rather to the explanatory context provided by the lecture as a whole. Although Stein asserts rather than argues for the coherence of her development as a writer, this claim occurs in the course of an intricately argued account of why her writing has created such interest among her contemporaries that student literary societies at Cambridge and Oxford should invite her to speak on it. (All of Stein's lectures were written for delivery in an academic context, and in this respect she participated in the general consolidation of literary criticism within the academy in the twentieth century.) Normally such literary societies would have displayed an entirely academic taste in art, not an interest in 'avant-garde' writing; the World War, however, had brought about an exceptional state of affairs in the relation between contemporary art and 'modern times'. 'No one is ahead of his time', Stein suggests,

it is only that the particular variety of creating his time is the one that his contemporaries who also are creating their own time refuse to accept. And they refuse to accept it for a very simple reason and that is ... because it would not make any difference as they lead their lives in the new composition anyway.[31]

[30] For an argument along these lines, see my introduction to Gertrude Stein, *The Making of Americans* (Normal, 1995), pp. xi–xxxiv.
[31] Stein, 'Composition as Explanation', pp. 27–8.

The difference between the ordinary person and the avant-garde artist arises, according to Stein, from the fact that the typical person, despite living in the present, understands present experience exclusively in terms of categories derived from the past. Hence one's explanatory framework is out of sync with one's experience. This may be viewed as a version of Eliot's analysis of modern 'dissociation of sensibility'; or, more exactly, Eliot's argument is a version of Stein's, since Stein quite sensibly makes such dissociation a general, although not inevitable, condition of human experience, rather than misleadingly giving it a precise genealogy, as both Eliot and Pound do.[32]

The explanatory framework provided by avant-garde art is the one the present demands, yet few individuals will recognise its pertinence. Why should this be so? It is here that Stein's notion of 'composition as explanation' comes into play, for avant-garde art (as distinct from academic or strictly generic art) requires explanation that emerges directly from the work, not from terms or categories derived from prior experience. Still, the imaginative art of a period and the general sensibility may be more closely in tune; this occurs when for social or political reasons, as in the advent of war 'actively threaten[ing]' one's nation or community, time speeds up. As 'Lord Grey remarked', Stein observes, 'the generals before the war talked about the war ... as a nineteenth century war although to be fought with twentieth century weapons'. Once the academic idea was replaced by actual war, conceptions of war necessarily 'became completely contemporary and so created the completed recognition of the contemporary composition', which

made every one not only contemporary in act not only contemporary in thought but contemporary in self-consciousness made every one contemporary with the modern composition. And so the art creation of the contemporary composition which would have been outlawed normally outlawed several generations more behind even than war, war having been brought so to speak up to date art so to speak was allowed not completely to be up to date, but nearly up to date, in other words we who created the expression of the modern composition were to be recognized before we were dead some of us even quite a long time before we were dead.

The difficulty that such recognition created for Stein was how to acknowledge it without viewing herself as already 'a classic' – 'the modern compo-

[32] Eliot locates the fall into dissociation in the poetry, most notably Milton's, which followed on the heels of the English metaphysical poets in the seventeenth century; Pound, in the transition from Guido Cavalcanti, the fourteenth-century Italian 'metaphysical' poet, to Petrarch. See T. S. Eliot, 'The Metaphysical Poets', *Homage to John Dryden* (London, 1924) and Ezra Pound, 'Cavalcanti', *Literary Essays*, ed. T. S. Eliot (1954; rpt. New York, 1968). On the tendentiousness of Eliot's historical claims, see Frank Kermode, *Romantic Image* (London, 1957), pp. 138–61 and Perry Meisel, *The Myth of Being Modern: A Study in British Literature and Criticism after 1850* (New Haven, 1987), pp. 75–80.

sition having become past is classified and the description of it is classical'
– and consequently dead before her time.[33]

Aside from stressing the mechanisms of writing in works like 'An
Elucidation' – which aim, by means of examples, to provide knowledge of
acquaintance rather than knowledge-about – how might she address her
writing without simply reducing it to an assortment of literary ideas? Her
solution in 'Composition as Explanation' focused on the complex temporality of composition, involving not just development from composition to composition and within individual compositions, but also the
relation of these to 'the contemporary composition' in which the artist and
her contemporaries 'lead their lives'. The writing, on this account, takes
the form of a genetic process, one that has no particular external aim but
operates instead on a Darwinian model of emergent evolution.[34] Even
'Composition as Explanation' doesn't put an end to this process, since the
lecture's explanatory mode proves inseparable from the particulars of its
composition, as when in the last lines Stein extends the account of her
writing to the present occasion – not, however, by expressly discussing the
lecture, but instead by addressing 'the thing that is at present the most
troubling', namely what she calls the distribution and equilibration of
time. Only through such distribution and equilibration can she bring
'Composition as Explanation' to a close in the present, both on the
occasion of its composition (despite its being composed for subsequent
delivery) and on the occasion of its delivery (despite its having been
composed on a prior occasion). 'And afterwards', she asks herself in the
penultimate line of the lecture. 'Now that is all', she concludes.[35]

Lectures in America: summer / fall 1934

That would be all until 1934, after the concentrated meditations on
writing of the late 1920s and early 1930s, after the self-publication of the
Plain Edition – five volumes published between 1931 and 1933 at 27 rue
de Fleurus, containing writing composed between 1911 and 1931 – after
the self-publicity of *The Autobiography of Alice B. Toklas*, a surprise

---

[33] Stein, 'Composition as Explanation', pp. 26, 28, 35–6, 27.

[34] 'I do still think that Darwin is the great man of the period that formed my youth', Stein
observed in a letter to Robert Haas dated 13 September 1937 in the Yale Collection of
American Literature; the letter is cited by Clive Bush in *Halfway to Revolution:
Investigation and Crisis in the Work of Henry Adams, William James, and Gertrude Stein*
(New Haven, 1991), p. 269. 'I began with evolution', she asserted several years later in
Wars I Have Seen. 'Most pleasant and exciting and decisive. It justified peace and justified
war. It also justified life and it also justified death and it also justified life'; see *Wars I Have
Seen* (New York, 1945), p. 61.

[35] Stein, 'Composition as Explanation', p. 38.

1933 best-seller, and after the equally startling success of *Four Saints in Three Acts* on Broadway in early 1934. That summer Stein decided, after considerable hesitation, to deliver a series of lectures during her upcoming visit to the United States, her first in thirty years, timed to coincide with the publication of a new volume of selected writings in early November. In a letter to a colleague she described herself as 'solemnly going on writing the lectures':

I have finished one about pictures, one about the theatre, and am now doing the one about English literature. Then there are three about my work, Making of Americans, 2 Portraits and so-called repetition and what is and what is not, 3 Grammar and tenses, I get quite a bit of stage fright while doing them but if one must one must.[36]

The lectures follow the same order in the published version, with the single exception that in *Lectures in America* 'the one about English literature' is moved to the beginning. The result is that at the outset Stein contextualises her writing externally, first in relation to English literature and then in relation to painting. In the transitional third lecture, 'Plays', she moves from a general consideration of dramatic writing as being, like the lectures themselves, 'either read or heard or seen', to an account of her own experience as a spectator of theatre – a narrative which parallels the preceding account of her experience as a viewer of paintings – and concludes with a narrative account of her own writing for the theatre.[37] Finally, each of the last three lectures sketches an alternative narrative of the development of her writing.[38] 'Composition as Explanation' had

[36] W. G. Rogers, *When This You See Remember Me: Gertrude Stein in Person* (New York, 1948), p. 116.

[37] Stein, 'Plays', in *Lectures in America*, p. 94.

[38] Whereas the account in 'Plays' only starts in early 1913, just after Stein has completed the pieces collected in *Tender Buttons*, the next lecture, 'The Gradual Making of The Making of Americans', moves back in time to the composition of *Making* and then forward only so far as the transitional works linking *Tender Buttons* and 'the Long Book', as Stein characterised *The Making of Americans* in a 1925 letter to Carl Van Vechten; for the text of this letter, see Edward Burns, ed., *The Letters of Gertrude Stein and Carl Van Vechten* (New York, 1986), I, p. 118. Stein had recently published several of these intermediate works in the final Plain Edition volume *Matisse Picasso and Gertrude Stein With Two Shorter Stories* (1933), In 'Plays' she recalls that 'for a long time' after moving to Paris, she 'did not go to the theatre at all. I forgot the theatre, I never thought of the theatre at all. I did sometimes think about the opera. I went to the opera once in Venice and I liked it and then much later Strauss' Electra made me realise that in a kind of a way there could be a solution to the problem of conversation on the stage'; see Stein, 'Plays', p. 117. In a letter to Mabel Dodge, written immediately following a brief visit to London in late January and early February of 1913 and shortly before she composed her first play, Stein comments on having just seen Richard Strauss's *Elektra* in London and describes her experience in nearly identical terms to those she would use in her lecture more than twenty years later. The opera, she writes, produced a 'deeper impression on me than anything since Tristan in my youth . . . [Strauss] has made real conversation and he does it by intervals and relations directly without machinery'; see Patricia R. Everett, ed., *A History of Having a Great*

offered a single, hesitant narrative, meant to dissuade her audience from regarding the writing as the expression of a single aim; Stein ran the risk, however, of making the writing appear the product of considerable confusion. Now, she took the alternative tack of providing multiple accounts of her writing's development. Each account concentrated on a particular 'literary idea', yet by including several complementary accounts she again made it difficult – at least for the reader of the entire set of lectures – to reduce her writing to a single aim, 'a central thing which has to move'. Together with the actual examples of her writing distributed through the lectures, this strategy countered the tendency of literary criticism to privilege certain ideas over others and one idea over all, a tendency which follows directly from a conception of knowledge as composed essentially of ideas.

It was to James's alternative form of knowledge, 'knowledge of acquaintance', that Stein referred when, in a brief work prepared on the occasion of her return to the United States, she commented that her lectures were 'to be a simple way to say that if you understand a thing you enjoy it and if you enjoy a thing you understand it'. 'And in these lectures', she continued, 'I want to tell so simply that anybody will know it and know it very well that you can enjoy the things I have been writing. And since you can enjoy them you can understand them. I always say in my lectures, knowledge is what you know, and I do want you to have knowledge and to know this that understanding and enjoying is the same thing.'[39] In her own presence it was relatively easy both to enjoy the

Many Times Not Continued to be Friends: The Correspondence Between Mabel Dodge & Gertrude Stein, 1911–1934 (Albuquerque, 1996), p. 174. Stein's fifth 'lecture in America', 'Portraits and Repetition', reverses the temporal perspective of the previous lecture. Instead of following the internal development of *Making*, it focuses on the portraiture that unexpectedly emerged as a by-product of her attempt in *Making* to 'describe … every possible kind of a human being'; see Stein, 'The Gradual Making of The Making of Americans', *Lectures in America*, p. 148. Here, in effect, *Making* is examined from the perspective of the writing that followed it. Even so, this correction of the unidirectional perspective displayed in 'The Gradual Making of The Making of Americans' didn't satisfy her; and the account in the concluding lecture, of her 'long and complicated life' with grammar and punctuation, is framed by an extended meditation on the relation between poetry and prose, a relation epitomised for Stein by the poetry of *Tender Buttons* and the prose of *The Making of Americans*; see Stein, 'Poetry and Grammar', *Lectures in America*, p. 216.

[39] The Yale Collection of American Literature contains three drafts – one manuscript, two typescripts of the piece of writing which opens with these lines. The manuscript, as well as one of the typescripts, is labelled 'Pathe', and the New York files of the Pathe News Library, now part of the Sherman Grinberg Film Libraries, record a 1934 News Flash on Stein's arrival in America: 'Gertrude Stein, Writer, Returns/ Close-up of Gertrude Stein reading some/ of her so-called famous descriptions.' (A copy of the actual newsreel is listed in the Hollywood-based collection of the Pathe News Library, but the soundtrack seems to have been destroyed.) This must have been the 'newsreel' that Stein referred to in the 1935 article 'I Came And Here I Am', when she wrote that 'the first thing that happened was what they call a newsreel'; see Stein, 'I Came And Here I Am', *How Writting Is Written*,

examples of writing she included in her lectures and to feel that one understood them. 'To hear Miss Stein read her own work', one journalist reported,

> is to understand it – I speak for myself – for the first time … [Y]ou see why she writes as she does; you see how from sentence to sentence, which seem so much alike, she introduces differences of tone, or perhaps of accent. And then when you think she has been saying the same thing four or five times, you suddenly know that she has carefully, link by link, been leading you to a new thing.[40]

Within its limits this statement is both accurate and admirably succinct. It certainly describes the effect of the remarks cited above on 'understanding and enjoying', in which one finds that after several repetitive equations of the two terms Stein has indeed led one to something 'new': the statement that 'understanding and enjoying is the same thing'. What would normally have seemed a solecism – plural subject mismatched with singular verb – offers instead an example of the point Stein is making. Yet not only does the reporter's testimony implicitly claim that Stein's writing generally took the form of the repetitive manner of 'Melanctha' and *The Making of Americans* – an impression that the merest glance at the dissociative compositions she produced from 1912 on quickly dispels – it also misleadingly collapses the distinction between *listening to* and *reading* her. 'It has been so often said', Stein already noted in *The Autobiography of Alice B. Toklas*, 'that the appeal of her work is to the ear and to the subconscious. Actually it is her eyes and mind that are active and important and concerned in choosing.'[41] Needless to say, hearing her read only strengthened the impression that she traded on the dark secrets of the psyche, that like so many American 'altars to the Unknown God', she was, as T. S. Matthews commented in a scathing editorial in *The New Republic*, something of a 'sideshow', a 'barker-priest … drumming up trade'.[42]

Stein, of course, *was* selling the public on her writing. Her lectures were meant to convince one that the writing was thoughtful and pleasurable rather than nonsensical and probably offensive, yet in the lecture format those aspects of the writing which appealed to the eye and not the ear would remain imperceptible or appear as nonsense, a kind of static. To the

ed. Robert Bartlett Haas (Los Angeles, 1974), p. 68. The two-page 'Pathe', which remained unpublished until 1996, would have been written for that occasion; see Edward M. Burns and Ulla E. Dydo, ed., with William Rice, *The Letters of Gertrude Stein and Thornton Wilder* (New Haven, 1996), pp. 351–3. It is unlikely, however, that it was used in full – News Flashes typically lasted no longer than thirty seconds, as the name would suggest.

[40] From a newsclipping, dated 2 November 1934, in the Yale Collection of American Literature. The name of the newspaper is illegible.

[41] Stein, *Autobiography*, p. 75.

[42] T. S. Matthews, 'Gertrude Stein Comes Home', *The New Republic*, 81 (5 December 1934), pp. 100–1.

listener, the textual relations which the words possessed to one another did not exist; at best they could be approximated in the translation from a visual to an oral register. Aside from its aural features, the writing remained as impenetrable as before, at least so long as the lectures were merely heard. With publication, however, the passages that Stein cited from her own writing became visible, as did those aspects of the lectures' writing which no oral presentation could convey. The opening lecture, 'What Is English Literature', begins, for example, with the line, 'One cannot come back too often to the question what is knowledge and to the answer knowledge is what one knows.'[43] Hearing this, one might imagine that Stein has indeed 'often come back' to this consideration, and that she was certainly doing so each time she repeated the lecture. The listener might thus contextualise the statement by putting it into a stream of events – narrativising it in terms of prior occasions, as well as simultaneous and projected ones. Upon reading the line, however, one is struck by the irony of the statement's placement. Where is one returning from if one is only just starting out? Isn't this precisely the territory that American, as distinct from English, writing has so persistently staked out for itself? Stein's 'lectures in America' begin with the question of just what English literature is because American literature, including her own writing, has evolved from the English example; at the same time, this process of evolution has produced an American literature quite distinct from its English counterpart. American writing thus represents both a continuation and a new beginning, and it is this particular narrative doubleness that Stein herself reenacts throughout the *Lectures in America*: a beginning again and again instead of a straightforwardly progressive narrative.

'The business of Art', Stein declares in 'Plays', 'is to live in the actual present, that is the complete actual present, and to completely express that complete actual present'; this, she acknowledges, is what she had 'tried to explain in Composition as Explanation'. In both 'The Gradual Making of The Making of Americans' and the concluding lecture, 'Poetry and Grammar', she further characterises 'living in the present composition of the present time' as a distinctively American trait.[44] 'Everybody knows who is an American', she asserts, 'just how many seconds minutes or hours it is going to take to do a whole thing. It is singularly a sense for combination within a conception of the existence of a given space of time that makes the American thing the American thing, and the sense of this space of time must be within the whole thing as well as in the completed whole thing.' From this perspective *The Making of Americans*, which Stein regarded as at once a work of science and of art, may be viewed as an attempt to overcome the double legacy of positivist science and realist fiction which nineteenth-century England had bequeathed the United States: in particu-

---

[43] Gertrude Stein, 'What Is English Literature', in *Lectures In America*, p. 11.
[44] Stein, 'Plays', pp. 104–5.

lar, the epistemological discrepancy between 'acquiring [one's] knowledge *gradually*' (in the form of knowledge-about) and subsequently
coming to possess a 'complete conception ... of an individual ... *at one
time*' (involving a sense of acquaintance). 'A great deal of The Making of
Americans', Stein proposes, was 'a struggle ... to make a whole present of
something that it had taken a great deal of time to find out, but it was a
whole there then within me and as such it had to be said'. The difficulty lay
in expressing this 'strictly American' conception of 'a space that is filled
with moving, a space of time that is filled always filled with moving' in a
medium, the *English* language, and within traditions of inquiry, the novels
of George Eliot, for instance, and Darwinian science, which so differently
conceived of time and space.[45] An American, Stein remarked in 'Poetry
and Grammar', 'can fill up space in having his movement of time by
adding unexpectedly anything and yet getting within the included space
everything he had intended getting'. As an example of this distinctively
American spontaneity she described the experience of 'a young french
boy[,] ... a red-haired descendant of the niece of Madame Recamier'. On
a visit to the United States, he initially found Americans 'not as different
from us frenchmen as I expected them to be', but changed his mind when
he saw a train 'going by at a terrific pace': 'we waved a hat the engine
driver could make a bell quite carelessly go ting ting ting, the way anybody
playing at a thing could do, it was not if you know what I mean professional he said'. The young Frenchman, with his strict lineage, is quite
unable to accommodate the engine driver's carelessness. It was Stein's
sense of the appropriateness of such whimsical behaviour – *non*professional, yet not *un*professional – which distinguished her from strict evol-
utionists like Darwin and Thomas Huxley as well as anti-evolutionists like
Louis Agassiz: a sense she shared with Emerson, who, 'shun[ning] father
and mother and wife and brother when genius calls', famously affirmed
that he 'would write on the lintels of the door-post, *Whim*. I hope it is
somewhat better than whim at last, but we cannot spend the day in
explanation.' With similar sang-froid Stein concluded her parable: 'Perhaps you do see the connection with that and my sentences.'[46]

In accounting for her gradual disillusionment with nineteenth-century
science in *Wars I Have Seen* (1945), Stein suggests that

to those of us who were interested in science then ... [e]volution was as exciting as
the discovery of America, by Columbus quite as exciting, and quite as much an
opening up and a limiting, quite as much. By that I mean that discovering America,
by reasoning and then finding, opened up a new world and at the same time closed
the circle, there was no longer any beyond. Evolution did the same thing, it opened

---

[45] Stein, 'The Gradual Making of The Making of Americans', pp. 160, 147, 161 (emphasis
added).
[46] Stein, 'Poetry and Grammar', pp. 224–5; Ralph Waldo Emerson, 'Self-Reliance', in *Essays
and Lectures* (New York, 1983), p. 262.

up the history of all animals vegetables and minerals, and man, and at the same time it made them all confined, confined within a circle, no excitement of creation any more.[47]

The experience of confinement described here exactly complements Emerson's 'I am ready to die out of nature, and be born again into this new yet unapproachable America I have found in the West.'[48] It is a sense of this unnatural America – an America which escapes any form of understanding premised on strict historical linearity, yet which Americans experience daily, an America continually being recreated – that Stein calls the 'essentially American thing', 'a space of time' which 'is a natural thing for an American to always have inside them as something in which they are continuously moving'. 'Think of anything,' she proposes, 'of cowboys, of movies, of detective stories, of anybody who goes anywhere or stays at home and is an American.'[49]

'How Writing Is Written' / *Narration*: winter 1935

Columbus's discovery of America, involving 'reasoning' as well as 'finding', recedes into the past, a merely historical event; yet the rediscovery of America occurs again and again, from present moment to present moment. Stein's six-month lecture tour of the United States, with its daily discoveries of a remarkably approachable America, presented an exemplary instance of this phenomenon. It is this very exemplarity which she stressed in *Everybody's Autobiography*, the 1936 account (published in 1937) of herself lecturing throughout the nation.[50] Only on two occasions

---

47 Stein, *Wars I Have Seen*, p. 61. In *Wars I Have Seen* Stein lumps Darwin together with Huxley and Agassiz: 'To believe in progress and in science', she writes, 'you had to know what science was and what progress might be. Having been born in the nineteenth century it was natural enough to know what science was. Darwin was still alive and Huxley and Agassiz and after all they all made the difference of before and after' (p. 61). It is of course still a matter of considerable controversy as to whether Darwin's evolutionary theory was as mechanical as the theories of either Agassiz or Huxley and how central to his theory those aspects were which, at least in retrospect, seem to allow room for the 'excitement of creation' and which have become central to much recent evolutionary theory.

48 Ralph Waldo Emerson, 'Experience', *Essays and Lectures*, p. 485; also see Stanley Cavell's 'work in progress', *This New Yet Unapproachable America* (Albuquerque, 1989).

49 Stein, 'The Gradual Making of The Making of Americans', pp. 160–1.

50 Beginning in New York, Princeton, and Chicago, Stein then lectured throughout the Midwest and the Northeast, heading South in early February, returning by way of New Orleans and St Louis to Chicago, then on to the Southwest and reaching California in the early spring. James Mellow, in his biography of Stein, cites a letter from Alice Toklas to W. G. Rogers, dated 18 November 1934, in which Toklas gives the schedule for a set of lectures in New England in January: 'the 7th, Springfield; 9th, Amherst; 10th, Northampton; 11th, Pittsfield; 12th, Wallingford; 15th, Wesleyan; 16th, South Hadley; 18th, Hartford; 21st, Providence; 23rd, Springfield'; see James R. Mellow, *Charmed Circle: Gertrude Stein & Company* (New York, 1974), p. 608.

did she vary her prepared script, the regimen of six lectures. The first was a talk she gave, in January 1935, at the Choate School in Connecticut, which was recorded by a stenographer and published a month later in the *Choate Literary Magazine* with the title 'How Writing Is Written'.[51]

Much more consecutively organised than her prepared lectures, the talk offered an updated version of 'Composition as Explanation', filtered through *Lectures in America*. 'What I want to talk about to you tonight', she remarked at the outset,

is just the general subject of how writing is written. It is a large subject, but one can discuss it in a very short space of time. The beginning of it is what everybody has to know: everybody is contemporary with his period... The whole crowd of you are contemporary to each other, and the whole business of writing is the question of living in that contemporariness.

In addition to this 'contemporary quality' – 'the thing you can't get away from[,] ... the fundamental thing in all writing' – Stein suggested that 'each period of time ... has a time-sense' as well. 'Things move more quickly, slowly, or differently, from one generation to another.'[52] Under the rubric of 'trying to make you understand... that every contemporary writer has to find out what is the inner time-sense of his contemporariness', she provided a clearly articulated summary of the main ideas of *Lectures in America*, even concluding, as she had in 'Poetry and Grammar', with a characterisation of herself as having reached a point where 'there is no essential difference between prose and poetry' – adding, for the benefit of this most contemporary of crowds, that 'this is essentially the problem with which your generation will have to wrestle'.[53] In removing

[51] The typescript of 'How Writing Is Written' in the Yale Collection of American Literature is labelled a 'copy of stenographic report of lecture at Choate school. January, 12, 1935'. Richard Bridgman cites letters in the Yale Collection of American Literature from Dudley Fitts to Stein which suggest, however, that the report is not entirely verbatim. Having observed on 18 January 1935 that the stenographer 'had difficulties' transcribing the talk, Fitts adds on 5 February 1935 that he 'had to "restore" a great deal of the lecture from memory... Sorry to have missed entirely what you said about the noun; but the text was so corrupt that I couldn't do anything with it'; see Bridgman, *Gertrude Stein in Pieces* (New York, 1970), p. 266. W. G. Rogers, in his memoir of Stein, describes the 'discussion periods' which followed her prepared lectures as often 'the most exciting features of those evenings[,] ... sometimes last[ing] an hour': 'At such moments Miss Stein appeared at her best. Instead of remaining a lecturer, she became a superb conversationalist; instead of being an abstruse writer, she became a rich, living voice, a quick and entertaining wit, a warm personality'; see Rogers, *When This You See Remember Me*, pp. 138–9. Although 'How Writing Is Written' is not a discussion – in *Everybody's Autobiography* Stein recalls that she only talked the next morning with the boys about what she had said the evening before – its delivery is that of the 'superb conversationalist' who, in her two months in the United States, had been interviewed repeatedly on the topic of her writing.
[52] Stein, *Everybody's Autobiography* (1937; rpt. Cambridge, 1993), p. 248; Stein, 'How Writing Is Written', p. 151.
[53] Stein, 'How Writing Is Written', p. 160. In 'How Writing Is Written' Stein discusses, in the following order, English writing in relation to American writing; the relation between the

herself from the ring to clear the way for these young pugilists, however, Stein was being somewhat disingenuous. As she made clear in her second deviation from *Lectures in America*, the set of four lectures she delivered later that winter at the University of Chicago, on the subject of 'what narrative has gotten to be now', she was still endeavouring to express the contemporary composition in her own writing and certainly did not regard herself as a relic from the past.[54]

In 'Poetry and Grammar' Stein had acknowledged that she found narrative 'a problem', and by the time she returned to Chicago in early March she was prepared to address her concerns.[55] It is useful to consider Stein's lectures in chronological order, as I have done here, precisely because from beginning to end she consistently made an issue of sequentiality, returning 'again and again' to the topic. Like so many writers of the period she had worked to disrupt the sense of a linear unfolding of time in her writing, an aim she attributed to a distinctively twentieth-century, and American, sense of composition. 'The Nineteenth Century', she suggested in 'How Writing Is Written', was 'roughly the Englishman's Century. And their method, as they themselves, in their worst moments, speak of it, is that of "muddling through". They begin at one end and hope to come out at the other.'[56] In Chicago she elaborated:

When one used to think of narrative one meant a telling of what is happening in successive moments of its happening the quality of telling depending upon the conviction of the one telling that there was a distinct succession in happening, that one thing happened after something else and since that happening in succession was a profound conviction in every one then really there was no difference whether any one began in the beginning or the middle or the ending because since narrative was a progressive telling of things that were progressively happening it really did not make any difference where you were at what moment you were in

nineteenth and the twentieth centuries; 'the element of punctuation' in writing; the American sense of movement; the struggle between 'the sense of time which belongs to [one's] crowd' or generation and 'the memory of what you were brought up with'; the attempt to get at 'present immediacy' in *The Making of Americans* and thereby to 'give the appearance of one-time knowledge' instead of 'mak[ing] it a narrative story'; the relation between her psychological experiments at Harvard and her effort in *Making* to 'make a description of every kind of human being'; her reasons for writing *Four Saints in Three Acts* 'about as static as I could make it' ('the better the play the more static', she observes near the end of the talk); the relation between portraiture and repetition; the fact that the 'immediacy' she 'was after' in her portraits was something that 'a single photograph doesn't give' and more like 'Making a cinema of it'; see Stein, 'How Writing Is Written', pp. 158, 153–6, 158–9.   [54] Gertrude Stein, *Narration* (Chicago, 1935), p. 17.

[55] 'I often wonder', Stein observed in 'Poetry and Grammar, 'how I am ever to come to know all that I am to know about narrative. Narrative is a problem to me. I worry about it a good deal these days and I will not write or lecture about it yet, because I am still too worried about it worried about knowing what it is and how it is and where it is and how it is and how it will be and what it is'; see Stein, 'Poetry and Grammar', p. 32.

[56] Stein, 'How Writing Is Written', p. 152.

your happening since the important part of telling anything was the conviction that anything that everything was progressively happening.

'But now', Stein added, and this was the source of the perturbing nature of narrative as a 'contemporary thing', 'we have changed all that we really have. We really now do not really know that anything is progressively happening.'[57] By contrast with the nineteenth-century piecemeal whole, merely the end-product of an orderly temporal process, the twentieth-century whole took the form of a process which, according to Stein, involved 'a feeling of movement' without a sense of succession or events following one another in a set order.[58] Every part was perceived as part of a whole, not a separable piece. In both 'How Writing Is Written' and *Narration*, Stein offered as an example of such non-progressive movement the behaviour of the American soldiers during the World War: 'standing, standing and doing nothing standing for a long time not even talking but just standing and being watched by the whole French population and their feeling the feeling of the whole population that the American soldier standing there and doing nothing impressed them as the American soldier as no soldier could impress by doing anything'.[59] Consequently, as Stein recognised, when the French talked to one another about what was happening around them, the 'quality of [their] telling' could no longer 'depend upon the conviction of the one [doing the] telling that there was a distinct succession in happening'. What now moved the 'passionately interested' populace, on the contrary, was the absence of successive movement, the fact that 'the average dough-boy', instead of religiously following orders – as soldiers, especially in time of war, might be expected to do – 'stand[s] on a street corner doing nothing': just 'say[ing], at the end of their doing nothing, "I guess I'll go home"'.[60] The typically American disinterest in succession, together with the newly acquired interest (if not yet conviction) of the French in the absence of succession – 'the Americanization of Europe', Stein would label it in *Everybody's Autobiography* – comprised the difference, as she proposed in Chicago, 'between narrative as it has been and narrative as it is now'.[61]

In each of her four lectures Stein examined a different aspect of this shift from 'a narrative of succession as all the writing for a good many hundreds of years has been' to the present state of narrative: first, in terms of the different ways that the English and the Americans 'tell their story in English'; second, in relation to prose and poetry; third, in relation to history and especially journalism; fourth, with respect to what Stein characterised as the historian's 'burden' – namely, the failure of history to repeat itself – and in terms of basic differences between writing and

---

[57] Stein, *Narration*, p. 17.   [58] Stein, 'How Writing Is Written', pp. 152–4, 157.
[59] Stein, *Narration*, pp. 19–20.   [60] Stein, 'How Writing Is Written', p. 157.
[61] Stein, *Everybody's Autobiography*, p. 245; Stein, *Narration*, p. 20.

lecturing.[62] Like *The Autobiography of Alice B. Toklas, Narration* seems to offer a relatively traditional narrative of one thing following another – in this case, *successive narrative* having been succeeded by *non-successive narrative* – yet, again as in the *Autobiography*, things are not quite so pat. Already at the beginning of the second lecture, Stein alerts her interlocutor, and herself, to the fundamental discrepancy between the 'conviction that anything that everything is progressively happening' and the contemporary experience of 'not really know[ing] that anything is progressively happening'. 'Does telling anything as it is being needed being telling now by any one does it mean cutting loose from everything', she asks: 'no because there is nothing to cut loose from'. The idea that scepticism concerning the progressive nature of experience makes it impossible for one to chart a movement of succession from old to new manner of thinking is itself a product of the earlier conviction. Only in the context of a genuine conviction of progressivity does the insistence that there is indeed something 'to [be] cut loose from', something which one has progressed from and, by the same token, is able to repress, make any sense at all.

Given the historian's necessarily non-contemporaneous perspective, Stein asks in her final lecture, 'how can history be writing that is be literature'. The same question pertains to her lectures as well: 'how can an historian', including, and perhaps especially, a writer telling the story of her own writing,

> who knows everything really knows everything that has really been happening how can [s]he come to have the feeling that the only existence the [wo]man [s]he is describing has is the one [s]he has been giving to him [her]. How can [s]he have this feeling, if [s]he cannot then [s]he cannot have the recognition while in the process of writing, which writing really writing must really give to the one writing.[63]

Stein had already done something like this herself in the *Autobiography*: 'making it the Autobiography of Alice B. Toklas made it do something, it made it be a recognition by never before that writing having it be existing'.[64] No one before her had written a combination third-person autobi-

---

[62] Stein, *Narration*, pp. 20, 6, 58; for an account of Stein's analysis of contemporary journalism and historiography, see my 'Gertrude Stein Shipwrecked in Bohemia: Making Ends Meet in the *Autobiography* and After', *Southwest Review*, Winter 1992, pp. 12–33.

[63] How can the historian, Stein adds, 'have the creation of some one who has no existing except that the historian who is writing has at the moment of writing and there has as recognition at the moment of writing being writing. The historian is bound to have with him all the audience that has known every one about whom he is writing. It is worse than the wailing of the dead soldiers in L'Aiglon'; see Stein, *Narration*, p. 61. Edmond Rostand's play *L'Aiglon (The Eaglet)* – the title refers to Napoleon's son, the Duke of Reichstadt – was first performed in March 1900 with Sarah Bernhardt in the lead role. The New York production later that year starred Maude Adams as the Duke; see *L'Aiglon: A Play in Six Acts* (New York, 1900).   [64] Stein, *Narration*, p. 62.

ography / first-person biography, but, equally important, the hybrid form enabled a reader to experience Stein's own sense of 'immediacy' – namely, the recognition in each sentence that she was writing of herself in the third person and of Toklas in the first person.[65] The reader's sense of the writer here is identical with the writer's own sense of the matter; and as such the writer of the *Autobiography* becomes a creation of Stein's, existing as a function of the self-recognition which occurs in the act of writing. The reader is able to 'feel [the] writing', much as Stein herself had in the process of writing the *Autobiography*, and first-person acquaintance is thereby imparted, overcoming James's strictures.

Stein concludes the last of her American lectures with the assertion that it should be possible to compose writing which is 'really writing' in the form of history 'as a mystery story', a *whodunit*:

I am certain so certain so more than certain that it ought to be able to be done. I know so well all the causes why it cannot be done and yet if it cannot be done cannot it be done it would be so very much more interesting than anything if it could be done even if it cannot be done ... [S]o perhaps history will not repeat itself and it will some to be done.[66]

The idea that history, which 'concerns itself with what happens from time to time', may come to an end ('come to be done'), and so 'not repeat itself', seems especially fitting at the conclusion of a series of lectures designed to call into question out-dated assumptions concerning the nature of time.[67] After *The Making of Americans* Stein was indeed done with history, at least in the form it had taken in the nineteenth century; it was the break with linear models of time and composition that enabled her to resolve the problem of how to move from descriptive knowledge to knowledge of acquaintance, from knowledge 'acquired, so to speak, by memory' to knowledge involving a 'sense of the immediate'.[68] Her solution was to bypass the nineteenth-century conception of knowledge entirely – as the assembly of discrete pieces, such as buttons on a shirt or words with fixed meanings, strictly succeeding one another according to the rules of grammar – and to replace it with the idea of 'whole[s] made up of [their] parts': 'tender buttons' and words 'gaily and happily alive ... excitedly feel[ing] themselves as if they were anywhere or anything'.[69]

---

[65] In addition to her use, cited above, of the term 'immediacy' in 'How Writing Is Written', Stein also uses the term in *Narration* in a description of Boswell's *Life of Johnson*: 'by the intensity of his merging himself in the immediacy of Johnson', she suggests, Boswell 'achieved recognition as Johnson himself was doing'; see Stein, *Narration*, p. 60.

[66] *Ibid.*, p. 62.   [67] *Ibid.*, p. 30.   [68] Stein, 'How Writing Is Written', p. 155.

[69] Stein, *Narration*, pp. 12–13, 10.

'An American and France' / 'What Are Master-pieces': winter 1936

A year later, in February 1936, Stein revisited Oxford and Cambridge to deliver a final pair of lectures, in which she addressed topics raised briefly in *Narration* and subsequently pursued in *The Geographical History of America or The Relation Between Human Nature and the Human Mind*. Human nature, for Stein, was at bottom a function of identity, constructed over time and experienced in temporal terms: 'you know who you are because you and others remember anything about yourself'. By contrast, 'when you are doing anything essentially you are not that': human activity could not be understood exclusively in terms of human nature.[70] Like so many modern writers, Stein recoiled at the naturalistic vision of inexorable forces determining every motion and emotion. Unlike Eliot, however, she didn't replace the ideology of progress with an ideology of loss; nor did she replace it, as Yeats did, with a sense of the rigorous cyclicality of history. Whereas her early writing was generally naturalistic – one has only to think of *Q.E.D.*, with its geometric interpretation of human relations, or the deterministic colour scheme of 'Melanctha' and the emphasis on 'bottom nature' of *The Making of Americans* – in 'An American and France' and 'What Are Master-pieces' she emphasises those aspects of her writing which remove it from the dictates of place and time. Although she may appear to reinstate an old-style idealism, her emphasis on the human mind seeming to confirm this impression, in fact she does nothing of the kind. Instead, she substitutes a dualism of function for the Cartesian dualism of substance; writing, no less than 'the human mind', is an activity, not substance, and both, in James's phrasing, are 'made of the same stuff as things are'.

Stein's explanation in 'An American and France' as to why Paris offered so appropriate a setting for her to write hinged on the spatial and temporal isomorphism of what she termed 'romance'. Just as there were only two ways that one could situate oneself spatially in relation to a place whose distance, or foreignness, one found compelling – either by 'making the distant approach nearer' (resulting in 'adventure') or by 'having what is where it is which is not where you are stay where it is' (resulting in 'romance') – so one could situate oneself temporally in modalities that were either 'historical' or 'romantic'. 'There always is romance and there always is history', Stein insisted, although the contemporary sense of just which persons or places were romantic and which historical varied over time. If, as she proposed, 'to us Americans England is historical' and

---

[70] Stein, 'What are Master-pieces And Why Are There So Few Of Them', in *What Are Master-pieces*, pp. 83–4.

France romantic, this was because 'the American and the Englishman' could 'to some extent progress together and so ... have a time sense together', namely, 'a past present and future together'. The flip side was that 'living in England' did not 'free the American the way living in France' did precisely 'because the french and the American' lacked 'the sense of going on together' and hence a sense of shared history, a common 'time sense'. Only by living, as an American could in France, with 'a complete other a romantic other another that stays there where it is' might one possess 'in it' – that is, living in this place which nonetheless remains separate from one – 'freedom in [one]self'. The romantic setting, according to Stein, 'is there but it does not continue it has no time it is neither past nor present nor future'; consequently, it provides an especially fitting environment for creative activity, as there is 'nothing that any one creating anything needs more' than to be able to regard oneself romantically, as a free, self-creating agent rather than an historically determined being. It is certainly easier to live 'in the complete actual present' in the midst of a 'civilization that has nothing to do' with you than in a community in which 'you are apt to mix yourself up too much with your [own] civilization'.[71]

Residing in Paris thus provided Stein with an environment which, because she didn't ordinarily 'come into contact' with it, readily served as a 'second civilization' for her in her 'business as a creator'. Having thereby accounted for her own experience, Stein then moved on in her lecture to suggest that writing might serve, in itself, as a means of acquainting one with an alternative civilisation when mobility between cultures, and even knowledge of other cultures, proved difficult or impossible. Commenting on the relative isolation of 'early civilizations', she proposed that 'the reason why they always had a special language to write which was not the language that was spoken' was that 'the writer could not write unless he had the two civilizations coming together the one he was and the other that was there outside him'. In suggesting that creation required the 'opposition' of writing and speaking, and that consequently 'the written thing' could not be identified with 'the spoken thing', Stein was returning to a concern with the status of her own lectures which had dogged her since 'Composition as Explanation'.[72] Although she had only recently

---

[71] Stein, 'An American and France', pp. 62–4, 63–5, 62–3.

[72] The full passage runs: 'In the early civilizations when any one was to be a creator a writer or a painter and he belonged to his own civilization and could not know another, he inevitably in order to know another had made for him it was one of the things that inevitably existed a language which as an ordinary member of his civilization did not exist for him. That is really really truly the reason why they always had a special language to write which was not the language that was spoken, now it is generally considered that this was because of the necessity of religion and mystery but actually the writer could not write unless he had two civilizations coming together the one he was and the other that was outside him and creation is the opposition of one of them to the other. This is very

begun to address explicitly the inadequacy of the lecturing format for conveying the 'feeling [of] writing' essential to her compositional practice, already in the opening paragraph of 'The Gradual Making of The Making of Americans' she had carefully, if not quite openly, acknowledged the ambivalence she felt. 'I am going to read', she had announced, 'what I have written to read, because in a general way it is easier even if it is not better and in a general way it is better even if it is not easier to read what has been written than to say what has not been written.'[73] The thin line she was straddling was the difference between speaking – 'saying what ha[d] not been written' – and reading something aloud which had been written with the intention of its being read aloud. If, as in a lecture, such writing was itself modelled on speaking, where did the difference lie?

This difference was crucial for Stein, given her insistence that 'talking essentially has nothing to do with creation', as she put it in her valedictory lecture, 'What Are Master-pieces And Why Are There So Few Of Them'.[74] Conversation supposed the simultaneous presence of both a speaker and a listener, whereas 'genuine creative ability' required a sense of the individual's self-sufficiency.[75] 'I was almost going to talk this', the lecture opens,

and not write and read it because all the lectures that I have written and read in America have been printed and although possibly for you they might even being read be as if they had not been printed still there is something about what has been written having been printed which makes it no longer the property of the one who wrote it and therefore there is no more reason why the writer should say it out loud than anybody else and therefore one does not.[76]

In 'What Are Master-pieces' Stein was able to understand and even enjoy, if not resolve, the dichotomy between writing and talking. When she announced that she 'was going to talk to you but actually it is impossible to talk about master-pieces', the apparent non sequitur called into question the very activity that lecturing demanded of her, namely, making writing seem like talking. She could not talk *to* her listeners because she could not say anything *about* her topic. Indeed, the only way she could say anything about masterpieces was by convincing her listeners that there was nothing to say. With this particular topic, talking would not suffice,

interesting. Really this is very true, the written thing is not the spoken thing and the written thing exists there because the writing that is in the old civilization was a something with which there was not really anything existing [that is, it did not correspond to any spoken language, native or foreign] because it existed there and it remained there and the one writing connected that with himself only by creating. That is what romance is and is not what history is'; see Stein, 'An American and France', pp. 64, 63, 65.

73 Stein, 'The Gradual Making of The Making of Americans', p. 135.
74 Stein, 'What Are Master-pieces', p. 84.
75 As Stein wryly noted in 1930, 'genuine creative ability' is the quality that 'the Guggenheim prize is always to be given for'; see Stein, 'Genuine Creative Ability', *A Primer for the Gradual Understanding of Gertrude Stein*, ed. Robert Bartlett Haas (Los Angeles, 1971), p. 104.   76 Stein, 'What Are Master-pieces', pp. 83–4.

for speech assumed that one had both an audience and a subject-matter, whereas it was precisely this assumption which masterpieces, like 'the human mind', managed to do without. As she had proposed in *The Geographical History of America*:

The human mind is the mind that writes what any human mind years after or years before can read, thousands of years or no years it makes no difference . . . And the writing that is the human mind does not consist in messages or in events it consists only in writing down what is written.[77]

In the American lectures she had typically found herself divided between saying one thing and doing another, between the writing she was interested in and the talk that was her medium; yet the only way she could acquaint her auditors with 'what master-pieces are' was by making them recognise that her lecture was itself writing and not just talk. The lecture format was quite appropriate for acquainting one's audience with *how* something had come to be – how Stein, for instance, had come to make Paris her home, how she came to write *The Making of Americans* as she did – but it was not designed to acquaint anyone with *what* something was apart from the historical, evolutionary process involved in its creation. This wasn't knowledge about anything, and therefore could not take the form of an historical account, an act of remembering. As such, it was 'frightening', she cautioned in 'What Are Master-pieces', self-knowledge that required one to 'let one's self go'.[78]

'It is necessary that there is stock taking', Stein had written several months after the publication of *Geography and Plays* and several years before writing 'Composition as Explanation'. Not only was taking stock of oneself and others an inevitable feature of human nature but human nature was itself a product of such stock taking. Still, the mere fact of such necessity did not require one to 'abandon individualism', along with the conviction that the existence of the human mind was at least functionally distinct from human nature, by 'critically' reducing individuals to accounts of their 'stock'. Nor did it require one to abandon criticism. The critic *qua* critic may be compelled to regard acts of creation as acts of construction, the contemporaneous as the historical, pieces of writing as the sort of thing one can speak about; yet nothing is remiss so long as one

[77] Gertrude Stein, *The Geographical History of America or The Relation of Human Nature to the Human Mind* (New York, 1936), p. 80. In the same passage Stein distinguishes between two forms of writing: 'all the writing that has to do with events has to be written over' – since it becomes obsolete when circumstances change – 'but the writing that has to do with writing does not have to be written again, again in this sense the same as over'.

[78] Stein, 'What Are Master-pieces', p. 92. I take the expression *letting one's self go* from Stein's description, in an undergraduate experiment at the Harvard Psychological Laboratory, of 'the habit of self-repression, the intense self-consciousness, the morbid fear of "letting one's self go", that is so prominent an element in the New England character'; see Gertrude Stein and Leon Solomons, *Motor Automatism* (New York, 1969), p. 31.

recognises that this is what one is doing, that 'those who concern themselves with aesthetic things critically and academically' are likely to be
'several generations behind themselves'.[79] Even so, one runs the risk, in
getting caught up in the act of writing, of persuading oneself that one has
indeed 'critically realise[d]' one's subject. Stein's lectures may consequently be said to offer, among other things, a double-edged criticism of literary
criticism: a bravura performance of self-criticism that, by the same token,
functions as an exemplary act of self-creation. Like the dicta of Boswell's
Johnson – of whom she observed in her concluding lecture on narration
that he 'say[s] those things as if he were writing those things that is
achieving recognition of the thing while the thing was achieving expression' – hers is at once a forbidding and a creative literary criticism.[80]

The initial significance of Stein's lectures was, as I have suggested,
twofold. In the first place, when 'Composition as Explanation' appeared
in the mid-1920s it served as a rallying-point for a new criticism that set
itself against the historicism dominant in academic study and which
remained central to Woolf's and Eliot's criticism. Composition as explanation, not historical explanation: this perspective informed the two most
important works of the nascent New Criticism, Riding and Graves's
Survey of Modernist Poetry (1927) and Empson's *Seven Types of Ambiguity* (1930). At the same time, 'Composition as Explanation' offered
writers like Williams an account of creativity and of modern writing that
seemed closer to their own experience than the more academic, if no less
self-interested, account provided by Eliot. Stein's subsequent lectures built
on the foundations laid down in this first effort, as she returned again and
again to issues of temporality and writing. Nor did 'Composition as
Explanation' provide a foundation for her alone; in composing his important essay 'Rites of Participation' in the mid-1960s, the poet Robert
Duncan repeatedly turned to it, much as Riding had forty years earlier.[81]

Although Stein prepared her lectures for academic delivery, they were
singularly free of the trappings of academic learning or knowledge-about.
Instead, she supposed that the incoming freshman, no less than the society
matron, was fully prepared for instruction in the mysteries of avant-garde
composition. If this meant that the tenor of her criticism ran counter to the
prevailing trend of increased specialisation and expert knowledge, it also
meant that a work like *Lectures in America* could be used in the late 1940s
and 1950s as an introductory text for undergraduates at Columbia. Like
Eliot, however, the reception of Stein's criticism has generally been tied to
the reception of her literary compositions, if for opposite reasons. Eliot

[79] Gertrude Stein, 'Thoughts on an American Contemporary Feeling', *Reflections on the
Atomic Bomb*, p. 160.   [80] Stein, *Narration*, p. 60.
[81] See Robert Duncan, 'Rites of Participation', in *A Selected Prose*, ed. Robert J. Bertholf
(New York, 1995), pp. 97–137.

offered a narrative of literary history which led ineluctably to his own work, although he was careful not to draw this conclusion himself. Stein, by contrast, rarely talked about anything but her writing and at the same time criticised the logic of succession which until recently remained the principal academic model for accounting for literary 'success'. In the last two decades this model has itself come in for a good deal of criticism and, not coincidentally, Stein's writing has found its way increasingly into print and into undergraduate and graduate curriculums. Long a favourite of writers as varied as Thornton Wilder and John Ashbery, Richard Wright and James Merrill, Marianne Moore and William Gass, she is now read by students of advertising and 'of movies [and] of detective stories', as well as of literature. The self-consciousness about writing and temporality which is the mark of her criticism has become a staple of late twentieth-century sensibility, as the academy has finally caught up with the lectures she delivered several generations ago.

4

Virginia Woolf

Maria DiBattista

For reasons soon to be enumerated, Virginia Woolf did not presume, nor openly aspire to take her place among the select company of writer-critics she admired. She would praise, but never mimic 'the downright vigour of a Dryden, or Keats with his fine and natural bearing, his profound insight and sanity, or Flaubert and the tremendous power of his fanaticism, or Coleridge, above all, brewing in his head the whole of poetry and letting issue now and then one of those profound general statements which are caught up by the mind when hot with the friction of reading as if they were of the soul of the book itself'.[1] Coleridge, indeed, was for her perhaps the greatest, certainly the *purest* of critics in his exemplary 'indifference to, in his hatred of, "mere personality"'. Affections may be, as Coleridge affirmed, the 'best part of humanity', but the pure critic mounts 'into an atmosphere where the substance of [human] desires has been shredded by infinite refinements and discriminations of all its grossness' and the light of criticism 'is concentrated and confined in one ray – in the art itself'.[2]

By such standards, Woolf does not rate highly as a pure critic of literature. Her criticism, as she openly confessed, was of the grosser sort, adulterated by personal likings or aversions, alloyed by doubts and perplexities. It was, in short, so intent on tracking 'the flight of the mind' in all its unpredictable coursings that to capture the soul of the book was an outcome devoutly to be wished, but never confidently expected: 'The critic may be able to abstract the essence and feast upon it undisturbed, but for the rest of us in every book there is something – sex, character, temperament – which, as in life, rouses affection or repulsion; and, as in life, sways and prejudices; and again, as in life, is hardly to be analysed by the reason.'[3]

The rest of us presumably are of the tribe which Woolf, after Dr Johnson, identified as the common reader, a being quite distinct in her mind from the mass audience. The common reader is the presiding spirit

---

[1] Virginia Woolf, 'How It Strikes a Contemporary', *The Common Reader: First Series* (London, 1925), p. 239.
[2] Virginia Woolf, 'Coleridge as Critic', *The Essays of Virginia Woolf*, ed. Andrew McNeillie, 3 vols. (London, 1986–9), II, pp. 222–3.
[3] Virginia Woolf, 'Indiscretions', *Ibid.*, III, p. 460.

and eponymous hero of her first collection of essays, whose early working title was simply *Reading* and which was originally to have contained an introductory chapter, 'Byron and Mr Briggs', depicting his character, habits and opinions. Mr Briggs, as Woolf described him, could be ruled by an 'unguided passion ... capable of doing enormous harm as a glance at [contemporary] literature [is bound to] prove'. Yet there was merit and attraction for her in a passion for reading so 'voluntary and individual', even 'lawless'.[4] Mr Briggs, as it transpired, is a person of discriminating, not socially conditioned tastes, who reads according to the promptings of two instincts Woolf believed were 'deeply implanted in our souls – the instinct to complete; the instinct to judge'.[5] Like Johnson, Woolf rejoiced to concur with the common reader, whose judgements, however prejudiced by feeling or marred by ignorance, ultimately supersede, as Johnson claimed, 'all the refinements of subtlety and dogmatism of learning'.

Woolf's respect for the untutored discernment of the common reader went deeper than Johnson's, however, and formed the core of her identity as a critic. It irradiates her vision of tradition as deeply embedded in the common life. It attracts her to the dim shades where the 'lives of the obscure' were huddled, silenced by the remorseless rule of history consigning them to oblivion unless the ventriloquising historian or critic restore to them, however briefly, 'the divine gift of communication'.[6] A pure critic, focused on the work and not on the circumstances in which it came to be written, might overlook or disregard the testimony of such mute, inglorious Miltons. 'A student of letters', Woolf not unreasonably objected,

is so much in the habit of striding through the centuries from one pinnacle to the next that he forgets all the hubbub that once surged round the base; how Keats lived in a street and had a neighbour and his neighbour had a family – the rings widen infinitely; how Oxford Street ran turbulent with men and women while De Quincey walked with Ann. And such considerations are not trivial if only because they had their effect upon things that we are wont to look upon as isolated births, and to judge, therefore, in a spirit that is more than necessarily dry.[7]

This sentiment is more succinctly expressed in the famous maxim that guides her researches and orients her speculations in *A Room of One's Own*: 'For masterpieces are not single and solitary births; they are the outcome of many years of thinking in common, of thinking by the body of the people, so that the experience of the mass is behind the single voice.'[8]

[4] Virginia Woolf, 'Byron and Mr Briggs', *Ibid.*, III, p. 478.
[5] *Ibid.*, p. 482. There is also an endearing portrait of a man of 'pure and distinterested reading', whose character and motives differ completely from the man of learning, in 'Hours in a Library', *ibid.*, II, p. 55.
[6] Virginia Woolf, 'Lives of the Obscure', *Common Reader: First Series*, p. 110.
[7] Virginia Woolf, 'Thomas Hood', *Essays*, I, p. 159.
[8] Virginia Woolf, *A Room of One's Own* (London, 1929), p. 68.

Tradition did not suggest to Woolf, as to T. S. Eliot, a panorama of pinnacles, a simultaneous order continually renewed and altered by the successive works of individual talents. Tradition encompasses the wide, undifferentiated expanses that lie between and lead up to the summits; it is enlivened by all the hubbub at its base.

To dramatise this view, Woolf places the four sketches that compose 'The Lives of the Obscure' at the very centre of the first *Common Reader*. We know this is not an accidental placement, given how carefully Woolf considered the symbolic relation of essays in ordering the collection, beginning with 'The Pastons and Chaucer' and concluding with 'How it Strikes a Contemporary'. No history, she seems to suggest, is complete without consulting the 'faded, out-of-date, obsolete library' where 'the obscure sleep . . . slouching against each other as if they were too drowsy to stand upright'. There is, as a further inducement, the special romance of feeling oneself 'a deliverer advancing with lights across the waste of years to the rescue of some stranded ghost'.[9] Woolf's common history accommodates what stricter histories deride: the gossip's tales, rich in the lore of eccentric persons like Margaret Cavendish, a keen but unfulfilled talent who 'loved wandering in the fields and thinking about unusual things and scored, so rashly, so unwisely, "the dull manage of a servile house"'.[10] These vivid personalities from a bygone age appealed to the novelist in Woolf, obsessed with character. Yet, also like a novelist, she places the obscure within a specific social context, thus satisfying both the annalist's interest in the social and cultural data of everyday life and the historian's justified fascination with epochal events – like the exploration of the new world, the cataclysm of war, or the writing of Shakespeare's plays.

Woolf's forays beyond the well-illuminated grounds of the 'great tradition' take us along overgrown trails where little-known or -honoured writers once struggled toward Parnassus, helping to create the common language and conventions that the great artist later put to lasting use. Still, those wishing to follow in her footsteps may find it hard going, for what she offers us is an approach, not a set itinerary. Woolf's criticism everywhere manifests the novelist's congenital distrust of systems. Perhaps the first title proposed for her last critical project, *Reading at Random*, best proclaims her belief that the mind's spontaneous interest, rather than a prescribed method, should dictate what and how we read. 'In literary criticism at least', she elsewhere maintains, 'the wish to attain completeness is more often than not a will o' wisp which lures one past the occasional ideas which may perhaps have truth in them towards an unreal symmetry which has none.'[11] Her conviction that truth is more likely to show itself in the unmolested part rather than the fabricated whole

---

[9] Woolf, 'Lives of the Obscure', p. 110.   [10] Woolf, *Room*, p. 64.
[11] Woolf, 'Coleridge as Critic', p. 223.

precludes her attempting prescriptive criticism in the more canonical manner of Eliot or F. R. Leavis. Although she does not hesitate to offer advice on 'How Should One Read a Book?', she stresses the interrogation at the end of the title, and insists, in her opening remarks, that 'Even if I could answer the question for myself, the answer would apply only to me and not to you.' Woolf comes as close to an unqualified libertarian line in this essay as she ever does in insisting that no law or authority be permitted to fetter the freedom of reading: 'Everywhere else we may be bound by law and convention – there we have none.'[12] We should not expect strict teachings from the critic who writes to demonstrate such a belief, nor hope for the inspired instruction exemplified in I. A. Richards's *Practical Criticism*, a book which methodically documents the 'protocols' governing the current state of culture. Richards and Woolf, however, the one relying on scientific, the other on subjective methods, share the same goal: 'to make men's spiritual heritage more available and more operative'.[13]

Woolf worked toward this goal by seeking to give what 'No critic ever gives' – 'full weight to the desire of the mind for change'.[14] Such, at least, was the desire of her own mind and she did not scruple to please herself. Her best essays nimbly juggle the throng of contradictory but dependably fertile suggestions the mind tosses up while reading until it settles, in the pensive aftermath of reading, upon a final, lingering impression. It is then that reading slides into criticism, then that it is possible 'to continue reading without the book before you, to hold one shadow-shape against another'.[15] In this second stage the contrary emotions aroused in reading are reconciled and rationalised until they subside into a literary judgement. There are, however, distinct limitations, even dangers in making the mind its own consultant, and Woolf acknowledges them in her testimonial to the rewards and insights that accrue to reading at random, 'Phases of Fiction'. Reading to satisfy the mind in its various moods does usher us into a world 'as inhabitable as the real world', but 'such a world ... is created in obedience to tastes that may be peculiar to one temperament and distasteful to another', so that any record of such a course of reading 'is bound to be limited, personal, erratic'.[16]

We are in a better position to understand and assess Woolf's literary views once we recognise that she speaks less as a critic of supreme and learned authority than as a reader of strong feeling and pronounced tastes. Never could it be said of Woolf what she offered of Hazlitt, that 'He is one

---

[12] Virginia Woolf, 'How Should One Read a Book?', *The Common Reader: Second Series* (London, 1932), p. 234.
[13] I. A. Richards, *Practical Criticism* (London, 1929), p. 291.
[14] Virginia Woolf, *A Writer's Diary* (London, 1954), p. 188.
[15] Woolf, 'How Should One Read a Book', p. 246.
[16] Virginia Woolf, 'Phases of Fiction', *Collected Essays*, 4 vols. (London, 1967), II, p. 56.

of the rare critics who have thought so much that they can dispense with reading.'[17] Everything could be dispensed with *but* reading. Etymologies may help clarify the distinction I propose. Criticism comes from the same origin as crisis; both potentially involve acts or moments of radical separation which demand absolute rather than qualified judgements. Woolf is thinking of criticism in this sense when she laments that the modern world lacks a great critic – the Dryden, the Johnson, the Coleridge, the Arnold – whom 'if you had taken to him some eccentricity of the moment, would have brought it into touch with permanence and tethered it by his own authority in the contrary blasts of praise and blame'.[18] Reading traces its roots to *reden*, to explain, and *raeden*, to counsel, thus establishing common cause between the work of interpretation and the search for wisdom.

Woolf is more likely to offer us the counsel derived from reading than report the determinate findings of 'pure' criticism. Her mind was speculative, but in an imaginative register, so that one is unlikely to find the fruits of her reading distilled in talismanic concepts, such as 'objective correlative', 'dissociation of sensibility', epiphany, or 'the phantom aesthetic state' that constitute central terms in modernist aesthetics. Her critical legacy consists rather in an image-repertoire rich in symbolic formations: 'a room of one's own', 'the androgynous mind', the leaning tower, granite and rainbow. Because of her we now appreciate not only the monetary significance, but the symbolic import of £500 and three guineas in underwriting the creative life and preserving the intellectual independence of women in a society where culture is bought and paid for. If Woolf survives as a true critic, as she herself would define one, who possesses 'the power of seeming to bring to light what was already there beforehand, instead of imposing anything from the outside',[19] she will do so by virtue of her necromantic powers to revive the neglected or underestimated ancestors of our literary heritage: the 'common reader', resuscitated and reinvested with the authority Johnson ascribed to him as the final arbiter of all claims to poetical honours; the Angel of the House, that wraith-like spirit of devotion, self-sacrifice, and submission immortalised by Coventry Patmore,[20] and her demonic counterpart, Milton's bogey, who obstructed one's view of tradition and of the world,[21] phantasms summoned from the shadows to be exorcised from the female imagination, freeing the woman writer to describe her body, depict her life, criticise her society or simply

[17] Virginia Woolf, 'Hazlitt', *Common Reader: Second Series*, p. 164.
[18] Woolf, 'How It Strikes a Contemporary', p. 238.
[19] Woolf, 'Coleridge as Critic', p. 222.
[20] Her reign and death are described in Virginia Woolf, 'Professions for Women', *Collected Essays*, II, pp. 285 passim.
[21] This hobgoblin appears at the very end of *A Room of One's Own*, as the incarnation of all that is oppressive and censorious in the regime of patriarchy. See Woolf, *Room*, p. 118.

gaze at the heavens; and, her *coup de théâtre* – the resurrection of Shakespeare's sister, restored to her name (Judith) and provided with a biography typifying the historical plight of the woman who possessed talent, even genius, but lacked money and education, was schooled only in the repressive codes of chastity, altruism, and anonymity, was in fact 'so thwarted and hindered by other people, so tortured and pulled asunder by her own contrary instincts, that she must have lost her health and sanity to a certainty'.[22]

Woolf might have argued in defence of her unorthodox, antinomian 'methods' of literary revivalism that the times made more orthodox methods virtually impossible. 'The scattered dinner-tables of the modern world, the chase and eddy of the various currents which compose society in our time', she maintained, 'could only be dominated by a giant of fabulous dimensions.'[23] Though she shared the common reader's suspicions of 'fixed labels and settled hierarchies', she was somewhat dazed, as both novelist and reviewer-critic, by the break up of the reading public into a 'bewildering variety' of audiences: 'the daily Press, the Weekly Press, the monthly Press; the English public and the American public; the best-seller public and the worst-seller public; the high-brow public and the red-blood public, all now organised self-conscious entities capable through their various mouthpieces of making their needs known and their approval or displeasure felt'.[24] The reading public had become the reading publics, with different rather than converging interests, and Woolf was by no means sure that reviewers, through whose ranks she first joined the literary estate, eased rather than intensified the confusion and contention among them. Her pamphlet, *Reviewing* (1939), which provoked Leonard Woolf into appending a dissenting note, contains the startling suggestion that reviewers abolish themselves as a class, and resurrect themselves as consultants, expositors, or expounders, that is, as sympathetic readers.[25]

For her part, Woolf assumed the position and persona of the outsider without a stake either in established hierarchies or the periodic agitations

[22] *Ibid.*, p. 51. [23] Woolf, 'How It Strikes a Contemporary', pp. 238–9.
[24] Virginia Woolf, 'The Patron and the Crocus', *Common Reader: First Series*, p. 212.
[25] Leonard Woolf defended the role of reviewers, and literary journalism generally, as a service to a reading public overwhelmed by the mass production of books. Woolf had already acknowledged the economic re-organisation of the literature in 'The Patron and the Crocus', observing how different was the patronage for the Elizabethan writer, whose audience was the aristocracy and the playhouse public, or, for the nineteenth-century authors writing for 'the half-crown magazines and the leisured classes'. Woolf admitted that for the modern writer, the question of 'audience' was less simple, and indeed constituted a 'predicament'. Still, she insisted that the reader and reviewer were not to concern themselves with the ephemera of popular and commercial successes, but with creating a fit and demanding audience for writers, that is, by becoming patrons in a meaningful sense of that term. See Woolf, 'The Patron and the Crocus', pp. 211–12.

of the marketplace, an outsider, of course, who, as the daughter of Leslie Stephen and an accomplished, esteemed author in her own right, had an insider's experience of the workings, as well as the singular personalities, of the literary world. To present herself as a common reader and literary outsider was not as disingenuous as might first appear. As an aspiring woman novelist who lacked a formal education, a fact she exploits for sharp humour and point in the opening pages of *A Room of One's Own*, she may have had no real choice in adopting such a strategy. Nevertheless, it served her well, or, which is not quite the same thing, she made the most of her outsider status. Woolf was one of the first critics to demonstrate to us the special authority and unique advantage of those stationed on the periphery of officialdom, exploiting an exclusion that had been imposed until it begins to appear that one *chose* to stand apart, in order to develop larger, impartial, less compromised views and to stiffen into less submissive attitudes. Hence her lifelong fascination with the itinerant figure of Anon, the nameless village poet, sometimes man, sometimes woman, who, though despised by master and mistress of the Manor and feared when not hated by the elders of the Church, enjoyed 'the outsider's privilege to mock the solemn, to comment upon the established'.[26]

As an outsider possessed of 'inside information', Woolf commands an authority of a peculiar sort. It is authority predicated on the virtual incontrovertibility of what Gertrude Stein called 'personal knowledge'. In 'What is English Literature', Stein proposes a distinction between two ways of thinking about literature, 'literature as it is a history of it and the literature as it is a history of you'. Stein and Woolf both wrote of literature as a 'history of you', that is, as primarily a history of reading: 'Any one of us and anyway those of us that have always had the habit of reading have our own history of English literature inside us, the history as by reading we have come to know it'.[27] Stein seems content, or principled, in simply declaring what she indisputably does know, whose truth anyone, as she might say, can see for himself. Woolf is more interested in the strange vicissitudes of our relation to books, which she assiduously follows through all their tortuous phases, beginning with initial reactions, including passing thoughts and irresistible digressions, and concluding with the ordered ideas – the judgements – with which reading ought to conclude. She does not immediately appeal, as Stein does, to what we know, what is inside us and in a sense remains there, open to periodic inspection, but recreates the scene of reading. Typically she chooses a niche close to a window where 'somehow or another, the windows being open, and the

[26] Virginia Woolf, '"Anon" and "The Reader": Virginia Woolf's Last Essays', ed. Brenda Silver, *Twentieth-Century Literature*, 25 (1979), p. 383.

[27] Gertrude Stein, 'What is English Literature', *Lectures in America* (New York, 1975), p. 13.

book held so that it rested upon a background of escallonia hedges and distant blue, instead of being a book it seemed as if what I read was laid upon the landscape not printed, bound, or sewn up, but somehow the product of trees and fields and the hot summer sky, like the air which swam, on fine mornings, round the outlines of things'.[28]

Woolf habitually measures what she reads against such vistas. The window may open out onto a complementary scene of human labour, or on a panorama of uncultivated Nature, or simply lead the eye outward onto the wide prospect of life where the outline of things may be clearly seen and adjudged. I do not mean that Woolf insists on referring what she reads to some abstract but emotionally compelling idea of Nature of Society or God that will endow a literary work with transcendent meaning or eternal relevance. For Woolf, literature was both mirror and sanctuary of reality, of things in themselves, and yet it was not to be identified with anything *but* itself.

For Woolf the realist was also a formalist who believed that literature constituted its own reality, was a transmutation, not a servile transcription of life. The writing of novels helped form this conviction, for a novelist, as Woolf once reflected, 'is bound to build up his structure with much very perishable material which begins by lending it reality and ends by cumbering it with rubbish'.[29] The artist solves this problem by putting life into conflict with something that is not life (what we commonly identify as 'form'). Thus, in the imaginary but typical instance she cites in *A Room of One's Own*, we might yearn for the success and unending happiness of the hero we admire, but we must yield to the hard necessity that the hero must die because the story requires it. In forcing this choice between what we desire and what truth demands, the novel confirms its 'integrity' both as a moral record and work of art. The 'integrity' of great art consists in holding together 'all sorts of antagonist and opposed emotions' so that the reader is left with 'the conviction ... that this is the truth'. Nor is this conviction to be lightly dismissed as readerly solipsism, since it is 'Nature, in her most irrational mood', who has 'traced in invisible ink on the walls of the mind a premonition which these great artists confirm'.[30] Masterpieces (Woolf was not embarrassed by that term or by the concept of unimpeachable greatness) survive because they possess this integrity of feeling and form, because they hold together the antagonistic forces of life and form that lesser books allow to split apart or tear themselves asunder. They attain and communicate 'a complete finality' that summons all our faculties in reading, so that 'some consecration

---

[28] Virginia Woolf, 'Reading', *Collected Essays*, II, p. 13.
[29] Virginia Woolf, 'Jane Eyre and Wuthering Heights', *Common Reader: First Series*, p. 159.
[30] Woolf, *Room*, p. 75.

descends upon us from their hands which we return to life, feeling it more keenly and understanding it more deeply than before'.[31]

The truth of things was not, then, to be contested, but rather to be *determined*, or, more precisely, redetermined in new acts of creation, new readings. Woolf does not hesitate to make these determinations about literary value and, without any ideological fuss, can dismiss bad writing for what it is – a revenge not against art, but against reality:

> The bad writer seems to possess a predominance of the day-dreaming power, he lives all day long in that region of artificial light where every factory girl becomes a duchess, where if truth be told, most people spend a few moments every day revenging themselves upon reality. The bad books are not the mirrors but the vast distorted shadows of life; they are a refuge, a form of revenge.[32]

Bad writing is bad in itself and bad for us because it contains not too much reality, but too little. Perhaps only a critic of Woolf's extensive reading and her declared interest in non-canonical works could understand the pleasures of bad books without feeling obliged to attribute to them imaginary merits.

These wider views of literature, afforded by open windows through which the outline of things appears in its shimmering reality, may break our concentration, but that is their purpose – to provide stimulants and correctives to the absorption of reading. However sinuous her prose, Woolf is actually of more disruptive temper than Stein, whom nothing seems to arrest as she advances her argument through the precisely modulated repetitions that eventually settle in a triumphant assertion of common and incontrovertible sense, as in the following grand definition of what is, in fact, English literature:

> As I say description of the complete the entirely complete daily island life has been England's glory. Think of Chaucer, think of Jane Austen, think of Anthony Trollope, and the life of things shut up with that daily life is the poetry, think of all the lyrical poets, think what they say and what they have. They have shut in with them in their daily island life but completely shut in with them all the things that just in enumeration make poetry, and they can and do enumerate and they can and do make poetry, this enumeration. That is all one side of English literature and indeed anybody knows, where it grows, the daily life the complete daily life and the things shut in with that complete daily life.[33]

Woolf, on the other hand, is the mistress of deferral, dilation, and delay. If she prides herself on being a highbrow who 'rides [her mind] at a gallop across country in pursuit of an idea'[34] she can alter her course in mid-

---

[31] Woolf, 'Hours in a Library', p. 60.
[32] Virginia Woolf, 'Bad Writers', *Essays*, II, p. 328.
[33] Stein, 'What is English Literature', pp. 17–18.
[34] Virginia Woolf, 'Middlebrow', *Collected Essays*, II, p. 196.

stride, detour an argument into unsuspected places, and so recreate the excitement, or the indignation, of arriving at a conclusion other than what one hoped to find on setting out. However much she blamed the 'tea-table training' inculcated at Hyde Park Gate for the 'suavity' and 'politeness' she detected in her *Common Reader* articles, she put her training to unexpected and good use in devising a rhetoric that allowed her to 'say a great many things which would be inaudible if one marched straight up and spoke out'.[35] We can see the benefits of this manner in the confiding first sentence of 'On Not Knowing Greek', where Woolf manages to create a community of (unscholarly) opinion simply by beginning with the utterly disarming:

For it is vain and foolish to talk of Knowing Greek, since in our ignorance we should be at the bottom of any class of schoolboys, since we do not know how the words sounded, or where precisely we ought to laugh, or how the actors acted, and between this foreign people and ourselves there is not only difference of race and tongue but a tremendous breach of tradition.[36]

Tradition is striated by historical ruptures, fatal ignorances. Such breaches could appear insuperable, discouraging any attempts at repair, were it not for the amending power communicated by that opening 'For', which reminds us that in picking up a book, whether in ignorance or in partial knowledge of our subject, we are resuming a discussion or dialogue already and still underway. This is what it means to enter into a tradition, to join up at the point of common conjunctions. Even when Woolf's singular and strategic use of conjunctions is startlingly abrupt, it still strikes the sociable note of resumed dialogue, as in the arresting opening of *A Room of One's Own* – 'But you may say, we asked you to speak about women and fiction – what has that got to do with a room of one's own?' We are not eased into an argument, but plunged immediately into its midst. The 'but' of expostulation already sounds a note of heated exchange, one that promises to leave the audience at the conclusion of her talk not only informed of the social, economic, and psychological factors that affect creativity, but equally important, instructed in the suggestive and persuasive powers of symbolic representations. Those who follow her through multiple changes in identity (she speaks first in her own person, while allowing that 'I' denotes a 'convenient term for somebody who has no real being', then as Mary Beton, who will conduct most of the research and conversation, finally returning to her 'real' identity as 'expert' woman of letters in time to deliver the peroration), who suffer with her the rebuff at the entrance to the College Library and persist through all the distrac-

[35] Virginia Woolf, 'A Sketch of the Past', *Moments of Being: Unpublished Autobiographical Writings*, ed. Jeanne Schulkind (London, 1976), p. 129.
[36] Virginia Woolf, 'On Not Knowing Greek', *Common Reader: First Series*, p. 24.

tions, digressions, ellipses, and interruptions that divert or retard her train of thought, but never – such is the providence that rules Woolf's mental world – derail it, will eventually learn what a room of one's own has to do with the question of women and fiction.

Woolf, then, might be said to have pioneered reader response criticism of a very sophisticated, if unmethodical kind. And yet it must also be said that the author of an essay advising 'How Should One Read a Book', or a review admonishing 'The Wrong Way of Reading', is already uneasily aware of some impending complication and crisis in the relation between the outer and inner life, imperilling the future of reading, hence of literature itself. Of course, to see modernity as a time of unprecedented, convulsive change was not unique to Woolf, but perhaps no modern critic put the crisis in such bold, mischievous terms as Woolf in her famous claim that on or about December 1910 human character changed.[37] She measured these changes as a novelist might be expected to – by noting the more open character of one's cook, by suggesting that Clytemnestra, and not Agamemnon, now elicits our sympathy, and by considering how the 'horrible domestic tradition' condemned Jane Carlyle, woman of genius, to scouring saucepans instead of writing books.

It was this change in character, manifested in the altered relations between 'masters and servants, husbands and wives, parents and children', that made modernity new. It is one of history's many ironies that human character may have changed so radically in the seventy-odd years since Woolf first hazarded this observation that for many it has ceased to exist entirely. Indeed, Woolf's fascination with Mrs Brown or 'character in itself' may seem old-fashioned, a quaint fiction easily repudiated by those who no longer believe in the reality of the self, much less the idea of character. But Woolf cherished human character as something *achieved*, not fantasised. Character was the supreme accomplishment of our social and cultural evolution and prose was its greatest expositor. Life was not always a 'luminous halo surrounding us from the beginning of consciousness to the end'. The Elizabethans, for example, did not have a sense of character in the modern understanding of that word, as one can see in comparing, as Woolf does, Annabella in *'Tis Pity She's a Whore* to

[37] The 'on or about' retains just enough of the liberal spirit of flexibility to indemnify the confident precision of December 1910. It is generally agreed that Woolf chose 1910 to mark these changes in social attitudes because that year saw the death of King Edward VII and the First Impressionist Exhibition. Less commonly remarked, but a literary fact Woolf did not fail to note, is that 1910 also saw the reissue and double printing of Samuel Butler's *The Way of All Flesh*, a book Woolf considered to have paved the way for modern characters, thus vindicating her faith in the sagacity of the common reader in deciding what deserves, over time, to survive. It should finally be remarked that 1910 saw the deaths of Mark Twain, William James, and Tolstoy, all great forerunners of the modern novel. See Virginia Woolf, 'Character in Fiction', *Essays*, III, pp. 421–2.

Anna Karenina. Anna is 'flesh and blood, nerves and temperament, has heart, brain, body and mind', in other words is a full incarnation of a human being. But of Annabella, who 'is flat and crude as a face painted on a playing card', we know very little, nor do we need to, since as a literary creation she 'is without depth, without range, without intricacy'.[38] By contrast, even the most ordinary mind of someone alive on or about 1910 would be host to 'a myriad impressions – trivial, fantastic, evanescent, or engraved with the sharpness of steel', that shape 'themselves into the life of Monday or Tuesday'. As a note in her last reading notebook attests, 'the modern . . . the growth of articulateness' remained synonymous phenomena in Woolf's mind.[39]

The growth in self-consciousness and the power of art to liberate 'us from the enormous burden of the unexpressed' are the twin themes that dominate Woolf's reading of history from her *Common Reader* essays, through the brilliant feminist revisionism of *Room*, to her last major critical project, which gives pride of place to two figures whose role in the making of the tradition Woolf was intent on commemorating. One is Anon, 'the common voice singing out of doors', who ushers us to the threshold of individuality and the print culture that memorialised the self. Without Anon's singing at the back door of the manor houses and his staging of dramas in churchyards and the marketplace, the English in the silent centuries before the advent of the book 'might be a dumb race, a race of merchants, soldiers, priests, who left behind them stone houses, cultivated fields and great churches, but no words'.[40] The other is, of course, 'The Reader', whom Woolf presents not as a convenient personification, but as an historical being who 'comes into existence some time at the end of the sixteenth century' upon the death of Anon, and whose life history 'could we discover it would be worth writing, for the effect it had upon literature'.[41]

The *Common Reader* may be regarded as the first volume of that life history. The plot unfolds in the family chronicle recounted in 'Chaucer and the Pastons': Margaret Paston, the mother, dutifully writes to her husband of the happenings on the estate, 'letters of an honest bailiff to his master, explaining, giving news, rendering accounts'; her son John, moving to London, establishes himself as a gentleman, a change in character marked by his desire to write of things that have no immediate practical importance and by the pleasure he finds reading Chaucer, where he might encounter 'the very skies, fields, and people whom he knew, but rounded and complete'.

In the growing inwardness of John Paston's character we witness the

---

[38] Virginia Woolf, 'Notes on an Elizabethan Play', *Common Reader: First Series*, p. 53.
[39] Virginia Woolf, 'Notes for Reading at Random', *Twentieth Century Literature*, 25 (1979), p. 376.   [40] Woolf, '"Anon" and "The Reader"', p. 383.   [41] *Ibid.*, p. 428.

shift in family and social relations that leads to the birth of the reader. Woolf's account of that momentous mutation sharply contrasts with Walter Benjamin's, who pictures the newborn reader as spiritually and morally stranded in the silence of the book, 'himself, uncounseled', and unable to counsel others.[42] Woolf attributes the reader's inward turn of spirit to habits developed in response or in reaction to the customs of the playhouse, where public concerns and private individuals worked out their destinies. 'The publicity of the stage and the perpetual presence of a second person', Woolf speculated, failed to satisfy a mind tired of company, a mind seeking 'to think, not to act; to comment, not to share; to explore its own darkness, not the bright lit-up surfaces of others'.

Such a mind belongs to the (newly born) reader. He will turn to Donne, Montaigne, Sir Thomas Browne, 'the keepers of the keys of solitude'.[43] To Montaigne alone belongs the art 'of talking of oneself, following one's own vagaries, giving the whole map, weight, colour, and circumference of the soul in its confusion, its variety, its imperfection'.[44] Montaigne, reading the book of himself, counsels us that 'Communication is health, communication is happiness',[45] a message the disordered mind of Septimus Smith makes the burden of his prophecy in *Mrs Dalloway*, even as he enacts the dark fate of modernity – the death of the soul. If Montaigne is the man who 'achieved at last a miraculous adjustment of all the wayward parts that constitute the human soul', Sir Thomas Browne, the first autobiographer, is a character in whom 'we first become conscious of impurities which hereafter stain literature with so many freakish colours that, however hard we try, make it difficult to be certain whether we are looking at a man or his writing'.[46]

All the writers who interested Woolf present this uncertainty: Donne, Defoe, Sterne, the Brontes, George Eliot, Meredith, Hardy, Henry James, Conrad, Lawrence, Proust, and Joyce, to name only a few who occasioned her most brilliant commentary. As *Persuasion* attests, even Jane Austen, exemplary in her impersonality and 'exquisite discrimination of human values', might, had she lived, 'devised a method, clear and composed as ever, but deeper and more suggestive, for conveying not only what people say, but what they leave unsaid; not only what they are, but what life is'.[47] She would have been a forerunner not only of E. M. Forster (and, of course, Woolf herself), but of Proust and Henry James.

[42] Walter Benjamin, 'The Storyteller', *Illuminations*, ed. Hannah Arendt (New York, 1968), p. 87.   [43] Woolf, 'Notes on an Elizabethan Play', p. 58.
[44] Virginia Woolf, 'Montaigne', *Common Reader: First Series*, p. 59.   [45] *Ibid.*, p. 69.
[46] Virginia Woolf, 'The Elizabethan Lumber Room', *Common Reader: First Series*, p. 48.
[47] *Persuasion* suggests this likelihood, since its famous outburst on woman's constancy 'proves not merely the biographical fact that Jane Austen had loved, but the aesthetic fact that she was no longer afraid to say so'. 'Jane Austen', *Common Reader: First Series*, p. 148.

Woolf does not strand her readers, as she stranded Orlando, in the modernist present, caught in the generational squabble between the Edwardian 'materialists' Wells, Galsworthy, and Bennett, who, according to Woolf, only told us where and how, but not why the modern character lived, and the 'spiritualist' Georgians, Joyce, Lawrence, and herself, seeking to capture the divagating 'spirit' of modern life, a task that necessitated their daring break with conventions. Her literary history sees beyond the modernist crisis when the mind's contradictory emotions will be subdued by 'the generalising and simplifying power of a strict and logical imagination'. The literature of the future, Woolf advised, would harness the power of poetry to abstract and exalt feeling so that we understand not just what we are, but what life is. Yet it would not lose its moorings in prose, where both the great and trivial facts of existence, the common sensations of the mind – including its humours, the emotions aroused by music, by crowds, by certain people, or merely by the play of light against the water – can be calibrated with a precision the poets might admire.[48]

Such a future will not materialise without a corresponding change in sex-consciousness, since for Woolf sex-consciousness is indistinguishable from the great problem of modernity: the mind divided against itself. Woolf's determination to include and credit the obscure, the common reader and Anon, who was probably a woman, as important figures in the history of English literature helped change not only the way we conceive of literary history, but how we understand women's relation to the art of writing. Modern feminist criticism is fundamentally an elaboration of Woolf's original insight that 'we think back through our mothers if we are women'.[49] Woolf is forced to trace this genealogy because women, denied the education and the material means to qualify as unconscious inheritors of the tradition, necessarily wrote not only differently, but also less expansively and confidently than men.

These feminist concerns were not ones she grew or stumbled into, but very early on determined her point of view as a critic. As early as 1918, in a review of *Women Novelists*, Woolf proposed that the question of women writers was 'not merely one of literature, but of social history':

---

[48] These ideas are adumbrated most concisely in 'Modern Fiction', 'How it Strikes a Contemporary', 'Mr Bennett and Mrs Brown', and 'The Narrow Bridge of Art'. These essays date to the twenties, when modernist practices were establishing themselves as indispensable innovations in view of the catastrophe of the Great War. By the thirties the aesthetic principles of modernism were challenged by a new generation who, seeing the conditions that led to the second great war of the century, began to question and often renounce the 'spiritualism' of their immediate forbears and to rely on 'materialist', politically and socially charged justifications for the work of art. Woolf's 'The Leaning Tower' is the most influential and important essay of the thirties addressing this issue, and *Three Guineas* her most important tract expressing her views on the relationship between patriarchy and war, literature and politics.   [49] Woolf, *Room*, p. 79.

What, for example, was the origin of the extraordinary outburst in the eighteenth century of novel writing by women? Why did it begin then, and not in the time of the Elizabethan renaissance? Was the motive which finally determined them to write a desire to correct the current view of their sex expressed in so many volumes and for so many ages by male writers? If so, their art is at once possessed of an element which should be absent from the work of all previous writers.[50]

These questions are today quite familiar, so much so that we might forget that their answers, which took a lifetime to formulate, are by no means definitive and, in some cases, are still incomplete. We are still seeking to resolve the major issues Woolf proposed for feminist inquiry: the social and economic conditions of creativity (or, as she puts it, how to feed the artist); the relation, if any, of gender and genre, the body and language. The most stubborn problem Woolf raised remains how to identify the element or elements which would theoretically allow us to recognise a work as distinctly female. As Woolf herself discovered, motive is no real clue, since women's reasons for writing are not consistent and uniform. Fanny Burney, 'the mother of English fiction', was not inspired 'by any single wish to redress a grievance', while her headstrong daughter, Charlotte Bronte, could barely contain her anger. A more reliable indicator of gender might be the pace and tread of the sentence. A woman's sentence would be likely to reflect the daily rhythms that marked and limited her life *whatever* she may have felt about it – happy or resentful, fulfilled or aggrieved. 'For interruptions there will always be' – women who write never escape the fatality of that sentence, which determines not only the way women write – sporadically, in short, not sustained bouts of concentration – but the way the world enters consciousness, in the intervals snatched from service to the children, duty in the sitting room, attendance at the family table.

Less credible but perhaps more interesting is Woolf's suggestion that we look for signs of sexual difference where we find it in life – not so much in the erotics of the text, but in its physiognomy. Woolf speculated that writing took its conformation from the proportions and nervous organisation of the body, the female's being shorter, more supple, shaped around a different centre of gravity, as it were. That a woman should write *as* a body and not as an angel of indeterminate or non-existent sex seemed a more important point for Woolf to make than to describe her literary anatomy. To renounce the vow of mental chastity imposed by patriarchy and tell the truth about the body was the first injunction for women seriously committed to writing.

Yet Woolf, who virtually taught us how to understand and interpret sex-consciousness in literature, is equally fervent in prescribing its subli-

---

[50] Virginia Woolf, 'Women Novelists', *Essays*, II, p. 314.

mation into more abstracted, impersonal modes of consciousness. For one thing, and it is the *main* thing, heightened sex consciousness limits imaginative capacity and thus distorts our view of reality:

To cast out and incorporate in a person of the opposite sex all that we miss in ourselves and desire in the universe and detest in humanity is a deep and universal instinct on the part both of men and of women. But though it affords relief, it does not lead to understanding. Rochester is as great a travesty of the truth about men as Cordelia is of the truth about women.[51]

Not surprisingly, it was Coleridge who guided Woolf to the 'soul' of the problem with his speculation that the creative mind is androgynous. Woolf interprets Coleridge as meaning that the 'androgynous mind is resonant and porous; that it transmits emotion without impediment; that it is naturally creative, incandescent and undivided'.[52] To confirm this theory Woolf turns to the one figure who represents for her the composure before reality, the emotional truth that literature has the power to convey – Shakespeare, whose mind had consumed all impediments and impurities so that it would be impossible to say what he personally thought of women or what causes he held most dear. The ordinary mind is riven by severances and oppositions, swayed by loves and aversions, but the creative, Shakespearean mind consummates these opposites, mates what is female to what is male in human consciousness until it expresses itself in perfect fullness, peace, and freedom.

All this talk of androgyny and the nuptials of the creative mind is, of course, a myth, as Woolf well knew. If Shakespeare was so incandescent of mind and feeling while he wrote, how did he create Cordelia, a travesty of woman? Still, and I would say more movingly, Shakespeare above all others stands for the writer who lives at enmity with unreality, who has fought the battles of the world and won. He is not a bogey blocking our view, but a continuous presence whose spirit animates every writer who fixes his vision on reality, determined not to let it disappear without a trace. Thus if it is absolutely indispensable to write, preferable to read, in a room of one's own, it is equally advisable that the windows not be shuttered so that the outline of things as they are can be kept in plain sight. For there is to be found the thing that endures change, survives catastrophe: there is the 'common life which is the real life and not the ... little separate lives which we live as individuals'.[53] There congregate Anon and the common reader, Shakespeare and his sister, Mary Beton and Mrs Brown, all busily conversing in the mind of those common and astute readers who pick up a book, and, taking one last glance out the window, resume their reading.

[51] Virginia Woolf, 'Men and Women', *ibid.*, III, p. 193.   [52] Woolf, *Room*, p. 102.
[53] *Ibid.*, p. 118.

5

Wyndham Lewis

Vincent Sherry

In 1929, in *Paleface: The Philosophy of the 'Melting Pot'*, Wyndham Lewis sets out to examine the operations of 'race-consciousness' in contemporary fiction and poetry. His subject entails methods and aims far more ambitious than those of 'literary criticism', a term he lifts away from his own prose on the tweezers of these inverted commas: 'these essays do not come under the head of "literary criticism". They are written purely as investigations into contemporary states of mind, as these are displayed for us by imaginative writers.'[1] Expanding the centre of attention from literary text to cultural context, Lewis augurs a change in critical ethic and practice that has continued, through the twentieth century, into the flourishing industry of 'culture studies'. As cultural *critic* more than cultural student, however, Lewis stands at the root of the contemporary discipline as a most provocative radical, a disturbing witness to the basic tendencies of socially and historically informed readings of literature. For Lewis's emphasis on the cultural grounding of art leads to a thoroughly determinist account, one which he promises, as that last passage continues, as the end and purpose of his inquiry. His essays are 'intended to set in relief the automatic processes by which the artist or the writer (a novelist or poet) obtains his formularies: to show how the formularies for his progress are issued to him, how he gets them by post, and then applies them'.[2]

If all literary expression is conditioned, as Lewis repeatedly avers, one issue asserts itself above all: to what measure of independence and authority may this critic lay claim? It is no rhetorical question. For Lewis, novelist (and painter) as well as critic, is a member of the same literary generation – with Joyce, Stein, Woolf, Pound, and Eliot – that comes most persistently and severely under his review. That he enjoys less critical distance on his subject than his pronouncements may concede is a fact that serves at once to limit the objective validity of his formulations and to explain their peculiar, sometimes luminous intensity. Detached visionary and local familiar, Lewis participates in the very energies he traces

---

[1] Wyndham Lewis, *Paleface: The Philosophy of the 'Melting Pot'* (London, 1929), p. 97.
[2] *Ibid.*, pp. 97–8.

through his contemporaries with such fierce intelligence. The fiery anatomy of folly he feels compelled to perform may itself be a performance, scripted by the same forces of cultural and political history that he seeks so assiduously to expose.

Hardly a predicament unique to Lewis, this contradiction resolves itself into a body of work that stands perhaps as the most telling record of his generation: *The Man of the World*. Under this provisional title he proceeded from 1919 until the early 1930s to write a single, multi-volume *oeuvre* on those 'contemporary states of mind', one which combines discursive and fictional prose and witnesses the kind of major syntheses of political and artistic history that his own brand of cultural determinism required. (The contents of this magnum opus will be read and cited here under the half-dozen titles into which Lewis finally parcelled it – on the advice of Eliot.)[3] But the severe and searching rebuke he extends here to the now characteristic features of literary modernism draws its authority from his own immersion in the matrix of political and cultural history that generated these developments. The exposition that follows here will take this contradiction as the first condition of the intensity that serves, finally, to legitimate Lewis's report. It is as though Jonah, still trapped in the dark belly of his whale, were suddenly able to describe, in incandescent detail, the structure of the exoskeleton that contained him.

The Lion and the Fox: The Role of the Hero in the Plays of Shakespeare (1927) appears in the 'Man of the World' sequence as one of a kind. Its subject – the influence of Machiavellian thought on the politics and literature of the English Renaissance – distinguishes it from the other books, which maintain nearly exclusively a contemporary frame of reference. Lewis argues here that the figures of lion and fox – the colossus and the strategist, the types of naked strength and covert cunning – define the opposite possibilities that the Machiavellian ruler must blend and balance, and he shows this challenge as the inciting force in the plays. Convincing and consistent as the argument is, it bears nowhere perceptibly on the critique of modernity that he conducts through the rest of the project. It seems to stand as an exercise in the methods of historically informed scholarship, as an attempt to demonstrate the writer's credentials in this newly adopted discipline. The historical narrative falters badly, however. Behind the rival political identities of lion and fox lies the shift from the feudal or chivalric values of *medium aevum* to the success-

---

[3] Of the six volumes published between 1926 and 1930, there were two novels – *The Childermass* and *The Apes of God* – and four discursive tracts: *The Art of Being Ruled*, *The Lion and the Fox: The Role of the Hero in the Plays of Shakespeare*, *Time and Western Man*, and *Paleface*. The aims and vision of the project are clearly extended through the mid-1930s in *The Diabolical Principle and the Dithyrambic Spectator*, *The Doom of Youth*, and *Men Without Art*.

ethic of early modernity, but this story stretches too thin and conventional a line to sustain the weight of documentation and elaborate referencing that Lewis asks it to bear. It is a revealing failure. When *The Lion and the Fox* is read against other volumes in the series, it suggests most forcefully that the main qualification for Lewis's claim to be an historically informed critic of literature is membership in the generation he is examining.

He demonstrates this membership through the signal failure of *The Lion and the Fox*. His indulgence of archival and esoteric detail over the needs of the argument moves the whole effort in the direction of historical romance – it is an academically stiffened version of the same temporal escapism he finds and censors most heavily among his contemporaries. This critique is part of a far-reaching commentary on the modern experience of time, one which is sufficiently complex to merit rehearsal through the next several paragraphs here, but it is clearly Lewis's own peculiar torque with the modern age that turns him into the most searching critic of (what he calls) its 'time-cult'.

In *Time and Western Man* (1927), ostensibly the centrepiece of the project and inarguably a major work in modern intellectual history, Lewis sees contemporary intellectual and popular culture under the sway of a distinctly modern attitude to time. This is typified for him by the philosophical writings of Henri Bergson and the theories of scientific relativism currently evolving through Albert Einstein. According to Bergson, models of history that emphasise sequence or linear pattern rely on a spatialising and distancing faculty that betrays the true nature of time, which must be experienced 'from within' to be grasped correctly. This ideal experience he brought under the heading of his signature doctrine, '*durée*', that is, an expanded moment, where past interpenetrates present in an intensive manifold, a living continuum free of the divisions the spatialising mind wrongly inserts. This attitude leaves its record in the visual arts, Lewis suggests, on the canvases of Cubism, where space is temporalised; where a single object, seen from a succession of viewpoints, stands in the end as the composite image of those perspectives (the resistance to fixed viewpoint also aligns this art with the theories of Einsteinian relativity). Cancelling distance, advocating immersion in the moment, Bergsonian and relativist models of time strike Lewis as 'fundamentally sensation[alist]; that is what Bergson's *durée* always conceals beneath its pretentious metaphysic. It is the glorification of the life-of-the-moment, with no reference beyond itself and no absolute or universal value.'[4]

Lewis's criticism of this time-view comes from the position of the plastic or visual intelligence: painter as well as man of letters, he seeks to reclaim what is for him the proper role and privilege of the eye, which relies on

---

4 Wyndham Lewis, *Time and Western Man* (London, 1927; rpt. Boston, 1957), p. 11.

distance and non-participation as the first condition of conceptual understanding. Lewis's own idea of time seems akin often to the classical view
of the past as an array of estimable models, a gallery of *exempla*, but he
builds a conceptual understanding of time in no sustained or systematic
way. Whether or not this is a major failure in the book, he is engaged
chiefly – expressly – in a diagnosis of the current malaise, a symptomatol-
ogy of (the) time. His representation of his insights clearly draws on his
primary skill as visual artist, specifically as caricaturist, but these cartoons
do not as a rule seem to lose much to veracity: they exaggerate certain
basic aspects of modernity and magnify the underlying reality to visionary
proportions.

His main target of rebuke is *Ulysses*. Its cultivation of local colour and
intricately detailed circumstances strikes him as a sign of Joyce's myopic
absorption in the Now, an indulgence that Bergson has preached and
sanctioned. Thus he sees Joyce bearing much less resemblance to a Dedalus than to a Dubliner, his art no aerial acrobatic escape from the
labyrinth of that city but a merely stylised form of his true Irish 'paralysis'
(a theme word in *Dubliners*). And so Lewis makes the case, surprising no
doubt to readers still under the thrall of *Ulysses* as a prohibited book, that
is, as a secret and mystic text, that Joyce's imagination was certainly not
breathtakingly novel. It was instead ultra-conventional, domestic, tied to
lower middle-class values and compelled to reenact those rites of shabby
gentility in his little punctilios of craft. In the end, the whole book
impresses Lewis as being sentimental in the conventionally wan, defeatist
fashion of that sunless northern province.

These unexpected perceptions offer perhaps the main measure of
Lewis's critical perspicacity: his ability to represent the emergent art of
literary modernism, on the surface the work of an elite coterie, as the most
characteristic expression of contemporary popular culture. Insofar as he
sees this culture dominated by Bergsonian values of flux and continuous
change, it is consistent – nonetheless surprising and revealing – to present
these as the standards informing the otherwise high, hierophantic priesthood of modernist 'technique'. For theirs is an emphasis on method, on
ways of doing things, and it shows to Lewis an immersion in process *qua*
process, timeful sensationalism of the sheerest kind. Thus the shoring of
fragments that Eliot and Pound undertook in *The Waste Land* (that
sacrament to the values of modernist craft), the recondite imitations of
period manners and styles in *Ulysses*, all strike Lewis as modes of 'composition'. This is a term he allows Gertrude Stein to define for his own
purposes, in a passage that turns the whole act of artistic making around a
temporal axis: 'In the beginning there was the time in the composition that
naturally was in the composition but time in the composition comes now
and this is what is now troubling every one the time in the composition is

now a part of distribution and equilibration.'[5] Using Stein's own prose
style to show the serious antics to which the detested time-values must
run, Lewis reduces the whole enterprise to the farcical example of that
'sausage-links prose song'.

   Modernists also show Lewis their immersion in the contemporary
philosophy of time in their exaggerated and aggravated sense of historical
period. Modern*ism*, the self-conscious sense of being modern, turns on a
feeling of separation between past and present, and for Lewis this feeling
of essential discontinuity in history stems from Bergson's own hyper-
valuation of the Now, in the idealised and expanded moment of *durée*
(Bergson's own assertions of continuity between past and present notwithstanding). Conversely, Lewis argues, the past acquires the value and
attraction of the Other, a distant and numinous locale, a far island in the
romance of strange lands – or times. (This is of course the same suscepti-
bility to which Lewis himself succumbs in the historical reconstructions of
The Lion and The Fox.) In Lewis's own severe but searching caricature:
the moderns' 'enucleation' of time results in the loathed 'glorification of
life-in-the-moment', so that the past, atomised and disconnected from the
present, is cheapened by the most 'meretricious' kind of 'exoticism',[6]
whereas the present, now uninformed by the past, enjoys a giddy but
empty hegemony. Thus Lewis offers the striking proposition that the two
apparently opposite aspects of literary modernism – its sometimes jazzy
contemporaneousness, its otherwise august traditionalism – derive from
the one source, the modern cult of time. Eliot's doctrines of canonical
literature and Stein's doxologies of the contemporary tongue are recited to
the same measure.

   Lewis engages another one of the structuring paradoxes of modernism
in the 'impersonality principle'. The mask of anonymity, he proposes, is
merely an inverted kind of personality, another mode of self-expression.
Eliot also conceded this contradiction, or at least revealed the reverse
purposes of impersonality, when he indicated that only a strong personality could make its suppression interesting. Lewis ignores this fact, however, for his aim exceeds that single tenet. He goes to the critical edifice
built around the impersonality principle, the whole set of related doctrines
that might be said to comprise a poetics of high modernism. Chief among
these is the notion of 'pseudo-statement', as formulated by I. A. Richards,
and renamed 'pseudo-belief' by Lewis, who sees it extending the principle
of authorial impersonality to nothing less than a voiding of thematic
content in literature. He traces this tendency back to the art-for-art's sake
movement in the 1890s, shows its progeny in the 1920s' attitude of

─────────────────────────

[5] From Stein's *Composition as Explanation*; as quoted and discussed by Lewis, *Time*,
    pp. 49ff.
[6] Lewis, *Time*, p. 131; Wyndham Lewis, *Men Without Art* (London, 1934), p. 72.

'life-by-style', and outlines attitudes that can be seen, in retrospect, to have augured Wittgenstein's formulation that 'aesthetics are ethics'. 'There you have it', he responds to the claim that poetry itself offers the supreme fiction: 'the agreeable, the life-giving, lies that we tell ourselves must be cut off from all embarrassing logical entanglements, and erected into autonomous systems – the *pseudo-belief* takes the place of *belief*.[7] Artists who turn their faith in pure art into structures of value, who thus *pretend* significance, seem to him to take the defeatism of modern (relativist) philosophy through its most cynical series of end-game manoeuvers.

Believer in no conventional or denominational sense, Lewis seems a surprising opponent of such faithlessness among his contemporaries. If this contradiction has gone unnoticed by commentators, it is perhaps because Lewis's own presentation of himself as 'the Enemy' – inveterate opponent of his chosen subjects – seems to make negation his only style. His objection to meaningless make-believe in literature, however, springs from passionate attachment to the possibilities of value and belief – a yearning no less valid for being esoteric rather than conventional in character, gnostic rather than orthodox in articulation. It connects him to a tradition of philosophical inquiry and political speculation that is chiefly Continental in background; that disciplines the content and methods of *ideology* to a meaning at once original and radical.

'Ideology' entered verbal currency through the *idéologues* of post-revolutionary France, intellectuals who used the word according to the exact sense of its Greek roots: *eidos-logos*, the study or science of images. Empirical inquiry into human physiology, in particular the faculties of perception and cognition, would provide truths about the human creature that might prove useful in formulating principles of government.[8] Whether or not such inquiry could remain free of preconception (these first *idéologues* were seeking 'objective' validation for the political principles of the Revolution), its high line of scientific inquiry insured its longevity in French intellectual culture. Its tendencies reemerged at the turn of the next century among a number of French critics commonly acknowledged as major figures in the European backgrounds of Anglo-American literary modernism, including Julien Benda and Remy de Gourmont. Their influence is most often told in terms of familiar phrases such as 'the dissociation of sensibility', but a deeper current of connection to

---

[7] Lewis, *Men Without Art*, p. 86.
[8] Good summaries of this tradition are by Emmet Kennedy, *A Philosophe in the Age of Revolution: Destutt de Tracy and the Origins of Ideology* (Philadelphia, 1978) and Keith Michael Baker, 'Closing the French Revolution: Saint-Simon and Comte', in *The French Revolution and the Creation of Modern Political Culture, 1789–1848*, ed. François Furet and Mona Ozouf (Oxford, 1989), pp. 325–31. Its relevance to Lewis is established and its import examined by Vincent Sherry, *Ezra Pound, Wyndham Lewis, and Radical Modernism* (New York, 1993), esp. pp. 24–30, 91–139.

Lewis (and Pound) lies in their extension of the original tradition of *idéologie*.

Drawing out the social implications of aesthetic – sensual – experience, Benda and Gourmont attend specially to the activities of ear and eye.[9] The ear, they find, is the most physical sense, tending to unite the listener with the physical stimulus of the sound and so, potentially, with other listeners. The empathy natural to hearing provides the channel for the fellow-feeling of mass democracy; the excitable crowd thus emerges as the social image – the direct result – of these susceptibilities of the ear. Whereas the ear merges democratically, the eye divides aristocratically. Relying on distance, the eye separates the viewer from the object of sight, achieving the distinctions on which clear conceptual intelligence depends. On the horizontal plane of sense perception the eye enacts the kind of discrimination that works, in a vertical scheme, in a hierarchical society. The visual sense thus locates the possibility in human nature of selective superiority, one which seeks fulfilment in the institutions of an echeloned State. It provides the instrument and emblem of a ruling intellectual elite.

Acknowledging Benda as author of 'the excellent *Belphégor*', conceding the relevance of 'le visuel' (Gourmont's term)[10] to his own thought and fiction, Lewis through his literary criticism extends the Continental science of the senses – to political polemic. Gertrude Stein provides his point of sharpest attack. She converts the visual frame of the page into an aural sensorium through heavy prose cadences, he proposes; thus she lifts the words into a fluent chant that hypnotises the inner ear. Merging with the physical body of her language, her reader mouths its sounds in a kind of silent echoing that obliterates the distance between the reading eye and the perceiving mind. This empathy provides the root experience of political collectivity: the whole enterprise, Lewis observes, is 'undoubtedly intended as an epic contribution to the present mass-democracy'.[11] Stein appears in Lewis's own democratic Dunciad as fellow-traveller with Ernest Hemingway (and Aldous Huxley), artists who have supplanted the well-born artifice of written prose for the bastard craft of a plebeian vocalese. Their fictional language is 'not written' at all; it is 'lifted out of nature and very artfully and adroitly tumbled out upon the page'; despite its stylised patina, 'it is the brute material of everyday proletarian speech and feeling'.[12]

Conversely, the faculty of visual discrimination marks the achievement of a superior art. The application of this essentially painterly value in the

[9] The main relevant works are Benda's *Belphégor* (1918), tr. S. J. I. Lawson (New York, 1929), and Gourmont's *Le Problème du Style* (Paris, 1902) and *Esthétique de la Langue Française* (Paris, 1905).
[10] Lewis, *Time*, p. 283, and Wyndham Lewis, *Satire & Fiction* (London, 1930), p. 46.
[11] Lewis, *Time*, p. 62.   [12] Lewis, *Men Without Art*, p. 35.

verbal medium remains problematic, however. Gourmont had addressed this issue in *Le Problème du Style* (1902), and argued that optical selectivity provided the rule of all fine writing, but this French critic enjoyed a sophistication much more specifically *literary* than Lewis's. In *Satire & Fiction* (1930), Lewis invokes Gourmont to endorse an art of visual grotesquerie, but he seems to find the preferred stance of 'le visuel' operating in no imaginative literature but his own – the highly visualised yet strained, indeed contorted surfaces of *The Childermass* (1928) and *The Apes of God* (1930), as in this passage from *Apes*, that largely plotless gallery of satirical portraits Lewis draws from Bloomsbury:

The impressive displacement (on the pattern of the heavy uprising from the pond-foam of the skull of a seal, with Old-Bill moustache, leaden with water, as exhibited at the Zoo) released the pinch of neck-flesh which had been wedged between the stud and shirt-band... Head lazily rolled to one side he considered it – with staring swimming eyes and moist pink muzzle, pulpily extended – plum locked in plum.[13]

The solitary (if questionable) eminence of this fiction provides testament at once to the limitations of Lewis's approach and the integrity with which he pursued it. All in all, the poetics of visual severity work best in his discursive prose, as ballast and support there for an enterprise chiefly critical, diagnostic. The values of the eye cede him the high ground, a vantage from which he seeks to expose the follies of contemporary, mass, 'musical society'.

Extending the principles of aesthetic experience into his far-reaching critique of modern politics, Lewis shows the true nature and aim of his work as culture critic. This politicisation of art reflects tendencies in literary and cultural history that were pronounced increasingly across the 1920s, developments that Benda himself would identify near the end of the decade and – his own earlier example notwithstanding – lament in *La Trahison des Clercs* (1928). Here he complained of the ways in which an artistic 'clerisy', having betrayed its high calling as witness to the superior imaginative 'spirit', had descended to the fury and mire of political partisanship. Lewis's response to Benda's book was ambivalent. He could ratify its censorship of his contemporaries, whom Benda portrays in the main as craven slaves to the demagogics of 'group feeling' and mass politics. But he must resist its challenge to his own locus of authority, the optical severity to which he laid claim as painter. This was a point of privilege he would not forsake, and its distinction seemed to carry the mantle of social responsibility, the duty of the civic commentator. While he believed that visual intelligence gave him a suprahistorical role, endowing him as political visionary, his main lines of thought are indeed

---

[13] Wyndham Lewis, *The Apes of God* (New York, 1930), p. 59.

thickened and enriched considerably by contemporary events. Chief among these is the major shaping force of his age: the Great War of 1914–18.

Modern*ism* turns for Lewis on a perceived discontinuity between present and past, and he draws the most vivid line of demarcation through the Great War. 'It is a totally novel world situation', he observes in *The Doom of Youth*; 'Our individual life is quite overshadowed by the machine, which separates us from all human life that has gone before us ... Even more than the age of Machines, this is the age of the machine-guns.'[14] This passage reads as a virtual topos in a new cultural rhetoric, an emergent myth, one which figures the technological character of the Great War as The Great Watershed in human history. The tersely finished eloquence of Lewis's remarks here may testify to their place in this contemporary convention, but he does more than polish received ideas. Whereas the war enforced this sense of disconnection between past and present on his generation, he uses the war, as cultural event, to explain their primary folly, the machinations of the modern cult of time. The absolute value of the Now, the compensatory attraction of the past as romantic. Then: these attitudes appear as symptoms on either side of the Great Divide that the war drove into Time. Yet the superiority of Lewis's own view here is of course open to question; the issue of his immunity from the forces he purports to analyse so objectively is once again relevant. 'Our chains rattle', Coleridge aphorised sardonically, 'even as we complain about the chains.' Lewis's attempts to reduce much of the work of his contemporaries to a manifestation of the war-forged time-mind may reveal the central, shaping connection between that historical experience and his own mature thought and art.

'Really the composition of this war, 1914–1918', goes Gertrude Stein's famed formulation,

> was not the composition of all previous wars, the composition was not a composition in which there was one man in the centre surrounded by a lot of other men but a composition that had neither a beginning nor an end, a composition in which one corner was as important as other corners, in fact the composition of cubism.[15]

Yes, a map of the Western line might well be redrawn as a Cubist structure. Multiple fronts, any number of battles being waged simultaneously and, it seemed, independently: these features embody those principles of relativism and poly-centric design that inform Cubism. But Stein's conceit goes to the larger concept of involvement between the art of a prewar avant-garde and the ethic and culture of the Great War, a nexus

---

[14] Wyndham Lewis, *The Doom of Youth* (London, 1932), p. 48.
[15] Gertrude Stein, *Picasso* (1938), rpt. in *Gertrude Stein on Picasso*, ed. Edward Burns (New York, 1970), pp. 18–19.

of troubled connection to which Lewis returns repeatedly. In his writings the Western front (Lewis was there, first as an artillery officer, later as a 'War Artist') assumes the shape of a cultural landscape, one which he repeatedly describes in terms of the temporalised spaces of Cubism and Futurism. The element linking the war to the values of the avant-garde for him is, predictably, Time. The signal word in Stein's account of the Cubist war, after all, is 'composition', an activity Lewis reduces elsewhere to the sheerest form of process-minded temporalisation; in his perception, the one errant dynamic of temporal sensation joins the strategies of mass-war and the practices of the artistic avant-garde. 'Once a crowd of hurrying shapes, a temporal collectivity', is 'put in place of the single object', he complains, the canvas opens – through the schemes and tropes of Lewis's analytical rhetoric – onto scenes from the Western front. 'In place of the characteristic static "form" of greek Philosophy', he observes, 'you have a series, a group, or as Professor Whitehead says, a *reiteration*. In place of form you have a "formation" – ... a repetition of a particular shape; you have a battalion of forms in place of one form.' And the disintegration of self that Lewis sees as the result of this emphasis on sequenced impressions is depicted in a way that might serve equally well to describe the welter of the Western Line, the atomised discontinuity of local frontages, where 'you are no longer a centralised self, but a spun-out, strung-along series'; '"you" become the series of your temporal repetitions'.[16]

No less true than severe, Lewis's cartoons of the prewar avant-garde miss only a declared sense of his own complicity in this situation as premier Vorticist, as editor of the short-lived but aptly titled journal, *Blast* (1914–15). For the title image of the Vortex, or whirlpool, denotes a form that is only a trace left by a force, a shape generated by a current that serves, at least in the early manifestos of Vorticism, as a primary point of interest and value. Vorticist designs like Lewis's *Plan of War* and *Slow Attack* (1913–14) show a kinetic architecture, a multiplication and variation of similar shapes across the canvas, and this kind of visual echoing is no less time-driven than the fluid progressions of Futurism, the serialised views of Cubism. Like these Continental artists, the Vorticists' form – once extended into time, and so multiplied and serialised – becomes 'formation', a proto-military advance. And while the general level of bellicosity in the style and content of Lewis's early pronouncements clearly matches that of the Futurists, the connection goes beyond the theatrics of violence. The temporal dynamism Lewis would later find as the one force binding avant-garde art to technological war is manifest centrally in his own kinetic designs.

That Lewis saw this link may help to explain major changes in the style

---

[16] Lewis, *Time*, p. 176.

of his prose fiction and visual art through the 1920s and 1930s. Yet he represses this awareness in his literary and artistic history, most notably, in his retrospective accounts of early modernism. In effect, he rewrites the artistic charter of Vorticism in order to write the movement – himself – out of alliance with the war-oriented dynamism of the avant-garde. To this point he constantly overemphasises the formalism of his prewar work, setting this value at odds with the war he presents as being inimical to it. There was a 'wave of formal enthusiasm that immediately preceded the War', his account begins by asserting: 'In the arts that movement brought imagination back once more, banishing the naturalist dogmas that had obtained for fifty or sixty years. Impressionism was driven out and the great ideals of structure and of formal significance were restored, to painting and sculpture, at all events. Sensationalism seemed to have been superseded in Europe by a new and severer spirit... But the War and Einsteinean physics have turned the scales once more ... all the tide of thought to-day ... is setting towards the pole of Sensation. But it carries with it as it goes a wreckage of disciplines and severities.'[17]

Lewis's need to alter or erase the attitudes of prewar Vorticism finds one of its most complex and interesting manifestations as he engages its connection with the 1890s. Of course the dandyism of fin-de-siècle may easily be seen to anticipate the theatrics of the avant-garde: *épater la bourgeoisie*, these two energies joined in crying. The convention-dismaying verve of *The Yellow Book* was signalled in the colour of its cover, and the same nerve was reproduced on and between the shocking pink boards of *Blast* 1, but the Vorticists mounted their challenge in an altogether different idiom: not the nudes of Beardsley but the abrasively angled machine. In view of these continuities and differences, Lewis's representation of Oscar Wilde seems an oddly contorted fusion of fin-de-siècle motives with avant-garde methods. For he figures Wilde's threat to Victorian moral normalcy under the unlikely image of the engine. 'That there could be anything "beautiful" about machinery, or anything "romantic" about industry', he proposes in this account of nineteenth-century attitudes, 'was never so much as entertained by the victorian mind. Wilde, I believe, was the first person to popularize the paradox that machinery could be beautiful.'[18] Lewis proceeds to associate Wilde with the decadence of high commercial culture, thus activating the now longstanding association – forged in the popular rhetorical culture of 1914 – between such decadence and the causes and misfortunes of the Great War. The link the ex-Vorticist has drawn between the dandy and the dynamo, then, is no more surprising than purposeful. Onto this sometime avatar of himself he is transferring his own earlier penchant for technology, for the sinister

[17] *Ibid.*, p. 152.   [18] *Ibid.*, p. 3.

beauty of the machine – the same faith that would meet its fateful disillusion in the Great War.

The shape of literary and artistic history that is generated by Lewis's need to obscure his involvement with the mechanisation and militarisation of culture in the prewar period is curious indeed. Notice his characterisation of the first fourteen years of the century in this account of the last forty years, in *Men Without Art* (1934):

> When the literary historian of the future comes to cast his eye over our little post-war age, he will not have to go very much to the heart of the matter to detect that he is in the presence of an ethos bearing a very close resemblance to that of the Naughty Nineties: he will see the trial of Wilde as the grand finale of the 'naughty' decade – then fourteen humdrum years of Socialist tract-writing – then the war – and then *more* 'naughtiness'.[19]

Here Lewis subdues the years of most violent activity in cultural and intellectual history to the ethos of humdrum prose, the sober poetics of 'Socialist tract-writing'. The characterisation catches the genre (if not the political creed) of the discursive project he himself undertook, but only *after* the war, and in large part as a function of the lesson it taught him about the disastrous consequences of theatrical dynamism. Rewriting the past in order to align it with his present, moreover, he displays a most revealing – and compromising – need for consistency. Here (and elsewhere) he shows his dependence on the same kind of totalising structures that the political culture of total war generates and relies on. His elaborate rewriting of history reveals the very connection it is designed to obscure.

The unwitting nature of this connection suggests that Lewis may indeed be one of those authors through whom history writes itself, that is, assumes an intelligible and revealing shape. In the contours of his prose, in the shape and pace of his critical argumentation, one may read a kind of history-in-miniature of nineteenth-century idealism and its twentieth-century sequel. If the great Victorian myth of progress through technology met its end in the Great War, which turned the engine of supposed advance into an instrument of unforeseen destruction, this belied ideal of gradual but inevitable improvement shows in more than Lewis's express rejection of meliorism. It appears in his chief argumentative mannerism: a tendency to court progressive logic, to think in the fashion of sequenced gradualism, but only up to a point, whereupon the reasoning falls away and cedes wholly to categorical assertion. This is a kind of intellectual and stylistic catastrophism, not only a rejection of gradualism but a reenactment of its fate, and it shows one of its most disturbing and revealing examples near the end of *The Art of Being Ruled* (1926). Here, after more than three hundred pages of closely reasoned engagement with opposite

---

[19] Lewis, *Men Without Art*, pp. 181–2.

political philosophies, this model exercise in dialectical progressivity flies apart into assertions of the sheerest kind. That Lewis asserts specifically the merit and necessity of dictatorial fascism is not arbitrary. The sudden turn in his performance aligns itself with the very reversal of humanist and rational and procedural values that fascism itself represented. This is a signal example of the claim to importance – unsettling or not – that Lewis must make on the attentions of the literary and cultural historian. He is at once a fiercely focused mirror on contemporary attitudes and a kind of crucible in which these forces enter into combinations equally representative and extreme.

If Lewis has enjoyed only an ambivalent distinction in most accounts of literary history in this century, the balance has shifted in his favour, in the last decade, with the growth and institutionalisation of cultural studies. This development has not profited other modernists: Eliot's early appropriation by the academy served mainly the purposes of the New Criticism and its more narrowly textual concerns, while Pound's wide-ranging considerations have remained compromised by his (mostly) unrepentant anti-semitism and fascism. Lewis's insistence on contextualising literary study has proved useful and indeed exemplary to contemporary critics as diverse as the New Historicists and Marxists such as Frederic Jameson. Beyond the vagaries of current appeal, however, Lewis may remain secure as a superior type of the cultural criticism that has remained a staple in modern intellectual history, a tradition that ranges from Matthew Arnold to Susan Sontag.

6

W. B. Yeats

Lucy McDiarmid

When the twenty-three year old W. B. Yeats praised Ruskin's *Unto This Last*, his father took offence, and 'we began to quarrel, for he was John Stuart Mill's disciple. Once he threw me against a picture with such violence that I broke the glass with the back of my head' (*Explorations*, 417). Some such encounter happens over and over in Yeats's criticism, whose rhetoric is animated by the language of conflict and combat:

[Dowden] has set himself upon the side of academic tradition in that eternal war which it wages on the creative spirit. (1895)   (*Uncollected Prose*, I, p. 353)

In no country has this independence of mind, this audacity I had almost said, been attained without controversy, for the men who affirm it seem the enemies of all other interests. (1908)   (*Explorations*, p.237)

I think that all noble things are the result of warfare; great nations and classes, of warfare in the visible world, great poetry and philosophy, of invisible warfare, the division of a mind within itself, a victory, the sacrifice of a man to himself. (1910)

(*Essays and Introductions*, p. 321)

Our first trouble was with the Unionists, but we have had to fight all parties, and are prepared to go on doing so. (1926)   (*Uncollected Prose*, II, p.463)

Not only in the Yeats family but in Ireland at large, literary opinions become fighting matters. Padraic Colum's father stood trial (in 1907) for 'shouting, hissing and booing and stamping his feet' and 'using obscene language to the annoyance of the audience' during one of the notorious first performances of *Playboy of the Western World* (*The Abbey Theatre*, p. 132). More recently, the publication of the *Field Day Anthology of Irish Writing* (1991) inspired public debate and private animosity, with its designation of some Irish writers as 'English', its lack of women editors, and its alleged 'Northern agenda'.

Yeats would have felt right at home in the arguments over *Field Day*, because most of his own criticism is inseparable from public, national debate about the nature of Irish culture. To write literary criticism in Ireland is to enter a continuing argument about what is truly 'Irish', about

151

the relation of Ireland to England, of Catholics to Protestants, religion to politics, politics to culture, the Irish language to the English language, and the State to the Arts. The argument takes place in any public arena; in the 1990s it has been heard in academic conferences and on television or radio, but it can always be found in newspapers, magazines, and quarterlies. Since the nineteenth century, a series of short-lived journals has constituted an unbroken tradition, so that at any given moment in the last 150 years one of them has provided space for cultural debate: *The Nation, The United Irishman, An Claidheamh Soluis, The Irish Statesman, The Bell, The Crane Bag, The Irish Review,* the *Field Day* pamphlets, the Attic Press Lip Pamphlets, and – the most recent addition – *The Irish Reporter.*[1] The 'tradition' is unbroken not because the journals agree with one another but because they don't: the ideas advocated in any one of these journals are not necessarily compatible with those advocated by any of the others, but each would consider itself oppositional to some current orthodoxy, 'suspicious', as Said says of oppositional criticism, 'of special interests, imperialized fiefdoms, and orthodox habits of mind' (*The World, the Text, and the Critic,* p. 29).

Although Yeats was not identified with any particular journal, he wrote in the combative style typical of Irish cultural debate, an agonistic rather than a belletristic criticism, never its own excuse for being. In an essay of this kind, large questions of national identity are always at stake in the review of any book, and the future of Ireland (not to mention its past) is brought to bear on the subject at hand. Because criticism is presumed to be a form of action, even quasi-political action, no issue is considered trivial or dilettantish or irrelevant. For one ironic moment, on occasion, some weary critic may condemn the debate as a national burden, but it is never called off and it never dies out.

Yeats wrote so much non-fiction prose that six 'collected' volumes (*Mythologies, Essays and Introductions, Letters to the New Island, Explorations, Memoirs, A Vision,* and *Senate Speeches*) and one thousand pages of 'uncollected prose' do not contain all of it; and many of his most telling comments on literary and cultural subjects occur in the fifteen hundred pages of his letters published to date.[2] These heterogenous pieces – book reviews, letters-to-the-editor, formal essays on spiritualism, magic, folklore, friends, eugenics, and education, introductions to his own books, introductions to other people's books, progress reports of the Abbey

---

[1] For a discussion of this tradition, see Richard Kearney, 'Between Politics and Literature: The Irish Cultural Journal', in *Transitions: Narratives in Modern Irish Culture* (Oxford, 1988), pp. 250–68.

[2] As copyrights for Yeats's books gradually expire, the non-fiction prose is being redistributed in different volumes by different publishers; see new editions published by Penguin Ltd. and by Macmillan (New York).

Theatre, prepared speeches, unprepared speeches, Irish literary gossip for
Americans, the anomalous 'Pages From a Diary Written in Nineteen
Hundred and Thirty', biographical sketches – include much 'literary
criticism', narrowly defined as commentary on literature, and much else.
In almost every case, the piece was prompted by some practical, immediate occasion – the need for money or the equally urgent need to defend his
name or his books or his friends' names or their books or his theatre
against attack. Prose, and especially criticism, was a 'low' genre for Yeats,
and in private letters he acknowledged it with apology. Of a piece on
Robert Bridges Yeats wrote to the author in 1897, 'You must not judge it
as you would judge an essay meant to be permanent. It is merely ...
journalism like all my criticism so far, and done more quickly than I would
like. One has to give something of one's self to the devil that one may live.
I have given my criticisms' (*Letters*, p. 286).

   Thirty-five years later Yeats was still apologising for his criticism. To
Horace Reynolds, who was editing Yeats's 1890s contributions to *The
Boston Pilot* and *The Providence Sunday Journal*, Yeats wrote in a
quasi-Platonic vein,

I was a propagandist and hated being one. It seems to me now that I remember
almost the day and hour when revising for some reprint my essay upon the Celtic
movement I saw clearly the unrealities and half-truths propaganda had involved
me in, and the way out. All one's life one struggles toward reality, finding but new
veils. One knows everything in one's mind. It is the words, children of the
occasion, that betray.   (*Uncollected Prose*, I, p. 34)

Yeats's assumption is that compromise with the 'occasion' means betrayal
of the truth, something that the prose words do as if on their own.
Commentators on Yeats's criticism tend also to believe that the 'low', less
truthful criticism stands in direct contrast to the higher, purer poetry.
Yeats 'propagandized, speechified, fund-raised, administered and poli-
ticked in the world of telegrams and anger', writes Seamus Heaney, 'all on
behalf of the world of vision.'[3] And John Frayne, the excellent editor of the
Uncollected Prose, summarises Yeats's apparent generic distinction: 'His
struggles as a propagandist were in prose, and he wished his poetry to be
unsullied by mere political opinions' (*Uncollected Prose*, I, p. 62).

   Frayne notes that Yeats's poems 'joined in the struggle' after 1910,
presumably becoming more sullied as they engaged in political issues.
Contemporary students of Yeats would maintain that a poetry 'unsullied
by mere political opinions' doesn't exist even in the 1890s: the corollary
might also be considered, that the criticism, no less than the poetry,
creates a world of vision, an imagined Ireland engaged in a grand national

[3] Seamus Heaney, 'Yeats as an Example?', *Preoccupations: Selected Prose, 1968–1978*
   (New York, 1980), p. 100.

artistic enterprise. However ephemeral the genres, all those letters to editors and contributions to long-dead controversies show Yeats attempting to build Byzantium in Ireland. His criticism is a Vision Militant. Like all the other participants in the continuing Irish cultural debate, Yeats argued about the circulation of culture in Ireland because he wanted to influence that hypothetical construct, the 'Irish mind'. Where or whether any collective Irish mind exists matters less than that, for centuries, Irish schools, churches, newspapers, writers, and politicians have gone after it.[4] As Yeats developed from the young hustler of the 1880s and 1890s struggling to establish his place in the literary scene, to the Abbey Director of the first two decades of the century, to the Senator and Nobel Prize winner of the 1920s, his criticism remained agonistic, but his models for the circulation of culture developed to allow a more active and intimate intervention in the formation of the Irish mind.

The Irish arts business (the 1890s)

In the middle of a 1937 *Irish Press* controversy that began over Roger Casement's diaries and grew to encompass the usual Irish topics, the novelist Francis Stuart took exception to a letter from Bernard Shaw. 'If any apology is needed for what I have written about a famous dramatist who did me the honour to invite me to become a member of the Irish Academy of Letters', Stuart began,

> founded by himself and Mr. Yeats, let me say this: It is only because he has in the past been considered in some respects the spokesman of what I may call the Irish Intelligentsia that as a writer I in this case repudiate any association with the views expressed in Mr. Shaw's letter.[5]

Hidden among the minor antagonisms and loyalties of the controversy, the invocation of 'the Irish Intelligentsia' makes the important assumption that such an entity exists. The relatively young (thirty-five) Stuart alludes to an institution, the Irish Academy of Letters, and its associated authorities, the Irish Intelligentsia, as T. S. Eliot's 'individual talent' might call on 'tradition' as a distinct, pre-existing parental body toward which he must define his relation – reverence, 'repudiation', or a little of each. But in the process of defining the relation Stuart discovers he has to give this body a name – 'what I *may call* the Irish Intelligentsia'.

---

[4] Yeats uses the phrase 'Irish mind' on numerous occasions. See, for instance, his remark that the 'Irish mind has still, in country rapscallion or in Bernard Shaw, an ancient, cold, explosive, detonating impartiality' (*Explorations*, 443). See also Richard Kearney, *The Irish Mind: Exploring Intellectual Traditions* (Dublin, 1985).

[5] Francis Stuart, 'Irish Novelist Replies to Mr. Shaw', *The Irish Press*, 13 February 1937, p. 8.

The naming of this collective shows how much change there had been in Irish intellectual life since 1892, when Yeats joined a newspaper controversy debating 'whether London or Dublin was the Irish intellectual capital', and soon (in response) founded the National Literary Society, in Dublin, to balance the Irish Literary Society, in London (*Uncollected Prose*, I, p. 222). Stuart's preference for Yeats's views over Shaw's privileges a Dublin-centred Irish Intelligentsia, as had Yeats and others in the 1892 controversy: *United Ireland* had called on 'exiled intellectuals' to come home to Dublin (*Uncollected Prose*, I, p. 222). Many of Yeats's efforts in the 1890s were devoted simultaneously to bringing such a body into existence and to claiming that it already existed. Defending Irish literature in 1895 against the criticism of Professor Ernest Dowden of Trinity, Yeats named those 'leaders of the "the Irish literary movement"' who expound 'what is excellent' in the literature, 'Mr. Stopford Brooke, Mr. Rolleston, Dr. Hyde, Mr. Ashe King, Mr. Alfred Perceval Graves, Mr. Lionel Johnson...' (*Uncollected Prose*, I, p. 347). This is an early version of that 'Irish Intelligentsia' Francis Stuart invoked, even if one of its members, Lionel Johnson, was English.[6]

It was not only the intelligentsia Yeats had to bring into being by proclaiming its prior existence, but the whole Irish arts business: producers, consumers, and products, had all to be set in motion at the same time. In *United Ireland*, in *The Freeman's Journal*, and in the English periodical the *Bookman*, Yeats urged on the circulation of culture in Ireland: 'Let it be the work of the literary societies to teach to the writers on the one hand', he asserted in 1892, 'and to the readers on the other, that there is no nationality without literature, no literature without nationality' (*Uncollected Prose*, I, p. 224). He had to create an audience for the work of the intelligentsia, or, in other words, declare a demand which their 'intelligence' could supply: 'our aim is to help to train up a nation of worthy men and women who shall be able to work for public good (*Uncollected Prose*, I, p. 206). The success of the much touted New Irish Library, Yeats argued in 1892, would depend on 'whether or not it keeps itself in touch with the young men of Ireland whom it wishes to influence, with those who represent them, and with the various organizations which they have formed or are forming through the country' (*Uncollected Prose*, I, p. 240).

Sometimes the vaguely imagined 'worthy' or 'young' men and women whose minds Yeats hoped his movement would train took on more concrete embodiment: sometimes he 'saw' the representative Irish mind. A

[6] My thinking in this paragraph has been influenced by Terence Brown's lecture 'Yeats as Victorian', delivered at the Yeats International Summer School, August 1993. I would also like to call attention to the title of Nina Fitzpatrick's *Fables of the Irish Intelligentsia*, a short story collection published by Fourth Estate Limited (1991).

noisy urban fisherman Yeats overheard in no way anticipated the quiet west-of-Ireland fisherman Yeats imagined in 1913. The ideal audience of 1892 was a person who desperately needed cultural products:

> One windy night I saw a fisherman staggering, very drunk, about Howth Pier and shouting at somebody that he was no gentleman because he had not been educated at Trinity College, Dublin... My drunken fisherman had a profound respect for the things of the mind, and yet it is highly probable that he had never read a book in his life... He is only too typical of Ireland. The people of Ireland respect letters and read nothing. They hold the words 'poet' and 'thinker' honourable, yet buy no books.   (*Uncollected Prose*, I, pp. 222–3)

Another kind of person might have recommended a temperance movement or a socialist government as a means of improving the fisherman's lot, but for the idealistic Yeats of the 1890s books would redeem the people of Ireland. Books were the most reproducible, portable, circulable form of culture: they must not remain in the urban centres of Dublin and London or in the private libraries of the 'leaders' of the 'movement', but must circulate throughout the country. Like wee folk in their feathered caps, books must go 'Up the airy mountain' and 'down the rushy glen'. They could triumph over the disadvantages of Irish geography: 'Is not the cause mainly the great difficulty of bringing books, and the movements and "burning questions" of educated life, to the doors of a people who are scattered through small towns and villages, or sprinkled over solitary hillsides...? The people have never learned to go to the book-shop' (*Uncollected Prose*, I, p. 223).

Describing the 'Young Ireland League', a precursor of the National Literary Society, Yeats set forth the details of an aggressive campaign to reach the 'Irish mind':

> Classes will be organized to teach the history and language of Ireland, lectures will be given upon Irish subjects, and reading rooms will be started in ... the various branches. It has been calculated that a reading-room, where the papers of all sides and the best magazines are taken, can be kept going in a country village for 4 ... or 5 shillings a week... For 4 or 5 pounds additional such a room could be stocked with a library containing, not only the best Irish books, but the master pieces of other countries as well... The Irish books in these reading-rooms should be before all else ... the books that feed the imagination.

> (*Uncollected Prose*, I, pp. 207–8)

All the issues involved in the circulation of culture came to the fore in the passionately contested New Irish Library, a publishing project whose editorship Yeats lost to Sir Charles Gavan Duffy in 1892. 'Will it publish the right books on the right subjects', Yeats asked, 'and if it does so, will it be able to put them into the hands of a sufficient number of Irish readers?' (*Uncollected Prose*, I, p. 240). Although a detached observer might have seen in this controversy a mere professional struggle for the control of a cultural network, for Yeats the future of Ireland was at stake: 'If we fail now to interest the people of Ireland in intellectual matters by giving them books of the kind they seek for, if we fail to enlist the sympathy of the young men who will have the building up of the Ireland of to-morrow, we may throw back the intellectual development of this country for years' (*Uncollected Prose*, I, p. 242). Considering how important linguistic, literary, and cultural matters were to Patrick Pearse and Thomas Mac-Donagh, Yeats may have been right: Standish O'Grady, another member of the Irish Intelligentsia, had (in a famously prescient drunken moment) predicted that the cultural movement would be followed by a political movement, and the political movement by a military movement (*Auto-biographies*, pp. 423–4). Although Yeats's failure to beat out Gavan Duffy had no noticeable retarding effect on the Easter Rising, he was not hyperbolic in his insistence that for the 'building up of the Ireland of to-morrow' books were important.

The right books, of course: and that meant the formation of a canon. In 1895 Yeats was busy making lists, responding to critics of his lists, and making more lists. His most significant such venture was a series of four articles on 'Irish National Literature' in the *Bookman*, in which he took up nineteenth-century literature from 'Callanan to Carleton', 'Contem-porary Prose Writers', and 'Contemporary Irish Poets', finishing with his canon, in October 1895, 'A List of the Best Irish Books' (*Uncollected Prose*, I, pp. 359–64, 366–73, 375–87). All this critical activity was predicated on the existence of 'a school of men of letters united by a common purpose, and a small but increasing public who love literature for her own sake' (*Uncollected Prose*, I, p. 373). Yeats saw his own canon-formation as a pioneering act of Irish literary criticism: 'In a literature like the Irish ... which is not only new, but without recognised criticism, any list, no matter how personal, if it be not wholly foolish, is a good deed in a disordered world' (*Uncollected Prose*, I, p. 382). Needless to say, Yeats's canon and lists were not wholly foolish. Some of his choices (Maria Edgeworth, William Carleton, Douglas Hyde, A. E.) are on syllabi one hundred years later; some are still considered important figures in the history of Irish folklore (Lady Wilde) and legend (Standish O'Grady). Some of the poets (Sir Samuel Ferguson, James Clarence Mangan, William Allingham, Emily Lawless) are only now, for the first time since Yeats reviewed them, receiving significant critical attention. Yeats's promotion of Katharine Tynan Hinkson and Nora Hopper, like his later support of Dorothy Wellesley, at least shows that he never assumed only male writers counted. And as Frayne points out, the greatest writer of the whole lot was one that Yeats, out of modesty, could not name.

Yeats's critical position required constant renegotiation. In his critical persona he spoke for Ireland, for a cultural nationalism whose value lay in the qualities of mind it would produce in future generations. His competitors tended to come in opposed pairs: London aesthetes for whom 'art and poetry are becoming every day more entirely ends in themselves', and Dublin patriots for whom 'literature must be the expression of conviction ... the garment of noble emotion and not an end in itself' (*Uncollected Prose*, I, pp. 248–9). As Frayne remarks, 'He tried to combine the best of both cities and thus pleased neither' (*Uncollected Prose*, I, p. 247). Dublin too had its binaries: Professor Edward Dowden and Trinity College professors denigrated Irish literature from the perspective of the English canon: 'Professor Dowden says that Irish literature has many faults, and this is indeed obvious; nor could it well be otherwise in a young literature ... a literature preoccupied with hitherto unworked material.' But Gavan Duffy's series anthologised Irish rubbish. Yeats quoted the worst of this stuff –

> Come, Liberty, come! we are ripe for thy coming;
>   Come freshen the hearts where thy rival has trod;
> Come, richest and rarest! come, purest and fairest,
>   Come, daughter of science! come, gift of the god!

– and, labelling it 'doggrel' (which he misspelled), asked of such literary taste, 'how can it do other than hinder a literary movement which must perish, or dwindle into insignificance if it do not draw into its net the educated classes?' (*Uncollected Prose*, I, p. 334). Although this was the period in which Yeats saw his critical writings as 'unrealities' and 'half-truths', Eliot (in a now famous passage) has described Yeats's compromises as an appropriate *via media*; he gives Yeats the benefit of the doubt Yeats didn't give himself. Yeats 'held firmly' to the 'right view' between 'Art for Art's sake' and art for social purposes, 'and showed that an artist, by serving his art with entire integrity, is at the same time rendering the greatest service he can to his own nation and to the whole world'.[7]

The arts in Dublin (the early years of the twentieth century)

Standish O'Grady's 'high nonsensical words' differentiated among literary, political, and military movements; but in the twenty or so years before 1913, when the military phase began, the literary and political were inextricably mixed in the flourishing activities of cultural nationalism. The most powerful of these activities flourished in societies and institutions, the ideological apparatuses of an emergent Irish state: the Gaelic League, founded in 1893 by Douglas Hyde, St Enda's School,

---

[7] T. S. Eliot, 'Yeats', *On Poetry and Poets* (New York, 1957), p. 262.

founded in 1908 by Patrick Pearse, the Fianna Éireann (Irish Boy Scouts), founded in 1909 by Constance Markievicz. The National University of Ireland was also established at this time (1908), and its Irish language requirement linked it culturally with the more alternative, proto-revolutionary institutions. Hugh Lane's Gallery of Modern Art, which opened in Dublin in 1908, was a national, though not nationalist, collection; its Protestant donor felt strongly about situating his paintings permanently in Dublin. For Yeats, after the instabilities of the various publishing projects of the 1880s and 1890s, the theatre seemed to offer a stable site from which to influence the Irish mind. As the Irish Literary Theatre (1899) became, in successive permutations, the Irish National Dramatic Company (1902), the Irish National Theatre Society (1903), and the National Theatre Society, Ltd. (Abbey Company) (1905), Yeats got to own a piece of Irish culture.

Yeats's involvement in the Abbey Theatre (the short name covering all permutations) and his active support of the Lane Gallery led to a closer focus on two elements in the circulation of culture, patrons, and audiences. Both turned out to be more irritable and more resistant to Yeats's ideals than his competitors in the arts business had been in the 1890s. Yeats's 1913 poem 'To a Wealthy Man Who Promised a Second Subscription to the Dublin Municipal Gallery If It Were Proved the People Wanted Pictures' urges an anonymous potential patron to imitate the Italian Renaissance patrons of the arts, for the sake of the Paudeens and Biddys not yet conversant with high culture. If the wealthy man would only spend some money and start the culture circulating, the (urban, Catholic) Irish people could be improved:

> Look up in the sun's eye and give
> What the exultant heart calls good
> That some new day may breed the best
> Because you gave, not what they would,
> But the right twigs for an eagle's nest!

> (*The Variorum Edition of The Poems of W. B. Yeats*, p. 288)

Through patronage those who give become god-parents of an improved society of cultural sophisticates. This is that 'nation of worthy men and women' in its twentieth century formulation.

In 'To a Wealthy Man' the role of the patron seems clearer than his effect on the Dublin world of Paudeens and Biddys; the ornithological metaphor fails to explain precisely the connection between paintings and eaglets. In a letter to the *Irish Times* written in the winter of 1913 Yeats's Paudeen took on more specific shape. Yeats heard (or says he heard) and immediately appropriated the response of a recipient of culture, someone who might build the nest. Urging municipal support of the gallery Lane hoped to see built on a bridge over the Liffey, Yeats observed of the National Gallery of Ireland,

I know how few visitors find their way there, and what a good portion of these are children and seemingly poor people, who must have come from a distance. The other day an old man who was painting a friend's bathroom spoke about Mancini's painting – how you had to stand some distance away, and how fine it was when you did stand so. The pictures once set up upon their bridge will be near to many men and women of his sort, and close to the doors of many business men and women . . . We have in Sir Hugh Lane a great *connoisseur*, and let us, while we still have him, use him to the full, knowing that, if we do, our children's children will love their town the better, and have a better chance of that intellectual happiness which sets the soul free from the vicissitudes of fortune. (*Letters*, pp. 579–80)

The old man's comment, if it wasn't a fiction, was a godsend to Yeats, because it gave him the response to museum culture of someone he had never heard of, a *poor* person, just the kind of person for whose benefit the gallery was intended. And there were many other 'men and women of his sort'. Yeats loved to invoke in his criticism the audience *trouvé*, like the drunken fisherman or any of a number of ordinary Irish people on whom Yeats eavesdropped to see how receptive they were to the culture circulated in their direction. The patriotic value of the gallery ('our children's children will love their town the better') is familiar from the 1890s, but in the newspaperese of the final phrase, 'that intellectual happiness which sets the soul free from the vicissitudes of fortune', Yeats tries to describe the autonomous soul he thinks art can bring to people of all classes.[8]

In the Abbey Theatre Yeats had even more opportunity to be on the front lines of reception, observing culture as it passed from performers to audience. As he records in *Samhain, Beltaine*, and *The Arrow*, 'occasional publications connected with the Irish Theatre', Yeats often caught reactions fresh from the mouths of the audience. After a performance of Lady Gregory's *Kincora*, in which Brian Boru is married to the warlike Queen Gormleith, Yeats overheard a man complaining to the person next to him, 'It's a great pity that he didn't marry a quiet girl from his own district' (*Explorations*, p. 185). On the opening night of Synge's *The Well of the Saints* the man who sat behind Yeats 'kept repeating "Blasphemy – blasphemy – more blasphemy"'. If he had only 'attended to the stage', Yeats scolded, 'he would have discovered . . . a possibility of life not as yet in existence' (*Explorations*, p. 302).

[8]   As everyone who studies Yeats or modern Irish history knows well, the Dublin Corporation did not give the money needed for the permanent gallery, and Lane gave the paintings to the National Gallery, London. After his death in the sinking of the Lusitania in 1915, a codicil to his will revealed that he wanted the paintings returned to Dublin. Because the signature to the codicil had not been witnessed, it was considered invalid. The division of the paintings between London and Dublin has been renegotiated periodically since 1959.

More often Yeats actively intervened by addressing or haranguing the audience from the stage; sometimes reception was quite audible, as when Padraic Colum's father (and many others) booed and hissed and used obscene language, or quite palpable, when the audience threw things at the actors. During that week of the *Playboy* riots, Yeats was of course trying to change the taste of the 'Irish mind', by force if necessary. He called in the police against the forty rioters because, as he asked at the debate at the Abbey the next week, 'What right had they to prevent the far greater number who wished to hear from hearing and judging?' As earlier Yeats had confirmed the existence of the emergent Irish intelligentsia, so in 1907 he claimed to have reached the Irish mind with Synge's plays: 'When the curtain of "The Playboy" fell on Saturday night in the midst of what the "Sunday Independent" – no friendly witness – described as "thunders of applause", I am confident that I saw the rise in this country of a new thought, a new opinion, that we had long needed' (*Uncollected Prose*, II, pp. 350, 352).

Between 1903 and 1910, Yeats was supplying the right twigs for the eagle's nest with the help of a wealthy woman, and the ideas of the theatre that he enunciates in those years must be studied with caution. Annie Horniman's patronage of the Abbey was dependent on a principle she iterated with orthographic care in her letters: 'NO POLITICS'. In his dramatic criticism at that time Yeats was in the position of someone receiving funds from a censoring arts agency. As Adrian Frazier observes, 'after learning that Horniman had money to spend and might well spend it on one of his theatre projects, Yeats came to know that she would never spend it on the Irish National Theatre Society until he could demonstrate that she would not thereby be making a contribution to an Irish uprising'.[9] Frazier notes of the statement of 'First Principles' in *Samhain: 1904* that Yeats 'elaborates on his vision of a national theatre, replying to his Irish critics while not offending his English patron's ban on politics'.[10] Statements like the following were written with Horniman's stipulation in mind:

Our plays must be literature or written in the spirit of literature ... Art delights in the exception, for it delights in the soul expressing itself according to its own laws and arranging the world about in its own pattern. (1904)

(*Explorations*, pp. 164, 168)

The antagonist of imaginative writing in Ireland is not a habit of scientific observation but our interest in matters of opinion ... All fine literature is the disinterested contemplation or expression of life, but hardly any Irish writer can

---

[9] Adrian Frazier, *Behind The Scenes: Yeats, Horniman, and the Struggle for the Abbey Theatre* (Berkeley, 1990), p. 75.   [10] *Ibid.*, p. 105.

liberate his mind sufficiently from questions of practical reform for this contemplation. (1905)   (*Explorations*, p. 197)

We have to free our vision of reality from political prepossession ... (1908)
                                                             (*Explorations*, p. 241

What, then, can be trusted, of Yeats's dramatic criticism? The central critical idea that begins before 1903 and endures after 1910 is the superiority of *voice* to *print* as a conduit of culture, and the purities of the former in contrast to the taint of the latter. 'Let us get back in everything to the spoken word', Yeats wrote rousingly in 1902, 'even though we have to speak our lyrics to the psaltery or the harp, for, as A. E. says, we have begun to forget that literature is but recorded speech, and even when we write with care we have begun "to write with elaboration what could never be spoken"' (*Explorations*, p. 95). The voice has aesthetic value because the 'only thing that gives literary quality' is 'personality, the breath of men's mouths' (*Explorations*, p. 95). It has nationalist value because from it the Abbey plays draw inspiration 'out of a study of the common people, who preserve national characteristics more than any other class, and out of an imaginative re-creation of national history or legend' (*Explorations*, p. 222). The theatre's work is 'full of the life of this country'. When the plays are written in 'that English idiom of the Irish-thinking people of the West', the theatre functions as a conduit of the best Irish speech, recycling the indigenous idiom and stories back to the indigenes (*Explorations*, p. 94).

In this period the printed word, which in the 1890s had been a vehicle to improve the Irish mind, through books and libraries that would convey the newly determined canon of Irish literature, is seen as an inferior influence. In 'Literature and the Living Voice' Yeats describes his disillusion when, after having paid homage to the blind Gaelic poet Raftery at his Killeenan grave, he saw in Galway a few days later signs of the competing print culture: 'halfpenny comic papers and story papers, sixpenny reprints of popular novels, and, with the exception of a dusty Dumas or Scott strayed thither ... and one or two little books of Irish ballads, nothing that one calls literature' (*Explorations*, p. 203). Even worse than the trashy novels is the journalism: 'Drama', writes Yeats, 'finds itself opposed, as no other form of literature does, to those enemies of life, the chimeras of the Pulpit and the Press' (*Explorations*, p. 119). Annie Horniman could not have disliked the conservative politics of the voice: the primitivising nostalgia for an illiterate peasantry and the antagonism to the proto-revolutionary writing of political journalism.

When Yeats made the gesture of rejecting the cultural politics of this Dublin period in 'The Fisherman' (June 1913), he did so in terms of the noisy voices of Dublin, impugning the Abbey plays: 'no knave brought to book / Who has won a drunken cheer, / The witty man and his joke / Aimed at the commonest ear, / The clever man who cries / The catch-cries of the clown'. The 'people' of Ireland were reinvented as the silent, rural fisherman, for whom the ideal art was not drama but 'one Poem'.

The classroom as cultural site (the 1920s)

If the Irish mind was recalcitrant, perhaps earlier intervention was necessary, so that by the time Irish people were old enough to go the theatre they knew good art when they heard it. Audiences needed to be trained *before* they went to the theatre. Looking back on those early Abbey years in 1926, Yeats said, 'It takes even longer to train an audience than a company of actors. You cannot have a natural theatre without creating a national audience, and that cannot be done by the theatre alone' (*Uncollected Prose*, II, p. 469). The theatres needed the help of schools. The importance of schools in circulating culture and training the Irish mind, and the metaphor of teaching, had always been present in Yeats's criticism: the Lane museum would be a 'nursing place for students', he had written in 1916 (*Uncollected Prose*, II, p. 418). Back in 1902, in an early *Samhain*, Yeats's ideas of living speech made his mind turn immediately to schools as a means of preserving the speech of the people:

I recommend to the Intermediate Board ... a better plan than any they know for teaching children to write good English. Let every child in Ireland be set to turn a leading article or a piece of what is called excellent English, written perhaps by some distinguished member of the Board, into the idiom of his own countryside. He will find at once the difference between dead and living words...

(*Explorations*, p. 95)

Even his early plans to get books and lecturers to the countryside were envisioned as compensation for the absence of universities. A parent for the first time in 1919, a senator in the Seanad of the new Free State in 1922, member of a senate committee on education in 1926, Yeats had many reasons to be concerned more specifically and practically about the education of Irish children. The classroom, he realised, was as influential a site as the theatre for forming the Irish mind. In a 1924 interview Yeats's vision of his ideal Ireland was one big art school: 'I should like to see the best teaching in architecture, in metal work, in mosaic work, and in everything else necessary for the establishment of a fine school of building here in Dublin. I should like to see the most competent teachers brought in from abroad, where necessary ... One thing we might do at once is to get proper teaching in the designing of lace' (*Uncollected Prose*, II, pp. 435–6).

In 'The Child and the State', a speech delivered to the Irish Literary Society in 1925 (later published in *The Irish Statesman*), Yeats develops in a new mode his ideas for improving the Irish mind. Just as thirty years earlier Yeats had envisioned an Ireland hungry for books, waiting to be redeemed with reading matter, so now he saw a 'plastic and receptive' nation needing 'discipline' and pedagogy. Now the canon of Irish literature appeared not as a publishing project but as a curriculum: 'Feed the immature imagination upon that old folk life, and the mature intellect upon Berkeley and the great modern idealist philosophy created by his influence, upon Burke ... and Ireland is reborn, potent, armed and wise' (*Senate Speeches*, p. 172). Now the schemes for which Yeats needed money and patrons were not libraries or theatres but schools:

> If societies like this interest themselves in Irish education and spread that interest among the Irish educated classes everywhere, money may be sent to us to cheapen the price of school-books for the poor, or to clothe the poorer children, or to make the school buildings pleasanter to a child's eyes, or in some way to prepare for an Ireland that will be healthy, vigorous, orderly, and above all, happy.
>
> (*Senate Speeches*, p. 174)

As once the urban intelligentsia had devised schemes to enlighten the backward rural Irish, and later the Abbey directors had striven to make sophisticates out of their Dublin audiences, so now 'the Irish educated classes' should attempt to educate poor Irish children, in order to make the nation healthy and happy. And just as Yeats had always worked to liberate Irish culture from the cruder forms of patriotic propaganda, so he sought such a condition for the new Irish schools: 'There is a tendency to subordinate the child to the idea of the nation'; he asserted in a 1926 senate speech. 'I suggest that whether we teach either Irish history, Anglo-Irish literature or Gaelic, we should always see that the child is the object and not any of our special purposes' (*Senate Speeches*, p. 112).

The Great McCoy (the 1920s and 30s)

But Yeats had a few of his own special purposes. In the last twenty years or so of his life, a quirky, outrageous self emerged, one with unapologetically fixed notions about what was good for the Irish mind – and the Irish race. Culture – so went one of those notions – circulates through the hormones and thence to the genes, and the formative powers of art are registered in the 'sexual choices' of men and women of reproductive age: the wrong kind of art may 'destroy' a family. In 1919, the year his first child was born, Yeats wrote,

> If the family is the unit of social life, and the origin of civilisation, which but exists to preserve it, it seems natural that its ecstatic moment, the sexual choice of man and woman, should be the greater part of all poetry. A single wrong choice may destroy a family, dissipating its tradition or its biological force, and the great sculptors, painters, and poets are there that instinct may find its lamp. When a young man imagines the woman of his hope, shaped for all the uses of life, mother and mistress and yet fitted to carry a bow in the wilderness, how little of it all is mere instinct, how much has come from chisel and brush. Educationalists and statesmen do their worst, but they are not the matchmakers who bring together the fathers and mothers of the generations.   (*Explorations*, p. 274–5)

In this kinky cast of mind, Yeats thought of the plastic and visual arts as conduits of culture, because statues and paintings were more like sexually attractive human beings. These works of art intervene more intimately in the formation of the Irish mind than books, or drama, or teachers, or politicians, because they are 'the matchmakers who bring together the fathers and mothers of the generations', and the family, Yeats the new *paterfamilias* argues, is the 'origin of civilisation'.

This line of thought places a large burden on artists to 'Bring the soul of man to God' so that God can 'fill the cradles right', as Yeats argues in 'Under Ben Bulben' and also in 'Long-legged Fly' and 'The Statues'. The word 'right', in those contexts, unambiguously implies that people ought to look the way European classical and Renaissance high culture represents them. In 'To-morrow's Revolution' (one of the pieces from *On the Boiler*), Yeats claims that shorter, stupider people, those 'gangrel stocks', are reproducing at a greater rate than taller, smarter ones (*Explorations*, pp. 421–5). The association of such ideas with the fanatical cruelty of German fascist ideology has long been noted and criticised: but these disturbing notions also represent a perversion of Yeats's idealistic belief of the 1890s, that reading would elevate the Irish mind and improve the future of the Irish nation.

To express the 'rage' that inspired his later criticism as well as his later poetry, Yeats created the persona of 'the great McCoy', that 'mad ship's carpenter' he had seen in his childhood. McCoy, as Yeats remembered him, would scull his boat in toward a crowd, 'denouncing the general wicknedness', and then leave, 'sculling it out amid a shower of stones' (*Explorations*, p. 407). For Yeats he is the voice of agonistic criticism, released from the context of cultural debate, or the voice of Protestant Yeats in the (predominantly) Catholic Irish Free State, released from the formalities of the Seanad. But not all Yeats's denunciations seem mad or irresponsible; a high-minded sense of cultural mission permeates the crankiest, most bigoted opinions. The Galway Library Committee, Yeats read in the paper,

had some years ago discussed whether 'the works of Mr. Bernard Shaw were works which should be kept in a public library, and on a division it was decided that the books of Shaw be not kept. It was suggested at the time that any book which was offensive should be burned. There was no other way of getting rid of them.'   (*Explorations*, p. 410)

Deploring the narrow Irish mind that the movements of the last half century helped educate, Yeats wants to take this Committee out of the culture business altogether: it seems 'probable that many men in Irish public life should not have been taught to read and write, and would not have been in any country before the middle of the nineteenth century' (*Explorations*, p. 411). Democracy is also to blame: 'Our representative system has given Ireland to the incompetent' (*Explorations*, p. 412). In these comments intellectual snobbery and elitist notions of class mingle with the visionary Yeats who wants to see a reading, thinking, painting, lace-making Ireland, a Celtic Byzantium, and looks up to find libraries burning books. Yeats's ideas about class may deserve a 'shower of stones', but how is one to disentangle them from his disgust with book-burning? This is classic oppositional criticism, and anticipates Sean O'Faolain's anti-censorship writings in *The Bell* in the 1940s.

'Not what you want but what we want' was Yeats's description of the Abbey Theatre's guiding principle in its selection of plays, and the division of the world of culture into a knowing 'we' and an ignorant 'you' constitutes a moral failing of Yeats's criticism. The Irish mind was preferable when it was located in silent fishermen, respectful, museum-loving house-painters, and schoolchildren; sometimes the improvement of the Irish mind seemed indistinguishable from indoctrination into the mysteries of high culture. Sometimes what 'we' wanted was what Annie Horniman wanted; and rarely was 'you' properly appreciative.

Arrogant, contentious, and cranky, Yeats's criticism may be an acquired taste, but it is never rarefied and never solipsistic. With its anecdotes, its gossip, its colour, its passion, the criticism could never metamorphose into an academic lecture or a scholarly article accessible only to a professoriat. McCoy denouncing the crowd on the shore is a transfiguration of Yeats on the Abbey Stage, haranguing the audience and belligerently insisting that his plays get a hearing. The stance of defence and defiance remains a stance of engagement in an Irish cultural debate that Yeats's energy and intellect helped keep alive.[11]

[11] Parts of this essay are taken from a lecture originally delivered at the Yeats International Summer School, August 1990.

7

The Harlem Renaissance

Michael North

If nothing else, the Harlem Renaissance was productive of controversy. During the relatively brief period of its active life, from the early 1920s to the early 1930s, it provoked a number of notorious literary battles. Contention ranged from specific works like Claude McKay's *Home to Harlem* and Carl Van Vechten's *Nigger Heaven* to the movement as a whole, which was characterised by its proponents as a new beginning in African-American life and by its critics as race betrayal or, in George Schuyler's words, mere hokum.[1] Thus the Renaissance, even more than most self-conscious literary movements, generated and depended upon literary criticism. Such criticism was even more crucial for the Harlem movement because the battle to judge and define its productions was a racial and political as well as a literary one. To a very great extent this remains true: disagreements about the Renaissance usually do not concern the particulars of individual works but rather the significance of the movement as a whole. Thus Houston Baker's polemical defence, *Modernism and the Harlem Renaissance*, is not about Langston Hughes, Jean Toomer, and Zora Neale Hurston, but rather about Booker T. Washington, W. E. B. Du Bois, and Alain Locke, polemical and critical writers whose importance lay in the way they interpreted and presented to the nation the achievements of African America.[2]

The most significant literary criticism of the Harlem Renaissance, therefore, has to do not with individual works but with the movement as a whole, not with matters of literary form and execution but rather with the role of literary art in the larger political and social world. In this area, the criticism of the Renaissance attained a significance that extends beyond its particular place and time. It touches on the perpetual rivalries between art and propaganda and between high art and popular culture. Finally and inevitably, it reaches the ultimate question about art and politics, one that was of immediate practical importance to African-American writers of the time: is art the highest expression of an achieved civilisation, or is it what a people has instead of political power? Most of the influential critical

---

[1] See Allison Davis, 'Our Negro Intellectuals', *Crisis*, August 1928, pp. 268–9, 284–6, and George Schuyler, 'The Negro Art Hokum', *The Nation*, 122 (16 June 1926), pp. 662–3.
[2] Houston A. Baker, Jr, *Modernism and the Harlem Renaissance* (Chicago, 1987).

writers of the Renaissance staked their own reputations and that of their race on the first of these two possibilities, and yet the entire movement was shadowed to the very end by the second.

One of the most eloquent and effective proponents of the orthodox view was James Weldon Johnson, who declared as early as 1922, 'The final measure of the greatness of all peoples is the amount and standard of the literature and art they have produced.' At crucial moments in the development of the Renaissance, Johnson reiterated this apparent truism. At the 1925 dinner celebrating the first literary awards given by *Opportunity*, house organ of the Urban League, Johnson told the audience, 'No race can ever become great that has not produced a literature.' In the landmark anthology *The New Negro*, he called Harlem a laboratory experiment that would determine if African Americans were such a race. In *Black Manhattan*, his panoptical survey of 1930, he used the same trope, but felt confident enough to declare that the spiritual and aesthetic achievements of the race were already such as to temper white racism.[3]

Johnson was clearly reasoning backward from one of the most persistent of all racist canards, that Africa lacked art, culture, even history, and that its descendants in the diaspora could never hope to achieve anything beyond a second-hand mimicry of Europe. With an altogether bracing faith in human reason, Johnson hoped that disproving this slander would disarm white racism: 'No people that has produced great literature and art has ever been looked upon by the world as distinctly inferior.'[4] Even more radically, Johnson's tropes suggested that only through art, through cultural production and possession, could African Americans come into full *self*-possession and thus emerge at last from the conditions of slavery. Over and over, in almost identical words, Johnson announced that the artistic productions of African Americans had shown that 'the Negro is a contributor to American life not only of material but of artistic, cultural, and Spiritual values; that in the making and shaping of American civilization he is an active force, a giver as well as a receiver, a creator as well as a creature'.[5] In this analysis, creation is the definitive act of the free and independent human being, the individual of the liberal state whose freedom is signified by the capacity to produce and own. Not to create is to be plunged into the status of the creature, who is created and therefore can be owned.

In one sense, Johnson's thinking can be seen as a shrewd realisation that

[3] James Weldon Johnson, 'Preface to Original Edition', *The Book of American Negro Poetry* (1922; 2nd edn., New York, 1931), p. 9; 'The Opportunity Dinner', *Opportunity*, 3 (June 1925), p. 177; *Black Manhattan* (1930; rpt. New York, 1968), p. 283.
[4] Johnson, 'Preface', p. 9.
[5] Johnson, 'Preface to the Revised Edition', *Book of American Negro Poetry*, p. 3. See also 'Preface', *Second Book of Negro Spirituals* (1926), in *The Books of American Negro Spirituals* (New York, 1940), p. 19 (separate pagination); and *Black Manhattan*, p. 283.

sheer political freedom in a situation of cultural domination amounts to very little. In another sense, however, this polemic can be seen as preparing a trap for the rest of the Renaissance writers. To 'write ourselves out of slavery', as Henry Louis Gates puts it, is both an impossible and an unnecessary task, unnecessary because literal slavery was sixty years dead even when Johnson wrote, and yet impossible because it presumed that the reasons given for the continued subjection of African Americans were amenable to reasoned demonstration. No other people, Gates points out, had ever been asked to prove its own humanity, by the production of art or any other test. To accept the terms of this test is already to give up that which success is supposed to confer.[6]

Therefore, Johnson's writing, which he intended as encouragement to greater artistic success, demonstrated despite his best efforts the painful dilemma that would confront, in one form or another, every writer of the Renaissance. Johnson was certainly the master publicist of the period, editor of *The Book of American Negro Poetry*, and the first and second *Book of American Negro Spirituals*, and author of *Black Manhattan*, which was in a sense the official history and guidebook to Harlem as a 'culture capital'. All of these works promote a single argument, that African Americans have already made significant contributions to American culture, that these contributions are likely to continue and to grow, and that white awareness of such contributions will lessen racial hostility. Even Johnson's novel, *The Autobiography of an Ex-Colored Man*, which was published anonymously in 1912, expounds the virtues of the Uncle Remus stories, the spirituals, the cakewalk, and ragtime, the four art forms that Johnson was to promote as the signal contributions of African America. In fact, Johnson was able to argue, with some justice, that these four forms are the source of virtually everything distinctive in American culture as a whole. What Johnson suggested ratherly modestly, 'that America is the exact America it is today' because of African-American influence, became one of the commonplaces of the Renaissance, as other writers realised that what the world considered distinctively American had been distinctively African American first.[7]

Despite Johnson's arguments, however, it seemed that this fact might be widely acknowledged without materially affecting the social or political position of the race. Such recalcitrance, of course, was hardly Johnson's fault, and yet there was a significant, perhaps even a paralysing, inconsistency in his own thinking. The declaration that a people achieves its full stature through art presumed that African Americans could be spoken of

---

[6] Henry Louis Gates, Jr, 'Writing "Race" and the Difference It Makes'; *'Race', Writing, and Difference* (Chicago, 1986), pp. 11–13.
[7] Johnson, 'Preface', *Book of American Negro Spirituals*, p. 19. See also V. F. Calverton, 'Introduction', *Anthology of American Negro Literature* (New York, 1929), pp. 2–12.

in terms previously applied, for example, to the Irish, whose cultural Renaissance was one very popular prototype for the Harlem Renaissance. Yet Johnson apparently never even considered the solution demanded by the most radical Irish cultural rebels: full political independence. Like the NAACP, of which he was a key official for many years, Johnson opposed Marcus Garvey and his plans for black independence in Africa. What Johnson hoped to achieve instead was 'the fusion' of the African-American contribution into American culture as a whole.[8] Art was therefore to demonstrate the particular gifts of the race and at the same time make possible its fusion into a largely white whole. The basic inconsistency between distinctiveness and fusion may be inescapable. But Johnson also seemed unaware of how easily the art that was supposed to demonstrate the full independent humanity of the race could, in a state of 'fusion', demonstrate just the opposite. The art that was supposed to mark the arrival of African America at the pinnacle of civilisation could be seen instead as nothing more than the sort of emotional and spiritual baggage that white civilisation had had to jettison in its march toward the top. Art was, in this analysis, not the finest expression of civilisation, but rather its opposite, the soul or spirit necessarily left out of the machine, or left behind until such time as a fully achieved civilisation might go back and pick it up, which is exactly what most white proponents of the Harlem Renaissance thought they were doing. Carl Van Doren, for example, declared quite forthrightly, 'What American literature decidedly needs at the moment is color, music, gusto, the free expression of gay or desperate moods. If the Negroes are not in a position to contribute these items, I do not know what Americans are.' This is not exactly the sort of contribution likely to establish the full humanity of the race. At the same 1925 awards dinner that Johnson addressed, Clement Wood, author of *Nigger*, welcomed the Harlem writers because they brought into American literature 'the hot, pelting passion of the jungle'.[9] Thus the very art that was to demonstrate the development of a distinctive African-American civilisation could be used to reinforce the racist notion that African Americans were uncivilised beasts.

Many of the polemical battles within the Renaissance were not so much real disagreements as attempts to break free of this irony. This is true even of the celebrated dispute between W. E. B. Du Bois and Alain Locke over the issue of propaganda. Du Bois, whose career, of course, predated and outlasted the Renaissance by many years, had been promoting the basic Renaissance credo since the turn of the century. In 1915 he declared, 'we

[8] Johnson, 'Preface', *Book of American Negro Poetry*, p. 42.
[9] Carl Van Doren, 'The Younger Generation of Negro Writers', *Opportunity*, 2 (May 1924), pp. 144–5; Clement Wood, quoted in an anonymous notice, 'The Opportunity Dinner', *Opportunity*, 3 (June 1925), p. 176.

should set the black man before the world as both a creative artist and a strong subject for artistic treatment'.[10] In a 1926 *Encyclopedia Britannica* article, he said that it was not through propaganda but rather through art that a renaissance in the status of the race would be achieved.[11] Here his reasoning precisely duplicated Johnson's. Greater attention to the art of African America would show, he believed, that the race had not been 'a passive victim or brute fact' but rather a major contributor to American culture. Nothing could demonstrate this contribution better than art: 'it has long been the consensus among the wise, that the great gift of the Negro to the world is going to be a gift to Art. This is quite contrary to popular opinion, to whom the Negro means labor, sweat of brow, the bent back and bloated eye, the beast and burdenbearer.'[12]

Thus Du Bois welcomed what he called 'The Younger Literary Movement', and he remained an active proponent throughout the 1920s.[13] The reputations of many of the Renaissance writers were promoted through *The Crisis*, which Du Bois created and edited and which he felt derived its greatest strength and popularity from its literary connections. Yet Du Bois is perhaps best known, at least insofar as this period is concerned, for two celebrated thunderations against the movement. In his review of *The New Negro* he takes issue with 'the idea that Beauty rather than Propaganda should be the object of Negro literature and art'. This warning is developed further in the address, 'Criteria for Negro Art', which contains the famous pronouncement 'all Art is propaganda and ever must be, despite the wailing of the purists'. The alternative, Du Bois warns Alain Locke and all other 'purists' and aesthetes, is 'decadence', not advance. Du Bois seemed to find his own prediction horribly confirmed in Claude McKay's *Home to Harlem*, the novel he found so filthy it made him want to take a bath.[14]

The uncompromising vividness of Du Bois's writing has given these pronouncements a kind of misleading fame, and they have made him seem far more curmudgeonly than he was. Though his tastes in art and literature were quite conservative, he was capable of welcoming Jean Toomer's *Cane* precisely *because* it might 'emancipate the colored world from the conventions of sex'.[15] And he argued elsewhere than in his fight with

[10] Quoted in Arthur P. Davis, *From the Dark Tower* (Washington, D.C., 1974), p. 18.
[11] W. E. B. Du Bois, 'Negro Literature', in *Writings by W. E. B. Du Bois in Non-Periodical Literature Edited by Others*, ed. Herbert Aptheker (Millwood, N.Y., 1982), p. 149.
[12] W. E. B. Du Bois, 'The Contribution of the Negro to American Life and Culture', and 'Can the Negro Serve the Drama?', in *Writings by W. E. B. Du Bois in Periodicals Edited by Others*, ed. Herbert Aptheker, 4 vols. (Millwood, N.Y., 1982), II, pp. 149, 210–11.
[13] See W. E. B. Du Bois, 'The Younger Literary Movement', in *Book Reviews by W. E. B. Du Bois*, ed. Herbert Aptheker (Millwood, N.Y., 1977), pp. 68–70, and 'A Negro Art Renaissance', in *Writings in Periodicals*, II, pp. 258–9.
[14] Du Bois, *Book Reviews*, pp. 79, 113–14; and *W. E. B. Du Bois: A Reader*, ed. Meyer Weinberg (New York, 1970), p. 258.   [15] Du Bois, *Book Reviews*, p. 69.

Locke that the younger writers were burdened by a 'black audience which wants no art that is not propaganda'.[16] Even in 'Criteria for Negro Art', Du Bois castigated the African-American reading public for what he thought was an unnecessary prudery, and he argued that it was this audience alone that could 'afford the Truth', whatever it might be. Unlike the white public, which depended on a tissue of lies to reinforce its hold on power, African Americans needed only honesty and candour.[17]

Du Bois's inconsistency on these issues is telling, because it showed how difficult it was to lay down any consistent principles to discriminate between the sort of literature that would advance the race and the sort that would plunge it into 'decadence'. Similarly, the demand for propaganda is simplifying only if propaganda is easy to define. Even Du Bois had a hard time describing precisely the difference between the sort of art that might serve as a positive testimonial and the sort that might be turned to slander. In part, this difficulty may be due to Du Bois's relative indifference to matters of literary technique, a conservative and even complacent indifference that left him helpless before one of the basic paradoxes of literary art: that a reader may well be uplifted and inspired by the artistic portrayal of death and degradation. Though Du Bois was at times willing to admit the possibility that the artistic genius of African Americans could be demonstrated even where the subject matter was less than flattering, in specific instances, most notoriously in the case of Home to Harlem, his resolve failed, and the distinction between technical accomplishment and pleasing subject matter collapsed. Yet even this distinction was finally of little moment if Art itself was defined not as the crowning glory of civilisation but rather as an escape from it. It was this possibility, that the literary productions regarded by Du Bois as indices of culture might be received by a white audience as so many momentary diversions, that cruelly shadowed his dispute with Locke and which called from this opponent and ally some of his subtlest reasoning.

Locke's own welcome to the younger literary group appeared in The Crisis immediately after Du Bois's, and in general he based his hopes for the new movement on the same assumptions. Locke told his classes at Howard that 'a people is judged by its capacity to contribute to culture', and he announced to the country as a whole that the Renaissance marked the moment at which the African American 'becomes a conscious contributor and lays aside the status of a beneficiary and ward for that of a collaborator and participant in American civilization'.[18] As the editor of

[16] W. E. B. Du Bois, 'The Social Origins of American Negro Art', Writings in Periodicals, II, p. 270.
[17] Du Bois, Reader, p. 259. For a discussion of Du Bois's inconsistency on this issue, see Arnold Rampersad, The Art and Imagination of W. E. B. Du Bois (Cambridge, Mass., 1976), pp. 190–1.
[18] Alain Locke, 'The Ethics of Culture', in The Critical Temper of Alain Locke, ed. Jeffrey C.

The New Negro, literary sponsor and mentor to many in the younger generation, and regular reviewer of fiction, poetry, drama, and art, Locke probably did more to advance this view than any other writer of the time. The very sophistication and subtlety of his apologetic shows how well aware he was of the potential pitfalls of his position.

Like Johnson, Locke drew a direct comparison between the cultural strivings of African America and the general cultural nationalism of the time. He appealed to the examples of Zionism and Czech nationalism as well as to Irish republicanism.[19] Thus he makes clearer than any other writer of the Renaissance the link between its essential assumptions and the cultural pluralism stemming from Herder.[20] Yet there was a significant difference between Harlem and Prague, unless one was willing to propose what no African-American intellectual of the Renaissance ever suggested, full political independence on American soil. Instead, Locke quite cleverly, and with perfect justification, included America itself within the movement toward cultural independence. Aware of the strong currents of Anglophobia in what was sometimes called the New York Little Renaissance, Locke suggested an analogy between 'America seeking a new spiritual expansion and artistic maturity, trying to found an American literature, a national art, and national music' and 'a Negro-American culture seeking the same satisfactions and objectives'.[21]

The beauty of this analogy lay in the way it dissolved one contradiction within the Renaissance project, which sought to demonstrate the distinctive gifts of African America only so that it could be 'fused' into its white counterpart. Unlike Du Bois, who had so vividly described back in 1897 the 'unreconciled strivings' of the African American, the 'warring ideals' of the 'double self', Locke held that the only way to be a true American was to be a true African American first. And the only way that America could realise itself was if all its parts were allowed full self-realisation of their own: 'So the choice is not between one way for the Negro and another way for the rest, but between American institutions frustrated on the one hand and American ideals progressively fulfilled and realized on the other.'[22] Like Dilthey, Locke proposed human variety as the ultimate, in fact the only, transcendent value, and he made this value synonymous with American political independence. Thus the accomplishments of the Harlem Renaissance were not just a success for a group hoping to become full Americans; they were also already a success *for* America.

In the same way, Locke resolved the other difficult issue raised by the

Stewart (New York, 1983), p. 421; 'The New Negro', in *The New Negro*, ed. Alain Locke (New York, 1925), p. 15.   [19] Locke, *The New Negro*, pp. xv, 7.
[20] Locke himself makes this connection explicit. See Locke, *Critical Temper*, p. 25.
[21] Locke, *The New Negro*, p. xvi.
[22] *Ibid.*, p. 12. See Du Bois, 'Striving of the Negro People', *Reader*, p. 20.

Renaissance, that of propaganda. In his most direct answer to Du Bois's challenge, he used language that may have seemed to confirm the older man's worst fears: 'Art in the best sense is rooted in self-expression and whether naive or sophisticated is self-contained.' Yet this was not perhaps the narrow aestheticism it seemed, for Locke conceived of the freedom and neutrality of art as an analogy for the freedom of his race. 'It is no longer true', he told the readers of *The New Negro*, 'that the Negro mind is too engulfed in its own social dilemmas for control of the necessary perspective of art, or too depressed to attain the full horizons of self and social criticisms.' Thus it was only by *avoiding* propaganda, by attaining to the full independence of the aesthetic attitude, that African Americans might demonstrate their arrival as free human beings. Because there was what Locke called an 'ethics of beauty' the most disinterested art could have the profoundest social effects.[23]

Thus Locke was able to take up an independent position on many of the issues that exercised debate within the Renaissance. Though the relation of African Americans to Africa could be a vexed and difficult issue because it raised the spectre of primitivism, Locke wholeheartedly celebrated African art both for itself and as a possible model for American artists. This was possible because Locke, influenced by European enthusiasm for African masks and sculpture, looked to these as examples for innovation not atavism. The African example might help American artists to break free from 'timid conventionalism' and thus attain the true freedom of the aesthetic. For the same reason, Locke was in general friendly to literary experimentation at a time when much of the African-American press was fiercely hostile to it. Freed from dialect, from racial stereotypes and apologetics, African-American writers, he felt, were experiencing a new exhilaration, 'a strange peace and ease', which allowed them to become 'at one and the same time more universal and more racial'.[24]

Whether this could ever have been more than a neat philosophical solution to a grindingly real political problem history does not allow us to tell. In any case, Locke frequently neglected the important distinction he himself had made, by which the aesthetic became an analogy for the full and free development of an independent African America. Instead, he often proposed, along with the rest of the Renaissance writers, that 'the Negro may well become what some have predicted, the artist of American life'.[25] Those who had proposed this were, of course, the Carl Van Dorens and the Clement Woods, who quite agreed with Locke's view that there was a 'complementary' relationship between 'the dominant Negro traits [and] those of the Anglo-Saxon Nordic'.[26] This psychic division of labour

---

[23] Locke, *The New Negro*, p. 53; Locke, *Critical Temper*, pp. 27, 23.
[24] Locke, *The New Negro*, p. 262; Locke, *Critical Temper*, p. 44.
[25] Locke, *The New Negro*, p. 258.   [26] Locke, *Critical Temper*, p. 448.

could be made perfectly congenial even to the most thoroughly racist of white Americans, as long as the artistic traits were put in clear subordination to those that built, sustained, and controlled civilisation. In this way, even the most thrilling of artistic successes would only cement African Americans more securely into a position of perpetual political weakness.

That something had gone wrong was certainly apparent to Locke by the early 1930s, and by the late 1930s he signified the collapse of his hopes by turning into W. E. B. Du Bois. Where he had once praised *Home to Harlem* as 'objective and balanced', Locke now denounced it and its author precisely for advancing the very arguments Locke himself had used against Du Bois. In his 1937 review of McKay's autobiography, Locke thundered against McKay's lack of loyalty, his 'escapism', his inconsistency and egotism. He adopted Du Bois's own terms to damn McKay's 'decadent aestheticism', his 'spiritual truancy and social irresponsibility'. Where Locke himself had once welcomed the attentions of the white intelligentsia, he now charged the whole of the Renaissance with selling out 'to the gallery of faddist Negrophiles'.[27] This intemperate language is directly proportional to Locke's fond hopes of the previous decade; the sins he charges McKay with are the virtues he once tried to inculcate into American literature. It would hardly be fair to take this bitter assessment as the last word on the Renaissance, but it does show quite clearly the ironic disappointment always implicit within the high hopes of its apologists.

A number of dissident critics had warned of this from the very beginning, and it would not be at all true to represent the Renaissance as a monolith ruled by the ambitions of the three critics so far discussed. There were a number of regular literary critics who did follow the lead provided by Johnson, Du Bois, or Locke; these would include Countee Cullen and Gwendolyn Bennett, both of whom had regular columns in *Opportunity*. Other publications could be devastating in their criticism. The *Independent* reacted to *The New Negro* with exaggerated but cutting indifference: 'If I had supposed that all Negroes were illiterate brutes, I might be astonished to discover that they can write good third rate poetry, readable and unreadable magazine fiction, and that their real estate in Harlem is anything but dilapidated slum property.'[28] There was also a rival literary circle centred on Marcus Garvey's *Negro World*. Though this publication, like Garvey himself, was frequently hostile to Du Bois, their literary policies did not in fact differ significantly. The one thing both men could agree on was that Claude McKay was a discredit to the race.[29]

[27] *Ibid.*, pp. 447, 65–6.
[28] Quoted in David Levering Lewis, *When Harlem Was In Vogue* (New York, 1981), p. 119.
[29] For a detailed discussion, see Tony Martin, *Literary Garveyism: Garvey, Black Arts, and the Harlem Renaissance* (Dover, Mass., 1983).

The most eloquent and persistent dissidence came from George Schuyler at the *Messenger*. It was Schuyler who denounced the whole movement as 'The Negro-Art Hokum'. This essay is now most usually remembered for its purposely scandalous assertion that 'the Aframerican is merely a lampblacked Anglo-Saxon' and for having preceded Langston Hughes's far more famous 'The Negro Artist and the Racial Mountain' in the same publication.[30] But Schuyler was also an acute observer of the ironic racial dynamics of the Renaissance. His essay, 'Our Greatest Gift to America', which was printed in the anthology *Ebony and Topaz* along with Locke's 'Our Little Renaissance', is a vicious satire on the whole Renaissance project and at the same time a very telling exposure of the weaknesses of Locke's position. For Schuyler argues that the real gift of the African American to white America is not art at all but rather the sense of superiority that keeps the white race efficiently unified. Schuyler thus reversed the whole argument of the Renaissance, upsetting the fond belief that a demonstration of African-American contributions could relieve racial hatred by arguing that acting as an object of racial hatred *was* the race's contribution.[31]

Schuyler was just as devastating where the white side of the Renaissance was concerned. In his satirical story 'At the Coffee-House', a down-at-heels bohemian is shown the road to literary success by his girl friend: 'Sketch in an African background with the throb of tom-toms, the medley of jungle noises, the mutterings and incantations of the witch doctor, the swish of javelins and the last lunge of the wounded rhinocerous. You've been in the Village long enough to know how to do this.' He has, as it turns out, and three months later has a house in the Hamptons and a black butler, who writes on the side but can't find a publisher.[32] The real irony of this situation, as Schuyler pointed out in 'Our White Folks', is that African Americans knew their white compatriots far better than whites knew them, and yet white writers were extravagantly rewarded for writing on African American subjects while African Americans were virtually forbidden to write about whites.[33]

Since Schuyler was primarily a satirist and not a creative writer himself, he was able to take a devil-may-care attitude toward the contradictions of the Renaissance. Certain of the writers of the time were, however, provoked to write eloquent criticism in sheer self-defence. Johnson himself had noted how difficult it was for an African-American writer to satisfy two audiences, one white and one black, demanding quite different things,

[30] George Schuyler, 'The Negro-Art Hokum', *The Nation*, 122 (16 June 1926), pp. 662–3.
[31] George Schuyler, 'Our Greatest Gift to America', in *Ebony and Topaz: A Collectanea*, ed. Charles S. Johnson (New York, 1927), pp. 122–4.
[32] George Schuyler, 'At the Coffee-House', *The Messenger*, 7 (June 1923), pp. 236–7.
[33] George Schuyler, 'Our White Folks', *American Mercury*, 12 (December 1927), pp. 385–92.

uplift and inspiration on the one hand and jungle realism on the other.[34] Claude McKay's finest non-fiction prose was devoted to an exposition of the same difficulty. McKay had written a good deal of political commentary in the earliest days of the Renaissance, some of it fused with literary criticism, as in the review 'He Who Gets Slapped'. Here the fact that McKay, though a bona fide drama critic, is nearly refused admission to the theatre turns Andreyev's play inside out, rewriting its title and turning it from brittle melodrama to allegorical tragedy.[35]

McKay's most significant piece of polemical criticism is, however, 'A Negro Writer to His Critics', in which he takes up the central issues that had exercised Locke, Johnson, and Du Bois. On the one hand a complaint against censorship, 'A Negro Writer' is also a denunciation of the 'guilty conscience' that race imports into literature. As McKay points out, the self-consciousness of the nation where race is concerned puts a peculiar and unfair burden on the African-American writer, whose work is picked apart and tested by standards never applied to white writers. McKay himself had been accused, he noted, of being too bitter and denunciatory and too irresponsible. Pulled apart by such contradictory standards, the writer found it difficult to create at all.[36] Langston Hughes made the same complaint in 'The Negro Artist and the Racial Mountain': '"Oh, be respectable, write about nice people, show how good we are", say the Negroes. "Be stereotyped, don't go too far, don't shatter our illusions about you, don't amuse us too seriously. We will pay you", say the whites.'[37] In such essays the practising writer complains against the basic contradiction of the Renaissance, that the same artistic production could be harnessed to the social project of the African-American intelligentsia and perverted to sustain white racist mythology. Between the two there was very little room for the writer to manoeuvre.

About the same time that McKay answered his critics, Zora Neale Hurston published 'Characteristics of Negro Expression', which was not strictly polemical or literary but rather anthropological. And yet this essay, along with the other non-fiction that Hurston published during her remarkable career, pointed a way out of the impasse of the Renaissance and toward a contemporary African-American literary criticism. Where Locke and the others had become entangled in a contradiction about the distinctiveness of African-American culture, Hurston argued that its originality lay precisely in its ability to take up and transform the cultural materials around it. Yet this propensity toward mimicry, embellishment,

[34] James Weldon Johnson, 'The Dilemma of the Negro Author', *American Mercury*, 15 (1928), pp. 477–81.
[35] Claude McKay, *The Passion of Claude McKay*, ed. Wayne F. Cooper (New York, 1973), pp. 69–73.   [36] *Ibid.*, pp. 132–9.
[37] Arthur P. Davis and Michael W. Peplow, eds., *The New Negro Renaissance: An Anthology* (New York, 1975), p. 474.

decoration, does not condemn African Americans to a secondary status, simply because no culture can ever claim to be truly original: 'What we really mean by originality is the modification of ideas.' Thus Hurston breezily dismissed the whole issue that had so exercised Johnson, Du Bois, and Locke, who were concerned to show that African America deserved the world's respect because of its original cultural productions. As Hurston realised, mimicry or artistic embellishment was itself an original accomplishment: 'Mimicry is an art in itself. If it is not, then all art must fall by the same blow that strikes it down.' In fact this art was so powerful that it was the one trait most often copied by whites. Yet this condemned the white American to secondary status as copies of copies, like William Vanderbilt copying the cakewalk that had originally been a modification of the dances of white plantation aristocrats.[38]

Even more subtly, Hurston dissolved the opposition between art and propaganda. She argued that the language used by African-American speakers was so vivid and actual that it became a kind of action in itself. She portrays an African-American society, most particularly a rural one, in which speech is such an important social activity that it becomes a kind of politics. There is no conflict between art and politics in such a society because the community is actually organised by its artistic productions, insofar as these are the verbal improvisations of citizens who are also in part performers. What Hurston suggests here is a principle that has become the core of contemporary theories of African-American literary criticism, such as those of Henry Louis Gates and Houston Baker, which make literary criticism, under the name of signifying, into the particular accomplishment of African-American culture. Where Locke and Johnson were concerned to show that the race had been creative, Hurston shows that it had always been critical. In this way, Hurston, who was not really a literary critic at all, raised criticism to the highest level, until it was in a sense synonymous with the verbal culture of the race.

[38] This essay, along with several others, was originally published in *Negro*, ed. Nancy Cunard (London, 1934), pp. 39–46. It is most readily found today in Zora Neale Hurston, *The Sanctified Church: The Folklore Writings of Zora Neale Hurston* (Berkeley, 1981), pp. 49–69.

The New Critics

8

I. A. Richards

Paul H. Fry

The prominence accorded to I. A. Richards in the present volume is owing in large part to his having pioneered and encouraged the scrupulous, verbally oriented teaching and reading of literature which has been standard practice in English and American secondary schools and colleges since the 1930s. Among academic critics the theoretical aspects of the Richards legacy have been passed along – with some alteration – through the writings of the American New Critics and such related figures as Kenneth Burke, R. P. Blackmur, and Richards's student William Empson. It is only if one emphasises his influence on the anonymous practice of classroom teaching, however, that one realises his full historical importance; and in so doing one brings to the fore his remarkably broad range of interests, which include linguistics, psychology, philosophy, and the theory of education.

Ironically enough from his own point of view, it was just when the influence of his early work on the theory of literary interpretation came most to be felt and admired, in the 1930s and 1940s, that Richards himself turned away from literary issues and diffused his attention across the much broader field of language and communication in general; and while his later work found new readers among such unified field theorists as the Encyclopedists of Unified Science, the General Semanticists, the United World Federalists, and the promoters of Basic English, Richards's original readers among the literary critics, who were devoted to what John Crowe Ransom liked to call the 'special ontology of the poem', tended to lose interest.

We must not be misled by the changes in Richards's audience, however, into supposing, as many have, that there were any decisive shifts in his thinking. Increasingly by implication, but as an announced programme first in *The Philosophy of Rhetoric* (1936), Richards expanded his theory of interpretation from the study of poetry to the entire domain of 'prose', ranging from propaganda to philosophy; and in such ensuing books as *Interpretation in Teaching* (1938) and *How to Read a Page* (1942) he did for prose what *Practical Criticism* had done for poetry, preparing the way in turn for a philosophy of teaching in still later books. But at no stage were any of these shifts in emphasis accompanied by a radical change of purpose. As I hope to make clear in the course of this essay, for Richards it was much the same to say, as he notoriously said in 1926, that 'poetry is capable of saving us' (*Poetries and Sciences*, p. 78), as to argue, in later years, that man's only hope lies in making the teachable art of interpretation the cornerstone of school curricula; already in *Practical Criticism* (316) a recommendation had been smuggled in that 'a Theory of Interpretation' be given 'the foremost place in the literary subjects of all ordinary schools'. His reformer's zeal for 'improved communication' remained constant – his literary writing, his psychology, his philosophy, and his linguistics were inseparable from one another and all jointly contributed to a programme for global betterment.

Such a grand vision may sound humourless, even cranky, and while Richards was capable of urbane and witty writing, solemnity of purpose lies rather heavily even on his playfulness. Many would argue (probably Richards himself would have argued in speaking of someone else) that his tonal and stylistic flaws perforce reveal his intellectual indiscriminateness. If this is so, the weakness in question can be generously understood as a public-spirited but self-disproving optimism – self-disproving because endlessly necessary – about the corrigibility of misinterpretation. Or, more churlishly, one could say that it consists in the violent repression of stock responses and irrelevant associations by a transcultural despot called Human Reason.

Ivor Armstrong Richards was born in Cheshire in 1893. He went to Cambridge in 1911 intending to study history, but soon switched to Moral Sciences, in which he took a First in 1915, variously influenced (if only to disagree, as he has said) by J. M. E. McTaggart and G. E. Moore. (Richards's relationship to Wittgenstein during this period is unclear. He claims, somewhat unconvincingly, to have been put off by Wittgenstein's intellectual preciousness, but he did eventually write an ambitious poem, 'The Strayed Poet', about the man who had achieved ascendency over Moore overnight, and there are fairly definite debts to Wittgenstein in his work.) His sojourns at Cambridge for the next few years were intermittent owing to recurrences of tuberculosis. During this period, in quest of quiet and clean air he took up mountaineering, an avocation he was to share with his future wife, Dorothy Pilley, until his old age. At Cambridge he studied the biological sciences to prepare for a career in medicine and psychoanalysis, but his plans changed again, this time decisively, when he was asked to lecture on criticism and the modern novel in the new English School. Cambridge had lagged behind Oxford in making an English degree available to undergraduates, and the English School was just then being formed along extremely innovative lines by the flamboyant don Mansfield Forbes under the distant but avuncular auspices of the historian of early literatures Henry Sidgwick and the legendarily insouciant professor of Modern English, Sir Arthur Quiller-Couch. Richards has told the story that he had gone to Forbes for letters of introduction to notable Scottish families with a view to becoming a mountaineering guide on the Isle of Skye. The conversation turned to Wordsworth, and two hours later Forbes offered Richards his lectureship.

While it has been truly said that a reaction against the narrowing and subdivision of disciplines in the later nineteenth century was then characteristic of intellectual life at Cambridge, the varied background I have just sketched can alone suffice to explain the precocious eclecticism of Richards's first, co-authored books, *The Foundations of Aesthetics* (1992; with C. K. Ogden and James Wood) and *The Meaning of Meaning* (1923; with C. K. Ogden). The first of these is notable as an early sign of Richards's lifelong interest in Chinese sources and culture (the epigraph from the *Chung Yung* was chosen by Wood, an art historian) and for its introduction of a technique Richards was eventually to describe as 'Multiple Definition', here involving sixteen definitions of the word 'beauty', most of them sponsored by one writer or another and all but the last airily dismissed as the projection of mental moonshine upon value-neutral objects (in *Principles*, pp. 11ff., Richards would write of 'the phantom problem of the . . . aesthetic state'). The last definition, favoured by the authors, presents a psycho-neurological phenomenon called 'synaesthesis', a heightened state of all the senses responding simultaneously to experience. This concept fully anticipates the equation of poetic value with the optimum reconciliation of disparate 'impulses'[1] which organises the next four books.

If *The Foundations of Aesthetics* offers a first, behaviourist version of Richards's aesthetics, *The Meaning of Meaning* performs the same function for his semantics. Having laid about them unsparingly once more, the authors set forth their own unitary 'meaning situation'. Here they are indebted to the psychology of Pavlov and to the semiotics of C. S. Peirce, whose correspondence with Lady Welby the authors cite extensively in an appendix.

I shall have more to say about the meaning situation, or 'triad', in Richards, because it provides the surest guide to his seemingly inconsistent understanding of 'thinking' and selfhood (states of being banished with ringing authority in Richards's youth by the Behaviourist J. B. Watson and by Bertrand Russell).[2] For the moment it is enough to say that for

---

[1] John Paul Russo has argued that Richards takes the confusing term 'impulse', and his neurological understanding of it, most directly from Sir Charles Sherrington ('Richards and the Search for Critical Instruments', in *Twentieth-Century Literature in Retrospect*, ed. Reuben Brower (Cambridge, 1971), p. 137).

[2] See Russell's review of *The Meaning of Meaning* (*Dial*, 81 (1926), pp. 116, 119), and also the opinion attributed to Wittgenstein in 'The Strayed Poet': '"The thinking . . . subject: there is no such thing"' (I. A. Richards, *Internal Colloquies: Plays of I. A. Richards* (New York, 1971), p. 185).

Ogden and Richards, when we hear the scrape of a match we expect to see a flame, a fact which suggests the existence of a 'sign' (the match-scrape) giving rise to a 'reference' (the expectation based on experience that a flame will ensue) which may or may not be confirmed by a 'referent' (the actual occurrence of a flame). The polemical thrust of this book involves the denial that signs point directly to referents, i.e., to real entities; they are either 'symbolic', pointing scientifically toward references that can be verified by referents, or they are 'emotive', pointing toward references which need not and perhaps cannot be verified by referents. (Except in the terms given by a few incautious passages, emotive signs are not necessarily untrue, as many critics of Richards's early work tried to argue; they may be verifiable but it is functionally unimportant whether they are true or not.)

Principles of Literary Criticism consolidates and develops the work of these first two books, and sets forth in one form or another, with one exception ('tenor and vehicle' first appears in *The Philosophy of Rhetoric*), the body of ideas that can be said to have influenced the later course of literary theory. This book was written as a general aesthetic. It was advertised in Ogden's 'International Library' as 'Principles of Criticism', and in fact it does include chapters on the other arts, but it is chiefly a *vade mecum* for literary critics. Every facet of interpretation and judgement is discussed with the general purpose of taking qualitative features out of poems and confining them to the minds of poets and readers. Richards dilates on the 'reconciliation of impulses' as the essential value of the poetry experience, producing in the reader a 'finer adjustment' (234) both psychologically and socially. In a chapter on 'The Two Uses of Language', Richards turns again to the emotive and (as he now calls it) 'referential' functions of language, recklessly claiming on this occasion that we 'require' distorted references ('fictions') as much as we require undistorted ones. This is the germ of his next and most controversial book, *Science and Poetry* (1926), which was prudently revised first in 1935 and again, with an apologetic introduction, much revisionary comment, and a new title suggesting the inversion and plurality of priorities, as *Poetries and Sciences* in 1970. Following Matthew Arnold's argument in 'Literature and Science' (1882) much more closely than he appears to realise, Richards argues that, science having once and for all destroyed the 'magical view' of the world and made the orthodox religions untenable, endangering man's integration with the surrounding world, poetry is more than ever needed as an expression of attitudes in which all the registers of human experience, including the old religious impulses, may be involved together. Depending for its justification on what the epistemologist would call 'coherence' rather than 'correspondence', poetry consists of 'pseudo-statements' whose referential truth or lack thereof has no bearing on their desired function and effect. Richards is well aware that Coleridge's 'disbelief' is not an easy thing to suspend willingly (hence it is, he feels, that many scientists to their detriment cannot read poetry at all), but he gets around this problem in his next book, *Practical Criticism* (1929), by arguing that 'the question of belief or disbelief, in the intellectual sense [he has said that poetry satisfies the need for 'emotional belief'], never arises when we are reading well' (p. 260).

Until *Practical Criticism*, his most lastingly admired book, Richards had written as though the success of the communication that is supposed to take place between poet and reader required only the sort of sympathetic cooperation of which the willingness to suspend disbelief would stand as a pledge. Hence the mental state of the poet, whom Richards had always followed Wordsworth in judging to be 'a man speaking to men', blessed with no faculty that is not present in all of us, could be treated as fully equivalent to, even indistinguishable from, the receptive mental state of the reader. But Richards must have suspected otherwise. For several years he had been conducting a classroom experiment with his Cambridge students that must surely have posed a constant challenge to his hopes for poetry. Every week he would bring in four poems of varying quality, withholding their titles and their authors' names, and ask his students to respond to them after repeated diligent readings. The resulting documentation, which Richards published piecemeal in *Practical Criticism*, was so appallingly incompetent that no comment was really necessary to alert teachers everywhere to the need for instruction in careful reading.

The students responded to thirteen poems ranging from canonical work by Donne, Hopkins, and Lawrence to ephemeral contemporary verses, with some interesting in-between examples – all of which are assigned authors and titles in an appendix to the book. From the chaos of their conflicting readings and judgements (another appendix shows that the students' preferences are roughly in inverse proportion to the canonical estimate, but even here anarchy prevails over symmetry) Richards extracts ten reading malfunctions for comment. Of these, 'stock response' and 'irrelevant association' are best known and remain interesting in the annals of reception theory because of their mirror opposition to each other: whereas the former distorts poetic meaning through the premature appeal to ready-to-hand ideas (Richards compares them to clothes bought off the rack and acknowledges that in much of our everyday experience we properly avoid overstrain on our nervous systems by making do with them), the latter distorts by retreating toward private images and autobiographical experience for which the poem provides no authorisation.

Between these excesses of herd-instinct and selfhood the other errors group themselves. The symmetrical pair Sentimentality and Inhibition can again be respectively referred, with obvious exchanges of position in certain cases, to public norms and private histories. These are followed by the problem of 'belief' again ('doctrinal adhesion'), and this time the criterion of success for the truth-neutral attitudes of poetry is called 'sincerity', a concept of mental equilibrium documented extensively from the *Chung Yung* and supplemented with five exercises in secular meditation which were quite devastatingly ridiculed by T. S. Eliot (*The Use of Poetry*, pp. 132–4). Eliot's correction of Richards's 'enormity' ('of the universe') to 'enormousness' was gleefully cited by Leavis in a savage *Scrutiny* attack; it bothered Richards so much more than straightforward disagreement that on later occasions he not only answered it sophistically in prose, but returned to the defence in poetry (*Tomorrow Morning, Faustus!* in *Internal Colloquies*, p. 278). Rounding out the list is a set of more technical problems: mishandling the logic of imagery; failures in the 'sensuous apprehension' of figure, rhythm, and the like; 'technical presuppositions' involving the belief that formal considerations are intrinsically valuable (sonnets are better than ballads, sonnets ought to be Shakespearian, etc.); and problems in 'making out the plain sense'.

In discussing this last difficulty, which Richards lists first among the ten 'reading malfunctions' because it is the most fundamental, he takes the occasion to augment his earlier twofold understanding of 'meaning' (as symbolisation and expression) with a subtler and nimbler fourfold with which he must have hoped obliquely to counter protests against his notion of 'pseudo-statement'. The first aspect, 'Sense', now carries the whole burden of 'statement', but extends also to cover the purely constative part of pseudo-statement as well, while the other three aspects, 'Feeling' (attitude toward the reference), 'Tone' (attitude toward the listener), and 'Intention' (purpose of the utterance) break up and redistribute the parts of pseudo-statement. Despite the unverifiability and arguable irrelevance of 'Intention', a category which continued to bedevil both Richards (for a time he dropped it) and his descendents among the New Critics, this is undoubtedly a more flexible poetics than the one he is better known for. It can be counted as a precursor, with important differences, both of the six functions of speech in Roman Jakobson's 'Linguistics and Poetics' and of the sevenfold – to be discussed below – with which Richards himself finally rested content.

During the next decade Richards was to divide his time between China, where he taught and lectured mainly in Beijing, and points west, including Harvard, which was to be his home university from 1939 until his death in 1979. His first year in China was devoted to the project which became *Mencius on the Mind*. The 'Foreword' to this book is dated 'Peking, New Year's Eve, 1930', but most of it must have been written later, as it was not published until 1932, and we have Richards's fascinating report that it was actually worked up from notes during a first teaching visit to Harvard, 'written out with much of the feeling one has in trying to scribble down a dream before it fades away' (*Speculative Instruments*, p. 17). It is in this and his next book, *Coleridge on Imagination* (1934), that Richards comes closest to modifying his rationalist understanding of the human universe – and it is in these books also that he introduces a degree of scepticism about language and thought which subverts the philosophical realism of scientific classifications without undermining their experimental validity.

Pitched rhetorically as a Malinowskian homily on the importance of cultural relativism, *Mencius on the Mind: Experiments in Multiple Definition* is also a theory of translation; and it offers, yet further, by way of its text from Mencius, what is at once a psychology and a physics. As a theory of translation put to the test, it must confront the question to what extent disparate minds are language-bound (see p. 5), thereby further threatening what Geoffrey Hartman has called Richards's 'dream of communication' (see Reuben Brower et al., eds., *I. A. Richards*, pp. 157ff.). Overriding these doubts, however, Richards struggles valiantly toward a 'meaning', which is, as he reads it, that for a disciple of Confucius, there is no difference between psychology and physics, given that 'Nature' (*hsing*) is always inextricably both mind and object. To put it another way, *Mencius* exposes crises both for the 'reference' and the 'referent': for the former, there may be no translation which effectively evokes the 'thought' of other words, and for the latter, there may be no 'thing' which is not a mental projection.

The latter crisis awaits the book on Coleridge and receives a complex response. The former receives what by comparison is a tellingly simple response (there could be no 'semantics', Ricardian or otherwise, without a simple response), in a book published before *Mencius* in 1931 called *Basic Rules of Reason*. The allusion in the title is to a simplified language called Basic English which was invented by Richards's early collaborator C. K. Ogden in 1929. This language consists of some 850 English words and their grammatical variants with which, so goes the argument, any thought can be clearly expressed. So much for the vertigo of translation – to fend off which, it is probable, Richards first became a staunch supporter of this ultra-positivistic assertion of the fixed, measurable distance between language and thought. He then proceeded, as the years passed, to devote more and more energy to the defence of the belief – at least ostensibly an unthinkable belief in his anti-idealistic youth – that the Ideas of Plato are the keystones of Western civilisation.

To return to *Coleridge on Imagination*: Watson and Pavlov were Richards's Hartley and Plato was his Schelling, but instead of turning the ideal against the material, as Coleridge did, he attempted to see whether these two immemorial and mutually dependent rivals could be reconciled

if properly viewed. Repeatedly in this book Richards returns to an issue he
first confronted in responding with due scepticism in *Mencius* (see p. 98)
to a question raised by Sir Herbert Read, the question whether apparently
radical disagreements are not merely terministic (each referring unawares
to the same 'thought'), but now his scepticism is set aside: 'in the forms in
which [realist and idealist – projective – concepts of Nature] conflict they
are both false; and . . . in the forms in which they are true they combine to
be a description of the fact of mind which is their ground and origin'
(*Coleridge*, p. 147).

'Imagination', or more precisely the Secondary Imagination of the
famous *Biographia Literaria*, chapter thirteen definition, is the 'fact of
mind' to which Richards here refers, and the content of Imagination is a
Nature which closely resembles that of Mencius. Richards turns to
Multiple Definition and tabulates four pertinent senses of Nature: (1) the
Behaviourist sense of 'the influences . . . to which the mind is subject' from
without; (2) the Idealist sense of the mind's projection, receiving but what
it gives; (3) a selection from (2) comprising the world as all people
construct it in common, intersubjectively (this version of 'stock response'
Richards supposes unwarrantably to be the work of the Primary Imagination in Coleridge); and (4) a narrower selection from (2) which enables
scientific hypothesis, as in the development of modern physics (see *ibid.*,
pp. 157–8).

With these distinctions in view we can attempt to gauge the difference
between the Richards of 1934 and the Richards of *Science and Poetry*.
The earlier Richards offended the literati by calling poetry 'pseudo-statement'. The later Richards will now offend the scientists by putting 'Nature
(Sense I)', formerly the object of 'statements', in brackets as one of the
hypotheses of 'Nature (Sense IV)', while insisting that the truly scientific
'Nature (Sense IV)' must remain, because it is projected by the observer, a
'myth': 'We can say nothing of it and think nothing of it without producing a myth' (*ibid.*, p. 181). It is not that science is unverifiable; its findings
are certainly valid, exerting an 'unrestricted claim upon our overt action'
(*ibid.*, p. 178); and because they are valid Richards feels that he is entitled
to remain a materialist; his point is only that as a 'fact of mind' science is
projected in the same way poetry is. Poetry is now the *whole* of nature,
'Nature (Sense II)', absorbing both common sense and science but without
the illusion of these latter that it is philosophically in the realist camp; and
thus, finally, Richards has achieved a way of saying far more plausibly
than in the books of the 1920s that '[p]oetry is the completest mode of
utterance' (*ibid.*, p. 163).

The cost to poetry in this triumph, however, is its abandonment as an
object of study – and also the loss, on most occasions, of its discrete
identity. With Coleridge and Shelley, Richards is now inclined to say that

all memorable discourse is poetry, a mythical projection sustained by the new object of study in his next book: metaphor, which courses at will through verse and prose alike. I mentioned above that Richards's latest influential concept, the resolution of metaphor into 'tenor' (what is thought of) and 'vehicle' (the expression of the thought), first appeared in the series of Bryn Mawr College lectures published as *The Philosophy of Rhetoric* (p. 96), and this is true, but it is important to realise also that this formulation scarcely departs in substance from the distinction between reference and sign in *The Meaning of Meaning*. The differences in emphasis now introduced are instructive, however. In the first place, the early Richards would not have called verifiable sign-reference relations metaphorical. Now it is the disparity between tenor and vehicle, hence the necessarily arbitrary nature of the relation, which receives emphasis, with no exemption granted for the scientific discourses. Accordingly, to an unprecedented degree in this book Richards finds himself talking about 'ambiguity' and wondering, as in *Mencius*, whether anything can be done to corral it. His answer and stay is Plato: however inadequate vehicular formulae may be, their basic occasion can and must be kept in view, without confusing 'the abstractness we . . . arrive at intellectually with the primordial abstractness out of which these impressions have already grown – before any conscious explicit reflection took place' (p. 36). And the last word is given to a rhapsodic passage from the *Timaeus*.

Interpretation in Teaching (1938) is a sprawling book that defies summary. Reverting to the 'protocol' method of *Practical Criticism*, now applied to passages of prose embodying wrongheaded approaches to the unfolding argument of this book (the Möbius Strip effect of this strategy is what makes the later Richards such difficult going), Richards brings all the techniques he has ever devised to bear on the deepening problem of meaning: multiple definition, restatements of earlier work done on metaphor, translation, doctrinal adhesion, and technical presupposition (a fallacy now ascribed to grammarians who promote 'usage' as a canon of value), and a theory of definition which insists rather desperately that statements of equivalence are not circular. This last enterprise touches on what is new and most revealingly problematic in this book, the division of its approach among the three topics of the Medieval Trivium. 'Rhetoric', by which Richards is always content simply to mean 'metaphor', is all too impressively comprehensive. 'Grammar' is not always clearly distinguished from rhetoric; the intended distinction between rhetoric as semantics and grammar as semiotics is difficult to maintain because of what I shall isolate below as a fundamental problem, the question whether the language–thought relations of rhetoric are not really themselves language–language relations differing from those of grammar merely in being paradigmatic rather than syntagmatic; but the discussion of grammar in any case provides a platform for an attack on norms. 'Logic', finally, by the time Richards gets to it, has nothing left to do. A long introductory discussion of 'The Interpretation of IS' wavers between rhetoric (metaphor) and grammar (predication), but none of the eight senses of 'is' (p. 321) requires or entails a third category.

The title *How to Read a Page* (1942), aimed at Mortimer Adler's carefree *How to Read a Book*, is itself an icon of the close reading Richards pioneered. Probably because one is indeed so eager to learn what its title promises, this book proves rather disappointing. Not so much a hermeneutics of but an argument with several quoted pages of metaphysical writing, the book eventually turns once more to multiple definition, this time of the hundred key words (listed pp. 22–3) one is likely to find on a page. Halfway through there is an interchapter on 'Specialized Quotation Marks', a set of custom-encoded brackets Richards would henceforth put around problematic terms in his own text. Apart from 'w … w', denoting the metalingual use of a word, and 'r … r', denoting a specialised usage which would need in any case to be clarified, the other five brackets are all thin-ice signals which could easily be subsumed under '! … !', the 'shriek mark' employed more broadly by Empson in *The Structure of Complex Words* (1951). The equivalent of nervous italics, these warning superscripts only codify Richards's pervasively annoying habit of suppressing insoluble problems by exaggerating the difficulty of soluble ones.

In 1950 Richards published a shortened translation of the *Iliad* called *The Wrath of Achilles*. This was among the first of the projects designed to consider the content as well as the method of school curricula. While the introduction to this translation is quite generous toward Homer, Richards was soon increasingly to use him as a foil to offset the cultural revolution marked (in the work of Werner Jaeger and Eric Havelock which most influenced Richards) by the emergence of Plato. These interests would culminate in a book called *Beyond* (1973), in which the Book of Job is exhibited alongside Homer as a pre-civilised contrast with the genius of Plato, and the *Divine Comedy* and *Prometheus Unbound* are brought in as later mythographic texts in the Platonic tradition. Appearances notwithstanding, this book is not designed as an exercise in literary criticism but as a kind of Rise of the West, a survey of human self-conceptions drawing a sharp division between the wars of incomprehension and the peaceful coexistence of communication via that ultimate and ultimately necessary Ricardian channel, the intersubjective Platonic Soul.

During the same period, only seemingly at the opposite pole of his concerns, Richards became interested in the use of the media, from audio-visual aids to computers, both as cybernetic models and as educational tools. First and last for Richards – and this is the source of continu-

ity in his thinking that has been frequently overlooked – the Soul remains
neurological, with intersubjectivity commandeered for biology as a form
of telecommunication mainly concerned with transmitting that 'common
sense' of which 'Nature (Sense III)' after all chiefly consists. Hence without qualm Richards can understand 'feedback' as the Platonic *anamnesis*,
with the *Meno* its urtext, and 'feedforward' as Aristotelian self-actualisation, with the *Physics* its urtext. The culmination of this thinking will be
found in a pair of 1968 books called *Design for Escape* and *So Much
Nearer*.

There are two other late collections of essays, both in the form of
uncollected remains, *Poetries* (ed. Trevor Eaton, 1974), and *Complementarities* (ed. John Paul Russo, 1976: reminiscent of Joyce's 'parallax'
and designedly a scientific parallel to Coleridge's 'interinanimation', the
name of the title essay is taken from Niels Bohr). An earlier and more
attractively balanced collection of essays called *Speculative Instruments*
had been published in 1955, and this was the book that Richards himself
considered his best. Here a great deal is reworded and introduced which
remains constant for the rest of his life: referential and emotive beliefs are
now neatly called 'truth' and 'troth' just as the proto-Kuhnian reconsideration of science in the early 1930s is now used avowedly to uncover
some of the common purposes of poetry and science.

An important essay in this collection called 'Toward a Theory of
Comprehending' expands the four functions of utterance to seven, represented as a wheel of six segments surrounding an inner seventh, 'Purpos-
ing', the old 'Intention' now more rigorously seen in a determinate rather
than a merely relational position. What is interesting about the remaining six functions, in contrast with Jakobson's better-known six (phatic,
conative, expressive, referential, metalingual, poetic), is that five are
oriented toward the reference, the thought to be expressed, only one,
'influencing', toward the addressees, and none at all, amazingly after all
Richards's work on poetry and rhetoric, toward the message: despite
Jakobson's very great influence on Richards at Harvard, there is no
equivalent in Richards of what Jakobson calls the 'poetic function'. What
the diagram makes us realise is that this had always been so for Richards,
that he had never believed language to have a self-referential dimension;
on the contrary, what he had always wanted to 'escape', to get 'beyond'
or at least 'nearer' to, was the boundary of language itself, the very object
of his study and medium of his message, which nevertheless casts its
shadow as a Nietzschean prison-house across his every breakthrough.
Richards turned to the writing of poetry and plays at roughly the time
when he stopped writing literary criticism. The name of his most interesting poem, 'The Screens', indicates the difficulty of escaping or getting
beyond sheltering camouflages and surfaces for projection, while holding

out the hope that these may also be somehow transparent, merely the contours of selfhood that make otherness visible.

I shall devote the remaining space to addressing some central issues and anomalies of Richards's thought in more consecutive fashion. To begin with his most fundamental premise: that there is a 'tendency' both in the mind and the world toward increased and more inclusive 'order'. This 'foundation' of his aesthetics, 'synaesthesis', he derives from his training in the psychological sciences. It also reflects a reigning taste in poetry. A summary passage in *Principles* (p. 184) about the links among the wheeling of pigeons in Trafalgar Square, the colour of water in the foundations there, and the tone and purport of a speaker in this setting obviously alludes to the 'Metaphysical taste' of Eliot on reading Spinoza, falling in love, the sound of the typewriter, and the smell of cooking (sceptical as he was on the whole, Eliot had conceded that Richards's synaesthetic theory was, as far as it went, 'probably quite true' ('Literature, science, and dogma', p. 243)); but we should not miss the somewhat more subversive influence of Walter Pater (from whom Richards attempts to distance himself in *Principles*, p. 132) on Richards's displeasure with 'wasteful organization'; 'Consider an hour of any person's life. It holds out innumerable possibilities' (*Poetries and Sciences*, p. 36. And further along (p. 38): 'Setting pain aside, we may perhaps agree that torpor would be the worst choice'). Pater too confessed the influence of science in the 'Conclusion' to *The Renaissance*, but his scientific model was different from that of Richards and in the event an equally prescient one: a *disorderly* atomism which makes the boundaries of both our inner and outer worlds indistinct, and 'clear, perpetual outline ... but an image of ours'. So it is that Richards's most cherished premise is permeated by its negation.

'Value', a term deliberately poised between sensuous and supersensuous uses, could be ascribed to the reconciliation of impulses because this fundamental idea of order was a progressive one. We 'know' that 'a growing order is a principle of the mind' (*Principles*, p. 50); fallibility and accident aside, there is in the mind *a tendency towards increased order* (*Practical Criticism*, p. 268; italics Richards's). And everywhere in these early books Richards seems also to be arguing, in generally Aristotelian (and Confucian) terms of 'self-completion', that poetry in repeated doses strengthens psychic potential just as exercise strengthens a limb.[3] And if synaesthetic order spreads upward in the mind, it also

---

[3] See W. H. N. Hotopf, *Language, Thought, and Comprehension: A Case Study of the Writings of I. A. Richards* (London, 1965), esp. p. 167. Richards cannot write wholeheartedly in these terms because what he supposes to be the non-figurative discourse of his Behaviourist training will not let him imagine a 'self' to be completed.

spreads outwards through other faculties and groups of impulses as a happy contagion, improving 'intimate relations with other human beings' (*Practical Criticism*, p. 295). While no causal inference can be drawn from this effect (it is wrong to assume 'that a man who is stupid with poetry *must* be stupid with life' (*ibid.*, p. 300)), Richards does imply in an article called 'The Lure of High Mountaineering' that the 'peculiar exhilaration' afforded 'by the mere sweet-running mechanisms of the nervous system' is much the same in endeavours of all kinds (*Complementarities*, p. 241).

It has been frequently pointed out, however, that if the benefits of synaesthesis are not to be merely personal, or at most interpersonal, there ought to be a means of realising them on a truly social scale. Plainly this is the intention of one whose thought forms itself according to 'the managerial imperative of what is now called Social Science' (Hartman, in Brower et al., eds., *I. A. Richards*, p. 163). And there are gestures in this direction, the most timid being the implicitly social interpretation of the reconciliation of the fear and pity impulses in Aristotle (see *Principles*, p. 245), a somewhat bolder one being the application of Bentham's blueprint for social welfare to the psyche: 'the conduct of life is throughout an attempt to organize impulses so that success is obtained for the greater number or mass of them' (*ibid.*, p. 46). Here indeed is a promising analogy: what Richards needs in order to reinforce it is a medium, an interconnectedness or evidence of affinity more compelling than the crude parallelism of the Hobbesian or Benthamite 'body politic' with which the persistently macrocosmic thinking of political philosophy is apt to justify itself. The hope of 'finer, subtler' responses to poetry brightens 'the world-picture' (*Practical Criticism*, p. 240), and – in a more intellectually conventionalised culture – the conceptions of one school have 'given both a fine and a very widely diffused civilization to the Chinese people' (*Mencius*, p. 64). But how? How can the contagion celebrated in Shelley's *Defence of Poetry* (see *Principles*, p. 67) seem plausible in a scientific age – an age which belittles the role of individual achievement (if, again, there is an individual) in history?

As an approving reader of Trigant Burrow's *The Social Basis of Consciousness* in Ogden's International Library (see *Mencius*, p. 78n.), Richards shares in these doubts. Arguably, for instance, both the model and the opportunity for self-completion originate in the freedom accorded the individual by a democratic polity (see *How to Read a Page*, pp. 146–7). Hence the best hope for realising the 'value' of the Ricardian aesthetic is to invoke a concept which is founded on analogy, like empirical social thought, but is also, as Coleridge would say, 'interinanimate', both productive and produced, continuous and one: i.e., the Republic of Plato. With this authority and its refusal to distinguish between the governing faculties of the soul and the modes of political government, Richards can envision a seriously punning 'United Studies' and posit a 'Supreme Ruler within us' which is itself 'the interests which, without such a Ruler, war with one another in shifting alliances forever' (*Speculative Instruments*, pp. 105, 142).

There are many trenchant criticisms of this position. As Eliot argued most eloquently, it is not at all clear that what is best for the human organism ('psychological value') is always or even ever consistent with ethical conduct: 'The two are incompatible, but both must be held, and that is just the problem' ('Literature, science, and dogma', p. 241).[4] At least in modified form, this view will seem damaging to that of Richards for anyone who does not hold that self-sacrifice and masochism are exact synonyms. From another standpoint, supposing the microcosmic view of the individual to be adequate, it is nevertheless far from 'complete'. Eliseo Vivas, citing Nietzsche, rightly called Richards's regimen 'Apollonian'. Whatever its social value, the Dionysian will to disorder can be judged at least as therapeutic for the individual as self-control (see 'Four Notes on I. A. Richards' Aesthetic Theory', p. 356). And suppose, finally, that conflict (doubtless in the interest of broader 'alliances') were essential to the health of the social order.[5] There is no place in Richards for civil war – or, less dramatically, for individual protest, which would have to be viewed on analogy with the rebellion of a single unassimilated impulse, breaking ranks like an unruly collar.

What all these criticisms amount to, and what aligns them with those contemporary protests against literary formalism which are also symptomologies of 'bourgeois humanism' from Arnold to the New Critics is the complaint that Richards's aesthetics of equilibrium is by extension an ethics of inaction. Whereas scientific belief can be defined as 'readiness to act as though the reference symbolized ... were true' (*Principles*, p. 277), but is not even itself, strictly speaking, an active or activist stance,[6] poetry on the other hand is defined as *a state of readiness for action* which *will take the place of action when the full appropriate situation for action is not present* (*Poetries and Sciences*, p. 29; italics Richards's); and Richards adds elsewhere that this form of readiness ('imaginative assent') will not conduce to 'success in meeting definite situations' (*Complementarities*, p. 33). Indeed, he is nowhere more Arnoldian than in his insistence that vigilance in the presence of art breeds a refinement which actually discourages knee-jerk responses of the sort which this view is

---

4 See also S. L. Bethell, 'Suggestions Toward a Theory of Value', *Criterion*, 14 (1934), p. 241.
5 This issue is raised most persistently by Jerome P. Schiller in *I. A. Richards' Theory of Literature* (New Haven, 1969).
6 As a proponent of revolutionary 'science', Max Eastman is tellingly witty on this point in *The Literary Mind: Its Place in an Age of Science* (New York, 1932), p. 312.

prone to equate with action in general: hence his endorsement of literary difficulty, in common with the early Eliot, T. E. Hulme, Pound, and Viktor Skhlovsky – of poetry which 'is necessarily ambiguous in its immediate effect' (*Principles*, p. 291) and cannot therefore suit action to its words.

It is obvious that the disinterestedness of Arnoldian culture theory can translate into relativism and tolerance up to a certain point only – a point which, to his credit, Richards most certainly reached. What it cannot countenance are those 'crude' states of mind (or language: see the attack on 'linguistic egalitarianism' in *So Much Nearer*, p. 74) which are programmed for action only. In the case of Richards it may not be improper to see this in personal terms as a revulsion against the oversimplifications of his own Behaviourism. Along these lines one could envision a feminist critique which began simply by noting that Richards nearly always calls the secondary-school teacher 'she', according her great respect and sympathy yet gender-marking her sphere of influence as a merely practical one, while indicating that her pupil, hope of the future, is a 'he' (see, e.g., *So Much Nearer*, p. 37; a man teaches a woman to teach a man). Such a critique would go on to notice that, in common with many of his peers, Richards finds ('somewhat unfairly', he admits (*Practical Criticism*, p. 198)) in the oft-invoked name of Ella Wheeler Wilcox a synecdoche for crude response and irrationality in poetry.

One could also isolate, even in the wonderfully cosmopolitan Richards, a strain of what Edward Said calls 'Orientalism'.[7] *Mencius*, for example, begins as an attack on Occidental provincialism but soon enough strongly suggests that the 'fixity, in unquestioned security, of a system of social observances' consitutes a '*terminus*' to Chinese thinking (p. 56; and see his critique of a Japanese description of 'freedom' in *Design for Escape*, p. 51). It is the flexibility of the word 'is' which should get 'a main part of the credit for the peculiar intellectual development of the West' (*Interpretation in Teaching*, p. 319), and it is English, after all, as Richards argues on behalf of Basic, which should provide a groundwork for world understanding. One might add to these evidences a 'Hellenism' exceeding Arnold's in the late attacks on Homer and the Hebrew Bible. However, as Pamela McCallum has shrewdly argued, a far more fundamental difficulty in Richards is not any alleged cultural nearsightedness but rather an unreflective commitment to the global unity of the human subject which denatures cultural difference: 'the pluralist referents of any particular instance are basically transcultural and atemporal' (*Literature and Method*, p. 59). It is not difficult to see

---

[7] This point is belaboured by William V. Spanos in 'The Apollonian Investment of Modern Humanist Education: The Examples of Matthew Arnold, Irving Babbit, and I. A. Richards (I)', *Cultural Critique*, 1 (1982), p. 67ff.

that the consistency of these seemingly opposite critiques of Richards, together with the feminist critique of disinterestedness and refinement, can be found in his underlying, enabling hypostasis of Reason – ultimately Platonic Reason – as Order itself.

And although the 'emotive' utterances of poetry, unmistakably gendered feminine, are to be judged for coherence (not correspondence), this fact does not undercut the ascription of order to reason because the value of such utterances does not inhere in their formal properties. Richards is an affective critic who differs most sharply from his successors among the New Critics – as John Crowe Ransom, Allen Tate, Cleanth Brooks, and W. K. Wimsatt themselves proclaimed in chorus – in displacing the desiderata of order and unity from the poem itself, considered as an iconic object, to the mental experience of the poet (at times) and, preeminently, of the reader. Thus typically Marshall McLuhan complains, against Richards, that 'a poem has external relations only accidentally' ('Poetic vs. Rhetorical Exegesis', p. 268). In defying this Formalist maxim Richards is a direct forebear of Wolfgang Iser, who suspends the 'literary work' between text and reader, and of Stanley Fish, who goes farther than Richards in insisting that even the apparently objective, value-neutral properties of texts are projected by the 'literary competence' of the reader. Richards does hold that such properties can be enumerated and exist as occasions giving rise to values they do not themselves possess, being only 'a range of possible effects', but he calls their description the '*technical* part' of criticism, which is to be kept separate from the '*critical* part' (*Principles*, pp. 136, 23; see also *Practical Criticism*, pp. 217, 338) in order that 'technical presuppositions' will not become prescriptive (see *ibid.*, p. 276).

In Richards's affectivism there are the seeds of an epistemological scepticism which, with his early reverence for positive science, he could scarcely acknowledge. The logical conclusion to which Fish has carried the Richards view is implicit even in the earliest attacks on 'intrinsic value' by one who would soon find himself driven to redefine science as myth. In any case, however, we can see that his merely instrumental attitude toward objective poetic structure makes his treatment of it rather perfunctory. In the chapter on 'The Sense of Musical Delight' in *Coleridge*, for example, which denies the semantic independence of metre from syntax, there is no indication that Richards would know how to account for the poetic *line*, either as a sound sequence or as a unit of meaning. Indeed, he is not even sure 'whether we find order in, or impose order *upon*, nature' – or, by implication, upon the literary artifact (*Mencius*, p. 119).

Speaking more broadly of all discourse in *Interpretation in Teaching*, Richards acknowledges in this vein that '[t]here is no metaphor which we cannot, if we wish, break down by over-development' (p. 87), and it is to close the door here left ajar for deconstruction that he does assign to the autonomous poem, in his later work, an intentional structure that is not a formal one: 'A poem is an activity, seeking to become itself' (*Poetries and Sciences* ('Commentary', 1963), p. 108). To this end, we find him actually exaggerating the circularity of certain poems, rather than speaking more accurately of their proleptic repetitions, in an essay called 'Reversals in Poetry' (*Poetries*, ed. Eaton, pp. 59–61); but at the end of another, much earlier practical exercise, 'Fifteen Lines from Landor', we find the distribution of order between object and interpreter to be poised with a convenient ambiguity which perhaps best represents Richards's position: 'We can say ... that inner and outer coherence is the correctness. When an interpretation hangs together ... we call it correct' (*Speculative Instruments*, p. 196).

What is never resolved in Richards, however, owing to his relative lack of attention to form, is the question whether there is a boundary between 'poetry' and other discourses (best called 'prose' here to let the distinction – if there is one – be made in formal terms), and whether within such bounds there may not be more than one kind of poem. It was the complaint first of F. R. Leavis, who blamed Richards's indifference to the very thing he claimed to admire, and later of R. S. Crane, whose 'Neo-Aristotelianism' of course made this objection inevitable, that there is no consideration in Richards of genre, of the purposeful choices formally and cognitively shaping the literary kinds (see Leavis, 'Dr Richards, Bentham and Coleridge', p. 389, and Crane, 'I. A. Richards on the Art of Interpretation', p. 124). Far from being given pause by these protests, Richards in fact moved, as we have seen, from 'literary' to 'rhetorical' criticism, to a theoretical standpoint from which not even the distinction between poetry and prose was any longer relevant to his interpretive pedagogy. The study of language itself, even the learning of a language, produces intellectual effects which 'can be of the very kind which the apologists for the study of Literature customarily allege to be its peculiar benefits' (*Speculative Instruments*, p. 98).

What finally disappears altogether, owing to this unification of the field, is the distinction between the symbolic and the emotive – except, of course, when these characteristics are viewed as functions, among others, of all discourse. It may be said in leaving this distinction behind that the problem had always resided in the question which was which rather more than in the question whether the distinction was valid. Obviously it was valid in some measure, but it prevented its wielder from seeing how often his own symbolisations – of neurological states, for example – were nonsense and how often his derisive citations of poetical rhapsody may after all have suggested something like the true state of things.

All we have to do to justify this last assertion, as Richards acknowledged in one of his last compositions, is to try 'substituting THE LANGUAGE for Apollo and the Muses and for whatever sources of inspiration were taken as speaking through the Prophets of the Old and New Testaments' ('Verse V. Prose', p. 9). But this is more daring than his normative view, which is aimed at the enforcement of a distance between Language and Thought which is broad enough to keep the dream of communication alive. For this, as for all solutions, he needs Plato, and for that reason it may be helpful to comment on an interesting slippage of allusion – and the uncertainty it betrays.

Like Hans-Georg Gadamer on a similar occasion, Richards was bemused by a passage in Aristotle's *Posterior Analytics* comparing a retreating army with the formation of a concept: '"It is like a rout in battle stopped by first one man making a stand and then another, until the original formation has been restored... When one of a number of logically indiscriminable particulars has made a stand, the earliest universal is present in the soul"' (*How to Read a Page*, p. 55). For Aristotle, the universal is the self-actualisation of particulars, and hence can be said to be arrived at cumulatively, as differently as may be from the always already determinate Idea of Plato. Aristotle is to some extent indulging the whim of his metaphor in speaking of an 'original formation', and it is pertinent for Gadamer to ask, just how many soldiers have to stop for the army to have 'made a stand'?[8] But Richards overrides such questions, and while Platonising later in this book, he silently transfers this by no means Platonic expression from Aristotle to carry his point: 'After studying a few [instances of a class] thoroughly, the parallel instances leap to the eye – ⌐ the universal; the one behind the many which is a single identity within them all ⌐ has made its stand' (*ibid.*, p. 137). From the time of his Peircean treatment of 'reference' until his last work, Richards never clearly decided whether thought fully transcends its appearance as sign.

Perhaps I can evoke Richards more clearly in conclusion if I compare him with three figures who are perhaps better known today. The first is Coleridge, whose catholic, continuously integrated interests, whose comparable if less tentative 'pilgrimage towards idealism' (Max Black), and whose brain aswarm with projects and bursting with the importance of futurity, reappear in Richards to a degree that is unique among modern intellectuals. The second is Paul Ricoeur, in whose Janus-faced hermeneutic in *Freud and Philosophy* the reader will recognise an analogue for the double understanding of the 'soul' in Richards: at once oversoul

---

[8] See Hans-Georg Gadamer, *Philosophical Hermeneutics*, trn. David E. Linge (Berkeley, 1976).

and nervous system. The third is a novelist, Thomas Pynchon, the striking similarity of whose mental furniture and world outlook to those of Richards will be obvious from a passage in *Coleridge* (p. 199) concerning the nature of poetry which requires no comment or sequel:

The metaphor is that of a path leading to some destination, or of a missile (arrow or boomerang) going to some mark; but let us exercise a trifling ingenuity in inventing journeys without destinations – movements of the earth, the pigeons' flight, the tacking of a boat, an ant's tour of the spokes of a wheel – or in considering the different trajectories which an arrow will take in shifting winds, or that most illuminating instance here, the rocket; and we shall see clearly how unnecessary, as applying to poems, the assumptions behind any division between a *way* and a *whither* may be.

9

The Southern New Critics

Mark Jancovich

Contemporary criticism tends to dismiss the New Criticism as a type of asocial formalism. The New Critics, it is claimed, disconnected the literary text from its social and historical context and were solely concerned with the practice of close reading. As Terry Eagleton has put it, close reading did 'more than insist on due attentiveness to the text. It inescapably suggests an attention to *this* rather than to something else: to the "words on the page" rather than the context which produced and surrounded them.'[1]

However, nothing could be further from the spirit of the New Criticism as a movement than this description. The figures who promoted and established the New Criticism as a mode of literary analysis were anything but asocial formalists, at least not in the ways that Eagleton and others define this term. Indeed the central preoccupation, and even the principal motivation, of those who championed the New Criticism was a concern with the condition of culture and society within twentieth-century America, and it was in order to disseminate their criticism of that condition that they developed and promoted the New Criticism as a mode of study. Through that development the New Criticism established the basis for later modes of academic literary criticism, altering, as it did, the definition of literary studies within the academy. It was the New Criticism which shifted the dominant forms of academic study from philology, source-hunting, and literary biography to textual analysis, literary theory, and what is now understood as 'literary analysis'.

The social origins of the New Criticism

While the New Criticism is often associated with bourgeois individualism and empiricism,[2] the New Critics who were central to its establishment within the academy were all explicitly anti-bourgeois in their politics. John Crowe Ransom, Allen Tate, and Robert Penn Warren were the three

---

[1] Terry Eagleton, *Literary Theory: An Introduction* (Oxford, 1983), p. 44.
[2] See, for example, Terence Hawkes, *Structuralism and Semiotics* (London, 1977).

critics who formed the core of this movement, and each of them came
from the American South, a region, which when they first began to
practice criticism, was distinguished by its lack of capitalist development.
Rather than accepting bourgeois individualism as an idealogy, they were
actually vocal critics of bourgeois society and culture, and it was during
their period of most intense social and cultural criticism that they developed the critical positions which would later be identified *as* the New
Criticism.

The three met in Nashville, where each was in one way or another
associated with Vanderbilt University. Initially, they came into contact
through the small circle of poets which became known as the Fugitive
group, after their small poetry magazine, *The Fugitive*, which ran from
1922 to 1925.[3] It was in the pages of this publication that their first
literary criticism was published, although they soon began to publish
more widely.

From its earliest days, one of the central features of the Fugitive group
was its interest in modernist poetry, a topic which provoked severe
disagreement. Indeed, as early as 1922, Tate and Ransom found themselves at odds over the publication of T. S. Eliot's 'The Waste Land'. For
Ransom, Eliot's poem was not 'realistic', by which he meant that literature must involve more than 'the first immediate transcription of the
reality', that reality must be subjected to analysis and the relationships
between its elements established. Ransom's objection to 'The Waste Land'
was therefore over a question of literary form. Like Lukács and others,
Ransom claimed that realism involved more than a mere transcription of
surface reality – an approach which Lukács distinguished from realism by
referring to it as naturalism – and claimed that realism proper should
involve a sense of the processes through which the details of surface reality
were produced.[4] He acknowledged that Eliot was 'trying for the form' but
also claimed that he 'hasn't got it'. Is it not, he asked, 'pure pretence ... to
write as if wisdom were not and pure blank tracts of experience – waste
lands – were all there is?'[5]

However, when these views appeared in published form, they sparked a
public row between Ransom and Tate. Tate argued that Ransom had
failed 'to discover the form of the poem, for, as he says, it presents metres
so varied, and such lack of grammar and punctuation and such a bewildering array of discrete themes, that he is at a loss to see the poem as one
poem at all'. However, as Tate retorts, Ransom's real failure was his

[3] For a history of the Fugitive group, see J. M. Bradbury, *The Fugitives* (Chapel Hill, 1958)
    and Louise Cowan, *The Fugitives* (Baton Rouge, 1959).
[4] For an account of Lukács distinction between realism and naturalism, see Georg Lukács,
    'Narrate or Describe?' in *Writer and Critic* (London, 1978).
[5] John Crowe Ransom, 'Letter to Allen Tate, 17th December, 1922' in *The Selected Letters
    of John Crowe Ransom* (Baton Rouge, 1985), p. 115.

inability to see that 'Whatever form may be, it is not, I dare say, regularity of metre.'[6]

The real debate therefore came down to a question of form, and the extent to which the modern period required a new form differing from that of previous periods. For both Ransom and Tate, the question was whether Eliot's poem provided an adequate formal solution to the situation of the modern poet. For Ransom, Eliot's poem lacked form, while for Tate, it offered a radical, new way of conceptualising the world, and one which was a necessary response to new circumstances.[7] Nonetheless, while members may have differed in their response to specific poems or poets, the attempt to get to grips with modernist poetry remained an important feature of the group and was of crucial significance in the development of the New Criticism.

However, although Ransom, Tate, and Warren were poets, they were also Southerners, and it was their concern with the South that established the next stage of their careers. In the aftermath of the Scopes trial of 1925, a series of debates raged within America over the character of the South and its relationship to modern American society as a whole, and these debates galvanised a new commitment in these writers.

Ransom and Tate, in particular, may have become champions of modernist poetry, but they soon became critics of modern, capitalist America and defended the South for its difference from the rest of the nation. The South, they claimed, was still not fully modern, and within it, one could therefore find the residual elements of an alternative way of life, a way of life which was preferable to that dominant in capitalist America.[8] As Ransom observed in a letter to Tate in the mid-1920s: 'Our fight is for survival; and it's got to be waged not so much against the Yankees as against the exponents of the New South. I see clearly that you are as unreconstructed and unmodernized as any of us, if not more so.'[9]

This new commitment led to a series of articles and books on the South and modern America, in which these critics re-examined the social and cultural history of both their local region and the American nation.[10] Throughout this work, the recurring feature is a developing critique of the relationship between capitalism and modernity, a critique which came to a head by 1929. By this point, the group had come to believe that any

---

[6] Allen Tate, 'Waste Lands', *Evening Post's Literary Review*, 3 (4 August, 1923), p. 886.
[7] See John Crowe Ransom, 'Waste Lands', *Evening Post's Literary Review*, 3 (11 July 1923), pp. 825–6; Tate, 'Waste Lands'; and John Crowe Ransom, 'Mr Ransom Replies', *Evening Post's Literary Review*, 3 (11 August 1923), p. 902.
[8] See, for example, John Crowe Ransom, 'The South – Old and New', *Sewanee Review*, 36 (April 1928), pp. 139–47.   [9] Ransom, *Selected Letters*, p. 166.
[10] See, for example, Ransom, 'The South – Old and New'; 'The South Defends its Heritage', *Harper's*, 159 (June 1929), pp. 353–66; Allen Tate, *Stonewall Jackson: The Good Soldier* (New York, 1928); Allen Tate, *Jefferson Davis: His Rise and Fall* (New York, 1929); and Robert Penn Warren, *John Brown: The Making of a Martyr* (New York, 1929).

coherent and organised response to the New South required an active community of Southern intellectuals, and as a first step in the formation of such a community they organised a symposium on the South which was to become known as *I'll Take My Stand: The South and the Agrarian Tradition*, a title which caused some ill feeling among the participants.[11] Despite the disagreements among members, what stands out as perhaps the central feature of this symposium is an awareness that cultural life is inseparable from the specific economic order within a given society. Indeed, as the statement of principles maintained, culture is a material activity which develops in relation to existing economic relations and as a result, a 'truly humanistic culture' cannot develop from a purely natural impulse, but only in relation to a whole way of life.[12]

These critics' objection to modern capitalist society was that it depended on a specific form of abstraction which was a necessary component of the commodity form. Objects (and people) were abstracted from their context and valued only as commodities to be bought, sold, or used to produce other commodities. The primary value in production became efficiency and productivity, and as a result, capitalism had fundamentally reorganised the relationships between the economy and culture, between humanity and nature, and between individuals. Within this situation, it was argued, culture became separated from economics. Instead of being a whole way of life that was intimately and inextricably bound up with economic activity, culture had been redefined as an alternative sphere, which existed as a mere diversion or distraction from other aspects of life. While economic life became associated with activity, cultural life became associated with leisure and passivity, concerned only with the consumption of commodities.

As Tate put it during a later stage of what was to become known as the Agrarian movement, society came to regard 'making a living' and 'a way of life' as quite different pursuits, and, as a result, culture was denied any real place within the whole way of life, so that it became a mere addition or complement to social and economic life. It lost its meaning and came to be seen as merely a series of fine and decorative forms – sterile, meaningless, and trivial.[13] It is for this reason that Tate was to claim that, as industrial capitalism developed in the North, 'New England became a museum'.[14]

---

[11] Allen Tate, for example, objected that this title 'emphasizes the fact of exclusiveness rather than its benefits; it points to a particular house but omits to say that it was the home of a spirit that may also have lived elsewhere and that this mansion was incidentally made with hands' (*I'll Take My Stand: The South and the Agrarian Tradition* (Baton Rouge, 1980), p. 155).   [12] John Crowe Ransom, 'Statement of Principles', in *I'll Take My Stand*.
[13] Allen Tate, 'A Traditionalist Looks at Liberalism', *Southern Review*, 1 (Spring 1936), p. 740.
[14] Allen Tate, 'Emily Dickinson', in *Essays of Four Decades* (London, 1970), p. 283.

As a result, these critics did not see literature and culture as separate from economics and society. On the contrary, they stressed that not only had the emergence of capitalism virtually destroyed culture in America, but also that culture could not be repaired without establishing a set of social and economic relations which were fundamentally different from those dominant within modern America. The Agrarian society was therefore proposed as such an alternative, but Ransom and others were careful to emphasise that agriculture did not offer a solution in itself. It could only offer an alternative if pre-capitalist economic relations were employed, relations which were not bound up with a market economy.[15]

Literature and social criticism

It was during the period in which Ransom, Tate, and Warren were developing this critique of modern America that they were also refining their literary theory and so developing the theories and methods which would later become known as the New Criticism. These theories and methods were largely shaped in opposition to two alternative approaches to literature: neo-humanism and Stalinist Marxism. However, they were also opposed to the emphasis on philology, source-hunting, and literary biography which was then dominant within the academy.

For all three critics, literary value could not be reduced to its rational content. Literature could not be simply assessed on the basis of the statements it might make or the positions it might take. Indeed, they argued that those forms of criticism that did judge literary value according to content were merely symptoms of the rationality and abstractions of modern society, in which literature, like all other forms, became valued for its 'utility'. Moreover, they claimed that the value of literature specifically lay in its difference from, and even its challenge to, scientific and rationalist discourses.[16]

For example, Ransom argues that the difference between aesthetic and scientific discourses lies in their different attitudes to the world, and he attempts to clarify this point through a distinction between work and play. Work, he claims, views its objects in purely economic terms so that they are only valued for their utility, while in play, the object is viewed in essentially aesthetic terms; play values the object in its totality, rather than

---

[15] John Crowe Ransom, 'The State and the Land', *New Republic*, 66 (February 1932), pp. 8–10.

[16] This position can be seen in the essays which these critics wrote during this period, many of which were collected in books during the mid-1930s. See John Crowe Ransom, *The World's Body* (New York, 1938) and Allen Tate, *Reactionary Essays on Poetry and Ideas* (New York, 1936). See also Robert Penn Warren and Cleanth Brooks, *Understanding Poetry* (New York, 1960) and *Understanding Fiction* (New York, 1943).

simply valuing it abstractly for some specific useful feature. As Ransom puts it, 'aesthetic forms are a technique of restraint, not efficiency'.[17] Aesthetic forms contemplate their objects in a disinterested manner. Indeed, the Southern New Critics also stressed that the attempt to value literature according to its statements or positions tended to ignore the formal features of literature, and even in those cases where these features were not ignored, they were dismissed either as mere decorative additions or as expressive of the statement: they had no value in themselves but were always subordinated to the rational content.

This position was not acceptable to Ransom, Tate, and Warren, but they were careful to emphasise that their own position was not merely an aesthetic hedonism. Literary form did have its value, they claimed, but this could not be identified as decorative or expressive in nature. On the contrary, as Ransom's distinction between *structure* and *texture* was later to clarify, they claimed that the value of form was the extent to which it offered a critique of the rational content. For Ransom, rational content was identified as the *structure* of a text, while the *texture* was seen as the patterns of sound which were the materiality of the text. By stressing and stylising this materiality, he claimed, the literary text did not simply distract attention away from the rational content, but actually worked to undermine that content. It tested and challenged its apparent transparency, and so revealed those aspects of language and discourse which rational discourses (such as science) sought to control and repress.[18]

This challenge, it was claimed, was also present in the literary emphasis on the figurative aspects of language and in the use of tropes. As Ransom puts it:

Figures of speech twist accidence away from the straight course, as if to intimate astonishing lapses of rationality beneath the smooth surfaces of discourse, inviting perceptual attention, and weakening the tyranny of science over the senses.[19]

In this way, it was claimed, literature drew attention to the limits of scientific discourse, to those aspects of language which threatened rational coherence and control and which therefore needed to be repressed by rational discourse. But in so doing, literature did not just differ from rational discourses, it also posed a fundamental challenge to their values.

Since literature issued its challenge to rationality not through its statements or positions, but through its form, the New Critics greatly valued

---

[17] John Crowe Ransom, 'A Poem Nearly Anonymous: II The Poet and His Formal Tradition', *American Review*, 1 (September 1933), p. 446.

[18] John Crowe Ransom, *The New Criticism* (Norfolk, Conn., 1941). See also Ransom, *The World's Body*; Tate, *Reactionary Essays*; and Warren and Brooks, *Understanding Poetry* and *Understanding Fiction*.

[19] John Crowe Ransom, 'Poetry: A Note on Ontology', *American Review*, 3 (Spring 1937), p. 784.

the term '*irony*' and saw it as the central feature of literary texts. If these critics were critical of those who saw literary form as simply a vehicle for the rational content of the text, they were just as critical of those who simply attempted to do without ideas or social concerns and who tried to concentrate solely on the formal features of language. Indeed, as Warren argued in relation to the poetry of Archibald MacLeish, poets who sought to purge their work of ideas and social concerns had actually accepted the same opposition and alternatives as those who simply saw literature as a form of propaganda. Furthermore, Warren claimed that, due to its lack of ideas and social concerns, MacLeish's poetry could not develop a coherent form, and for this reason, he rejected MacLeish's claim that 'a poem should not mean, but be'.[20] As Tate also stressed, poets should not do away with ideas but, on the contrary, they must use them '*ironically*'. They must examine and interrogate them through linguistic form.[21]

On analogous grounds, the New Critics were opposed to what later became known as the '*heresy of paraphrase*'.[22] They claimed that the meaning of the text was inseparable from its linguistic form, and therefore could not be reduced to a simple extractable meaning. The meaning of the text was the totality of its elements and their inter-relations, and it was in this sense that they saw literary texts as self-sufficient and even autonomous objects. However, it is also the reason that they do not see these 'self-sufficient' or 'autonomous' objects as fixed objects. Although they valued meaning and unity, they also stressed that the literary text was never a stable structure. Its inter-relations were so complex that it was quite literally a process of productivity, and hence could never be resolved into a simple paraphrasable meaning.[23]

It was in this sense that the New Critics claimed that the literary text was '*organic*' in nature.[24] Literature could not be identified with any one stylistic feature or subject matter, but rather with the way in which all the elements of a work inter-related. For example, it was claimed that the relationship between meaning and form cannot be a mechanical one in

---

[20] Robert Penn Warren, 'Twelve Poets', *American Review*, 3 (May 1934), pp. 212–27.

[21] Tate, *Reactionary Essays*. Indeed, all three critics wrote essays which explicitly criticised poetry which tried either to rely on abstract ideas or to reject abstract ideas. See John Crowe Ransom, 'Poetry: A Note on Ontology' *American Review*, 2 (March 1934), pp. 172–200; Allen Tate, 'Three Types of Poetry' in *Essays of Four Decades* (London, 1970); and Robert Penn Warren, 'Pure and Impure Poetry', *Kenyon Review*, 5 (Spring 1943), pp. 228–54.

[22] This term was coined by Cleanth Brooks, a friend of Ransom, Tate, and Warren, who worked with them as a member of the Fugitive group, the Agrarian movement, and the New Criticism, and it has become strongly associated with the New Criticism as one of its central tenets.

[23] See Ransom, *The World's Body*; Tate, *Reactionary Essays*; and Warren and Brooks, *Understanding Poetry* and *Understanding Fiction*.

[24] The clearest statement of this position is in the introduction to Warren and Brooks, *Understanding Poetry* and *Understanding Fiction*.

which form exists to express meaning; form cannot be seen as an object or vessel which contains meaning, but rather as a process through which meaning is produced. Nonetheless, the struggle for unity which the New Critics valued was not merely a formal, technical process. Instead it was a deeply moral one. Literature, it was argued, did not offer easy or abstract solutions, but acknowledged paradoxes and contradictions. For this reason, the New Critics stressed that there can be no ideal literary form. Each text must struggle for its own sense of unity and coherence.

Hence when these critics claimed that the literary text was 'iconic',[25] they did not mean that it simply resembled that to which it referred, but that it presented 'an object in the round, a figure of three dimensions, so to speak; in technical language a singular and individual object'.[26] In contrast to rationalist discourses, which were said to view their objects as instances of some abstract feature or quality, aesthetic discourse was said to present the object in its full complexity and individuality, and so provide a sense of the world which scientific discourses neither have nor desire. However, it achieves this not through rationalist notions of mimesis, but through its form. It is the form of the text that provides this sense of complexity and individuality, and as a result, the text is 'iconic' exactly because it *is* what it represents; it does not simply refer to the complexity and individuality of some external object but rather its form is itself an example of such complexity and individuality. It is in this sense, then, that Wimsatt was later to associate the New Criticism with the concept of the text as a *'verbal icon'*.[27]

However, this did not mean that these critics denied that aesthetic discourse had a cognitive dimension.[28] On the contrary, they maintained that aesthetic discourse was a form of knowledge, but one which was fundamentally at odds with scientific and rational discourses. As Tate put it, poetry 'is merely a way of knowing something: if the poem is a real creation, it is a kind of knowledge that we did not possess before. It is not knowledge "about" something else; the poem is the fullness of that knowledge.'[29] Aesthetic discourse gives a knowledge of the world by

---

[25] See, for example, Ransom, *The New Criticism* (Norfolk, Conn., 1941); Allen Tate, 'Literature and Knowledge', *Southern Review*, 6 (Spring 1941); and Warren and Brooks, *Understanding Poetry* and *Understanding Fiction*.

[26] John Crowe Ransom, 'Editorial Note: The Arts and the Philosophers', *Kenyon Review*, 1 (Spring 1939), p. 198.

[27] This term was coined by W. K. Wimsatt in the title of his book, *The Verbal Icon: Studies in the Meaning of Poetry* (New York, 1958). While Wimsatt was not a member of the original group, this book was to be one of the most famous and influential New Critical texts, re-presenting the movement to a new audience.

[28] See, for example, Robert Scholes, *Semiotics and Interpretation* (New Haven, 1982), p. 23.

[29] Allen Tate, 'Narcissus as Narcissus', *Virginia Quarterly Review*, 14 (Winter 1938), p. 110.

emphasising that which scientific discourse represses, and in so doing, it offers a critique of the modern world.

The New Criticism and the academy

While the cultural criticism of Ransom, Tate, and Warren developed alongside their involvement in the Agrarian movement and was intimately bound up with their social and economic criticism, it is often claimed that their attempt to establish the New Criticism within the academy represented a loss of interest in social and economic criticism.[30] But this concern with the academy can be seen very differently. Far from being a break with their Agrarian concerns, it can simply be seen as a change in strategy and tactics.

The New Critics had stressed that culture cannot exist independently of social and economic relations, and from the outset of the Agrarian movement they had emphasised the necessity of specific institutional conditions that would enable the establishment of a community of Southern intellectuals. As Tate had argued in 1929, what was needed was:

1. The formation of a society, or an academy of Southern *positive* reactionaries made up at first of people of our own group.

2. The expansion in a year or two of this academy to this size: fifteen active members – poets, critics, historians, economists – who might be active enough without being committed at first to direct agitation.

3. The drawing up of a philosophical constitution, to be issued and signed by the academy, as the groundwork of the movement. It should be ambitious to the last degree; it should set forth, under our leading idea, a complete social, philosophical, literary, economic and religious system. This will inevitably draw upon our heritage, but this heritage should be valued, not in what it actually performed, but in its possible perfection. Philosophically we must go the whole hog of reaction, and base our movement less upon the actual Old South than upon its prototype – the historical social and religious scheme of Europe. We must be the last Europeans – there being no Europeans in Europe at present.

4. The academy will not be a secret order: all cards will be on the table. We should be *secretive*, however, in our tactics, and plan the campaign for the maximum of effect. All our writings should be sign 'John Doe, of the – ,' or whatever we call it.

5. Organised publication should be looked to. A Newspaper, perhaps, to argue principles on the lower plane; then a weekly, to press philosophy upon the passing show; and thirdly, a quarterly devoted wholly to principles. This is a large scheme, but it must be held up constantly. We must do our best with what we get.[31]

---

[30] See, for example, John Fekete, *The Critical Twilight: Explorations in the Ideology of Anglo-American Literary Theory from Eliot to McLuhan* (London, 1978).
[31] Thomas D. Young and John Tyree Fain, eds., *The Literary Correspondence of Donald Davidson and Allen Tate* (Athens, Ga., 1974), pp. 229–30.

However, these conditions never materialised and by the mid-1930s, the New Critics were becoming disenchanted with the South.

They still saw the region as one which continued to contain the residual elements of an alternative way of life, but they were frustrated by its failure to support them as intellectuals, frustration which came to a head in 1937, when Ransom was offered a post at Kenyon College, an offer which the Southern institution of Vanderbilt University refused to match. The move from Vanderbilt proved advantageous. Ransom was given the opportunity to edit a new journal, the *Kenyon Review*, and this journal, along with the *Southern Review* which Robert Penn Warren had been editing with Cleanth Brooks since 1936, began to fulfil some of the conditions that the group had considered necessary to the formation of a community of critical intellectuals. Indeed, Tate stated this explicitly in an article published in the *Southern Review* in 1936, an article entitled, 'The Function of the Critical Review'.[32]

Other processes in the 1930s also moulded the group's changes in tactics. In 1937, Ransom published 'Criticism, Inc.', an article which acknowledged the growing crisis over the teaching of English in America and which proposed the New Criticism as a solution to that crisis.[33] Indeed, in 1938, he wrote to Tate about the meeting of the Modern Language Association, from which he had just returned. As Ransom commented:

The professors are in an awful dither, trying to reform themselves and there's a big stroke possible for a small group that knows what it wants in giving them ideas and definition and showing them the way.[34]

Indeed, Ransom was quite explicit about the possibilities which this crisis offered to them as intellectuals:

Shall we be independent Chinese war lords, or shall we come in and run the government? Another question of strategy. There's so much congenial revolutionary spirit in the MLA that there's really something there to capitalize.[35]

The shift to the academy was not therefore an abandonment of the interests which had underpinned the Agrarian movement, but an alternative way of promoting their interests and of establishing support for social change.

The crisis which faced the teaching of English in the mid-1930s needs to be understood as the product of deep-seated tensions that date back to the emergence of literary studies within the American academy. As Gerald Graff has pointed out, literary studies established itself as an academic discipline only during the last quarter of the nineteenth century 'as part of

[32] Allen Tate, 'The Function of the Critical Review', *Southern Review*, 1 (Winter 1936), pp. 596–611.
[33] John Crowe Ransom, 'Criticism, Inc.', *Virginia Quarterly Review*, 13 (Autumn 1937), pp. 586–602.   [34] Ransom, *Selected Letters*, p. 236.   [35] *Ibid.*

a larger process of professionalization by which the old "college" became the new "university"'.[36] Furthermore, as it emerged as a discipline, literary studies were not defined in the same ways as those which are now current. Indeed, as Graff has argued, 'the profession of "literary studies" was established before it began to consider literature as its subject'.[37] Instead of concentrating on questions of aesthetics and textual analysis, the profession defined itself as a discipline through its concentration on 'scientific research' and the philological study of language. In this period, literature was used to document changes in language.

However, that model of literary study did not go unchallenged, and an alternative model was posed by figures who Graff refers to as the 'generalists'. Generalists argued that the study of literature should not be limited to the narrow specialisms of the philologists, that it should be concerned with values rather than facts. For the generalists, literature was 'a moral and spiritual force and a repository of "general ideas" which could be applied directly to the conduct of life and the improvement of national culture'.[38] Nonetheless, even these critics were not concerned with aesthetics, or questions of literary form.

From its outset, then, the profession of literary study was dogged by conflict and crisis. It faced the problem of reconciling the traditionalism of liberal culture on the one hand with the criteria of professional secularism on the other. The very scientism of the philologists, while it enabled them to establish their credentials as professionals within the academy, actually prevented them from making the humanistic claims which might have justified the study of literature outside the academy. The problem became increasingly acute as the universities expanded from the late-nineteenth century and into the twentieth century. It was one thing for the philologists to defend their specialism while the university population was relatively small 'by protest[ing] that mass education was not their business', but 'as universities expanded such disclaimers seemed irresponsible'.[39] The move to mass education required the scholars to question their practices and to find ways of justifying their activities in social, rather than strictly technical, terms. Indeed, with the depression of the 1930s, this requirement assumed still greater urgency.

Unfortunately, such a justification was difficult for the profession to produce. Its claim to professionalism had been based on the distinction between research and criticism in which the former was defined as the objective, scientific search for 'certifiable facts' and the latter was simply dismissed as a matter of 'subjective impressions'. By the end of World War

[36] Gerald Graff, *Professing Literature: An Institutional History* (Chicago, 1987), p. 55.
[37] Gerald Graff and Michael Warner, 'Introduction' in Gerald Graff and Michael Warner, eds., *The Origins of Literary Study: A Documentary History* (London, 1989), p. 5.
[38] *Ibid.*, p. 6.   [39] Graff, *Professing Literature*, p. 144.

I, some researchers did attempt to revise this assessment of criticism, and they argued that it was not criticism *per se* which was a problem, but criticism which was not informed by scholastic groundwork. However, as Graff points out,

> these concessions were hollow as long as most scholars still conceived of criticism as an affair of subjective impressions opposed to certifiable facts. As long as that assumption prevailed, there was little chance that criticism could become accepted as part of a literature student's necessary concerns.[40]

The distinction made it virtually impossible for the discipline to incorporate a discussion of cultural values within itself. It opposed the accumulation of historical information on the one hand with the interpretation of texts on the other, and so prevented any attempt to connect these activities in a significant or convincing way.

Here was the very distinction that the New Criticism attacked in its attempt to establish itself within the academy. As Tate argued, for example, in 'Miss Emily and the Bibliographer':

> The historical method will not permit us to develop a critical instrument for dealing with works of literature as existent objects; we see them as expressive of substances beyond themselves. At the historical level the work expresses its place and time, or the author's personality, but if the scholar goes further and says anything about the work, he is expressing himself. Expressionism is here a sentiment, forbidding us to think and permitting us to feel as we please.[41]

As a result, Tate argued that by concentrating on the text as a linguistic construct the problem of subjectivity could be overcome. If language could be seen as a public medium which determined both the production and the consumption of texts, then the analysis of linguistic forms could become not just a matter of subjective impressions, but a means of assessing the validity and significance of specific readings.

As a result, the New Critics concern with the 'objectivity' of the text was a way of overcoming the philologist's distinction between the objectivity of the historical background and the subjectivity of the critic's analysis.[42] Indeed, it went further and allowed the New Critics to overturn the distinction altogether. It was not the text which had no meaning

---

[40] *Ibid.*, p. 137.

[41] Allen Tate, 'Miss Emily and the Bibliographer' in *Essays of Four Decades*, pp. 146–7. Similar positions can also be found in Ransom, *The World's Body* and *The New Criticism*; and Tate, *Reactionary Essays*. However, it is more clearly and directly stated in Robert Penn Warren and Cleanth Brooks, 'The Reading of Modern Poetry', *American Review*, 8 (February 1937), pp. 435–49; and Warren and Brooks, *Understanding Poetry* and *Understanding Fiction*.

[42] Indeed, this position can be identified in the early writing of both Ransom and Tate. See Ransom, 'A Poem Nearly Anonymous: II The Poet and His Formal Tradition' and Tate, 'Emily Dickinson'.

except as a transparent expression of its background, they argued, but, on the contrary, it was the background which had no meaning (for literary studies) except in so far as it informed the processes of literary production. Defining the literary process of production as a linguistic process allowed Tate and the others to define a basis for aesthetic evaluation and judgement which could also establish the credentials of criticism as a professional discipline. The New Critics were therefore able to maintain that responses need not be a matter of 'subjective impressions', but could be fully public and social. If responses were defined in relation to a linguistic process that was both public and social, such responses could be produced and evaluated through a particular disciplined method.

It was in this sense that the New Critics took issue with the approaches which W. K. Wimsatt would later describe as 'the Intentional Fallacy' and 'the Affective Fallacy'.[43] For Ransom, Tate, and Warren, the linguistic forms of the text should be the object of study and should be identified as the process through which the meaning of the text was produced. Hence they took issue with those approaches that saw meaning as the product of authorial intention because they claimed that all authors have to work with the public medium of language and that, as a result, the meaning of the text will finally escape their control during the process of writing. For the New Critics, texts cannot be purely transparent forms through which authors express themselves, but must always be more complex linguistic objects whose productivity and materiality will exceed and even contradict the intentions of their authors.[44]

This concern with the materiality and productivity of the text also led the New Critics to challenge those who saw the meaning of the text as simply a matter of individual, subjective responsive. For Ransom, Tate, and Warren, while subjective responses to texts may be affected by a range of social and cultural factors, the meaning of a text cannot simply be reduced to subjective responses. Again, they emphasised that language was a public medium and that as such a text's meaning was both objective and social. This meaning might be endlessly complex and therefore ultimately indeterminate, but for this very reason it not only exceeded the intentions of its author but also the responses of its readers. Thus, the intentional fallacy and the affective fallacy were both said to be reductive, and to ignore the objective materiality of the text as a linguistic object.

As we have seen this focus on textuality was not intended to define criticism as a type of asocial formalism in which critics explicated texts

---

[43] See Wimsatt, *The Verbal Icon*. However, this position is more clearly articulated by Warren in 'The Reading of Modern Poetry', and Warren and Brooks, *Understanding Fiction* and *Understanding Poetry*.

[44] Similar positions can also be identified in John Crowe Ransom, 'Shakespeare at Sonnets', *Southern Review*, 3 (Winter 1938), pp. 531–41; and Allen Tate, 'Narcissus as Narcissus', *Southern Review*, 6 (Spring 1941), pp. 108–22.

without reference to social or cultural concerns. On the contrary, by establishing the New Criticism as the dominant mode of literary study within the academy, the New Critics hoped to disseminate their critique of modern America, a critique that was fundamentally embedded in their literary theory.

The activities which established the New Criticism within the academy were various. Journals such as the *Southern Review* and the *Kenyon Review* helped to develop a community of intellectuals and to promote the New Criticism as a movement, while essay collections made up of materials which they had published during the early 1930s enabled them to identify the coherence of their approach.[45] They also delivered papers at the Modern Language Association meetings which argued a case for their approach and demonstrated its application.[46] However, perhaps the most important and influential event was the publication of Cleanth Brooks and Robert Penn Warren's *Understanding Poetry* in 1938.[47] *Understanding Poetry* was to become the first of a series of textbooks that not only clarified the ideas of the New Criticism, but also presented a clear practice through which this mode of literary analysis could be applied to the teaching of English. Finally, in the early 1940s, the *Southern Review* and the *Kenyon Review* jointly published a symposium on the study of literature within the academy in which it was argued that literary studies should be preoccupied with the analysis of the formal features of literary texts, and that literary theory should also become an independent activity within the departments of English; that it was not just necessary to study literary texts according to their formal features, but that it was also necessary to study the constitutive forms of literary activity at a more general and abstract level.[48]

The success of these various activities changed the American academy and laid the foundation for contemporary criticism, but it did not just change *how* literature was studied but also which literature was studied, revising and transforming the literary canon in fundamental ways. Most significantly, it introduced modernist literature into the academy and rewrote literary history in the process. The status of a whole series of writers changed. Some passed out of favour and others, such as Henry James, became enshrined in a position of prestige which they had not

---

[45] See, for example, Ransom, *The World's Body* and Tate, *Reactionary Essays*.
[46] See for example, Allen Tate, 'Modern Poets and Conventions' and Robert Penn Warren and Cleanth Brooks, 'The Reading of Modern Poetry'. Both essays were originally delivered as papers at the conference of the Modern Language Association in 1936 before being published in the *American Review*, 8 (February 1937).
[47] Warren and Brooks, *Understanding Poetry*.
[48] 'Literature and the Professors' appeared in the *Southern Review*, 6 (Summer 1940) and the *Kenyon Review*, 2 (Summer 1940).

enjoyed before.[49] Indeed, the New Critics' publications explicitly addressed the case of modern literature, defending its forms as a response to the social and cultural context of modern America, and so arguing that despite its use of non-traditional forms, modern literature remained traditional in its values – most specifically its opposition to the rationalism of modern society.

The New Criticism and the critique of pure aesthetics

It is here that the problems of the New Criticism become evident. The theory of 'literature' produced by these critics was in fact a claim about what constituted 'real' literature. That is, it did not discuss literature itself (whatever that might be), but rather it privileged one particular definition over others. In one sense, of course, the New Critics were well aware of this, but in another, they were also obliged to suppress its implications to themselves and others. The term 'literature' (even when it is used in its more specialised sense rather than simply referring to writing in general) has been used in a variety of ways with a variety of different meanings. By defining it in a particular way, the New Critics implicitly and even explicitly sought to displace and even exclude certain meanings. In so doing, they not only excluded certain forms of writing which had hitherto been seen as literature, but more to the point, they excluded certain forms of reading. It was not simply a question of what texts could actually be defined as 'literary', but also about what types of reading could be defined as 'literary'. As we have seen, readings of a 'literary' text which concentrated on its content were deemed inappropriate, and hence the issue was less about the text itself and more about the legitimate mode of its appropriation.

This is a point made by the French sociologist of culture Pierre Bourdieu in a different context. As Bourdieu argues:

If the work of art is indeed, as Panofsky says, that which 'demands to be experienced aesthetically', and if any object, natural or artificial, can be perceived aesthetically, how can one escape the conclusion that it is the aesthetic intention [of the viewer] which 'makes' the work of art . . ., that it is the aesthetic point of view that creates the aesthetic object.[50]

Indeed, the New Critics' definition of literary study conforms to what Bourdieu refers to as 'the aesthetic disposition' or 'the pure gaze'. This

---

[49] Indeed, the *Kenyon Review* even devoted an issue to a reappraisal of James as a writer (*Kenyon Review*, 5 (Autumn 1943)).

[50] Pierre Bourdieu, 'The Aristocracy of Culture,' in Richard Collins *et al.*, eds., *Media, Culture and Society: A Reader* (London, 1986), p. 173.

mode of perception is preoccupied with form over function, and privileges disinterested contemplation over use or utility.

However, as Bourdieu points out, this mode of perception is not, as is commonly supposed, universal or free from history. On the contrary, it is specific to the social conditions of specific groups at specific historical moments. As Bourdieu puts it:

> it suffices to note that the formalist ambition's objections to all types of historiciz-ation rests on the unawareness of its own social conditions of possibility. The same is true of a philosophical aesthetics which records and ratifies this ambition. What is forgotten in both cases is the historical process through which the social conditions of freedom from 'external determinations' get established; that is, the process of establishing the relatively autonomous field of production and with it the realm of pure aesthetics or pure thought whose existence it makes possible.[51]

For Bourdieu, the pure gaze is directly related to the economic situation of dominant social groups. It is based on a refusal of 'simple' or 'natural' pleasures, which is itself the product of a 'distance from necessity'. The ability to value form over function, or to engage in practices which have no functional purpose, depends upon 'an experience of the world freed from urgency'[52] – that is, the disinterested contemplation of art depends upon a position of social and material privilege, but tends to forget this fact and to present itself as though it were merely a natural inclination instead.

This mode of perception not only forgets these historical conditions, but also acts to re-enforce the legitimacy of the dominant groups. Its refusal of function in favour of form is also implicitly and explicitly a refusal of the tastes of those social groups who do not share a position of material privilege. As Bourdieu puts it, the pure gaze explicitly asserts its 'superiority over those who, because they cannot assert the same contempt for ... gratuitous luxury and conspicuous consumption, remain dominated by ordinary interests and urgencies'.[53] It is for this reason that aesthetics so often makes the distinction between the self-evident, transparent, and easy pleasures which are supposedly offered by popular culture and the complex, difficult, and active processes which are associated with the consumption of high culture. It is also the reason that aesthetics can be seen as 'a sort of aggression [or] affront' to the culture of subordinate classes. However, what Bourdieu finds most worrying is that while these cultural distinctions are the most classifying of all social differences, they also have 'the privilege of appearing to be the most natural'.[54]

[51] Pierre Bourdieu, 'The Historical Genesis of a Pure Aesthetics' in *The Field of Cultural Production: Essays on Art and Literature* (New York, 1993), p. 266.
[52] Bourdieu, 'The Aristocracy of Culture', p. 190.   [53] *Ibid.*, p. 191.   [54] *Ibid.*, p. 192.

For these reasons, the New Critics faced severe problems which they could never finally resolve or even admit. On the one hand, their definition of literature could not have the universal status which they claimed for it. Their attempt to define literature is a clear case where what purports to be an essence is in fact a norm: that is, while the New Critics claimed to be identifying the essence of literature, they were actually simply attempting to impose one specific definition as *the* definition. Hence their claims were not about what constituted 'Literature', but rather what 'really' constituted 'Literature', or to put it yet another way, what constituted 'real' literature. However, as Bourdieu points out,

the word 'real' implicitly contrasts the case under consideration to all other cases in the same category, to which other speakers assigned, although unduly so (that is, in a manner not 'really' justified), the same predicate, a predicate which, like all claims to universality, is symbolically very powerful.[55]

In other words, the New Critics were attempting to establish the superiority of the pure gaze over other modes of cultural appropriation, to present 'disinterested contemplation' as the legitimate and authorised way of consuming cultural texts.

Indeed, as Bourdieu also makes clear, it is for this reason that the term literature is inherently unstable and undeterminate: that it is incapable of uncontested definition:

Because they are inscribed in ordinary language and are generally used beyond the aesthetic sphere, these categories as taste [such as the term literature] which are common to all speakers of a shared language do allow an apparent form of communication. Yet despite that, such terms are always marked – even when used by professionals – by an extreme vagueness and flexibility which (again as noted by Wittgenstein) makes them completely resistant to essentialist definition. This is probably because the use that is made of these terms and the meaning that is given to them depend upon the specific, historically and socially situated points of view of their users – points of view which are quite often perfectly irreconcilable.[56]

As a result, the New Critics' project was inherently doomed to failure. It did succeed in establishing itself in a position of dominance and legitimacy, but it could not finally resolve the problem of defining the essence of literature. Its definition was limited by issues such as class and national origin, and was also largely dependent on the aesthetics of a specific literary movement – literary modernism. Indeed, many of its key terms were centrally at odds with other literary movements – such as Romanticism – and were often developed in direct opposition to them.[57] As a result, the New Critical definition of literature was not only inapplicable

---

[55] Bourdieu, 'The Historical Genesis of a Pure Aesthetics', p. 263.   [56] *Ibid.*, p. 261.
[57] For example, the concept of the Intentional Fallacy was developed in direct opposition to the romantic focus on individual artistic expression.

to other periods and movements, but it was often deliberately defined in order to exclude them.

This is most centrally the case with its relationship to popular literature and culture which is rarely openly discussed exactly because these critics assumed it to be 'non-art' or even 'anti-art', to borrow Dwight Mac-Donald's description of popular culture.[58] Like most mass culture theorists of the period, the New Critics unproblematically assumed that due to its production within (or at least its entanglement with) capitalist commodity production, popular culture was forced to rely on the easy or abstract solutions against which they define literature – that it was not complex in form or content and that its consumption involved the complete inverse of 'disinterested contemplation'. However, as Bourdieu suggests, this assumption is not simply inappropriate, but it is actually structurally essential to the legitimisation of the pure gaze. It is an assumption which is necessary in order to assert the superiority of that which the New Critics wanted to be defined as 'real' Literature.

Indeed, what is perhaps even more troubling is that while the New Criticism was intended as a critique of bourgeois culture and capitalist society, it was quickly and easily transformed to quite different ends. As Bourdieu has noted, the position of the cultural bourgeoisie has usually made it explicitly anti-bourgeois in its politics, dependent as it is on the dominant, economic sections of the bourgeois class. The cultural bourgeoisie reacts against its dependent status by seeking to assert the autonomy of aesthetic discourse in order to protect its own activities from the demands of the economic bourgeoisie, and also in an attempt to assert the authority and value of itself and its activities. Unfortunately, while this usually results in an anti-bourgeois politics, Bourdieu also stresses that it ironically ends up reaffirming the authority and superiority of the pure gaze and bourgeois culture. What presents itself as a critique of bourgeois society usually results in its affirmation.[59]

The problem for the New Criticism was that while it was neither bourgeois in its origins or its ambitions, its success was in part a product of its appropriation by the cultural bourgeoisie rather than its displacement of them. As mass education increasingly became central to literary study within the academy, the academy needed to justify literary study in humanistic terms. However, while it is usually the case that, as Bourdieu argues, this justification is articulated through a left-wing, anti-bourgeois politics, the context of the 1940s and 1950s made this option difficult.

[58] Dwight MacDonald, 'Masscult and Midcult' in *Against the American Grain* (London, 1963), p. 4.
[59] Pierre Bourdieu, *Distinction: A Social Critique of the Judgement of Taste*, (London, 1984); see also Nicholas Garnham and Raymond Williams, 'Pierre Bourdieu and the Sociology of Culture', in Nicholas Garnham, *Capitalism and Communication: Global Culture and the Economics of Information* (London, 1990).

Not only did the Cold War politics which was emerging after 1945 make left-wing politics increasingly difficult to legitimate and maintain, but the politics of Stalinist Marxism allowed little opportunity for those hoping to assert the autonomy of aesthetic discourse. Indeed the experience of the 1930s was, for many, one of disillusionment in which the promise of left-wing politics had turned instead into a nightmare in which the turn to the left had not enabled intellectuals to assert the autonomy of the aesthetic from the economic, but rather had resulted in the subjugation of the aesthetic by the political. In this context, then, the promise of a traditionalist, anti-bourgeoisie rhetoric was not just appealing, but a necessary solution to a fundamental problem. However, as with the appropriation of left-wing critiques, the appropriation of the New Criticism did not finally undermine the authority and legitimacy of the bourgeoisie, but ultimately reinforced it. If offered a means of asserting the superiority, authority, and legitimacy of bourgeois culture, even as it criticised bourgeois economics.

Ultimately, then, while the New Critics did dramatically transform the academy, their definition of literature was based on a fundamental repression of the very social and historical conditions which had produced it, and this problem not only made their position contradictory, but also left it open to appropriation by groups with quite different interests and ambitions.

10

William Empson

Michael Wood

> Do words make up the majesty
> Of man, and his justice
> Between the stones and the void?
>
> Geoffrey Hill, 'Three Baroque Meditations'

William Empson's first book, *Seven Types of Ambiguity*, begun while he was an undergraduate at Cambridge, was published in 1930, when he was twenty-four. It established him at once and permanently as one of the two most brilliant practitioners of what he called verbal analysis, more commonly known as close reading. Only R. P. Blackmur had equal (if differently angled) gifts, and the two men were often grouped together as the critics who, as Stanley Edgar Hyman said, 'did the work' of intricate literary exploration, where others had preached or proposed it.

'Close reading' is a familiar phrase now, but we need to pause over it for a moment, since its implications have shifted rather drastically over the years, as those of catchphrases often do. I. A. Richards, Empson's teacher at Cambridge, later said his former pupil's 'minute examinations ... raised the standards of ambition and achievement in a difficult and very hazardous art'. The art was reading, and Richards himself had discovered (and reported in *Practical Criticism* (1929)) how inattentive and prejudiced even apparently serious reading could be. Close reading was rigorous reading, the opposite of loose or distant or offhand appreciation or criticism, and its appetite for detail produced many surprises. It was meant to complement historical knowledge, indeed might be said itself to offer historical knowledge, since the behaviour of words is an aspect of social life. Close reading then became a major instrument of the New Criticism, and the technique gradually came to suggest, in the minds of its detractors and sometimes even in the minds of its proponents, a concentration on the text to the exclusion of all context, as if words in literature had a separate, exclusive, self-contained life. Both half-truths are half-true, of course: literary language is different from and entangled in the ordinary language of its day. At present close reading, as a fading slogan, seems chiefly to mean a radical refusal of history, a vision of the literary text as a perfected and unalterable verbal structure, a paradise of poised irony and ambiguity, invulnerable to time or politics. Empson and Richards would have been shocked, were shocked at this development; and much of Empson's later work takes issue with what he sees as a concerted academic attempt to take literature away from lived experience.

Empson himself later saw his first book as caught in two cross-currents, leading him, as he thought, away from verbal analysis: the work of Eliot and the work of Freud. In Eliot he found an authority for his enthusiasm for Donne and the Metaphysical Poets, and more generally for writing in which intellect and feeling are inextricably mixed. In Freud Empson discovered a series of hints about the mind's ingenuity and its capacity for complicated, multi-layered thought; and about the possible revelations of mind in language.

These are very large currents, affecting not only Empson but the whole age; and they seem in fact to have led Empson back to analysis rather than away from it. To them we should add the specific influences of Richards, a man always wanting to know how language worked, and of a quirky and interesting book by Robert Graves and Laura Riding called *A Survey of Modernist Poetry* (1927), to which Empson attributed the 'invention' of the method he was using.

'The method of verbal analysis is of course the main point of the book', Empson remarks with gruff bluster. 'Method' is one of Empson's favourite words, along with 'trick' (sometimes 'trick of thought'), 'machinery', and a whole series of images for oblique or reclusive locations in the mind: 'the back of your mind', 'the back of his mind', 'wandering about in your mind', 'lying about in his mind'. These words are used in various ways – the 'trick', for example, is usually in the language of the poem, the 'method' and the 'machinery' belong to the critic, the 'mind' is the poet's or the reader's or both – but taken together they tell us quite a bit about Empson's stance, as indeed does the cool, laboratory-tinged word 'analysis'. Their brusqueness or apparent casualness indicates an allegiance to Richards and the 'psychologists' of literature: no truck with the refined or merely aesthetic approach, the sniffing of poetic posies.

But Empson's favourite words also reflect further and not entirely compatible assumptions and movements of thought. The words are strenuously modest, down-to-earth, almost dismissive of their high objects. Of course it is because he cares so much about those objects – literature, language, the mind, the project of understanding ourselves and others – that Empson can afford to seem dismissive, but we shouldn't ignore the stylistic signal. It suggests, among other things, that technical languages, whether scientific or literary, cannot bring us closer to the language of poetry; that with any luck we shall already know what he means; that criticism is a lumpish, clumsy, secondhand business and had better not try to be anything else; that Empson urgently wishes not to add to the stock of the world's nonsense. There is a certain amount of delusion here, a dandyism in the very modesty of the verbal means, and Empson's later vocabulary dips further and further into apparent negligence, off-hand assaults on what he takes to be scholarly decorum. But the delusion is a generous one, and in any case scarcely affects the general stance. Empson mentions Wittgenstein in a poem, but doesn't speak of him otherwise; yet his position here has real affinities with that of the philosopher. 'What *we* do', Wittgenstein said, 'is to bring words back from their metaphysical to their everyday use.' Empson also thinks the everyday use of words may take us further than we ordinarily assume, and should help to diminish our intellectual arrogance. 'Philosophy', Wittgenstein memorably remarked, 'is a battle against the bewitchment of our intelligence by means of language.' Empson's brand of literary criticism is precisely that – except that *being bewitched* by language is also part of the struggle, so that to be entirely cured would be to have lost rather than won the battle. The bewitchment is to be understood, reasoned about; but not banished.

Empson's use of the word 'method' is thus a serious linguistic gesture, but not a serious promise. We might say the dazzling *performance* of verbal analysis is the main point of the book, *is* the book. Empson describes a famous speech in *Macbeth* as 'words hissed in the passage where servants were passing, which must be swaddled with darkness, loaded as it were in themselves with fearful powers':

> If th'Assassination
> Could trammell up the Consequence, and catch
> With his surcease, Success . . .

His may apply to Duncan, *assassination* or *consequence*. *Success* means fortunate result, result whether fortunate or not, and succession to the throne. And *catch*, the single little flat word among these monsters, names an action; it is a mark of human inadequacy to deal with these matters of statecraft, a child snatching at the moon as she rides thunder-clouds. The meanings cannot all be remembered at once, however often you read it; it remains the incantation of a murderer, dishevelled and fumbling among the powers of darkness.

This is criticism which attends to the behaviour of words, but also evokes the dark rich world of the words, analysis which is also appreciation, and the book is crammed with such instances. Reading *Seven Types of Ambiguity* we discover (even if we know them already) poem after poem, passage after passage, swarming verbal life everywhere: in Pope, Sidney, Nashe, Dryden, Eliot, Donne, Herbert, Shakespeare, Hopkins. *Macbeth* is a kind of touchstone, provides recurring examples, as if murder and ambition were ambiguity's particular home. 'Light thickens', Macbeth says, and Empson writes:

there is a suggestion of witches' broth, or curdling blood, about *thickens*, which the vowel sound of *light*, coming next to it, with the movement of stirring treacle, and the cluck of the k-sounds, intensify; a suggestion, too, of harsh, limpid echo, and, under careful feet of poachers, an abrupt crackling of sticks.

But to insist only on the critical performance is to miss the interest of Empson's theory, and to enter too far into the diffidence about the intellect which is so much a feature of intellectual life in our century. It is true there is a great deal of confusion surrounding Empson's conception of ambiguity, and Empson does little to help us, indeed he positively fuels the confusion. He later said the term had been 'more or less superseded by the idea of a double meaning which is intended to be fitted into a definite structure', and his critics have always thought he merely meant to talk about multiple meaning. Empson invited this response by being hazy about his types ('In a sense the sixth class is included within the fourth') and by indulging in dizzying afterthoughts about whether he had placed his examples where they needed to be ('the last example of my fourth chapter belongs by rights to the fifth or to the sixth').

The effective order of *Seven Types of Ambiguity* is finally neither logical nor psychological, but dramatic: a rising order of intensity of contradiction, a movement from mild to desperate ambiguities. An ambiguity in Hopkins, for example, is said to give 'a transient and exhausting satisfaction' to two opposed desires, provoked by 'different systems of judgement'; 'and the two systems of judgement are forced into open conflict before the reader': 'Such a process, one might imagine, could pierce to regions that underlie the whole structure of our thought; could tap the energies of the very depths of the mind.'

Even the mild versions of ambiguity, though, involve serious conflict or hesitation about meaning, and Empson could legitimately have made much larger claims for his word than he did. 'Effects worth calling ambiguous', Empson says, 'occur when the possible alternative meanings of a word or grammar are used to give alternative meanings to the sentence.' He also speaks of 'alternative reactions'. In practice ambiguities are interesting or important only when the alternative meanings clash in some way, allow language to enact a puzzle or a problem which is bothering a person or a culture. We may borrow one of Empson's early and much discussed examples, from a Shakespeare sonnet, in which the branches of an autumn forest are called 'Bare ruined choirs, where late the sweet birds sang'. The birds may be literal, singing late among the branches/ruins. Or they may be the choristers who used to sing when the church was not a ruin – before the Dissolution of the Monasteries say. *Late* would then mean *lately*. *Sang* (rather than *sing*) gets a touch of lament into both readings: even if the birds are literal and really sang late, their summer song is over now. Empson finds a host of other implications in the metaphor, and says 'there is a sort of ambiguity in not knowing which of them to hold most clearly in mind'. Such 'machinations of ambiguity are among the very roots of poetry'. But the energy in the line surely comes from our hesitation between radically different meanings rather than from a general uncertainty. A picturesque ruin, birdsong at evening: the image is drastically at odds with the other possibility, the haunted memory of an unruined time. Shakespeare is talking of age in this sonnet ('That time of year thou mayst in me behold/When yellow leaves, or none, or few, do hang/Upon those boughs'), and rival emotions about the prospect fight it out in the imagery. Acceptance or regret? Are the yellow leaves gracefully fading, or angrily withered? Empson's poems offer good examples of ambiguity in just this troubled sense, conundrums about courage and patience and love. *Flight* means soaring and grandeur, but also escape, running away, and both sets of intimations are active, worried at. *Seven Types of Ambiguity* ends by evoking the most spectacular ambiguity of all, drawn from George Herbert: the crucified Christ, weighed down with the sins of the world, is also a mischievous child in the orchard of Eden, climbing a forbidden tree.

There is a word which covers much of this ground, which includes ambiguity and a number of other, related practices. The word is irony, but we need to understand it, not only as a stance or a structure, but as the reflection of a frame of mind, a complex cultural achievement. 'Human life', Empson says, 'is so much a matter of juggling with contradictory impulses (Christian–worldly, sociable–independent, and such-like) that one is accustomed to thinking people are probably sensible if they follow first one, then the other, of two such courses.' I'm not sure how accustomed 'one' is to making this assumption about 'people'. I'm sure one was even less accustomed to it in 1930 than one is now; and Empson acknowledges that such behaviour may merely seem foolish. But that makes his claim all the more striking, an instance of literary criticism reaching out into speculative social psychology.

I might say, putting this more strongly, that in the present state of indecision of the cultured world people do, in fact, hold all the beliefs, however contradictory, that turn up in poetry, in the sense that they are liable to use them all in coming to decisions.

There is a nervous, distinctly modernist flavour to this statement, but it also has Empson's own pluralising note. It's not that we have lost our beliefs but that we have so many; not that truth is gone but that 'absolutely anything ... may turn out to be true'.

Irony in this sense is a global name for what Empson calls the 'shifts and blurred aggregates of thought by which men come to a practical decision'.

It is close to Henry James's sense of irony as a projection of 'the always possible other case', and also to Eliot's notion of wit as involving 'probably, a recognition, implicit in the expression of every experience, of other kinds of experience which are possible'. Empson's formulation, characteristically, evokes a hesitation which is absorbed rather than simply overcome:

> people, often, cannot have done both of two things, but they must have been in some way prepared to have done either; whichever they did, they will have still lingering in their minds the way they would have preserved their self-respect if they had acted differently; they are only to be understood by bearing both possibilities in mind.

Meaning then may include not only a communicated message but a barely communicated (or unconsciously communicated) indication of the self's relation to the self, the trace not only of the mind's decisions, but of the way it watched itself deciding.

The mind here begins to sound like a character in Henry James, or like a poem by Marvell. Perhaps we should say that these mental and linguistic processes, however swift and familiar and ordinary, *are* complicated and delicate, but so thoroughly taken for granted that any extended talk of them is bound to seem strangely refined and teasing. In what is perhaps the most spectacular (and amusing) passage in *Seven Types of Ambiguity*, Empson argues that he has not discovered ambiguity, or overrated it, but simply persuaded an old cultural habit to dare to speak its name. Some of his readers, he hopes, 'will have shared the excitement' of the writing,

> will have felt that it casts a new light on the very nature of language, and must either be all nonsense or very startling and new. A glance at an annotated edition of Shakespeare, however, will be enough to dispel this generous illusion; most of what I find to say about Shakespeare has been copied out of the Arden text. I believe, indeed, that I am using in a different way the material that three centuries of scholars and critics have collected . . .

We may feel that Empson has 'copied out' this material in a peculiarly provocative or imaginative fashion, rather as Borges, say, 'copied' the work of Stevenson or Chesterton or Wells; but Empson himself is doggedly straightfaced on the subject.

> The conservative attitude to ambiguity is curious and no doubt wise . . . the reader is encouraged to swallow the thing by a decent reserve; it is thought best not to let him know that he is thinking in such a complicated medium.

Empson then quotes the Arden editor on the subject of all the things the word *rooky* does *not* mean in *Macbeth* (it doesn't mean murky or dusky or damp, misty or gloomy, and 'has *nothing* to do with the dialectic word "roke"'), and we seem suddenly to have entered the world of *Catch-22*

('When didn't you say we couldn't punish you' 'I always didn't say you couldn't punish me, sir'). Empson comments, 'There is no doubt how such a note acts; it makes you bear in mind all the meanings it puts forward'; and possibly the Arden editor 'secretly believed in a great many of his alternatives at once'. That secret belief, and the strenuous insistence on the public properness of only one of the alternatives, provide a model for what we might call the enabling fiction of understanding. We simplify for our convenience and our sanity; the muffled memory of how much we have simplified preserves something of the richness of our relation to the world.

Empson glances at the subject of pastoral once or twice in *Seven Types of Ambiguity*. The pleasure of pastoral, he says, arises from a 'clash between different modes of feeling', specifically the feeling that 'the characters of pastoral ... are at once very rustic and rather over-civilised'. In this phrasing pastoral looks like a broad mode of ambiguity, but it seems to serve more generally as a flexible structure of irony, with meanings sometimes clashing and sometimes converging and sometimes being held in suspension, like elements of a metaphor. In his next book, *Some Versions of Pastoral* (1935), Empson argues that the genre works by 'putting the complex into the simple', a characteristically offhand formulation for an extraordinarily various and complicated process. Pastoral assumes 'that you can say everything about complex people by a complete consideration of simple people'. It assumes this, but doesn't, we may guess, usually believe it; it is a strategy or a gesture, not an assertion.

The essential trick of the old pastoral ... was to make simple people express strong feelings (felt as the most universal subject, something fundamentally true about everybody) in learned and fashioned language (so that you wrote about the best subject in the best way).

Empson then traces the trick into areas we are not likely to think of as pastoral at all, but where the same play between the complex and the simple occurs; in proletarian literature, for example, in a Shakespeare sonnet, in Shakespearean and other double plots, in commentaries on Milton, in *The Beggar's Opera*, in *Alice in Wonderland*. Marvell's poem 'The Garden' is perhaps the only instance in the book where we *expect* pastoral ideas to be at work, and Empson begins his chapter on Marvell with a comparison to Buddhism. The conception of pastoral grows very large in this process, larger than a genre and certainly larger than a trick, becomes something like a cluster of related ideas, scattered over various cultures, and characteristically expressed in a particular set of tones and registers. Christopher Norris speaks of its 'ironic latitudes' and calls it 'more a species of extended dramatic metaphor than a definite form or distinctive structure of meaning'. 'It is the very queerness of the trick', Empson says, 'that makes it so often useful in building models of the human mind.'

'The waste remains', Empson writes in a poem called 'Missing Dates' (1937), 'the waste remains and kills.' The ideas which are 'naturally at home with most versions of pastoral' are those associated with limitation and underemployment, what Empson calls 'the inadequacy of life', the sense that the world may fall short of even fairly modest demands, and these ideas are what gives unity to this book – by far the most fluent and coherent and attractive of Empson's works, although not, I think, the most powerful or the most suggestive. There is some splendidly jaunty paraphrase of difficult texts, and there are several moments where the prose flies as high as critical prose is likely to get. The Classical Faunus in Milton's Eden is 'a ghost crying in the cold of paradise', and the reader of a Donne poem is 'safely recalled from the interplanetary spaces, baffled among the cramped, inverted, cannibal, appallingly tangled impulses that are his home upon the world'. A cold paradise and a tangled safety: no place quite like home. In this book Empson also finds the perfect metaphor for the mind as he sees it, an image which takes us further than any analytic definition could. He speaks of the different shades of opinion to be found in an Elizabethan, and presumably any audience; of the audience as 'an inter-conscious unit' trying to understand a play. An audience is thus a working-model of ambiguity, a set of unlike minds in communication, and Empson remarks that the difference between the theatre and the psyche is 'only a practical one': 'Once you break into the godlike unity of the appreciator you find a microcosm of which the theatre is the macrocosm; the mind is complex and ill-connected like an audience'. Ambiguity is the audience allowed to be itself.

But the most significant feature of *Some Versions of Pastoral* is probably its brilliant sketch of a theory of irony in the context of the double plot, along with certain afterthoughts which come up in the *Beggar's Opera* chapter. 'An irony', Empson says, 'has no point unless it is true, in some degree, in both senses': we don't merely mean something other than what we say, we mean what we say as well.

The fundamental impulse of irony is to score off both the arguments that have been puzzling you, both sets of sympathies in your mind, both sorts of fool who will hear you... The essential is for the author to repeat the audience in himself, and he may safely seem to do nothing more. No doubt he has covertly, if it is a good irony, to reconcile the opposites into a larger unity, or suggest a balanced position by setting out two extreme views, or accept a lie ... to find energy to accept a truth, or something like that...

Empson goes on to speak of the 'machinery' of irony as a 'dramatic ambiguity', but I think this confuses the issue slightly. As Empson's examples make clear ('the skyline beyond skyline' of irony in *Don Quixote*), an irony doesn't require a clash or hesitation among implications, yet must be more than a simple multiplication of meaning. There is irony whenever two or several meanings are felt to be indispensable; irony specialises therefore in the unspoken, in mobilising all the thoughts or feelings which belong inseparably to a situation, which can't and shouldn't be made to go away, but which can't directly be expressed. Irony in this form not only involves the unspoken but hints at the unspeakable, and is the most haunting of all the versions of pastoral. We find it in modern literature, in Günter Grass and García Márquez, for example, when the language of decency and humanity is required to encompass the obscenity and inhumanity of history. 'Many years later, as he faced the firing squad, Colonel Aureliano Buendía was to remember...'. Violence hides in the very casualness of the interpolated clause.

If there was a tilt toward psychology in *Seven Types of Ambiguity*, there is in *Some Versions of Pastoral* a leaning toward sociology. It's true that Empson says the book 'is not a solid piece of sociology' but we may be a little surprised to find him thinking of it as a piece of sociology at all. Pastoral itself though is a social idea, a means of negotiating, among other things, matters of class and visions of alternative social orders, and it is in this context that the question of waste arises.

Commenting on what he calls the ideology of Gray's *Elegy*, its slightly fraudulent claim that certain social arrangements are unfortunate but unalterable, and have plenty of parallels in nature – the hidden gem and the flower that blushes unseen don't *care* about their lack of opportunities as a man or woman may – Empson sees the fraud but also the rather desolate continuing truth:

it is only in degree that any improvement of society could prevent wastage of human powers; the waste even in a fortunate life, the isolation even of a life rich in intimacy, cannot but be felt deeply, and is the central feeling of tragedy.

Of course we may feel, as Empson himself no doubt did, that degrees of improvement are always important, and that the entire abolition of waste can't really be imagined, not even when the state has withered away. But the waste will always sadden us when we think of it or experience it, and may induce in us at times what Empson calls a 'generous distaste for the conditions of life', a 'feeling that life is essentially inadequate to the human spirit, and yet that a good life must avoid saying so'. It is important to see that Empson is not preaching here, not telling us that life *is* inadequate to the human spirit. He is inviting us to recognise a widely shared human feeling, and one for which pastoral seems the ideal expression. The ideal positive expression, we should perhaps add. Tragedy is the

mode where the horror of waste finds its full accounting; and comedy
redeems waste, recycles it for renewed and integrated use. Pastoral acknowledges waste and allows us to place it, to find room for it and to
remember what else there is in life. We can be 'torn by feelings', in
Empson's words, without being torn apart; there is a form of wit, of irony,
which survives horror without reaching redemption. We can learn a style
from a despair, as Empson says in his best-known poem, 'This Last Pain'.
This wouldn't have to be a pastoral performance, but it would have the
pastoral's mixture of submerged distress and resolute gaity.

Empson's next critical book, *The Structure of Complex Words*, appeared
in 1951. Its interesting theoretical proposals are cluttered with busy
symbols for the notation of meaning and mood (A for sense, (A) for sense
at the back of the mind, + and – for warmer and colder intimations, £ for
mood, ? for covert reference, and so on). It's as if there were two Empsons
at work here: the critic (and poet) of subtle, generous, even reckless mind;
and some sort of linguistic auditor, anxiously hovering with his tables and
his abacus. Empson recognises this distinction in the organisation of his
book ('The reader interested in literary criticism will find his meat' in the
central chapters), and hopes we shan't be too impatient with his linguistic
theory. He is of course right to suggest that 'even a moderate step forward
in our understanding of language would do a good deal to improve
literary criticism'. Still, the book is an odd affair; and the implied, or
scattered theory seems more significant than the one so concentratedly
insisted on.

Cleanth Brooks, reviewing *The Structure of Complex Words*, said
Empson was 'the incorrigible amateur, the man with a knack', but he is
trying very hard to be professional here, or at least to tidy up the mess the
professionals have left. Empson's chief topic is what he calls 'equations'
among the senses of a single word, and he proposes four types of equation
(1 where the context calls for a meaning which is not the chief or usual
meaning of the word, so the chief meaning is there but not in the foreground; 2 where the chief meaning *and* a series of implications are
invoked; 3 a reversal of 1, so that the chief meaning is in the foreground *as*
meaning, but not immediately applicable to the object, the usual mode of
metaphor; 4 where the different meanings are offered as the same meanings, as in many forms of paradox). He readily agrees that 'a classification
... can cover a field without telling us anything important about it'; we
may wonder whether this almost impenetrable classification isn't actually
distracting. What is fascinating here, of course, is not the classifying but
the very idea of an equation, which both narrows down Empson's continuing inquiry into language and the mind, gives him a closer field to work
in, and broadens its social implications.

Empson's engagement is now with words rather than images or idioms or pieces of grammar. And with words rather than what writers make of them. This distinction seems rather dodgy in practice, since Empson is using so many literary examples, but has a real theoretical interest. We might not be able to tell in any given case whether Pope or Shakespeare was personally bending the meaning of a word or exploiting a contemporary shift in its sense, but that would not be a reason for thinking the activities are not different. It is the old puzzle, in Saussure's terms, of *langue* and *parole*: Empson wants us to look at points where *parole* reaches into *langue*, begs its blessing and its grace.

It is in this spirit that he studies 'wit' in Pope's *Essay in Criticism*, 'all' in *Paradise Lost*, 'dog' in *Timon of Athens*, 'honest' in *Othello*, 'sense' in *The Prelude*, and so on. *All* the meanings of a word are its history. They may not be present in any particular poem or speech act, and of course they may die and no longer be available at all; but language lives through the changing traffic of such meanings, and we could, in such a world of riches, scarcely *not* say more than we intend. Indeed Empson argues that our small jokes, and the deck of thoughts and feelings we take for granted, perhaps scarcely recognise, 'carry doctrines more really complex than the whole structure of [our] official view of the world'. We do much of our most significant moral and emotional business through 'these vague rich intimate words'. So much for the Elizabethan (or Renaissance, or Medieval) world-view, which now needs conflating with our intuitions about the unspoken (but still linguistic) underworld, or what Empson calls the 'shrubbery of smaller ideas'. 'This may be an important matter for a society, because its accepted official beliefs may be things that would be fatal unless in some degree kept at bay.'

'Doctrine' is a key word here. True to his pursuit of reason even into the heartland of feeling, Empson insists that words say things, even when they are emotionally or confusedly employed, that they imply whole doctrines which we must attend to. 'Talkers are casual and often silly but they are up to something.' 'Doctrine' is used with slight irony, since Empson's whole point is that the doctrines he is interested in are not formulated as such; but even in this sense a doctrine is quite a long way from a trick, and *The Structure of Complex Words* is certainly Empson's most ambitious work. His 'critical *summa*', as Norris says? The book lacks the sheer thrill of *Seven Types of Ambiguity*, the sweep of argument of *Some Versions of Pastoral*, and Empson himself compares it to a lumbering old aircraft, rather slow to get off the ground. But it flies him over rich and rough and genuinely uncharted linguistic territory, and it contains what is no doubt his single most powerful piece of literary criticism, an essay where worrying about language, the old habit of 'verbal analysis', leads to the most daunting questions raised by one of the most difficult plays in the world.

Empson prefaces his study of *King Lear* with an examination of Erasmus's *Praise of Folly*, and of related images of foolishness. Folly has a
circle of meanings running from simple-mindedness to sanctity, taking in
the senses of *dupe, clown, lunatic, jester, knave*, and so on. Erasmus
suggests that certain forms of folly may be the ultimate wisdom. Shakespeare touches on this feeling, but more often, Empson argues, he makes
the equation fool = clown, often in intensely painful contexts, where the
clown is also some kind of madman. How are we to read Macbeth's 'Why
should I play the Roman fool, and die/On my own sword'? Is he asking
whether he should play the fool or not, or is the stress, as Empson wants to
think, on '*Roman* fool', 'so as to make him imply that he has got to play
some kind of clown's part anyway'? Either way the sense of the clown is
prominent.

In *King Lear* a sort of simplicity is learned through madness, that is, 'not
merely through suffering, but through having been a clown'. This seems
like a demonised version of Erasmus's thought: Christian theology as a
form of sublime farce. *King Lear*, Empson suggests, is about incomplete
renunciation, about an old king who 'has made a fool of himself on the
most cosmic and appalling scale possible; he has got on the wrong side of
the next world as well as on the wrong side of this one'. More than half the
chief characters in this play become fools in one sense or another (and
often in several), and the famous 'ripeness' of 'Ripeness is all' suggests not
calm maturity, but an exhausted blossoming into madness and death,
Lear as dying fool rejoins Erasmus's figure of folly, but his wisdom is of a
strange and depleted, almost dazed kind:

And the scapegoat who has collected all this wisdom for us is viewed at the end
with a sort of hushed envy, not I think really because he has become wise but
because the general human desire for experience has been so glutted in him; he has
been through everything.

'Everything' includes experiences we can scarcely imagine, since we have
learned among other things that 'there is no worst', because 'the worst' is
nameable, and there may be even worse in store for us than that. Even the
madmen (fools, clowns, jesters) 'cannot tell us directly what the worst is,
but they allow us to peer into the abyss for knowledge about the bases of
the world'.

Empson's essay on *Tom Jones*, first published in *The Kenyon Review* in
1958, and reprinted in *Using Biography* in 1984, returns to the question
of irony, but applies it to a reading of the novel which is both close and
broad, a 'defence', as Empson says, which seeks to show the intelligence
and moral grandeur of a work is often seen as enjoyable but merely
'hearty'. The result is a revision of a masterpiece which amounts to a
reinstatement; and includes the startling claim that a thorough-going

ironist must at last not know the answers to the questions he is asking. Irony at this point becomes not poise or mastery but the deepest kind of doubt. The case at issue is Christ's command to forgive our enemies. Tom Jones does this and is rebuked by the apparently all-perfect Allworthy. Is this another chink in the good man's armour (there have been others), or is Fielding himself hesitating about how far the Gospel should be followed in practice? What is attractive is Empson's notion that a thoughtful writer would do well to be uncertain on such a point; and his insistence that Tom himself rises to quite genuine ethical heights anyway, whatever Fielding's possible hesitations. The essay offers an important counterbalance to the *Lear* essay, as indeed Empson might say *Tom Jones* does to *King Lear*: the celebration of goodness needs to acknowledge everything that might wreck the occasion; but the dark night of the worst (which is not the worst) can be lit, at least for those who have survived it, by the example of a world of generous impulse.

'God is on trial', Empson says in his next book *Milton's God* (1961), 'and the reason is that all the characters are on trial in any civilized narrative.' Empson's sense of justice requires that even Satan (especially Satan) should have a fair trial, and he writes persuasively, here and in earlier works, about the ruined grandeur of the fallen angel. Satan has responded to what Empson calls 'an intellectually interesting temptation' – he wasn't right to have rebelled but he could have been – and the same is true of the temptation of Adam and Eve. We need to realise that Milton, 'here as in all the other cases, pitches a temptation staggeringly high'. In *Some Versions of Pastoral* Empson found the Fall crazily heroic, a difficult question addressed to God – 'It is a terrific fancy, the Western temper at its height; the insane disproportion of the act to its effects implies a vast zest for heroic action' – but he now seems to have answered the question once and for all. 'The Christian God the Father, the God of Tertullian, Augustine and Aquinas, is the wickedest thing yet invented by the black heart of man', because Christianity, alone among the world religions, 'dragged back the Neolithic craving for human sacrifice into its basic structure'. Christianity celebrates the torture of a son by a father, and the effect, Empson argues, must be 'morally corrupting' – the worshipper has to think of his/her god as a sadist. This imputation seems fairly wild, and Empson himself supposes that 'most present-day Christians of all sects feel sure that they may reject it'; but then he brings us up short by citing Aquinas on a particular aspect of the 'beatitude' of the blessed: they get to watch the damned being tortured. Why aren't we more shocked by this? As Empson says, it really is close to the spirit of the concentration camp. The difficulty with the book is that Empson's awful God is so real that it takes an effort of the will to think of him as a human invention, and that the *invention* of such a creature, such an extraordinary image of goodness and love, is what Empson defines as a moral evil.

Milton's God is rousing stuff, as Empson said of one of his own early poems. Students of Milton will always want to read it and argue with it, and many of us will retain a firm affection for it, gratitude even, for its courage and its extravagance. But it does not enlarge or alter Empson's place in the history of criticism and we need to note a new crudeness in many of Empson's arguments, an air of impatience and contempt, a hurry to win arguments even before they have started. What used to be breezy paraphrase has become tilted summary, a bullying of the reader. It is true, for example, that Milton says he has set out to 'justify the ways of God to man', and that 'justify' may indicate more uncertainty about the outcome than modern Christians like to contemplate. But Milton does *not* say he is 'struggling to make his God appear less wicked'; or that he has written his poem 'to justify God for creating a world so full of sin and misery'. This is Empson the ventriloquist speaking, keen to convict God, repeatedly breaking his own splendid rule about all the characters being on trial in a civilised narrative.

Faustus and the Censor, a manuscript patiently recovered and edited by John Henry Jones, and published in 1987, three years after Empson's death, shows Marlowe going one better than Milton, refusing God's orders and inventing a Faustus who is not damned, a Mephistopheles who is not a demon but a middle spirit, the sort who steals children and whisks them off to the fairies. Mephistopheles wants Faustus's soul, and Faustus wants to become a middle spirit himself and then die like a beast, rather than be damned eternally. Faustus therefore won't need his soul in the end, so Mephistopheles can have it – a reasonable deal, and neither God nor Lucifer get a look-in. Mephistopheles plays various tricks, to be sure, but finally Faustus, having feared hell and hoped for heaven, realises that what awaits him is oblivion, and 'dies in the arms of his deceitful friend with immense relief, also gratitude, surprise, love, forgiveness, and exhaustion. It is the happiest death in all drama.'

This, Empson argues, is the play Marlowe wrote, and traces of it are everywhere in the texts we have. 'It makes a wonderful play, once allowed its full variety of incident, with the soggy weight of sanctimonious horror removed.' Unfortunately, it was too radical, and too unbelieving, the censor took it in hand, and either Marlowe or someone else gave it the conventional slant, demonised the spirits, Christianised Faustus's fault, and made sure he was damned. For good measure Empson includes a guess at how the missing parts of the play went.

There is, as far as I know, no evidence at all to support this brilliant theory. Some scholars have found it eccentric or worse; others have found it entirely plausible, the beginning of a new understanding of Marlowe and his age. The writing has an extraordinary energy and power of persuasion, none of the hectoring which mars *Milton's God*, and I am tempted to think of the work as a remarkable historical novel, or a narrative poem along the lines of Pound's translations or reconstructions of Provence. There is more, though.

The unspoken was always Empson's realm, and he reminds us that we need to consider not only what a book says but 'what it leaves lying about'. The *Dr Faustus* we have, in any version, is fragmentary, a 'ruin', as Empson puts it; and some of the fragments 'gloat' over the fate of the man whom other fragments seem to celebrate. The standard answer to this riddle is to say Marlowe wrote only the good bits, but Empson will have none of this, since it rests on 'the mandarin superstition that one can always "spot" an author, as if he were a glass of port'. What Empson 'spots' here with the aid of the translation of the German *Faustbook*, which Marlowe must have worked from, is the sort of energy which makes a popular work reach into a whole array of sentiments in a culture, and therefore become dangerous. Another superstition, perhaps, but a demotic one.

Empson has trouble with Mephistopheles. If he's not a devil really, he must be pretending to be one in order to scare Faustus into the right frame of mind. We can reject this argument at once on Empson's own grounds: because it trivialises some of the best lines in the play. 'Why, this is hell, nor am I out of it', Mephistopheles says in answer to Faustus's question on the whereabouts of hell. Hell is not a place, but a condition, and it is dim of Faustus to be so literal about it; Mephistopheles is actually frightened by the degree of Faustus's dimness, which is a form of frivolity in the face of horror. We may not like the Christian hell, but it gives a tremendous power to this confrontation, as the notion of Mephistopheles merely borrowing the Satanic vocabulary doesn't.

Faustus himself is another matter, and he does speak of 'eternal death' where we might expect him to speak of hell or damnation; and he does call Lucifer 'Chief Lord and regent of perpetual night', which sounds rather peaceful for a realm of endless torment. Empson's reading gives real dignity to the Faustus who says he doesn't believe in hell, and it catches the flickering grandeur of *some* of Faustus's claims about magic. We need to note that whatever Empson himself believes he is doing, his idea of evidence is really critical rather than historical: 'the best evidence for this theory of the play is that it gives point and thrust to so many of the details'. 'All this part is so brilliant when restored that I feel I cannot have gone wrong.' Well, he can have gone wrong, and probably has, if 'right' means plausible or correct. But he has written a critical fable of considerable power, a *counter-Faustus* which multiplies the possibilities of understanding a troublesome text, and which raises the question of what this text or any text is. Not least of the challenges Empson sets us is where we are to stand if we want to contradict him. We can almost certainly get closer to historical probability than he does, but not if we smugly think we are already there. Empson ended his career as he began, rattling at the comfort of a consensus, and finding meanings no one else had thought to look for.

11

R. P. Blackmur

Michael Wood

> And as you cry, Impossible,
> A step is on the stairs.
>
> Randall Jarrell, 'Hope'

'Form is a way of thinking', R. P. Blackmur wrote, and form was one of his cherished, recurring words. Yet he cannot plausibly be called a formalist, and it is entirely characteristic of his criticism that he should use an apparently smaller concept – technique – to get him into even larger territories. His approach, he said in 1935, in an essay called 'A Critic's Job of Work', was

> primarily through the technique, in the widest sense of that word, of the examples handled; technique on the plane of words and even … linguistics … but also technique on the plane of intellectual and emotional patterns … and technique, too, in that there is a technique of securing and arranging and representing a fundamental view of life.

It may help to suggest that Blackmur's early work concentrated on technique in the first sense, with plenty of glances at the others, while his later work examined technique chiefly in the last sense; and that the middle sense never left him, early or late. This grouping corresponds very roughly to a focus on poetry and poets in the first books – e.g., *The Double Agent* (1935), *The Expense of Greatness* (1940) (much of this work reappearing in *Language as Gesture* (1952) and again in *Form and Value in Modern Poetry* (1957)) – and on prose and society in the later ones – e.g., *The Lion and the Honeycomb* (1955), *Eleven Essays in the European Novel* (1964), *A Primer of Ignorance* (1967). Henry James and Henry Adams, however, were permanent presences, in success as in failure, heroes and saints, instances and admonitions. Blackmur's essays on James have been gathered as *Studies in Henry James* (1983), and an eloquent fragment of his unfinished work on Adams, a selection from some seven hundred pages of manuscript, appeared as *Henry Adams* in 1980.

Blackmur was born in 1904 and, largely self-taught, became one of the most erratically learned critics of the century. In later life he was a highly regarded if not always easily understood professor of English at Princeton, showered with national and international honours. He died in 1965. Criticism, he said, was like walking: 'a pretty nearly universal art'. Both arts 'require a constant intricate shifting and catching of balance; neither can be questioned much in process; and few perform either really well'. Most of us, he thought, 'prefer paved walks or some form of rapid transit – some easy theory or outmastering dogma'.

The advantage of what he called the technical approach, he suggested, was that it 'readily admits other approaches and is anxious to be complemented by them', and that it doesn't confuse technique with other matters. It is able to see, for example, as Blackmur does in his work on Yeats and Eliot, how a system of beliefs, magic or religion, can function technically in a poem, and how, in a poem, that is all a system needs to do: 'not emotion put into doctrine from outside, but doctrine presented as emotion'. Conversely, Hardy, for Blackmur, was a poet who was likely to lumber his verse with the ready-made intellectual baggage of his time, 'a thicket of ideas, formulas, obsessions, indisciplined compulsions'. Hardy's poetry was therefore at its best when it shed these ideas or found more personal, technically manageable ones, converted them into a style, which in turn was 'reduced to riches'.

The great modern heresy, according to Blackmur, was the cult of spontaneity, of 'despotically construed emotions' which went, he thought, with fanaticism in politics. The heresy's favourite shape was the 'plague', the 'stultifying fallacy' of expressive form: 'the faith ... that if a thing is only intensely enough felt its mere expression in words will give it satisfactory form'. On the contrary, Blackmur argued, mere expression produces mere litter, a sentimental gesture toward the poetry we have not managed to create. 'Poetry, if we understand it, is not in immediacy at all ... Poetry is life at the remove of form and meaning; not life lived but life framed and identified.' Form for Blackmur was thus neither the antidote to habit and function proposed by the Russian Formalists, nor the high Aristotelian structure erected by the Chicago School; neither estranged nor monument. It was a chastening of the heart, in Yeats's phrase; but as Eliot would have said, only people with hearts can need the chastening.

It is true that Blackmur's chastening could sound stuffy, and that it didn't always find the words it needed. The 'rational imagination' ('rational art', 'a rational bias and a rational structure') is an odd motto for someone interested in 'unconscious skills' and sure that 'any good poet' must 'issue in ambiguity'. Bafflement, bewilderment, and contradiction are the poet's (and the critic's) proper companions; the 'logic of art' is not the 'logic of the textbooks'. 'Rational' therefore must mean disciplined by perceptible form, amenable, at the end of whatever subtle and intuitively pursued detours, to reasonable discourse. But the term still manages to seem both emphatic and hesitant, suggests a romance of reason being pursued beyond the odds. Blackmur acknowledges that reason is humanity's 'great myth', but only to clutch all the harder at what the myth offers. One of his poems hints at a history for such clutching, a melancholy reason for reason's rule. It is possible, the poem suggests, to avoid 'surprise,/ resentment, or despair', and 'the murky homage of shared injuries'. 'Knowledge without contact' is possible.

> Or so we plead – we who have married reason
> on desperate cause, when the heart's cause was lost.

Perhaps this is how one comes to be, as Blackmur once called himself, a tory anarchist: 'Let us say that we have not so much of reason that we can afford to lose any of it.'

Eliot, the Eliot of the early criticism backed by the poetic practice from 'Prufrock' to *Four Quartets*, was a crucial figure in Blackmur's development – more important in many ways than James and Adams, who recur more frequently as objects of affection and attention. Yet much of Eliot's criticism, however significant, was emphatic and rudimentary in its language, and casual about its examples. Blackmur was exact about his examples and, at his best, scrupulously tentative in his language. He was ready to follow not only Eliot but Arnold in the matter of touchstones, but dared to 'hope the pace is lighter and comes out in another world'. He saw criticism as 'consciously provisional, speculative, and dramatic': 'What we make is a fiction to school the urgency of reading; no more', 'the best we can do is a doubtful scaffold of terms'. He described Eliot's concept of tradition as a fiction in this sense, even 'if not consciously so contrived':

Used as Eliot uses it, it is an experimental conceit and pushes the mind forward. Taken seriously it is bad constitutional law, in the sense that it would provoke numberless artificial and insoluble problems.

'A mind furnished only with convictions', Blackmur sharply said, 'would be like a room furnished only with light.'

'Blackmur loved thought', Denis Donoghue writes, 'but he felt that it was nearly always premature... He was interested in explanations, subject to the qualification that he thought them ultimately beside the point.' Blackmur himself said that criticism was 'not a light but a process of elucidation'; and his own shifting, turning prose tests even flat-looking, dogmatic-seeming critical terms for the promise of glow or movement that is in them.

Poets find in poetry, he says, 'the only means of putting a tolerable order upon the emotions'. The very wording implies the possibility of intolerable orders. Order for Blackmur – another of his talismanic words – is always precarious and local, an encounter with particular confusions.

'Chaos is not what we must exclude; it is what we do not know ... of the behaviour which ... forms our lives.' It is even possible, Blackmur speculates at one point, that order may *require* distress (his italics), may regularly need the test of an engagement 'with the violence and strangeness of the actual'. Order would thus reflect a demand for knowledge or adventure rather than mere control; would represent an aspiration rather than a repression. 'The only sound orders are those which invite as well as withstand disorder.'

Similarly, concepts like form, frame, meaning, rational imagination are not dictates for Blackmur but soundings, attempts to reach what is in words and beyond words, a way of thinking, the way and the thinking.

When I use a word, an image, a notion, there must be in its small nodular apparent form ... at least prophetically, the whole future growth, the whole harvested life; and not rhetorically nor in a formula, but stubbornly, pervasively, heart-hidden, materially.

The motions of the words

'Poetry is idiom', Blackmur repeatedly and rather cryptically insists. 'A poem is an idiom and surpasses the sum of its uses.' Blackmur is in part telling us, as Ransom and Brooks and countless other modern critics also tell us, that poetry can't be paraphrased, that it is 'a special and fresh way of saying, and cannot for its life be said otherwise'. His slogan concerning 'the words and the motions of the words' means much the same thing. Words have rich lives of their own, their motions in poems, plays, and novels are 'all the technical devices of literature', and the successful meeting of words and motions makes an irreplaceable event. What the reader has to do is submit, 'at least provisionally, to whatever authority your attention brings to light in the words'. Attention is active in this dictum, and Blackmur uses the word reading, as he says on the subject of Hart Crane, in the strong sense. Somewhere around here the New Criticism might well claim credit for what was later called the invention of the reader. Or several readers. There is a reading ('our best reading', Blackmur perhaps prematurely says) which 'takes poetry in its stride'. But there is also a reading which chooses to 'arrest the stride or make slow motion of it'.

However, 'idiom' goes further than warning us against paraphrase and reminding us, with Mallarmé, that poems are made of words. It suggests culture and usage, a continuing linguistic life, a form of expression which is both quirky and solid, as idiomatic speech understands the reason and the unreason of a language, the difference between *at war* and *in war*, for example, or between *in-laws* and *outlaws*. To say a poem enters the language is to say it becomes a new language habit, or the promise of a habit. It makes nothing happen, as Auden said, but it becomes a feature of what's happening. Idiom is 'language so twisted and posed in a form that it not only expresses the matter in hand but adds to the available stock of reality'. It is also what might happen, a potentiality; it surpasses the sum of its uses because it awaits its future uses, like a parable whose meaning may deepen with time and history.

Blackmur is an eager believer in 'the radical failure of language (its inability ever explicitly to *say* what is in a full heart)', but also sees occasions, in Shakespeare and Wordsworth for example, when that fail-ure is 'overcome': these writers find small words, common words ('The rest is silence', 'But oh, the difference to me!') to say what no large or special words could say, they liberate the meanings which are already in the words, they both find and underline an idiom. Stevens similarly 'makes you aware of how much is *already* condensed in any word', although his words *are* special, a more rarified idiom, aligned by what Blackmur calls the magic of elegance. We are 'lonely in words', as a poem of Blackmur's has it, 'but under words at home'. Or lonely in grammar, and at home in idiom. In *The Lion and the Honeycomb* Blackmur remembers a Harvard lecture on Indian Philosophy, which he thinks Eliot too must have heard: 'The reality in words, gentlemen, is both superior to and anterior to any use to which you can put them.' The formation (belonging to a Professor Wood) is no doubt too lofty, too entangled in a faded philosophical idealism, and in a strong interpretation (*any* use?) is probably meaning-less: what could this unusable verbal reality be? But for Blackmur it caught what we might think of as the embedded history of words, the sense of our serving them rather than their serving us – the treasure of the *langue*, in Saussure's sense. Idiom would be not the knowledge of but the practice, the furtherance of such history, a magical crossing of *langue* and *parole*.

When a word is used in a poem it should be the sum of all its appropriate history made concrete and particular in the individual context; and in poetry all words act *as if* they were so used . . .

It is in this spirit that Blackmur traces echoes and ghosts in words; he sees the unwritten *haunted* appear between the lines of a Shakespeare sonnet as 'a kind of backward consequence' of the presence in the poem of *hunted* and *hated*, and comments on Crane's line 'Thy Nazarene and tinder eyes' as revealing

how Crane could at once isolate a word and bind it in, impregnating it with new meaning. Tinder is used to kindle fire, powder, and light; a word incipient and bristling with the action proper to its being. The association is completed when it is remembered that tinder is very nearly a homonym for tender, and *in this setting*, puns upon it.

This sort of critical practice recalls Empson, and Blackmur used to say that *Seven Types of Ambiguity* was a book he couldn't keep away from. He also spoke of his debt to Empson's mentor I. A. Richards: 'No literary critic can escape his influence; an influence that stimulates the mind as much as anything by showing the sheer excitement as well as the profundity of the problems of language.' But Blackmur, far more than either Empson or Richards, was engaged in the assessment and exploration of the work of his contemporaries (and often compatriots) – Crane, Stevens, Cummings, Eliot, Pound, Marianne Moore – and his besetting interest was not literature as irony or ambiguity, not language as an instrument or problem, but words as vivid idiom, as the compacted, functioning record of our passage, the place where our knowledge and our ignorance meet. 'Idiom is the twist of truth, the twist, like that of the strands of a rope, which keeps its component fictions together. History is old and twisted beyond our reach in time.' Or not quite beyond our reach. In the following quotation Blackmur comments on 'peregrine', in Eliot's 'Little Gidding'. The performance is a little arch and distinctly mandarin, and has none of Empson's bluffness about it; but it is also subtle, complex, and coherent, a brilliant critical poem, unmistakably fervent (but not solemn) about the riches it unravels.

Here is the American expatriate; the uprooted man in a given place; the alien making a home; man the alien on earth; man as the wanderer becoming the pilgrim; and the pilgrim returning with the last and fatal power of knowing that what was the pilgrim in him is only the mature and unappeasable state of the first incentive... In the Republic and the Empire, *Peregrini* were, in Rome, citizens of any state other than Rome... The Shorter Oxford Dictionary says of 'peregrine': one from foreign parts, an alien, a wanderer; and goes on to say that in astrology (that ironic refuge of Eliot as of Donne and of Dante) a peregrine is a planet situated in a part of the zodiac where it has none of its essential dignity...

Blackmur then quotes Dante on the contrast between the true City and a peregrine Italy, *Italia peregrina*, and concludes:

I do not know how much nearer home we need to come, but if we think of Arnold's Grande Chartreuse poem, surely we are as close to the quick of the peregrine's home as we are likely to come. There looking at the old monastery Arnold felt himself hung between two worlds, one dead and the other powerless to be born. I do not think this is too much to pack into a word, but it is no wonder that it should take the attribute unappeasable, for it is the demands of the peregrine, whether outsider or pilgrim, that cannot be met. I will add that the peregrine is also a hawk or falcon found the world over but never at home: always a migrant but everywhere met, and, wherever found, courageous and swift.

The theory of failure

The most alluring and problematic aspect of Blackmur's criticism is its dedication to the idea of failure. Is it really a 'radical failure of language' that it should never be able 'explicitly to *say* what is in a full heart'? Doesn't the heart have its own implicit language, and doesn't Blackmur's practice, if not his theory, endorse Wittgenstein's suggestion that what can't be said may be shown? We can say yes to both questions, but if we go no further we shall miss the pathos and the austerity of Blackmur's idea. Failure for Blackmur is a form of distinction, a sign that one was trying for what mattered.

Whitman and Dickinson fail in spite of their occasional greatness, Crane and Cummings fail in spite of their gifts, and Blackmur's essay on Crane ends with a celebration of 'the distraught but exciting splendour of a great failure'. Still, these are perhaps expected misses in Blackmur's critical universe, the result of an adherence to the fallacy of expressive form. It is a little more startling to see Blackmur include *The Waste Land* among the century's exemplary failures, remind us that Yeats cannot be placed among the greatest poets, and that Stendhal 'was not great enough'. Only Dante and Shakespeare, it seems, don't fail, and (at least once) Wordsworth. In fact, even Dante comes under suspicion, and is said to be, rather absurdly, 'of all poets least *manqué*'. With failure like that, who needs success? Still, the absurdity shows the degree of Blackmur's attachment to his idea; and the effect of such near-success as Dante's was to remove a writer from our world, to make him a measure but not a model.

Our writers, the great modern writers who so preoccupied Blackmur, are incomplete, 'like ourselves', experts in the difficult and honourable art of failure.

Most failures we have the tact to ignore or give a kinder name... Most failures come too easily, take too little stock of the life and forces around them; like the ordinary failure in marriage, or business, or dying; and so too much resemble the ordinary success... A genuine failure comes hard and slow, and, as in a tragedy, is only fully realized at the end.

Blackmur thinks criticism may be 'the radical imperfection of the intellect striking on the radical imperfection of the imagination', and in an essay on T. E. Lawrence associates radical imperfection with original sin. There is a dark dandyism here, a will to find failure absolutely everywhere, scarcely tempered by the 'almost' in a phrase like 'Well, all of us are defeated almost to the degree that we try.'

Success is not the propitious term for education unless the lesson wanted is futile... Surely the dominant emotion of an education, when its inherent possibili-

ties are compared with those it achieved, must strike the honest heart as the
emotion of failure ... failure in the radical sense that we cannot consciously react
to more than a minor fraction of the life we yet deeply know and endure and die.

Even the honest heart might want to quarrel here. The passage too easily
dismisses all kinds of honourable success, and seems wilfully self-torment-
ing. If we *always* fail, the thought of those inherent (im)possibilities is
mere flagellation. The 'radical sense' of failure surely overrates the role of
consciousness (what of the deep knowledge so casually mentioned?) and
offers a familiar limitation as if it were a calamity, as if our inability to fly,
for example, were a tragic lack. What is happening, though, as the tone of
all this makes evident, is that Blackmur is using failure less as a philosophy
than as a metaphor, a strenuous reminder of work yet to be done. Against
all logic, the right kind of failure just *is* success for Blackmur, as he says
ignorance is 'the humbled form of knowledge'. In any realm but metaphor, ignorance is no form of knowledge at all, and dying is a feat at which
we all, fatally, succeed. The remarkable force of the following aphorism,
literally both banal and false, lies in its figurative reach, its appeal to our
fear, our miserliness and our generosity. 'As it is a condition of life to die,
it is a condition of thought, in the end, to fail. Death is the expense of life
and failure is the expense of greatness.'
     Henry James initially posed a problem for Blackmur's theory, troubled
the grandeur of the metaphor. The first James novel he read – at age
seventeen – was *The Wings of the Dove*, and he knew, he said, that a
master had laid hands on him. Later (in 1934) he argued that James's
Prefaces were 'the most eloquent and original piece of literary criticism in
existence'. Not much scope for failure in either mode. Later still Blackmur
came to find a certain 'thinness' in James's work, but also to write much
more subtly about him. It was a matter perhaps not of a 'decreasing
admiration', as one scholar suggests, but of an increasing awareness of
James's desperation, of the lean failure lurking in the rotund success.
'Whoever wins, in this novel', Blackmur says of *The Ambassadors*, 'wins
within a loss.' What are all those ghosts in James but 'the meaning that
pursues us or is beyond us'; 'moral images of possible life', 'unused
possibilities ... unfollowed temptations of character'? Unused and perhaps unusable possibilities, Blackmur seems to suggest, at least in any
material or historical life we are likely to live – rather like the reality in
Professor Wood's words. The novels themselves, Blackmur thought by
1952, have a 'fabulous air': 'we believe in them only as we believe in
hellish or heavenly fables, as we might believe in some fabulous form of
the uncreated shades of ourselves'. For Isabel Archer, in *The Portrait of a
Lady*, it is 'as if knowledge ... could never be quite *yet*!' Blackmur
construes the question (James's question) of whether she could be rich

enough to meet the requirements of her imagination as a darker question still, involving not unreachable but maybe non-existent riches: 'That there may be no such riches is perhaps what the look in the eyes of this portrait of a lady is saying.'

None of these bleak thoughts, however, can dispense us from picturing riches and possibilities, and nothing is more American than Blackmur's reading of James in this respect. James understands 'the swindle in human relations' – Blackmur even compares him with Swift – but he chooses to work through social conventions rather than against them:

> He took the best face values of society . . . as principles and seriously applied them, in much the same sense that people have in mind in making the assertion that no one knows whether Christianity will work because no one has ever tried it.

Society for James doesn't work even when we do try it – at its best – and that is the grand and poignant failure the novels reveal to us. In spite of its apparent conservatism James's work for Blackmur 'constitutes a great single anarchic rebellion aginst society', a 'rebellion of the ideal' puzzlingly conducted through the very social norms that fail us, but unmistakably a rebellion all the same. James and his father were 'basic dissenters to all except the society that was not yet', a secular, humane community that many (European) cultures don't even bother to promise themselves. Even more memorably Blackmur writes of James's 'deep, almost instinctive incentive to create the indestructible life which, to his vision, must lie at the heart of the actual life that has been hurt'. Failure here can rightly be called the expense of greatness, and it will scarcely be paradoxical to write, as Blackmur does, of failure being 'won'.

Blackmur first uses those phrases, though, not of Henry James but of Henry Adams. Both men engaged in what Blackmur called 'a specialized form of autobiography in which the individual was suppressed in the act only to be caught in the style'. Both achieved, that is, a considerable measure of form; both were 'obstinately artists at bottom'. But their failures, and their interest in failure, were different. If James had to fail as dissenter and idealist, just as Isabel Archer had to fall short of the requirements of her imagination, he did of course succeed splendidly as a writer. That 'obstinate finality', as James called the artist, was not the very end but he worked hard and slow and he arrived somewhere, offered a serious mitigation of failure. Adams, in Blackmur's view, laboured at the very perfection of failure, made himself not a craftsman but an emblem, not a dissenter but the mind's martyr, a figure in whom society could read the ruin of its best intentions. Adams too saw 'what life needed but never provided' but didn't create a dramatic form for that need. He created instead a brilliantly intelligent record of neediness, which is why Blackmur could regard him and James as 'two extreme – and therefore deeply related – types of American imagination'. The extremes, as Blackmur saw them, were a tilt toward intellect and a tilt toward sensibility, and are perhaps related to Blackmur's sense of Americans (his sense of the European sense of Americans) as 'both abstract and hysterical: we throw away so much and make so much of the meager remainder'. Adams throws and James makes.

The importance of Adams for Blackmur – an importance so great that Blackmur seems at times literally haunted by Adams's values and style, by the tone of his mind – lay in his 'complex ... allegiance': to medieval art and imagination, to an eighteenth-century politics, and to modern scepticism. Nothing was his to have and keep, not even his own education, but he fully retained his loyalty to what he had lost or failed to find. Associating Adams with Montaigne, Blackmur writes eloquently of the *riches* (his italics) of a scepticism which 'in reconciling two points of view into one ... manages to imply the possibility of a third and quite unadjusted point of view'. Much humour and modesty in such scepticism – necessarily, we may think, if the unadjusted point of view is not to drive one to despair. Adams, like Blackmur, could not believe, but he knew what faith was. Asked why he wouldn't allow Sargent to paint his portrait, Adams said, 'I knew too well what he would do to me, and I was too much of a coward.' He then – Blackmur describes the scene with admiring tenderness – offered as a picture of himself a postcard of a sculptured panel from Chartres Cathedral, a Nativity with Virgin, Joseph, baby, a sheep, a donkey. 'That is my portrait', Adams said. 'It is the donkey sniffing the straw.'

Schools of insight

Fame and security brought out the oracular in Blackmur. His criticism in the 1950s was often contorted, dipping into arcane vocabularies, driving words like 'gesture' rather too hard, harrying metaphors to ugliness, as in (from *The Lion and the Honeycomb*) 'Most of these steps are second nature to five thousand years of the mind's feet.' In this period he travelled widely in Europe and the Middle East, became a roving cultural commentator, an inspector of the postwar world. Much of his writing in this line is rather vapid and meandering, although there are flashes of epigrammatic wit. St Peter's, for example, is said to be 'the Grand Hotel on the beach of Christianity', and Blackmur thinks 'Kafka could have invented Versailles.' There are interesting speculations too, like the vision of American abstraction and hysteria I have mentioned above, which Blackmur discovers even in American styles of ballet. He sees (in 1958) the 'long moment in creeping imperialism which so preoccupies us' – which didn't then preoccupy us enough, we might say – and he must be (dubious distinction) among the first writers to use the term post-modern.

He saw the West, and notably America, as newly illiterate, that is, not ignorant but devoted to 'fragmented and specialized knowledge'. There was an 'industrialization of intellect'; we had invented smart new academic subjects, 'malicious techniques' like psychoanalysis, anthropology, sociology, biology, much modern philosophy, 'those great underminers of belief, those great analyzers of experience'. 'It is thus that we *become* our problem when we ought to exemplify some effort at the solution of it.' Much of this sounds merely querulous, but the first-person plural suggests Blackmur hasn't forgotten that he is himself a quirky symptom of the condition he is describing. The broad attack on modern disciplines ('we had psychology which dissolved the personality into bad behavior, we had anthropology which dissolved religion into a competition, world- and history-wide, of monsters, we had psychiatry which cured the disease by making a monument of it and sociology which flattened us into the average of the lonely crowd') is bland and glib, itself a piece of pop sociology; but the attempt to point to the elusive but undeniable historical effect of these disciplines is striking. One of the most notable features of modern writing, from Eliot to Borges, is what it *reads*, its interest in forms of understanding once thought to lie 'outside' literature.

Much of this argument occurs in the four lectures ('Anni Mirabiles 1921–1925') which Blackmur gave at the Library of Congress in 1956, and although the drift of the discussion is despairing, Blackmur does implicitly modify his doctrine of failure. All these explicit knowledges are a threat not in themselves but because they crowd out other modes of knowing. 'We have invented so many ways of formularizing consciously what we know that it sometimes seems we know, by nature, nothing at all.' In context, this is a dizzying thought: our difficult, conscious modern writers and critics, not only Yeats and Eliot but Mann and Gide and Empson and Tate, would be seeking, by every means they had, to remind us of our unformularised knowledge, to send us back to all we scarcely know we know. The earlier Blackmur had respected magic and religion, but felt they had to be made readable, intelligible. 'We are all, without conscience, magicians in the dark. But even the poems of darkness are read in the light.' The suggestion now seems to be that we have tried too hard for the light, have forgotten the magic and the dark. Conscience is still crucial, but consciousness – Blackmur must have intended the double meaning, must earlier have hoped the two meanings would stay together – can betray us by becoming too glaring, too confident and demanding and divisive. 'What', Blackmur wrote in a fine fit of petulance, 'should we get rid of our ignorance, of the very substance of our lives, merely in order to understand one another?'

There is a tell-tale slippage in Blackmur's memorable phrase 'techniques of trouble', which at first clearly refers to the dangerous new disciplines, 'all the new forms into which our knowledge has segregated and incriminated itself': 'These are our techniques of trouble, and if there were no troubles we would invent them or would find new ways of looking at old troubles.' Later, though, the phrase seems to shift toward a suggestion of techniques *for* trouble, the scrupulous artist's brave but partial use of 'the technical resources of the humane imagination' to cope with, precisely, the troubles that other techniques have located or magnified. This is all rather murky, but can be glossed as saying, perhaps, that the modern, whether in science or society or art, has gone beyond welcome and nostalgia, but not beyond question or worry, has become irresistible but also incurable. 'Technique' in its shifted sense would mean what 'form' used to mean for Blackmur, and what technique, as we saw at the beginning of this essay, could always mean – except that technique itself would now be in trouble: tackling trouble, but also troubled.

Blackmur's major later criticism, and much of the most agile and brilliant of any of his criticism, concerns the European novel. He found there a new/old way into trouble, and a new sense of form. The novel as genre, Blackmur suggests, unconsciously meeting up with Lukács, does not place its characters 'into relation with some received or religious or predicted concept of significance', as the characters in Sophocles, Virgil, or Dante are placed.

We are working the other way round: we have to find out in the process of experience itself. We are about the great business of the novel, to create out of manners and action motive...

When Blackmur suggests that the novel 'is the form most appropriate to an intolerable society', he is thinking of Dostoevsky, with his borrowing of crime fiction, but the remark will carry further. 'Art shows the human cost of society', Blackmur says of *Madame Bovary*, 'or if we want to be arrogant about it we can say that art shows the criminality of society from the point of view of every individual within it.' Blackmur finds in Tolstoy, Flaubert, Dostoevsky, and Thomas Mann – he writes less well on Joyce, in spite of his great admiration, perhaps because Joyce is not a tragic humanist or a baffled believer – spectacular, inverted forms of the rebellion so discreetly conducted in Henry James. It is a rebellion *against* the ideal, a vision of life as the betrayal of desire and the future, as the discovery of motives we might prefer to leave undiscovered. Politics in *The Possessed*, for instance, 'is a transgression against the good to come – but only as life itself is; to a novelist especially as life itself is'. American ghosts give way to European devils: 'the devil is always what happens to the ideal'; 'the devil is God gone to the devil'. Hope itself is an 'affliction', and Dostoevsky takes us even further into the great business of the novel than Tolstoy does, since he not only creates motive but loses it.

Dostoevsky is the great master of the unmotivated and nowhere more so than in *The Brothers Karamazov*: in him you see how hard it is to achieve lasting or adequate motive, how almost impossible to escape from evil into the good and yet live, but also how deep is the affliction of hope within us that we may do so.

In such a world, in such a novel, heroism and humanity lie not in victory or even failure or damnation but in perseverance, the dedication to the evoked details of hope and transgression, the ability to make and hear the music of what Blackmur calls, in relation to Mann's *Dr Faustus*, 'the long human howl'.

Blackmur found in a finger trapped in a door in Dostoevsky 'a whole school of insight', and he became the most gifted of teachers in just such a school. The concrete features of a (usually foreign) fiction – gesture, speech, place, time – allowed him, as the behaviour of words in English and his own cultural generalisations had not, to connect social and psychological behaviour, to see an intricate history in motion. 'Not only do the guilty flee when none pursue, the innocent flee so that all may pursue. It is a deep habit either way.' This brief comment – and there are many such scattered about Blackmur's essays on the novel – offers a glimpse of a whole modern pathology, an altered social relation, Kafka hidden among the Karamazovs.

Blackmur's late idea of form might almost be a recantation: 'there seems a kind of mutilating self-determinism about what we call form'. He means English and American form, any sense of form which cannot acknowledge the mastery which lies in Dostoevsky's apparent form-lessness. It is appropriate that he should, as a critic, finally come upon such verges of disorder, write so intimately about them, and cling so fervidly to lucidity as the complications rose. 'Criticism is the rashest of acts', he wrote. His risk and his achievement were to perform that rash act slowly.

12

Kenneth Burke

Eugene Goodheart

Nothing human is alien to Kenneth Burke. He is the least confined of modern critics. It is not simply that he writes about everything: he tries to encompass everything within a system or systems of explanation that have the effect of conservation. In the narrow political sense, Burke is by no means a conservative, and yet one might say, that he is the most 'conservational' of critics. The trajectory of Burke's career from the first collection of essays *Counter-Statement* to *The Rhetoric of Religion* is a movement of increasing encompassment of all branches of knowledge: literature, sociology, philosophy, linguistics, theology etc. 'Branches of knowledge' is misleading, because of the peculiarly idiosyncratic appropriation of them.

How to encompass this most encompassing, yet most personal of critics? The question has been raised, particularly by writers hostile to his enterprise, about whether indeed Burke qualifies as a literary critic. Thus Marius Bewley, one of his severest critics, has noted, 'how easily, without an exacting critical conscience, Burke's theory moves through art to propaganda, how easily the literary merges into the revolutionary critic'.[1] The occasion for the charge is an extended passage in *Attitudes Toward History* of which the following sentences should serve: 'Our own program, as literary critic, is to integrate technical criticism with social criticism (propaganda and didactic) by taking the allegiance to the symbol of authority as our subject... And since the whole purpose of a "revolutionary" critic is to contribute to a change in allegiance to the symbols of authority, we maintain our role as "propagandist" by keeping this subject forever uppermost in our concerns.'[2] Burke's role as revolutionary critic may be only a phase or aspect of his total performance, but it is taken to be expressive of a characteristic disposition in the performance. Thus, for instance, Burke's neo-Aristotelian medievalist regard for theology as the unifying discipline (whether or not the theology is Marxist) becomes evidence for Bewley and others of Burke's incapacity 'to conceive of literary criticism as a central discipline'.[3]

It should be noted that Bewley's response is to an early work in which

[1] Marius Bewley, *The Complex Fate* (London, 1952), p. 219.
[2] Kenneth Burke, *Attitudes Toward History* (Los Altos, 1959), p. 331.
[3] Bewley, *The Complex Fate*, p. 223.

the Marxist element (a product of the thirties) seemed much more prominent that it seems now in retrospect. One is indeed surprised by the
Marxist element, coming to *Attitudes Toward History* after a reading of
late work like *A Grammar of Motives* and *The Rhetoric of Religion*.
Burke doesn't react against Marxism, he outgrows it. Bewley's point,
however, is not to charge Burke with being a Marxist, but to show how his
ecumenism, his catholic embrace of all disciplines, his pragmatic inclination to turn everything to use puts in question his role as a literary critic.
   What is at work is an assumption, shared by Bewley, Ransom, Tate,
and other modernists, about the separate integrity of the disciplines and in
particular the literary or aesthetic disciplines. New Critics resisted the
contamination of discussions of poems and even novels by political or
moral considerations. Political and moral themes were interesting only
insofar as they were transformed into literary structures. The effort of
separation and purification of the disciplines belongs to a classic modernist desire to overcome Victorian moralising and a Marxian politicising of
literature. The effort at separation has proven to be problematic. A
rigorous scrutiny of the literary or the aesthetic shows how often the term
conceals moral, political, and spiritual interests. The literary is itself an
amalgam. Consider, for instance, Bewley's praise of Burke, for whom
'poetry becomes, not a segregated experience, but an experience at one
with all human action . . . Poetry is therefore seen to be ethical, and of the
deepest influence in shaping our structures of orientation.'[4] The issue is
not whether the critic preserves, so to speak, his literary chastity, but
whether his sensibility remains literary while responding to the amalgam
that constitutes literature. Burke does not put in question the very idea of
literature as some post-structuralists have done, but his lack of aesthetic
purism leads to disciplinary interactions that make him a modernist in a
sense in which his New Critical peers were not.
   Burke transgresses with impunity disciplinary boundaries; he also ap-
propriates subjects traditionally deemed unworthy of serious intellectual
and aesthetic consideration. As a result it has sometimes been charged that
Burke's method could be applied with equal fruitfulness to Shakespeare,
or Marie Corelli, and Dashiell Hammett, a charge which presupposes a
distinction between higher and lower forms of cultural life that Burke did
not explicitly disavow, but in practice disregarded. He is a forerunner of
those critics, now legion, who engage all forms of cultural expression with
an uninvidious interest, at once aesthetic and sociological. The weakening, if not dissolution, of the high–low distinction, makes it possible for
critics now to discover not only the sociological conditions shared by a

---

[4] *Ibid.*, p. 217.

variety of artistic and cultural forms, but to consider as well aesthetic value in popular forms of cultural life.

Unlike his contemporaries (Ransom, Tate, Blackmur, among others) Burke is not to be approached *simply* as a literary critic, analysing individual works of literature. It is not, however, enough to say that literary criticism is one among many of the activities that Burke engages in. He is not an eclectic of disciplines. He is a critic with systematic ambitions, though I think it inaccurate to represent him as a systematic critic. His work is marked by a tension between the effort to systematise and the need to resist the stultifying consequences of such an effort. Indeed, Burke's work gives the impression of waywardness rather than the rigour of step-by-step construction characteristic of the system building of, say, Northrop Frye.

We can see the contrary tendencies in Burke's thought in his definition of man, from which many of his ideas and observations flow. 'Man is a symbol-using animal, the inventor of the negative, separated from his natural condition by instruments of his own making, goaded by the spirit of hierarchy and rotten with perfection.'[5] The definition suggests a number of affinities and inspirations. Man as a symbol-making animal evokes the American pragmatist George Mead and the anthropologists Leslie White and Alfred H. Kroeber. In stressing the separation from the natural (elsewhere he will speak of transcendence), we should also recognise the secularising humanist (a legatee of the nineteenth century) interested in preserving spiritual ambition in a materialising world. Hierarchy and perfection evoke Burke's affinities with the classical tradition and in particular with Aristotelian teleology. The definition also suggests the scepticism that informs Burke's work: the idea of the *negative*, the problematic *separation* from the natural condition, the *rot* of perfection, that threatens all hierachies.

In *Permanence and Change*, Burke makes it clear that he wants to unsettle things, not tidy them into a neat system. He is concerned with 'how an "orientation" (or general view of reality) takes form. How such a system of interpretation, by its very scope and thoroughness, interferes with its own revision. Why terms like "escape", "scapegoat mechanism", "pleasure principles", and "rationalization" should be used skeptically and grudgingly.'[6] No interpretation is secure: 'We may also interpret our interpretations.'[7] Burke's desire to keep things open, to question the terms of the structures and activities he scrutinises, is homeopathic (cathartic) rather than destructive. In his first book, *Counter-Statement*, he contrasts

---

[5] Kenneth Burke, *Language as Symbolic Action: Essays on Life, Literature and Method* (Berkeley, 1966), p. 16.
[6] Kenneth Burke, *Permanence and Change*, rev. edn. (Berkeley, 1984), p. 3.
[7] *Ibid.*, p. 6.

Platonic censorship to Aristotle's homeopathic 'lightening' rod poetics, which he prefers. 'Lightening rods are designed, not to suppress danger, but to draw it into harmless channels.'[8] Scepticism may be viewed as a way of venting (not suppressing) dangerous energies, so that the work of structure-making can continue.

But Burke is also keenly aware of the radical and corrosive tendency in modern art, which he finds in Mann and Gide, writers whom he admires but about whom he feels a certain ambivalence. 'There is an art, a questioning art, still cluttered with the merest conveniences of thinking, a highly fluctuant thing often turning against itself and its own best discoveries. How far it will go, how well it can maintain its characters, I should not venture to calculate. But working in the traditions of such art are two conscientious, or corrupt writers, Thomas Mann and Andre Gide.'[9] Burke's commitment to the constitutive impulse in human life sets him apart from the tendency of modernist thought to demystify all structures, to deflate pretensions, to dissipate illusions. Demystification is the most powerful method of the modern intellectual's will to power, and Burke is the most penetrating critic of modernist debunking. What he tries above all to do is to account for the motives which impel men to construct and constitute the structures that fill the space of *human* life.

Our resistance to a purely 'debunking' vocabulary of motives is made clear if we imagine a thinker who chose to 'debunk' such a motive as 'solidarity'. There are unquestionably ways in which one may 'cash in on' it, in the purely selfish sense of the term – but if *all* acts of 'solidarity' were interpreted in the light of this possibility, its 'reality' would be dissolved out of existence . . . quite as Democritus' atomism resolved the gods out of existence . . . Those who cooperate with the help of this concept must leave its 'euphemistic' nature as a motive intact.[10]

Even a debunker like Freud acknowledges the necessity and value of 'mystery and mystification'. 'Every man has his "secret", an awe too deep for the boldness and shrewdness of rational verbalization. There is the "trembling veil" of sleep, which he cannot draw without risk.'[11] Debunking works against such understanding, and indeed, as Burke cunningly suggests, is susceptible of the same demystifying treatment it accords all other activities, structures, and motives. 'While leading you to watch his act of destruction at one point, the "unmasker" is always furtively building at another point, and by his prestidigitation, he can forestall accurate observation of his own moves.'[12]

How does Burke the anti-debunker avoid a falsifying mystification, surely a bad thing in the realm of thought? Sidney Hook believes that

[8] Kenneth Burke, *Counter-Statement* (Los Altos, 1953), p. xii.   [9] *Ibid.*, p. 106.
[10] Burke, *Attitudes Toward History*, p. 74.   [11] *Ibid.*, p. 180.
[12] Burke, *Permanence and Change*, p. 294.

Burke is a mystifier, and he discovers it in particular in Burke's fellow-travelling communism. Hook focuses on Burke's habit of finding a central metaphor in a work or action in order to understand its achievement. He cites the instance of Burke's review of Henri Barbusse's idolatrous biography of Stalin. Burke characterises the biography as a 'public monument', in effect extenuating if not justifying the extraordinary mystification and falsification of Stalin's life by Barbusse. Hook mischievously suggests 'the dung hill' as another appropriate metaphor for the book. 'Why one metaphor rather than another?', Hook asks.[13] Hook implies that the metaphor is not adventitious, that is, it reflects a political allegiance to communism, and communism in its Stalinist version.

There is certainly substantial evidence in Burke's early work of that allegiance. But the instance of Barbusse's *Stalin* is in a sense a diversion from a full and generous understanding of what Burke is up to. He does a similar thing with Hitler's *Mein Kampf* and one can hardly impute Nazi motives to him. Burke's way is always to enter into the spirit of the work, to try to grasp its rhetorical, that is to say its persuasive power. (Who would deny the persuasiveness of *Mein Kampf?*) We need to keep in mind that rhetoric is one of Burke's main subjects and that mystification is inescapably implicated in rhetorical performance. The issue is not necessarily truth, but belief. Burke means to examine the myriad ways in which language leads people to conviction and action. His virtuosity both as rhetorician and as student of rhetoric consists in his extraordinary awareness of 'the endless catalogue of terministic screens'[14] in and through which human beings live. 'Screen', of course, is an image of concealment and mystification, but the image can be one of discovery and illumination as well.

If you decree by secular prayer that man is 'essentially' a warrior (as did Nietzsche) you may then proceed, by casuistic stretching, to discern the warlike ingredient present even in love. If on the contrary you legislated to the effect that man is essentially a communicant, you could discern the co-operative ingredient present 'essentially' even in war. Capitalism is 'essentially' competitive (on this point, both opponents and proponents agree). But despite this essence, we note the presence of many non-competitive ingredients (there are many examples of true 'partnership') in the competitive struggle.[15]

Burke means to revive the ancient reputation of casuistry, which the Shorter Oxford Dictionary defines in its non-contemptible sense as 'the science, art, or reasoning of the casuist; that part of Ethics which resolves

---

[13] Sidney Hook, 'The Technique of Mystification' (review of *Attitudes in History*), in William H. Rueckert, ed., *Critical Responses to Kenneth Burke 1924–1966* (Minneapolis, 1969), p. 93. Reprinted from *Partisan Review*, IV (December 1937), pp. 57–62.
[14] Burke, *Language as Symbolic Action*, p. 52.
[15] Burke, *Attitudes Toward History*, p. 261.

cases of conscience, applying the general rules of religion and morality to particular instances which disclose special circumstances, or conflicting duties'.

The danger of terministic screens and casuistic stretching is a relativism, with truth, whatever it may be, as the casualty. The difficulty arises (and here Hook's criticism is relevant) in the indiscriminateness with which Burke treats all intellectual and imaginative structures, literary, philosophical, political. It is not enough for a critic to provide a metaphor for the intention of Barbusse's *Stalin* or Hitler's *Mein Kampf*; he must evaluate it in moral terms as well. He must *transcend*, to use a favourite Burke term, the merely rhetorical.

But Burke's insufficiency in the case of certain texts, those with momentous political consequences, does not undermine the essential value of Burke's resistance to debunking as a pervasive activity. Indeed, it suggests that Hook and others have exaggerated the significance of Burke's allegiance to Marxism, since he is after all so antipathetic to its demystifying spirit.

What distinguishes Burke is not so much his allegiance to a particular 'symbol of authority' as his negative capacity for sympathetically grasping allegiances to a variety of symbols of authority to the point of undermining his moral credibility. As between Marx, the dyslogist, and Carlyle, the eulogist, for example, Burke remains suspended in indecision as if he wants it both ways: the mystery and the 'truth' that lies concealed beneath the mystery, without evaporating the mystery. In a discussion of Carlyle's 'Philosophy of Clothes' in *Sartor Resartus*, Burke says that he has 'not been trying to abolish, or debunk, or refute, or even to "approve with reservations". Above all, we are not trying to decide whether mystery should be considered dyslogistically, as with Marx, or eulogistically, as with Carlyle. For we need not decide here whether there should or should not be reverence (hence "mystification").'[16] If not here, certainly elsewhere and in many places, Burke almost always prefers the eulogist. (More recently, Roland Barthes in *Mythologies* has, in a way that recalls Burke, addressed himself to the poverty of demystification, lamenting 'the drift between the object and its demystification, powerless to render its wholeness'.)[17]

Burke's stance against debunking is consistent with the role of literary critic. While debunking may be an essential activity of sociology, for instance, it is more often than not inimical to the practice of literary criticism. What counts above all for the literary critic is the language that constitutes the work. Words are at once the surface and the reality of literature, to which the demystifier's suspicious view of the spoken or

[16] Kenneth Burke, *A Rhetoric of Motives* (New York, 1950), p. 122.
[17] Roland Barthes, *Mythologies*, tr. Annette Lavers (New York, 1957), p. 159.

written word is inimical. Burke shares with his modern contemporaries a belief in language as the essential subject of literary study. In contrast to his contemporaries (Brooks, Ransom, Empson, Tate) who focus most of their critical activity on individual works, lyric poems in particular, in order to discover the ambiguities and paradoxes of language and the *sui generis* character of the individual work, Burke attempts a more systematic understanding of the workings of language.

The master discipline for the study of language is theology. It is an emergent idea throughout Burke's late work and receives its most complete expression in *The Rhetoric of Religion*. 'A close study of theology and its forms will provide us with good insight into the nature of language itself.'[18] In *Language as Symbolic Form*, Burke writes: 'Everything that can be said about "God" has its analogue in something that can be said about *language*. And just as theorizing about God leads to so-called "negative theology", so theorizing about language heads in the all-importance of the Negative.'[19] Theology is not simply the language of human transcendence, it reveals the telic, transcending properties of language itself. Burke refers to a word like honour as a god term, because it represents an aspiration toward a kind of perfection.[20] The ultimate term, of course, is God himself. Analogy may be too weak a term to describe the relationship between theology and language. For Burke theology represents the essence of language itself.

Theology, of course, cannot be reduced to language. Thus the study of language requires another name, for which Burke provides the neologism, logology. And he specifies the difference between theology and logology. 'Logology fails to offer grounds for the *perfection* of promises and threats that theology allows for.'[21] Burke's secularising project, a version of the secularising humanism of the nineteenth century, is distinguished by an attention to the rhetorical constitution of theology, a concern with the relation of the Word to words. As William Rueckert puts it: 'Burke offers a logological ("naturalistic and empirical", he calls it) explanation of the Christian drama of creation, disobedience, fall, expulsion, expiation and redemption which, from a theological point of view, is an extended reversed analogy since he moves from "words" to the "The Word"; or from the natural, verbal and socio-political to the supernatural as an analogical extension of the first three.'[22] In *The Rhetoric of Religion*, Burke's main text is Augustine's *Confessions*. But Burke should not be read as an apologist for Christian orthodoxy. Though he works exclusive-

18 Kenneth Burke, *The Rhetoric of Religion: Studies in Logology* (Boston, 1961), p. vi.
19 Burke, *Language as Symbolic Action*, pp. 469–70.
20 See Burke, *A Rhetoric of Motives*, p. 110.
21 Burke, *The Rhetoric of Religion*, p. 300.
22 William H. Rueckert, 'Burke's Verbal Drama', in Rueckert, *Critical Responses*, p. 348. Reprinted from *The Nation*, 194 (February 1962), p. 150.

ly within a Christian framework (a radical unconsidered limitation to his logology) he attempts to encompass and in a sense validate all the heretical and even antinomian tendencies within the theological project and modern secular versions.

There are, underlying the Church, many ingenious heresies so thoroughly silenced by the sword that they survive only in the refutations of the faithful. There are subtle schemes deriving the best of human insight from Cain, or centering salvation upon the snake, or lauding the act of Judas Iscariot which procured for uneasy mankind a God as scapegoat. To look back upon them is to consider a wealth of antinomian enterprise extended in ways which seem excessive, troublesome, and unnecessary, their gratuity being surpassed only by the same qualities among the orthodox. But let one not be misled into thinking that the heresies have perished.[23]

Burke does not identify himself with any single tendency, orthodox or heretical, or rather through a suspension of disbelief he is able to identify himself at different times with all tendencies. This is what is meant by 'perspective by incongruity'. Burke has been compared to Coleridge for his philosophic range, but his closest affinity, it seems to me, is with Keats, the 'theorist' of Negative Capability.

For all the insights Burke's logology offers, it has not played a central role in contemporary literary discourse. The advent of post-structuralism, in particular deconstruction, has revived interest in Burke's logology. Burke anticipates the emphasis in deconstruction on logocentricism, but with a wholly different intention. Whereas Burke attempts to show the ways in which language unfolds motives and constitutes structures, deconstruction tries to undo structures and expose the illusoriness of motives (origins). Burke represents a powerful modern version of the nineteenth-century higher criticism, which deconstruction with its powerful anti-theological animus is trying to undo. The fact that Burke commands respectful attention from post-structuralists is a sign not necessarily of agreement, but of similar preoccupations.

The theological analogue represents Burke's distinctive contribution primarily to linguistic speculation. As a literary theorist and critic, Burke's perspective may be fairly characterised as neo-Aristotelian, though not of the Chicago school. He calls his version dramatism, which is composed of the pentad 'scene', 'act', 'agent', 'agency', and 'purpose'.

In *A Grammar of Motives*, where each term is exposed in a separate chapter, Burke's interest is in the dramatist implications of philosophy and reciprocally the philosophical implications of dramatism. His subjects are Aristotle, Aquinas, Spinoza, Leibnitz, and Kant, among others (in short, 'The Philosophic Schools'). In Aristotelian fashion, Burke attempts

---

[23] Kenneth Burke, *Towards a Better Life* (New York, 1932), p. 195.

to show how narrative unfolds the logic of an idea through time, 'temporizes essence' in Burke's phrase.

Thus the search for 'logical' priority can, when translated into temporal, or narrative terms, be expressed in the imagery of 'regression to childhood', or in other imagery or ideas of things past. This concern with the statement of essence in terms of *origins* (ancestry) [may be complemented by] the statement of essence in terms of *culminations* (where the narrative notion of 'how it all ends up' does serve for the logically reductive notion of 'what it all boils down to'). In either choice (the ancestral or the final) the narrative terminology provides for a *personalizing* of essence.[24]

Above all, Burke is a cognitive critic for whom the intellectual form of a literary work and the dramatic form of an idea are the main concern. Burke tries to discover the active principle of an idea, a character, a lyric.

John Crowe Ransom's placing of Burke as a dialectical critic is right, but it is connected with a somewhat misleading distinction. 'There are two kinds of poetry (or at least of "literature") and Burke analyses one kind with great nicety, and honors it, but shows too little interest in the other. The one he honors is the dialectical or critical kind, and the one he neglects is the lyrical or radical kind.'[25] Burke doesn't neglect the lyric: his interest is in its dialectic. Thus Burke reads Keats's 'Ode to a Nightingale' as an argument in which spirit is liberated from the 'scene' of bodily fever in order to achieve a new 'immortal' or 'heavenly' scene associated with death in which the earthly contradictions no longer obtain. Burke's reading is based on biographical speculation about Keats's illness and his love affair with Fanny Brawne, something of a heresy in the world of New Criticism. 'Linguistic analysis [Burke insists] has opened up new possibilities in the correlating of producer and product – and these concerns have an important bearing upon matters of culture and conduct in general that no sheer conventions or ideals of criticism should be allowed to interfere with their development.'[26] The analysis can be read as an illustration of the scene/act ratio (an essential feature of dramatism), but it can also be read independently as an illumination of the poem.

As is the case with every Burkean perspective, limited as it is in one sense, it is all-consuming and totalising in another. If Burke is the adversary of all forms of reduction and demystification, he nevertheless proves himself to be an obsessive translator of forms of thought into his own privileged *dramatistic* vocabulary. Thus other terms that have had powerful explanatory or descriptive functions in other discourses are subsumed under the pentad: for example, idealism under agent, mysticism under

[24] Burke, *A Rhetoric of Motives*, pp. 14–15.
[25] John Crowe Ransom, 'An Address to Kenneth Burke', in Rueckert, *Critical Responses*, p. 154. Reprinted from *The Kenyon Review*, IV (Spring 1942), pp. 219–37.
[26] Kenneth Burke, *A Grammar of Motives* (Berkeley, 1969), p. 451.

purpose, realism under act, pragmatism under agency.[27] This is not reduction, because the intention is not to show the illusoriness of the terms that are being translated, but rather their functional or active roles in the world. Nothing in Burke's system precludes the possibility of translating his pentad into another system for other purposes.

Burke's pragmatic/perspectival approach implies the possibility of other perspectival approaches. Indeed, he encourages 'the heuristic or perspective value of a planned incongruity', what the Russian formalists called defamiliarisation, 'depriving yourself of the familiarity of a particular perspective ... in the interest of a fresh point of view'.[28] But the question remains: Why should the pentad have the superior or privileged status that it does have in Burke's discourse? Burke's own scepticism about the provisionality of other people's intellectual and imaginative structures leaves him open to Max Black's criticism.

It is perfectly clear that he is *not* faithful to his recommended ironical and compassionate contemplation of the foibles and embarrassments of human thought: it does not take long to find out that 'dramatism' is an alias for neo-aristotelianism, and that materialists, pragmatists, positivists and naturalists are going to take a beating for neglecting essential aspects of the mystic pentad. But how is this preference for the five-fold description of human motives grounded?[29]

In *Criticism of Culture and the Cultural Criticism* (1987), Giles Gunn rightly stresses the openness of Burke's system or systems, his comic and playful sense of the vulnerability of all essentialist categories, his willingness to revise and to abandon in the light of new situations.[30] Burke's stance is pragmatic, 'strategic', ever alive to the instance at hand. Yet the fact remains that Burke's dramatistic pentad and his logological commitments persist essentially undisturbed throughout his work.

I am not sure that a philosophically justifiable ground for Burke's dramatism can be discovered. One may speculate, however, about the reason or reasons for Burke's attraction to dramatism. It is clear from the beginning of his career that, as Bewley puts it, 'poetry [one might emend it to verbal discourse in general] becomes, not a segregated experience, but an experience at one with all human action'.[31] Dramatism serves Burke's activist, propagandistic, didactic needs. But dramatism goes beyond propaganda and didactism.

Dramatism is a vision of life and its textual embodiment as a contention of character, voices, moods. 'We contend that "perspective by incongruity" makes for a *dramatic* vocabulary, with weighting and counter-

---

[27] *Ibid.*, p. 128.   [28] Burke, *Permanence and Change*, p. 121.
[29] Max Black, 'A Review of "A Grammar of Motives"', in Rueckert, *Critical Responses*, p. 168. Reprinted from *The Philosophical Review*, LV (July 1946), pp. 487–90.
[30] Giles Gunn, *Criticism of Culture and Cultural Criticism*, pp. 63–90.
[31] Bewley, *The Complex Fate*, p. 216.

weighting, in contrast with the liberal ideal of *neutral* naming in the characterization of process.'[32] But the contention avoids mutual destruction through a comic framing, which Burke benignly proclaims to be 'most serviceable for the handling of human relationships'.[33] The comic view implies an awareness of limitation of each character's claim. It acknowledges the egoistic, materialistic drive in human beings, but it 'avoids the ... dangers of cynical debunking' by 'promoting the realistic sense of one's limitations'.[34] For all of Burke's eschewing of the liberal idea of neutrality, he is very much attached to the liberal idea of accommodation. Burke's revolutionism is toothless. Burke's dramatism invites comparison with Bakhtin's dialogism, but it is considerably more benign, perhaps a sign of the difference in the historical situations of the two writers.

The ungroundedness of Burke's pentad suggests the permanent tension in his work between the modernist perspectivalist and the nineteenth-century totaliser. How does one harmoniously encompass the world while respecting the differences within it, an especially problematic task if the individual perspectives are incongruous and not complementary.

The effect of contradiction and incongruity in Burke is to produce a new kind of non-synthetic writing. Burke's deepest moral and political ambition is to revolve murderous conflict in order to create a kind of global unity in difference. In *Language as Symbolic Action*, Burke describes his development in the following way: 'Basically, the situation is this. I began in the aesthete tradition. In *Counter-Statement*, I made a shift from "self expression" to "communication", happiest when I can transform dyad into triad – "consummation".'[35] The dyad (or what structuralists call binary opposition) contains positive and negative terms, but Burke is careful to protect the idea of the negative from connotations of evil or inferiority. Triad suggests synthesis: the dialectical totalising of Hegelian or Marxian thought. Perspective by incongruity suggests a resistance to ultimate reconciliations. I am not sure whether we are in the presence of a fundamental contradiction in Burke's view, or an unresolved tension. Perhaps encompassment is the appropriate word for Burke's intention. He wants to encompass the world without dissolving difference. He wants world government without eliminating nations. The last sentence is not intended as a metaphor, for Burke's speculations have the political ambition of world peace.

The very movement of this exposition shows the impossibilities of confining Burke to the role of mere literary critic. His perspective encompasses the world. There remains however an unworldliness in Burke's approach. He cultivates the illusion of linguistic solutions to problems of

---

[32] Burke, *Attitudes Toward History*, p. 311.   [33] *Ibid.*, p. 106.   [34] *Ibid.*, p. 107.
[35] Burke, *Language as Symbolic Action*, p. 305.

ideology and power (the approach of semanticists contemporary with him like Stuart Chase). Unlike post-structuralists, who continually stress the insurmountable gulf between word and world, Burke sees the world in the word, though not in the aesthetic sense of depriving the world of its physical, biological, political, and social substance.

In *Criticism and Social Change*, Frank Lentricchia uses Burke's activism as a club to beat modernist 'theories of aesthetic autonomy'[36] and the 'debilitated criticism' of Paul de Man's deconstructionism 'whose main effect is political paralysis'.[37] Against the background of the radical scepticism of deconstructive theory, Burke's engagement with the world seems salutary indeed. But the placing of Burke against de Man, the aligning of him with Gramsci, is itself an exercise in ahistorical abstraction, a sign of a felt despair about the current state of literary studies rather than a true assessment of Burke's status as an activist thinker and a political theorist. What this latest effort to redeem Burke for contemporary literary politics overlooks is not only the attractive and archaic Aristotelian devotion to rational coherence (to hierarchy and perfection), but also the scepticism that runs counter to all reifications (to use a contemporary jargon word) that make him so powerful a player with ideas. It is no service to Burke's extraordinary achievement to enlist him in causes for which he was not equipped to fight.

[36] Frank Lentricchia, *Criticism and Social Change* (Chicago, 1983), p. 85.
[37] *Ibid.*, p. 20.

13

Yvor Winters

Donald Davie

In 1983 Donald E. Stanford, the justly esteemed editor of Edward Taylor's poems, published *Revolution and Convention in Modern Poetry*. Subtitled 'Studies in Ezra Pound, T. S. Eliot, Wallace Stevens, Edwin Arlington Robinson, and Yvor Winters', Stanford's book rates the five poets in this sequence on a rising scale of merit from first to last. The book went largely unnoticed, as was customary with critics of Stanford's persuasion: the judgements that he arrived at were so far from those commonly accepted, that the majority seemingly could not find any common ground that would make dispute profitable. Yet Stanford reached those judgements out of a coherent understanding of the poetic tradition in English over the centuries. As he declared in the *Southern Review* in 1987:

the 'meditative short poem', written from a fixed mental point of view but not necessarily from a fixed point in the landscape, that achieves coherence and unity of thought and feeling by means of rhythms derived from traditional meters (in English usually the iambic), that speaks in a single, not a multiple voice, is I believe the finest instrument available for examining and evaluating human experience, simple or complex. It has been employed by such poets as Donne, Herbert, Vaughan, Valéry, Wallace Stevens, Winters, and Cunningham. I think they are better role models for the future than Jeffers, Whitman, Pound...

Winters would have named Ben Jonson along with Herbert, and would have reversed the rankings of Pound and Eliot in Stanford's hierarchy. Yet we hear in these comments Yvor Winters still speaking twenty years after his death. Before dismissing such views as merely crotchety, it must be noticed that they come to terms with certain figures that the current consensus is uncertain about. One such is Edwin Arlington Robinson. Another is J. V. Cunningham. And a third is Paul Valéry. More generally the consensus is uneasy with the assumption that poetry is an instrument for *evaluating* experience; and it is reluctant to legislate for the future, as Stanford does with his concern for 'better role models'.

All these emphases are characteristic of Winters: he devoted a book to Robinson (1949); he never ceased to applaud his own younger contemporary, Cunningham; he was sure that a good poem evaluates (morally) the experience that it deals with; and the readers that he had in mind were always, in the first instance, beginning poets. The French name, Valéry, is particularly significant. Though Winters refused to travel outside the USA, he was sure that an understanding of poetry derived only from poems in English must be deficient. Not only did he in his youth study Renaissance poetry in some Romance languages before he turned to English, but in the first issue of his magazine *Gyroscope* (August 1929) he cited as required reading, along with Allen Tate, I. A. Richards, Irving Babbitt, and (surprisingly) T. S. Eliot, René Lalou (*Défense de l'homme*, 2nd edn. (1926) and Ramon Fernandez (*Messages*, tr. Montgomery Belgion (New York 1927)). Winters, after his college days in Chicago, hardly ever moved far from the Pacific Coast, but he was neither provincial nor chauvinist. On the contrary, when he embarked in the 1930s on a sustained examination of his American cultural heritage (*Maule's Curse* (1938), dealing with prose fiction and historiography more than poetry), provincialism was what he convicted his inheritance of, in its undue reliance on what he thought the baleful bequest of Emerson. And among the neglected twentieth-century poets whom he campaigned for, there figure the non-American names of T. Sturge Moore, Robert Bridges, and Bridge's daughter Elizabeth Daryush. Because the case to be made for Bridges and Daryush, for Robinson and Cunningham, for Fulke Greville and Frederick Goddard Tuckerman, nowadays mostly goes by default, the Wintersian strain in criticism, still alive and vigorous, cannot be weeded out of the garden as a querulous and eccentric off-shoot, but must be seen as in many ways more generous than the accepted wisdom it seeks to supplant.

Winters in his lifetime was not at once, nor for several years, relegated to that outsider status which a successor like Donald Stanford has learned to endure with hard-earned equanimity. On the contrary, in the 1920s Winters wrote for what were recognised as the mainstream periodicals of the avant-garde: *The Dial, Transition*, and especially *Poetry*. And he was corresponding with Marianne Moore, Allen Tate, and Hart Crane. True, from the first there was a characteristic fearlessness in passing judgement; and Francis Murphy, who collected his early criticism, was surely right to remark, of these pieces as of later ones, that 'Evaluation is so infrequent in criticism that any act of judgment seems to most readers harsh and surprising.' But in this early criticism, because we cannot detect what principled position the judgements are delivered from, the judgements often seem perky or cocky, the licensed extravagances of a recognised *enfant terrible*. What was new on the other hand, and would always characterise Winters's procedure, was a determination to discriminate inside a writer's *oeuvre* between pieces where he was at the top of his bent and others where he wasn't – Winters was always at pains to point to the weaker performances of a writer whom on the whole he fervently admired, notably at this period Robinson. In other words, from the first he was more interested in poems than in poets. However, his youthful animadversions at their most caustic were still delivered from a position undefined indeed but securely within a set of assumptions that may be called 'modernist', even 'Poundian'. And this is in line with the poems that Winters was writing in those years, which he thought of, not implausibly, as 'Imagist'. Robinson, he thought in 1922, was one founder of 'a tradition of culture and clean workmanship that such poets as Messrs. Stevens, Eliot, and Pound, as H. D. and Marianne Moore, are carrying on'; and though by 1928, reviewing the anthology *Fugitives*, he declared 'the poetry of Mr Eliot is a catastrophe', the alternative that he recommended was still 'modernist': 'the tremendously energetic forms of such writers as Williams, Pound, and Miss Moore'. As Eliot in poems like 'Ash-Wednesday' began to struggle mournfully with questions of religious belief and unbelief, he alienated many more unbelievers than Winters; but Winters, at this time still devoted to 'perceptions' and distrustful of 'generalities and concepts', remained within the world of that Eliot who praised Henry James for having a sensibility too fine to be violated by ideas. The Winters of 1928 was very far from the critic whose precepts Donald Stanford was still swearing by in 1983.

That later Winters first appeared in several contributions to *The Hound and Horn*: 'Traditional Master' (about Bridges, 1932); 'The Objectivists' (1932–3); and 'T. Sturge Moore' (1933) – to which may be added his short story, 'The Brink of Darkness' (1932). The essay on Sturge Moore is often cited to show how perversely wrong-headed Winters could be. And certainly the verses by Moore chosen for approbation by Winters reveal how deaf he could be to diction, especially British diction. Moreover Winters here exposes a sort of racism that would always colour his comments on W. B. Yeats, applauding Moore in his dramas for choosing Greek or Hebrew themes, whereas Yeats 'has chosen most of his subjects from the formless and sentimental myths of Celtic tradition'. The essay on Bridges stands up much better. But the sting of these pieces is in the Anglo-American comparisons, as when Winters says that 'the diction of Dr. Bridges is as fresh and living as that of Dr. Williams; his meters allow him greater freedom, or rather greater range; he is in general a more civilised man'. Again, having detected in J. M. Synge 'a vast excess of mannerism', he remarks that 'the verse and prose of writers so varied in talents and aims as Carl Sandburg, Ezra Pound, Marianne Moore, and Elizabeth Madox Roberts, suffer rather seriously from the same vice'. Sturge Moore and Bridges provide a smoke-screen behind which Winters can launch an attack on American modernism in poetry, an attack which thenceforward he never flinched from, but pressed home with special acerbity because he judged he had himself been deluded by it for ten years or more. He discerns, first, that despite coat-trailing gives at romanticism by Eliot and others, American modernism was deeply romantic. (This others have noticed since, but equally, quite without Winters's sense of betrayal.) Secondly – and in this he is original and still disconcerting – he diagnoses romantic *irony* as a manoeuvre in writers since Jules Laforgue which enables them 'to correct the stylistic defects of looseness and turgidity tolerated by the Romantics, *without understanding the conceptual confusion which had debauched Romantic style and Romantic character alike*' (italics added). This reveals first that with Winters's condemnation of what he calls 'romanticism' is an ethical judgement, but secondly it shows how seriously by 1933 he was taking those 'concepts' which ten years before, writing of Robinson, he had airily dismissed as 'generalities'.

His review of *An 'Objectivists' Anthology* shows how incapable Winters was at this stage of showing any sympathy for the Poundian cause in which he had soldiered himself not many years before. His story, 'The Brink of Darkness', has been made much of by his admirers, as showing that Winters had personally experienced those gulfs or gusts of irrationalism which thereafter he never ceased to warn against. But who ever doubted this? Those who most strenuously urge us to be reasonable are those with most cause to fear the irrational. Samuel Johnson is one case in point; and Winters shared with Johnson more than an admirably lucid and trenchant prose-style. Johnson however, it may be thought, was clearer than Winters about the difference between rationality and rationalism.

In this momentous turn-around Winters was impelled by considerations partly practical, partly theoretical, but also in part religious. Affronted by how Eliot, in poems like 'Ash-Wednesday' and 'Marina', recorded with a curious passivity the processes which might, and again might not, lead him into the Christian church, Winters adumbrated a morality, 'stoic', which left to the individual will far more margin to decide its own destiny. The crucial document here is an essay, first published in *The New American Caravan* (1929), which, drastically revised, became 'The Experimental School in American Poetry'.[1] The hero of this essay in its first version was Charles Baudelaire. And though Winters cannot have been unaware of the argument that Baudelaire cannot be understood except as a believing Roman Catholic, Winters presents him, as he does also that hymn-writer and hymn-translator, the Anglican Robert Bridges, as a *stoic*:

---

[1] See *Primitivism and Decadence* (1937). Temperate and judicious, this essay, when reprinted in *In Defense of Reason* (1947), became probably the most influential piece that Winters wrote.

The man who, through a dynamic and unified grasp on life, lives fully and to the point of being able to renounce life with dignity, having known it, achieves something vastly more difficult and more noble than the immediate evasion and denial of the mystic or the whimper of the nihilist. It is in the consideration of this fact that we find the true function of the poet...

Though in subsequent years this message would be cloaked in the vocabulary of the literary historian or literary critic, this is the strenuous and heroic vision of man that Winters would henceforward promulgate alike in his verse and his prose.

It was the strenuousness that set him at odds with John Crowe Ransom. Ransom it was who coined the slogan-label, 'The New Crticism'. And Winters's none too civil arguments with Ransom – notably in *The Anatomy of Nonsense* (1943; later comprised in *In Defense of Reason*) – explode the still common misconception that Winters was himself a 'New Critic'. Ransom's distinction between 'structure' and 'texture' in poems affronted Winters's conviction that a genuine poem was, or came out of, a unitary act of the mind. That conviction he arrived at not theoretically but out of painfully personal experience: the suicide of Hart Crane in 1932. Winters along with Tate had been at great pains to keep Crane on an even keel and productive. And Terry Comito is surely right to say that there is no passage in modern criticism more moving (or more flagrantly in breach of academic convention) than the pages in which Winters contrasts Professor X, who toys with irrationalist theories of literature, to Crane, who took such notions seriously enough to live them out to their logical conclusion. For, he declared in *In Defense of Reason*, 'the doctrine of Emerson and Whitman, if really put into practice, should naturally lead to suicide'. Winters's bad manners in *The Anatomy of Nonsense* toward Eliot and Ransom, less noticeably toward Henry Adams (a 'nominalist') and Wallace Stevens (a 'hedonist'), should be seen in the light of the grief and indignation he felt at the wasteful extinction of Crane's genious. Wrong ideas, he thought (and thought he had seen), could *kill*; hence his vehemence in exposing them.

Though Winters's ear for diction was faulty – like his friend and contemporary Tate, he was oddly susceptible to high-flown archaisms – his ear for rhythm and cadence was incomparably fine. And it is the nicety of his discriminations about metre which makes him irreplacable. The distinctions that he made in 'The Experimental School in American Poetry' between syllabic, accentual, and accentual-syllabic metres, ought to constitute (though it's plain that they don't) a rudimentary primer for every reader. They are plain and commonsensical, in an area where common sense is hard to come by. His attempt to scan the short-lined unmetred verse of William Carlos Williams must be judged a failure; it represents one stage in a dogged but ultimately hopeless rearguard action on behalf of the author of *Sour Grapes* (1921), who in every collection after that early one disappointed Winters more than he found it, until the very end, possible to acknowledge. The essential supplement to Winters's prosody is 'The Audible Reading of Poetry' which, originally a lecture to the Kenyon School of English in 1949, was reprinted with four other essays (one on Hopkins, one on Frost) in *The Function of Criticism* (1957). The fine discriminations that Winters could make in metred verse – in unmetred also, though there he never found a terminology for registering his perceptions faithfully – were possible only to a reader who acted on the principle, idly subscribed to by many, that the rhythmical character of a poem is near to the heart of it; who thought moreover that that 'character', perceptible to us as deviations from a norm of expectation, could emerge only when that norm was firmly established and not transgressed lightly. One sees clearly why Winters was outraged by Ransom's supposition that at a late stage in composition a poet might choose to 'roughen' the metre of a poem so as to make it more 'interesting'.

Winters's last book, *Forms of Discovery* (1967), has been thought by intemperate admirers to crown appropriately his solitary and embattled career as a critic. But it is hard to agree: leaving aside the justified resentments at ill-treatment which colour its pages to those in the know, it seems to represent a sadly instructive instance of how *not* to combine literary history with the history of ideas. In *Maule's Curse* and elsewhere Winters had powerfully called on intellectual history to buttress his strictly literary judgements. But, dealing with American writers, he could safely assume in himself and his readers (it might not be a safe assumption today) sufficient knowledge in the broadest terms of other dimensions of American history – political, social, economic, demographic. Winters had no such inwardness with these dimensions of the history of the British Isles, and reading that history through the single lens of the history of ideas brings about such anomalies – alike in *Forms of Discovery* and the associated anthology *Quest for Reality* (1969, completed by Kenneth Fields) – as finding no British poet of merit between Charles Churchill (1731–64) and Thomas Hardy (b. 1840). One may sympathise with Winters's distrust of 'romanticism', whether in its British or its American versions, and yet doubt whether it was a misconception dreamed up in poets' or philosophers' studies without some pressure from extra-intellectual developments like the Industrial Revolution. The strength of *Forms of Discovery* is all in its first chapter, where Winters showed all over again his sensitivity to what he first isolated as 'the plain style' in Elizabethan poetry; but that style, and the principles that inform it, were not, as Winters would have us believe, lost to sight between the seventeenth century and the twentieth.

The critic
and the institutions of culture

14

Criticism and the academy

Wallace Martin

In concluding his *History of Criticism* (1900–4), Saintsbury remarked that 'the *personnel* of Criticism' had been 'enlarged, improved, strengthened in a most remarkable degree' during the preceding fifty years. Citing Sainte-Beuve and Matthew Arnold as the most distinguished practitioners of 'this New Criticism', he looked forward to its dissemination and to the 'possible institution of a new Priesthood of Literature, disinterested, teaching the world really to read, enabling it to understand and enjoy' (III, pp. 606–7). As Saintsbury all but says, that priesthood could only be the professoriate. During the next fifty years, 'criticism, once the province of nonacademic journalists and men of letters, became (with exceptions) virtually the monopoly of university departments' (Graff, *Professing Literature*, p. 14).

At the beginning of the century, the distinction between men of letters and professors was not so sharp as to prevent movement from one occupation to the other. Later, universities served as occasional havens for writers and poets who also happened to be critics. In these cases, the academy was simply a site for the production of criticism that might incidentally reflect the circumstances of its creation. There was a more integral relation between the site and the activity in the criticism of those who spent their entire careers in universities, but within this encompassing category, discriminations are necessary. Some were also poets whose critical interests were related to their creative practice (Richards, Empson, Blackmur, and Winters, for example). Scholar-critics (A. C. Bradley, C. S. Lewis) constitute another category, and scholar-theorists (René Wellek, R. S. Crane, W. K. Wimsatt) a third. And a few made signal contributions as editors – such as Leavis and Ransom, who, in *Scrutiny* and *The Kenyon Review*, brought together the practical criticism that is the most noteworthy innovation of academic criticism in the first half of the century.

When history is conceived as a narrative in which some new force challenges existing structures, gradually grows stronger, eventually achieves dominance, and becomes in its turn an institutional structure that defends itself against new challenges as its powers wane, it is understandable that the story most frequently recounted about criticism and the academy in the first half of the century is that of the rise and incipient decline of practical and new criticism. For critics and scholars who were not adherents of these schools, however, this account explains only a few of the significant changes in literary study during these years. As other evidence is adduced, the coherence of the story is threatened by subplots, embedded narratives, and the retelling of episodes from different points of view. Other protagonists emerge, and the middle of one critic's history becomes the beginning or end in a tale told by another.

Least frequently recounted is the story in which philologists and advocates of modern literatures were the heroes who established a place for English studies as a discipline despite the opposition of classicists and those who would either subordinate such study to the acquisition of literacy and inculcation of morality, or equate it with criticism as practised in literary and political journals. Pedagogy and criticism stood opposed to scholarship as the basis of a professional formation. For those committed to the educational ideals of the traditional college, the introduction of English studies was a defeat: it marked another stage in the decline of humanism. Conservative and radical critics viewed the professionalism of scholarly specialists as an unacknowledged commitment to positivist, materialist, and capitalist values. To exclude 'criticism' from English studies was, from either point of view, to exclude cultural as well as literary judgement from the core of the curriculum.

For the man of letters, the 'bookman', and the literary journalist, disputes between scholars and critics proved to be less important than a more fundamental change: a gradual shift of literary consumption and production from the public to the academic sphere. By mid-century, even contemporary literature had entered the academy. Poets and novelists, when not themselves teachers, carried lessons learned as undergraduates into their writings, which found acceptance from reviewers similarly trained. Only a handful of columnists and critics could thenceforth maintain themselves independent of university support or purely commercial publication.

Viewed in a more encompassing perspective, the rise of English studies, the resultant disputes between scholars and critics, and the shift of literary activity from the public to the institutional sphere can be seen as byproducts of a socioeconomic formation that has extended its sway and maintained its stability since the mid-nineteenth century. Within this formation, government-sponsored commissions have accelerated the rate of educational change, usually attempting to subordinate literary study to the ideological and technological objectives of capitalism. But once institutionalised in schools and universities, English studies attained an autonomy that made them relatively impervious to governmental pressures, public dissatisfaction, and critiques from within the profession. Although of little use in accounting for specific developments in literary study, this perspective helps explain why substantive changes have occurred only during periods of expansion, when new programmes have been introduced or new universities created. Such was the case in the late nineteenth century and again after World War II, with the proliferation of doctoral programmes in the United States and the creation of new universities in Britain. It also helps explain why, institutionally as well as intellectually, English studies in the two countries have developed along similar lines.

Although the differences between British and American universities may make it seem that no history of literary studies encompassing both can be useful, their common characteristics become apparent when they are contrasted with the universities on the Continent. In the English-speaking world, most educational institutions were products of sectarian and municipal enterprise. Differences between universities (between Oxford and Cambridge, between them and other British universities, between British and American, or privately endowed and state supported) are the norm, whereas the educational systems of the Continent have a uniformity ensured by State control. Because governments did not institute study of the vernacular literature at the university level in the English-speaking world, it emerged as an alternative to the classical curriculum in the latter part of the nineteenth century, as part of the curricular reform that also introduced degrees in the natural sciences. Consequently, proponents of English studies sought allies among the advocates of other modern subjects in the curriculum – thus setting themselves and their disciplinary methods in opposition to the classicists. The resulting tensions, unknown on the continent, tended to relegate the study of classical languages to the secondary curriculum, from which, in our time, they have almost disappeared.

Given the difficulty of reconciling these disparate accounts of criticism and the academy, the most prudent strategy is not to merge or oppose them, but to divide and concur – to sort out the conditions, forces, and intentions that shaped English studies during the first half of the century, assess their importance, and determine how they interacted. The founding of English studies will be the first topic treated in the pages that follow. The shape of this story is determined by politics, economics, demography, and the character of universities as institutions. Governmental decisions led to the rapid expansion of education, and of English as a subject, until the 1930s, after which enrolments increased slowly for a decade, dipped during the war, and then again began increasing rapidly. The subject of study, examinations, and degree requirements put in place early in the century survived until the 1950s with only minor changes. Admitting the importance of these changes, one is nevertheless forced to recognise the stability of this institutional formation, despite the continual criticism that attended its survival.

The second section of this account concerns the critiques of the philological and historical emphasis of English studies that appeared between the 1890s and 1930s. These critiques not only serve as an index of the distance between criticism and the academy at the time, but also prompt reflection on the diversity of interests – social, political, pedagogical, theoretical – that contended for possession of the subject. Most of the reforms urged by these critics were not adopted, despite widespread agreement that some of them were desirable. It is remarkable that, in the face of institutional inertia, one pedagogical innovation did secure a foothold in some universities during the 1930s – practical criticism or 'close reading', a development discussed in the third section.

In most studies of twentieth-century criticism, the introduction of practical criticism at Cambridge under the aegis of Richards and Leavis, and its gestation at Vanderbilt, where Ransom was mentor to a noteworthy collection of writers that included Brooks and Warren, are taken to mark a new beginning of English studies. Granting the importance of these events, I think they have been better understood in intellectual than in institutional histories. We know which critics were teaching in universities, and what they wrote; though the definition of 'New Criticism' becomes fuzzy as it is expanded, the phrase can plausibly be used to designate a general tendency in critical history. Within English studies, however, the effects of this critical movement are difficult to trace. Contemporaneous observers provide contradictory evidence concerning its influence in universities. Through reference to discussions of pedagogy and commission reports prepared in the 1930s, I shall argue that such success as practical criticism identifiably achieved in the academy resulted from its compatibility with pedagogical changes initiated independently within the profession.

Practical criticism was not of course the whole of new criticism, nor did the latter encompass all academic criticism. What in retrospect is most striking about the critical ferment and professorial polemics of the 1930s is the redefinition of 'criticism' which they initiated. Until then, the critical terms most prominent in debates had concerned judgement and taste. For critics from Arnold to Irving Babbitt, literary judgements were primarily assessments of meaning and of ethical significance; for Pater and what Saintsbury referred to as 'aesthetic criticism', taste was an informed but ultimately individual response not implying an objective ranking of merit. In either case, as Saintsbury said in describing his 'New Critic', the great danger was 'dogmatic' criticism, any response based on principles or rules. In the academic criticism of the 1930s, 'judgement' and 'taste' are often opposed or simply disregarded as constituents of criticism. Though 'rules' find no advocates, principles, theories, and philosophy loom large. The practical criticism of some twentieth-century critics (Leavis and Winters, for example) preserves an affiliation with that of Arnold through an emphasis on judgement and ethical values. But in the main, the theoretical criticism produced by academics is something quite different and augured a reorientation of literary study.

The last two sections of my account discuss this change and the accommodation between criticism and scholarship that it facilitated in the 1950s. What is here viewed as an accommodation is not an absence of polemics, but the use of a new vocabulary that manifests a shared understanding of English as a discipline and new ways of disagreeing about it. So long as they doggedly insisted on the importance of values and taste, in opposition to the positivistic conception of knowledge defended by scholars, critics had little to contribute to the institutionalised study of literature. What they opposed, ultimately, was not simply the scholars, but the conception of knowledge on which the modern university is based. In their turn toward principles and theory, they found a means of legitimating criticism as a form of knowledge; and in doing so, they revived the disciplinary domains that had dominated the study of literature in all earlier academies: rhetoric and poetics.

In 1895 there were about thirty-five teachers of English language and literature in the ten leading colleges and universities of the United States, and roughly the same number in Great Britain.[1] Many institutions on both sides of the Atlantic offered a degree in the subject, which three decades before had been obtainable only at the University of London. In Great Britain, this change was a byproduct of governmental efforts to modernise the universities. Between 1858 and 1889, commission reports and legislation intended to facilitate curricular change had led to the creation of chairs of English in Scottish universities. Those at Edinburgh, Glasgow, and Aberdeen were in 1895 occupied by Saintsbury, A. C. Bradley, and H. J. Grierson, respectively. At University College, London, W. P. Ker had succeeded to the chair held by David Masson from 1852 to 1865 and then, until 1889, by Henry Morley. Walter Raleigh was at Liverpool.

In some cases, as at Edinburgh, a chair of rhetoric and belles lettres had simply been renamed to accommodate English literature. In others, division of an existing chair that combined English with another subject such

---

[1] The American estimate is from Michael Warner, 'Professionalisation and the Rewards of Literature: 1875–1900', *Criticism*, 27 (1985), p. 16, and from William M. Payne, ed., *English in American Universities* (Boston, 1895), excluding instructors in composition. The British estimate includes lecturers in England and assistants to professors in Scottish universities. Where not otherwise noted in the following pages, figures concerning the United States are from *Historical Statistics of the U.S.*, 2 vols. (Washington, D.C., 1975). For less precise statements about growth, decline, and the like, I rely on Fritz K. Ringer, *Education and Society in Modern Europe* (Bloomington, 1979), and *The Transformation of Higher Learning, 1860–1930*, ed. Konrad Jarausch (Chicago, 1983).

as history (Liverpool and Manchester) or logic (Aberdeen) created the new position. Similar changes were in progress in the United States, where Frances Child, who had been the Boylston Professor of Rhetoric and Oratory, became Harvard's first professor of English in 1876.

The careers of these figures provide a representative profile of the earliest members of the profession. Half of the British professors here named – Masson, Morley, and Saintsbury – had supported themselves as writers before becoming academics. Because the stipend of professors at London, based on student fees, was less than that earned by enterprising journalists, Masson and Morley had continued their commercial editing and writing while occupying the chair. Morley and Saintsbury had been schoolmasters before becoming journalists. Masson, like W. W. Skeat (professor of Anglo-Saxon at Cambridge), had planned to be a clergyman. Some members of the profession originally secured academic positions in another field and moved into English when the subject became available; such was the case with Skeat and Child, who began their careers teaching mathematics. In Great Britain, a degree in English from London or a Scottish university, followed by one in classics or history from Oxford or Cambridge, provided a typical academic background, one shared by Raleigh, Ker, and Grierson.

For many of the early American professors of English, a bachelor's degree based on the traditional curriculum – Greek and Latin, mathematics, history, logic, theology, some natural science – was the only academic preparation. A few punctuated their academic careers with extended absences for writing and editing. M. C. Tyler, author of the first important history of American literature, resigned his professorship at the University of Michigan to become literary editor of the *Christian Union*. When the university offered to increase his salary to $2,500 in 1874, he returned, despite the fact that he had been earning $1,000 more as an editor (Vanderbilt, *American Literature and the Academy*, p. 87). Such alternation of academic and journalistic occupation remained common in the early twentieth century. The most noteworthy difference between British and American professors of English in the 1890s was that about a third of the latter had studied in Germany, and another third had higher degrees in English from American universities (Warner, 'Professionalisation', p. 17).

The proliferation of doctoral programmes in the United States, most of them modelled on the Germanic pattern introduced by Johns Hopkins University in 1876, gave rise to a professionalism that was one of the most obvious differences between English studies in the two countries. Another important difference was in numbers of institutions and students. In intellectual history, comparison of the leading institutions of America with those in Great Britain as a whole is justifiable. But hundreds of colleges dotted the American landscape, over which regional accrediting agencies exercised little control. In these circumstances, with enrolments rising rapidly, the creation of higher degrees, offered at only a few universities, and the formation of professional organisations such as the Modern Language Association of America, founded in 1883, provided useful standards of certification as well as serving the more self-interested end of establishing distinctions that would enhance status and improve salaries.

In the early history of the American MLA, as Wallace Douglas has shown, pedagogical interests were soon discarded, and exhortations by presidents of the association to prevent literary study from dwindling into philology and pedantry, beginning with James Russell Lowell's address in 1890, were ineffectual in the face of increasing scholarly specialisation. In Great Britain, no such professional organisation existed to promote scholarly interests at the university level. The British Modern Languages Association, founded in 1892, consisted mainly of school teachers of foreign languages, and when the English Association was organised in 1906, a motion to seek affiliation with the Modern Language Assocation was narrowly defeated; neither group exercised a significant influence on the development of the profession (Hawkins, *Modern Languages in the Curriculum*, p. 122; Smith, *The Origin and History of the English Association*, p. 5).

These differences are sometimes cited to argue that English studies in America turned in the direction of scholarship while those in Great Britain remained broadly humanistic. But it is surprising to find that, in the 1890s, the book that led professors and the public of both countries to react against philology and historical scholarship was John Churton Collins's *The Study of English Literature* (1891), in which Oxford and Cambridge, not a newly instituted professionalism, were represented as the main impediments to the appreciation of literature (Palmer, *Rise of English Studies*, pp. 83–7; Pattee, *Tradition and Jazz*, pp. 201–5). Among the factors shaping English studies, the American doctoral degree and the control exercised by the classicists in Great Britain were less important than the character of the modern university and the purposes that the study of English was intended to serve.

In Great Britain, the earliest and most practical purpose of literary study was to prepare for examinations requiring knowledge of English literature – the scholarships for apprentice pupil teachers, beginning in 1846; the East India Company Civil Service examination, after 1855; the Oxford and Cambridge Local Examinations, instituted in 1858. Macaulay and Benjamin Jowett were members of the commission that recommended this change in the East India Company examinations (Palmer, *Rise of English Studies*, pp. 46–7); Matthew Arnold was among those who graded them, lamenting the cramming they required; Austin Dobson was one of several who wrote textbooks for them; Churton Collins, among others, tutored those preparing for them. After 1903, there were English papers in the government's Civil Service examinations (Tillyard, *Muse Unchained*, p. 52).

Preparation in English literature, important for pupils who took the Oxford and Cambridge or the University of London preliminary examinations, became essential in the United States after 1870, when admission to the better institutions became dependent on the results of entrance examinations requiring knowledge of set texts (see Applebee, *Tradition and Reform*; Hook, *A Long Way Together*). Latin was of course a prerequisite for admission to all British and many American institutions; over half the secondary pupils in America were enrolled in Latin courses in 1900, less than forty per cent in English. Teachers in British public and grammar schools, like those in American high schools, had usually completed a BA that enabled them to teach classical languages. Since most were responsible for more than one subject, those who taught Latin and Greek were often expected to teach English when it entered the curriculum.

English became a 'specific subject' (thus qualifying for government subsidies) in British secondary schools in 1871, and the education act of 1907 required that funded schools offer instruction in English language and literature. In the United States, a court decision in 1874 upheld the legality of using local taxes to support high schools, which soon outnumbered the private schools that prepared students for college. To prepare teachers for the rapidly expanding schools in both countries, English instruction in colleges and universities was thus desirable. Most of the arts students in the municipal colleges of England became teachers after a fourth-year course leading to a degree in education. At Oxford, a petition signed by over a hundred members of Congregation in 1891 pointed out that an English School was desirable because there was 'an increasing demand for teachers or lecturers competent to handle the subject' (Palmer, *Rise of English Studies*, p. 107).

In this brief account of the rise of English studies, the differences between American and British universities appear less important than the similarities resulting from the parallel development of secondary education in the two countries. Long before they offered degrees in English, colleges and universities set entrance examinations to test a candidate's writing ability, literature being the subject of the essays. Once such tests had been created, teachers perforce prepared pupils to take them, leading in turn to the necessity to prepare teachers to offer such instruction. That tests should lead to the creation of a course of study, rather than vice versa, may seem paradoxical. But in the United States, this conclusion is inescapable: histories of English in the secondary schools begin with accounts of college entrance examinations and the protest against them that led to the founding of the National Council of Teachers of English in 1911 (see Hook, *A Long Way Together*).

Other factors deserve mention in connection with the introduction of English in British universities. The desire for wider access to higher education led to the creation of university extension-programmes (most of them introduced in the 1870s), through which the teaching staffs of Oxford, Cambridge, and London, as well as lecturers that these institutions employed for the purpose, offered courses at other locations. It was the extension-courses that paved the way for the founding of university colleges in the midlands and north of England. To serve the needs of women, the Ladies' Education Association sponsored its own extensions. English literature proved to be the most popular subject not only in the extensions but in the working men's colleges and mechanics' institutes. For the acceptance of English in universities, however, its popularity among women and the lower and middle classes played an ambiguous role: even among those 'preachers of culture' who made extravagant claims for the importance of the subject, English was perceived as a surrogate for the classics, appropriate for those who could not enter university (see Mathieson, *Preachers of Culture*).

English, to be accepted as something other than a secondary school subject, needed allies within the university, and they were to be found not among the classicists, who considered their own discipline quite adequate for providing a humane education, but among scientists, modern historians, and those who taught medieval and modern languages. At one level, the conflict was between two models of education described by Jonathan Culler: 'The first makes the university the transmitter of a cultural heritage, gives it the ideological function of reproducing culture and the social order. The second model makes the university a site for the production of knowledge' (*Framing the Sign*, p. 13). Those who think of Matthew Arnold as an advocate of the first model may not know that he endorsed the second at the university level: 'The secondary school has essentially for its object a general liberal culture ... It is the function of the university to develop into science the knowledge a boy brings with him from the secondary school, at the same time that it directs him towards the profession in which his knowledge may most naturally be exercised. Thus, in the university, the idea of science is primary, that of profession secondary' (Arnold, *Schools and Universities*, p. 254).

The growth of science and professionalism in the universities of Great Britain was a byproduct of legislation in 1858 and 1877, which facilitated the reorganisation of teaching and hence the introduction of new degrees. The philological and scholarly cast of English studies was an integral part of their claim for acceptance as a university subject. What Palmer says concerning Oxford was true throughout the English-speaking world:

rather than proposing English as an alternative to the classics for transmission of the cultural heritage, proponents of the subject allied themselves 'with those who wished to introduce more specialisms and direct
emphasis from undergraduate teaching towards scholarship and research'
(*Rise of English*, p. 83). In the United States, the 'elective' curriculum
instituted at Harvard during the latter part of the nineteenth century
served as a model for curricular expansion in other colleges and universities and paved the way for the creation of new degree programmes. In
joining forces with teachers of other modern languages, proponents of
English were aware that, as a member of the American MLA put it, 'the
question is, will the classics as taught in our colleges make any concessions
of their amount of time to the modern languages appealing for such time?'
(Douglas, 'Accidental Institution', p. 43).

At Oxford and Cambridge, proposals to allow substitution of French
and German for Greek in preliminary examinations were rejected repeatedly between 1902 and 1905; the founding of the Classical Association in
1903 appears to have been prompted in part to organise opposition to
such changes. The strategic advantage of alliances between English and
other modern languages was apparent at Cambridge, where the Medieval
and Modern Languages tripos gained acceptance in 1878. Until 1890,
students combined English with French or German in the tripos. After that
date, they could substitute Old and Middle English, Gothic, and either
Anglo-French or Icelandic for French or German, but few chose to do so.
As late as 1922, after another revision in the tripos, only one candidate
obtained the degree entirely in English (Holloway, *Establishment*, p. 1).

Except at London, the provincial colleges, and the Scottish universities,
the degree in English was preceded, on both sides of the Atlantic, by what
was in effect a degree in modern languages and literatures. Most American colleges offered barely enough courses to constitute a 'major' in
English (consisting of about a fourth of the student's work in four years),
and the elective system allowed for flexibility in course selection. As
undergraduates at Harvard early in the century, T. S. Eliot and Wallace
Stevens studied French and German as well as English literature; they did
not complete a major in the modern sense of the term. Ezra Pound's
amalgam of linguistic and literary interests can be seen as a product of this
curricular flexibility. His call for 'a literary scholarship which will weigh
Theocritus and Yeats with one balance', like Eliot's conception of the
'simultaneous order' of 'the whole of the literature of Europe', was a
product of an undergraduate curriculum in which students moved from
one epoch and language to another in successive class hours.

At Oxford, the attempt to establish a school of modern European
languages and literature prompted an eight-year debate, which ended in
1894 with approval of an English school; but all candidates for the degree

were required to take classical moderations (the first part of the examination for the degree in classics), or complete another honours degree,
before studying English. The belatedness of the Oxford degree stimulated
public discussion of a question that had seldom been posed: what course
of study would be appropriate to a degree in 'English'? John Churton
Collins's answer to this question, accompanied by attacks on the philological emphasis in the teaching of literature, appeared in British newspapers and periodicals between 1886 and 1893, prompting response on
both sides of the Atlantic. The participants in this debate, summarised by
D. J. Palmer in *The Rise of English Studies*, explored in detail the problems that continue to confront attempts to join languages and literature in
a single discipline.

Three conceptual structures, and combinations thereof, proved attractive to advocates of English. Historical organisation was the most obvious,
but it was marked by the great divide between the medieval and the
modern. One could argue that literary studies should honour this division,
and draw the societies and languages on either side of it into two courses
of study. The philological conception of the discipline, however, insisted
on the continuity of those epochs and emphasised their origins in Gothic,
Icelandic, Old High German, and Anglo-Saxon, which for ideological as
well as linguistic reasons was henceforth to be known as Old English.
Finally, there was the conception of literary study that emphasised the
continuity of classical and modern civilisation, the Renaissance figuring as
the renewal of a humane understanding lost in the interregnum.

History and philology, the only branches of humanistic study that could
claim to be sciences, dealt with their subject matter as a chronological
continuum; they studied laws of succession. The attitude toward history
of those who envisioned a degree based on classical and modern literature
(Collins and E. M. W. Tillyard in Great Britain, Irving Babbitt in the
United States) was similar to that held by the Nuer of the Sudan. They
claim to remember personal genealogies back to the beginning of time.
Anthropologists investigating this claim discovered that the first few
generations of ancestors remain constant, but those in the middle are
discarded as new generations are added. This method of maintaining a
culture's continuity with its origins is reasonable and perhaps necessary,
when history extends so far that it cannot be contained in memory. Since
no course of study can include all literature, one can begin with Greece
and Rome, then continue from the Renaissance to the present, dropping
medieval literature into the chasm of forgetting that consumes the middle
generations of Nuer. But the result is not 'English', and at the turn of the
century there was no academic discipline for the study of 'literature'. At
Oxford, there was a professor of Anglo-Saxon, and the Merton professor
of English Language and Literature was a German-trained philologist, A.

S. Napier. Understandably, then, the new English school was largely based on the disciplinary focus provided by philology; Gothic was required.

Philology was an important part of the degree in all British universities and remained so in the 1950s. In 1917, a proposal at Cambridge that would allow students to read English without studying Old English prompted an objection from the English Association (Tillyard, *Muse Unchained*, p. 62). But after World War I, the tide had turned against German philologists and the Germanic sources of the language. A government committee appointed to study the teaching of English recommended, in its report *The Teaching of English in England* (1921), that students be allowed to substitute medieval Latin or French for Old and Middle English. Again, members of the English Association objected, and the committee's report had no identifiable influence on University requirements. Only at Cambridge, in 1926, was there a substantive change in the degree (a subject to be discussed later in connection with practical criticism).

Because the examinations for British degrees allowed few options, students pursued similar courses of study. The elective system in the United States allowed students to combine different courses (units of study) for the degree, and as enrolments increased, course offerings became more varied. From rhetoric and belles lettres, the modern curriculum inherited courses in composition. As in Great Britain, philology – Anglo-Saxon and Middle English – was the next curricular stratum to appear. When courses in Shakespeare and post-medieval literature entered the curriculum, they were often philological rather than literary in character. A maxim frequently quoted before the turn of the century was that 'English should be studied like Greek', through painstaking grammatical and lexical analysis.

Realisation that history should be the organising principle of the English curriculum appears to have arrived late, to judge from a description of how J. M. Manly changed the course structure at the University of Chicago when he arrived there in the 1890s: 'Manly's reorganisation of the English Department involved a change from the aesthetic to the historical approach in the study of literature. Hitherto our discussions had turned on such questions as: what is literature? Is Macaulay literature? Manly defined the basic discipline in six period courses each occupying a quarter, running from the sixteenth century through the nineteenth. The Harvard group in the department was enthusiastically in favor of the plan, and we boldly divided the field' (Lovett, *All Our Years*, p. 92).

Descriptions of American programmes in English that appeared in *The Dial* in 1894 show they had little in common. At Yale, the available English courses did not constitute the equivalent of a year's full-time study of the subject. Greater variety was available at Harvard and the University of Chicago, in part because both had substantive graduate programmes; at the University of Iowa, there were only two advanced courses in literature. In the variety of subjects taught in the ten institutions represented, the principles that would lead to expansion of the curriculum are already apparent. Historical periods are obviously subject to division, a course in nineteenth-century literature at one university corresponding to separate Romantic and Victorian courses at another. Given the existence of courses on individual authors – usually Chaucer and Shakespeare – other possibilities spring to mind (Columbia offered one on Tennyson). Separation by genre or type (English drama to 1640; nineteenth-century prose) was common. There was also, at that early date, overlapping: Milton might appear in both a survey of English literature and a course on English poetic masterpieces.

A survey of one hundred English departments in 1930 showed that they offered well over a hundred different courses in literature (see Davidson, 'Our College Curriculum'). The only restraint they seemed to exercise was that they had few offerings in American literature, contemporary literature, and the novel; addition of courses in these areas was the most significant curricular change of the next three decades. About half of the departments offered courses in literary criticism, a proportion that had increased only slightly by the 1960s (Gerber, *College Teaching of English*, p. 184). (In England, by 1909, there were papers on literary criticism in the examinations at Manchester, Liverpool, Leeds, and Sheffield, but proposals for similar papers at Oxford and Cambridge had not been approved.)

From the wealth of available courses, American students in English selected those that would constitute their major. Many institutions required them to choose courses in certain historical and generic categories, in order to ensure their 'coverage' of the subject. A report prepared by the Curriculum Commission of the National Council of Teachers of English, published in 1934, recommended that students majoring in English take five year-long courses in the subject, but did not make any suggestions concerning their selection. It was more specific about language requirements, recommending four years of Latin and two of a modern language at the secondary level, and at the college level one year of Latin or Greek, continuation of the modern language studied earlier, and commencement of another (Campbell, *Teaching*, pp. 61–4).

The haphazard character of the American BA and of departmental course offerings resulted from the purposes they did and did not serve. Because most students working for degrees in other subjects were required to take one or two courses in English, the discipline inherited, at the lower levels, the function of transmitting the cultural heritage once performed

by the classics; hence it did not become as narrowly professional as it
might have been in other circumstances. Given the structure of the elective
system, departments found it advantageous to offer varied advanced
courses that would appeal to the entire student body, and at the same time
allow faculty, who now had to read a great many student papers, an
opportunity to teach a subject that interested them. Limitation of the
curriculum to a few courses taken by all those majoring in English would
have been absurdly narrow and pointless, given the lack of any standard
of certification requiring such uniformity. Once American colleges of
education acquired the authority to certify secondary teachers, the BA in
English did not qualify one for any particular employment, though many
were able to use it as a teaching qualification early in the century. As in
Great Britain, the degree appealed more to women than to men (in 1941,
the first year for which American statistics are available, the ratio was
three to one).

In completing a master's degree, American students acquired a knowledge of English literature comparable to that provided by the British BA,
though with much less emphasis on philology. By the turn of the century,
the PhD had become the normal qualification for new faculty at the best
universities, and subsequent commission reports and surveys of the profession refer to the MA as a degree with no identifiable function. That
conclusion is odd, in view of the fact that until 1960, the proportion of
faculty holding the PhD was well below forty per cent (see Axelrod,
Graduate Study; Gerber, *College Teaching of English*, p. 230). Understandably, accounts of English studies emphasise the important institutions and critics; colleges and faculties of the hinterland have seldom
altered the course of intellectual history. But it is useful to remember, amid
generalisations about the doctoral degree and its effect on literary study,
that they apply only to the most prestigious universities and colleges.

For the PhD, knowledge of Latin, French, and German was presupposed, and until the 1950s, much of the study was philological – Old and
Middle English, Old French, Gothic, and perhaps Old High German,
Icelandic, or Old Norse (Campbell, *Teaching*, p. 147). Douglas Bush's
memories of Harvard in the 1920s are representative: 'Oral examinations,
after the first thirty or forty minutes on philology (which reduced many
minds, including mine, to pulp), were wholly concerned with the facts of
literary history, chiefly medieval; if the Middle Ages left any time, there
was a hop, skip, and jump through the modern centuries' ('Memories',
p. 596). In this factual and philological emphasis, we find what English
studies in Great Britain and the United States (at the doctoral level) had in
common. It persisted despite the efforts of critics, professors, and even
professional organisations to dislodge it. It originated in part as a means of
adding intellectual rigour to an inchoate discipline, but its ultimate sanc-

tion, as critics from Arnold to Leavis recognised, was an academic system based on examinations.

One of the earliest objections to degrees in English had been that an academic subject is by definition one in which it is possible to examine, and English is not such a subject: literary appreciation can neither be taught nor objectively tested, and although one can ask questions about the facts of literary history, these do not constitute knowledge of any particular 'discipline'. Avoiding the accusation that they tried to assess taste, examiners stuck to matters of fact. L. C. Knights's 'Scrutiny of Examinations' (1933) and Stephen Potter's *The Muse in Chains* (1937) show how examinations dominated the teaching of English in British schools and universities. In America, a factual emphasis prevailed not only in graduate education but in national admissions tests such as the College Board Examinations and (beginning in the 1940s) the Graduate Record Examinations. Institutionally, the debate about the kinds of teaching and testing appropriate to English was one between representatives of different conceptions of knowledge. Scholars allied themselves to canons of truth current in the natural sciences, whereas critics inside and outside the academy, as we shall see, proposed alternative models of understanding. The most compelling reasons for the use of factual examinations were, in the end, social and political.

Objective examinations in English became the norm, McMurtry suggests, because they were unbiased: 'If opportunities were to be given to the most able, then that ability should be measured in an open and visible manner; if, for example, civil service jobs in India and elsewhere were to be filled by the best qualified candidates rather than the candidates who happened to know the people who made the decisions, then an examination would produce results against which a charge of favoritism might be harder to make' (*English Language, English Literature*, p. 49). From this point of view, questions about the nature of literature, its role in education, and the proper way to teach it dwindle in importance. Equality of opportunity being the purpose, what is crucial is the fairness of a test, not its adequacy in relation to the subject matter.

Though the examination system does not provide any basis for inferring what students experienced when they read literature, it does at least provide a concrete basis for discussion of the social effects of English studies. The aims of British advocates of English, discussed in Margaret Mathiesen's *The Preachers of Culture* and Chris Baldick's *The Social Mission of English Criticism, 1848–1932*, were varied and often unrealistic, if not absurd. If English studies could achieve the social and political objectives envisaged for them by government commissions, Great Britain would have had a patriotic populace free of social tension resulting from class differences that devoted much of its leisure to high culture. On the other hand, some hoped, and others feared, that literary study would lead to dissatisfaction and social unrest.

It is impossible to determine the effects of literary study on politics and the national psyche, but one can assess its more immediate consequences in relation to economic opportunity and social status. As McMurtry suggests, the use of competitive examinations to fill government positions marks the emergence of the bureaucratic state and a new means of attaining social status – one based not on family or money, but on certification. On the Continent and in the United States, this system included the professoriate; British universities, particularly in the humanities, resisted that extension of professionalism.

The most obvious obstacle to equality of educational opportunity was the requirement of Latin and desirability of Greek for admission to higher education. The British Newbolt report of 1921 recommended English for all students, without really questioning the superior status and enhanced opportunities available to those who studied classical languages. Two American reports issued but not prepared by the United States Office of Education, *Reorganisation of English in Secondary Schools* (1917) and *Cardinal Principles of Secondary Education* (1918), made it clear that Latin would be forced to the periphery of the curriculum, and that as a result it would not continue to be a college entrance requirement. As we have seen, Latin survived as a requirement or a recommended language for those reading English, especially at the better universities; in the 1930s, students at Yale were not allowed to major in English unless they had completed four years of Latin at the secondary level. Though it entered the curriculum as a modern and hence 'progressive' subject, English found its interests allied with those of the classics when the natural and social sciences became increasingly influential in the university.

As part of the history of education, which itself is a byproduct of political and economic forces, the rise of English studies is scarcely distinguishable from that of the modern curriculum. Features of the discipline that critics have found objectionable, such as the character of examinations, specialisation in the curriculum and in scholarship, and the tendency to reduce literature to linguistic and historical fact, are precisely those features that made English acceptable to others in the university. In representing institutions, professional organisations, and governments as the agents that brought English studies into being, I have not done justice to the individuals whose interventions were important to the development of the discipline. For example, W. W. Skeat ingeniously facilitated acceptance of English at Cambridge by establishing an annual prize for an extracurricular examination in English in 1866, and by publishing *Questions for Examination in English Literature* (1873; by 1890, the book was in its third edition). Recital of such facts would extend this account inordinately. Granting their importance, one finds that the most significant acts of individuals were those that fulfilled tendencies already implicit in the discipline or the university.

The conjunction of institutional possibility and individual initiative in the rise of English studies was not accidental. Many founders of the discipline were aware of the ways in which class interests, ideology, and social change afforded them certain opportunities while foreclosing others. Such awareness is evident in an essay on 'The Higher Study of English' by Albert Cook, a professor at Yale, which appeared in *The Atlantic Monthly* in 1901. Contrasting the acceptance of English in American universities with the resistance it encountered in England, he said the difference was 'in some measure due to the aristocratic traditions which cling to the ancient seats of learning in that country. And, with exceptions here and there, the representatives of the classics have ignored, depreciated, or opposed the progress and extension of English study. The reason is plain: these classes have been the representatives of prescription and authority, and have therefore felt in the advance of English the approaching triumph of a natural foe. On the other hand, the allies of English have been democracy and individualism, the spirit of nationality, the methods of physical science, and the sensational and utilitarian philosophy, to which may be added the growing influence of women' (pp. 40–1).

In allying himself with democracy and casting aspersions on the study of Latin ('more easily learned than Greek', he said it therefore served 'for those who wish cheaply to acquire an aristocratic tincture'), Cook did not pretend to sympathise with the masses. Drawing on his own classical education, he described the rapidly expanding student body 'rushing upon the domains of culture like the hordes of Attila upon the plains of fertile Italy ... What they clamored for was less the garnered wisdom precious to the ripe scholar than such enginery of science as would empower them to extort riches from the soil and the mine, or assist them in levying tribute upon the labor of others, together with such smattering of letters as would enable them to communicate with precision and brevity their wishes and commands, or would embellish the rare social hours ... Here was the opportunity, the problem, and the pitfall of English' (pp. 46–7).

Given his views of the upper and middle classes, Cook's conception of the social position occupied by professors, who seem to perform functions imposed on them by society, is especially interesting. Like others, the professor responds to the intellectual 'forces' and 'agencies' of the age, which in his time were 'scientific zeal, insistence upon the doctrine of evolution ... the club spirit, and devotion to the cause of humanity'. Rather than opposing these, the English professor should channel the energies they represent into forms of study appropriate to the subject. 'Take first science. This can be made an instrument of training, and a producer of useful results, by means of the elaboration of indexes, glossaries, catalogues, phonological and syntactical monographs, and the like... The subsequent publication of the results should also gratify the social instinct – the instinct to associate oneself, at least in thought, with the life of humanity – and confer the sense of benefiting mankind.' There are also practical reasons for publication: 'Without this he cannot count on the respect of his professional brethren in other institutions, and without their respect he cannot, in general, hope to secure and hold the highest respect of his immediate colleagues in other branches, of his departmental subordinates, of his students, of the discerning public – or even, I may add, of himself' (pp. 121–6).

Here a new form of social organisation emerges within the academy – one that secures public acceptance through its appeal to the scientific spirit of the age, but which stands apart from social classes in an institutional hierarchy based on research and publication. The respect of colleagues in other disciplines is a crucial element in this structure, and it too depends upon a shared commitment to science. Not just the respect of others, but one's self-respect, one's identity, is conferred by this system of authentification. For those who share the spirit of the age, the scientific study of literature, perhaps based on historical principles derived from 'the doctrine of evolution', is not an imposition but an opportunity.

Pedagogues and pedants have been targets of criticism since the formation of academies. Spokesmen for the aristocracy, from Aristophanes to Irving Babbitt, charge them with substituting ethical relativism and naturalistic explanation for the sanctioned hierarchies and values on which society must be based. Advocates of social change accuse them of conservatism, of sustaining the prevalent system of values by representing it as a collection of facts and cutting literature off from its critical bearing on the present. Authors have had reason to see academics as opponents of innovation, always ancients in relation to literary modernism. To the enjoyment and understanding that the public and men of letters seek in literature, the scholar often seems irrelevant. The scholarly activity that accompanied the rise of English studies prompted these objections and others from the new humanists, liberal critics, proponents of modernism, and journalists who voiced popular opinion.

In the late nineteenth century, professors and men of letters engaged in the same kinds of scholarly activity – editing texts and writing biographies, appreciative essays, and literary histories. It was often on the basis of such activities that the man of letters became a professor. Morley's editorial activity produced Cassell's Library of English Literature, Cassell's National Library, Morley's Universal Library, and Carisbrook's Library – over three hundred volumes between 1875 and 1892. Public demand for cheap reprints continued in the first decade of the twentieth century, prompting the appearance of five new series, including Dent's Everyman's Library and Temple Classics, the latter edited by Israel Gollancz of the University of London. For information about authors, there were the thirty-nine volumes of the English Men of Letters, also edited by Morley, to which Henry James contributed his book on Hawthorne. Saintsbury edited a series on Periods of English Literature, to which other professors (Ker, Grierson, and Oliver Elton, Professor at Liverpool) contributed. In the United States, beginning in 1881, there was the American Men of Letters series, and later the Riverside Literature series, which by 1911 comprised over two hundred volumes (Bliss Perry of Harvard was among the editors).

On entering the academy, men of letters often turned toward scholarship. The journalism of Arnold and Sainte-Beuve yielded the criticism that Saintsbury admired; their professorships gave us *The Study of Celtic Literature* and *Étude sur Virgile*. The same pattern is apparent in other careers, including that of Saintsbury, who began writing multivolume histories on assuming his chair, and returned to journalism after retiring. The most striking alternations between academic and journalistic activity are found in the United States, where Paul Elmer More, Bliss Perry, Ludwig Lewisohn, Stuart Sherman, Henry Seidel Canby, and Carl Van Doren resigned academic positions to become editors, usually at a higher salary. From such figures the philologists and scholars were clearly distinguishable, but not all of the latter were academics. The most renowned scholarly projects of the nineteenth century – the publications of the Early English Text Society (founded by F. J. Furnivall), the *Oxford English Dictionary*, and the *New Variorum Shakespeare* (initiated by H. H. Furness, a Philadelphia lawyer) – were largely the work of enthusiastic amateurs.

The publication of works addressed to the academic audience marked the differentiation of the roles of the professor and man of letters. *The Cambridge History of English Literature* (1907–17) and *The Cambridge History of American Literature* (1917–21) exemplify this change, though both had some appeal to the general public. The same cannot be said of the scholarly journals that served as the standard gauge of professional achievement. In the United States, *Publications of the Modern Language Association*, the *Journal of English and Germanic Philology*, *Modern Philology*, and *Philological Quarterly* were founded between 1884 and 1922; in England, the *Modern Language Review*, *The Year's Work in English Studies*, and *Review of English Studies* appeared between 1905 and 1925. The older generation of professors and men of letters, writing copiously on the entire range of literature, had often blundered; research and specialisation were necessary to set things right. The existence of scholars performing that task and of journals to disseminate their work within the discipline need not have disturbed the public or literary critics. They prompted a wrath out of proportion to their impingement on public consciousness.

A more popular target of criticism was the teaching of English literature. Commenting on a speech given by the novelist Gilbert Parker in 1912, an editorial in the *Manchester Guardian* deplored the 'mandarin learning that tends to settle on English literature... Badly taught, it accumulates a minute lore of small facts and allusions, and worse still, it has settled exactly the relationship of every writer to every influence, and exactly what the student ought to think of him.' Stuart Sherman, then a professor at the University of Illinois, quoted this passage because it had so much in common with complaints about the teaching in American colleges. 'When the professor and the literary man fall out', he remarked, 'the public, which has its own grievances, is likely to side with the man of letters as probably the more valuable, and certainly the more entertaining, member of the commonwealth' (*Shaping Men and Women*, pp. 59–60).

The most obvious occasion of widespread dissatisfaction with the teaching of English was a vastly expanded student body that had been exposed to it. Many of the writers who gained prominence after 1900 had attended college, unlike the generation that preceded them. Jack London and Frank Norris were among the American novelists, and Van Wyck Brooks, Randolph Bourne, and John Macy among the younger critics, who complained of the historical emphasis, the piecemeal readings in survey courses, and the dull lectures characteristic of the discipline (Pattee, *Tradition and Jazz*, p. 178; Vanderbilt, *American Literature and the Academy*, pp. 199–208). On the other hand, the universities that these writers attended had one or two prominent critics in their faculties who were themselves opposed to a philological and historical emphasis in English studies; one might have expected them to escape the wholesale censure to which the profession was subjected. But the character of most criticism written by professors was such as to make it particularly objectionable to the younger generation.

Not wishing to give offence, most academic critics eschewed value judgements and espoused a genial tolerance of all literature. The three principles that Saintsbury proposed for the 'new critic' were: 'he must read, and, as far as possible read everything... Secondly, he must constantly compare books, authors, literatures ... but never in order to dislike one because it is not the other. Thirdly, he must, as far as he possibly can, divest himself of any idea of what a book *ought to be*, until he has seen what it is' (*History of Criticism*, III, p. 609). Walter Raleigh, who became Oxford's first professor of English literature in 1904, endorsed this avoidance of evaluation in his comments on the 'new criticism' (probably included in his lectures of 1910–11): 'we do not judge our poets; we diagnose their cases' (*On Writings and Writers*, p. 219). Arthur Quiller-Couch, Cambridge's professor of English literature, said in his inaugural lecture in 1911 that he would be guided by these principles: first, to study a work 'intent on discovering just what the author's mind intended'; second, 'since our investigations will deal largely with style', always to study concrete examples, eschewing 'all general definitions and theories'; and finally, to recognise that English literature was 'still in the making' ('Inaugural', pp. 11–22).

The American critics Bliss Perry of Harvard and George Woodberry of Columbia said that there were three types of criticism – interpretive, judicial, and appreciative. Their distinction between the first two was a legacy from the German philologist Boeckh, for whom interpretation meant understanding of an individual work, and judgement meant comparison of works, principles, and opinions (Cooper, *Methods and Aims*, pp. 45–52). Perry and others disparaged judicial criticism because it was associated with insistence on adherence to rules; principles, rules, and theories were suspect, as they were to Saintsbury and Quiller-Couch. In 'The New Criticism' (1910), Joel Spingarn of Columbia argued that traditional criticism, as represented by these three categories, should be discarded, and the Crocean theory of expression take their place. His essay was the occasion of Raleigh's sympathetic reference to the 'New Criticism'.

It was less the principles than the practice of the academic critics that irritated the younger generation. Perry, Woodberry, Brander Matthews of Columbia, and William Lyon Phelps of Yale were distinguished from their colleagues by the periodicals to which they contributed – not the scholarly journals, but *Scribner's Magazine*, *The Atlantic Monthly*, *The Nation*, and *The Century Magazine*, among others. Raleigh and Quiller-Couch had stopped writing for the periodical press when named to their chairs, but British professors of the next generation – Lascelles Abercrombie, B. Ifor Evans, and Geoffrey Tillotson, for example – appeared in *The London Mercury*, *The Fortnightly*, and *Nineteenth Century and After*. The critical writings of the professors were scarcely distinguishable from those of other contributors to these journals, which were strongholds of conventional taste.

On the rare occasions when they ventured opinions of current literature, the professors revealed their own conventionality. Arnold Bennett was truculent: 'For their own sakes, professors of literature ought to bind themselves by oaths never to say anything about any author who was not safely dead twenty years before they were born. Such an ordinance would at any rate ensure their dignity.' As writers of criticism, he dismissed 'the whole professorial squad – Bradley, Herford, Dowden, Walter Raleigh,

Elton, Saintsbury' (*Books and Persons*, pp. 44, 269). For the radical critics of Van Wyck Brooks's 'young America', professors were those who worshipped English literature and the past, disregarding all American literature after the 'good grey poets' of the nineteenth century. The main impediments to social change, according to Brooks, were the professor and the business man; to Waldo Frank, they were the professor, the Anglophile, and the industrialist; to John Macy, the professor, the puritan, and the capitalist (Vanderbilt, *American Literature and the Academy*, pp. 199–216).

For these American critics, whose views of literature and society owed more to Wells and Shaw than to their undergraduate education, the crucial issues in criticism involved aspects of evaluation that most academic critics tried to avoid. American critical polemics between 1910 and 1930 were less aesthetic than ideological. Authors and literary epochs served as representatives of social and political tendencies, philosophic positions, and ethical attitudes, to be praised or condemned accordingly. The refusal of the professoriate to admit that its purportedly factual scholarship and critical impressionism were based on unacknowledged ideological commitments was what proved so irritating to its critics – then as now. Van Wyck Brooks and Irving Babbitt recognised that contemporary literature was only one of the sites of contention. To make their views prevail, it would be necessary to change the literary canon, as part of a larger project of rewriting history in order to create what Brooks called 'a usable past'.

The most noteworthy assault on English studies early in the century was mounted from within the academy by the new humanists, beginning in 1896 with articles that Babbitt contributed to *The Atlantic Monthly* and later included in *Literature and the American College* (1908). When Paul Elmer More, another leading humanist, became editor of *The Nation* in 1909, he solicited contributions from Stuart Sherman, who had been one of Babbitt's students at Harvard. During the second decade of the century, Sherman continued the critique of English studies and contemporary culture while Babbitt and More elaborated the humanist creed in their writings on earlier literature. As Sherman drifted away from humanist orthodoxy in the 1920s, Norman Foerster, another of Babbitt's students, became the movement's chief spokesman on criticism and the academy.

Babbitt recognised that the difference between the traditional college and the modern university was not simply one between the transmission of culture and provision of specialised training, but represented a clash between two forms of social organisation. The college had attempted to create 'a social élite', an 'aristocracy of character and intelligence that is needed in a community like ours to take the place of an aristocracy of birth, and to counteract the tendency toward an aristocracy of money'.

Through the expansion of undergraduate enrolments, society was 'trying to elevate youths above the level to which they belong, not only by their birth, but by their capacity'; graduate education was directed toward 'professionalism and specialisation, by the almost irresistible pressure of commercial and industrial influences' (*Literature*, pp. 75–116).

Institution of the doctorate, with its emphasis on philology and medieval literature, tended to 'dehumanise literary study', 'to substitute literary history for literature itself', and to push candidates into specialities irrelevant to their subsequent teaching. Babbitt, Foerster, and More did not complete the PhD; Sherman, who did so, was even more outspoken in his criticism of the degree. The attitude of the new humanists was shared by critics of the left and by William James, who in 'The Ph.D. Octopus' (1903) referred to 'the doctor-monopoly in teaching' as 'a sham, a bauble, a dodge whereby to decorate the catalogues of schools and colleges' (p. 71). Babbitt accused professors of either reducing literature to facts, in the name of an objectivity sanctioned by science, or making it an occasion of emotional indulgence. His importance as a critic results from his insistence that the study of literature cannot be separated from questions of value and from the learning, wit, and consistency with which he sustained his thesis in his excoriations of almost all literature since the enlightenment.

From their distinction between the natural and human orders, the new humanists derived their opposition to materialism, relativism in philosophy and social thought, science in the service of technology, and naturalism in literature. Babbitt's animus against romanticism was related to his tacit rejection of theistic religions, in that the unrestrained idealism and associated egotism, egalitarianism, sensualism, and optimism of the romantics were in his view derived from what M. H. Abrams aptly termed natural supernaturalism. Through their intellectual debts to Pierre Lasserre, Ernest Sellière, and others associated with the Action Française, Babbitt and T. E. Hulme developed similar critical principles, and after Hulme's turn away from Bergson, they occupied comparable ideological positions in the polemics of their time. The new humanists provided American critics with occasion to identify the academy as a stronghold of conservatism. However, as Richard Ruland (*Rediscovery*, p. 56) and others have pointed out, radical and conservative critics were united in their condemnation of contemporary society and their opposition to an academic professionalism that, in avoiding the hazards of critical judgement, reduced literary study to factual scholarship and appreciative impressionism.

Although the emphasis of the new humanists and their opponents on the importance of critical evaluation may now seem a salutary critique of a discipline that was dwindling into pedantry, professors had theoretical as well as practical reasons for rejecting it. Some of them genuinely believed that politics and belles lettres had little to do with each other. Quiller-Couch was apparently named to the King Edward VII chair at Cambridge because of his services to the liberal party (Tillyard, *Muse Unchained*, p. 38), but one cannot infer his politics from his lectures. Oliver Elton described Saintsbury thus: 'If there is a single seat of honour, among those who discourse of church and state, that is *beyond* the extreme right, there, surely, sits Saintsbury' (*Essays and Addresses*, p. 24); yet he tried to maintain a strict demarcation between political and literary commentary. Spingarn, attacked by critics of both left and right because of his insistence on art's separation from ethics and politics, lost his professorship at Columbia because he protested the dismissal of a colleague; thereafter, he served as chairman of the National Association for the Advancement of Colored People (Van Deusen, *J. E. Spingarn*, pp. 46–60).

There were also practical reasons for professors to avoid commenting *ex cathedra* on social and political issues. In 'College Professors and the Public' (1904), Bliss Perry described the wrath unleashed in the press and even from the pulpit when professors took political positions at odds with popular opinion (pp. 106–8). English had attained its disciplinary identity by accepting the conception of knowledge current within the university. From that conception, opinions and contested values were excluded; standards of scholarship based on criteria allied to those of the sciences provided a method of assessing and certifying professional achievement. The profession of English was thus in accord with the form of social organisation then emerging, in which specialised competence – that of the engineer, psychologist, and administrator as well as the professor – rather than social affiliation was the source of status.

This was but one of the practical reasons that the profession tried to maintain its distance from some functions that others would have it perform. Exhorted by some to instil traditional cultural values, by others to produce citizens committed to one or another ethic, or simply to provide linguistic skills useful for employment, English studies were also beset from within the academy by pressures that would have reduced them to purely instrumental status. It was all very well for James Bryant Conant, president of Harvard, to assert in *The Atlantic Monthly* (1935) that 'the clash of opinion is the essence of such subjects', and that 'in this side of the field of learning a university must be concerned not with providing for cooperation but rather with arranging an area of combat' ('Free Thinking', p. 439), but such proclamations were of little use to professors in less liberal institutions.

Only by claiming to stand on the neutral territory of knowledge, as an equal of other disciplines, could English remain independent of the pressures applied by the trustees of private colleges, the governing bodies of state universities, and the populace. Secure in that position, it could leave opinion (values, taste, ideology – in short, criticism) in the hands of the institution that since the eighteenth century has thrived on such diversity: the press. This distinction between institutions is based on their functions: in the university, the production of knowledge and its transmission to a professional class; in the schools, paideia; in the periodical press, criticism and social, political, and cultural debate.

Justified in its refusal to make literary study a site of ideological and political controversy, the profession was unable to persuade the public or even its own members that it should occupy itself exclusively with philology and historical scholarship. During the 1920s, as the American Modern Language Association increased its commitment to research, dissatisfaction with that emphasis reached its height (Graff, *Professing Literature*, pp. 136–44). In 1927, E. E. Stoll, himself a well-known scholar, complained of the 'fallacies and irrelevances' of current scholarship in an article that appeared in *Studies in Philology*. A year later, Henry Seidel Canby, a former Yale professor, ridiculed the triviality of scholarly publication in a lead article in *The Saturday Review of Literature*, of which he was editor. William A. Nitze replied to Canby in his presidential address to the Modern Language Association in 1929, deriding literary critics and asserting unequivocally the organisation's commitment to scholarship. His remarks on the aims of the discipline ('Horizons', p. vi) corroborate a charge made by Norman Foerster in *The American Scholar: A Study in Litterae Inhumaniores* (1929): 'not satisfied with abandoning literature in favour of literary history and its facts', scholars were 'abandoning literary history in favour of general history' (p. 20).

Having dealt with the scholars, Foerster attacked impressionists, 'journalistic critics', and radical critics in *Towards Standards* (1930); he was editor of *Humanism and America*, published the same year, in which the targets of humanist assault were modern literature and modern civilisation. Edwin Greenlaw of Johns Hopkins replied to Stoll and Foerster in *The Province of Literary History* (1931), arguing that the dispute between critics and scholars was in a deeper sense a repetition of the battle between the ancients and the moderns, between an enlightenment belief in timeless universals and a pragmatic recognition of historical change. A new generation of American critics replied to *Humanism and America* in a collection of essays entitled *A Critique of Humanism* (1930). The latter volume augured the direction that criticism was to take in succeeding decades, and the tendencies it represented bore little relation to the polemics between academic critics and scholars in the preceding three decades.

Most contributors to *Humanism and America* were professors, and their comments on modernism (Joyce, O'Neill, Dos Passos, Stevens, and

Williams) were simply extensions of their earlier complaints about Dreiser and other naturalists: when not unintelligible, modernists represent sensory experience, instincts, and consciousness untrammelled by the 'inner check' that can raise one to the properly human level, and elevate art to a properly classical form. Contributors to *The Critique of Humanism*, when not questioning the scholarship of the humanists (Edmund Wilson), uncovering fallacies in their arguments (Allen Tate), or calling attention to their reactionary affiliations (Kenneth Burke), argued that the humanists did not recognise the morality and discipline embodied in modern literature (R. P. Blackmur) or the ethical dimensions of the act of composition (Yvor Winters). All but two of the thirteen contributors were under thirty-five, and only two had academic affiliations. Despite their political differences, they were drawn together by their commitment to modernism.

Historians of criticism note that the humanist controversy, which reached its height in 1930, subsided soon thereafter and was all but forgotten within a few years. With the onset of the depression, the humanist conception of society proved irrelevant. The southern Agrarians inherited the conservative mantle of the humanists and began contributing to periodicals sympathetic to humanism (*The Bookman* and its successor, *The American Review*); the socialists of Van Wyck Brooks's generation were succeeded by the Marxists of the 1930s. In criticism, humanism was not defeated, but simply displaced by practices more germane to literary understanding. It is in the judgements and justifications of modern literature that criticism, in the first half of the century, achieved its most vital expression. Even when the ostensible subject was poetics or earlier literature, the implicit theme in the writings of the best critics was the bearing of the past on the literature of our time. Here criticism assumes functions different from those performed by the man of letters or the pedagogical humanist. Given the difficulties that modernism presents to readers, the critic's task is to posit principles that will make texts accessible. It involves poetics and interpretation, as well as evaluation and clarification of the bearing that modernist content has on modern life.

Linked together outside the academy, modern literature, poetics, and interpretation gained a foothold therein through the activities of a generation of critics who gained entrance into the academy but remained outside the profession. Few had completed the PhD; many established their reputations in the little magazines and, after 1930, the new critical quarterlies: *Partisan Review* (founded in 1934), *The Southern Review* (1935), *The Kenyon Review* (1939), and *Hudson Review* (1948). Of equal importance in England were *The Calendar of Modern Letters* (1925), *Scrutiny* (1932), *Horizon* (1940), *Essays in Criticism* (1950), and

Encounter (1953). All but *Scrutiny* and *Essays in Criticism* (edited by Leavis and F. W. Bateson, respectively) included poems and short stories; most had columns on the arts and the cultural scene in other countries; and many of the contributors were not academics. Of particular interest for institutional history is the fact that the impetus to create *The Southern Review* and *The Kenyon Review* came not from the editors, but from the Presidents of Louisiana State University and Kenyon College; and that the Rockefeller Foundation supported these two and *The Hudson Review*, the funds being devoted to payments to contributors. The tenacity of Leavis and Bateson in keeping their periodicals alive with little financial support reminds one of the extent to which the success of new criticism in America was a product of institutional largesse.

Like the men of letters who preceded them, the critics who entered the academy after 1930 were distinguished from their colleagues by the fact that they edited or contributed to periodicals addressed to the general public. But the little magazines and quarterlies associated with modernism appealed to a much smaller audience than the magazines in which the men of letters had appeared. It was seldom possible, after the onset of the depression, for a professor to leave the academy for an editorial position. Henceforth it would be the universities in the United States that offered positions and financial security to writers whose publications served as substitutes for the doctorate.

The influence of these critics and the critical journals on English studies is difficult to assess. Some can still remember dutifully attending lectures as undergraduates but pursuing what seemed a more significant course of study in the periodicals room of the library. The quarterlies' occasional attacks on professors and their irreverence toward established reputations invited student agreement and nourished a sense of superiority and participation in a literary world outside the college. That most of one's fellow students did not share this interest was of course part of its attraction.

That the critiques of English studies by humanists, critics, and the public did not lead to changes in the curriculum or pedagogy is hardly surprising. A conception of knowledge endorsed by the profession, inculcated in graduate schools, and propagated in scholarly journals is unlikely to change at the behest of outsiders. Within the profession there was, however, recognition of a need for pedagogical methods that would be suitable for the expanding student body at the secondary level in Great Britain, and the college level in the United States. To suggest that practical criticism entered the curriculum because of its usefulness in teaching English at the introductory level is not to denigrate the method, but simply to identify the main source of its success. Although discussions of modern poetry in the 1920s contain examples of close reading, the use of practical criticism as a pedagogical method clearly stemmed from the work of

Richards and was transplanted in the United States by Americans who studied with him or learned of his work when they were Rhodes Scholars.

In 1925, I. A. Richards gave his first series of lectures on 'practical criticism' at Cambridge. In 1926, the university approved a revision of the English Tripos that contained new examination papers on the English moralists and 'passages of English prose and verse for critical comment' (what became known as the 'practical criticism' paper). These two were combined with papers from the earlier examination (on tragedy, criticism, special subjects, and modern languages) to constitute a new section of the Tripos (Tillyard, *Muse Unchained*, pp. 106–9). One result of these changes, as D. J. Palmer notes (*Rise of English Studies*, p. 153), was to reinforce the orientation toward 'life, literature, and thought' that had become part of the Cambridge degree in the Tripos revision of 1917. The paper on the English moralists gave birth to an emphasis on cultural and intellectual history, Basil Willey's lectures and books on seventeenth- and eighteenth-century backgrounds being one of its products. Another result of the new examinations was to institutionalise practical criticism, which might not otherwise have survived at Cambridge after Richards's departure (he was seldom in residence after 1929).

The practical criticism paper helped solve a long-standing problem: that of relating teaching to examinations. As Tillyard observed, 'it was a tonic to the teachers to know that the close study of actual texts, which they believed was the most profitable substance of supervision, led up to actual papers in the Tripos; there was no longer the uneasy feeling that in this study you were minding the good of a man's soul at the price of his examination results' (*Muse Unchained*, p. 117). It is doubtful whether this belief in 'the close study of actual texts' was something that did not exist before Richards's lectures and won universal assent immediately thereafter. At Cambridge, as at other universities, there were set texts for examinations, and the papers students wrote for weekly tutorials were often on a single text.

In discussing the educational applications of practical criticism, Richards said that 'exercises in parsing and paraphrasing are not the kind of analyses I have in view' (*Practical Criticism*, p. 313). His method was a form of 'interpretation', but *'only the actual effort to teach such a subject can reveal how it may best be taught'* (p. 317). Others may not have found much to guide them in his early writings. In Leavis's view, 'the show of actual analysis' in *Practical Criticism* was 'little more than show', and Richards's later work, 'with its insistent campaign against the "Proper (or One Right) Meaning Superstition" and its lack of any disciplinary counter-concern has tended ... to encourage the Empsonian kind of irresponsibility' (*Education*, p. 72).

The views of Tillyard and Leavis are here adduced to enforce a point that would presumably be obvious, if recent histories of criticism had not repeatedly overlooked it: practical criticism was never a monolithic methodology, on the basis of which one can infer its beneficial or deplorable effects on the study of literature. As conceived by Richards, practical criticism facilitated psychic adjustment to a society in which science provided the standard of truth, and literature helped people live with it. As conceived by Leavis, it became a means of exposing the shortcomings of that society in comparison with the organic community that purportedly preceded it.

Detailed study of individual texts, some say, is inherently anti-historical, and Richards, in asking students to discuss poems without knowing the authors, simply demonstrated how necessary historical information is for literary understanding. But as anyone knows who has taken examinations that require discussion of unidentified passages (such questions were set at Yale and by Winters at Stanford in the 1950s), they put a primacy on historical knowledge, in that one must be able to infer the date from the text. The emphasis on social and intellectual backgrounds at Cambridge was not at odds with practical criticism; in Leavis's view, the two were inseparable.

Leavis's views entered British secondary schools as a result of the missionary zeal he inspired in those of his students who went on to become professors of education (Boris Ford and G. H. Bantock) or teachers of English and writers of books on the subject (Denys Thompson, Frank Whitehead, and David Holbrook). Here practical criticism found expression in another form, one affected by the needs of lower- and middle-class students for imaginative and creative experience (Mathiesen, *Preachers of Culture*, pp. 117–18, 137–40). But the innovations at Cambridge had practically no influence in other British universities before the 1960s. In the United States, the dissemination of practical criticism was just the opposite: it had little effect on secondary education, in which the history of English and American literature, as anthologised by scholars (especially Greenlaw's *Life and Literature* series) held sway (Vaughn, *Articulation in English*, p. 25). In colleges and universities, the early progress of practical or new criticism – altered again to suit the conditions of its use – can be traced in the careers of a few critics.

During Cleanth Brooks's first year at Oxford (1929–30), Robert Penn Warren, another Rhodes scholar, called his attention to *Principles of Literary Criticism* and *Practical Criticism*. Brooks 'read both books eagerly' – *Principles* 'perhaps a dozen times during that first year of acquaintance' – trying to absorb Richards's mode of thought while seeking an alternative to 'the new psychological terminology as well as the confident positivism of the author'. Later, in letters to Allen Tate and John Crowe

Ransom (who had also been a Rhodes Scholar and, like the others here named, did not complete the DPhil), Brooks attempted to persuade them that despite their objections to his theories, Richards was worthy of their attention (Brooks, 'I. A. Richards', pp. 487–9). Building on Richards's emphasis on tension and 'inclusion' in poetry, but rejecting his positivist dichotomy between subject and object, Brooks and Warren produced an organicist version of practical criticism in their textbook *Understanding Poetry* (1938).

Brooks and Warren eventually joined the Yale faculty (in 1947 and 1950 respectively), where W. K. Wimsatt had taught since 1939, and René Wellek since 1946. According to Douglas Bush, one of the scholars most vocally opposed to the new critics, their only representative at Harvard (his institution) was Reuben Brower ('Memories', p. 603). After going abroad to complete a second BA at Cambridge, where he came to know both Richards and Leavis, Brower taught at Harvard and then Amherst before returning to Harvard as a professor in 1953. There he supervised the introductory course 'The Interpretation of Literature', in which graduate students served as teaching assistants. According to Paul de Man, who was one of them, the course was based on a precept derived from *Practical Criticism*: students 'were not to say anything that was not derived from the text they were considering' ('Return', p. 23). Between 1930 and 1955, about one in eight American doctorates in English was granted by Harvard or Yale; the transmission of practical criticism through their graduates began toward the end of that period.

To identify other paths by which practical criticism entered the American curriculum, it is necessary to collect evidence concerning curricula, textbooks, professional organisations, and the experiences of teachers at institutions remote from the critics and universities that understandably serve as the focus of attention in intellectual history. Changes in the teaching of literature did not result from the publication of essays or books so moving or compelling that professors set aside lifetime habits and embraced new pedagogical methods; they were not imposed on faculties, or effected by national committees. But there were areas of the curriculum vulnerable to changes that were either in accord with traditional practices or were particularly suited to the solution of problems that arise in teaching. A survey of the evidence available about these matters will establish a context for discussion of the changes that did take place.

Faculty who had not completed the PhD usually taught the introductory courses in composition and literature that were required of students who would not major in English. Because this area of the curriculum was the most troublesome and least interesting to scholars, it afforded the greatest opportunities for innovation, and it was here that alternatives to historical study first appeared – without any reference to the discussions of practical criticism then current among critics. Scholars and professional organisations that took an interest in these courses recognised that the historical approach was not well suited to the needs of students whose college 'introduction to literature' was in fact the conclusion to their dealings with the subject.

In 1930, the National Council of Teachers of English organised a Curriculum Commission to prepare reports on the teaching of language and literature at all educational levels. The collegiate group was chaired by Hardin Craig, and other leading scholars were members of the committee (A. C. Baugh, Ernest Bernbaum, R. S. Crane, Marjorie Nicholson, and Karl Young). Their report, *The Teaching of College English* (ed. Campbell, 1934), provides a useful picture of professional attitudes toward the curriculum at the time. Although Karl Young of Yale held that the introductory course in literature should be a historical survey, the committee as a whole made the following recommendations: '1. The first course or courses in literature should be planned to meet the needs not only of those seeking an introduction to advanced courses in the subject' – this being the obvious function of the survey – 'but also of those desiring to discover the essential values in the reading and study of literature. 2. The conventional survey course does not adequately serve the ends of the ideal first course in literature, since it is too heterogeneous in its contents and too little capable of promoting thought and interpretation'. They recommended instead 'courses which permit a fairly prolonged study of individual works and individual authors' (pp. 56–8).

About the form such a course might take, opinions were divided. Some advocated concentration on major authors or the literature of one period or genre. Professors Raysor of Nebraska and Noyes of Yale favoured the 'eclecticism of the French *explication de textes* [sic] – historical, intellectual, esthetic' (p. 57). In this connection, it is interesting that in discussing the MA, which it viewed as a teaching degree, the committee recommended that 'at least one course in the M.A. curriculum should be devoted to some modification of the method that the French call the *explication de textes* [sic]' (p. 126).

Complaints about the introductory survey regularly appeared in the college edition of the *English Journal* in the 1930s and in its successor *College English* (both published by the NCTE), but all evidence indicates that only the 'major authors' course, chronologically ordered, made significant inroads into its curricular dominance. A study of one hundred representative institutions in 1931 showed that eighty-six offered the survey; in 1941, a detailed questionnaire submitted to fifty colleges indicated that about a third had introductory courses involving 'types'; by 1955, the emphasis on major authors appears to have displaced the true survey, but colleges offering non-chronological introductory courses usually made them an option for students not majoring in English (see Davidson, 'Our College Curriculum'; French, 'Introductory Course'; Wray, 'Modern Odyssey'). Reversing the recommendation of 1934, a commission reporting in 1959 declared that 'literature for the *college freshman* and sophomore should survey the English and American tradition' ('Basic Issues', p. 15). The ambiguities of the sentence mark it as the product of a committee; however interpreted, it signals a reaction against alternative approaches. The most reliable data on course offerings are from 1967–8, at which time three-quarters of the departments polled required that English majors take an introductory survey course (Wilcox, *Anatomy of College English*, p. 136).

The 'types' courses considered especially appropriate for non-majors usually treated the novel and short story, poetry, and drama in one course, or separated them in three courses from which students could choose. At least six textbooks appropriate for poetry courses were published between 1934 and 1936; *Understanding Poetry*, by Brooks and Warren, appeared in 1938. 'There must be a great demand for textbooks of this kind, or new ones would not be appearing with such rapidity', remarked the reviewer of *Understanding Poetry* in the *English Journal*. After criticising the length of the commentaries on poems that it contained, he concluded that 'a teacher using this book would be glad to have so much assignment work done for him', and that those 'who will fall in with the spirit of this book will be strong for it' (see Haber).

According to Brooks (in 'The New Criticism' (1979)), *Understanding Poetry* was written because he and Warren could not find a satisfactory textbook for a course in 'literary types and genres' that they were assigned to teach when they moved to Louisiana State University in 1934. By 1936, they had (with Jack Purser) produced *An Approach to Literature*, which included sections on the essay and on biography and history, as well as on the short story, novel, poetry, and drama. Originally published by the university, it was issued by a commercial press in 1938. The order in which they presented poems in the two books – three sections on types of poetry, beginning with narrative, followed by sections on elements of poetry – combined the two methods of presentation then most common. But as the reviewer noted, their method was unconventional in two respects. Most introductions to poetry did not include detailed analyses, which even today some view as intrusions on the teacher's authoritative commentary in the classroom. Second, there are many who find any negative assessment of poems, especially those written by canonical poets, objectionable. For students cloyed with the sweets of poesy as purveyed in schools, the suggestion that a poem could be criticised was a liberation; for many professors, it was a desecration.

Given the prevalence of survey courses and the tendency to admit alternative approaches to literature only in introductory courses designed for students who would not major in English, the influence attributed to *Understanding Poetry* – commonly said to have brought New Criticism into the curriculum – is as difficult to question as it is to substantiate. How widely was the book used? The only reliable information available on this subject is from a compilation of textbook orders by sixty colleges and universities during the 1958–9 academic year. At that time, ten – mostly southern and western state universities – ordered *Understanding Poetry*; an equal number used Perrine's *Sound and Sense*, a simpler, more traditional introduction to poetry first published in 1956 (see Clapp, *College Textbooks*). Princeton, Dartmouth, Northwestern, Johns Hopkins, and Amherst, which are among the institutions that enrol many students who go on to complete the PhD in English, did not use Brooks and Warren.

In the late 1950s, the Modern Language Association, in conjunction with the NCTE, the College English Association, and the American Studies Association, undertook a study of the discipline similar in scope to the one completed in 1934. The resultant report on higher education, *The College Teaching of English* (1965), contains interesting testimony concerning the entry of practical criticism into the curriculum. 'What has made the new critical approaches to literary study so vital and exciting over the last thirty years', wrote John H. Fisher in the introduction, 'has been not their addition to knowledge but their contribution to *teaching*. The new criticism with its emphasis upon form, structure, and meaning, is essentially a brilliant method of pedagogy' (Gerber, *College Teaching of English*, p. 10). It would be fairer to say that a pedagogy could be extracted from new criticism, apart from the principles on which it was based. William C. DeVane, a representative of the older generation at Yale, remarked that the New Critical method 'is actually an old one whose novelty lies only in its emphatic reinstatement in America' (p. 22). What his further comments imply is that it was a version of translation and paraphrase exercises descending from the teaching of Latin. Just as Brooks had accepted Richards's practical criticism but rejected his theories, so the American teacher made use of the interpretive method of Brooks and Warren, separating it from their organicist theorising.

Practical criticism was clearly the most important innovation in English studies in both Great Britain and America. That those at Cambridge who disagreed with Leavis on most matters could still endorse the practical criticism question in the examinations is evidence that in most minds it was not attached to any critical theory or ideology. Bateson's view was probably acceptable to his colleagues at Oxford: 'At the lower level a degree in English should be a guarantee of the ability to read English (of any period) at least as closely and accurately as the Classics man is expected to read Greek (from Homer to Lucian) and Latin (from Ennius to Ausonius)' (*Essays*, pp. 174–5). Although he opposed the philological emphasis that persisted at Oxford, as it did at London and other civic universities, Bateson thought that 'the Cambridge system' was 'vitiated by its unhistorical bias'. About such matters, disagreement persisted, but all accepted practical criticism, and other universities added a question modelled on the one at Cambridge to their examinations.

A few American graduate programmes had tested the doctoral candidate's 'ability to pass esthetically sound judgements upon selected passages of poetry and prose' in the early 1930s, before New Criticism gained currency (Campbell, *Teaching*, pp. 140–1), and the qualifying examinations at Harvard and Iowa in the 1960s included a 'written test of the student's ability to explicate a text' (Gerber, *College Teaching of English*, p. 238), but such tests were incidental in relation to the examinations as a whole. During the three decades separating the two reports on English studies in America, the philological emphasis that had characterised the PhD and prompted criticism in 1934 had disappeared, leaving only Old and Middle English as requirements in most programmes. The earlier recommendation that those planning to enrol for the BA in English should study Latin for four years before entering college (a requirement at Yale in the 1930s) was not repeated in the later report, nor was the recommendation of two modern foreign languages at the undergraduate level.

More important than doctoral programmes, commission recommendations, or introductory courses in bringing criticism into the curriculum was the infiltration of courses in contemporary literature. In 1931, a survey of one hundred institutions indicated that a third of them offered such courses (Davidson, 'Our College Curriculum', p. 411). The commission report of 1934 said that 'opinions for and against including contemporary literature in the major as an elective are almost equally divided', and the same was true of courses in American literature (Campbell, *Teaching*, p. 64). Students clearly preferred to take such courses when they were available; the usual method of restricting enrolments was to offer only one or perhaps two (modern poetry and the modern novel). In discussing this topic, Graff cites a comment by Ransom in 1938 that suggests why the presence of these courses affected the fortunes of criticism: contemporary literature 'is almost obliged to receive critical study if it receives any at all, since it is hardly capable of the usual historical commentary' (Ransom, *World's Body*, p. 336).

By 1930, amply annotated anthologies of English literature through the Victorian period, containing biographical sketches and bibliographies, were readily available. The teacher of contemporary literature had to rely on trade editions or unannotated collections of poetry. Avid readers of modern critics and the new quarterlies could draw on those resources in teaching; others might have recourse to M. D. Zabel's *Literary Opinion in*

America (1937), an anthology of twentieth-century criticism taken mostly from periodicals, in which two thirds of the essays were devoted to particular authors and many of the others to the poetics of modernism. Although the complexity of much modern poetry makes it understandable that courses in the subject should have emphasised poetics and interpretation, this emphasis also gave professors something to teach. Simple lyrics that require no biographical or historical commentary leave all but the subtlest readers with little to say.

Historians of modern criticism have understandably attached considerable importance to revaluations of the poetic canon between 1930 and 1950: Milton suffered from the onslaughts of Eliot and Leavis, lavish attention was accorded the metaphysical poets, Shelley was a fading coal and Coleridge's criticism a rising star (despite Wellek's defence of Shelley in 1937, in response to Leavis's *Revaluations*). Granting the importance of these changes, which were reflected less in the pages accorded to each poet in anthologies than in the number of articles written about them, one can still argue that they were ultimately less consequential for conceptions of 'the canon' than the entry of modern literature, the novel, and American literature into the curriculum (the last of which is discussed in detail in Vanderbilt's *American Literature and the Academy*). So long as these three subjects were not included among the courses acceptable for the American BA in English, students could be guided into a reasonably coherent understanding of the British literary tradition from the Renaissance to the Victorian period. By 1950, that coherence was strained; by 1965, it had disappeared.

Most modernist fiction in English, apart from that of Joyce and Faulkner, was less in need of professorial clarification than modern poetry. But narrative technique, as discussed by James and elaborated by Percy Lubbock (*The Craft of Fiction* (1921)), J. W. Beach (*The Twentieth Century Novel: Studies in Technique* (1932)), Joseph Frank, Mark Shorer, and Leon Edel, provided ample materials for classroom discussion. To secure for fiction a status equal to that enjoyed by poetry in the canon, critics apparently felt it necessary to show that novels, like poems, were thematically and technically complex. For the increasing emphasis on form at the expense of content, which was characteristic of academic criticism after World War II, these theorists of the novel were as responsible as the New Critics. The distinction between 'the extrinsic approach' and 'the intrinsic study' of literature (the nouns are as significant as the adjectives), set in place by Wellek and Warren in *Theory of Literature* (1949), marked not only a separation of historical from theoretical study but a detachment of both from concerns of criticism as traditionally conceived. In the chapter on 'Literary Theory, Criticism, and History', the first term is defined as 'the study of the principles of literature, its categories, criteria, and the like'. 'Studies of concrete works of art' are either literary criticism or literary history.

Granting that many critics in the academy tended to separate literature from its social and ideological entailments after World War II, one can ask whether their activities diminished some prior concern with these topics. The commission report of 1934 said that introductory courses should present literature 'as a criticism and revelation of life rather than as a developing art or as an esthetic experience', and the introduction called attention to the importance of higher education in providing 'guidance to our social and political life in time of crisis' (Campbell, *Teaching*, pp. 56, 3). Had such attitudes characterised the profession as a whole until the post-war period, academic critics might be held responsible for changing them. It appears, however, that the changes took place before World War II.

In the early years of the depression, many members of the profession were willing to consider ways of making English studies more relevant to social issues than they had been in the past. One instance among many is an editorial in the *English Journal* entitled 'Training for the New Social Order' (1934), prompted by publication of a report sponsored by the Carnegie Corporation. 'The important point for us as teachers of English is that both radical and conservative social-studies experts seem to *expect* the advent here of some (possibly new) form of collectivism', raising the question of how teachers might help prepare students for this change. The resultant suggestions, most of which concern positive reinforcement of collective rather than individual effort and selection of socially relevant reading materials, are less important than the tenor of the editorial, which was echoed in articles appearing in the following two years.

Having endorsed the view that literary study should have social relevance, English teachers found that they were acceding to the same pressures that had led to the substitution of English for Latin in the curriculum; in this case, it was English that was in jeopardy. 'Social studies', a relatively new school subject, were obviously more relevant than English, and some schools merged the two or substituted the former for the latter (see Lyman, 'English'). The hostilities resulting from this curricular struggle were 'often undercover and unadmitted', according to one writer. 'Some English teachers accuse social-studies teachers of trying to crowd them out of the curriculum; some social-studies teachers accuse English teachers of greater concern with vested curricular interests than with the education of boys and girls' (*Essays on the Teaching of English*, p. 52).

These tensions probably prompted the statement on 'The Aims of Literary Study' prepared by a joint committee of the NCTE and the MLA and published in *PMLA* in 1938. The first section is entitled 'The

Humanities and the Social Studies', the following three 'Literature as Delight', 'Literature as Imaginative Experience', and 'Literature as Document'. In response to 'the insistent current demand that literary study should primarily inculcate "social values"', the committee expressed its belief that 'there is a considerable danger that "social values" may be overstressed at the expense of those values of individual enrichment without which the democratic state cannot long endure . . . Whatever the errors of rugged individualism in the economic sphere, the concept of political democracy assumes the efficacy of rugged individualism on the plane of the spirit'. In prompting imaginative identification 'with all sorts and conditions of men', literature contributes to a sympathetic understanding relevant to democracy; as a document, it provides insight into history and 'the potentialities of the human race'. And 'through heightened perception of the artistic excellence of more difficult material', the purpose of literary study 'is to create in the student an appetite for a more subtle, rich, and complex enjoyment than is possible on the naive level'. In lending itself to this last purpose, New Criticism was in accord with the objectives of the profession.

The pressures acting on literary study in 1940 are well represented in an essay by Merritt Hughes entitled 'Our Social Contract'. After alluding to the purely instrumental functions that university administrations would impose on English departments, he discusses 'the three-sided attack which is threatened upon the historical approach in elementary instruction'. The first threat is 'types courses', which 'have been universally shaped (and shaped very much to its good) by the principles of Messrs. Richards and Ogden'. They are an understandable reaction 'against the crass ignorance of grammar and lexicography of our students', but may divert us from the proper study of literature. In focusing on language, such courses make 'immunization to propaganda' their main object: 'they are intent on making the world safe for democracy, and they would give every student a sure antitoxin against false dialectics'.

The second and third threats come from Marxists and humanists. 'The social and ethical approaches to both the criticism and the teaching of literature make a strong appeal to those of us who are sensitive to the obligations of our profession to society', but 'a preoccupation with either of them is likely to interfere with our contract with society to teach as much representative, great literature as we have time to teach'. The best defence against all three threats is maintenance of the historical survey, which can also 'keep the balance even between the claims of Chaucer, Shakespeare, and Milton, on the one hand, and what in America is called "modern literature", on the other'.

As Hughes recognised, a shift from the truly historical survey to a study of complete works in historical sequence may appear to be a small change, but its implications are far-reaching. In the former case, extracts are chosen to serve as strands in the tenuous thread of chronological continuity spun by a lecturer. Once entire works are treated, they solicit a different order of attention, and if the continuity of the lecturer's presentation is interrupted, the historical thread is likely to break. 'One of the great solvents at work in the destruction of the survey course has been the gradual encroachment upon its lectures of the tutorial groups which alternate with them in most institutions', he wrote. 'In more than one way the tutorial method has radically changed the objects as well as the methods of teaching literature.'

For the many in American institutions who taught twelve to fifteen hours a week and graded compositions or prepared lectures when not in class, tutorial or discussion classes offered some relief. Because of pedagogical demands on their time, they usually met pressures to provide evidence of scholarly activity by preparing their dissertations, or extracts therefrom, for publication. Once that resource had been exhausted, further scholarly publication was difficult for those not located near large libraries that would facilitate research. In any case, historical research is time-consuming and often unproductive. The possibility of other kinds of publication, perhaps stemming from the interpretive possibilities that came to light in the discussion of individual literary works, thus proved tempting.

Intellectual history runs ahead of the institutional history in which ideas register their social effects; it takes less time to change one's mind than to persuade others to change theirs, or to change the curriculum. Absorption of practical criticism into the curriculum was a slow process, one which was completed only by the end of the 1950s. Though in the eyes of many it helped resolve the problem of how literature might best be taught, its applications in American New Criticism and in *Scrutiny* exacerbated the polemics between scholars and critics that, in the 1930s, moved from the literary weeklies and monthlies to the professional journals and New Critical quarterlies. What emerged from the debate was not a victory for one or another party but, as Raymond Williams points out (*Writing*, p. 182), 'a redefinition of criticism' that altered its relations with other disciplinary domains and opened new areas of literary study.

At the beginning of the century, definitions of scholarship and criticism were grouped by family resemblances around a distinction of positivist origin between 'fact' and 'value'. For those who construed value as an ethical concept, literature served a didactic function; those who associated it with enjoyment and taste looked to aesthetics rather than ethics for founding principles. Literary kinds, styles, and techniques constituted one area of criticism, journalistic assessments of merit another. This terminological network did not disappear after 1930. It survived intact, for example, in Hardin Craig's *Literary Study and the Scholarly Profession* (1944) and nearly so in G. B. Harrison's *Profession of English* (1962); many of its elements are preserved by Helen Gardner and Graham Hough around 1960. To say this is not to imply that these writers should have accepted other conceptions of criticism, but simply to point out that meanings added to the word did not necessarily encompass or cancel its traditional senses. Although increasingly varied usage of the word some-times led to misunderstandings, it had a more important consequence: 'criticism' expanded to include almost anything that might be said about literature in one or another connection.

A group of articles on criticism and the academy that appeared in the 1930s exemplified the ways in which the meaning of the word was narrowed, extended, or reconstituted for polemical purposes. For Edwin Greenlaw, whose book *The Province of Literary History* (1931) was the most noteworthy reply to the humanists, scholars studied literature as 'the reflection of a certain period in human history', whereas criticism saw it as 'evidence of what are called the immutable laws of literature and of the timeless and changeless character of the human spirit' (p. 121). He defined 'criticism' as a term equally applicable in history and science, any other sense being 'peculiar'. In reply, Norman Foerster (1936) reinterpreted the conflict as one between scholarship based on scientific naturalism and criticism rooted in the human realm of values and judgement. Foerster pounced on attempts to define criticism in ways he found unacceptable. In his MLA presidential address in 1933, John Livingston Lowes had attem-pted to mediate the dispute by construing criticism as 'interpretation, in the light of all our researchers can reveal, of the literature which is our field' ('Modern Language Association', p. 1403). Foerster would have none of it; values had disappeared in this definition, making criticism merely another word for that which 'gives form to our data' ('Literary Scholarship', p. 227).

The most decisive reorientation of the debate was instituted by the terminological innovations in Richards's *Principles of Literary Criticism*. There is nothing unusual in the title, for 'principles' and 'elements' had been staple terms in criticism since the eighteenth century. But the first chapter, 'The Chaos of Critical Theories', presupposes a conception of the subject almost without precedent in the English-speaking world. The 'chaos' Richards discovers results in part from the fact that for centuries, benighted philosophers, critics, rhetoricians, and writers on poetics had not realised that they were trying to produce 'theories', many of them not knowing what the term entailed. Here was a word around which assump-tions and speculation could gather, while remaining within the sphere of literary study. Previously, such activities had been the purview of aesthetics as a branch of philosophy. Other disciplines had 'theories'; literary study was now one of them. Furthermore, theory brought its opposite into existence – 'practice', along with practical criticism, these two sufficing to describe critical writing. With his usual terminological scrupulousness, Richards noted in the index where readers could find his definitions of 'aesthetic', 'beautiful', 'technical', 'value', and the like. 'Theory' does not appear there, probably because he thought he had used the term in its usual sense, which we all understand.

By introducing Richards's distinctions into the American debate between scholars and critics, R. S. Crane changed it from one in which fact and value had been the opposed terms into one in which literary history, as a theory of narrative, was opposed to criticism conceived as a combination of theory and practice. The first part of his essay 'History versus Criticism in the Study of Literature' (1935) concerned the presuppositions of historiography. The second part begins with the following definition of criticism: 'any reasoned discourse concerning works of imaginative literature the statements in which are primarily statements about the works themselves and appropriate to their character as productions of art' (p. 11). This definition separates criticism from 'literary appreciation' on the one hand, and any discourse or theory that does not treat 'literary works in their character as works of art' on the other. Discussion of the author behind the work is biography or psychology; personal responses are autobiography; the use of literature 'as a means of enlarging and enriching our experience of life or of inculcating moral ideals' is 'not criticism but ethical culture'. Any theory of 'the art of literature' is acceptable in criticism, but 'not a theory of ethics as with the New Humanists or of politics as with the Marxians'. Finally, Crane insists that no critic can escape the distinctions he draws by steering clear of theory and sticking to common sense. All critical writing is based on assumptions, hence on a theory; every critic has one, but some are not conscious of their presuppositions (pp. 12–13).

After making these distinctions, Crane discusses the relation between theory and practice. As in Richards, these two terms put criticism within the sphere of the scientific paradigm. But Crane altered the conceptual framework of Richards in two crucial respects. First, he cancelled, and then redefined and reinstituted, Richards's positivist distinction between the subject and the object in criticism. According to Richards, a critical statement has two parts: one that describes the object, 'the *technical* part', and another that describes the value of the experience, 'the *critical* part' (*Principles*, p. 23). Criticism, concerned with experiences, thus becomes a branch of psychology. Crane denies the substance of this distinction: the sensory, imaginative, and emotional experience of literature, as such, is ineffable and poorly represented in criticism, which is by definition a discursive form directed to a shared understanding based on reason. Criticism is therefore 'about' the object, not the experience, and what Richards sets apart as the technical is in fact its essence, 'value' being (by implication) peripheral.

This revision of Richards is related to another that has far-reaching consequences. Institution of the 'theory–practice' paradigm had the advantage of making it appear that criticism might be corrigible, rather than being a haphazard collection of impressions, speculations, arguments, and judgements (which scholars with some justice accused it of being). Philosophy, ideology, experience, and art could be reduced to a relation between hypotheses or theories and facts or experiences (practical criticism) that confirmed or disconfirmed them. By accepting this model and then pointing out that different theories – psychological, sociological, political, and ethical, for example – could be employed to study any cultural object, Crane set in place a philosophical level of critical discourse, comparable to the 'philosophy of science', that could clarify and assess the claims of theories. This conception was most fully realised in Wellek's and Warren's *Theory of Literature* (1949), in which theories are classified in relation to their disciplinary affiliations. Richards had made criticism a branch of psychology; the new model opened criticism to as many interdisciplinary affiliations as its practitioners wished to develop.

In concluding his article, Crane proposed 'a thoroughgoing revision' of English studies that would put aesthetic theory and critical practice (explication) at the centre of the curriculum and associate literary history with course work in other departments. This suggestion prompted the enthusiastic endorsement of Ransom in 'Criticism, Inc.' (1937; republished the next year in *The World's Body*). Like Crane, he put 'appreciation' and 'personal registrations' outside the domain of criticism because they are products of the subject rather than statements about the object. He also accepted Crane's exclusion of history, philology, and ethics from criticism, referring to the New Humanists and Marxists as 'moral diversionists'. (The tactic of citing these two as unacceptable extremes was common, since it left the writer occupying some generally acceptable middle ground.) Criticism, he said, 'must become more scientific, or precise and systematic'; it would be a hardheaded intellectual enterprise comparable to other disciplines.

Having freed 'criticism' from most of its traditional meanings, Ransom, like Crane, accepted 'studies in the technique of art' as part of the subject. But he did not accept synopsis, paraphrase, or even interpretation (practical criticism) as integral to criticism proper (pp. 344–6). These were menial tasks, the staples of high-school classes, women's clubs, and reviewers. The implication of this exclusion is that Ransom did not accept the theory–practice paradigm as the basis of criticism. For it he substituted

other antitheses (texture–structure, and particular–universal) that involved 'ontological or metaphysical' issues. The problem that Ransom
considered central to criticism – how does a poem differ ontologically
from non-literary prose? – is in part an answer masquerading as a question: they differ ontologically, and we must supply a philosophical explanation of this difference.

This was the third and final redefinition of criticism proposed before
World War II; elaboration of these definitions occupied academic critics
until the late 1950s. Schematically, the three can be characterised as
positivist (the stage of theory and practice instituted by Richards), pluralist (theories being subjected to philosophic assessment, under the aegis of
Crane's Aristotelianism and the *Theory of Literature*), and ontological (a
competition of philosophies, positivism, and Aristotelianism being challenged by the organicism of Brooks, Wimsatt, and Beardsley, who denied
that the subject–object, fact–value, form–content, and particular–universal dichotomies applied to the language of poetry). The existence of these
strata of critical discourse – practice, theory, philosophy, metaphilosophy
– contributed not only to the complexity of criticism but to the confusion
of critical controversies.

The systems generated by these conceptions of criticism are discussed in
other chapters; the purpose of bringing them together here, in all too
cursory a fashion, is to give some sense of how the debate concerning the
place of criticism in the academy progressed in the 1930s. The centre of
this debate in America was the *English Journal*, distributed to college and
university teachers who were members of the NCTE. Several of the
articles I have cited (including Crane's), and many of the subjects that
have not been mentioned, appeared there, each writer endorsing or
criticising other participants. A more complete account of the debate
would include discussion of a symposium on 'Literature and the Professors' that appeared in the *Southern Review* and the *Kenyon Review* in
1940, another on 'The Teaching of Literature' in the *Sewanee Review* in
1947, and a third entitled 'My Credo: A Symposium of Critics' in the
Kenyon Review in 1950–1. The second and third of these included contributions from Leavis, L. C. Knights, and Empson.

From the speculative side of the debate, most British critics preserved
themselves, despite attempts to elicit their participation. In response to
Wellek's insistence, in 'Literary Criticism and Philosophy', that a critic
should state and defend his assumptions, Leavis replied, in 1937, that he
was a literary critic, not a philosopher, and therefore under no obligation
to do so. Increased awareness of American criticism after the war did not
lead British critics to endorse its theoretical ambitions. In 1953, Bateson
remarked that Richards had 'always been more interested in critical
theory than in criticism proper' ('Function', p. 4); discussing the Chicago

critics, John Holloway said that they had produced 'history, theory, and criticism of criticism', but 'very little criticism proper' (*Mirror*, p. 199). In each case, the postpositive adjective appears to protect 'criticism', discussion of literary works, from an improper terminological expansion. The difference between the British and American traditions is exemplified in controversies about the relevance of biographical information to literary interpretation. *The Personal Heresy*, a collection of essays written by C. S. Lewis and E. M. W. Tillyard in the 1930s, is a witty and reasonably exhaustive treatment of the subject. 'The Intentional Fallacy' by Wimsatt and Beardsley (1946), the first in a seemingly endless series of American treatments of the subject, is also witty, but uncompromisingly philosophic. Their position is based on an organicist theory that entails an ontological distinction between poetry and other uses of language, and much else besides.

The cogency of some British arguments against theoretical criticism may be lost on readers who infer that an anti-theoretical position must also be anti-philosophical. A group of essays written by Holloway in the 1950s and republished in *The Charted Mirror* exemplifies the critique of theory at its best. He argues that the shortcomings of the New Critics result from their attempt to combine a respect for science with a desire to set poetry outside its purview. The scientific attitude was associated with the belief that complexity is in itself not just a virtue but an adequate index of value; to uncover it, critics were led to undertake minutely detailed analyses, uncontrolled by any sense of tact or plausibility. The claim that there is a categorical difference between poetic and scientific language led some New Critics to put ordinary usage on the scientific side of the distinction. But this made it difficult to account for the place of meaning in poetry. In making these points, Holloway, who read Modern Greats at Oxford before turning to literature, is consistently untechnical and colloquial, but his style and thought sometimes remind one of ordinary language philosophy as practised in British universities. In this instance, an untheoretical stance is a product of a very sophisticated philosophy.

Holloway was a member of the generation sympathetic to what he calls the 'revolution in literary criticism' that began in the 1930s (*Charted Mirror*, p. 204). Others at Oxford and Cambridge remained resolutely opposed to it. The persistence of an earlier conception of criticism and literary studies is clear in Helen Gardner's *The Business of Criticism* (1959), C. S. Lewis's *An Experiment in Criticism* (1961), and Graham Hough's *The Dream and the Task* (1963). They shared a distaste for the professionalism increasingly evident in the publications and vocabulary of critics. They objected to evaluation of literature because it could be based only on personal preference and might limit a student's propensity to read widely. Especially objectionable was any connection between literature

312 The critic and the institutions of culture

and ethical values. Their animus against Leavis is apparent: Lewis and
Gardner represent him by caricature, whereas Hough at least names him.
The greatest threat to English studies, in their view, was practical criticism, especially when it took the form of interpretation – trying to do the
reader's reading for him, as Hough and Gardner said. A literary work may
'suggest to us many interesting reflections', but they are not really part of
it; 'each attributes to his chosen author what he believes to be wisdom'
(Lewis, *Experiment*, pp. 84, 87). 'The heart of the matter', says Hough, 'is
not something that can be taught' (*Dream*, p. 80). Although one or
another of these ideas can be found in Eliot, within whose criticism they
take on a different meaning, their real source is the attitude of the man of
letters turned professor early in the century – Raleigh or Quiller-Couch.

The accelerated absorption of critics and criticism into universities in the
decade after World War II resulted as much from the massive influx of
students and attendant changes in the character of English studies as from
the influence of the theoretical critics. After some years of reading literature without supervision, returning veterans were not easily channelled
into the conventions of the discipline. For many students, the most vital
literary experience of the post-war years was extra-curricular – arguing
about poetry, writing for and producing college literary magazines, steal-
ing time from course work to read *Penguin New Writing* and literary
periodicals. In America, as Graff points out (*Professing Literature*,
pp. 196–7), the expansion of enrolments led to an increase not just in the
number but in the variety of courses offered, most of the new ones
involving contemporary and critical rather than scholarly interests. Faculty, students, and university libraries constituted an identifiable literary
audience large enough to support the publication of books and periodicals
that had little appeal to the general public; the character of critical and
literary production could not but be affected as a result.

  With the publication of Stanley Edgar Hyman's *The Armed Vision: A
Study in the Methods of Modern Literary Criticism* (1948) and William
Van O'Connor's *An Age of Criticism, 1900–1950* (1952), the critical
ideas that had been scattered in essays and books before the war took on
the appearance of a coherent history of innovation and debate. Five
anthologies of modern critical essays, intended primarily for classroom
use, appeared between 1948 and 1952; there were also textbooks on
criticism, such as David Daiches's *Critical Approaches to Literature*
(1956). Awareness of criticism was not circumscribed by the curriculum;
anyone interested in current literature would find criticism alongside it in
the older and newer quarterlies. Many reviewers in British weeklies were
members of the new generation who taught for a living but were professional authors – if not poets or novelists (Kingsley Amis, John Wain,

Donald Davie, and D. J. Enright) then social as well as literary critics.

For those interested in critical theory, the post-war decade brought a clarification of the differences that had emerged in the 1930s. In *Critics and Criticism* (1952), the Chicago critics registered their philosophical objections to Richards, Empson, and New Criticism, while adumbrating their Aristotelianism. The organicist theory of Brooks and Warren found its most complete theoretical formulation in Wimsatt's *The Verbal Icon* (1954), which contained a reply to the Chicago critics and the essays on the intentional and affective fallacies written in collaboration with Beardsley. In *The New Apologists for Poetry* (1956), Murray Krieger provided an incisive summary of the tradition that began with T. E. Hulme, seemed to end with the American New Critics, and traced its origins to Coleridge and German idealism. There is a sense in which the ultimate achievement of a theory is to secure acceptance of its version of history; it disappears as an object of current contention and re-emerges as a fulfilment of trends implicit in the past. By recounting the history of criticism as 'a history of ideas' separable from social history, and doing so from a particular 'point of view' (pp. vii–ix), Wimsatt and Brooks, in *Literary Criticism: A Short History* (1957), helped secure the place of new criticism in the academy. The first two volumes of Wellek's *A History of Modern Criticism, 1750–1950* also appeared during these years.

Apart from Beardsley and Eliseo Vivas, those who developed the theoretical aspects of the New Criticism were not philosophers. A revival of interest in the relation between aesthetics and literary criticism was evident in the *Journal of Aesthetics and Art Criticism*, founded in 1941, and (after 1960) in the *British Journal of Aesthetics*. R. G. Collingwood, Susanne Langer, Stephen Pepper, and contributors to the collection of essays *Aesthetics and Language* (1954) deserve mention because of their importance to the few who were not satisfied with the theoretical syntheses provided by any school then current. Without doubt, as many critics said in the 1950s, theirs was an age of criticism, but it was one in which theories were more often embraced or polemically rejected than subjected to philosophical analysis. In America as in England, critics generally condemned the 'criticism of criticism', abstractions pursued beyond their anchoring in immediate literary experience, and the use of a specialised critical vocabulary.

What the critics had achieved in their debate with the scholars was not a victory of theory over history, or value over fact, but a merging of one kind of practice with another. To substantiate this conclusion, it will be useful to review, if only briefly, the scholarship of the period. *Contemporary Literary Scholarship* (1958), a collection of essays sponsored by a committee of the National Council of Teachers of English, provides a representative account of the scholarly achievements of the preceding three decades, and it serves as a reminder that, in terms of quantity, criticism was an almost negligible part of academic publication during that period. The literary histories that appeared in 1948 – *A Literary History of England*, edited by Albert Baugh, and the *Literary History of the United States*, edited by Robert E. Spiller and others – may not have been entirely satisfactory as histories, but they remain valuable as collections of essays that winnow the scholarship then available and preserve much of it in readable form. Several volumes of the Oxford History of English Literature appeared during these years, and the seven-volume Pelican Guide to English Literature (1954–61), edited by Boris Ford, provided what many considered a useful combination of literary history and practical criticism.

Lewis Leary, the editor of *Contemporary Literary Scholarship*, asked two hundred and fifty scholars and critics 'to list the ten or fifteen scholarly or critical works published within the past thirty years which seemed most important' as contributions to an understanding of the area in which they specialised, and another ten or fifteen that had 'contributed most to an understanding of literature in general' (p. 463). In the latter category, five books stood out (there was little difference in the number of nominations each received): Eliot's *Selected Essays, 1917–1932*, Lovejoy's *The Great Chain of Being*, C. S. Lewis's *The Allegory of Love*, F. O. Matthiessen's *American Renaissance*, and M. H. Abrams's *The Mirror and the Lamp*. What in this context seems interesting about the list is that these books fit easily into the category 'literary history', except for Eliot's *Selected Essays* – and even there more than half the contents concern Elizabethan and seventeenth-century writers. Yet at the same time, reviewers referred to the works by Lewis, Matthiessen, and Abrams as 'criticism', and all three can also be characterised as contributions to intellectual history, if not to the 'history of ideas' more narrowly defined.

Intellectual history, as exemplified in Willey's *The Seventeenth-Century Background*, Theodore Spencer's *Shakespeare and the Nature of Man*, Hardin Craig's *The Enchanted Glass*, Tillyard's *The Elizabethan World Picture*, and Bredvold's *The Intellectual Milieu of John Dryden*, blends into the history of criticism, as represented in Abrams, Samuel Monk's *The Sublime*, and Bate's *From Classic to Romantic*. The 'unit-ideas' (Lovejoy) and 'archetypal analogies' (Abrams) of intellectual and critical history find imaginative embodiment in the 'elements' of literature identified by criticism – topoi, motifs, images, metaphors, symbols, and themes. In the meeting of these two currents, it is often difficult to classify particular works as belonging to one or the other. Spurgeon's *Shakespeare's Imagery and What It Tells Us* (1935) which, according to G. E. Bentley in *Contemporary Literary Scholarship*, 'did much to spread imagery study into the epidemic it became in the forties and early fifties' (p. 61), is not quite scholarship, nor is it criticism; Clemen's *The Development of Shake-speare's Imagery* is critical, but not New Critical; and if, with Bentley, we would classify G. Wilson Knight's studies of Shakespeare's imagery as 'criticism', we should take into account Knight's assertion that 'literary criticism has always been my peculiar *bête noire*; and for twenty-five years now I have been offering something in its place' ('New Interpretation', p. 382). So far as Knight was concerned, criticism entailed 'the intention of valuing, of assessing'; his own writing was 'interpretation', something 'very different'.

There is a sense in which Knight's distinction is entirely in keeping with established usage: criticism entails judgement. But once a writer has been accepted as canonical, the problem of evaluation has already been settled, according to Helen Gardner, and therefore it need not occupy the academic critic, though it remains important for journalists and reviewers (*Business of Criticism*, pp. 7–8). What appears to have happened in the 1950s, if not earlier, is that on entering the academy, 'criticism' lost most of its associations with theory and value, at a time when the most interesting scholarship on 'literary history' involved the history of ideas, rather than social and political issues. Intellectual history and practical criticism meet in 'interpretation': meanings found in particular works tend to form larger patterns that can be correlated with world views or philosophies, more persistent configurations based on myths and archetypes, the underlying attitudes that characterise a national consciousness, or stages in the evolution of culture and literature.

Myth and archetype criticism will be treated in the next volume of this history. Charles Feidelson's *Symbolism and American Literature* (1953) and R. W. B. Lewis's *The American Adam* (1955) show how a nation and its art can be characterised by the use of interpretive techniques fostered by the convergence of New Criticism and cultural history. The New Critics left the literary tradition in disarray – especially the latter part of it, as a result of their tendency to disregard the affiliations of romanticism and modernism, or to oppose the two. In works such as Kermode's *Romantic Image* (1957) and Robert Langbaum's *The Poetry of Experience* (1957), which restored connections between them, we see how poetics can contribute to literary history. As Jonathan Arac notes in *Critical Genealogies* (which contains an invaluable account of modern treatments of Romanticism), Kermode's work is indebted not to the New Critics but to Lovejoy, the historians of the Warburg Institute, and Curtius and Auerbach. Yet what he drew from these traditions seems to merge with critical interests in the 1950s – another instance of the productive confluence of criticism and scholarship.

Instances are no substitute for argument, but the works here cited, and others that could be named, serve as evidence that criticism in the acad-

emy during these years had not, as many claim, entered into a period of
decline. Graff cites comments by Wellek, Brooks, Jarrell, and others
concerning the proliferation of overingenious interpretations during the
1950s; they felt that New Criticism had dwindled into a pointless routine
(*Professing Literature*, pp. 226–9). Yet it is worth recalling that scholars
had registered the same objection to scholarship in the 1920s: driven by
the conventions of the discipline to make a 'contribution to knowledge',
writers proposed preposterous interpretations (see Stoll, 'Certain Fallacies'). Admittedly, there had been a change in the provenance of interpretive activity. Instead of asserting that Bottom was James VI (an
example Stoll cites), the modern exegete would discover an archetype or
paradox. Interpretation of individual works, which can be considered the
lowest common denominator of scholarship and criticism, need not be
used as an index of the value of either.

In 'The New "Establishment" in Criticism', published in 1956 and
collected in *The Charted Mirror*, John Holloway found in British practical
criticism a pattern of vitalising innovation followed by institutionalisation
and decline similar to the one some critics discerned in the United States. A
later essay that appeared in *The Colours of Clarity* registers a more
disturbing assessment of the changes in literary study: 'suppose the major
"reforms" of recent decades in "English" were listed. Both their champions and their opponents would include (their accounts would be different, of course) such things as freeing the student from the ... unrewarding
labour of Anglo-Saxon texts; from the burden of "useless knowledge" in
matters of "lit. hist.", or "textual study" (variant readings, Shakespeare
quartos); from an entrance requirement in Latin (the one in Greek went
long ago); and on the other hand, encouraging him both to give time to
modern literature, and to read earlier literature in the spirit he reads
modern... Can one support these changes, and yet be perturbed by
something common to them?... They all specifically *limit* knowledge.
They streamline knowledge of the past, until the student has just as much
of it as clearly makes its mark on the present' (p. 13).

Holloway traces a similar narrowing of awareness in modern poetry,
from Pound, Eliot, and Yeats (and for that matter Morris and Doughty) to
the Apocalyptics and the Movement poets. One paradoxical result of the
emphasis on recent literature in the curriculum, at the expense of courses
in earlier periods, was that it created a situation in which modernism was
scarcely intelligible to students: an attempt to explain the allusions that
puzzle them in Pound and Eliot becomes a pointless effort to reconstruct
the entire literary tradition in brief. Desperate remedies, such as courses in
world literature, the Bible, and the epic, merely add to the randomness of
a curriculum already replete with attractive alternatives. If surviving
literary historians, products of an earlier age, say that they warned us

about this eventuality, the ghosts of their predecessors, the classicists, would whisper that the problem began with the founding of English studies.

Some would hold critics responsible for the fragmentation of the curriculum. Though this is something critics may have abetted, even when they did not advocate it, decisions about the curriculum during this period were in the hands of the scholars, who seem to have been unable to forestall changes they opposed. Throughout its history, the study of English literature has grown through popular demand; even the administrators of the working men's colleges were troubled by the popularity of the subject (Palmer, *Rise of English Studies*, pp. 31–5). Despite all attempts to ensure disciplinary rigour, English studies succumb to the desires of students who, when given a choice, flock to courses in modern literature and the novel.

Another charge that has been registered against the critics is that by emphasising formal aspects of the novel, they drew attention away from its representation of society. The genre that might have preserved an awareness of the inseparability of literature and history became, in the classroom, an occasion to identify literary techniques, 'point of view' replacing 'realism' as the defining feature of narrative. In reply, one can only say that it was not the critics who brought about this change, but some critics, opposed by others; and that while the desire to raise the novel from its lowly status in relation to other genres by proving it their artistic equal was one motive for the emphasis on technique, another motive – withdrawal from social engagement – originated not in criticism, but in the political situation after World War II.

The changes that critics brought about in the curriculum apparently did not affect or reflect changes in the political commitments of the profession. Between 1930 and 1960, those who taught English tended to come from families that were conservative politically, but they became preponderantly liberal during their undergraduate years, and increasingly liberal as time passed. Faculty in English were more liberal than those in history or philosophy. The most productive faculty members and those that taught at the most prestigious institutions were more liberal than their colleagues (Ladd and Lipset, *Divided Academy*, pp. 26–30, 67–81, 127–40).

The critiques of the influence of criticism in the academy, most of which appeared in the 1950s, were responses to trends evident in publications but only incipient in the curriculum. Anthologies of essays emphasising technical aspects of the novel, designed for classroom use, did not appear until the 1960s. It is difficult to gather information about what went on in the classrooms of colleges and universities more or less remote from centres of innovation. One member of the profession who visits more

American institutions than most (Stanley Fish) says that the experience can be compared to time travel in science fiction: one faculty will embody the intellectual attitudes of the mid-1970s, another may be firmly anchored in the 1950s. The same disparities probably existed in the 1950s. Holloway's apprehension about the disappearance of the traditional curriculum might have been allayed by the descriptions of English studies at Liverpool, London, and Durham which appeared in a series of articles on 'The State of English' in the *Times Literary Supplement* in 1972. The articles on Oxford and Cambridge evoked letters to the editor from Leavis, Bateson, L. C. Knights, Raymond Williams, and George Steiner (3–17 March) which record some of the personal passions and animosities associated with English studies during the preceding decades.

Whatever the shortcomings of English studies in the 1950s, they could not be remedied by returning to some prior state of the discipline, and even in favourable circumstances, university procedures and faculty differences make curricular change an arduous process. The most efficient method of changing a course of study is to build a new university. Organisation of the new universities in Britain began in the late 1950s. The resultant programmes in literature fall outside the purview of this discussion, but they do serve to indicate the ways in which literary study might be strengthened through interdisciplinary allegiances (see 'The Newer New Universities', *Critical Survey*, 2 (1966)). Because students of English in American institutions take most of their course work in other departments, there has always been a potential for a cross-fertilisation of disciplines, but few English departments seem inclined to design their programmes with this in mind.

The creation of the literature departments in the new British universities during the 1960s can be seen as the final phase of a movement that began with the writings of Eliot, Richards, Leavis, and the New Critics. In the United States, the institutionalisation of New Criticism did not take so concrete a form; it was absorbed into existing structures, rather than being monumentalised in new ones. A history of criticism in the academy organised along these lines has the virtues of simplicity and clarity. But in equating 'criticism' with practical or New Criticism, it can account for only a small portion of the relevant evidence.

The difficulty of writing a history of criticism is similar to one identified by Lovejoy in his discussion of 'romanticism': we are confronted not with one meaning of 'criticism', but many, each of which can be seen as a villain from one point of view, and a hero from another. As we have seen, many academic critics defined the word so as to exclude its associations with both 'appreciation' and 'value'; Richards reconceived it as a combination of 'theory' and 'practice'; Wellek and Warren shifted the 'theory' to 'literary theory', defining criticism as a judgement of an individual work;

several British critics identified it with 'practical criticism', by which term some meant explication, and others meant the totality of intellectual, emotional, and evaluative response; Gardner would exclude both evaluation and interpretation from criticism; for Knight, it meant the antithesis of interpretation, and for many others, it meant nothing but interpretation. Ransom, on at least one occasion, took the position that criticism was theory or philosophy, not explication or interpretation; but the view that appears to have prevailed was just the opposite: theory, 'criticism of criticism', is not 'criticism proper'.

But the metamorphoses of the word do not end there. On the first page of *The Armed Vision* (1948), Hyman defined modern criticism as 'the organised use of non-literary techniques and bodies of knowledge to obtain insights into literature'. He cited the use of psychoanalysis and semantics as examples and later referred to 'biographical criticism' and 'psychological criticism'. The principle underlying this generative semantics is clear: change the name of any subject or discipline to an adjective and combine it with 'criticism'. Hence: sociological criticism, psychoanalytic criticism ... and, in Frye's *Anatomy of Criticism* (1957), historical, ethical, archetypal, and rhetorical criticism. 'By criticism', Frye wrote, 'I mean the whole work of scholarship and taste concerned with literature.' Here was a terminological innovation more audacious than that of Richards. Scholarship and literary history had found a place, alongside the whole gamut of interpretive possibilities afforded by other disciplines, within the embrace of 'criticism', the latter term having sacrificed only its connection with value judgements in order to achieve this hegemony. Evaluative or judicial criticism, Frye asserted in a pamphlet produced by the Modern Language Association, should be 'entirely confined to reviewing, or surveying current literature or scholarship: all the metaphors transferred from it to academic criticism are misleading and all the practices derived from it are mistaken' ('Literary Criticism', p. 58).

The interpenetration of criticism and literary history discussed earlier had created a situation in which Frye's terminological fusion was plausible, and the opposition of the two, in the writings of American humanists and New Critics, had been exaggerated for polemical purposes. Although the protean usage of 'criticism' was sometimes a terminological shuffle intended to secure a rhetorical advantage, more often it records the attempts, within English studies, to adapt to new social and institutional circumstances. As paraphrase and explication, criticism was an essential exercise at the introductory level for many students then undertaking higher education: they lacked linguistic skills, and any preservation of the tradition required that they be taught to read pre-Enlightenment English. The transfer of a portion of the production and consumption of literature from the commercial to the academic sector brought criticism with it. But within the academy, transmission of the cultural heritage was clearly opposed to a critique of culture, and evaluative aspects of criticism were therefore discarded. Furthermore, it was not the political and social aspects of the past that, in the social formation of the post-war years, seemed most important as 'heritage'. Intellectual history, national consciousness as myth, the changing relation of the self to reality – these, and not history in the old sense, were a heritage that was in the process of formation, and 'criticism' seemed as appropriate as 'history' or 'scholarship' to name them.

Within an institutional framework, a dispersal of the meanings of 'criticism' and 'historical scholarship' was necessary for a reorganisation of knowledge that would bring literary study into relation with recent developments in other disciplines. 'Biographical criticism', for example, is a thesis without a predicate: it disengages biography from its traditional place within historical scholarship, joins it to a realm in which opinions vary, and opens it to varied theories, psychological and psychoanalytic, that might explain a life. Richards was of course the precursor of this cross-fertilisation or miscegenation of disciplines; by the 1950s, other disciplines were penetrating the perimeter of literary study, and critics were adopting their methods. The difference between the narrow meanings of 'criticism' that gained currency in the 1930s and the inclusive ones that emerged in the 1950s is epitomised in a remark Graham Hough made in 1963. Matthew Arnold's conception of the function of criticism, he said, was 'an odd one. By criticism he seems to have meant the whole intellectual culture of a nation, the mental soil from which creative work can spring' (p. 58). In retrospect, Hough's usage seems dated, and Arnold's the path of the future.

Even Hough's reference to the 'mental soil' of creation is appropriate to those years (the social and ideological side of Arnold's criticism would not resurface until later). In 1958, Jacques Barzun called attention to the way in which, after *'explication de texte'* or 'close reading' had freed literature from its historical and social moorings, other disciplines encouraged an exploration of the depths on which it drifted: 'the "hidden-meaning" postulate was a derivative of the new physics and the new psychology, which could also be seen at work in anthropology, semantics, philosophy, mythology, and folklore. Indeed many experts in these disciplines, themselves caught by the new hunger for fine art, fell upon its products like starved augurs, dismembering each specimen to show by their several methods what it *really* meant' (Leary, *Contemporary Literary Scholarship*, p. 6).

The following decade witnessed the untrammelled pursuit of interpretation; and the problems raised by what appeared to be a radical indeterminacy of meaning led in turn, during the 1960s, to a revival of the one aspect of criticism that, according to Murray Krieger and Raymond Williams, had been shunted aside during this period: 'theory', a term stretched to include the philosophy of language and ontology, as well as hermeneutics and the scrutiny of disciplinary practice (Graff, *Professing Literature*, p. 191; Williams, *Writing in Society*, p. 183). In relation to subsequent changes in the curriculum and in degree requirements, the 1950s appear to mark the end of an epoch that commenced with the founding of English studies; from another perspective, that decade was one in which the reorganisation of knowledge established a groundwork for new modes of literary understanding.

15

The critic and society, 1900–1950

Morris Dickstein

Surveying the state of criticism in 1891, Henry James wrote: 'If literary criticism may be said to flourish among us at all, it certainly flourishes immensely, for it flows through the periodical press like a river that has burst its dikes. The quantity of it is prodigious... Periodical literature is a huge, open mouth which has to be fed – a vessel of immense capacity which has to be filled.' Filling this maw, James found, was a great deal of uninspired chatter of a generalised, mechanical kind, a deluge of 'reviewing' that 'in general has nothing in common with the art of criticism': 'What strikes the observer above all, in such an affluence, is the unexpected proportion the discourse uttered bears to the objects discoursed of – the paucity of examples, of illustrations and productions, and the deluge of doctrine suspended in the void.'

Besides this periodical literature there was also academic scholarship that was either genteel-Arnoldian, concerned with upholding certain moral and social values, or historical-philological, oriented toward establishing literary facts, mainly biographical, and exact texts, some of which – the poems of Donne and other metaphysical poets, for example – would prove essential to the critical revolution that followed. But especially in America, there was little that we today – with our ingrained emphasis on close reading, with our view of literary commentary as professional discourse yet also as a political and social argument – would describe as criticism. Two longtime antagonists, the humanist Paul Elmer More and his iconoclastic opponent, H. L. Mencken, could agree on one thing: the sheer paucity of genuine aesthetic criticism in the first decade of the twentieth century, when each began writing. 'When I did most of my work', wrote More, 'there was almost a critical vacuum in this country and in England... It was something of an achievement – I say it unblushingly – just to keep going in such a desert.' Mencken said much the same thing. 'When I began to practice as a critic, in 1908, ... it was a time of almost inconceivable complacency and conformity.'

By midcentury complacency and conformity were again a problem, but no one could complain, as James had, of a criticism that failed to take account of the concrete literary fact. In a 1949 lecture on 'The Responsibilities of the Critic', F. O. Matthiessen described how Eliot and other

modern writers, in the face of their wrenching experiences during and
after the First World War, had set out 'to use a language that compelled
the reader to slow down', a more difficult, more densely physical, more
disjunctive language that also demanded a different kind of reading. I. A.
Richards called it 'practical criticism' in his famous book of the twenties
that had an especially strong impact on American critics. 'What resulted
from the joint influence of Eliot and Richards', noted Matthiessen, 'was a
criticism that aimed to give the closest possible attention to the text at
hand, to both the structure and texture of the language.'

F. O. Matthiessen had developed mixed feelings about this emphasis on
language, technique, and close reading, which was rapidly establishing
itself as a new orthodoxy in American universities. He himself had given
great impetus to the academic study of American literature with his
epochal *American Renaissance* (1941), a book that applied a variety of
analytic approaches – mythic, psychological, linguistic, and social – to a
sharply defined canon of five of America's greatest writers. Though Matthiessen was a leftist and Christian socialist who insisted on his subjects'
'devotion to the possibilities of democracy', his influence was pedagogic,
not political. Just as D. W. Griffith had invented cinematic narrative by
perfecting the close-up, Matthiessen scanned the physiognomy of his
writers through a lens borrowed from the study of difficult modern
literature.

But by 1949 he was disenchanted: 'As we watch our own generation
producing whole anthologies of criticism devoted to single contemporary
authors and more and more detailed books of criticism of criticism, we
should realize that we have come to the unnatural point where textual
analysis seems to be an end in itself.' A movement that had come to
challenge the old undiscriminating journalism, caught up entirely in the
hubbub of the present, and the old historical scholarship, which left the
writers of the past safely immured in the past, had itself become pedantic,
mechanical, predictable. The little magazines, after they had raised the
banner of criticism against the journalists and the scholars, had declined
into 'a new scholasticism' and were 'not always distinguishable from the
philological journals which they abhor. The names of the authors may be
modern, but the smell is old.'

Matthiessen's discontent highlights many of the changes that had occurred in criticism since the twenties, and their limitations. His essay itself
is part of the flood of 'criticism of criticism' that gathered steam in the
forties with John Crowe Ransom's *The New Criticism*, Stanley Edgar
Hyman's *The Armed Vision*, and René Wellek and Austin Warren's
Theory of Literature. The shift he describes from general commentary to
close reading reflects the overall turn from periodical journalism and
belles lettres toward academic criticism, which resulted from the great

expansion of higher education all through the twentieth century, but especially after the Second World War. Few modern writers had much use for democracy; they saw in the extension of literacy the degradation of art, the decay of language. Indeed, the difficulty of their work can be seen as a reaction against the late-Romantic style of their predecessors, the Victorians, but also against the hackneyed conventions of an expanding mass culture still Victorian in its idiom. The New Criticism built an exegetical bridge between the modern writers and their rejected audience, but it did so at the expense of some larger, less instructional aims of criticism.

The generation of 1910

If the prevailing criticism of 1950 was analytical, the criticism of 1900 was predominantly social, moral, and historical, whether it dealt with older writers or with the new realists who challenged them. From Hegel and Marx to De Sanctis, Taine, and Brandes, history was the secular god of the nineteenth century. It was natural for a critic like Matthew Arnold to shape his criticism into a narrative of periods and of generations, to think in loosely Hegelian terms of 'epochs of expansion' followed by 'epochs of concentration', and to say that 'for the creation of a masterwork of literature two powers must concur, the power of the man and the power of the moment'.

In the eyes of the Young Turks who appeared on the scene before the First World War, the social and historical vision of those great critics had decayed, among their followers, into a fussy moralism, hard to distinguish from the ordinary prejudices of their compatriots. 'We have done with all moral judgments of art as art', said Joel Spingarn in his once-famous manifesto 'The New Criticism', a lecture delivered at Columbia University in 1910. 'It is not the inherent function of poetry to further any moral or social cause', he added. 'The historian, the philosopher, the legislator may legitimately consider a work of art, not as a work of art, but as a social document... The poet's only moral duty, as a poet, is to be true to his art, and to express his vision of reality as well as he can.' Spingarn considered American critics especially prone to confuse moral and aesthetic judgements. 'Critics everywhere except in America have ceased to test literature by the standards of ethics.'

Spingarn followed Croce in insisting that every work of art was the unique expression of an individual vision, not a document of its times or the manifestation of a certain genre, convention, or style. To the scholar he said, 'we have done with all the old Rules... We have done with the *genres*, or literary kinds... We have done with the comic, the tragic, the sublime, and an army of vague abstractions of their kind.' To the rhetorical critic he announced, 'we have done with the theory of style, with metaphor, simile, and all the paraphernalia of Graeco-Roman rhetoric. They owe their existence to the assumption that style is separate from expression ... instead of the poet's individual vision of reality, the music of his whole manner of being.'

Spingarn continued his litany of rejection until he reached the Tainean historical critic: 'We have done with the race, the time, and the environment of a poet's work as an element in criticism. To study these phases of a work of art is to treat it as an historic or social document, and the result is a contribution to the history of culture or civilization, with only a subsidiary interest in the history of art.'

The generation of 1910 was an iconoclastic one, deeply influenced by English critics of Grundyism and Victorianism like Shaw and Wells, impressed above all by their sparkling manner, their attacks on puritanism, their faith in progress. It was a much more cosmopolitan generation than its Victorian predecessors, whose idea of a European writer was a classic figure like Dante or Goethe, or a minor one like Sénancour or Amiel. The new generation in America had been introduced to Ibsen and Wagner by Shaw, to Zola by Howells and Norris, to impressionism and the *fin de siècle* by James Gibbons Huneker, to Nietzsche by H. L. Mencken, to Freud by G. Stanley Hall, who had invited Freud and Jung to the United States in 1909. Much of the acquaintance with these radical figures was superficial but, with the added impact of new ethnic voices just beginning to be heard, it made Anglo-Saxon insularity much harder to sustain.

One typical history of a young rebel was written by Randolph Bourne in his third-person 'History of a Literary Radical', published posthumously in 1919. Bourne describes how his alter ego, called Miro, a young man with a strict classical training, was stunned and converted after hearing a lecture on modern writers by – of all people – William Lyon Phelps, the popular Yale bookman. After reading some of these moderns, including Turgenev, Tolstoi, and Hardy, 'Miro returned to college a cultural revolutionist. His orthodoxies crumbled. He did not try to reconcile the new with the old. He applied pick and dynamite to the whole structure of the canon. Irony, humor, tragedy, sensuality suddenly appeared to him as literary qualities in forms that he could understand. They were like oxygen to his soul.'

Miro joins a group of young radicals who start a new college paper. 'Social purpose must shine from any writing that was to rouse their enthusiasm ... Tolstoi became their god, Wells their high priest. Chesterton infuriated them. They wrote violent assaults upon him which began in imitation of his cool paradoxicality and ended in incoherent ravings... The nineteenth century which they had studied must be weeded of its nauseous moralists... In a short time Miro had been converted from an aspiration for the career of a cultivated "man of letters" to a fiery zeal for artistic and literary propaganda in the service of radical ideas.'

Eventually Miro comes to a more balanced position. He learns to develop critical discriminations even among the radical writers – the naturalists, the muckrakers, the pamphleteers – making judgements his perplexed teachers are unable to provide. 'Miro had a very real sense of standing at the end of an era. He and his friends had lived down both their old orthodoxies of the classics and their new orthodoxies of propaganda.' He looks to critics henceforth to be as boldly unconventional as the writers they discuss, just as Spingarn had called for a criticism as creative and expressive as literature itself ('a unity of genius and taste'). 'To his elders', writes Bourne, 'the result would seem mere anarchy. But Miro's attitude did not want to destroy, it merely wanted to rearrange the materials. He wanted no more second-hand appreciations. No one's cultural store was to include anything that one could not be enthusiastic about.'

Spingarn and Bourne were two versions of the young radical intellectual of 1910. Though Spingarn attacked literary scholarship, he himself was a superb scholar of Renaissance criticism. Though he appeared to renounce politics and society for aesthetics, he was a founder, patron, and for three decades a leading figure in the NAACP, working closely with W. E. B. Du Bois. Bourne, who seemed, during World War One, to leave literature behind for political controversy, was a forerunner of the kind of cultural radical who brought aesthetic concerns into politics itself. Progressivism, Christopher Lasch has noted, 'was for the most part a purely political movement, whereas the new radicals were more interested in the reform of education, culture, and sexual relations than they were in political issues in the strict sense'. If Spingarn was the prophet of a recoil into aesthetics which, as his later essays show, he came partly to regret, Bourne was the forerunner of the adversary intellectual alienated from the temper of American culture, determined to put it on a wholly new footing.

The attack on the Gilded Age: Van Wyck Brooks and H. L. Mencken

Neither Spingarn nor Bourne made their impact strictly as critics; neither pursued much extended commentary on contemporary writers. For members of this generation, the line between literary criticism and social or cultural criticism was very hard to draw. They saw writers and artists as exemplary figures – allies or enemies in their struggle for cultural renewal;

they saw them as representing either the wave of the future or the dead hand of the past. Other members of the class of 1910 were more directly political, including Greenwich Village radicals like John Reed and Max Eastman, who put out *The Masses* (founded in 1911), and the progressive intellectuals who began publishing *The New Republic* in 1914, among them John Reed's Harvard classmate Walter Lippmann. (T. S. Eliot was another classmate, but that belongs to a different part of the story.)

The two men who eventually had the greatest impact as socially oriented critics were H. L. Mencken and Van Wyck Brooks, Mencken as editor of *The Smart Set* from 1914 to 1923 and the more widely read *American Mercury* from 1924 to 1933, Brooks for a decade after the publication of *America's Coming-of-Age* in 1915, perhaps the single most influential diatribe against the culture of the Gilded Age. The following year, in one of a series of essays in *The Seven Arts*, Brooks sounded the keynote of a generation and an entire era: 'How does it happen that we, whose minds are gradually opening to so many living influences of the past, feel as it were the chill of the grave as we look back over the spiritual history of the last fifty years?'

Everything about this passage is typical of the early Brooks: the doleful prophetic note sounded more in sorrow than in anger; the sinuous poetic flow of the sentence itself, appraising an entire culture in a single interrogative nod; the emphasis on spiritual history rather than material life since Brooks, far from rejecting the past, insists on its quickening influence – this was the 'usable past' that he would spend his life trying to recreate. *America's Coming-of-Age* is best known for its attack on the division between Highbrow and Lowbrow in America, but where these terms have come down to us as aspects of an entertainment culture, a putative hierarchy within the arts, for Brooks they stood for a grievous split in the culture as a whole. Though Brooks tags one with the name of Jonathan Edwards (and calls it Puritan), the other with the name of Benjamin Franklin (and calls it practical), his real subject is the business civilisation of post-Civil War America, with its division between a brash entrepreneurial culture resourcefully bent on acquisition, and a rarefied intellectual culture which has devolved from puritanism and transcendentalism to a thin-blooded gentility.

Brooks took his main argument and even some of his examples from George Santayana's seminal 1911 lecture on 'The Genteel Tradition in American Philosophy'. (Other notable sources include Carlyle's exhortations to Emerson to be less abstract and more worldly; Henry James's 1879 study of Hawthorne, with its stress on the thinness of American life; and Matthew Arnold's contrast between the practical, activist spirit he calls Hebraism and the more reflective, aesthetic mode he labels Hellenism.) In his lecture Santayana found America 'a country with two mentalities, one a survival of the beliefs and standards of the fathers, the other an expression of the instincts, practice, and discoveries of the younger generations'. He suggested that 'one half of the American mind, that not intensely occupied in practical affairs, ... has floated gently in the backwater, while, alongside, in invention and industry and social organization, the other half of the mind was leaping down a sort of Niagara Rapids'. While the American *mind* looked back toward Europe and to the secular remnants of its own Calvinist past, American energy was hurtling forward into the modern world.

As Brooks develops this argument, he comes close to the spirit of Max Weber's and R. H. Tawney's work on the Protestant Ethic and the Spirit of Capitalism. (Weber, of course, also uses Benjamin Franklin as his prime exhibit.) Brooks writes that 'the immense, vague cloud-canopy of idealism which hung over the American people during the nineteenth century was never permitted, in fact, to interfere with the practical conduct of life'. But it's not enough for him to invoke the split between culture and society, mind and practical life. To him, as to any nineteenth-century historicist, the great writer is not simply an individual but a crystallisation of his time and place. Brooks is concerned, for example, with the relation between Emersonian individualism and America's economic individualism. For him Emerson's thought reflected the spirit of the pioneers. It went back to a period of genuine mobility in American life: 'It corresponded to a real freedom of movement and opportunity; pioneers, inventors, men of business, engineers, seekers of adventure found themselves expressed and justified in it.'

Though Emerson himself eventually travelled West on the new transcontinental railroad, to Brooks he presides over this new world like a rarefied spirit, hovering above it but scarcely part of it. Here Brooks follows Santayana, who had found 'a certain starved and abstract quality' in Poe and Hawthorne as well as Emerson. ('Life offered them little digestible material', said Santayana, 'nor were they naturally voracious. They were fastidious, and under the circumstances they were starved.') Brooks too insists on the abstractness of Poe and Hawthorne, which flies in the face of Hawthorne's abundant historical detail and Poe's richly embroidered Gothic fantasies. Brooks may also have been influenced by John Jay Chapman's brilliant account of the 'anaemic incompleteness of Emerson's character', with its astonishing peroration: 'If an inhabitant of another planet should visit the earth, he would receive, on the whole, a truer notion of human life by attending an Italian opera than he would by reading Emerson's volumes. He would learn from the Italian opera that there were two sexes; and this, after all, is probably the fact with which the education of such a stranger ought to begin.'

Brooks himself was a man whose inhibitions, grounded in his own genteel upbringing, drove him to identify with Emerson as well as to criticise him. (According to Brooks, a typical American grows up 'in a sort of orgy of lofty examples, moralized poems, national anthems and baccalaureate sermons; until he is charged with all manner of ideal purities, ideal honorabilities, ideal femininities'.) Chapman, a severe, idiosyncratic moralist as well as a cultural critic of great distinction, thought Emerson dangerous reading for the impressionable young, for 'his philosophy, which finds no room for the emotions, is a faithful exponent of his own and of the New England temperament, which distrusts and dreads the emotions. Regarded as a sole guide to life for a young person of strong conscience and undeveloped affections, his works might conceivably be even harmful because of their unexampled power of purely intellectual stimulation.' Like Brooks's treatment, this attack is also a rare tribute, and undoubtedly an autobiographical one.

Edmund Wilson, a literary heir to both Chapman and Brooks, wrote a striking study of Chapman's personality in *The Triple Thinkers*, as well as several shrewdly balanced reviews of Brooks's later work. Brooks himself was subject to recurring bouts of depression, which no doubt impelled him toward the psychological approach of one of his best books, *The Ordeal of Mark Twain* (1921). But the position of the alienated outsider critical of American culture, which finds its fullest expression in his treatment of Twain, was personally difficult for him to sustain. It led to a nervous breakdown later in the 1920s, which kept him from working for five years – significantly, just as he was completing a biography of Emerson.

As he recovered, Brooks abandoned criticism and social prophecy for a more anecdotal kind of literary history – a 'pageant of genius', he later called it. His biography of Emerson turned lyrical. He celebrated much about American life that he had once denounced, and, in his best-selling Makers and Finders series (1936–52), wove a richly detailed tapestry of the usable past he had once been so hard pressed to discover. By the early forties, he was attacking Eliot and other modernists in vituperative terms as 'Coterie-writers', as if only the past had produced any literature of value. As Wilson drily noted, for Brooks the 'modern' writers were still the writers of the Wells and Shaw generation who had excited him before the war. The man who had once looked to Europe as a standard now became an uncritical promoter of American literary nationalism. The aging Young Turk wrapped himself in the Great Tradition. 'A homeless generation has obvious needs', he wrote in a 1934 preface to his earlier work. 'It needs to be repatriated. It needs to find a home.'

Brooks criticised his early books without entirely renouncing them. In his later preface he attributed their pessimism to the Oedipal vivacities of youth. Puritanism, he says with some justice, 'has ceased to menace any

sentient being; and, properly apprehended, it stands for a certain intensity
that every writer values'. The bold new scholarship of Perry Miller was
just over the horizon, and the rebel causes of 1915 seemed remote. In
America's Coming-of-Age he had followed Santayana in finding this
special intensity in Whitman. In Emerson he then saw only the vaporous
idealism of someone 'imperfectly interested in human life'. Looking for a
writer more grossly embodied, a writer with more *mud* on him, he settled
on Whitman, who, though 'saturated with Emersonianism, ... came up
from the other side with everything New England did not possess: quanti-
ties of rude feeling and a faculty of gathering humane experience almost as
great as that of the hero of the Odyssey ... He challenged the abnormal
dignity of American letters ... Whitman – how else can I express it? –
precipitated the American character.'

   Can any writer ever really do this much, or even stand for this much?
Brooks's early books, beautifully written, remain of permanent interest,
yet it's hard to escape the impression that he is using a method inherited
from Matthew Arnold to work out his own inner conflicts – Arnold's
'dialogue of the mind with itself'. Like Arnold he turns writers into
cultural emblems, projecting the divisions of his sensibility into a historical dialectic. He was no practical critic; he never got close to writers in the
intense formal way the New Critics would teach everyone to do. Despite
his fame and influence, his name goes unmentioned in W. K. Wimsatt's
and Cleanth Brooks's hefty history of criticism (1957). At the end of his
essay 'On Creating a Usable Past' he writes, rather lamely, that 'the real
task for the American literary historian ... is not to seek for masterpieces –
the few masterpieces are all too obvious – but for tendencies'. Even more
than Arnold, he turned criticism into a form of cultural diagnosis, an
examination of the national mind.

H. L. Mencken was older than Brooks but his greatest fame came afterward, when the young men of the twenties devoured *The American
Mercury* and lived by his cynicism, wit, and satirical gusto. Mencken was
protean; he was a force of nature. He learned to write not among pale
Harvard aesthetes like Brooks but in the hurly-burly of Baltimore journalism and at smoke-filled national conventions. If Brooks's weakness was a
poetic vagueness, as if he were sometimes mesmerised by the soulful flow
of his own voice, Mencken's writing was almost too clear and sharp. Like
all great caricaturists he sacrificed nuance for vivid exaggeration. He
could be blunderingly unsubtle, elephantine, ponderously Germanic. But
like his master, Shaw, Mencken was never vague, never in doubt. In a
perfectly Shavian put-down of the man he calls 'the Ulster Polonius',
Mencken writes that much as he enjoys reading Shaw's works, 'so far as I
know, I never found a single original idea in them'. No, he says, Shaw is an

immensely entertaining set of rhetorial tricks. Shaw is 'quick-witted, bold, limber-tongued, persuasive, humorous, iconoclastic, ingratiating... It is his life work to announce the obvious in terms of the scandalous.'

In other words, Shaw, like Mencken himself, is a style – a dazzling high-wire act, an endlessly resourceful iconoclasm: 'He has a large and extremely uncommon capacity for provocative utterance; he knows how to get a touch of bellicosity into the most banal of doctrines; he is forever on tiptoe, forever challenging, forever *sforzando*. His matter may be from the public store, even the public junk-shop, but his manner is always his own. The tune is old, but the words are new.'

Mencken was not primarily a critic, though he wrote a great deal of criticism between 1910 and 1920. But as these scintillating lines on Shaw demonstrate, Mencken wrote about books with exactly the same kind of sweeping brush strokes he used to attack politics, morals, and manners. His portrayal of Shaw, supposedly the most intellectual of writers, is simply a piece of Shavian paradox: just the way Shaw might have eviscerated anyone who dared influence *him*. Mencken's style is his rhythm; he repeats himself, courses his theme through endless variations, but he is never boring. As a satirist he relishes strut and pretension, adores folly and stupidity on a grand scale. No one would say he's 'fair' to his subjects, but outsized characters such as William Jennings Bryan, Anthony Comstock, and Henry Cabot Lodge give him the material for vivid cartoons as no literary subject could; unlike merely bad writers, these men cut a figure in the world. They unwittingly synthesised the prejudices and pomposities of others; their excesses amplified the mood of the moment.

Despite this turn toward social satire, Mencken did his work as a critic. He took up the causes initiated in Howells's and Norris's campaign for realism by tirelessly promoting the work of Dreiser and Conrad. He shared his friend Huneker's cosmopolitan taste and loved to lampoon American provinciality. He was a working editor as well as the key advisor to Knopf, one of several new publishing houses that began to bring out bold new European writers along with young, unconventional Americans. 'The publication of Mencken's *Book of Prefaces* in 1917, with its remarkable essay on Dreiser and its assault on "Puritanism as a Literary Force", was a cardinal event for the new American literature', Edmund Wilson later wrote. As late as 1950 Wilson would pay tribute to Mencken's old battle against 'the genteel-academic culture that had done so much to discourage original American writing from about 1880 on', adding, 'he was without question, since Poe, our greatest practicing literary journalist'.

Yet Mencken's essay on Dreiser is more vivid on Dreiser's faults, such as his style, than on his virtues. He offers up a small anthology of Dreiser's sins with the note that 'every reader ... must cherish astounding specimens'. Dreiser's worst novel, *The 'Genius'*, sends him building toward a Homeric riff: 'There are passages in it so clumsy, so inept, so irritating that they seem almost unbelievable; nothing worse is to be found in the newspapers.' The book's structure fares no better: it 'is as gross and shapeless as Brunnhilde. It billows and bulges out like a cloud of smoke, and its internal organization is almost as vague ... The thing rambles, staggers, trips, heaves, pitches, struggles, totters, wavers, halts, turns aside, trembles on the edge of collapse.' But Dreiser is not to be dismissed. Mencken, a great stylist himself, never mistakes style for greatness. Keeping his balance, he criticises Dreiser's vision of the world but without confusing the philosophy with the fiction.

Along with Brooks and Wilson, Mencken was one of our last true men of letters. He takes us back to a world where newspapermen could be more literate than most academics and could write far more intelligently about American literature and the American language. He loved baiting professors, especially heavy-handed moralists like the New Humanists, and in a piece called 'Criticism of Criticism of Criticism' he praised Spingarn's demolition of all the usual academic ways of pigeonholing writers, especially troublesome and innovative writers. He attacked most critics for 'their chronic inability to understand all that is most personal and original and hence most forceful and significant in the emerging literature of the country'. 'As practiced by all such learned and diligent but essentially ignorant and unimaginative men, criticism is little more than a branch of homiletics.' If the writer is 'what is called a "right thinker"', if he devotes himself to advocating the transient platitudes in a sonorous manner, then he is worthy of respect'.

Warming to his theme, Mencken writes that 'we are, in fact, a nation of evangelists; every third American devotes himself to improving and lifting up his fellow citizens, usually by force; the messianic delusion is our national disease'. Mencken, of course, cannot resist intensifying, exaggerating; settled into his pulpit, caught up in the swell of his surging prose, he exemplifies the very evangelism he loves to pillory. Moreover, though he detests moralism, he cannot accept a purely aesthetic attitude: 'Beauty as we know it in this world is by no means the apparition *in vacuo* that Dr. Spingarn seems to see. It has its social, its political, even its moral implications ... To denounce moralizing out of hand is to pronounce a moral judgment.'

We remember Mencken the entertainer rather than Mencken the critic. He had a plain bluff way with books, as with everything he wrote about, but his mind was never so simple or so eager for effect that it left no room for qualification. The offensive but fairly routine racism and anti-semitism of his post-1930 diaries were contradicted by his actual behaviour toward blacks and Jews, including his strong patronage of young black writers.

The serious issues of the Depression ploughed Mencken under, made him seem cranky and irresponsible, and he subsided gracefully into autobiography, like Edmund Wilson in his final years. As a critic he had no role to play in the Age of Eliot, when terms like 'beauty' and 'sincerity' lost their meaning, and modern literature became Hemingway, Joyce, and Proust rather than Ibsen, Shaw, and Wells. The struggle against Victorianism was over; the battle for modernism had hardly begun.

As Americans became less provincial, more cosmopolitan, Mencken lost his subject. He had some imitators but no successors, certainly not the brash right-wing journalists of the 1980s who worshipped at his shrine. Perhaps the many-sided work of Dwight Macdonald came closest. He too was a sharp critic of language, a witty and destructive polemicist, a brave editor, a political gadfly, and a ruthless but entertaining mocker of cultural sham and pomposity. But he was more purely the intellectual, a nemesis of middlebrows and a critic of ideology, in a style that originated with the thirties generation. Like Mencken he could be obtuse and unsubtle; he could simplify for effect. But he lacked Mencken's wider interest in the whole American gallery of rogues and fools.

The New Critics hated Mencken for his mockery of the South and his refusal to take literature with their kind of gravity, as a special, complex realm of aesthetic discourse. Yet it was Mencken's criticism that provoked them to define their social views in *I'll Take My Stand*, the youthful manifesto they published in 1930. The radical intellectuals of the thirties, not notable for their sense of humour, modelled themselves on Brooks and Bourne and the cultural radicals of *The Masses*, not on Mencken. (Macdonald wrote perhaps the sharpest attack on Brooks for his defection from the highbrow camp.) The younger critics were as theoretical, as remote from the cynical *Front Page* world of daily journalism, as any of the professors. The work of Edmund Wilson and Malcolm Cowley bridged the yawning gap between the Mencken world of the teens and twenties and the radical thirties.

The critic as man of letters: Edmund Wilson and Malcolm Cowley

In a career that spanned five decades, Wilson became the paradigm of the twentieth-century literary intellectual in America. He came of age in the twenties, a friend and contemporary of F. Scott Fitzgerald – 'my literary conscience', Fitzgerald once called him. He earned his living as a book editor and literary journalist, first for *Vanity Fair*, then for *The New Republic*, finally for *The New Yorker*. Wilson's work was rooted in the historical criticism of an earlier era. In *Axel's Castle* (1931) he wrote: 'The old nineteenth century criticism of Ruskin, Renan, Taine, Sainte-Beuve, was closely allied to history and novel writing, and was also the vehicle for all sorts of ideas about the purpose and destiny of human life in general.' In contemporary criticism he found too much of 'a detached scientific interest or a detached aesthetic appreciation which seems in either case to lead nowhere'. By 'nowhere' he seems to have meant nowhere beyond the text itself. Yet Wilson's advance over Brooks and Mencken lay precisely in his ability to get a good deal closer to books and writers without detaching himself from a larger social and intellectual framework. In the fewest, clearest words, he could tell you exactly how a book was put together, could compare it effortlessly to other books of its kind, to other things that weren't books. He practised the New Criticism without taking any notice of it.

By our standards today, Brooks and Mencken seem to be pursuing their own agendas when they write about literature. Their critical personalities are too strong, their prose too unbending, their prescriptions for the culture too urgent and pressing. Lewis Mumford's 1926 book on the American literary tradition, *The Golden Day*, shows how the diagnostic Brooks approach could lead a potentially strong critic astray. Though Mumford strikingly anticipates the canon Matthiessen would later carve out in *American Renaissance*, he canvasses the major figures all too briefly and distantly before wielding them as a club against the writers of the Gilded Age. It was not until he dealt with architecture in *The Brown Decades* (1931) that his own feeling for the city landscape and its designers – men like Olmstead, the Roeblings, Sullivan, and Wright – could break free of Brooks's abstract polemic against the post-Civil War period, which altogether missed the ruggedly expansive energy of the era.

Reviewing Brooks's book on Henry James in 1925, Wilson complained that 'Mr. Brooks has completely subordinated Henry James the artist to Henry James the social symbol, with the result that James's literary work, instead of being considered in its integrity on its own merits, has undergone a process of lopping and distortion to make it fit the Procrustes bed of a thesis.' Determined to protest 'the spiritual poverty of America and our discouragement of the creative artist', Brooks 'cannot help expecting a really great writer to be a stimulating social prophet'. In a later review Wilson expressed amazement that Brooks had been able 'to develop into one of the first rate American writers of his time' without learning to appreciate 'other writers save as material for cultural history'. For Wilson, as for the New Critics, some notion of aesthetic autonomy is essential, even for the cultural historian. Brooks's appropriation of James shows evidence of 'the critic's failure to be fully possessed by his subject'.

It may be significant that *Axel's Castle*, the only critical work of Wilson's that feels partly dated today, is also the only book of his driven by a thesis: the origins of modernism in the French symbolist movement. Moreover, Wilson was converted to radicalism in the course of writing the book, and this obliges him finally to condemn the aesthetic ideas he had first expounded with more sympathy. This gives some individual chapters – those on Valéry and Proust, for example – a slightly schizophrenic quality. (Besides undergoing a political conversion, Wilson was recovering from a nervous breakdown as he composed this book; the text reflects some of the unresolved tensions of his personality.) In addition, Wilson had little feeling for verse, which he had already begun to consider 'a dying technique'. Though Wilson was never fully committed to modernism – his chapter on Gertrude Stein is at best perfunctory – his engagement with Proust and Joyce, writers who speak to his strong social interests, was far stronger than his limited empathy for Yeats or Valéry. With some polemical verve, he taxes Valéry for his obscurity, his withering attack on Anatole France, and his abandonment of the common reader, showing his own preference for a classical French clarity.

Like the nineteenth-century critics he praises in the book, Wilson writes criticism which is allied to history and biography. But his crystalline narrative method, the very hallmark of the public critic and literary journalist, is controlled by his acute literary judgement. He had a feeling for art as art that Brooks never had – a feeling which, in Eliot, excluded all other critical considerations. Wilson was a great reader; as an evaluative critic, his literary taste holds up better today than the judgements of any of his contemporaries except F. R. Leavis. But he was a far more catholic reader than Leavis, whose strength lay in selection, exclusion, canon-formation, certainly not in wide-ranging curiosity or enthusiasm. And Wilson, in his longer works, aimed at panoramic effects and social visions that belonged more to the critics of the nineteenth century.

In the opening essay of *The Bit Between My Teeth* (1965) Wilson describes how enthralled he was at the age of fifteen by Taine's *History of English Literature*, impressed above all by Taine's scenic and dramatic method: 'He had created the creators themselves as characters in a larger drama of cultural and social history, and writing about literature, for me, has always meant narrative and drama as well as the discussion of comparative values.' And Wilson adds: 'I had also an interest in the biographies of writers which soon took the bit in its teeth.' But 'the bit between my teeth' also alludes to the specific writer, the particular book he must chew over, that he can neither swallow nor spit out. Though his sensibility scarcely resembled Wilson's, Eliot was a writer he could not put by; the chapter devoted to him in *Axel's Castle* is balanced between cultural history and Wilson's very personal kind of literary judgement.

(One example: 'I am made a little tired at hearing Eliot, only in his early forties, present himself as an "aged eagle" who asks why he should make the effort to stretch his wings.')

In 'The Critic Who Does Not Exist', a virtual manifesto written in 1928, Wilson reviews the critical scene in acerbic terms reminiscent of James's 1891 screed: 'It is astonishing to observe, in America, in spite of our floods of literary journalism, to what extent the literary atmosphere is a non-conductor of criticism.' What he finds instead are separate schools that pursue different methods and collect adherents but have nothing to say to each other. (He cites the school of Mencken and the school of Eliot as two examples.) Wilson's essay is a prescription for a critic very much like himself: a writer who practises criticism for its own sake, who can write knowledgeably about the past in terms of the present, a professional reviewer who can 'deal expertly with ideas and art, not merely tell us whether the reviewer "let out a whoop" for the book or threw it out the window'. Unfortunately he finds that although many people write criticism with their left hand, 'no such creature exists as a full-time literary critic – that is, a writer who is at once first-rate and nothing but a literary critic'.

Wilson himself should have been an ideal candidate – in one sense it was exactly the critic he ultimately became. But in 1928, when his literary ambitions still covered a wider field, this would have been a bitter pill for him to swallow. A year later, about to publish his first novel, *I Thought of Daisy*, a portrait of the Village bohemian scene and his friend Edna St Vincent Millay, Wilson rereads *The Great Gatsby*, 'thinking with depression how much better Scott Fitzgerald's prose and dramatic sense were than mine. If I'd only been able to give my book the vividness and excitement, and the technical accuracy, of his!' (*Letters on Literature and Politics*, p. 173). Though he tries to reassure himself that 'writing, like everything else, is partly a matter of expertness' – as if technique were separable from talent – the honest critic in him, holding to high standards, is beginning to tell him he's not really a novelist. Nevertheless, his journals of the 1930s are largely composed of material he was collecting for his second novel, *Memoirs of Hecate County*, which he perversely singled out, much later, as 'my favorite among my books – I have never understood why the people who interest themselves in my work never pay any attention to it'.

Socially oriented critics are often blocked novelists, just as formal critics, critics of language especially, tended in this period to be moonlighting poets. Lionel Trilling's ambition was to write great novels, but he published no more fiction after *The Liberal Imagination* fully established his standing as a critic in 1950. In his journals in 1948 he complained that he paid for his professorial life 'not with learning but with my talent ... I draw off from my own work what should remain with it.' At moments he envied wilder, more 'irresponsible' writers like Hemingway and Kerouac for their lack of balance, inhibition, decorum, even their wild romantic attraction to adventure, criminality, deviance. Fifteen years earlier, while still a young man, he had already lamented 'how far-far-far- I am going from being a writer – how less and less I have the material and the mind and the will. A few – very few – more years and the last chance will be gone.' His criticism, as he recalled publicly in 1971, had begun as a something 'secondary, an afterthought: in short, not a vocation but an avocation'.

George Orwell was a failed novelist who later returned to write political fables more closely related to his critical essays than to his earlier fiction. On the other hand, Eliot, Pound, Ransom, Tate, Blackmur, Winters, Warren, and Empson wrote about poetry as practising poets. The first kind of critic shows an elective affinity not only with fiction but with the social and political issues that often animate fiction. The other critic is more often drawn to questions of form and structure that turn literature in upon itself, that sunder it from its social matrix.

A concern with technique, with methodology, is a major theme of twentieth-century thought, from post-Newtonian science and post-Weberian social science to analytic philosophy and modernist art, which searchingly interrogates the forms it inherits. The advanced criticism that responded strongly to modern art sometimes became the discursive projection of its self-consciousness, its anxiety, or its technical exuberance. Toward the middle of the twentieth century, a few critics tried to apply the same formal approach to fiction that had dominated the new poetry criticism. They found antecedents in the letters of Flaubert and the late prefaces of Henry James, which R. P. Blackmur assembled into an influential book in 1934, but also in the Russian formalists and the Chicago Aristotelians. One well-known example from a modernist viewpoint was Mark Schorer's 1948 essay 'Technique as Discovery', which appeared in the first issue of the *Hudson Review*. But there was also a brilliant rebuttal from a historicist viewpoint in Philip Rahv's 1956 essay 'Fiction and the Criticism of Fiction', which reflected the spilt Marxism of the *Partisan Review* circle.

Schorer argued that unlike the naturalists, who struggled aimlessly within received fictional forms, modern writers like Joyce, Faulkner, Lawrence, and the early Hemingway *were* their styles: books like theirs are 'consummate works of art not because they may be measured by some external, neoclassic notion of form, but because their forms are so exactly equivalent with their subjects, and because the evaluation of their subjects exists in their styles'. (Fresh from a study of Blake, a strongly historical study, Schorer might have been more sceptical about this fearful symmetry, this 'fitting & fitted' that Blake decried in Wordsworth.) Rahv, on the other hand, argued for a looser, more open, more Bakhtinian sense of the novel, insisting that formal rigour was often less important than the work's interactions with a wider world. He pointed out that inferior or unimpressive stylists like Dreiser, Tolstoy, or Dostoevsky could still be great novelists, since their effects 'are achieved not locally, in the short run, but in the long run, by accumulation and progression'.

The New Critics were generally in Schorer's camp, while the socially oriented critics were allied with Rahv. The New Critics, when they wrote about fiction at all, were drawn to patterns of metaphor, myth, and symbolism, while their antagonists commonly made fiction their vehicle for writing social and cultural history. The work of certain writers became a virtual battleground. F. R. Leavis – who published a continuing series of essays in *Scrutiny* on 'The Novel as Dramatic Poem' – excluded all but one of Dickens's novels from his Great Tradition. Echoing Henry James's disparagement of Tolstoy and Dostoevsky, he found most of Dickens teeming with 'irrelevant life'. When Leavis later retracted this judgement, or when R. P. Blackmur shifted his attention from the close analysis of poetry to the modern European novel, especially Dostoevsky, it marked a significant turn from formal criticism to social prophecy. Long before Leavis changed his mind (without acknowledging he had done so), Wilson, Orwell, and Trilling wrote signally important essays on Dickens, reclaiming him as a social critic but also, in Wilson's and Trilling's case, as a modernist whose dark, neglected later novels achieved depth and intensity through a profound symbolic organisation.

Thus Dickens became a meeting ground between historical criticism, focused on social conflict in Victorian England, and a modernist poetics, which emphasised radical departures from strict realism. At about the same time, Erich Auerbach's great study of the genesis of realistic representation, *Mimesis* (1946), combining philology with a European tradition of *Geistesgeschichte*, demonstrated that style itself was socially and historically conditioned. Just as Montaigne had argued that each man bears the whole form of the human condition, Auerbach showed how local details of syntax, description, and dialogue could be understood in historical terms, for writers of each period constructed reality in different configurations of language.

It was the call of history that kept Edmund Wilson from becoming either the exponent of modernism implied by parts of *Axel's Castle* or the purely literary critic conjured up in the manifesto of 1928. Thanks to the crash and the onset of the Depression, by 1931 – when Frederick Lewis Allen published *Only Yesterday*, when Wilson finished *Axel's Castle*, when Fitzgerald wrote 'Babylon Revisited' – the twenties already seemed like another world, an unimaginably distant time. The Depression drew many writers, including Wilson, into the larger world beyond the arts. It brought the expatriates home; it interested them for the first time in what was happening in the American heartland; it made journalism and politics more pressing than aesthetics; it made the Menckenite cynicism and sophistication of the twenties seem thin and brittle.

Even before the Crash, writing early in 1929, Wilson had praised his friend Dos Passos – one of the first of his contemporaries to be radicalised – for keeping his eye trained on the larger social picture, not simply his own small corner of the field. Wilson contrasted this not only with other writers of their own generation but with the reigning wit, Mencken. Despite Mencken's brilliance as a social critic, Wilson complained, 'the effect of Mencken on his admirers is to make them wash their hands of social questions. Mencken has made it the fashion to speak of politics as an obscene farce.' Dos Passos, on the other hand, 'is now almost alone among the writers of his generation in continuing to take the social organism seriously'. Yet he complains that Dos Passos gives far too monolithic a picture of life under capitalism. Dos Passos's own characters are deformed by it, their lives are too unrealistically constricted by it. 'No human life under any conditions can ever have been so unattractive. Under however an unequal distribution of wealth, human beings are still capable of enjoyment, affection and enthusiasm – even of integrity and courage.' Instead, Dos Passos's 'disapproval of capitalist society seems to imply a distaste for all the beings who go to compose it'.

This 1929 article shows that before the Depression Wilson's social interests had already prepared him to favour a radical shift. But in Dos Passos he also identifies the limits of that radicalism as applied to literature. As he later discovered, he would always remain a man of the twenties, would always believe that people were capable of enjoyment, affection, courage – whatever the larger public forces affecting their lives. Nevertheless, the 1930s were a turning point for Wilson. In 'An Appeal to Progressives', a widely discussed manifesto published anonymously in 1931, he found a striking change not only in the economy but in the national psyche. The Horatio Alger belief in enterprise and opportunity had waned: 'American optimism has taken a serious beating; the national morale is weak. The energy and faith for a fresh start seem now not to be forthcoming: a dreadful apathy, unsureness and discouragement is felt to have fallen upon us.' He urged radicals and progressives to 'take Communism away from the Communists' but to take it seriously, for some form of socialism seemed the only solution. By 1932 he joined a group of intellectuals endorsing William Z. Foster, the Communist candidate for president.

Wilson's days as an agitator and organiser were short-lived; so was his enthusiasm for the Soviet Union. He was a genuinely independent radical, with little affinity for movements and causes. Wilson was transformed as a writer – in the subjects he chose, the way he approached them – not as a political activist. The same cannot be said about Malcolm Cowley, his successor as literary editor of *The New Republic*, who was an ardent fellow traveller all through the thirties and an early victim of red-baiting when he was appointed to a minor government job in 1942. In the thirties Cowley was perhaps the most influential literary critic in America, thanks to his limpid and beautifully crafted weekly articles in *The New Republic*. Except for Wilson himself, no one could say so much, so gracefully, in so brief a compass. His literary judgement was good; he kept a remarkably even temper through a tumultuous era; collections of his reviews still hold up as literary chronicles of their time.

But by the second half of the thirties he also became a functionary of the literary left, signing petitions, chairing front organisations, and learning to tell less than the whole political truth in his weekly pieces. In several stinging letters, his friend Wilson accused him of 'plugging the damned old Stalinist line ... at the expense of the interests of literature and to the detriment of critical standards in general', and even, on one occasion, of writing 'Stalinist character assassination of the most reckless and libelous sort' (*Letters on Literature and Politics*, pp. 311, 358).

Cowley later made some attempts to come to terms with his 'sense of guilt' about this unhappy period, most notably in – *And I Worked at the Writer's Trade* (1978). His memoir of the thirties, *The Dream of the Golden Mountains* (1980), stops short in the middle of the decade, and its promised sequel never appeared. Apart from this lamentable episode, Cowley's long career must be seen as a remarkable chapter – some would say the last chapter – in the rise and fall of the man of letters in America. Despite his productivity over nearly seven decades, his body of work was a less adventurous version of Wilson's. If Wilson was the literary journalist and public critic par excellence, Cowley, like many English reviewer-critics, was *only* the journalist, without Wilson's breadth and range as an intellectual historian, travel writer, and restless student of other cultures, languages, and literatures. Yet Cowley too was a cultural critic of considerable importance whose first book, *Exile's Return*, published in 1934 and revised in 1951, remains our most revealing portrait of the Lost Generation.

Cowley's book is deeply indebted to *Axel's Castle*, a book it praises, imitates, criticises. Cowley takes note of Wilson's shift of attitude midway through the book, yet *Exile's Return* is itself a divided, ambivalent work – part recollection and celebration, part demolition – which views the modernist writers of the twenties through the political prism of the 1930s. Where Wilson, playing the Poundian role of the village explainer, had taken the whole sweep of international modernism as his field, Cowley stays closer to home, confining himself to the expatriate writers of his own generation. And where Wilson took the symbolists as prototypes, Cowley looks to the influence of the French Dadaists, the ones he himself knew in his Paris years.

In his chapters on Joyce, Proust, and Eliot, Wilson, despite his growing political commitment, had managed to strike a balance between sympathetic exposition and political criticism. Cowley is more heavy-handed. His main theme is the self-destructive madness, the social irresponsibility, of the bohemian writers of the teens and twenties. Wilson, though alert to the risks of decadence, the pitfalls of the purely aesthetic attitude, was attuned to the social basis of modernism. He saw Proust, for example, as 'perhaps the last great historian of the loves, the society, the intelligence, the diplomacy, the literature and the art of the Heartbreak House of capitalist culture'. Wilson could be amusing on his own apostasies to modernism. As early as 1925 he wrote to Cowley, 'I am contemplating myself experimenting in a vein so journalistic and optimistic that admirers of Eliot will never speak to me again' (*Letters on Literature and Politics*, p. 127). Cowley, on the contrary, is determined to condemn the writers of the twenties for their pessimism and escapism, for taking refuge from real life in a 'religion of art'.

Bohemianism and Dada are Cowley's emblems of rebellion, escape, *épater le bourgeois*; his book culminates with the suicide of Hart Crane and Harry Crosby – the dead end to which these movements inexorably lead. Even earlier, in Flaubert's Paris, 'the religion of art very quickly expressed itself as a way of life, and one that was essentially anti-human'. Later, 'the Dada manifestations were ineffectual in spite of their violence, because they were directed against no social class and supported no social class'. Though he would always identify with this generation, Cowley was by temperament a survivor, a man who moved with the times: he had signed on for the new puritanism and moral uplift that thirties Marxism offered. From this new vantage point, Dada violence could only be seen as futile and self-destructive. Cowley insists on a social ethic, an ethic of responsibility, not the values of the lone Romantic artist. 'The young man who tried to create a vacuum around himself would find in the end that he could not support it. He would find that the real extremes were not that of Axel's lonely castle, or Gauguin's Tahiti, or Van Gogh's fanatical trust in the Sun: they were inertia, demoralization, delusions of persecution and grandeur, alcohol, drugs or suicide.'

There is drama in watching Cowley play sober Polonius to Hart Crane's wild, erratic Hamlet, trying to convince the poet, as he tells us, to give up 'the literature of ecstasy' for 'the literature of experience, as Goethe had done'. Instead, Hart Crane chose the path of young Werther, not the

Apollonian course of the elder German sage. Rather than taking his advice, Crane ran off with Cowley's wife, Peggy, Crane's first heterosexual lover, who was with him on a ship from Mexico in 1932 when he took his leap into the sea. Meanwhile, back home, Cowley became the superego to the Lost Generation.

Especially in its 1934 edition, *Exile's Return* propagates a myth of social responsibility that belongs strictly to the thirties, but this shouldn't obscure the book's enduring value. Cowley's ambivalence gives the book its personal anchor and internal drama. His description of bohemianism could be applied with few alterations to the counterculture of the 1960s. So could the book's remarkably original account of how easily this rebellion was commercialised into a toothlessly hedonistic culture of consumption. Indeed, Cowley's account of the way a *'production* ethic' gave way to a *'consumption* ethic' has been widely accepted by historians of the 1920s (such as William E. Leuchtenburg in *The Perils of Prosperity*). And Cowley's finely wrought pattern of exile and return is axiomatic for any understanding of the cultural history of the years between the wars. Even his appeal to a 'literature of experience' – his insistence on the social and personal basis of art – must, in a more subtle way, define the historical critic's understanding of the relations between literature and life, between art and its audience. Critics like Cowley and Wilson remained anchored to this social view of art throughout their careers.

Wilson spent most of the decade wrestling with political and economic issues rather than literary matters. While Cowley took over his duties at *The New Republic*, Wilson took to the road to report on how ordinary Americans were coping with the Depression. The results were collected in *The American Jitters* (1932), one of the best of many valuable books of Depression reportage, including works by older writers like Dreiser and Sherwood Anderson and by newcomers like John Steinbeck, Erskine Caldwell, and James Agee. In 1935 Wilson travelled to Russia to do research for the history of Marxism and revolution that proved to be his masterpiece, *To the Finland Station* (1940). Though first published like all his books as a series of essays, it was a unified work that dramatically extended his critical range.

Marxism was an improbable subject for a 'literary' treatment. Unlike Marx and Engels themselves, most of its adherents had written about it in terms of dry dialectics and pseudo-scientific historical 'laws'. In the work of these sectarian believers, the intellectual antecedents of Marxism were hazy; the founders' lives were a closed book. Though many had lived and died for these ideas, the moral passion and excitement of revolutionary history were strangely absent from this literature. Some intellectuals would sniff at Wilson's mastery of theory, but this was not his goal.

Instead, he set out to apply the methods of criticism to both the writing and *acting* of history, imparting a vigorous narrative thrust to what these radicals said as well as what they had done.

More than any other book of Wilson's, *To the Finland Station* called upon a novelistic talent missing from his fiction but vital to his critical essays, with their lucid recapitulations of his wide reading. Wilson needed characters who were given to him, outside of him; he had little gift for introspection but great feeling for social history as it expressed itself in individual lives and idiosyncratic ideas. *To the Finland Station* is essentially a narrative work, a series of lives in their historical settings. It applies the scenic method of Michelet and Taine to the history of ideas and their impact in the world. The earlier historians themselves play cameo roles in Wilson's book, perhaps as his own surrogates. Michelet's discovery of Vico, Taine's shock at the suppression of the Commune, become part of the drama of the book. Taine's belated effort to master politics and economics becomes a parable of Wilson's own conversion.

Through it all Wilson remains the critic – weighing, assimilating, expounding – above all, making his material come alive, as few students of Marxism ever did. To Wilson's detractors this was a form of fabulation: Wilson was the populariser, the magazine journalist, the 'introductory' critic, as he had been in *Axel's Castle*. Yet Wilson's way of drawing connections by shaping his story line and assimilating his sources is always at the service of his strong interpretive bent. It is never simply the middlebrow 'story of philosophy' or 'story of civilization', or the kind of potted popular biography that elides all the crucial questions. In fact, Wilson was a pioneer in applying new literary techniques to nonliterary texts, including the psychoanalytic approach and the analysis of rhetoric and imagery. Not only did he examine Marx's youthful poetry for clues to his emotional life but in a later chapter, 'Karl Marx: Poet of Commodities', he isolated Marx's vivid and violent imagery as a way to 'see through to the inner obsessions at the heart of the world-vision of Marx'. At about the same time, Kenneth Burke was applying his own critical methods to Hitler's *Mein Kampf* in 'The Rhetoric of Hitler's "Battle"' (1939).

Wilson's conversion to Marxism did not long endure. The purge trials and the Hitler–Stalin pact tore the mask off Stalinist Russia for all but the most loyal and myopic believers. By 1940, the year his book appeared, Wilson would say that 'Marxism is in relative eclipse. An era in its history has ended.' What never ended for Wilson was an acute historical awareness, insistent in its human concern, that had been intensified by the Depression and by his encounter with Marxism. The Marxism of the thirties, because it was conceived so mechanically and applied so dogmatically, because it remained at the service of a political movement, produced little criticism of lasting value in the English-speaking world. Even Malcolm Cowley later condemned 'the ideological vulgarity of what passed for Marxian criticism in the 1930s'. But the encounter with Marxism, as part of the experience of the Depression, was the forge in which the historical criticism of the next generation was tempered.

Some writers, disillusioned or deradicalised, lost their bearings, retreated into silence or slipped back toward the kingdom of art for art's sake. But others, deprived of their comfortable Marxist certainties, were immensely invigorated, forced to think for themselves in difficult, intuitive ways. It would be hard to imagine the work of Wilson, Orwell, Cowley, Burke, Trilling, Rahv, Meyer Schapiro, or Harold Rosenberg without the Marxist moment early in their lives, a moment from which they never entirely recovered despite their later anti-Communism.

Compared to these writers who would follow him, Wilson's ingrained historicism took him in an unexpected direction. In his *New Republic* years, in *Axel's Castle* and *To the Finland Station*, in his two great collections of longer essays, *The Triple Thinkers* (1938; revised 1948) and the psychoanalytically oriented *The Wound and the Bow* (1941), with its full-scale monographs on Dickens and Kipling, Wilson was very much the cosmopolitan critic. This was an insular period in American culture. The refusal to ratify the Treaty of Versailles or join the League of Nations expressed more than a diplomatic isolationism. Wilson's feeling for European culture had been fostered by Christian Gauss at Princeton. In literature at least, he had something of an expatriate's sensibility, and his criticism did much to introduce the new writers of the twenties and to broaden America's literary taste.

But the Depression, while it turned intellectuals toward Marxism, also turned them inward, toward their own country, where people were suffering through unprecedented calamities. Just when the American Dream appeared more distant than ever, the United States came to seem like a precious enigma. Individual American lives could be scrutinised as keys to a national mystery. Though any excess of subjectivity was sure to be condemned by radical critics, a wave of autobiography followed the success of books like Michael Gold's *Jews Without Money* (1930) and *The Autobiography of Lincoln Steffens* (1931).

Some of these books were immigrant sagas, as if a whole new class of Americans suddenly realised that they too had a story to tell. But Edmund Wilson came of old American stock – he was distantly related to Cotton Mather – and as he became more disaffected with America as it was, his turn toward autobiography became an inquiry into the American past, an archaeology of a country that no longer existed, that lay buried under the new 'transnational' America the children of immigrants were helping to create.

The same journalistic impulse, the same restless curiosity, that took him to Harlan County also brought him to Talcottville, in upstate New York, where his mother's family had lived and he had spent some of his childhood and youth. 'The Old Stone House' (1933) initiated a vein of autobiography in Wilson that led eventually to his remarkable portrait of his father at the end of *A Piece of My Mind* (1956) and to the best of his late books, *Upstate* (1971), a collection of journals, family memories, and comments on regional culture. This retrospective turn inspired his major postwar work of cultural history, *Patriotic Gore* (1962), a collection of studies of the literature of the Civil War era that had occupied him for nearly two decades. Wilson's criticism after 1940 became, in a sense, the extension of his autobiographical impulse. His excursions into family history spilled over into cultural history and brought out a strength that had been muted in his work on modernism – his subtle, instinctive sense of time and place, of the relationship between individual lives, individual books, and the enveloping flow of the culture around them, something we rarely find in most 'textual' criticism. But his work also became a recoil from what America had become.

At the end of *A Piece of My Mind* Wilson had wondered whether he too, like his brilliant but neurotic father, like the old stone house in Talcottville (to which he, like his father, had grown so attached), was now a quaint artifact of an earlier era: 'Am I, too, I wonder, stranded? Am I, too, an exceptional case? When, for example, I look through *Life* magazine, I feel that I do not belong to the country depicted there, that I do not even live in that country. Am I, then, in a pocket of the past?' He marvels that his father, despite the tragic foreshortening of his career, had 'got through with honor that period from 1880 to 1920', for he himself feels just as alienated from the life of his time.

This hadn't been the case in the twenties and thirties. If Wilson's attraction to the drama of the Finland Station was a form of vicarious revolutionary excitement, it was also a way of living in the present, for Wilson, like all good historical critics, saw the past as the embryo of the present, its intrinsic, revealing prehistory. But in *Pariotic Gore* a reader feels that Wilson simply prefers to dwell among the granite-jawed republican figures of the past, men like Lincoln, Sherman, and Grant – or like Alexander Stephenson, the extraordinary vice-president of the Confederacy, and Oliver Wendell Holmes, the long-lived Supreme Court justice, who sit for two of the book's most vigorously detailed portraits. Wilson's long introduction, far from bringing this material together or connecting past and present, is a sweeping dismissal of the political history of the twentieth century, above all the two World Wars and the cold war. Its tone of patrician aloofness and disdain recalls Henry Adams at his worst, though the canny Adams was never simply dismissive. Part radical, part simply cranky, this astonishingly olympian essay, which sees nations as 'sea slugs' who devour each other as if by biological law, is Wilson's grim farewell to the modern world.

For all of Wilson's sense of isolation, his turn inward toward history was characteristic of American critics starting with the 1930s. The decade began with an agrarian manifesto against industrial society by the same men, including John Crowe Ransom, Allen Tate, and Robert Penn Warren, who would eventually make their mark as New Critics. Their book, *I'll Take My Stand* (1930), was first to be called *Tracts Against Communism*, but the Communists themselves soon began to encourage an interest in the American past. After 1935, during the Popular Front period, they fostered a sentimental cultural nationalism that had wide ramifications in the arts, especially in music and dance, and in government-sponsored arts programmes which fed the mural movement, the oral history projects, and commissioned guides to each of the forty-eight states. Studies of the American past flourished as a patriotic prehistory to the New Deal. Common-man versions of Tom Paine, Jefferson, Lincoln, and Whitman, as well as semi-legendary figures like Paul Bunyan and Davy Crockett, became staples of popular biography and populist literary history.

Like the younger *Partisan Review* critics who admired him, Wilson had little sympathy for this middlebrow populism, which was more a form of ersatz folklore and 'progressive' mythmaking than criticism. In *Patriotic Gore* he wrote, 'there are moments when one is tempted to feel that the cruellest thing that has happened to Lincoln since he was shot by Booth has been to fall into the hands of Carl Sandburg. Yet Carl Sandburg's biography of Lincoln, insufferable though it sometimes is, is by no means the worst of these tributes.' Wilson had far more tolerance for the intricate if mannered embroidery of Van Wyck Brooks's literary histories, beginning with *The Flowering of New England* in 1936, for they reminded him of the Taine model that still appealed to him. In a succession of reviews in *The New Yorker* he dissected their weaknesses as criticism but they encourged his own explorations of American cultural history. Wilson's turn from modernism and Marxism, the twin beacons of his earlier books, was never as sharp as Brooks's recoil from modernism, but it led in the same direction, toward a renewed interest in the American past.

The rise of American Studies

The same period saw the growth of the American Studies movement, which provided some academic parallels to the later development of Wilson and Brooks. Influenced by the prophetic writings of the early Brooks and his circle, but also, to a degree, by the new work of linguists and cultural anthropologists, this was an effort to overcome the hardening disciplinary boundaries of literature and history and to see American culture as an organic whole. In book after book, starting with V. L. Parrington's *Main Currents of American Thought* (1927–30), Constance Rourke's *American Humor* (1931), and F. O. Matthiessen's *American Renaissance* (1941), critics and historians set out to determine the essential character of American life. Avoiding the diagnostic, polemical vein of Spingarn, Santayana, Mencken, Brooks, and Mumford, they set out to construct a central core of American masterpieces that would differ strikingly from the canon of the genteel critics and their radical successors. Their work was inspired not by the new realists of the prewar years, such as Dreiser, but by the modernists of the postwar period, including Eliot and the New Critics. 'In their hands', says Gerald Graff of the new Americanists, 'the New Criticism became a historical and cultural method.'

Parrington's unfinished work laid out in monumental detail the viewpoint of the progressive Old Guard against which these later Americanists would react. Though Parrington was not a Marxist, his social and economic determinism was congenial to the Marxist decade. (Still, even a Marxist critic, Bernard Smith, found it 'crude and vulgar'. Smith's 1939 volume, *Forces in American Criticism*, was in fact one of the best-balanced, least programmatic pieces of Marxist literary history, far superior to Granville Hicks's better-known work on American literature, *The Great Tradition*.)

Though Parrington was a professor of English, he chose in this work 'to follow the broad path of our political, economic, and social development, rather than the narrower belletristic'. In the foreword to his second volume he was even more explicit: 'With aesthetic judgments I have not been greatly concerned. I have not wished to evaluate reputations or weigh literary merits, but rather to understand what our fathers thought, and why they wrote as they did.' He insisted that he was writing as a historian, not a critic, and he defended the kind of omnivorous antiquarianism that has often brought literary history into disrepute: 'The exhuming of buried reputations and the revivifying of dead causes is the familiar business of the historian, in whose eyes forgotten men may assume as great significance as others with whom posterity has dealt more generously. Communing with ghosts is not unprofitable to one who listens to their tales.'

Such a ponderous approach, though welcomed by sociological critics and economic determinists in the thirties, could not survive the decline of radical politics after 1940 and the ascendency of new forms of aesthetic analysis. Parrington is at his best as an intellectual historian, not as a critic of any kind. He insisted that minor works, documents, sermons, and theological polemics were as relevant as works of art. He was the first to carve out a large cultural space for the Puritans, enabling Perry Miller and his successors to correct his own hostile account of them. He explored revolutionary thought in great detail, and paid moving tribute to the progenitors of American liberalism, such as Roger Williams and Theodore Parker, but he was at his worst in his discussions of America's greatest writers, from Poe to Henry James. He could deal only with the typical, the representative, never with the singular, the idiosyncratic. His sardonic side enabled him to take the measure of the literary lights of the Gilded Age such as Holmes and Lowell, for they belonged entirely to their cultural moment. But he disposes of Poe in two pages, declaring: 'The problem of Poe, fascinating as it is, lies quite outside the main current of American thought, and it may be left with the psychologist and the belletrist with whom it belongs.' Poe's psychological problems, he says, 'are personal to Poe and do not concern us here. And it is for the belletrist to evaluate his theory and practice of art.' But he grudgingly adds that 'whatever may be the final verdict it is clear that as an aesthete and a craftsman he made a stir in the world that has not lessened in the years since his death, but has steadily widened'.

No student of American culture could fail to learn from Parrington, but few could be happy with what he gave them. As Alfred Kazin wrote in a balanced epitaph in *On Native Grounds*: 'What ailed him, very simply, was indifference to art; an indifference that encouraged him to write brilliantly of General Grant but lamely of Hawthorne; Grant had made "history"; Hawthorne merely "reflected" a tradition.' Parrington pointed criticism in the direction of social history, only to dissolve social history into the history of ideas, so that even the academic left, when it revived decades later, found little use for him. His successors were liberal historians like Henry Steele Commager, whose lively biography of Theodore Parker (1936) and broad survey, *The American Mind* (1950), were directly inspired by Parrington.

Constance Rourke offered quite a different alternative to formalist criticism in her study of popular culture, *American Humor*. The difference between Rourke and Parrington, and later between Rourke and Matthiessen, was almost a textbook illustration of the split described by Santayana and Brooks between the upper and lower reaches of the American mind. Instead of attacking the genteel tradition, Rourke looked behind and beneath it. Her sources lay not in novels, sermons, or political pamphlets but in the popular arts. Though Rourke was no anthropologist, she did her work in the early, pioneering years of that discipline; she has a highly diversified, strongly ethnological sense of American culture.

Whitman in *Democratic Vistas* had attacked a class-bound, European sense of culture, and argued for 'a programme of culture drawn out, not for a single class alone, or for the parlors or lecture-rooms, but with an eye to practical life, the west, workingmen, the facts of farms and jack-planes and engineers, and of the broad range of women also of the middle and working strata'. Santayana and Brooks had invoked Whitman as the key figure, but Rourke had a genuinely Whitmanesque sense of American culture, which for her was essentially an oral culture composed of frontier humour, legends and folktales, the performances of strolling players, and ethnic or regional stereotypes. She turns popular jokes about Yankees or black people, tall tales about Mike Fink or Davy Crockett, into the equivalent of a national mythology, and shows how much serious American literature 'has had its roots in common soil ... an anterior popular lore that must for lack of a better word be called folk-lore'. Thus she is able to move on from primitive versions of the Yankee and the backwoodsman to the fictional protagonists of James and Howells, Twain and Bret Harte, right up through the up-to-date satirical figures of Sinclair Lewis. Her emphasis is on the archetype, not the individual work.

Rourke's populism predates the Popular Front. In its handling of recurrent myths, formulas, and narrative motifs, it foreshadows many later explorations of popular culture. Her aim, like Brooks's, was to define the national character: this was part of Brooks's legacy to American Studies. But unlike Brooks she had 'no quarrel with the American character; one might as well dispute with some established feature of the national landscape'. Rourke accepts what she finds because she enjoys it; the foibles of popular culture seem rich to her, not crude or ragged. Her book has a lightness of touch that makes Brooks feel dour, that leaves Parrington and Matthiessen looking elephantine.

For almost the same reason, her work was less usable than theirs to the burgeoning academic study of literature. Parrington gave his readers a sweeping overview that helped dislodge the genteel canon; he helped them see American literature as a progress toward the triumph of realism. But his work was deficient in critical judgement and out of touch with both the literature and criticism that developed after the first world war. Rourke's approach, on the other hand, required an unusual kind of learning that was hard to pass on: it was not centred on masterworks that were accessible to criticism, and it could scarcely be refined into a method. Yet its cultural emphasis gave an invaluable grounding to American Studies – even after 1945, when the new formalism began to dominate literary study. Here Matthiessen proved to be the greater influence, for he not only set up a pantheon of a few select writers, as Leavis did in England, but offered a method by which they could be closely read – a canon and a method that proved remarkably in tune with the literature and criticism of the postwar era.

Matthiessen's work is a tissue of contradictions, but they are rich and interesting contradictions, for his mind never settled into a single groove. His last work on Dreiser is hard to reconcile with his lifelong devotion to James. At the height of the radical thirties, his Christian socialism did not prevent him from writing a pioneering study of T. S. Eliot, as well as withering critiques of Marxist volumes on American literature by V. F. Calverton and Granville Hicks. He was close to the New Criticism yet he attacked it in his last major essay, 'The Responsibilities of the Critic', for bogging down in pedantic exegesis, with its terms used not 'as the means to fresh discoveries but as counters in a stale game'. He demolished Parrington's method in the preface to *American Renaissance*, arguing (like Leavis) that as a historian 'you cannot "use" a work of art unless you have comprehended its meaning'. But by 1949, when Parrington's influence was fading, he described him as 'our greatest recent cultural historian', whose 'instinct was right, in insisting on the primacy of economic factors in society'.

It may simply be, as some scholars have suggested, that his literary method was inconsistent with his radical politics, just as he himself, as a serious Christian, would never be fully reconciled to his own homosexuality. Or it may be that he simply swam against the tide, pursuing a formal approach in the turbulent 1930s, partly under the impact of modernism, but turning leftward, disaffected, in the 1940s as he saw the New Criticism becoming routinised into pedagogy. Here Matthiessen's own work weighed tellingly, for *American Renaissance* gave a mighty push to the formal and academic study of a handful of American writers who were quite different from the Longfellows, Bryants, and Lowells who once held a key place in American literary history. Matthiessen's canon – Emerson, Thoreau, Melville, Hawthorne, and Whitman – was not original: it was indebted to the previous attacks on the genteel tradition, especially the polemical work of Brooks, Mumford, and Parrington, which cleared the ground that he would build upon. But none of the earlier critics focused on texts in the close analytical way Matthiessen did.

Matthiessen's orientation is not exclusively formal. *American Renaissance* includes cultural history, political analysis, biographical criticism, and even comparisons of writers with painters like Mount and Eakins. But the influential new element is suggested by sections like his close study of the language of Emerson's essays, or his prefatory assertion that all interpretation 'demands close analysis, and plentiful instances from the works themselves'. He continues: 'With few notable exceptions, most of the criticism of our past masters has been perfunctorily tacked onto biographies.'

His treatment of Thoreau begins: 'Thoreau has not ordinarily been approached primarily as an artist.' On Hawthorne, a similar overture: 'A total impression of one of Hawthorne's tragedies, in its careful and subtle gradations, demands a closer reading than most critics have apparently been willing to give.' The chapter on Whitman is called, somewhat ironically, 'Only a Language Experiment', after a remark by the old poet to Traubel about *Leaves of Grass*, to which Matthiessen adds: 'It will be interesting, therefore, to begin by seeing how much we can learn about Whitman just by examining his diction.'

Matthiessen was uncommonly interesting on all these subjects: on the syntax of Emerson's sentences and paragraphs, on Thoreau's or Melville's imagery, on Whitman's diction, on Hawthorne's fictional structures as well as his tragic vision. To a remarkable degree, Matthiessen created American literature as a subject for academic study. He did this by establishing the formal complexity and tragic seriousness of a few key writers in a way that appealed to the age of modernism – which was also an era of mass instruction, when the journalistic critic and the 'common reader' were giving way to the academic expert and his classroom charges. Unlike some who followed him, Matthiessen had an extraordinary depth of feeling for the writers he discussed. He could hardly have imagined that his way of inhabiting these writers, which was not simply analytical but had an intimate spiritual dimension, would soon be turned into a cottage industry. When he writes of Melville that 'he plunged deeper into the blackness than Hawthorne had, and needed more complex images to express his findings', he surely could not have guessed that this would let loose a flood of studies of light and dark imagery in Hawthorne, Melville, and Poe. This was the kind of sterile, mechanical work he criticised in 1949, the year before he took his own life.

Thus, even as Matthiessen helped create American Studies by giving it a critical method, he also helped derail it from its cultural mission, which was to focus on a single culture in all its complexity, to overcome the widening gap between literature and history, literature and politics, literature and the other arts. Against his own beliefs and intentions, he helped dehistoricise literature for an age that was already turning away from the historical awareness of the twenties and thirties. Ironically, Matthiessen, like D. H. Lawrence in his *Studies in Classic American Literature*, gave American writers tremendous currency by making them seem more contemporary, more powerfully up-to-date. Boldly examining his writers through the prism of modernism, he rescued them from the stuffy official versions of their work.

'The first awareness of the critic', he later wrote, 'should be of the works of art of our own time. This applies even if he is not primarily a critic of modern literature.' Matthiessen came to his work fresh from his pioneering study of Eliot, and Eliot is only one of the modern writers whose names are sprinkled throughout his text. Just as Perry Miller drew a line from the Puritans through the Transcendentalists to the moderns, Matthiessen compares Thoreau's style to Hemingway's, Hawthorne's allegory to Kafka's, connects Hawthorne through James to Eliot, invokes Lawrence frequently, and compares Whitman not only to Hart Crane and Pound, to Carl Sandburg and Archibald MacLeish, but also, at much greater length, to a key modernist icon, Hopkins, as if that improbable linkage could somehow validate Whitman's poetry. (In this sense, the rediscovery of Melville in the 1920s made Matthiessen's project possible, for Melville and Emily Dickinson were the Hopkins and Donne of American literature, the 'metaphysical' writers who were too advanced, too difficult for their own contemporaries, only to be redeemed from neglect and incomprehension by a new post-Victorian aesthetic.)

As a result, the American Renaissance writers were reshaped into modern writers, bristling with irony, ambiguity, and the tragic sense of life; other American writers who scarcely fit this pattern, such as the naturalists, were greatly devalued. Here Matthiessen's work dovetailed with the influence of the New York intellectuals who, as anti-Stalinists, disagreed with him politically. Most of the early *Partisan Review* writers began as Marxists in the 1930s before breaking with the Communist Party. Schooled in fierce political debate, they retained enough of their Marxist grounding to continue writing historical criticism throughout the New Critical era. But their sense of history was quite different from Wilson's or Brooks's. Their sensibilities were formed by the modern writers, but they were oriented toward Europe, and only a few had strong interests in earlier American writers. But the impact of those few, especially the work of Lionel Trilling, as seconded and developed by Richard Chase, ultimately proved decisive.

Trilling as a cultural critic

Trilling's career had begun with an intellectual biography of Matthew Arnold and a brief study of E. M. Forster. But even before and during this English phase, he made his mark on contemporary American writing as a poised and accomplished reviewer for *The Menorah Journal, The Nation, The New Republic*, and, after its revival in 1937, *Partisan Review*. While still an undergraduate, Trilling grappled in print with Dreiser's newly published *An American Tragedy*, and later he contributed two distinctly harsh essays, on Eugene O'Neill and Willa Cather, to Malcolm Cowley's *After the Genteel Tradition* (1937), a revaluation of the insurgent writers of the 1910–30 era. With a few exceptions, Trilling disliked the new American realists, whom he compared unfavourably to the great European novelists, above all Balzac and Stendhal, Jane Austen and George Eliot, writers who occupied a key place in his teaching at Columbia.

Trilling's most important and influential book, *The Liberal Imagination* (1950) can be seen as a meeting point between the important historical work he had done on English culture and the journalistic chores he had undertaken in his essays on recent American writers. Trilling's study of Matthew Arnold and his strong identification with Victorian culture are almost never given their due in discussions of his work, except for the customary observation that Trilling later assumed an Arnoldian pose and even, eerily, an Arnoldian prose in his own criticism. (Someone cannily observed that in his anthology *The Portable Matthew Arnold*, it was at times difficult to tell the introductions from the selections.) Trilling called his first book 'a biography of Arnold's mind', but it was also saturated with history. It brings to life the mental and political atmosphere of the whole age, centring on the predicament of one critic – as concerned with society as he is with literature – who is caught up in a period of political and cultural upheavals, including the decline of religious sanctions, the shifting positions of poetry, criticism, and fiction, the beginnings of mass education, the sharpening of class antagonisms, and the popular agitation that culminated in the second Reform Bill of 1867, which called forth Arnold's famous polemic *Culture and Anarchy*.

In his notes for an autobiographical lecture written toward the end of his life, Trilling reveals that he was first drawn to Arnold's poetry, not his prose: 'The Arnold that first engaged my interest was ... the melancholy poet, the passive sufferer from the stresses and tendencies of his culture. When the book was finished my concern was with the man who had pitted himself against the culture, who had tried to understand the culture for the purpose of shaping it – with the critic, with (perhaps it can be said) the first literary intellectual in the English-speaking world.' Trilling had begun the book, he tells us, as a Marxist but concluded it as an Arnoldian, an engaged cultural critic in the Arnold–Brooks–Bourne mould, impelled to question liberal and progressive views from within the liberal, humanistic consensus. 'No sooner was the book out of the way', Trilling adds, 'than I found myself confronting a situation that I had inevitably to understand in Arnold's terms.' Like Arnold during the battle for Reform or Brooks and Bourne in the waning days of the Progressive era, Trilling saw himself confronting a debased, instrumental liberalism, descended from Stalinism and the Popular Front, whose cultural icons were figures like Dreiser and Parrington, the writers he attacks with unusual polemical vigour in the opening essay of *The Liberal Imagination*.

To labour over a book on Arnold, a dissertation no less, all through the Marxist decade was itself a dissenting gesture. Trilling later expressed gratitude to Edmund Wilson for a moment of warm encouragement; indeed, the book is his closest parallel to Wilson's historical studies. Much later Trilling even attributed a dialectical purpose to his slim 1943 study of Forster, suggesting that it was undertaken as part of his 'quarrel with

American literature' of that moment, that he had 'enlisted Mr. Forster's vivacity, complexity, and irony' against 'what seemed to me its dullness and its pious social simplicities'. This is precisely the argument that unifies *The Liberal Imagination*: that literature, especially the great tradition of the novel, could enrich the liberal mind with a human and emotional dimension it had lost, could provide it with a model of complexity, variousness, and possibility. Though friendly critics like R. P. Blackmur and Joseph Frank demurred that no actual politics could ever sustain such a nuanced literary vision, that the book was implicitly a blueprint for quietism and aesthetic retreat, Trilling's exquisitely modulated prose itself proposed a model of dialectical tension and reflective inwardness for critics who had long been disenchanted with radicalism.

Trilling's book, composed all through the 1940s, gives us some essential markers for the passage of criticism from the boisterous Depression decade to the more purely literary world of the 1950s. When he began writing it, the cultural nationalism of the Popular Front, with its preference for harsh realists like Dreiser and protest writers like Steinbeck, still held sway, while the cosmopolitan, modernist outlook of the *Partisan Review* critics seemed at best a marginal force. But after the war, as America assumed its position on the world stage, the old rebels and naturalists, who were still reacting against a bygone Victorian America, gave way before the growing influence of the great modernists, including Hemingway, Faulkner, and Fitzgerald, as well as Kafka, Joyce, and Proust. Problems of style, along with the brooding concerns of the inner life, became more important to the younger writers than the social documentation of a Farrell or a Dos Passos, or the grandiose, inchoate yearnings of a Thomas Wolfe. American literature was undergoing one of its periodic shifts of sensibility. Thanks in part to Trilling, who forwarded this momentous reconsideration in the closing pages of *The Liberal Imagination*, a large segment of American criticism would soon be making this modernist turn.

Yet Trilling's book was not all of a piece. In promoting writers like Kipling, Twain, Henry James, and Fitzgerald over Dreiser and Sherwood Anderson, in giving his primary allegiance to a more Freudian, more introspective literary sensibility, Trilling was in tune with powerful trends in postwar American culture. Though Trilling is usually thought of as a cultural critic far removed from formalism, his emphasis on the complexity and irony of the imagination is quite compatible with the New Critics, with whom he remained on graciously respectful terms all through his life. For all their differences, there was a considerable measure of common purpose between the New York intellectuals and the New Critics; both tended to cast the issue in terms of art against politics, modernism against naturalism, the autonomous imagination versus the politics of commitment. Philip Rahv's 'political autopsy' on proletarian literature first appeared in the *Southern Review*; Trilling's harsh farewell to Sherwood Anderson, along with other essays of his, came out in John Crowe Ransom's *Kenyon Review*. Both Rahv and Trilling joined the New Critics to help found the Kenyon school of English, an important summer institute.

Yet the New York critics were far more politically explicit, more historically oriented, and more touched by the immediate concerns of contemporary culture. Even in its reasoned recoil from politics, *The Liberal Imagination* was Trilling's most political book, the one he grimly located at 'the dark and bloody crossroads where literature and politics meet' – perhaps a deliberate allusion to the crossroads at which Oedipus slays his own father, the place where Trilling enacts his own rebellion against the radical generation, including the radical father in himself. Trilling was above all a reactive critic, finely attuned to the contradictions in his own mind, given, as his published notebooks show, to writing against himself, even against the grain of a consensus he had helped establish. Within a few years of *The Liberal Imagination* he could write that 'the American intellectual never so fully expressed his provincialism as in the way he submitted to the influence of Europe. He was provincial in that he thought of culture as an abstraction and as an absolute. So long as Marxism exercised its direct influence on him, he thought of politics as an absolute. So long as French literature exercised its direct influence upon him, he thought of art as an absolute.' In the same reactive vein, Trilling would eventually express deep reservations about modernism and, later still, about the uninflected way some neoconservatives had appropriated his own ideas.

Thus in *The Liberal Imagination* it is never possible to tell how much Trilling is reacting against liberalism, or against political criticism in general, and how much he is making the case for a more finely honed political outlook. A certain cordiality toward the New Critics doesn't prevent him, in one essay called 'The Sense of the Past', from making a strong case for historical criticism, reminding the formalists 'that the literary work is ineluctably a historical fact, and, what is more important, that its historicity is a fact of our aesthetic experience'. On the other hand he cautions that 'the refinement of our historical sense means chiefly that we keep it properly complicated'.

Trilling, with his gift for inclusive and suggestive formulations, even anticipates the scepticism of the deconstructionists by adding that history, like art itself, like all interpretive thinking, is an abstraction from the flux and multitudinousness of experience – in other words, a set of choices: 'Try as we may, we cannot, as we write history escape our purposiveness. Nor, indeed, should we escape, for purpose and meaning are the same thing. But in pursuing our purpose, in making our abstractions, we must be aware of what we are doing; we ought to have it fully in mind that our abstraction is not perfectly equivalent to the infinite complication of the events from which we have abstracted.'

These cautionary lessons for historical critics were inspired by the excesses of a vulgar Marxism, but Trilling typically framed them in cogently general terms that acquired new resonance decades later, when post-structuralist theorists, retreating to the barricades of a new formalism, lodged similar complaints against all historical criticism. Trilling never considered himself a theorist, but he loved ideas and always pushed from specific cases toward general formulations. In a stern review, he objected to the elder Brooks's version of the American past because 'ideas and the conflict of ideas play little or no part in it'. By contrast, Trilling's interior dialogue proceeds by ironies and undulations that set up conflicting viewpoints and the interplay of general ideas from sentence to sentence. The opening lines of his essay on Wordsworth, a piece unusual for him in concentrating on a single poem, provide a neat instance: 'Criticism, we know, must always be concerned with the poem itself. But a poem does not always exist only in itself: sometimes it has a very lively existence in its false or partial appearances.' With an elegant bow to the text, he proceeds to open it outward to its many contexts.

Writing about the novel in his influential 'Manners, Morals, and the Novel' and its sequel, 'Art and Fortune', Trilling drives home the historicity of the literary text strikingly, by emphasising money, manners, and class as the very substance of great fiction. Discussing the kind of novel that was no longer dominant in an age of modernism, Trilling shows his strong debt to Marxist criticism but also his significant divergence from it. Nothing could be further from the vapid idealisation of the 'timeless values' of a classic than Trilling's remark that 'every situation in Dostoevski, no matter how spiritual, starts with a point of social pride and a certain number of rubles'. But Trilling focuses on money not simply as an economic fact but as the coin of human interaction, expressed in minute details of status, feelings, and social style. 'Money is the medium that, for good or bad, makes for a fluent society.' His discussion of manners contradicts both the hard Marxist stress on class and the trivial academic stereotype of the novel of manners, which is blind to the deeper links between manners and morals. Manners for him are 'a culture's hum and buzz of implication', a subtle aura of intentions and moral assumptions that is more psychological than behavioural. Trilling even deals with class as an element of mind and will, a dimension of character, arguing that 'one of the things that makes for substantiality of character in the novel is precisely the notation of manners, that is to say, of class traits modified by personality'.

Trilling called this a tradition of 'moral realism', perhaps to distinguish it from more strictly economic definitions of realism. His values in fiction closely resemble those of F. R. Leavis, whose work on George Eliot and Henry James forms part of the ground for Trilling's later essays on Jane Austen. Leavis, like Wilson, had welcomed Trilling's book on Matthew Arnold, and Trilling in turn handsomely reviewed *The Great Tradition* in the pages of *The New Yorker*. Meanwhile, some of Trilling's more promising students at Columbia went on to study with Leavis in Cambridge (including Norman Podhoretz, whose first published essay was a 1951 review of *The Liberal Imagination* in *Scrutiny*). Both Leavis and Trilling had flirted with Marxism in the early thirties, and both maintained a lifelong interest in connecting literature to social history. Some of Leavis's colleagues, especially Q. D. Leavis in *Fiction and the Reading Public* and L. C. Knights in *Drama and Society in the Age of Jonson*, made valuable contributions to a modest sociology of literature that figures significantly in the early volumes of *Scrutiny*. Long before the mantle of Blakean and Lawrentian prophecy settled on him in his old age, Leavis's studies of seventeenth-century prose and eighteenth-century poetry were strongly bound up with social questions including class. In his teaching at Cambridge he made the social history of English style one of his specialities.

For all his emphasis on practical criticism – the precise configuration of the words on the page – Leavis, like Van Wyck Brooks and Trilling, like T. S. Eliot himself, had deep roots in the Victorian tradition of cultural criticism, as Raymond Williams demonstrated so effectively in *Culture and Society*. Throughout the twentieth century this tradition provided some notable critics with an alternative to both aesthetic formalism and Marxist determinism, offering them both a social strategy and a way of making literature matter in a world in which it seemed to be sinking into insignificance.

Leavis included two essays in *The Common Pursuit* (1952) which defined the relationship between criticism and society in a rough but useful way. In 'Literature and Society' he argues that Eliot's notion of tradition, far from being ahistorical, requires us to read literature in contextual terms, 'as essentially something more than an accumulation of separate works'. In Eliot's name, Leavis insists on a criticism that stresses 'not economic and material determinants, but intellectual and spiritual, so implying a different conception from the Marxist of the relation between the present of society and the past, and a different conception of society. It assumes that, enormously – no one will deny it – as material conditions count, there is a certain measure of spiritual autonomy in human affairs, and that human intelligence, choice and will do really and effectively operate, expressing an inherent human nature.' This 'measure of autonomy' leaves considerable latitude for the Romantic individualism he felt Eliot's work had undermined.

In the companion essay, 'Sociology and Literature', Leavis, saluting the work of Leslie Stephen and G. M. Trevelyan, cautions literary people that practical criticism cannot confine itself to 'intensive local analysis ... to the scrutiny of the "words on the page" in their minute relations, their effects of imagery, and so on: a real literary interest is an interest in man, society and civilization, and its boundaries cannot be drawn'. On the other hand, he warns historians and sociologists that 'no use of literature is of any use unless it is a real use; literature isn't so much material lying there to be turned over from the outside, and drawn on, for reference and exemplification, by the critically inert'. This was precisely the point Matthiessen had made against Parrington in the introduction to *American Renaissance*, in a passage saluted by Trilling in *The Liberal Imagination*. All three critics were trying not simply to define a select company of great writers – this is a reductive view of their work – but to make cultural history more inward with literature itself, while grounding formal criticism in moral and historical awareness.

But where Leavis remained resolutely insular, almost never leaving Cambridge – where he encountered (and often provoked) frequent rejection – and confining his work largely to English literature in relation to English society, Matthiessen and Trilling helped create an American parallel to Leavis's Great Tradition. After defining the novel of manners and moral realism, Trilling writes that 'the novel as I have described it never really established itself in America... The fact is that American writers of genius have not turned their minds to society. Poe and Melville were quite apart from it; the reality they sought was only tangential to society. Hawthorne was acute when he insisted that he did not write novels but romances... In America in the nineteenth century, Henry James was alone in knowing that to scale the moral and aesthetic heights of the novel one had to use the ladder of social observation.' Trilling's point was coupled with his assault on the social realists America did have, such as Dreiser.

Just as the Marxist critic George Lukács had attacked the naturalism of Zola in the name of the 'critical realism' of Balzac and Stendhal, Trilling dismissed American realism as a factitious imitation of an essentially European tradition. This was partly a political judgement – many of the American naturalists had been radicals – but ultimately a comment on American society itself, on the lack of social texture which Henry James had observed in his life of Hawthorne. (There James had drawn the lesson that 'the flower of art blooms only where the soil is deep, that it takes a great deal of history to produce a little literature, that it needs a complex social machinery to set a writer in motion'.) Trilling even argued that American novels 'have given us very few substantial or memorable people': mythic figures like Captain Ahab or Natty Bumppo, yes, but few real characters: 'American fiction has nothing to show like the huge, swarming, substantial population of the European novel, the substantiality of which is precisely a product of a class existence.'

Not all the critics who took up Trilling's point shared his nostalgia for a class-bound culture, the kind in which he himself might never have attended a university or gained a professorship. Richard Chase's 1957 book *The American Novel and Its Tradition*, modelled on Leavis but more indebted to Trilling, traces the American romance from Brockden Brown to Faulkner, and Leslie Fiedler's more Freudian *Love and Death in the American Novel* (1960) emphasises the popular stereotypes of Gothic melodrama, going back to eighteenth-century works like *La Nouvelle Héloïse* and *The Monk*. Both Chase and Fiedler had contributed to the vogue of myth criticism in the postwar decade, and their books have a close connection to key works of American Studies which, using the same literary canon, tried to identify certain essential myths and symbols of American culture – books like Henry Nash Smith's *Virgin Land* (1950), R. W. B. Lewis's *The American Adam* (1955), and Leo Marx's *The Machine in the Garden* (1964).

Ultimately all these works beginning with Matthiessen's *American Renaissance* would come under attack from younger scholars as examples of 'consensus' history or cold war criticism, as books seeking common ground, a unified vision, yet ignoring fundamental conflicts and tensions in American culture. This had been Trilling's point against Brooks and Parrington, but where Trilling stressed the clash of ideas, the younger critics, returning to the spirit of thirties Marxism, insisted on the conflict of classes and economic forces. With the rise of academic Marxism, feminism, and third-world cultural studies among younger Americanists, this new historicism also put more emphasis on popular authors, women writers, black writers, and non-literary texts, along with the problems of ideology such works reflected. Much of the attention that had been focused for decades on the American romance was now directed toward the more progressive and critical tradition of American realism that Trilling, Matthiessen, and their followers had helped to banish. Yet many of the older myth-and-symbol critics, though they had reacted against the doctrinaire historicism of the 1930s, helped keep alive a social and cultural perspective on literature during the period of New Critical ascendence.

Kazin, Rahv, and *Partisan Review*

One major work on American literature that appeared shortly after *American Renaissance* stood apart from these trends. Alfred Kazin was

the early exception among the New York intellectuals in the depth and
intensity of his interest in the American past. He was only twenty-seven in
1942 when he published his prodigious book *On Native Grounds*, a study
of American prose writers since 1890. Trilling saluted his book in *The
Nation* as 'not only a literary but a moral history', but Kazin's acknowledged models, who became part of the story itself, were Edmund Wilson
and Van Wyck Brooks, critics already considered old-fashioned by 1942,
when Ransom, Tate, Blackmur, Burke, and Cleanth Brooks had published
their first major works. The son of Yiddish-speaking immigrants in the
Brownsville section of Brooklyn, Kazin had begun an illustrious career as
a reviewer – and a love affair with American literature – while still a
student at City College in 1934.

Like many other cultural critics in this tradition, Kazin was not simply a
critic but also a remarkable writer. He brought to criticism an almost
preternatural vividness, a breathless aphoristic brilliance that was far
more than a reviewer's facility: he could light up a writer's life and work in
a single phrase. His aim, always, was to cut through the verbiage of
commentary to find the figure in the carpet, the imaginative core or flow.
On Mencken: 'Mencken's technique was simple: he inverted conventional
prejudices.' On Steinbeck: 'Steinbeck's people are always on the verge of
becoming human, but never do.' On Wilson: 'Unlike most critics, he
seemed to be taking the part of the reader rather than talking at him;
thinking with the reader's mind and even, on occasion, at the reader's
pace.' On Van Wyck Brooks: 'Brooks's conception of the Gilded Age was
not false; it was a great literary myth... But as he applied it to Mark
Twain it rested on a curious amalgamation of social history and a literary
psychoanalysis that was so dazzling and new that it was at once uncon-
vincing and incontestable.' And this longer comment on Sinclair Lewis:
'What is it about Lewis that strikes one today but how deeply he has
always enjoyed people in America? What is it but the proud gusto behind
his caricatures that have always made them so funny – and so comfortable? Only a novelist fundamentally uncritical of American life could have
brought so much zest to its mechanics; only a novelist anxious not to
surmount the visible scene, but to give it back brilliantly, could have
presented so vivid an image of what Americans are or believe themselves
to be.'

This is a young man's work, highly rhetorical criticism of an unusual
freshness, energy, and intensity. Proud of its effects, it hurtles along
impatiently, certainly not 'at the reader's pace'. Yet, dispatching author
after author in a stunningly definitive way, Kazin's criticism reveals a gift
for atmosphere and portraiture that would later make his volumes of
memoirs, *A Walker in the City*, *Starting Out in the Thirties*, and *New
York Jew*, so polished and lapidary yet turbulently emotional. Kazin

published no fiction but composed his criticism, as Wilson did, in narrative terms. The first chapter of *On Native Grounds*, 'The Opening Struggle for Realism', is built around the transformation of William Dean Howells from the young midwestern acolyte of the genteel tradition to the serious radical and social novelist. Just as Wilson and Brooks built their criticism around narrative moments which were also cultural turning points, Kazin used Howells's move from Boston to New York as the emblem of a shift of cultural power from the old New England Brahmins to the new urban realists.

This is scarcely a new idea, but it sharply contradicts the direction that Matthiessen and Trilling were giving to students of American culture. Their new canon centred on the American Renaissance writers, on James, and on the young modernists of the 1920s, and it defined the academic syllabus in American literature for the next three decades. Kazin, on the other hand, though dealing with a period that could be seen as a triumph for modernism, returned to an older critical plot by tracing the progress of realism from Howells's early campaigns to the revival of naturalism during the Depression years. Like James Agee's *Let Us Now Praise Famous Men*, *On Native Grounds* is a belated work of the 1930s, a synthesis of cultural nationalism, modernism, and an idiosyncratic radicalism. Its final chapter, 'America! America!', dealing with Depression journalists, biographers, and documentarists like Agee, completes the full arc from alienation to integration that is part of the essential thirties myth – a way of coming home. (In his next book, *A Walker in the City*, Kazin would deal with ethnic New York and his own Jewish background as Trilling's generation, still set on leaving home, could not do.)

Like his mentors Wilson and Brooks, Kazin made his mark not as a close reader but as an omnivorous one. In the period of academic consolidation that followed, Kazin's vast panorama of major and minor talents, including not only novelists but nearly all the critics discussed in this chapter, was largely set aside. A few key writers dominated the courses and the scholarship alike. Kazin's sensibility could not be taught; the writers he discussed were going out of style; the historical method was losing favour. In Trilling's books even academics eventually found some unifying ideas they could use: the liberal imagination, the adversary culture, the role of biology in Freud, or the ideology of modernism. In Kazin they found only a welter of brilliant impressions and quicksilver insights. Kazin's mind, ignited by passion and enthusiasm, was always on individual writers and their world, not on ideas. Unfashionably, he still practised criticism as an extension of biography and cultural history, evoking major figures like Wharton and Dreiser through their milieu and their psychological formation, not through the details of individual works. His intuitive, epigrammatic manner was quite inimitable. Moreover, Kazin remained a staunch defender of Dreiser even as his reputation bottomed out in the 1950s, after Trilling's devastating attack – a Dreiser who yielded nothing to a New Critical or modernist approach.

Yet for all his tolerance for Dreiser's stylistic and intellectual flaws, for all his instinctive historicism, Kazin had an unabashed love of art for its own sake that brought him closer to Trilling than to the young academic radicals who returned to Dreiser and realism in the 1970s. For him literature was not an expression of ideology and cultural attitudes so much as a drama of momentous inner struggle and verbal achievement. 'What was it he had missed?' Kazin says of Howells's limitations at the end of his first chapter. He answers by evoking James, who, for all his own limitations, 'had somehow lived the life of a great artist, had held with stubborn passion to the life of art and the dignity of craft'. James too was a social realist but, unlike Howells, James had managed to achieve 'an inscrutable deceiving intensity, an awareness of all the possible shades and nuances and consequences of art, an ability to wind himself deeper and deeper into the complexities of consciousness'.

Kazin wrote this *before* the James revival of the early 1940s, and it helps define his distance from the 1930s social tradition in which he remains fundamentally grounded – the tradition Trilling's work set out to counteract. Perhaps *On Native Grounds* is 'explained' by *A Walker In the City* and *Starting Out in the Thirties*, for they show how much Kazin had remained the outsider, the working-class immigrant's boy, compared to Trilling, who honoured the values of the middle class, and who reserved for England – really, the idea of England – the kind of ambivalent but all-embracing love that Kazin lavished on American literature, American history, even the American landscape. Thus Kazin and Trilling struck a different balance between art and social consciousness, between modernism and populism. Though Kazin called the thirties in literature 'the age of the plebes', he also felt a peculiarly strong connection to patrician critics like Wilson and Brooks, as well as deeply American writers like Howells and Henry Adams, who depended less on sensibility than on their abiding roots in the culture they so often criticised.

If the strength of Wilson and Brooks was their sense of place, their sense of the past, Trilling's forte was his sense of the present, his remarkable intuition for the mood and temper of the cultural moment. When Kazin wrote about Howells, he made him the archetype of the outsider turned insider who, almost by choice, turns himself into an outsider again: a socialist, an unpopular writer, a man deeply shaken by the 'civic murder' of the Haymarket anarchists, a patron of unpleasant young artists and radical causes. This is Howells as the thirties might have seen him. When Trilling wrote about Howells ten years later, at the start of the fifties, he praised him as the chronicler of the ordinary world of the middle class, an antidote to the modern sense of extremity and apocalypse. Apart from what this reveals about Trilling's own values, and the deradicalised literary sensibility of the 1950s, it underlines his propensity for dialectical thinking, his instinctive gift for highlighting the moment by way of something that contradicts it or sets it off.

This kind of diagnostic cultural criticism, which had been developed by the early Van Wyck Brooks, who had learned it from the Victorians, was a speciality of all the *Partisan Review* critics, especially in their periodic symposia like 'The New Failure of Nerve', 'Religion and the Intellectuals', and, best known, 'Our Country and Our Culture'. The mark of these symposia was their emphasis not so much on the country at large as on the changing views of intelligentsia, above all the literary and political intellectuals who formed the circle and audience for *Partisan Review*. This was the intellectual class that Trilling embraced, often ironically, in his capacious first-person plural, that he later described as an 'adversary culture' at just the time it entered the academic and national mainstream. Other New York critics made their mark as shrewd and biting analysts of intellectual trends, including Harold Rosenberg in the early essays collected in *The Tradition of the New* and *Discovering the Present*; the novelist and critic Mary McCarthy; the exquisite stylist F. W. Dupee, once the literary editor of the *New Masses*, who wrote a superb book on Henry James and many finely sculpted reviews and essays; the young Irving Howe, who in essays like 'This Age of Conformity' (1954) preserved a radical stance that put him at odds with other New York intellectuals; and, especially, Philip Rahv, the longtime co-editor of *Partisan Review*, who, with William Phillips, broke with the Communist Party in the mid-1930s yet continued brilliantly to defend a more eclectic historicism against each new development on the critical scene.

Rahv was perhaps the strongest theorist, the most adept ideologue among the New York critics. Schooled in modern European literature, language, and political controversy, Rahv was a ponderous but adroit polemicist who adapted Marxist methods to anti-Stalinist arguments and to special American problems. He made his debut as a theorist of proletarian writing, but even in the Communist phase of *Partisan Review* from 1934 to 1936, Rahv and Phillips expressed discontent with the narrow limits of proletarian criticism and fiction. Later, in 1939, one of Rahv's first important essays was a devastating attack on proletarian literature as 'the literature of a party disguised as the literature of a class'. In the same year he published 'Paleface and Redskin', a well-focused restatement of Brooks's thesis about the split between highbrow and lowbrow in American culture.

In this essay it was unfortunate that Rahv singled out James and Whitman as his two emblems, and not only because the elder James came to be deeply moved by Whitman's poetry, as Edith Wharton testified; in fact, both writers were too large and comprehensive to suit Rahv's allegorical scheme. (Indeed, Santayana and Brooks had pointed to Whitman as the figure who best transcended the split.) This schematic, even dogmatic quality was one of the drawbacks of Rahv's criticism. Trilling had cloaked his polemical intentions in sinuous dialectics and graceful euphemisms, as when he described Stalinism enigmatically as 'liberalism'. This gave his terms far wider application, so that they proved at once slippery and challenging to other critics. But Rahv, whose range was far narrower, whose work was often complex but never ambiguous, could write as if he were drawing up a position paper for a party meeting, excommunicating writers rather than criticising them.

Yet when he wrote about Dostoevsky, Kafka, Tolstoy, Gogol, or Chekhov, Rahv, besides proving himself a virtuoso at ideological analysis, revealed a robust, finely tuned sense of literary judgement; above all, he zeroed in decisively on the right critical issues. Like Wilson and Kazin (though far more brusquely), he had the good reviewer's gift for grasping the imaginative core of a writer's work. Chekhov was not someone whose sensibility, measured and delicately ironic, appealed to him as readily as Dostoevsky's. Yet Rahv turns a review of Chekhov's selected letters into a terse, powerful statement. Denying that Chekhov leaves us with no more than a mood of 'delicious depression', but also dismissing the heavier view that takes him 'simply as the critic of Russian society at a certain stage of its development', he perfectly grasps the combination of gaiety, pessimism, personal will, and empathy in Chekhov's humane outlook. Thus Rahv seeks out a middle ground in his critical method – between a wholly detached impressionism and a mechanical, deterministic historicism; his writing, though often abstract, attends closely to the concrete world of the author.

Rahv loved art too much to remain a strict Marxist, yet he was far too steeped in history and politics to settle for formalism, aestheticism, or art for art's sake, as a few *Partisan Review* writers like Clement Greenberg did. In his final years – he died in 1973 – Rahv became even more of a character and curmudgeon than he had always been, issuing marching orders to the New Left, delivering execrations against the counterculture and even against writers *Partisan Review* had built up, such as Norman Mailer – in short, behaving like the cultural commissars he had brushed aside in his youth. But in the forties and fifties he was an active opponent of the new formal and technical criticism, including rhetorical criticism, myth criticism, and poetic exegesis as applied to prose fiction. Though never as enthusiastic about Henry James as his most fervent admirers, he not only helped forward the James revival but, in wide-ranging essays like 'Notes on the Decline of Naturalism' and 'Fiction and the Criticism of

Fiction', contributed to James's goal of putting the discussion of fiction on a firmer theoretical basis.

Rahv has often been seen as the quintessential *Partisan Review* critic. His work, situated even more than Trilling's at the 'bloody crossroads where literature and politics meet', combines a relatively conservative modernism, which is suspicious of the wilder flights of the avant-garde, with an anti-Communist Marxism, ever alert to signs of his colleagues' backsliding into some form of accommodation with the American scene. Thus Rahv took note acerbically of 'the ambiguous, if not wholly conservative, implications' of Trilling's 'extreme recoil from radicalism'. Yet Rahv's essays on fiction run fundamentally parallel to Trilling's: he calls up the classical tradition of European realism as a way of attacking naturalism, and he appeals to the great modernists against their contemporary successors, the would-be inheritors of the avant garde. But where Trilling came to see modernism in increasingly apocalyptic terms, as a regression to the primitive and a rejection of the common life, Rahv saw it as a later stage of realism, an attempt to do justice to the disruptions and contradictions of the modern world. Modernism was the realism of the twentieth century; postmodernism was its nihilistic caricature. The greatest writers were those who shed light on the general crisis by exploring their own inner conflicts.

Thus Rahv, in true Hegelian fashion, emphasised the concrete universal, the impact of history as felt through the experience of individuals. Where Trilling came to see modernism as a form of spiritual violence, Rahv saw it as the final moment of the great tradition, the inevitable self-realisation of a turbulent era. While Trilling located realism essentially in the nineteenth century – to be invoked as an antidote to modernity – to Rahv, as to the novelist Saul Bellow, the principle of realism remained 'the most valuable acquisition of the modern mind'. And he directed his salvos against critics who, in his view, retreated from this 'sixth sense', the sense of history solidly grounded in realism. These opponents included myth critics, who failed to see that symbols and allusions were never the core of a novel but 'its overplus of meaning, its suggestiveness over and above its tissue of particulars'.

Like Bakhtin and Trilling, indeed like Henry James and D. H. Lawrence before them, Rahv saw the novel as the form of literature most open to experience. Deeply hostile to religion, he considered the vogue of symbolic interpretation as 'some kind of schematism of spirit; and since what is wanted is spiritualization at all costs, critics are disposed to purge the novel of its characteristically detailed imagination working through experiential particulars – the particulars of scene, figures, and action: to purge them, that is to say, of their gross immediacy and direct empirical expressiveness'. Along with Trilling and other New York intellectuals,

Rahv was a reactive critic, arguing in the militant thirties against extreme forms of naturalism, arguing in the depoliticised fifties against 'the reactionary idealism that now afflicts our literary life and passes itself off as a strict concern with aesthetic form'. As Rahv sums it up, 'if the typical critical error of the thirties was the failure to distinguish between literature and life, in the present period that error has been inverted into the failure to perceive their close and necessary relationship'.

Similarly, Rahv attacks the stylistic and formal criticism of fiction as 'the superstition of the word', the result of an 'infection of the prose sense by poetics'. Some formal critics are 'inclined to overreact to the undeniable fact that fiction is made up of words, just like poetry'. But, he argues, the language of fiction 'only intermittently leads itself to that verbal play characteristic of poetic speech, a play which uncovers the phonic texture of the word while releasing its semantic potential'. If indifferent stylists like Tolstoy and Dostoevsky can be greater novelists than Turgenev or Jane Austen, he says, this shows that other formal elements predominate over local effects of language: 'character creation, for instance, or the depth of life out of which a novelist's moral feeling springs, or the capacity in constructing a plot (plot, that is, in the Aristotelian sense as the soul of an action) to invest the contingencies of experience with the power of the inevitable'.

Style is simply the narrative rhythm that best suits the writer's imagination of reality. 'A Dostoevsky story cannot be appropriately told in the style, say, of Dreiser, as that style is too cumbersome and the pace too slow.' And Dreiser, whom Rahv had once attacked, he now sees as unquestionably a better novelist than Dos Passos, who is the better writer. As for Dostoevsky, 'Dostoevsky's style has a kind of headlong, run-on quality which suits perfectly the speed of narration and the dramatic impetuosity of the action... The principle of Dostoevsky's language is velocity; once it has yielded him that it has yielded nearly everything that his dramatic structure requires of it.'

Formulated more theoretically than Trilling's essays on fiction, Rahv's views add up to a powerful statement that could speak for many of the socially oriented critics of the first half of this century, including many Marxists like Georg Lukács and the Frankfurt school, who also combine a conservative epistemology, a traditional sense of form, with left-wing politics. Whatever their degree of sympathy for the avant-garde, their work is firmly rooted in the ethics and aesthetics – and above all in the historical outlook – of the nineteenth century. They see literature essentially as a reflection of reality, a reconstitution of immediate experience that has the power to criticise that experience. They focus on realism as a weapon of social criticism, an instrument of self-examination.

While the Marxist critics usually insist on a close correspondence between life and literature, between history and literary history, the Anglo-American culture critics, estranged from Marxism, insist on the relative autonomy of the individual and the crucial mediations of literary form – which, in Rahv's words, can 'invest the contingencies of experience with the power of the inevitable'. They show the influence of Freud and Anglo-American empiricism and individualism. As the phrase suggests, their 'sixth sense', the historical sense, is more often a matter of intuition and sensibility than hard theory; they rarely pursue such exact parallels between literature and history as we find in Lukács's *Goethe and His Age*, *The Historical Novel*, or his essays on Balzac and Stendhal, though their understanding of fiction has been formed around many of the same writers. Thus, when Edmund Wilson connected the 'inexorable doom' of Edith Wharton's protagonists with 'the mechanical and financial processes which during her lifetime were transforming New York', he was making a suggestive analogy – invoking a social fact which gives individual fates their resonance – not describing a direct cause and effect.

By and large, the Marxist critics were anti-modernist, profoundly suspicious of what they saw as a literature of decomposition and disintegration. On the other hand the culture critics, especially those born in the twentieth century, saw modernism as a further development of realism, an acute reflection of contemporary life, marked by what Rahv calls 'the crisis of this dissolution of the familiar world', the decay of the old rational order of nineteenth-century science and stability. Yet their modernism was essentially conservative: the same accusations their elders levelled against modernism – charges of incoherence, irresponsibility, frivolous pessimism – they direct against late modernism and postmodernism. If Lukács and Wilson would attack Kafka, so Rahv, an acute student of Kafka, could direct his fire (as early as 1942) at Kafka's imitators: 'To know how to take apart the recognizable world is not enough, is in fact merely a way of letting oneself go and of striving for originality at all costs. But originality of this sort is nothing more than a professional mannerism of the avant-garde.' Of the 'genuine innovator' he insists, almost classically, that '*at the very same time that he takes the world apart he puts it together again*'. This is perfectly consistent with his attacks on formal criticism, his emphasis on art as experience.

These socially oriented critics generally showed far more affinity for the political novel than for the experimental work of the avant-garde. Wilson and Rahv, both fluent in Russian, were entranced by the spiritual intensity with which the Russian writers grappled with social, moral, and political issues but, resolute secularists themselves, paid much less attention to their religious concerns. Rahv's first essay on Dostoevsky dealt with *The Possessed*, Dostoevsky's feverish assault on the radical generation of the 1860s. Wilson brilliantly illuminated Flaubert's *Sentimental Education* in his essay on 'The Politics of Flaubert'. Both essays projected the political concerns of the 1930s back into the nineteenth century. Trilling was drawn to the anti-radical politics of James's most atypical novel, *The Princess Casamassima*; other critics, including Leavis, focused on similar themes in Conrad's *Secret Agent*. Trilling himself wrote a novel of ideas and ideologies, *The Middle of the Journey*; its most compelling character was modelled on the Dostoevskian figure of Whittaker Chambers. The first major critical work by Rahv's colleague at Brandeis University, Irving Howe, was an influential collection of essays, *Politics and the Novel* (1957). This book identified a whole tradition of political or ideological fiction extending from Stendhal to Orwell, from bourgeois realism to anti-utopian fable. Showing how the novel had become a vehicle for exploring ideas about political action, not simply 'manners and morals', Howe was trying to reclaim for the independent left what Trilling had mobilised for his critique of ideology. Always a socialist, never a Communist, equally at home in politics and literature, Howe eventually became both the inheritor and the historian of the New York intellectual tradition.

Orwell: politics, criticism, and popular culture

This new interest in political fiction, like many of the novels themselves, including Trilling's *The Middle of the Journey*, was the fruit of the encounter with Marxism; indeed, it was a consequence of all the political traumas of the twentieth century, especially the rise of totalitarian dictatorships. This minor but engrossing literary tradition embraced writers like Arthur Koestler and Victor Serge, who had themselves been revolutionaries and whose books, like the famous essays in *The God That Failed*, exposed the grandiose hopes and bitter betrayals that inevitably beset intellectuals in politics. One of these novelists, George Orwell, who had fought with the anarchists in Spain, was also an avid student of this political writing. Almost alone among English critics, who showed little interest in intellectuals and ideology, he was repeatedly drawn to the work of ex-Communists like Koestler and to anti-utopian novels such as Jack London's *The Iron Heel* and Zamyatin's *We*, which became the model for his own *Nineteen Eighty-Four*.

After his disillusionment with Communism in Spain, Orwell became more of a political writer than any critic we have discussed here. He would later say that 'every line of serious work that I have written since 1936 has been written, directly or indirectly, *against* totalitarianism and *for* democratic Socialism, as I understand it'. As a result, Orwell, much discussed as a novelist, praised and damned as a prophet, widely imitated as a transparent stylist and essayist, revered as a man of exceptional probity and decency, has been comparatively neglected as a critic. His name figures in none of the standard histories of criticism. Yet Orwell's combination of quasi-novelistic journalism, political controversy, and what he called 'semi-sociological literary criticism' is strikingly characteristic of the American critics we have already considered and of the continental intellectuals they most admired, as Orwell himself did.

Orwell corresponded with Rahv and contributed a regular London Letter to *Partisan Review* from 1941 to 1946. Rahv, Trilling, and Diana Trilling were among those who acclaimed *Nineteen Eighty-Four* on its first appearance. Trilling helped shape American perceptions of Orwell as a truthful, decent man, a man of conscience and virtue, with his 1952 introduction to *Homage to Catalonia*, Orwell's book on the Spanish war. Irving Howe wrote frequently about Orwell over several decades and described him as one of his models: 'For a whole generation – mine – Orwell was an intellectual hero.'

Much of this identification with Orwell was political. The Trillings, Rahv, and Howe had long been embattled against Stalinism and its intellectual sympathisers. Orwell's book on Spain offered the kind of first-hand evidence of Communist perfidy that fellow travellers always worked to ignore. Many years later Orwell essays attacked the wilful blindness of the left-wing intelligentsia, their preference for ideological abstractions over concrete realities and simple moral imperatives. Orwell's conversion in Spain had given him a cause bordering on a passion. By 1946 he could write that 'looking back through my work, I see that it is invariably where I lacked a *political* purpose that I wrote lifeless books'.

Since Orwell's literary criticism has received so little attention, its close relationship to his political writing has rarely been noted. Even Trilling, in passing, expresses only a reserved approbation: 'His critical essays are almost always very fine, but sometimes they do not fully meet the demands of their subject – as, for example, the essay on Dickens.' With considerable point, though not without a touch of condescension, Trilling adds: 'And even when they are at their best, they seem to have become what they are chiefly by reason of the very plainness of Orwell's mind, his simple ability to look at things in a downright, undeceived way.'

While Trilling doesn't pause over the political implications of this last statement, his point is clear enough: Orwell is no 'genius'; his common sense, though not a sufficient basis for literary criticism, enabled him to avoid the traps of more brilliant, more theoretical minds, the occupational pitfalls of intellectuals. But apart from Dickens, who was one of Trilling's special authors, few of Orwell's critical subjects truly interested Trilling. Nor was he genuinely drawn to the kind of allegorical fable Orwell wrote in *Nineteen Eighty-Four* and *Animal Farm*, which belonged neither to nineteenth-century realism nor to twentieth-century modern-

ism. Trilling's own criticism showed little affinity for this kind of message
novel, which ran counter to his view of fiction as an open, unencumbered
form.

The most striking and, ultimately, influential feature of Orwell's literary criticism is his fascination with popular culture. By the end of the
1950s, Orwell's work in this field, combined with the continuing impact
of *Scrutiny* and of working-class English Marxism, would help bring
forth a new kind of socio-cultural criticism from Raymond Williams,
Richard Hoggart, Stuart Hall, and the Birmingham school of cultural
studies. Yet when Orwell was alive, nothing could have appealed less to
the modernist New York intellectuals than a serious critical approach to
popular culture.

There were a few American echoes of Orwell's work. It would be hard
to imagine Robert Warshow's essays on gangster films and Westerns as
fundamental American myths, or his pieces on comic books and on
Chaplin, without Orwell's example. But by and large the New York
viewpoint on popular culture was more influenced by the haughty attitude
of emigré intellectuals who recoiled almost viscerally from the American
scene. It was best articulated by Clement Greenberg in 1939 in 'Avant-
Garde and Kitsch' and by the early work of Dwight Macdonald: a
sweeping denigration of mass art and thirties populism in the name of
modernist intransigence, abstraction, and aesthetic complexity. On the
other hand, Orwell's complicated involvement with popular culture
wasn't confined to his famous essays on boys' weeklies, penny postcards,
and hard-boiled crime thrillers. If we adjust our lens slightly, nearly all his
other critical writings can be seen as 'Studies in Popular Culture', the
subtitle of one of his collections.

Orwell's first book of criticism, *Inside the Whale* (1940), which was
favourably noticed by Q. D. Leavis in *Scrutiny*, contained three long
essays – on Dickens, on boys' weeklies, and (the title essay) more or less on
Henry Miller. Orwell's Dickens, to Trilling's evident dismay, was not the
modern Dickens uncovered by Wilson but the popular Dickens long
beloved by ordinary English readers, above all, the preternaturally vivid
Dickens characters that all English children had grown up with. Acutely
attuned to class differences, Orwell draws up a social and moral inventory
of the Dickens world, extracting a tendency or 'message' from each of the
writer's works. This emphasis on argument, not form – on social, not
verbal texture – was guaranteed to curl the hair of any New Critic – or, for
that matter, any New York critic, since Orwell's rationale is that 'every
writer, especially every novelist, *has* a "message"' and, anyway, 'all art is
propaganda'.

Though radicals since Ruskin and Shaw had made free use of Dickens's
attacks on English society, Orwell shows that Dickens's social criticism is

'exclusively moral', not Marxist. Yet he argues that it is no less subversive: 'A good tempered antinomianism rather of Dickens's type is one of the marks of Western popular culture.' Thus Orwell turns Dickens – and popular culture generally – into the epitome of the common man outlook, as opposed to the inhumane absolutism of the typical intellectual. 'The common man is still living in the mental world of Dickens', a world of instinctive human generosity and indignation, of simple pleasures and dastardly abuses, 'but nearly every modern intellectual has gone over to some or other form of totalitarianism'.

Thus, just as Trilling appealed to the novel for its anti-ideological character, its openness to experience, Orwell's essays invoke popular culture as a rebuke to the abstract thinking of intellectuals, especially their worship of power, whether Marxist or Fascist. Popular culture was simply one facet of Orwell's affinity for the 'lower depths'. V. S. Pritchett described him as a man who had 'gone native in his own country'. Of the mildly pornographic penny postcards Orwell writes: 'Their whole meaning and virtue is in their unredeemed lowness... The slightest hint of "higher" influences would ruin them utterly. They stand for the worm's-eye view of life.' Robert Warshow later made a similar point about the tramp figure in Chaplin.

Orwell exalts writers who create a sense of limitless human abundance, like Shakespeare and Dickens, but also others like Swift, Gissing, Smollett, Joyce, and Henry Miller who specialise in the unpleasant truths most writers leave out. We cherish Dickens, he says, because of his 'fertility of invention'; the Dickens world is like life itself. 'The outstanding, unmistakable mark of Dickens's writing is the *unnecessary detail*.' Shakespeare he defends against the puritan moralism of the aged Tolstoy who, no longer content with a writer's 'interest in the actual process of life', demanded a literature of 'parables, stripped of detail and almost independent of language'. Like a modern ideologue, Tolstoy wants puritanically 'to narrow the range of human consciousness'.

Yet Orwell is even more attracted to writers who, though strikingly limited themselves, descend obsessively into the lower depths that polite literature shuns. Swift was 'a diseased writer', a permanently depressed figure whose worldview 'only just passes the test of sanity'. Yet he possessed 'a terrible intensity of vision, capable of picking out a single hidden truth and then magnifying it and distorting it'. This is in line with Orwell's oft-stated belief that 'for a creative writer possession of the "truth" is less important than emotional sincerity'. Orwell's criticism itself is less interesting for its explicit arguments, where he himself can sound like a Tolstoyan ideologue, than for the way he fleshes them out; his best work as a novelist can be found in the descriptive vividness of his essays. Thus he likens Tolstoy's scorn for Shakespeare's profligate abundance to the reaction 'of an irritable old man being pestered by a noisy child. "Why do you keep jumping up and down like that? Why can't you sit still like I do?" In a way the old man is in the right, but the trouble is that the child has a feeling in his limbs that the old man has lost.' Hostile to all forms of spirituality, sceptical of empty idealisms, Orwell grounds ideas in the physical basis of life. 'Saints should always be judged guilty until they are proved innocent', he wrote of Gandhi in *Partisan Review* in 1949, shortly after his assassination. 'The essence of being human is that one does not seek perfection.'

The same insistence on the grossly physical helps explain Orwell's affinity for Swift, including the Swiftian disgust that surfaces often in his own work. Again, Orwell's version of this is intensely concrete and deliberately shocking: 'Who can fail to feel a sort of pleasure in seeing that fraud, feminine delicacy, exploded for once? Swift falsifies his picture of the world by refusing to see anything in human life except dirt, folly and wickedness, but the part which he abstracts from the whole does exist, and it is something which we all know about while shrinking from mentioning it.' Thus, in a single sentence, Swift epitomises both the (bad) abstracting intellectual and the (good) concrete imagination, reminding us of unpleasant facts, as Orwell prided himself in doing. Orwell on Swift is also Orwell on Orwell, exposing himself as he drives his point home: 'In the queerest way, pleasure and disgust are linked together. The human body is beautiful: it is also repulsive and ridiculous, a fact which can be verified at any swimming pool. The sexual organs are objects of desire and also of loathing, so much so that in many languages, if not in all languages, their names are used as words of abuse.'

Orwell has it both ways: he is the student of language yet also the spokesman for the common wisdom; the Freudian intellectual, anticipating Norman O. Brown on Swift, but also the critic of intellectuals; the common man but ever the iconoclast. For Orwell, the unregenerate popular mind – filled with irregular bits of ordinary patriotism, decency, common sense, lust, and even a touch of heroism – *is* a species of iconoclasm. His long essay 'Inside the Whale' is the most naked example of a dialectic that underlies Orwell's criticism. Beginning and ending with Henry Miller, this is an acidulous history of the relation between writers and politics between the wars. Miller embodies the standard of ordinary experience by which the political follies of intellectuals, such as the Auden-Spender group, can be judged.

Orwell had reviewed *Tropic of Cancer* and *Black Spring*, corresponded with Miller, and even visited him on his way to fight in Spain, when Miller supposedly called him an idiot for risking his own skin. In his essay Orwell compares him to Joyce, Celine, and especially Whitman for his passivity toward experience, his rejection of 'higher' goals. Just as Joyce's 'real achievement had been to get the familiar on to paper', so 'what Miller has in common with Joyce is a willingness to mention the inane squalid facts of everyday life'. Thanks to his passive acceptance of life, 'Miller is able to get nearer to the ordinary man than is possible to more purposive writers.' As writers like Auden, on the other hand, grew increasingly politicised, they fell into casual complicity with tyranny and violence. In Auden's hard-boiled poem on Spain, the phrase 'necessary murder', says Orwell, 'could only be written by someone to whom murder is at most a *word*... Mr Auden's brand of amoralism is only possible if you are the kind of person who is always somewhere else when the trigger is pulled.' A master polemicist as well as a master of the plain style, Orwell can devastate a writer with one or two well-chosen phrases. Like Howe and Rahv, he brings the habits of political controversy into literary criticism – but also the subtleties of a literary sensibility into political writing.

'Inside the Whale' is something of a mess; it's really two essays, one on Miller, the other on the left-wing English intelligentsia. The parts come together only by an act of will. Yet it is precisely the *kind* of piece that socially oriented critics often produce: diagnostic, polemical, using writers as emblems of larger cultural attitudes. Orwell touches on a dozen writers from Housman and Eliot to Auden and Miller, connecting each with his social moment, his class, and the historical burden of his message. He identifies the pastoral writing of Housman and Rupert Brooke with the disillusionment that followed the war, and links the radicalism of Auden and Spender with their soft, middle-class, public school education, their inverted snobbery, their 'sense of personal immunity'. The narcissistic, bohemian spirit of Henry Miller becomes one of Orwell's literary masks, enabling him to strike the pose of the common man, the enemy of intellectual cant.

As a critic Orwell is better when he explores the common man more directly, not as an adjunct to social prophecy. As direct observation *The Road to Wigan Pier* (1937) is a masterpiece; as analysis it's often cranky and absurd. But Orwell grew rapidly as an essayist. His classic pieces on boys' weeklies and penny postcards ('The Art of Donald McGill') are evocative and shrewdly observant. They affectionately explore these sub-cultural materials as reflections of the popular mind but also as specimens of ideology, little doses of safe, conformist thinking with which the masses are always being inoculated. Thus Orwell anticipates both the sociologists of mass culture, who take bestsellers and hit songs as an index of public attitudes, and the ideological critics of the Frankfurt school and, later, the Birmingham school, who see modern mass culture as part of a process of 'hegemonic' indoctrination.

Orwell's essays combine a remarkable tenderness toward popular art (especially in its older, Edwardian forms, which take him back to his own childhood) with a detached insight into its social and political outlook. By the end of 1941, as he himself turns less radical, he sees its 'antinomianism' less as a form of radical criticism than as a safety valve within an essentially conservative society. The McGill postcards give us something like 'the music-hall world where marriage is a dirty joke or a comic disaster, where the rent is always behind and the clothes are always up the spout, where the lawyer is always a crook and the Scotsman always a miser, where the newlyweds make fools of themselves on the hideous beds of seaside lodging houses', and so on. 'Like the music halls, they are a sort of saturnalia, a harmless rebellion against virtue.'

Conclusion: England and America

Orwell is an unlikely but useful figure to round off this survey of the largely American cultural criticism of the first half of the twentieth century. Though his disillusionment with Communism enabled him to forge strong links with American intellectuals and to win a large cold-war audience, he was the kind of writer only England could have produced. He was also something of a loner, certainly a less typical English critic than his school friend Cyril Connolly, who edited *Horizon* all through the 1940s. Despite his aesthete's pose as an indolent sybarite and self-confessed failure, the boorish but well-connected Connolly was a prolific, influential reviewer and baroque man of letters. Connolly's mandarin style was remote from Orwell, who believed that 'good prose is like a window pane'. But both men came of age under conditions that never existed in America and gradually passed even in England as the century wore on.

England had a number of traditions that made the careers of writers like Orwell or Connolly or V. S. Pritchett possible. Since the founding of the great reviews like the *Edinburgh* or the *Quarterly* at the beginning of the nineteenth century, England had a long, rich, and uneven history of literary journalism, which expanded dramatically at the turn of the century with the effects of compulsory education. But despite the growth of a mass audience, England remained to a significant degree a class-bound society in which literature still mattered. Though Orwell, in a grim moment, likened the professional book reviewer to someone 'pouring his immortal spirit down the drain, half a pint at a time', it was far easier for a literary journalist to survive in England than in America, where book reviewing was a more marginal, more mechanical pursuit and, except for a brief period in the thirties, government support for culture or communications was nonexistent. (Orwell worked unhappily for the BBC during the war years.)

More than in England, book reviewers in America tended to be functionaries of the marketplace rather than guardians of literary values, a role which fell more and more to the growing professoriat. A surprising number of important English writers were also supple, assiduous reviewers, supporting themselves with literary journalism while enlarging the literary culture. Though their pieces were impressionistic and unsystematic, Arnold Bennett, Virginia Woolf, E. M. Forster, and D. H. Lawrence all did significant work as critics; the same could be said about few American novelists after James and Howells. (The sparkling criticism of Mary McCarthy and John Updike were rare exceptions.) This crosshatching with the world of the novel enlivened the prose and the creative insight of English criticism and sharpened its social perspective. The kind of attention to class and manners we find in Orwell was a staple of English criticism left and right. In America, a more open society, the novel of manners was an extremely minor enterprise. As literary criticism became more formal, analytical, and academic, social criticism was left to the old-style historians and pop sociologists. For critics it was a minority pursuit bordering on the unpatriotic.

The growth of higher education, with its need for a new mass pedagogy, proceeded far more slowly in England than America. Only after World War II did a university education become more widely available. The New Criticism as machinery for the production of close readings was never institutionalised in England; it lacked the necessary industrial base, the academic factory. In England, aestheticism was long hobbled by its associations with upper-class decadence, symbolised by the fate of Wilde, Beardsley, and the *Yellow Book*. It took a brilliant generation in the 1920s to gain approval for the formal study of English literature in Cambridge, a more modern university than Oxford. The interwar figures who stood for criticism as against historical scholarship – critics like Eliot, Leavis, Richards, and Empson – were anything but pure formalists. Their close attention to language and style was saturated with historical considerations. The same could be said of the first American New Critics, before their work was routinised.

By 1950, the year Orwell and Matthiessen died, the year Trilling published *The Liberal Imagination*, the year Edmund Wilson, at the low ebb of his reputation, collected his *New Yorker* pieces under the deliberately casual title of *Classics and Commercials*, historical criticism was far more beleaguered in America than it would ever be in England, a nation with a longer moral tradition and a more ingrained, more conservative sense of the past. Victorian cultural criticism remained a living body of work, especially for the English left. Always suspicious of modernism, the English, bereft of empire, began turning inward. The welfare state, the Movement (in poetry), and the Angry Young Men became cultural features of Little England. For many young postwar writers, Thomas Hardy became the man of the moment, not Proust, Kafka, or Joyce.

Historical criticism in America was by then primarily a counter tradition, a minority enterprise, but it was also far less insular and more cosmopolitan than its English counterpart. Trilling's subjects in 1950 ranged from Tacitus to the Kinsey Report, from Kipling and Scott Fitzgerald to Freud. Wilson's book, though not as various as his earlier work, included a delicious evisceration of *Brideshead Revisited*, an iconoclastic assault on detective stories, and a book-length study of the new California hard-boiled writers.

Both books avoided the kind of technical criticism already fashionable in the academic world. Like most traditional criticism from Johnson to Arnold, they offered the distilled effect of close reading, not the minute record of it. They were the work of public critics: essayistic, conversational, accessible to any intelligent reader. Their concerns were contemporary, not antiquarian, but their methodology, if they had one, was rooted in the familiar essay of the nineteenth century. As if to highlight his somewhat old-fashioned allegiance to social history, Wilson included no less than three reviews of his friend Van Wyck Brooks's Makers and Finders volumes, pieces more sympathetic to Brooks than his earlier dissection of *The Pilgrimage of Henry James*. Though Wilson again emphasised Brooks's shortcomings as a practical critic, he was most impressed by the quality of the writing, by the intricately patterned mosaic of major and minor figures, and by the keen sense of time and place that enabled Brooks to locate American literature so firmly in the American landscape. Brooks's own goal, as he tells us in his 1953 *envoi*, *The Writer in America*, was 'to show the interaction of American letters and life'. This was a goal Wilson admired without sharing Brooks's nationalism and anti-modernism. Like every other critic we have considered here, Brooks and Wilson would have agreed with Leavis that 'one cannot seriously be interested in literature and remain purely literary in interests'.

16

The British 'man of letters' and the rise of the professional[1]

Josephine M. Guy and Ian Small

Today most literary criticism takes place in institutions of higher education, and most literary critics, by virtue of their academic qualifications and institutional employment, are considered (and consider themselves) to be members of a profession. Indeed the widespread use by publishers of the term 'academic writing' is an acknowledgement that most of what is called literary criticism is now written for professional and pedagogic purposes. It is rare for the professional critic to address a general (that is a non-academic) audience. A hundred years ago, however, matters were rather different. The professional procedures with which we are now so familiar were then being put into place for the first time, and reaction to them was mixed. In *The Importance of Being Earnest* Oscar Wilde has Algernon Moncrieff deflate Jack Worthing's intellectual pretensions with the comment: 'literary criticism is not your forte my dear fellow. Don't try it. You should leave that to people who haven't been at a University.' Wilde was referring to the newly professionalised academic literary critic, a species from which he constantly and strenuously tried to distance himself. Moreover, he was not unique in his antagonism to professionalisation. For the next thirty years or so a number of critics, located for the most part outside institutional structures, also attempted to resist the discourses of the new academic professionalism. They did so in a variety of ways: they adopted different styles and objectives, wrote on different topics, but principally they addressed their work to a different audience. For the first few decades of the twentieth century these 'amateur' critics managed to co-exist with their professional colleagues, but as the century progressed they became more and more marginal, until by the late 1930s they had to all intents and purposes disappeared. Historians of the universities and of university education have tended to ignore these dissenting voices, and have described the transition to professionalisation as an inevitable and smooth progression. But in English studies at least the resistance of the amateur critic, although historically unsuccessful, is still

---

[1] The argument of this essay draws substantially on Josephine M. Guy and Ian Small, *Politics and Value in English Studies* (Cambridge, 1993).

significant; indeed it raises some serious issues about the function of criticism in society, and the relationship between professional critics and the public which supports them. These issues are as important now as they were then.

The removal of literary criticism from the arena of educated public debate to that of academic institutions began in the late nineteenth century. It was part of a large set of changes in the structure and organisation of knowledge which took place at that time and which is generally characterised in terms of the twin processes of professionalisation and specialisation. Briefly, during the nineteenth century developments in science and the growth of technology led to knowledge becoming abundant but, as a consequence, also becoming increasingly complex and diverse, and thus increasingly specialised. To claim competence in a particular field, individuals had to narrow their interests and undertake specialised training. One consequence was that the authority of the Victorian sage – that of the cultural critic or distinguished 'man of letters' (and they were nearly always men) – began to give way to that of the expert who specialised in one particular area. To have any widespread social utility, however, expert knowledge (now as well as then) had to be formalised and policed, and alongside specialisation developed the parallel process of professionalisation.[2]

Professionalisation can be usefully understood as those institutional and intellectual structures which define and authorise what will count as expert knowledge. Two of its features are particularly important for the history of literary criticism. The first concerns the reciprocal nature of the relationship between the universities and the professions. Nearly all professions need universities, for they train future practitioners for a particular profession and they formally test competence through examinations. They also ensure the maintenance of standards by the continual modernisation and improvement of knowledge through research. Hence nearly every well-established profession is located in some form or other within the university structure; and nearly all aspiring professions seek to locate themselves within it. But universities themselves were and are affected by the criteria (of competence, accountability, relevance, and so forth) which the professions were instrumental in establishing. The pressure to con-

---

[2] The literature on professionalisation in both Britain and the United States is immense. For a basic account of professionalisation in Britain, see W. J. Reader, *Professional Men: The Rise of the Professional Classes in Nineteenth-Century England* (London, 1966). For further examples of the large body of sociological work devoted to the professions, see the edition of *Daedalus*, 92 (1963); A. H. Halsey and M. A. Trow, *The British Academics* (London, 1971); J. A. Jackson (ed.), *Professions and Professionalization* (London, 1970); Magali Sarfatti Larson, *The Rise of Professionalism: A Sociological Analysis* (London, 1970); Andrew Abbott, 'Status and Strain in the Professions', *American Journal of Sociology*, 86 (1981), pp. 819–35.

form to such criteria resulted in the widespread university reforms which took place over the second half of the nineteenth century. These reforms concerned the implementation of formal examination procedures and changes to entrance requirements, but in social terms the most important change took place in the curriculum, which was greatly expanded to accommodate the interests of those groups who wished to see their particular practices given the prestige and authority which only the universities could confer.[3]

The other important (and closely related) aspect of professionalisation concerns the changes it brought about in the concept of intellectual authority. Prior to professionalisation, authority tended to reside in the prestige of the individual; so the authority of the Victorian 'sage' – figures such as John Stuart Mill, Matthew Arnold, or Thomas Carlyle – derived principally from who they were. With the advent of professionalisation, however, authority came to be located instead within a scholarly community, that of a professional peer-group: research was deemed valid only insofar as it was acceptable to this community. This new way of defining what was to count as legitimate research clearly required new structures – that is, new mechanisms of intellectual authority. In other words, collective judgements had to be validated by a socially agreed body of criteria and procedures. At one level this process involved a recognition by scholars that they had to locate their work in relation to the normative standards of a scholarly community. As a result, procedures to formalise those standards began to emerge. These chiefly concerned the corroboration of evidence, its presentation and agreed forms of reference, including conventions for citation and quotations. As a consequence what we now understand as the 'literature' on an academic subject came into being. Initially this impetus to formalise academic discourses in order to facilitate scholarly communication and verification came from the natural sciences. But the scientific 'paradigm' very quickly spread to inform the social sciences and then the humanities. This process is most obvious in the changes which took place in the discipline of history. A requirement of its professionalisation in the 1880s was a systematic way of referring to sources and evidence: hence in the late nineteenth century there was a move to adopt what was then thought to be a more 'scientific' approach to the subject. It involved a greater attention to the sources of historical evidence and to a discrimination between kinds of evidence. Practically this resulted in the institutionalisation of archival and source material, a

---

[3] The widespread changes which took place in British universities in the late nineteenth century have been described by Sheldon Rothblatt in *The Revolution of the Dons* (London, 1968) and in *Tradition and Change in English Liberal Education* (London, 1967); and by T. W. Heyck in *The Transformation of Intellectual Life in Victorian England* (London, 1982).

process most easily seen in the editing of texts in the Rolls Series by William Stubbs, professor of history at Oxford from 1866, and a prime mover in its professionalisation.[4]

One of the less welcome results of the introduction of these new mechanisms of intellectual authority was the increasing inaccessibility of academic writing to a non-specialist audience. The whole apparatus of citation and verification which the newly professionalised academic community valued so highly presupposed an intimate and detailed knowledge which in practice existed, and could only exist, within that community. In this sense academic writing became increasingly self-regarding and esoteric. The days of the sage who could write on any serious subject for a generally educated audience had, by 1900, virtually disappeared. But so too had his medium. The generalist periodicals, such as the *Edinburgh Review* or the *Cornhill Magazine*, which in the middle of the nineteenth century carried articles on a wide range of subjects from science and politics to fiction and geography, were in the process of being superseded as forums for intellectual debate by the advent of the specialised professional academic journal, such as *Mind* (begun in 1870 by the academic psychologist Alexander Bain).

Given the cultural preeminence of literary criticism in the nineteenth century, it was more or less inevitable that the study of literature would be caught up in the general drift toward professionalisation. Indeed from the early 1880s onwards enthusiasts such as John Churton Collins lobbied for the institutionalisation of literary criticism.[5] But initially there was strong resistance to the proposal that criticism should become the main practice of the new academic discipline of English studies. Indeed the first professors of English were philologists, for they could more easily claim a scientific basis for their subject and thereby fulfil the generally accepted criteria for professionalisation. But by the turn of the century, literary criticism had been incorporated into the new discipline, although the range and nature of its practices had undergone considerable changes in order to answer to the imperatives of the new academic forms of intellectual authority. At a general level, the move toward professionalisation involved paying much greater attention to the nature and status of literary judgements. Indeed, the principal task of the academic critic was to make explicit (and thereby to formalise) the knowledge underlying judgements about literary value, and to do so in ways which corresponded to the new

---

[4] For an account of the professionalisation of history, see Doris Goldstein, 'The Professionalization of History in the Late Nineteenth and Early Twentieth Centuries', *Storia della Storiografia*, 1 (1983), pp. 3–23.

[5] For an account of Churton Collins's attempts to establish English as a university discipline, see Anthony Kearney, *John Churton Collins: The Louse on the Locks of Literature* (Edinburgh, 1985).

standards of scholarly rigour which professionalisation had engendered. This large objective in its turn resulted in the establishing of two relatively new areas of critical practice: the formalisation of the procedures of text-editing and of literary history.[6] The late nineteenth and early twentieth centuries saw a systematic attempt to build an archive of authoritatively edited literary works similar in function to those archives being established in other newly professionalised humanities disciplines, particularly, as we have suggested, in history. The works of the *Early English Text Society*, or early scholarly editions of Shakespeare, treated literary works as sourced, and paid due attention to matters such as the authenticity of documents and the integrity of the literary text. In this way the role of individual editors and large editorial projects became a key element in the academic study of literature; and specialised knowledge of the textual history of a work became an important element in judgements about literary value. So it was not uncommon for critical re-evaluations of particular writers to be accompanied or brought about by new modern editions of their work. For example the work of textual scholars, such as Herbert Grierson's pioneering edition of John Donne, did much to change the reputations of neglected writers. A similar role was found for the writing of literary history in that knowledge of a work's historical relationships with its predecessors came to be seen as an important element in forming literary judgements. But literary history also mapped the subject-area for the newly professionalised discipline; in terms more familiar today, it made explicit the literary canon – that formal expression of the literary values which a particular community holds. In the process, literary history was itself transformed. In a way unknown in the early part of the century, under the direction of professional academics, it became both systematic and comprehensive, borrowing many of its conceptual tools and narrative paradigms from history proper. The new academic literary historiography placed a premium on verifiable evidence, especially in the form of biographical and bibliographical detail, a strategy which in its turn drew upon a traditional element in British historiography, that of the primacy of individual agency. A representative example of the consequences of these developments in literary history for literary criticism is to be found in the 'Great Writers Series' established by Eric S. Robertson in 1887. It was a set of studies by distinguished critics on what were seen to be major literary figures. The aims of 'this series of little monographs' were, in Robertson's introductory note, to provide 'a chronicle of the chief events in a famous author's life; ... a critical history of that author's

---

[6] The editing of texts and the writing of literary histories had of course existed prior to the late nineteenth century; but they had been practised in unsystematic or eclectic ways. The achievement of professionalisation was to begin the process of theorising both practices.

works; ... a full bibliography of these works; and ... an analytical Table of Contents, that will summarize the biography on a new plan'.[7]

In all these ways the professionalisation of literary criticism was, by the turn of the century, transforming critical practice and redefining what it meant to be a literary critic. And it was precisely these processes which amateur or (to use the pejorative Victorian and Edwardian phrase) bel-lettrist writers were opposed to. Their hostility to professionalisation focused on the issue of specialisation – more particularly, on the professional assumption that literary judgements involved specialised knowledge which it was the task of literary criticism to formalise and make available. The obvious response to this argument was to redefine the nature of literary value such that it drew upon 'common' (that is, non-specialised) knowledge and experience. And indeed a prominent feature of amateur criticism of this time is a strong (and, at times, almost messianic) emphasis on the *moral* nature of literary judgements, for moral knowledge by definition cannot be specialised. Clear examples of this strategy are to be found in the work of amateur critics such as A. R. Orage and John Middleton Murry.

In his weekly literary column in *The New Age*, for example, Orage, a reviewer and journalist, defined the function of the 'good critic' as finding 'the truth about things', and 'propagating' it. He went on:

I can conceive an artist writing with no propaganda in mind ... but I can imagine no critic worth his office who does not judge with a single eye to the upholding of the moral laws. Far from being an offence to literature, this attitude of the true critic does literature honour. It assumes that literature affects life for better or for worse.[8]

In a later piece in the same periodical, Orage went on to describe the nature of the authority which permitted the critic to make such large claims. He began by disputing two common prejudices of the time: that literary judgements were either subjective and personal or, alternatively, 'scientific'. They were not the latter because 'truth' – the basis of literary judgements – was not, according to Orage, capable of scientific verification; but neither was 'truth' relative to the individual and therefore personal. Rather 'truth' had an 'essential character' which is accepted as authoritative when it is recognised by a community. In abstract terms, Orage is claiming that moral judgements are absolute and non-negotiable, but that their authority requires communal assent. It ought to be noted that there is a contradiction here; if a truth is absolute, then by definition its authority is independent of *any* individual or communal assent. How-

---

[7] Eric S. Robertson, *Life of Henry Wadsworth Longfellow* (London, 1887), 'Introductory Note'.
[8] *The New Age*, 13 (1913), p. 634. Quoted in Wallace Martin, *Orage as Critic* (London, 1974), p. 83.

ever, this *non-sequitur* allowed Orage to claim (without any awareness of its illogicality) that the critic can individually perceive 'truth', but also that his literary judgements may not be accepted as authoritative until his community is persuaded of that truth. This strategy in turn permitted Orage to retain a central role for the critic which exists in his privileged and unique access to truth, while at the same time grounding the authority of literary judgements in common experience:

There is nothing in the nature of things to prevent men arriving at a universally valid (that is, universally accepted) judgment of a book, a picture, a sonata, a statue or a building any more than there is to prevent a legal judge from arriving at a right judgment concerning any other human act. And, what is more, such judgments of art are not only daily made, but in the end they actually prevail and constitute in their totality the tradition of art. The test, however, ... is not scientific; but as little, I protest, is it merely personal. Its essential character, in fact, is simply that it is right; right however arrived at, and right whoever arrives at it. That the judge in question may or may not have 'studied' the history of the art-work he is judging is a matter of indifference. Neither his learning nor his natural ignorance is of any importance... All that matters is that his judgment, when delivered, should be 'right'. But who is to settle this, it may be asked? Who is to confirm a right judgment or to dispute a wrong one? The answer is contained in the true interpretation of the misunderstood saying: De gustibus non est disputandum. The proof of right taste is that there is no real dispute about its judgment; its finality is evidenced by the cessation of debate. Or, as it may be simply stated, a judge – that is to say, a true judge – is he with whom everybody is compelled to agree, not because he says it, but because it is so.[9]

A similarly fallacious set of assumptions underwrote the copious literary criticism of a contemporary critic, John Middleton Murry. A decade later in 'A Critical Credo' he made them explicit. Like Orage, he subscribed to the view that literary judgements did possess a moral basis, and that the task of the critic is to illustrate and explicate this moral value: 'Criticism ... should openly accept the fact that its deepest judgements are moral. A critic should be conscious of his moral assumptions and take pains to put into them the highest morality of which he is capable.'[10] Moreover Murry believed, once more like Orage, that critics had a privileged access to this moral knowledge, but that their literary judgements, to be considered authoritative, had to receive communal assent:

[The critic] begins like any other writer, with the conviction (which may of course be an illusion) that his views and conclusions on the subject-matter which is literature are of importance in themselves and to others; and he proceeds to promulgate and propagate them. Like any other writer, he stands or falls in the long run, by the closer or more remote approximation of his views to the common

[9] *The New Age*, 24 (1918), pp. 25–6. Quoted in Martin, *Orage as Critic*, pp. 77–8.
[10] John Middleton Murry, *Countries of the Mind: Essays in Literary Criticism, First Series* (Freeport, N.Y., 1968), p. 189.

experience of that comparatively small fraction of the human race which itself comes to conclusions about life and literature.[11]

The strategy of these amateur critics had three basic elements. The first was an attempt to ground literary values in non-specialist – that is, moral – knowledge. The second was an appeal to a common experience to authorise the judgements of literary critics. The third claim, which works to undermine the first two, was the proposition that the critic had a privileged access to the 'truth' of literature.

Of course, the general argument that correct literary judgements embody a common moral truth was not new. In fact the idea had its origins in Romanticism and was the foundation of pre-professional mid-Victorian aesthetics. In the work of the Victorian sages the moral basis of literary value, and therefore the social and cohesive function of literature, was constantly asserted. As early as 1833, John Stuart Mill had pithily claimed, 'poetry, when it is really such, is truth'.[12] But in the same essay he had also been concerned to describe the role and function of the critic. For Mill, the problem with poetry was that its truth was of a special kind – it was 'intuitive' or 'symbolic'. Indeed it was precisely the ability to apprehend and express this special kind of moral knowledge which defined the poet as poet. A consequence of this special knowledge, however, was that it tended to make poetry inaccessible – a limitation which had haunted the Romantic aesthetic which Mill was invoking. Mill sought to overcome this difficulty by assigning a special role to the critic. For Mill, the critic's job was to explicate the 'higher' truth of poetry and make it accessible to a larger reading public; and it was the critic's knowledge of logic or metaphysics (Mill called criticism 'the office of the logician' or 'metaphysician') which equipped him for this task. In this way, Mill's ideal critic was not unlike the new professional academic, in that his role was to make explicit the knowledge underlying judgements about literary value; but he was also not unlike the new amateur critics in that they too saw a mediating role for the critic which existed by virtue of his special sensibility. But in one important respect both Mill and the new amateurs differed from the professionals; it concerned the ways in which such special knowledge could be acquired. Mill tends to assume that the critic's understanding of

---

[11] *Ibid.*, p. 184.
[12] John Stuart Mill, 'Some Thoughts on Poetry and Its Varieties', in John M. Robson and Jack Stillinger (eds.), *The Collected Works of John Stuart Mill: Autobiography and Literary Essays* (London, 1981), p. 346. The full context makes Mill's point more strongly: 'The distinction between poetry and what is not poetry, whether explained or not, is felt to be fundamental: and where everyone feels a difference, a difference there must be ... Poetry, when it is really such, is truth; and fiction also, if it is good for anything, is truth: but they are different truths. The truth of poetry is to paint the human soul truly; the truth of fiction is to give a true picture of life' (*ibid.*, pp. 343–6). In this respect it is interesting to compare Orage's claim in *The New Age*, 13 (1913), p. 297, that 'the value of a work of art lies in its expression of truth' (quoted in Martin, *Orage as Critic*, p. 73.)

metaphysics is simply a given of his natural intelligence; in this sense critics, like Romantic poets and artists, are born and not made. Matthew Arnold made exactly the same assumption when he too defined critics in terms of their knowledge of what was the 'best', where the definition of 'the best' derived from the critic's superior intellect. (This is also true of Orage's and Murry's idea of the 'truth'.) For professional critics at the end of the century, however, the knowledge which they thought made literary judgements possible, although specialist, was *not* mysterious in origin. Like any other kind of professional knowledge, it could be investigated (in part empirically), codified and, most importantly, it could be acquired through appropriate education and training. In principle (but not, of course, in practice), with the right teaching and the right ability, anyone could become a professional critic.[13]

The real difficulty faced by the amateur critics lay in the ambiguous ways in which they identified the origins of their authority. In order to justify their status and role, they found that (just like their professional colleagues) they had to give criticism some kind of specialist component. After all, if criticism required no specialist knowledge or skills, then everyone could be his or her own critic. But at the same time they were intent on resisting specialisation on the grounds of its association with professionalisation and academia – more specifically, they objected to the fact that the esoteric nature of professional criticism alienated it from a general audience. Hence their attempt to invoke the values of the common reader to authorise their judgements. This desire to invoke a common realm of experience while at the same time holding to the privileged (and mysterious) sensibility of the critic presented a dilemma which could not be resolved on logical grounds; but it could be disguised through rhetoric. The amateur critics therefore self-consciously resurrected the prose style of the Victorian sage. Eschewing the paraphernalia of scholarly discourse, which drew attention to scholarly knowledge, they attempted rather to persuade through 'personal' authority. In so doing amateur critics established themselves as literary personalities whose superior taste gave them a privileged insight into literary values. In this sense there is a continuity of strategy from later nineteenth-century writers, such as Walter Pater and Oscar Wilde through to Middleton Murry and Orage; all adopt an oracular, *ex cathedra* tone in their writing where the reader is given little opportunity to disagree with (let alone debate the assumptions of or evidence for) the judgements in question. This tone is produced by a variety of rhetorical devices which all have the same end. They range from Pater's endlessly attenuated sentences which make dissent difficult, to

---

[13] It is worth noting here that the principles of professionalisation in theory permitted women to become professional critics. In practice, professionalisation has helped in the degendering of literary criticism.

Wilde's use of epigrams which make his critical precepts incontestable, to the biblical tone of Murry's literary judgements and his use of the magisterial 'we', to Orage's construction of a plausible narratorial presence – the intrusive 'I' which invites only assent from his readers.

As we suggested earlier, the authority of the Victorian sage had largely depended upon a public recognition of his worth as an individual. In this respect, his authority was intimately related to his readership. The real problem for the amateur critics in the early decades of the twentieth century was to find a comparable audience. To whom did critics such as Murry and Orage address themselves? One of the general consequences of professionalisation is the way it removes intellectual debate from a public arena: academic research tends to be written chiefly for an academic community, and the newly professionalised discourses of literary criticism were no exception. The scholarly materials which the nascent discipline of English produced were not primarily intended for the general reading public. In the words of a contemporary academic, one Professor Dewar of the University of Leeds, there was a crucial distinction between what he called 'home reading' and that scholarly activity undertaken within and for his own profession.[14] In this sense, the readership for professional literary criticism was very different from that invoked by the Victorian sage. Moreover the difference was not simply one of numbers. Both readerships were restricted, for the Victorian reading public was also an élite by dint of money, class, and education. Rather, it was the nature of the constituency which had changed. Professional critics addressed themselves to a small but highly specialised and judgemental peer group; the work of Arnold and Mill, on the other hand, was directed to a generally educated audience of diverse interests and values, who were not invited to judge their work in the same way. The amateur critics of the early twentieth century initially attempted to write as if they were addressing that generally educated Victorian reading public, self-consciously proposing themselves as modern sages. However, since the advent of professionalisation two important areas of social change had made this ambition impossible to realise.

The first concerns the splitting of the relatively homogeneous Victorian reading culture into a variety of forms, most easily and crudely character-

---

[14] For Dewar's comments, see the *Proceedings of the English Association Bulletin*, 22 (February 1914), p. 12. Dewar recognised that for English to justify its disciplinary status, and to be reckoned the intellectual equal of other university subjects, it had to possess a set of specialist practices which would produce specialist knowledge: 'The real university graduate in English is one who not only knows English, but also the method, the procedure, to adopt with a view to increasing knowledge upon the subject. He must have some sense, some power, of what is nicknamed in other studies "research". If we are going to produce students who will advance the knowledge of the subject, then our first year must include something ... to enable [the student] also to understand how a scholarly critic goes to work in editing a text or in making a study of some author or period' (*ibid.*).

ised as high and popular culture. This fragmentation was in turn brought about by a number of larger demographic, educational, legal, and economic changes. They included the advent of mass literacy, rapid developments in the technology of book publication and distribution, as well as new legislation affecting the length of the working-day and the concomitant growth of what has now come to be known as leisure and the leisure industry. These developments have all been well documented; their importance for the professionalisation of English studies and the history of literary criticism concerns the way in which they redefined the relationship between the critic and the reading public. The growth of the reading public, actual and potential, in the years between 1880 and 1920, resulted in a specialisation and diversification of markets – what a modern economist would understand as the growth of new market sectors. Broadly speaking, most of the 'new' reading public was engaged by a very different kind of literature. The enormous growth in the sales of various Victorian and Edwardian sub-genres, such as detective fiction and ghost stories, both answered to and helped to create these new kinds of readers. The same developments also produced the crisis in sales experienced by many 'high' (or serious) literary artists of the time, and the inability of novelists such as Henry James and George Gissing to find anything other than a coterie readership. Given this market diversity, the difficulty for the amateur critic was who to address. In practice their chosen subject of inquiry (so-called 'high' literature) had a readership which was now more marginal and which served a different constituency from the 'literature' studied by the Victorians. In simple terms, the readership which had supported the sage was simply no longer available to the new amateur critic. Indeed, this limitation was tacitly recognised in the ways in which they were forced to publish. Most amateur literary criticism appeared in small or coterie literary magazines, such as *The New Age*, or in limited runs of fairly expensively priced books.

The second large area of social change which made the strategy of the amateur critic problematic concerned the gradual displacement of cultural authority from the realm of art and the aesthetic generally to that of other discourses, principally the natural and social sciences. In the mid- and late nineteenth century, the centrality of the role of culture in general and literature in particular was almost taken for granted. This can be seen in a variety of ways. Most visibly there was the enormous financial commitment to public institutions such as art-galleries and museums in the major Victorian cities. There was also the widespread building of public libraries, the easy accessibility of paperback editions of classic writers, and the prestige which attached to an arts-based education, which at one extreme encompassed an Oxford Greats degree and at the other the simple social grace of being 'well-read'. It was precisely these kinds of values which produced a work such as Matthew Arnold's *Culture and Anarchy* in which art and literature were seen as fundamental to the structure of society. In other words, the social significance of literary criticism was simply self evident, and the freedom and authority of writers such as Arnold to comment on large-scale social issues were also assumed. Hence, too, their ability to address a general audience – the kind of audience which today might be compared to the readership of the 'serious' newspapers. But by the turn of the twentieth century the displacement of the authority of the arts by the natural and social sciences had all but destroyed this authority. A generally educated audience no longer looked to literary critics, and to literary criticism, to tell them about problems in society. Rather they looked to specialists in the new professions – figures such as John Maynard Keynes and Sidney and Beatrice Webb.

One of the ironies for the amateur critics, then, was that, given these social changes, professionalisation probably functioned to preserve literary criticism in that it provided a protective if limiting environment in which critics could continue to operate. At the same time the paradox of professionalisation (which the amateurs rightly recognised) was that in the process literary criticism became more and more removed from the general public. And hence the rationale, that of the social utility of literature, which had permitted the professionalisation of literary studies in the first place, was put in jeopardy.

17

F. R. Leavis

Michael Bell

F. R. Leavis was one of the most potent single influences on English studies in the earlier and middle part of the twentieth century. He is best known for his radical revaluation of the accepted canon of English literature, and his impact lies in the revaluative activity itself as much as in the particular set of judgements it involved. His principal concern was with English literature as the expression of a distinctive culture. His radical revaluations, along with his sense of what it means to belong to a particular tradition, rest upon a comprehensive conception of literature and language. Furthermore, his career spanned the rise, and the subsequent renewed questioning, of English as an independent academic discipline. He maintained a passionate and intellectually grounded belief in the distinctiveness, and the cultural centrality, of English as a critical discipline, a belief which cannot be adequately described as liberal humanist, even if he would not have repudiated either term. The main purpose of the present essay will be to explicate his central belief as it is manifest within his critical judgements. Accordingly, there follow in turn: a career survey covering the main Leavisian themes and occasions; a summary account of his conception of literature and language; an examination of his idea of social tradition of which the literary tradition is an integral part; a principled look at his rereading of literary tradition in respect of poetry and the novel; a brief look at some of the critics associated with Leavis including fellow contributors to *Scrutiny*: and finally a comment on the limitations and continuing significance of Leavis's thought about literature and criticism as he has himself become more distinctly an historical figure.

Career and themes

Frank Raymond Leavis was born in 1895 in Cambridge, England where, apart from his years as a stretcher bearer in the Great War, he lived throughout his life. After the war he started a degree in history, changing at the end of the first year to English (available as a degree subject in the University of Cambridge only since 1917). This change of subject prefigures the central conviction of his later career that imaginative literature provides the most significant, and inward, understanding of the past and ultimately, therefore, the present.

In 1927 he became a probationary lecturer and his criticism was crucially formed, both in style and in substance, by a pedagogical purpose, his goal of educating his students as future common readers with an essential, but not reductive, understanding of literature as a holistic expression of the culture at large. His acerbic critical judgements and authoritative style should be understood, at least partly, in the light of this pedagogical commitment, his practical concern with what a student should concentrate on within the limited time of a three-year degree.[1]

In 1929 he married a former student, Queenie Roth, who became his most important, and his only life-long, collaborator. Particularly well read in the history of English fiction, she influenced his increasing preoccupation with the novel over the course of his career, and her effect can already be seen in his first important publication, the pamphlet *Mass Civilization and Minority Culture* (1930), which set out the Leavises' cultural historical vision and affirmed the central function of literary criticism.

As will be seen, the Leavises developed a critique of modern culture as radical in its way as those of Flaubert or Nietzsche in theirs. In the more immediate social historical foreground, they believed that widespread literacy, combined with the commercial exploitation of popular reading matter, had led to a debasing of public sensibility which slighted serious creative work and coarsened public capacity to recognise it. The intellectual clerisy of those was not just a minority, it was itself largely, if more subtly, permeated by the commercial and social values of the wider world. But unlike Flaubert or Nietzsche, who treated modern bourgeois culture of the right and left with supreme contempt, the Leavises wished to work for a truly educated and critical democracy which could only be achieved in the face of almost all institutionalised culture, including the universities.

Since the newly founded English School at Cambridge was a group of remarkably talented individuals, several of whom consciously emphasised the importance of contemporary literature and criticial judgement of the past, the Leavises hoped it would prove a collaborative centre for the cultural self-examination they had in mind. In the event, their ideal 'Cambridge' became increasingly isolated from the actual university. Considerable acrimony developed between the Leavises and many of their

---

[1] The responsibility involved in recommending reading to students is a primary emphasis, for example, in Leavis's essay 'Coleridge in Criticism', *Scrutiny*, 9, pp. 57–69. See also F. R. Leavis, *English Literature in Our Time and the University: The Clark Lectures* (London, 1969), pp. 168–9.

established colleagues, although it is difficult to assess to what extent their isolation was personal and circumstantial and to what extent it was intrinsic to their endeavour. Even with good will, their radical vision was hard to institutionalise.

Leavis's early publications bring out how his essential vision remained constant, despite changes in particular emphases and judgements. In *Mass Civilization and Minority Culture*, for example, Dickens's sentimental populism was seen as evidence of the lowering of public taste (although the Leavises later reversed this view). Similarly, Leavis's pamphlet of the same year, *D. H. Lawrence*, was his first attempt to come to terms with another author, in this case only recently dead, who was to become increasingly central to his understanding of ethical and creative imagination. But the chief interest of the pamphlet now is the extent to which Leavis shared the general perception of Lawrence as a talented but extreme figure on the margin of the culture, a view which accepted the conventional objections to Lawrence's work. Leavis's gradual re-assessment of Lawrence and Dickens, who became his most positive cultural exemplars, is part of his increasing preoccupation with the novel as the preeminent form of cultural and ethical critique.

In 1932 Leavis became director of studies in English at Downing College where he taught for the next thirty years. The Cambridge critical journal *Scrutiny* was founded in the same year, and Leavis was soon responsible for its combative and influential stamp. *Scrutiny* provided the indispensable public forum for the Leavisian critical project. It reviewed contemporary literature; it conducted a systematic revaluation of the English literary canon; and it debated more general questions, among which a campaign for British educational reform and a critique of Marxism were the most important.[2]

Also in 1932 Leavis published *New Bearings in English Poetry* and *How to Teach Reading: A Primer for Ezra Pound*. Leavis's critical understanding was shaped by his attempts to come to terms with the modern movement and particularly, at first, contemporary poetry. He recognised that the terms of earlier criticism were not adequate to the new literature. The three figures on whom he concentrated most positively in this volume, Hopkins, Yeats, and Eliot, are seen to have a peculiarly complex and creative relation to the English tradition. Pound comes in for more negative treatment and in the separate short volume, offered as a reply to Pound's *ABC of Reading*, Leavis explains why. Although Leavis admired *Hugh Selwyn Mauberley*, and endorsed Pound's iconoclastic impact on

---

[2] In the first volume of *Scrutiny* Leavis attacked what he saw as the reduction of culture to economics in 'Under which King, Bezonian?', *Scrutiny*, 1, pp. 205–14. Replies by H. B. Morton and Herbert Butterfield appeared respectively as 'Culture and Leisure', *Scrutiny*, 1, pp. 324–6 and 'History and the Marxian Method', *Scrutiny*, 1, pp. 339–55.

the literary ambiance of Edwardian Britain, he saw Pound's cosmopolitanism as rootlessly synoptic and too narrowly technical. Pound was too much concerned with novelty in its own right, rather than as the outcome of a specific creative struggle with past forms and meanings. By Leavis's conception, Pound did not really know what tradition was.

The positive value of tradition is stressed in Leavis's title for a collection of his *Scrutiny* essays published in 1933, *For Continuity*. In 1934 he edited a collection of *Scrutiny* essays by various hands under the title *Determinations*, followed in 1936 by one of his most influential books, *Revaluation*, in which he drew on previous essays to redraw the significant lines of development in English poetry from Shakespeare to the Victorians. Along with *New Bearings*, it articulated his essential understanding of English poetic tradition as an index of the broad changes in sensibility which had led to the condition of modern culture.

In 1943 he drew again on previous *Scrutiny* material for *Education and the University*. He was effectively summarising *Scrutiny*'s long campaign for educational reform just before the Educational Act of the following year, although his own interest was in university rather than school teaching. The *Scrutiny* campaign sought to liberalise educational methods and syllabi: it emphasised personal judgement in tutor and student, and encouraged relating literary study to other cultural disciplines. Many of his specific proposals were to be embodied later in the new generation of British universities founded in the sixties. (Ironically, Leavis was opposed to this massive expansion of tertiary education, which did not reflect his ideal of an intellectual clerisy with a common critical purpose.)[3] *Education and the University* is the last volume in which his social writing is animated by a hopeful, if not optimistic, sense of his possible influence on public consciousness or the direction of public affairs.

In the event, the greatest influence of Leavis and *Scrutiny* in Britain was not in university departments, but in the school teaching of literature. With their attempt to create an intellectual clerisy to replace the old class order of British society, the 'Leavisites' sought goals which coincided with the era of the 'grammar' schools, academically selective, but economically and socially open schools which gave an academic education to the top thirty per cent or so of the secondary school population. This system lasted from the 1944 'Education Act' until the early to mid-sixties, when the selective system came to be politically intolerable as well as educationally controversial. There is no simple cause and effect to be inferred here so much as a recognition that Leavis was of his time, one in which the older hierarchical assumptions of social leadership overlapped with a new openness as to who might perform this function.

---

[3] See his seven specific proposals in 'Education and the University', *Scrutiny*, 9, pp. 98–120.

Perhaps the most influential and controversial of Leavis's books, *The Great Tradition: George Eliot, Henry James, Joseph Conrad*, appeared in 1948. His rereading of the English novel showed how narrative language and structure are inseparable from the quality of moral vision, at least in the great writers. Rather than judging 'artistic' works from a 'moral' standpoint, as has been changed, Leavis was demonstrating the interdependence of these dimensions. But his intensive appreciation of these authors involved a comparative dismissing of others, including the whole of the comic and formally self-conscious line in English fiction. *The Great Tradition* poses a question repeatedly raised by Leavis's criticism: is the intentness of his reading undermined by the exclusiveness on which it is predicated?

In 1950 he edited *Mill on Bentham and Coleridge*, with an introduction setting out the historical significance of utilitarian thought. Bentham became Leavis's instance of the malaise of modern culture, with its narrowly scientific conception of instrumental reason. It is a significant if in some ways unfair critique. Bentham, for example, could be defended as seeking appropriately generalised premises, and a corresponding discourse, for public legislation. But Leavis wished precisely to bring out the radically symptomatic meaning of his feeling able to do so, an impulse which points to a recurrent problem with Leavis's rhetoric, if not his essential thought. He uses synoptic phrases such as 'technologico-Benthamite' which signify an elaborate and specific historical analysis, but which can well be taken as offering self-evident truths, or even mere catch-phrases, and often one must read a significant body of Leavis's *oeuvre* to assess the force of particular expressions.

In 1952 there appeared one of Leavis's best-known collections of critical essays, *The Common Pursuit*. The introduction borrows T. S. Eliot's definition of criticism as the 'common pursuit of true judgement' to affirm Leavis's model of collaborative disagreement. Critical statements, however authoritatively expressed, implicitly invite a reply of 'Yes, but...'.[4] As a pragmatic description of critical activity the essay is still a classic and useful statement. Of course, there remains a problem about the shared premises of the collaborative community in which constructive disagreement can occur – a problem which is thrown into relief by the iconoclasm of Leavis's own judgements and the personal contempt they frequently entailed for those who oppose them. The collection also contains his most famous statement on the nature of criticism. In reply to René Wellek's invitation to give a principled formulation of his critical procedure and criteria, he declined on the grounds that such formulations would only be banally generalised and actively damaging to cogent

---

[4] Leavis appeals to this formula, for example, in *English Literature in Our Time*, p. 47.

thought about literature. As Leavis's essay shows, the question of the critic's general 'criteria' in reading is inextricable from that of the poet's 'beliefs' within the poems. There is no such thing as an abstract 'belief' except *as* an abstraction which has ceased to be a commitment. The same 'belief', held by two different people, is not the same belief. It is the interest of literature to engage questions of belief and value in this holistic, subliminal and creatively questioning way, and it is the function of criticism to understand this without reimposing the very reductions against which imaginative expression has struggled.

At stake here is the significant locus of commonality. For Leavis, all imaginative literature is an attempt to embody in language, and thus make commonly available, some new complex of value or realisation. When language is used creatively it is being used against its inevitable tendency to find the largest common denominators of meaning. Hence within the ideal of the 'common pursuit' there lurks importantly the ghost of the common reader. For despite the democratic objections sometimes made to Leavis's 'minority' conception of culture, it is significant that he sought always to use the common tongue rather than a specialised terminology, an effort which put his language under great strain, since he had sophisticated and difficult things to say. There is an important connection between Leavis's use of the common tongue and his attempt to understand the kind of commonality at stake in great creative literature. Wellek's well-meaning offer to set out Leavis's general principles would be likely only to preempt the Leavisian commonality.

The Common Pursuit includes several of Leavis's essays on Shakespeare, whose work he considered the consummate expression of creative thought within the English language. 'Shakespearean' English offered a concrete criterion for the reading of later poets such as Milton and Dryden, as well as a clue to the essential genius of apparently less-related writers like Dickens. Several *Scrutiny* contributors, including Leavis, effected a revaluation of Shakespeare as a poetic dramatist in contrast to the 'character'-based criticism associated with Andrew Bradley.[5] (Seen from a later vantage-point, the *Scrutiny* emphasis on '*poetic* drama' missed the theatrical dimension of Shakespeare which became evident in the sixties.)

In 1953 *Scrutiny* ceased publication. In a valedictory note, Leavis

[5] A. C. Bradley, *Shakespearean Tragedy* (London, 1904). L. C. Knights's pamphlet *How Many Children had Lady Macbeth?* (Cambridge, 1933) gave a decisive force to this distinction. The books of G. Wilson Knight were likewise extensively, if critically, reviewed in *Scrutiny* (although Leavis absorbed Wilson Knight's influence and still appealed to it late in his career; see Leavis, *English Literature in Our Time*, p. 162). Leavis's own essays on Shakespeare were part of this movement. See 'Antony and Cleopatra and All for Love', *Scrutiny*, 5, pp. 158–69; 'Diabolic Intellect and the Noble Hero: A Note on *Othello*', *Scrutiny*, 6, pp. 259–83; 'The Greatness of *Measure for Measure*', *Scrutiny*, 10, pp. 234–47; 'Criticism of Shakespeare's Late Plays', *Scrutiny*, 10, pp. 339–45; 'Tragedy and the Medium', *Scrutiny*, 12, pp. 249–60.

observed that the journal had been difficult to produce since the beginning of the war years as economic pressures were compounded by the dispersal of key contributors, and there is a discernible loss of quality over the second decade of its publication. Although he was not one of its founders, the journal had come to be effectively identified with Leavis. Yet during the later years of *Scrutiny*, Leavis had written a number of essays elsewhere, some as introductions, on American literature. He criticised Van Wyck Brooks's history of American literature as uncritically compendious and approvingly introduced Marius Bewley's *The Complex Fate*, which was an attempt, by an American, to identify the major tradition of American literature in a Leavisian spirit. Bewley and Leavis particularly urged that the greatest achievements in American writing were not those which most overtly expressed an especially American experience, such as the frontier, but those which explored the 'complex' double identity of a transported European heritage.

In 1955 he reworked material from earlier essays to produce *D. H. Lawrence: Novelist*, the first work to argue that Lawrence was a 'normative' figure within an ethical and literary tradition coming from Wordsworth and George Eliot. Later, he came to see Lawrence's significant forebears as Blake and Dickens. Leavis saw, from his own experience, that a major adjustment in consciousness was required to appreciate the radical significance of Lawrence, and the inability of many representative figures in academic and other intellectual spheres to make this adjustment gave Lawrence an increasingly strategic importance to Leavis throughout the latter part of his career. For him, Lawrence's break with Bertrand Russell in 1915 epitomised his relation to academically educated culture at large,[6] and he recognised the cost to Lawrence, as a writer, of his marginal position. As Leavis himself became more embattled and isolated in his final years, he increasingly affirmed Lawrence's significance in the synoptic, apparently uncritical, manner to which his rhetoric was susceptible. In his own way, the late Leavis also suffered the loss of a collaborative community. To hostile readers, Leavis's Lawrence came to seem an obsessional totem.

In 1962 Leavis acquired a public notoriety when his Richmond lecture, 'Two Cultures: The Significance of C. P. Snow', initially delivered at Downing College, was published in *The Spectator*. Snow's *The Two Cultures and the Scientific Revolution* (1959) had proposed that, as a matter of educational policy, practitioners of the scientific and humanistic disciplines should have some intelligent awareness of each other's specialisms. But when he proposed that science and the humanities were two

---

[6] Three essays on this theme are in F. R. Leavis, *The Common Pursuit* (London, 1952): 'Wild Untutored Phoenix', pp. 233–9; 'Mr Eliot, Mr Wyndham Lewis and Lawrence', pp. 240–7; and 'Keynes, Lawrence and Cambridge', pp. 255–60.

separate, equal cultures, so that ignorance of twentieth-century physics was comparable to an ignorance of Shakespeare, he ran afoul of Leavis's conception of a common culture based on the collective creative achievement of language. And it was evident to Leavis, from Snow's presentation of 'scientific' culture as enlightened and 'literary' culture as obscurantist, that literature for Snow meant little more than a conventional cultivation of polite letters. Snow's much reprinted views, his assured condescensions, and his assumed authority as a novelist, all represented for Leavis an orthodox establishment which belittled imaginative literature and denied its critical function just as Britain was about to embark on a massive expansion of university education. In Snow's tone and language Leavis saw the 'technologico-Benthamite' world view. He attacked Snow's central notion of the two cultures, derided his standing as a novelist, and savaged the whole nature of his discourse. The result was a summary of Leavis's understanding of criticism and an indication of how the personal dimension, the 'attack' on Snow, was intrinsic to its case. Leavis, in a public arena, had given intellectual convictions greater weight than considerations of politeness, and although Leavis's strictures were no more than a telling and timely statement of the emperor's lack of clothes, the affair signalled his general isolation.

The same significance can be seen in his response to the 1960 'trial' of *Lady Chatterley's Lover*.[7] In this case, the British establishment, as it was perceived in the prosecution, advertised its own absurdity. Leavis naturally believed that the book should be published as being part of Lawrence's *oeuvre*, but he refused to have anything to do with a defence based on the intrinsic quality of the novel. Leavis had come to see it as a travesty of the Lawrence who mattered, and he was appalled to see that the assimilation of Lawrence as a major modern author had been effected so uncritically. Lawrence was the very last author to be read uncritically or as representing some acceptable body of doctrine.

In 1962 Leavis reached retirement age and his university and college posts were terminated, although he had visiting positions for some years in other British universities. Besides the volume *'Anna Karenina' and Other Essays* (1967), he gave in the late sixties a series of Clark lectures published as *English Literature in Our Time and the University* (1969) and a joint visit to the United States with his wife resulted in their combined *Lectures in America* (1969). In 1970 came another joint study with Q. D. Leavis, *Dickens the Novelist*, which reversed the generally negative view of Dickens that Leavis had maintained as late as *The Great Tradition*. The moral fable of *Hard Times*, previously seen as the exception that proves the rule, was now exemplary of Dickens's poetically

---

[7] F. R. Leavis, 'The Orthodoxy of Englightenment', *'Anna Karenina' and Other Essays* (London, 1967), pp. 235–41.

concentrated social vision, his intricate elaboration of theme, and his psychological penetration. Dickens, like Lawrence, embodied and thematised the peculiar impersonality which enables a great artist to speak, 'for the race, as it were'.[8]

Leavis's last decade was characterised by attempts to defend his activity in some more principled terms. Though still far from seeking a methodology or set of principles to encompass critical practice, he did want to ground the activity of criticism on an explicit conception of language and creative thought. Hence, of his three final volumes, *Nor Shall My Sword: Discourses on Pluralism, Compassion and Social Hope* (1972), *The Living Principle: English as a Discipline of Thought* (1975), and *Thought, Words and Creativity: Art and Thought in Lawrence*, (1976), the last two shift their emphasis from the *practice* of cultural criticism to a meditation *on* it. He drew at this point on Marjorie Grene and Michael Polanyi, whose principal titles, *The Knower and the Known* (1966) and *Personal Knowledge* (1958), indicate his own emphasis on the personal dimension in knowledge.

But as his guarded use of these comparatively minor figures suggests, he maintained his suspicious relation to philosophy. He was offering, as he well knew, a philosophical view of language and creativity, but refused to be drawn on to philosophical ground, a strategy that constitutes his strength and his vulnerability. The late writings make explicit the conception of language underlying his *oeuvre* at large, and whether or not one agrees with it, it is complete, coherent, and sophisticated. But his conscious adoption of a middle position between the disciplines of philosophy and literary criticism, a viewpoint clearly intended to challenge each, resulted for the most part in his conception remaining invisible to both.

This philosophical invisibility compounds an even more crucial aspect. Leavis's continuing importance, or the reason he remains a nagging presence in the academy, is that he expressed in a forceful and considered way the implicit commitment of many intelligent common readers and teachers of literature who do not have a publicly thought out position. That, of course, leaves his conception open to being equated with the most generalised and sentimental beliefs in the humane value of literature. His active commitment to an ideal of the common reader has left him vulnerable to reduction to the lowest common denominator, and his very representativeness, which is the key to his importance, makes him invisible.

F. R. Leavis died in 1978 and Q. D. Leavis in 1981.

[8] Leavis quotes this phrase from a Lawrence letter in *English Literature in Our Time*, p. 51.

Literature and language

Leavis's encompassing conception of literature, literary history, and criticism rests upon a prior conception of language. A recognition of language as the radically governing medium of thought is a defining characteristic of twentieth-century thinking in a range of fields. Leavis shared this recognition, but in a sense that ran counter both to the structural, semiotic linguistics arising from Saussure and to the analytic, positivist concerns of British philosophy in his day. The important qualities of language for him were its flexibility, its indeterminacy, its moments of individual creativity, and its resulting capacity for dynamic development as the expression of a particular culture. From this viewpoint Saussurean and post-Saussurean modes of analysis err not because they are untrue but because they are unable to discuss what really matters about language precisely, insofar as any generalised or theoretical account of what does matter will be equally empty.

When Leavis attempts to define his creative sense of language, his difficulty can be felt in the straining of the prose:

The nature of livingness in human life is manifest in language – manifest to those whose thought about language is, inescapably, thought about literary creation. They can't but realize more than notionally that a language is more than a means of expression: it is the heuristic conquest won out of representative experience, the upshot or precipitate of immemorial human living, and embodies values, distinctions, identifications, conclusions, promptings, cartographical hints and tested potentialities. It exemplifies the truth that life is growth and growth change, and the condition of these is continuity. It takes the individual being, the particularizing actuality of life, back to the dawn of human consciousness, and beyond, and does this by fostering the *ahnung* in him of what is not yet – as the as yet unrealized, the achieved discovery of which demands creative effort. Blake was speaking out of the 'identity' when he said 'Tho I call them Mine, I know they are not Mine.' He was referring to his paintings and designs, but he would have said the same of his poems. One's criterion for calling an artist major is whether his work prompts us to say it, emphatically and with the profoundest conviction for him – to put the words in his mouth and impute to him that rare modesty which makes the claim that is genuinely a disclaimer.[9]

Leavis found nothing in the philosophy he knew to ground his sense of what matters in language, and his personal acquaintance with Wittgenstein leaves a teasing sense of unrealised possibility, in that Wittgenstein's later interests were closer to Leavis's preoccupation with the elusive, tacit processes of meaning in language.[10] Instead, his conception is best under-

---

[9] F. R. Leavis, *The Living Principle: 'English' as a Discipline of Thought* (London, 1975), pp. 44.
[10] See Leavis's 'Memories of Wittgenstein', *The Human World*, 10 (February 1973).

stood in relation to important currents of contemporary philosophy of which he was unaware. His late interest in Grene and Polanyi indicates the true philosophical analogue which might indeed have helped him had he known of it: the continental phenomenological tradition from which Grene and Polanyi partly derive.

It is particularly instructive to see the close analogy between Leavis and Heidegger. Heidegger also criticises radically the whole metaphysical tradition in Western philosophy and, in his later writings, draws increasingly on poetry to explain the general significance of language as a creative medium.[11] To see Leavis as the English analogue of Heidegger has a double value: it brings out the positive claims and coherence of Leavis's work as a body of thought, rather than an arbitrary set of attitudes, and it highlights the important differences between them, which Leavis would certainly have seen as reflected in their respective disciplines of philosophy and literary criticism.

At the centre of Heidegger's thinking is his concern with Being, a term he regularly capitalised to indicate the inadequacy of its ordinary usage. For Heidegger, the history of Western thought since Socrates had been an increasing incapacity to respond to Being, and one important aspect of this failure is the metaphysical assumption of an 'external' world, whether as an object of epistemological investigation or an object of instrumental use. Response to Being is lost precisely when consciousness is conceived as separable from its 'world', a term which he insisted on putting in quotation marks to deny this separability. Any human 'world' exists only in the human response. Although Leavis used the phrase 'human world' similarly, the centre of his thinking lies in the comparably difficult, yet equally inescapable, term 'life',[12] which serves the same function of denying the radical dualism of Western thought, culture, and language, but points to vital values, as opposed to the more meditative implication of Heidegger. In this respect Leavis's thought is closer to Nietzsche's than to Heidegger's.

Heidegger endorsed Neitzsche's fundamental recognition that the question of value was prior to the question of knowledge but, he argued, the question of Being is more radical again.[13] Leavis is somewhere between the two. His understanding of the positive and creative function of lan-

---

[11] See especially *What is Called Thinking*, tr. F. P. Wieck and J. Glenn Gray (New York, 1968); *On the Way to Language*, tr. Peter D. Herz (New York, 1971); *Poetry, Language and Thought*, tr. Albert Hofstadter (New York, 1971); and *The Question Concerning Technology and other Essays*, tr. William Lovitt (New York, 1977). A late and indirect connection with this tradition is suggested by Leavis's extended quotation from Rilke in *English Literature in Our Time*, p. 188.

[12] For Leavis's use of the phrase 'human world' see, for example, *Living Principle*, pp. 43–4.

[13] See Heidegger's essay 'The Word of Nietzsche', in *The Question Concerning Technology and Other Essays*, pp. 53–112.

guage is thoroughly Heideggerean, as will be seen, but his critical spirit, and his awareness of the paradoxes of any critical posture, are Nietzschean. Hence his insistence that '"life" is a necessary word' is to be understood within the Nietzschean recognition that there can be no meaningful judgement of the value of life itself.[14] As Nietzsche insisted, there is no 'life' to be judged separable from individual living beings. One can, certainly, affirm or deny the value of life, but this will be an expressive rather than a referential utterance. Any general judgement on the value of life has meaning only as an expression, or symptom, of the quality of life in the utterer.[15] The centrally inescapable term is not itself a matter of argument. The radical nature of the Nietzschean and Leavisian critique of their respective cultures made each of them peculiarly aware of its essential inarguability. This is reflected in their personally challenging rhetoric which, far from being a sign of inability to argue in a more conventional way, is itself an important, and thoroughly conscious, aspect of their meaning. To see Leavis as the English analogue of Nietzsche and Heidegger is to see that, while lacking their philosophical weight and sophistication, he had the root of the matter in him and understood the essential questions in a more balanced and pragmatic way.

This may explain why Leavis, although aware of Nietzsche from early in his career, seems not to have been fundamentally influenced by him; and, of course, in Leavis's formative years Nietzsche was frequently taken up in reductive and damaging ways. Leavis's own formation was through reflection on the English critical tradition, which he examined in a series of essays covering particularly Johnson, Coleridge, Wordsworth, and Arnold.[16] He saw the difficulty of maintaining this tradition in the intellectual, as well as social, context of the new century. In a world of broadly accepted values it had been possible to see poetry as essentially the vehicle of meanings which could be conveyed by other means. Such a conception is evident in Pope's formula 'True Wit is Nature to advantage dressed/ What oft was thought but ne'er so well expressed.' Arnold's essay 'Literature and Dogma' places a different burden on imaginative literature as the ultimate values of the community come to be seen as collective cultural creations with no metaphysical sanction beyond their own expression. Hence the importance for Arnold of learning and propagating the 'best that is known and thought in the world'.[17] But as Arnold's use of the

[14] F. R. Leavis '"Life" is a Necessary Word', *Nor Shall My Sword: Discourses on Pluralism, Compassion and Social Hope* (London, 1972), pp. 11–37.
[15] See Friedrich Nietzsche, *Twilight of the Idols*, tr. R. J. Hollingdale (Harmondsworth, 1990), p. 40.
[16] F. R. Leavis, 'Johnson as a Critic', *Scrutiny*, 12, pp. 187–204; 'Coleridge in Criticism', *Scrutiny*, 9, pp. 57–69; 'Wordsworth', *Scrutiny*, 3, pp. 234–57; 'Arnold as a Critic', *Scrutiny*, 7, pp. 319–32.
[17] The phrase is from 'The Function of Criticism at the Present Time', *Matthew Arnold*, ed. R. H. Super, vol. 3 (Ann Arbor, 1962), p. 283.

present tense implies, his cultural 'touchstones' still reflect classicist and universalist assumptions. Leavis saw that this was no longer adequate, as the 'great hiatus' of the war had made particularly evident.[18] Though Leavis shares much with Heidegger, he understood himself within an immediate cultural-historical context, and his creative conception of language was attached to a controversial vision of decline from the 'organic community' of the past. (Heidegger's broader sweep over Western thought enabled him to place post-Cartesian modernity within a less historically vulnerable account.) Still, his enduring interest lies in a comparable attempt to understand the dynamic manifestation of life values in language. And, as with Heidegger, it is crucial to recognise the anti-Cartesian conception of language in which this occurs. Without that, many of Leavis's judgements seem arbitrary.

Leavis's very comparable vision can be seen in the passage already quoted. Leavis is explicitly concerned with the collective creative process that arises from the efforts of countless individuals – efforts which are uncoordinated except in so far as they pass into the language and thereby become a resource for future speakers. It is particularly emphasised that the individual exists in language, is almost a focusing of the language itself, so that much of the process described takes place, as it could only take place, in a twilight zone between the individual and the collective, the conscious and the unconscious. Hence the capacity of the language to prompt or suggest, and the capacity of the individual to learn from its promptings. Heidegger described the same creative interaction as 'listening' to language,[19] an account of language which enforces the impossibility of regarding individual consciousness as separable from its linguistically constituted world. The insistence on language as the medium in which self and the world jointly inhere, rather than as a referential system mediating between the separate zones of consciousness and an external world, is crucial to Leavis and helps explain several controversial features of his critical readings, such as the appeal to an 'enactive' aspect in poetic language.

Leavis emphasised this 'enactive' quality, for example, in his reading of Keats's 'Ode to Autumn'. In following the sounds, rhythms, and pauses of the poem, he claimed, we are led to simulate muscular actions akin to those being described at the semantic level: 'In the step from the rime-word 'keep', across (so to speak) the pause enforced by the line division, to 'Steady' the balancing movement of the gleaner is enacted.'[20] We may note how Leavis's own syntax in turn reenacts, as if instinctively, the enactive

---

[18] Leavis used this phrase to refer to the war in 'T. S. Eliot as Critic', *Commentary* (November 1958). The essay is reprinted in Leavis, *'Anna Karenina' and Other Essays*, pp. 177–96.
[19] See 'On the Way to Language' in Heidegger, *On the Way to Language*, pp. 123–4.
[20] Leavis, *Common Pursuit*, pp. 16–18.

quality he is seeking to bring out in Keats. But the increasing dominance of semiotic conceptions of language has led us to dismiss such claims. Sounds have no intrinsic meaning and it is a sentimental illusion to speak of language as enactive.[21] The dismissiveness arises from the absence of common terms, and the real usefulness of this debate about a small question of poetic technique is to focus the radical difference in linguistic conceptions.

To the instrumental, dualistic conception it is self-evident that sounds cannot 'enact' features of the external world. But against that conception, Heidegger argued insistently: 'It is just as much a property of language to sound and ring and vibrate, to hover and to tremble, as it is for the spoken words of language to carry a meaning.'[22] What language 'enacts' on this view, one which Leavis shares, is not some aspect of the external world but the inner process of response, the constant movement of a living being in affirmation and recoil by which its 'world' is created and sustained. Far from being a mere system of signs, or the register of a neutral epistemological act, language is itself the medium in which Being or life is experienced as value.

The Heideggerean conception of language as a continual creative evolution helps to explain another controversial aspect of Leavis's criticism: his apparent exclusiveness. It is evident that Leavis's interest in literature is largely as a means to something else. His attention, like Heidegger's, was on a long-term, and for the most part necessarily sublimal, process of creative change within language. Great writers are those in whom this process is decisively manifest. In such cases, personal expression within language becomes rather an impersonal function of the language itself. As Leavis insists in the long passage which defines his sense of language in these are moments rare, yet so important, that the difference is appropriately treated as one of kind rather than degree. Heidegger made the same point:

It is precisely in great art – and only great art is in question here – that the artist remains inconsequential as compared with the work, almost like a passageway that destroys itself in the creative process for the work to emerge.[23]

So too when Leavis judges a work to be 'major' he means something more specific than 'best'; and indeed within his conception the major artist may well have *less* artistic finish than distinguished minor ones. Leavis's own revaluations were certainly a matter of considered judgement, but they were not just a question of 'taste', even in the sense of educated taste. They identified a specific, and rare, form of creativity.

---

[21] For example, Peter Barry, 'The Enactive Fallacy', *Essays in Criticism*, 30 (April 1980), pp. 95–104.
[22] 'The Nature of Language' in Heidegger, *On the Way to Language*, p. 98.
[23] 'Origin of the Work of Art' in Heidegger, *Poetry, Language, Thought*, p. 86.

Leavis brought this radical awareness of language to the Victorian cultural debate associated with such figures as Matthew Arnold, a context which accounts for the special inflection he gave in his criticism to the term 'sincerity'. Ian Robinson has suggested that it signals his original contribution to thought.[24] 'Sincerity' is the personal dimension of feeling that underwrites creative impersonality, and the word is meant to be a corrective to widespread, post-romantic misapprehensions about the nature of feeling in poetry. Leavis used it to challenge any simple confusion of its critical implication with its everyday meaning, but also maintained its crucial connection with everyday usage – another instance of his using the common tongue rather than a specialist terminology. Hence the following typical usage:

I don't myself believe that Blake had any comprehensive guiding wisdom to offer, but it was his genius to be capable of a complete disinterestedness, and therefore of a complete sincerity. He had a rare integrity, and a rare sense of responsibility as a focus of life. His experience was *his* because only in the individual focus can there *be* experience, but his concern to perceive and understand was undeflected by egotism, or by any impulse to protect an image of himself.[25]

'Sincerity' appears as an aspect of disinterestedness. Like 'egotism', it is a key term of Victorian moral and critical discourse which was to become deeply problematic in the new century. While G. H. Lewes, for example, could use the term unself-consciously as a marker of good writing, the modernists were highly aware that personal sincerity was no guarantee of literary quality and could indeed sentimentally impede it.[26] And so T. S. Eliot enforced the distinction between 'sincere' and 'significant' feeling:

There are many people who can appreciate the expression of sincere emotion in verse... But very few know when there is an expression of *significant* emotion: emotion which has its life in the poem and not in the history of the poet.[27]

Counter-emphasis on the quality of feeling as inhering in the poem, and only knowable from the text, can become merely the complementary error to the original one; the 'poetic' emotion is a technical creation of the poem, irrespective of the poet's personal experience. As Lionel Trilling suggested, the change is part of a long modern shift in emphasis from sincerity to authenticity, or, as a matter of critical procedure, from the biographical to the textual.[28]

Leavis fully endorsed that general shift, but saw the technical emphasis in the modernist movement as losing the baby with the bath-water.

[24] Ian Robinson, *The Survival of English* (Cambridge, 1973), p. 39. See also Leavis's 'Reality and Sincerity: Notes in the Analysis of Poetry', *Scrutiny*, 19, pp. 90–8.
[25] F. R. Leavis (with Q. D. Leavis), *Lectures in America* (London, 1969), p. 77.
[26] G. H. Lewes, *The Principles of Success in Literature* (London, 1869).
[27] T. S. Eliot, *Selected Essays* (London, 1932), p. 22.
[28] Lionel Trilling, *Sincerity and Authenticity* (Cambridge, Mass., 1972).

Technique was becoming not just an inextricable aspect of the achievement, but its cause.[29] For Leavis, instead, the personal matrix from which the work was created remains an integral aspect of its finished meaning. Though entirely committed to an inductive reading whereby all significance is found within the text, his interest lies in the artist's achievement of creative sincerity, however fleeting and uncharacteristic, for which the text is the index. Leavis is not interested in personal sincerity as a value *per se* or an explanation of the poem. His usage combines the holism of Lewes with the rigour of the modernists, a critical criterion more testable than the former and more testing than the latter. It transcends the 'biographical' and the 'technical' fallacies by properly understanding, and incorporating, their respective truths.

The Heideggerean parallel, therefore, explains Leavis's special emphasis on the impersonal dimension of great art as a personal achievement. The 'impersonality' of the artist was a great theme of modernist writers, part of a necessary reaction to the aftermath of romanticism. But for Leavis the technical, formalist concern with impersonality in some modernists writers, such as Joyce, was not necessarily a sign of creative impersonality; it might, as in the case of T. S. Eliot, even indicate a radical difficulty or failure in this area. And as Mikhail Bakhtin was discovering over the same period, through a comparable meditation on the novel as a genre, it is precisely an author like Dostoevsky who most evidently lacks the formal trappings of impersonality, who proves the most truly impersonal.[30] Impersonality is achieved by engagement, not by seeking to 'escape'[31] personality.

For Leavis, 'impersonality' has inextricable moral and artistic dimensions that distinguish it from the narrowly egotistic concern for protecting a self-image, whether in writing or in life. He expressed this distinction through the words 'self' and 'identity', terms which he derived from Blake, as in the passage quoted, although the force of the distinction is really Leavis's. But why did he not more distinctly claim it as his own and highlight, as Heidegger's idiom implicitly did, the radical significance of what he was saying? Leavis always saw the critic as a midwife whose function is to deliver the baby, not to claim it. His criticism, as part of its own impersonality, seeks to create an intense focus of attention rather than a fresh interpretation. Hence it was part of his point that this important recognition was truly there in the creative achievement of Blake, who emerges as a classic instance of how wisdom or understanding

[29] Mark Schorer's essay 'Technique as Discovery', reprinted in *The World We Imagine* (London, 1969), pp. 3–23, makes this pervasive modernist implication fully explicit and in doing so unwittingly reveals its limitation.
[30] See Mikhail Bakhtin, *Problems of Dostoevsky's Poetics*, tr. R. W. Rotsel (Ann Arbor, 1973).
[31] This was T. S. Eliot's word; *The Sacred Wood* (London, 1920), p. 58.

is to be found in literature, not at the level of general ideas or portable truths, but as experience to be recovered only in the act of reading. Indeed, Leavis may well have wished this distinction of 'self' and 'identity' to remain meaningless, or empty, when separated from the reading of the appropriate author, a strategy to protect it from banality and reduction. Of course, Leavis was far from thinking that Blake or Lawrence always exemplified this quality. But once the quality and its importance are recognised, even the limitations of these authors may actually come to highlight, rather than undermine, their achievement, calling attention to their personal struggle. In every fully attentive reading of the work, just as in the original creation, the meaning lies in the emotional quality.

Paradoxically, it is seriously misleading to call Leavis a literary critic, and more so to call him anything else. For him, imaginative literature has a unique and crucial significance within a larger conception of human creativity in language. True, he endorsed T. S. Eliot's view that literature must be seen 'as literature and not another thing'. The creative dimension in great art must not be confused with its referential aspects, and literature must not be confused with history, philosophy, or ethics. Yet he denied that there were specifically literary values.[32] The creative achievement is a new value won in, and for, the language as a whole. In Wittgenstein's phrase, it modies the 'form of life' implicit in that language.[33] In short, Leavis's unwillingness to present himself philosophically, or even to develop a technical vocbulary, was part of a considered relation to common speech which he found underlying the great imaginative achievements of the past. But how did this essential conception manifest itself in his social historical critique?

Social tradition and the 'organic community'

Leavis's conception of language stood in a problematic relation to philosophical statement. It was intrinsically philosophical, yet he feared, with reason, its reduction to a set of ideas. In his social historical critique he was even more firmly resistant to political discourse, which likewise threatened, whether in a hostile or a helpful spirit, to traduce his conception. And once again, this resistance has produced its own traductions.

Scrutiny contributors largely shared the belief that the slow changes coming over English life in the preceding five centuries could not be fruitfully understood within a myth of progress. It was a story of loss as well as gain. The widespread assumption of progressive criteria was itself

[32] Leavis, 'Anna Karenina' and Other Essays, p. 195.
[33] Ludwig Wittgenstein, *Philosophical Investigations*, tr. G. E. Anscombe (rpt. Oxford, 1968), p. 88.

evidence of the loss. Progress, while evident and beneficial in many technical domains, had increasingly become an end in itself, which supplanted the examination of humane ends in the conscious development of society. Accordingly, they emphasised the values of a customary society. The writings of George Sturt (George Bourne), such as *Change in the Village* (1912) and *The Wheelwright's Shop* (1923), had stressed the rapid disappearance of patterns of rural life which had lasted, with only gradual modification, for centuries. The 'organic community' evoked by Sturt has been dismissed by progressives as a nostalgic conservative myth. But if it was a myth, it was partly offered as a counter myth. The *Scrutiny* group did not oppose change or progress, but a pervasive myth of progress which obscured, and colluded with, the real problems of modernity.

Objections to the idea of the 'organic community' have been most influentially expressed by Raymond Williams in *Culture and Society* (1958). The belief in a lost communal way of life is a persistent feature of English culture from at least *Piers Plowman* down through Cobbett,[34] as old as the enclosures and the early rural capitalism to which it is partly a response. It is significant as a 'structure of feeling', rather than historical fact, and the 'organic community' is a dangerous modern myth which denies the miseries of earlier generations and resists change in the present. Leavis, however, was not denying unjust economic relations in the past so much as applauding the cultural achievement of earlier generations as this was embodied for him in the English language and in the impact of ordinary folk culture on English literature. He was concerned with 'quality of life' rather than 'standard of living' and, without suggesting they were to be separated, resisted populist absorption of one into the other.

As in the argument against C. P. Snow, much hinges on the force of the word 'literary'. Initially influenced by Leavis, Williams developed a Marxist critique of the too 'literary' emphasis in Leavis's cultural analysis. Yet Leavis saw great works of literature as instances of contemporary *language*, and, as such, both representative and self-validating. They embodied the criteria by which they, and anything else, could be judged.

The nub of the question lies in how we use literary texts as historical evidence – particularly when genius is in question. Genius undoubtedly expresses a general potentiality of its culture, but the very fact of genius makes it hard to know what inference can be drawn for the average quality of the culture. Leavis thought that genius transcends individuality, makes available what until then was an inchoate potential, and he drew the stronger inference. Bunyan, for example, was not an average thinker, yet the quality of popular speech and sensibility in his work is profoundly representative.[35] Great literature is representative, although it requires

---

[34] See Raymond Williams, *Culture and Society* (London, 1958), pp. 246–57 and the early chapters of his *The Country and the City* (London, 1973).
[35] Leavis, 'The Pilgrim's Progress', *'Anna Karenina' and Other Essays*, pp. 33–48.

effort, more than just 'literary-critical' insight, to respond to this subliminal aspect of its significance.

But there is another difficulty that affects Leavis's whole vision of the
past and its implications for the present. In the past, the gradual evolution
of collective sensibility had to have been, in its overall direction, a largely
unwitting process arising from the myriad interactions of individuals or
groups, all espousing their own particular commitments and systems of
belief. But to transform that unconscious process into a conscious project
is necessarily to reveal both the limits of consensus and the lack of
metaphysical sanction. The very act of making it conscious is one with its
disintegration exposing its difficulty as a conscious project and exacerba-
ting it to the point of impossibility. Leavis had no answer to this: his merit
was rather to see that there was a problem. In a later terminology, he has
frequently been seen as an 'essentialist' by opponents wishing to expose
his ideological commitments, but the reverse is nearer the mark. He saw
fundamental values precisely as cultural creations and was impressed
more by their fragility than their power.

Which is why he resisted a political terminology. If Leavis's idea of
culture was too 'literary', Williams wished to make 'culture' a political
term. Leavis could see well enough that politics pervades everything, but
he resisted the Marxist and neo-Marxist inference that it constitutes the
ultimate horizon of human meaning and purposes. Ideological exposure,
from his viewpoint, collapses his complex recognition into a one-sided
half-truth. (In his reading of modern English culture the significant hegemony was not in the ruling class but in the pervasive reductionism of
neo-Benthamite sensibility, of which much would-be progressive thought
was itself a prime manifestation.)

The phrase 'organic community', like 'dissociation of sensibility', is a
vulnerable term, open to damaging questions as to when it existed and
how it is defined. But it had little practical working in his criticism and
should not distract from his essential critique of modernity. Leavis's
strength lay in his critical appreciation of particular complexes of vital
values expressed in language, his vulnerability in his historical extrapola-
tion from such moments, his tendency to place a theory of cultural decline
in the immediate historical foreground. Imaginative literature undoubtedly has a representative value of some kind, and Leavis's merit was to keep
this enigmatic aspect constantly in the foreground and always to ask what
it 'represents' for us now.

The literary tradition: poetry

Leavis's reading of English poetry followed the lead of the early Eliot.
Eliot found his own poetic voice by a critique of his romantic and

Victorian forebears and a recovery of qualities he found in early seventeenth-century verse. In the earlier period, Eliot thought, even a comparatively minor poet could provide a significant example, since the qualities
in question were those of the culture rather than of the individual. Eliot
saw in this period an integration of experience, such that intellect and
feeling, the noble and the everyday, the spiritual and the physical, were
not felt as separate realms requiring different discourses. By contrast, the
poetry of the succeeding centuries reflected a progressive 'dissociation of
sensibility' as the scientific, religious, and sociological etc. became separate discursive realms.[36] This affected poetry generically as it came to be
only one more specialised discourse among many and poets could no
longer be expected to encompass all the contemporary ways of responding
to the world. Milton was a crucial figure in this story since he belonged to
the same period as the founding of the Royal Society and was a poet of
such manifest stature. For Leavis, Milton's latinate style in *Paradise Lost*
represented a crucial remove from the contemporary spoken tongue and
provided a powerful, almost hypnotic, influence on later poets.

Despite its early influence on literary studies, the idea of the 'dissociation of sensibility' has been increasingly questioned and quietly discarded.[37] Eliot himself abandoned it and adopted a more positive view of
Milton once the question ceased to be important to his own creative
evolution. But Leavis continued to see something crucial at stake in the
intuition it encapsulated, and he remained deeply critical of Milton.
Leavis's own remark that he carried a copy of Milton throughout his years
on the Western Front suggests he was also struggling with a great puritan
forebear. It was the acknowledged power of Milton that aroused Leavis's
opposition. What he found damaging in Milton was not just the artificiality of the language, its alleged lack of relation to spoken English, but the
artistic will-power invested in this style. Milton's 'style' was not one
through which he could, as Heidegger would say, 'listen' to the language.

If Leavis's generally damaging critique of Milton is taken as his balanced reading, then he must be said to have lost the argument.[38] But in so
far as the intended 'dislodgement' sought to put the reading of Milton on a
different basis, to differentiate his stature sharply from Shakespeare's, for
example, it can be claimed that it succeeded, that it did put the appreciative reading of Milton on a more sophisticated footing.[39] Milton's

---

[36] Eliot developed this idea in 'The Metaphysical Poets'. See *Selected Essays*, esp. pp. 287–
90.

[37] Eliot came to dissociate himself from the phrase in, for example, his remarks on Donne in
'Lancelot Andrewes', *Selected Essays*, pp. 341–53. The idea was influentially criticised in
F. W. Bateson, *Essays in Critical Dissent* (London, 1972), pp. 142–52 and in the eighth
chapter of Frank Kermode, *Romantic Image* (London, 1957).

[38] Leavis always insisted there was a positive, or balanced, case to be made, as in his essay 'In
Defence of Milton', *Scrutiny*, 7, pp. 104–14.

achievement is an impressive one within its own terms, but Leavis was seeking to question the terms themselves. He read the poem rather as a novelistic narrative in which the author's artistic will, endorsed by theocratic and patriarchal authority, allows no truly questioning countervoice. This connection with the novel is borne out in Leavis's repeated contention that the strength of the English language eventually went into the novel rather than poetry.[40]

If a certain kind of conscious artistic will, as Leavis believed, could block a truly creative relation to language, then there is a related, if apparently opposite, danger in a poetic musicality which allows the author, and reader, to drift on a current of sounds and associations. This was the vice he saw preeminently in Tennyson. Though Tennyson was a substantial talent, his relation to language was vitiated by the adoption of this specially 'poetic' manner. Hopkins likewise invoked Tennyson as an instance of the 'parnassian' mode which takes over when creative thought is in abeyance.[41] For Hopkins and Leavis, this was not just a matter of personal 'taste'. They were resisting a power that was seductive but damaging, a surrender to language and a simulacrum of poetic thought. It parodies, and preempts, a truly creative 'listening' to language.

These complementary vices of will-power and musicality lead to a broader question. Leavis's reservations about Milton or Tennyson are related to his consistent suspicion of the word 'aesthetic', a term which almost invariably signalled a lack of critical grip in his view.[42] That suspicion has led some critics to charge him with being moralistic and literalistic, or with inappropriate conflation of artistic and non-artistic viewpoints. But within Leavis's conception of language, the charge is based on a false distinction. Just as he denies the Cartesian dualism of self and world, so there can be no specially aesthetic creativity separable from the creative dimension of language at large. His appeal to 'enactive' qualities in language is actually at the opposite pole from a naive literalism; they are expressive as much as mimetic and are always spoken of by Leavis as having an 'analogous' relation to the experience in question. For Leavis, all language is expressive and symbolic and therefore carries at all times a radical burden of creativity. Of course, most of us live within the habitual structures of thought and feeling imbibed from the language and are, as later critical theory came to realise, more created than creating in our relation to language. But language is nonetheless a continual act of

[39] For example, Arnold Stein, *Answerable Style* (Minneapolis, 1953); Christopher Ricks, *Milton's Grand Style* (London, 1963); Louis Martz, *The Paradise Within* (New York, 1964). [40] For example, in *'Anna Karenina' and Other Essays*, p. 145.

[41] See the letter to A. W. M. Baillie, 10 September 1864. The essential elements are in *Gerard Manley Hopkins: A Selection of His Poems and Prose*, ed. Helen Gardner (Harmondsworth, 1953), pp. 155–61.

[42] F. R. Leavis, 'The Dunciad', *Scrutiny*, pp. 12, 75.

self creation, individually and collectively, and Leavis's recognition of a permanent creative responsibility implicit in all uses of language preempts the attribution of any special value to a specifically aesthetic domain. Within his conception, any special claims of the 'aesthetic' suggest rather a deadness to the creative dimension of language *per se* and to the responsibility it entails.

The suspicion of the 'aesthetic' in relation to creativity can be seen in Leavis's respective treatments of Yeats and Eliot. Despite his increasingly critical view of Eliot, Leavis continued to recognise him as the major poetic intelligence of his day.[43] The resulting ambivalence can be seen in the extended close reading to which Leavis subjected Eliot's *Four Quartets* in *The Living Principle*. His central theme is Eliot's exploratory treatment of a spiritual intuition. Whatever Eliot's personal religious faith, he argues, the poem is not contingent upon Christian belief, and it therefore exemplifies the kind of creative *Ahnung* mentioned in the passage already quoted. Traditional Christian language and symbolism are being used to create a spiritual form for post-Christian modernity. Leavis applauds this achievement, and his almost line by line reading brings out its *being* an achievement. The poem does not express a pre-existing, or otherwise statable, conception, but one which exists only as it emerges in the poem's own terms. And the creative achievement is further set off by the moments when it fails to occur, moments when the personal limitations of the poet are so evident within it.

By contrast, although Yeats had written a handful of supreme poems, such as 'Among School Children', his fundamental mode was not, in Leavis's view, so profoundly creative. If Eliot was personally exposed in his poetry, this was also a condition of his success. By contrast, Leavis drew on the common comparison of Yeats with Blake to stress how Yeats was always concerned with his own self-image in a way that Blake was not. Yeats was undoubtedly vulnerable in this respect, particularly in late poems such as 'Under Ben Bulben'. But what Leavis could not see, or accept, in mature Yeats was a positive form of self-dramatisation, a dramatic 'as if' which has aestheticist roots and radically conditions the 'meaning'. Yeats's dramatic posture can help us to define the limits, in principle, of Leavis's reading. Since all conscious existence for Leavis is a constant struggle within the symbolic medium of language, any such deliberate remove, or bracketing, of meaning is a weakening and evasion, a *trahison de poète*. In short, with Yeats as with Milton, Leavis had a

[43] Leavis, *English Literature in Our Time*, pp. 136–7. For a different view see Bernard Bergonzi, 'Leavis and Eliot: the Long Road to Rejection', *Critical Quarterly*, 26 (1984), pp. 21–43; reprinted in *The Myth of Modernism and Twentieth Century Literature* (Brighton, 1986). I differ from Bergonzi in seeing Leavis as essentially right about Eliot and the final essays on him in *The Living Principle* as corrective rather than dismissive. For Leavis, Eliot was the one modern poet to merit this sustained attention.

radical objection to the artistic self-consciousness as blocking a more fundamental creativity. The term 'aesthetic' is a recurrent focus of this unease, but the objection is not to the 'aesthetic' *per se* so much as to what it implies for the nature of language at large.

The literary tradition: the novel

Although Leavis's creative conception of language bears most directly on the reading of poetry, his developing interest in the novel expressed essentially the same conception on a larger narrative scale. More generally Leavis typically read poetry by a partial criterion of realism and read fiction by a criterion of poetic discovery. When he coined the formula 'novel as dramatic poem', he was primarily seeking in a tactical way to highlight the radical significance of symbolic and metaphorical, as opposed to narrative or doctrinal, structures.[44] Yet the phrase points to the nature of his interest in literature at large, characteristically probing the zone where the traditional expectations of these two generic terms overlap.

Several commentators have criticised *The Great Tradition* for shifting uncertainly between an 'expressive' and a 'mimetic' conception of fiction.[45] It is true that the centre of gravity was shifting, but Leavis's *creative* conception necessarily encompasses both aspects: mimetic in so far as the felt reality of the world constitutes its theme and its discipline; expressive in that there *is* no simply 'external' world, in that the creative discovery of values is 'world' forming, a recognition to which the novel as a genre preeminently lends itself.

Even more than his criticism of poetry, his studies of the novel constantly engage the question of genre. This is partly because the novel was still only becoming a serious focus of critical attention at the time of Leavis's maturity, but also because of the special problems of relevance and attention posed by its greater length and characteristic verisimilitude. But most importantly, Leavis's reading of fiction stresses the impossibility of rendering its meaning in abstract or generally stable terms. The meaning of the novel lies in its apprehension of a 'world'. Therein lies the truly symbolic activity of the novelist.

The common reductive account of Leavis's criticism of fiction is to see it as 'moral' – in other words, to see it as judging by an overriding criterion

[44] Leavis's first *Scrutiny* essays under this heading were those on *Hard Times* in 1948 and *The Europeans* in 1949. His subsequent essays on Lawrence in the early fifties kept the same general title.
[45] Edward Greenwood, *F. R. Leavis* (London, 1978), p. 40 and P. J. M. Robertson, *The Leavises on Fiction: An Historic Partnership* (London, 1981), p. 28.

of moral maturity and complexity. There is a certain rough truth in this, but it fails to recognise the Nietzschean inflection in Leavis whereby the term 'moral' encompasses essentially *vital* and creatively *dynamic* values. It confuses Leavis's reading with a simply moralistic one. But Leavis's reading demonstrates the inextricability of the 'moral' and the 'artistic' intelligence within great fiction. Common parlance rightly tells us we may distinguish these as aspects but, Leavis shows, it is a mistake to suppose they can therefore be separated. Or, more accurately, they can be separated, but with fatal consequences. In Leavis's view, the discriminating embodiment of vital values within a fiction is in itself an act of testing and exploration.

Leavis, of course, was well aware that much fiction is merely a second-order representation of known values. But as noted, already, he was interested only in major imaginative achievement – or at least felt it necessary to distinguish sharply that kind of importance. Great fiction was marked by its capacity to test, modify, or rediscover living values. Hence in much of his criticism he places himself within the viewpoint of the creator – not in a literal biographical sense, but in the awareness of the work as something that had to be brought into being. The finished work is read in a way that recreates the struggle of its production. The tactical effort of his commentary on fiction (one would not call it a methodology) is to communicate this creative 'real-ising' of the novel's world.

Hence also the transparency of his critical rhetoric. This transparency is partly literal. He gives extended quotations from the text and repeatedly exhorts the reader simply to reread it. But the effect of transparency also arises from a more strategic and pervasive method of *bricolage* whereby other authors and critics provide him with constantly shifting standpoints to be endorsed or rejected. He typically circles around the work in question, setting up a number of comparative coordinates by means of which the reader comes to see the work afresh rather than in some obviously 'different' way. The wide but ambiguous influence of his criticism doubtless arises partly from this. Underlying the trenchant and authoritative tone he has a way of making his best criticism seem merely obvious. We seem simply to see the work with our own eyes.

That is why Leavis was so dismissive of academic symbol-hunting.[46] Of course, he was also deprecating the massive expansion of professional academic writing on literature that grew up over his working lifetime. But he was not just objecting to this as empty jobbery: he saw it as actively flattening the radically symbolic nature of fiction into a two-dimensional 'meaning'. On the same grounds, he attacked the notion of fresh interpre-

---

[46] See, for example, his deflection of a 'symbolic' reading of *The Shadow Line* in *'Anna Karenina' and Other Essays*, pp. 108–9.

tation, 'new readings' which provide another academic staple.[47] The artist's 'world' is what should command attention. Leavis fully endorsed the importance of the Jamesian 'figure in the carpet', but only as an aspect of the true mystery, the fictive carpet itself.

Indeed, in *The Great Tradition*, *D. H. Lawrence: Novelist*, and *Dickens the Novelist* the rhetorical procedure reflects the critical perception at the heart of each book. For George Eliot, Lawrence, and Dickens all had a transparency which left them largely invisible as *artists*. Leavis sought to bring out the true nature of their art without losing the invisibility, or transparency, which was its most important quality. In his discussion of George Eliot, therefore, Leavis developed a sustained comparison with James to bring out her specifically artistic command against James's own view of her comparative lack of artistry. He then moved on, having given a very positive account of James's quite different artistry, to show how James, in Leavis's view, suffered in his late phase from an over-attention to the artistic 'doing' at the expense of a sense of proportion about the value of what was being 'done'. George Eliot, we begin to realise, was a greater artist in being less overtly artistic, whereas James was a lesser artist when he was most overtly concerned to be one.

Leavis may be partly unfair to James's late novels, since James does recognise the inadequacy of their human material, in such figures as Chad Newsome, the Prince, or Charlotte Stant – although Leavis is right, perhaps, that James does not sufficiently 'detect' the Ververs and Kate Croy. What Leavis cannot acknowledge in *The Ambassadors* particularly is the poignancy of wasted life in Strether and the way the lives of admirable individuals may be inextricably bound up with less admirable ones. Nonetheless, Leavis's broader point is strongly communicated. Except that it is not a 'point'. It is a growing recognition of the relative proportions of Eliot and James, one in which the characteristic strength of each novelist emerges in the comparison and any note of limitation is equally integral to the positive sense of proportion.

The confrontation between Leavis and late James illuminates the fundamental commitments underlying Leavis's criticism. Most obviously, their shared conviction of the inseparability of 'life' and 'art' took the form in James of an apparent assimilation of 'life' to 'art' and in Leavis of an apparent assimilation of 'art' to 'life'. But I am thinking also of the commitments embodied in their very styles. For Leavis's own critical style seems partly derived from James, though modified by a different personality and purposes. He shares James's endlessly self-qualifying plasticity of thought, whereby anything so crude as a detachable idea is constantly

---

[47] See his dismissing of a critic's 'psychological gloss' on the same Conrad tale; *'Anna Karenina' and Other Essays*, p. 107.

dissolved in the process of thinking.[48] The highly familiar, even intimate, but austere prose which is thereby created is highly unrhetorical yet continually achieves a delayed or oblique eloquence. There is a constant testing compliment to the reader in the way the meaning is to be picked up by inference.

In James's case, this arises in significant measure from the attempt to honour simultaneously the order of truth and the order of charity. His nephew Billy remembered him saying 'three things in human life are important. The first is to be kind. The second is to be kind. And the third is to be kind.'[49] The subtlety of his prose, in criticism and in fiction, is to make the necessary judgements while avoiding the damaging effect of direct statement. As in good therapy, the reader comes to see the point more inwardly for *not* being told it. The unstated knowledge at the centre of *The Golden Bowl* is an overt culmination of this pervasive principle of educative and protective obliquity.

In *Dickens the Novelist*, artistic invisibility becomes an overt theme; perhaps this is the form in which Leavis's own belated conversion to Dickens is implicitly recognised. In his discussion of *Little Dorrit*, Leavis draws once again on Blake to indicate the impersonal spirit in which Dickens conducts what is effectively a psychological investigation. But, he argues, Dickens spreads his theme around a number of characters, none of whom seems individually to be the bearer of anything very complex. Complexity arises, as in Shakespearean sub-plots, from the interaction of these figures within the overall theme. The complexity, the growing weight of norms being significantly questioned and adjusted, comes from the way we are led to perceive the individual cases. As a web of mutually testing coordinates, the method of *Little Dorrit* is similar to that of *The Great Tradition* as already outlined. Great art and good criticism have an apparent obviousness after the event.

Yet for all its transparency, Leavis goes on to indicate how the positive significance of Dickens's own artistry is nonetheless figured within the book. This is not invested in the central consciousness, and still less in an artist figure within the narrative. Henry Gowan suggests the dangers of that sort of self-consciousness. Instead, Dickens allows his own vital expression to flow through the language of characters such as Pancks and Flora Catesby while expressing his own most essential standpoint in the technical inventor, Daniel Doyce. Daniel, rather than Flora's father, the seeming 'Patriarch', proves to be the true prophet.

The etymology of the word 'invention' suggests its ultimate inseparability from 'discovery', and whether or not the Circumlocution Office grants

---

[48] In T. S. Eliot's memorable phrase, James had 'a mind so fine that no idea could violate it' ('In Memory of Henry James', *Egoist*, 5 (1918), pp. 1–2).
[49] Leon Edel, *Henry James*, vol. 2 (Harmondsworth, 1977), p. 457.

Doyce a personal patent, the principle on which his invention is based remains an objective truth. He never saw it as merely 'his' in the first place; the practical exploitation of the principle would be for the general good. What Leavis shows in *Little Dorrit*, as in other Dickens novels, is that an important conception of the artistic function is hidden within it; and precisely in its being hidden, it reflects on the nature of Dickens's own art.

It is indicative that Leavis should have responded so warmly to Doyce as an unrecognised talent, but he also saw why it is in the nature of such genuine ability to remain unrecognised. This in turn helps to explain his increasing, almost crusading, commitment to D. H. Lawrence as a cultural exemplar in his later years. For Lawrence is the most striking and polarising instance of the way in which genuinely creative thinking may be unrecognised because it has to break down the given terms. Leavis came to see that Lawrence's way of thinking was indeed eccentric, undisciplined, and enthralled by his notorious obsessions. Yet despite and because of these obsessions, Lawrence offered a direct, powerful, and conscious challenge to conventional forms of thought. In Lawrence, more than in any other modern writer, Leavis saw a truly creative adjustment of vital values in language and in fiction. He saw also how Lawrence's artistry is, by the same token, so completely integral as to be virtually invisible to the conventional eye. Lawrence, therefore, brought to the fore what is implicit in all Leavis's criticism: a concentration on the act of reading as an existential test. Just as Leavis was not ultimately interested in literature *per se* so much as in the critical apprehension of vital values which it enables, so his criticism is ultimately concerned not with the work but with the reader's capacity (or lack of it) to respond appropriately. Leavis's final book on Lawrence was an attempt to articulate this directly: there is no point in discussing Lawrence's supposed 'thought', or assessing his 'art', until one has understood what is meant by 'thought, words and creativity'. At the same time, the existential challenge in Leavis's commitment to Lawrence reveals the strains always latent in his ideal of collaboration.

Criticism and collaboration

Leavis's essays on Johnson, Coleridge, and Arnold recognise the limited applicability of these forebears to the new historical circumstances. Leavis, therefore, formed his own critical practice through direct meditation on the act of creation and through the criticism of crucial creative writers such as Eliot, James, and Lawrence. If creation is an heuristic act arising from an unusual responsive capacity both to a subject and to the promptings of language, then criticism is likewise predicated upon a responsive, inward recreation of the original creative act as embodied in the text. Such a conception does not, of course, mean an uncritical acceptance of the artist's terms, and indeed Leavis would see the initial creative act as being itself inextricably an act of criticism. It is, after all, a complex weighing of values.

The need to devise an appropriate rhetoric for the participatory nature of criticism helps explain his well known hostility to making criticism a matter even of conscious principle, let alone of theory or system. The very fact of making the principle conscious, and therefore allowing it an incipiently guiding function, would be damaging to the openness of critical response just as it would be to the act of creation.

To anyone schooled in the modern 'hermeneutics of suspicion' such a posture immediately suggests ideological bad faith, an unwillingness to examine one's own ideological premises.[50] There is an incommensurable gulf here between what one might call the Sartrean and the Heideggerean conceptions of authenticity. For the former, the authentic is that which is fully conscious and critically examined. For the latter, the authentic is that which is able to attend to other centres of life outside of personal consciousness, including a less conscious domain, perhaps, within the self. Leavis opens himself up to a recreative identification with the author. Once again, it is not a question of being uncritical. Criticism is necessarily a commitment and Leavis once commented approvingly on the focus of Eliot's criticism arising from its having an evident 'axe to grind'.[51] The point is rather that Leavis's best criticism is characterised by the way even his negative comments stem from a standpoint within the creative struggle of the author concerned. By the same token, when he is unable to enter the terms of an author, such as Sterne, his criticism has little purchase. Even more than most critics, he is acute on the faults of authors he admires, but less so on those he does not.

It is perhaps already apparent that, even apart from questions of personal temperament, the consciously challenging commitment of his reading, coupled with its normative claims, would not lend itself to easy collaboration. Indeed, his relations with other major contributors to *Scrutiny* may partly be traced through his increasing distance as such critics came to develop, or overdevelop, particular recognitions at the expense of the representative holism at which Leavis himself always aimed.

I. A. Richards, two years older than Leavis and one-time supervisor to Queenie Roth, was a significant early influence. The Cambridge English School was founded at a time when the claim of English to be a distinct

[50] The phrase is from Paul Ricoeur, *The Rule of Metaphor*, tr. Robert Czerny *et al.* (London, 1978), p. 285.
[51] Leavis, *English Literature in Our Time*, pp. 85–6.

discipline with its own rationale was still not broadly accepted. Leavis argued strongly that it was such a discipline, and his period of maximum influence roughly coincides with the period, from the Second World War to the 1960s, in which English was a dominant and self-confident subject within the humanities. In the early days, Richards provided something more than the example of a good critic and teacher; he thought closely about the fundamental rationale of literary criticism as a discipline. His exercises in practical criticism, commonly using anonymous or ephemeral pieces, dislodged the act of reading from conventional evaluations and became permanent models for literature teaching around the English-speaking world.

But Richards's fruitful iconoclasm was increasingly linked to a desire to put the understanding of literature on a quasi-scientific, psychological basis, and also to emphasise the peculiar status of literary utterance as 'pseudo-statement'.[52] The scientificising and speculative interests of Richards were to prove representative of much later academic activity and Leavis soon signalled his distance from them. In his view, they could not help with the essential business of criticism, and insofar as they were active in the mind of a critic they would distract from the holism and commitment of the critical response. Hence Leavis's positive assimilation of Richards is suggested in his own preferred phrase 'criticism in practice', rather than 'practical criticism', to suggest the nature of such exercises with students.

D. W. Harding, a regular contributor to *Scrutiny*, was a psychologist and provides, in that respect, a counter case to Richards. With less theoretical ambition than Richards, his criticism is illuminated by his psychological interest without this standing out in a separable way from the critical occasion. His essay on 'regulated hatred' in Jane Austen is a case in point and exemplifies the kind of fruitful interaction between disciplines which Leavis promoted.[53]

William Empson, originally a student of mathematics and then a graduate student of I. A. Richards, was another *Scrutiny* contributor who thought in more speculative terms about the nature of the discipline. His emphasis, like Leavis's, was on the nature of language, and in his influential *Seven Types of Ambiguity* (1930) he likewise explored the implications for criticism of the modernist recognition that indeterminacy of meaning may have a positive expressive function.[54] Several interrelated, or mutually questioning, significances can be suggested within the same form of words. But as the title suggests, the emphasis on ambiguity was rather

---

[52] See the bibliography for Richards's principal titles.
[53] D. W. Harding, 'Regulated Hatred: An Aspect of the Work of Jane Austen', *Scrutiny*, 8, pp. 346–62.
[54] See the bibliography for Empson's principal titles.

programmatic and appears to invite an open-ended ingenuity. Empson's subtle and well-stocked mind responded readily and widely to verbal associations while the notion of poetic language as characteristically polyvalent and subliminal in its workings made it difficult to define a limited horizon of significance for the given poem. The effect of Empson's readings, it should be said, was generally stimulating, as they tended to open up texts rather than box them into personal interpretations. Even so, Leavis came to see Empson's critical practice in this period as having too much undirected ingenuity.[55] It was as if one important aspect of the Leavisian sense of language was overdeveloped at the expense of falsifying the whole.

L. C. Knights co-wrote the original manifesto for *Scrutiny* and published very regularly in it. His special interest in the seventeenth century, expressed most notably in his *Drama and Society in the Age of Jonson* (1937), gave him a crucial importance to Leavis's vision of cultural history.[56] He was, therefore, Leavis's most significant collaborator. Apart from his own influential essays, he contributed some acerbic reviews – for example, of C. S. Lewis, the Oxford literary historian whose conservative Christian humanism became a recognised anti-type to Leavis's urgently contemporary judgement.[57]

Other *Scrutiny* contributors included Martin Turnell, who wrote on French literature, as in his later *The Novel in France* (1950), and John Speirs, who wrote on medieval literature and later produced *Chaucer the Maker* (1951). The poet D. J. Enright regularly reviewed contemporary German writing. Wilfrid Mellers wrote on contemporary music. G. H. Bantock participated in the running debate on education.

Leavis undoubtedly had an inspiring effect upon several generations of school-teachers, mainly in Britain, and upon lecturers in universities and colleges around the English-speaking world. Many, like Speirs, had a vivid sense of purpose which communicated itself to students. But the authoritative transparency of the Leavisian method, when grafted on to a lesser personality, could readily dwindle into a self-confident banality. The strenuously achieved judgements of the master then survive as the assertive postures of the disciple. Such figures undoubtedly contributed to the decline and disrepute of Leavisian influence. To that extent it was to Leavis's personal credit perhaps that he had almost as short a way with disciples as with dissenters. Like Nietzsche he was a compelling, even

---

[55] For an appreciation of Leavis's holism as compared to Empson and Richards see H. M. McLuhan 'Poetic and Rhetorical Analysis: The Case for Leavis against Richards and Empson', *Sewanee Review*, 52 (April 1944), pp. 266–76.

[56] See the bibliography for Knights's principal titles.

[57] F. R. Leavis, 'C. S. Lewis and the *Status quo*', *Scrutiny*, 8, pp. 88–92 and 'Milton Again', *Scrutiny*, 11, pp. 146–8.

prophetic, figure whose central significance entailed a rejection of imitative discipleship.[58]

His criticism never disguised the force of personality on which it was based. Seeing the reading of literature as an existential test, he demonstratively enacted the running drama of his own response and, despite the principle affirmed in the phrase 'the common pursuit', the Leavisian critical arena became increasingly exclusive rather than collaborative. The running 'drama' of Leavis's response suggests that the question of collaboration may indeed be reflected in his attitude to theatre. For his well-known indifference to theatre, and his hostility to the histrionic character as he saw it in Joyce, Yeats, or Shakespeare's Othello arise from a related concern for inwardness and authenticity of response.[59]

Criticism and interpretation, for Leavis, are subsumed into a sensitive reading. And the compelling image here is the theatrical performance of a dramatic text. But while Leavis's reading is enactive, it is not histrionically projected. It is essentially *his* reading *in the mind*. He seeks to let us share an exemplary reading in which the functions of director, actor, and audience are all aspects of an imaginary reenactment within a single consciousness. There is thus a tension between Leavisian reading and theatre proper, and the collaborative and vicarious nature of theatre must surely have been part of his unease with it. The problem with theatre is that, as an act of reading, it is not only vicarious, it is literally directed by someone else.

But if theatre focuses the tension of Leavisian collaboration, the root of the problem lay in his essentially prophetic purpose, for Leavis could not have been more accommodating without risk to his own vision. Indeed, the question of 'collaboration', in something like its wartime usage, is precisely what was at stake. He was animated by an ethical loathing of a central and chronic feature of English life, the corruption of critical and artistic values by those of class and careerism. The phenomenon is universal, of course, but it has its particular national forms. And Leavis, as well as feeling that anyone's commitment has to be to his or her own tradition, saw another English heritage, that of Bunyan and Lawrence, as being actively stifled.

Isaiah Berlin has distinguished the intellectual types of the hedgehog and the fox. The fox knows many different things, while the hedgehog understands one big thing. Leavis was clearly the latter type, and this may be why discipleship and the continued running of *Scrutiny* were ultimately

---

[58] See Nietzsche's aphorism on disciples: 'You want to multiply yourself by ten, by a hundred? You are seeking followers? Seek Naughts!', Nietzsche, *Twilight of the Idols*, p. 34.

[59] For comments on this aspect of Joyce and Yeats: see 'Yeats the Problem and the Challenge'. *Lectures in America*, p. 75. On *Othello* see 'Diabolic Intellect and Noble Hero', *Common Pursuit*, pp. 136–59.

problematic. It is hard to go on saying the same large thing without becoming, or appearing, reductive and stale. Furthermore, by the end of the sixties, the increasing dominance of Marxist analysis, the impact of feminist and minority ethnic writing, and the globalising of literary influence and creation, all made Leavis's methods and concerns seem outdated and parochial. The new academic area of 'cultural studies' was a direct displacing of his idea of cultural self-examination. Rather than the adjacent disciplines being drawn into the holism of critical response, literary texts are assimilated to other kinds of inquiry.

By a supreme yet logical irony, he came for many in a new generation to represent the liberal humanist order because, in being the iconoclastic critic of its institutional forms, he had been obliged most profoundly to understand its fundamental position. That is why, despite being treated as a by-word for a naive and outdated conception, he has remained a nagging ghost. In the longer term his very unpopularity points to his permanent and classic significance. As his historical moment recedes, and that likewise of the necessary reaction, so his essential reflection on the nature of creativity and the act of reading stands out as his true contribution.

Conclusion: the prophet and the word

Leavis's refusal to theorise explicitly the act of reading has led to his being perceived as theoretically naive. His conception, and his practice, are indeed fraught with problems from a speculative standpoint, but they are not problems arising from naiveté. The central problem of justifying a fundamental judgement in the moral or artistic domains is there for everyone who exercises such judgement. The problem is only more visible, and vulnerable, as the judgement differs more radically from that conventionally accepted. Leavis's pecularity was that he went out of his way to highlight that dilemma as part of the ongoing specific business of criticism. And that, in turn, sharpened his awareness of how often the issue is silently evaded. Even when his assessment coincided with that of others, he still wished to make the act of judgement a freshly grounded one. His characteristic play on the term 'commonplace' draws attention to this; what ought to be a shared judgement is frequently a hackneyed acceptance.[60]

The problem can be given a pseudo-objectification by treating it as a matter of ideology. But setting out an ideology, although useful enough in itself, does not solve the problem of commitment – that is to say, why you

---

[60] As, for example, *Scrutiny*, 9, p. 57.

adopt, or don't adopt, a particular ideological stance. Leavis understood, with an intentness that allies him more to creative artists than to most academic critics, that this must always be so. Those who object to his theoretical inconsistency or ideological naiveté often have a point, but they have frequently not seen how much it is part of Leavis's own point.

Likewise, he has been attacked by later generations for seeking to establish an authoritative 'canon' of literature in English. But his radical achievement was significantly to address the question of the canon. He brought home the recognition that the body of books we choose to pass on in teaching is a matter for vital, grounded contemporary judgement. The inextricability of fundamental judgement in all reading was an unavoidable truth for him because of the peculiar sense in which he was a prophet; he was radically critical of his contemporary culture and found his primary task in seeking to change it, yet literature for him was never merely the expression of a pre-existing moral vision. The fact of creativity in language was essential, not adventitious, to his vision, and he sought to discriminate the vital and the dead in specific uses of language. He was a prophet of the word rather than the Word.

His agnosticism, that is to say, was every bit as crucial as his religious *Ahnung*. This German term was central to *The Living Principle*, as in the passage quoted earlier. The word *Ahnung*, which means the first stirrings of an obscure understanding yet to be clarified, is actually derived from *Ahnen*, meaning 'ancestors'; its etymology implies a now obscure reference to the remote past, experienced as a creative groping into the future. So, too, Leavis's almost reverential attention to the past is teleologically open.

Of course, his view of language is not itself susceptible of proof, although it seems to me more persuasive, more inward, and more encompassing than most of the post-Saussurian theory which grew up over the course of Leavis's career and after. It seems likely therefore that significant changes in Leavis's reputation will only accompany larger shifts of fashion with respect to the perception of language.

If by his later years Leavis was increasingly undiscriminating about contemporary life in ways that Raymond Williams and others have noted, the problem seems to be partly one of squaring an impossible circle.[61] As a critic of modernity, Leavis gave voice to a deep, almost visceral, loathing. It is as if this intense rejection is the overwhelming point which he could not afford to dilute with overmuch discrimination, although those who share his feeling can often make the necessary distinctions for themselves. And the moral feeling is by no means unique; the uniqueness lay in the securing of a platform for so many years and giving it such telling

---

[61] Williams, *Culture and Society*, pp. 253–4.

expression. If, on the other hand, one does not share or understand this feeling, then the vulnerability of his 'position' looms very large and appears to have merely a personal ill will as its motive. In this respect, he reenacts, without benefit of comedic containment, the predicament of Molière's Alceste.

Cogent reasons can always be adduced for professional cooperation. But the effect of such collaboration may be to lose the radical and long-term value for the short-term benefit and convenience. At the same time, the corresponding vice of isolation is to lose an educative interaction and become fixed in a self-fulfilling posture. Leavis suffered this effect of isolation, much as he recognised Lawrence to have done, and yet, as he likewise saw in Lawrence's case, the underlying critique which led to this isolation still had the root of the matter in it.

It seems to me a matter of shame that British public life, and his own university, did not make more positive use of Leavis, however 'difficult' he may have been. He still comes closest to expressing the impulse that leads so many people seriously to read, study, and teach literature, and he has therefore become the repressed bad conscience of the academy. Yet it was also in the nature of his critical vision that the collaborative community was so much, and tragically, within his own mind. The necessary condition of reading him is that the reader be drawn into the Leavisian world view. Nonetheless, it is precisely this uncompromising intentness which makes him an exemplary and a necessary figure to come to terms with for anyone who is seriously interested in the nature of imaginative literature and critical reading.

18

Lionel Trilling

Harvey Teres

One of the profound ironies of contemporary academic criticism is that, though its practitioners describe themselves as producers and distributors of cultural values, they have been patently unable to acquaint the culture at large with the content of the work they do. There are, of course, many reasons for this, some of them beyond the control of academics. The 'public sphere', after all, despite some pockets of freedom and rigour, bears little resemblance to the classical public sphere of eighteenth-century Britain as described, for example, by Jürgen Habermas and Terry Eagleton. Given the prevalence of advertising, publicity, mass media, and manufactured public opinion and consent, little opportunity exists for academics or others to transform the public sphere into a site of 'communicative action', Habermas's term for open and invigorating discourse that brings scientific, moral, and aesthetic evaluation to bear in order to democratise and transform the polity. Nevertheless, despite these difficulties, academics have been increasingly interested in exploring their relationship to the public sphere, perhaps more so than at any time since the 1960s. This is due in no small measure to the attacks that have been made on the academy by conservatives, who have alleged that contemporary criticism is responsible for an assault on the canon, on taste, on values, on shared beliefs and practices, and on common sense. In part, too, the renewed interest in the public sphere is the result of frustration following more than two decades during which the dramatic politicisation of literature and criticism has been largely confined to the politics of theory alone, as if such activity could be separated from the politics of the critic as citizen – as voter, as a community member with political beliefs and commitments, as activist. Often the highly politicised debates that have taken place in the academy over modernism and postmodernism, discourse and ideology, high and low culture, canons and conventions, and even issues of race, class, and gender, have occurred largely without crucial references to concrete political events, movements, causes, or constituencies outside the academy. Thus there is renewed interest among some academic critics who espouse a generally leftist or left-liberal perspective to pursue the consequences their views might have for a democracy of informed citizens. The attacks by the political right have presented the academic left with an opportunity to think seriously about addressing a broad public audience and make its critical interests known to citizens who would benefit from fresh perspectives.

Any serious consideration of how to reorient academic criticism would profit enormously from a careful, critical analysis of the role played by the New York intellectuals, arguably the most powerful formation of public intellectuals in twentieth-century America. Through such influential publications as *Partisan Review*, *Politics*, *Commentary*, *Dissent*, and the *New York Review of Books*, this circle addressed a relatively wide non-academic audience on a range of cultural and political matters and did a great deal to shape the taste, attitudes, and beliefs of educated Americans from the 1940s to the 1970s. Among the important members of the formation were Hannah Arendt, F. W. Dupee, Clement Greenberg, Elizabeth Hardwick, Sidney Hook, Irving Howe, Alfred Kazin, Dwight Macdonald, Mary McCarthy, William Phillips, Norman Podhoretz, Philip Rahv, Harold Rosenberg, Meyer Schapiro, Diana Trilling, and Lionel Trilling.

It is Lionel Trilling who ought to be considered the most representative, the most compelling, and the most instructive of the New York intellectuals by critics interested in renewing public discourse today; yet in a nation of critics of literature and critics of culture, no secure place has yet been found for Trilling, a consummate critic of literature *and* culture. This is not to gainsay his reputation as one of the country's foremost 'men of letters' during the twentieth century – indeed, along with Edmund Wilson and T. S. Eliot, Trilling was among a small number of powerful and public cultural arbiters who fought successfully to canonise certain romantic and modernist works and thus profoundly shape literary taste in the postwar period. But Trilling was not a literary critic in the usual sense of the word: he was not primarily interested in exegesis and the formal complexities of the literary work as were, for example, Blackmur or Ransom; nor was he, like Wilson and Leavis, mainly interested in generating brilliant but miscellaneous moral and social insights whose apparent sources were encounters with individual works. Trilling was unique because his chief concern was always to illuminate a contemporary cultural, moral, and ultimately political problem. His relationship to individual works was consciously generated by his sense of his historical surroundings and his role as citizen in a flawed industrial democracy with serious cultural and spiritual difficulties. For Trilling the critical enterprise could be explained only partially as an engagement between a reader and a text; in actuality this was merely one pairing, albeit an essential one, among many in the ongoing processes of acculturation and change involving critic, text, and an array of social forces. Characterising his highly contextual approach to literature, he wrote '[M]y own interests lead me to see literary situations as cultural situations, and cultural situations as great elaborate fights about moral issues, and moral issues as having something to do with gratuitously chosen images of personal being, and images of personal being as having something to do with literary style' (*Beyond Culture*, p. 12). His meticulously crafted essays move easily from one level of analysis to another, and nearly always compensate for the itineracy of interdisciplinary work with arresting juxtapositions and syntheses.

Trilling was very much a pragmatic, situational critic, which makes it difficult to generalise about the conclusions he reached. Cultural needs, as Trilling assessed them, shifted over time, and he adjusted his critical emphases accordingly. Many of his apparently inconsistent judgements can be counted as altered responses to changed circumstances. History may not have vindicated Trilling in all of these judgements, and several of the poorer ones will be identified below, but what is remarkable in retrospect is how impressively flexible his responses remain when understood in context. If we allow ourselves to see how thoroughly history impinged upon his criticism, we are bound to take note of the care expressed through nuance, subtle qualification, and dialectical precision which made him the foremost contextual critic of his time. His life's work nicely exemplifies Brecht's remark that the survival of cultural artifacts depends on the degree to which they are immersed in their time, not the degree to which they transcend it. He belongs in the line of the worldly citizen-critics, which extends from Plato and Aristotle to Hazlitt and Arnold, critics who gave pronounced attention to literature's connection to the well-being of the polity, and who portrayed that connection, as well as the nature and interests of the polity, with unusual specificity and insight.

Trilling considered himself part of the liberal culture which he spent a lifetime trying to strengthen. The point bears emphasis because among fellow inhabitants of this culture Trilling's position as ally came under increasing suspicion during the 1960s and 1970s as his critique of the counter-culture intensified. Since the 1970s, in fact, his legacy has been abandoned by many progressives and claimed by such neoconservatives as Hilton Kramer and Norman Podhoretz. But his work will not remain compelling if, ironically, it becomes associated with traditional values – not because traditional values cannot be compelling, but because such an association diminishes Trilling's role as social critic, as well as the actual complexity and challenge of renewing the liberal-radical culture which was at the heart of his engaged criticism. Broadly speaking, Trilling's lifelong critical work can best be understood as a critical humanist challenge to the culture and politics of liberalism, or, as he occasionally and more accurately referred to it, the 'liberal-radical culture' of the 1930s and the post-war period. He defined liberalism as 'a large tendency rather than a concise body of doctrine' (*The Liberal Imagination*, p. ii) held by an 'educated class' whose Enlightenment legacy of overly rational, prosaic habits of mind and utilitarian attitudes was manifested in 'a ready if mild suspiciousness of the profit motive, a belief in progress, science, social legislation, planning, and international cooperation, perhaps especially where Russia is in question' (*The Liberal Imagination*, p. 93). Trilling did not mean by such a broad definition the political viewpoint of a section of the Democratic Party; rather, he meant the whole spectrum of viewpoints which then went under the category of 'progressive' and more or less still does today, and included liberals, social-democrats, socialists, and Communists. Although it is certainly true that for much of his career his immediate target was Stalinism, his insights had, and continue to have, direct relevance to wide areas of social and ideological life in any capitalist democracy.

He described this larger social realm, and literature's relation to it, in the preface to *The Liberal Imagination*:

It is one of the tendencies of liberalism to simplify, and this tendency is natural in view of the effort which liberalism makes to organize the elements of life in a rational way. And when we approach liberalism in a critical spirit, we shall fail in critical completeness if we do not take into account the value and necessity of its organizational impulse. But at the same time we must understand that organization means delegation, and agencies, and bureaus, and technicians, and that the ideas that can survive delegation, that can be passed onto agencies and bureaus and technicians, incline to be ideas of a certain kind and of a certain simplicity: they give up something of their largeness and modulation and complexity in order to survive. The lively sense of contingency and possibility, and of those exceptions to the rule which may be the beginning of the end of the rule – this sense does not suit well with the impulse of organization.   (p. vi)

The function of criticism in such a society must be 'to recall liberalism to its first essential imagination of variousness and possibility, which implies the awareness of complexity and difficulty' (*The Liberal Imagination*, p. vi). It does so through its reliance on literature, which is uniquely relevant 'not merely because so much of modern literature has explicitly directed itself upon politics, but more importantly because literature is the human activity that takes the fullest and most precise account of variousness, possibility, complexity, and difficulty' (*The Liberal Imagination*, p. vii).

Trilling's own political experiences were decisive in establishing the framework and direction of his criticism. Soon after receiving his BA from Columbia, he began contributing to the *Menorah Journal*, a secular and humanist journal dedicated to the advancement of Jewish culture. It had been founded in 1915 by Henry Hurwitz of the Menorah Society, and placed under the managing editorship of Elliot Cohen in 1926, at which time it began moving steadily in the direction of cosmopolitanism and later, in the 1930s, of internationalism. From Cohen, a loquacious, witty, and charismatic figure, Trilling and others within the Menorah group learned to 'live [their] intellectual lives under the aspects of a complex and vivid idea of culture and society ... I have long thought of him as the greatest teacher I have ever known' (Eulogy for Elliot Cohen, Riverside Chapel, New York City, 31 May 1959). Trilling published his first piece, the short story 'Impediments', in the *Menorah Journal* in 1925, and subsequently contributed book reviews, essays, and stories. None of the pieces reveals evidence of direct influence by traditional Jewish religious and intellectual thought, a point Trilling later emphasised when discussing his career:

I cannot discover anything in my professional intellectual life which I can specifically trace back to my Jewish birth and rearing. I do not think of myself as a 'Jewish writer'. I do not have in mind to serve by my writing any Jewish purpose. I should resent it if a critic of my work were to discover in it either faults or virtues which he called Jewish.

(*Contemporary Jewish Record*, 7 (February 1944), p. 15)

Nevertheless Trilling's refined Anglophilia, which he derived from his London-born mother, was supplemented in some significant measure by the moral seriousness and respect for the word that emanated outward into the Jewish community from the Talmudic tradition. This background equipped Trilling and a legion of young Jewish writers for the strenuous, unprecedented journey toward respectability and eventually authority within the dominant American culture, notwithstanding the degree to which they may have suppressed aspects of their ethnic heritage as part of the established processes of assimilation.

Like others within the Menorah circle, Trilling was drawn to the political radicalism of the Communist Party in the early 1930s. Although he never joined the Party, for a relatively brief period he was involved with the National Committee for the Defense of Political Prisoners, an affiliate of the Party's International Labor Defense, and during the 1932 presidential campaign he signed a statement, along with fifty-two other intellectuals, supporting the Party's ticket. In May 1933, Trilling and other Menorah intellectuals resigned from the NCDPP, and less than a year later he signed an open letter opposing the Communist Party's violent disruption of a Socialist rally at Madison Square Garden (the letter also rejected reformism, capitalism, and fascism, and affirmed the signers' support for the working-class movement). Although Trilling's involvement with the Party and its auxiliary organisations was relatively short-lived, he continued to write for the liberal and left-wing press, including the *Nation, The New Republic, Partisan Review*, and V. F. Calverton's *Modern Monthly*. From the mid-1930s to the early 1940s, his anti-

Stalinist leftism focused on the intellectual bankruptcy of the Party, and the lively and often overlooked polemical writing of the period represents some of his best work. Trilling's polemical work has been overlooked partly through his own devices. More than once he excluded incendiary passages from later versions of his essays. One may compare, for example, 'Parrington, Mr. Smith and Reality' (*Partisan Review*, 7, 1 (January–February 1940), pp. 24–40) with its later, tamer incarnation as 'Reality in America' in *The Liberal Imagination*. Trilling's polemical skills were at their delightfully destructive peak in his 1937 review of Robert Briffault's Marxist novel, *Europa in Limbo*. Having disposed of the author's historical account of the bourgeoisie's oppression of the masses through sexual depravity, which Trilling labelled 'the license and rape theory of social upheaval', he turned to Briffault in the realm of thought, where he was said to be 'quite as seminal'. Here, observed Trilling, 'his great enemies are defunct ideas. Under his lash every extinct notion of the nineteenth century lies perfectly still. Ruthlessly he banishes our last stubbornly-held illusions about the survival of the fittest, the immutability of human nature, liberal democracy, the idealistic philosophies of reaction, Fabian socialism, the aesthetics of Ruskin. Supererogation, though dull, is not dangerous' (*Speaking of Literature and Society*, pp. 101–2).

Trilling opposed political litmus tests in 'Hemingway and His Critics' (1939), attributing the inferiority of *To Have and Have Not* and *The Fifth Column* to a critical community that had encouraged Hemingway 'the man' to usurp Hemingway 'the artist':

> Upon Hemingway were turned all the fine social feelings of the now passing decade, all the noble sentiments, all the desperate optimism, all the extreme rationalism, all the contempt of irony and indirection – all the attitudes which, in the full tide of the liberal-radical movement became dominant in our thought about literature. There was demanded of him earnestness and pity, social consciousness, as it was called, something 'positive' and 'constructive' and literal... One almost wishes to say to an author like Hemingway, 'You have no duty, no responsibility. Literature in a political sense, is not in the least important.'
>
> (*Speaking of Literature and Society*, pp. 125–6)

Trilling went on to discuss Hemingway's virtues as a writer, offering perhaps the best account of his style we have, and putting to rest the charge of mindlessness by drawing the important distinction between resisting reason and resisting rationalisation: '[I]n the long romantic tradition it never really *is* mind that is in question but rather a dull overlay of mechanical negative proper feeling, of a falseness of feeling which people believe to be reasonableness and reasonable virtue' (*Speaking of Literature and Society*, 129). In a particularly audacious essay, an appreciation of Eliot entitled 'Elements That Are Wanted', Trilling scorned the elitism of *The Idea of a Christian Society*, yet maintained that Eliot was asking pertinent questions ignored by the left, such as what the good life might consist in, what the morality of politics should be, what 'the spiritual and complex elements in life' might yield to politics. What Eliot and other modernist writers seemed to be recommending to the liberal culture of both bourgeois capitalism and its left opposition was 'the sense of complication and possibility, intensification, variety, unfoldment, worth. These are the things whose more or less abstract expressions we recognise in the arts; in our inability to admit them in social matters lies a great significance' (retitled 'T. S. Eliot's Politics', *Speaking of Literature and Society*, p. 166).

Trilling's willingness to enter the opposition's camp and admire some of what he found there was certainly an act of dissent among the dissenters, but he felt that liberalism would be doomed if it gave credence only to its own advocates. He was fond of quoting John Stuart Mill's famous essay on Coleridge in which he urged his fellow liberals to welcome the critical insights of this 'powerful conservative mind'. What made such solicitude absolutely essential for contemporary liberals was the fact that arrayed against them was every major writer of the modern period. 'Our liberal ideology has produced a large literature of social and political protest', Trilling noted, 'but not, for several decades, a single writer who commands our real literary imagination.' To 'the monumental figures of our time' – Trilling listed Proust, Joyce, Lawrence, Eliot, Yeats, Mann, Kafka, Rilke, and Gide – 'our liberal ideology has been at best a matter of indifference'. The lack of a connection between liberalism and 'the best literary minds of our time' meant that 'there is no connection between the political ideas of our educated class and the deep places of the imagination' (*The Liberal Imagination*, p. 94). As did the entire circle of New York intellectuals who contributed to *Partisan Review*, Trilling advocated an uneasy alliance with modern literature because liberalism seemed incapable of sustaining a culture autonomous and imaginative enough to produce incisive self-critique. This caused Trilling and others to diminish the importance of reactionary ideology in modernist works – roughly in proportion to the degree that Popular Front critics exaggerated its importance; instead they emphasised the modernists' adversarial stance. 'Any historian of the literature of the modern age', Trilling claimed, 'will take virtually for granted the adversarial intention, the actually subversive intention, that characterizes modern writing... [A] primary function of art and thought is to liberate the individual from the tyranny of his culture in the environmental sense and to permit him to stand beyond it in an autonomy of perception and judgment' (*Beyond Culture*, pp. iv–v).

This passage is among several from the preface to *Beyond Culture* sometimes cited by Trilling's critics as proof that, like Arnold, he opted ultimately for a transcendent notion of culture. It is charged that Trilling's culture is a high culture whose achievements are ultimately spiritual, whose perfection is realised to the degree that it escapes society, and whose beneficiaries are a select elite capable of purely aesthetic contemplation. It is, of course, perfectly true that Trilling had little respect for popular culture (at least in print: Diana Trilling has testified that he was an avid moviegoer), and that, like so many of his generation, he did entertain uninformed, undifferentiated, and frankly elitist opinions alleging its relative worthlessness. Thus he had nothing to say about achievements in film, television, theatre, or popular forms of literature: he was simply unwilling to challenge the Popular Front critics and their successors by staking out his own claims in these areas. Figures such as Hitchcock, Kovacs, or Blitzstein elicited no response whatsoever. The furthest Trilling went in this direction was no negligible distance, but it was, finally, inadequate: he did chastise Arnold for his exclusion of Chaucer from the first rank, observing that 'if Chaucer is not serious, then Mozart is not serious and Molière is not serious and seriousness becomes a matter of pince-nez glasses and a sepia print of the Parthenon' (*Matthew Arnold*, p. 375). He also defended Howells and Orwell precisely for their responsiveness to the details of actuality and the attributes of those who must get along in it – in other words, for their *lack* of solemn seriousness, greatness, and genius.

Nevertheless, the charge that Trilling held to a transcendent notion of culture is false, as a careful reading of the preface will reveal. Moving 'beyond culture' for Trilling could never mean transcending 'a people's technology, its manners and customs, its religious beliefs and organization, its systems of valuation, whether expressed or implicit' (*Beyond Culture*, p. iii). Culture taken in this sense, and this is the sense in which we take it today, can never be left behind. No person may escape his or her culture – on this matter Trilling is unequivocal:

[I]t is not possible to conceive of a person standing beyond his culture. His culture has brought him into being in every respect except the physical, has given him his categories and habits of thought, his range of feeling, his idiom and tones of speech. No aberration can effect a real separation: even the forms that madness takes ... are controlled by the culture in which it occurs. No personal superiority can place one beyond these influences ... Even when a person rejects his culture (as the phrase goes) and rebels against it, he does so in a culturally determined way.

(*Beyond Culture*, pp. iii–iv)

It is only when we think of culture as exclusive rather than inclusive, as 'that complex of activities which includes the practice of the arts and of certain intellectual disciplines' (*Beyond Culture*, p. iii), that we see what

Trilling wished to acknowledge by speaking of modern literature's adversarial stance. The ability to go beyond culture was nothing other than the continuing possibility, against great odds, of human agency manifesting itself in intelligent revolt against existing artistic and intellectual practices. This view was consistent with Trilling's cultural materialist perspective: critics may demur when it comes to endorsing the particular forms of revolt that appealed to Trilling, but it seems illogical for advocates of social change to condemn him as an idealist because he thought it possible for literature to be a locus of rejection and innovation. Trilling did privilege literature, of this there can be little doubt, but if one wants to avoid such privileging, it would mean identifying adversarial impulses in nonliterary realms of experience rather than denying their existence in literature by regarding literature or subjective experience in general as wholly imprisoned by established conventions, power, and authority.

Trilling's first book, one of only two full-length studies he produced, was the intellectual biography *Matthew Arnold* (1939), still the definitive work on Arnold. Here Trilling's direct engagements with sectors of the left were significantly amplified, a fact that belies the common assumption that Trilling took from Arnold's 'gospel of culture' an unsavoury mandarinism. It is much closer to the truth that Trilling valued Arnold for his refusal to remain aloof, for his aggressive political interventions, for his wish to spread superiority, as it were, and thereby ennoble the masses. For Trilling, if in theory Arnold's definition of literature as 'a criticism of life' meant that it 'illuminates and refines' Reason, literature's function was ultimately political because it prepared Reason by bringing to mind 'some notion of what is the right condition of the self' so that 'man might shape the conditions of his own existence' (*Beyond Culture*, p. 138). Following Arnold, Trilling considered literature capable of enabling the fullest imagination of that which the political will then strives to realise. Where Arnold's 'touchstones' failed to offer such a vision, or where they seemed too abstracted to help erode social prejudice, Trilling was quick to point it out. He upbraided Arnold, for example, for his intemperate response to mass agitation for the vote, and it is testimony to his own political engagement that the biography was laced with remarks connecting his subject matter with the current struggles against anti-semitism and fascism.

Although Trilling's admiration for E. M. Forster waned somewhat in later decades, during the 1940s he argued strenuously for the author's major status, again within a very definite political and ideological context. In *E. M. Forster* (1943) he based his claim on the novelist's rare combination of social understanding, particularly where money and class were concerned, and his intimate knowledge of how these conditioned the closely rendered moral lives of his characters. According to Trilling,

Forster's intense attachment to tradition allowed him to shun the eschatological belief in the future in favour of 'belief' in the present. He was
worldly because he accepted 'man in the world without the sentimentality
of cynicism' (*E. M. Forster*, p. 23). He could deal with the momentous
changes hastened by industrial capitalism – urbanisation, economic and
cultural imperialism, scepticism with regard to history and tradition –
without the lugubrious piety that, for Trilling, detracted from so many
American efforts at social criticism. Indeed, contrary to what might be
expected from a critic noted for his unrelenting seriousness, Trilling
praised Forster precisely for his lack of seriousness – for his comic manner,
playfulness, and 'relaxed will'. Forster's ease permitted him to remain
content with both human possibility and limitation, and to confront the
stark conflicts of his often melodramatic plots with a saving ambivalence.
Trilling referred to this ambivalence as 'moral realism': 'All novelists deal
with morality', he explained, 'but not all novelists, or even all good
novelists, are concerned with moral realism, which is not the awareness of
morality itself but of the contradictions, paradoxes and dangers of living
the moral life' (*E. M. Forster*, pp. 11–12). Forster's ease penetrated all
absolutes, casting doubt upon both sides of an issue, and upon that side of
character most constrained by social expectation. Montaigne-like, he
caught by surprise the subtlest of private hesitations. Such a disposition
was of particular use to middle-class liberalism, to which Forster appealed
'from the left' (*E. M. Forster*, p. 31), because it inured liberalism to the
surprise which, for lack of imagination, it habitually faced before giving
way to 'disillusionment and fatigue'. In place of the simple logic of good
versus evil, Forster presented a third possibility, an understanding of
'good-and-evil' (*E. M. Forster*, p. 14). This acceptance of contingency and
interconnection might have gone under the name of dialectical understanding had not the term been wrongly appropriated by doctrinaire
Marxism, the 'intellectual game of antagonistic principles' (*E. M. Forster*,
p. 15), which Forster so effectively repudiated.

    The sixteen essays composing *The Liberal Imagination* were devoted to
the project that Trilling, in 'The Function of the Little Magazine', attributed to the journal with which he was most closely associated, *Partisan Review*: the goal was 'organiz[ing] a new union between our political
ideas and our imagination – in all our cultural purview there is no work
more necessary' (*The Liberal Imagination*, p. 95). Trilling opened the
volume with his first widely influential essay, 'Reality in America'. Along
with two of Philip Rahv's essays ('Paleface and Redskin' (1939) and 'The
Cult of Experience in American Writing' (1940)), the essay's withering
and at times injudicious attack on progressive critical standards provided
the death knell for the liberal-radical version of a usable American past.
'Parrington', claimed Trilling, 'expressed the chronic American belief that

there exists an opposition between reality and mind and that one must enlist oneself in the party of reality' (*The Liberal Imagination*, p. 10). In Parrington writers who refused to join up were denigrated for their elitist concern with private experience and literary form – they included Hawthorne, Poe, Melville, and James; writers who dealt directly with economic, political, and social matters, and who did so, moreover, in a manner compatible with certain instrumental notions of democracy, were profusely praised. Applying a version of Eliot's dissociated sensibility to the American scene, Trilling (and Rahv) argued that the progressive critics were merely sustaining the American bifurcation of experience by insisting on a reality defined as fixed, given, and material. They were meeting 'mind' – contemplation, imagination, creativeness, *active* thought – with a settled hostility, as though these experiences were somehow antidemocratic. One of the writers the progressives favoured was Dreiser, whom Trilling disparaged in this essay and again in 'Manners, Morals, and the Novel', for his inability to portray a single interesting subjective life whose 'electric qualities of mind' involve the whole personality in ideas, and for, ironically, his pedantic ignorance of colloquial speech. In Dreiser and writers like him, Trilling maintained, ideas were merely 'pellets of intellection', whereas in actuality ideas arose out of emotional responses to social situations and were therefore 'living things, inescapably connected with our wills and desires', as he argued in 'The Meaning of a Literary Idea' (*The Liberal Imagination*, p. 284).

Not only did Trilling seek a way to link ideas with emotion and action – he also sought mediation on the fundamental question of the relation between subjective experience and the objective world, between being and consciousness, as Marx had put it. Trilling claimed that the Stalinists and progressives were wrong in giving absolute priority to material factors and in refusing to grant the reciprocal power of human agency in making history. The progressives' failure to provide a dialectical understanding of a question that went to the heart of a proper understanding of the novel caused Trilling to provide an intermediary category, which he called manners. 'What I understand by manners', he wrote in a famous definition,

is a culture's hum and buzz of implication. I mean the whole evanescent context in which its explicit statements are made. It is that part of a culture which is made up of half-uttered or unuttered or unutterable expressions of value . . . In this part of culture assumption rules, which is often much stronger than reason.

(*The Liberal Imagination*, pp. 194–5)

Manners were the constantly changing, conflicting system of styles and actions that a society made available to its members and, in turn, its members evolve through conscious and unconscious reproduction and modification. Trilling contended that liberalism's objectivist understanding of reality caused it to respond condescendingly and often with hostility to manners. He challenged the view that the complex of experience 'below all the explicit statements that a people makes' could be described by the sociologically top-heavy and overly cognitive term 'ideology', by which Trilling meant 'the habit or ritual of showing respect to certain formulas ... [to which] we have very strong ties of whose meaning and consequences in actuality we have no clear understanding' (*The Liberal Imagination*, p. 269). For Trilling it was quintessentially the novel that corrected such a view by demonstrating that the world of explicit statement and 'ordinary practicality' was not 'reality in its fullness'. It did so – and here he applied a notion akin to Marx's commodity fetishism – by exposing the obfuscatory effects of money and class relations on perception and behaviour. Trilling acknowledged that the novel's common coin was, precisely, ideology. But he claimed the novel was not *confined* to the analysis of ideology: by virtue of its focus on 'quality of character' as expressed by the ideas, attitudes, and styles that accompany action, it also traded in manners. Trilling's analysis of Hyacinth Robinson, the would-be activist and assassin in *The Princess Casamassima*, is instructive here. Robinson's 'superbness and arbitrariness', his intense response to art and his heightened sensitivity to the suffering masses that followed, and above all his final, heroic acceptance of responsibility for both the ideal of revolution and the ideal of civilised life – the quality of character that these attributes exemplified may have negated immediate practical necessity (Robinson chose suicide over assassination and, it is less often observed, over life after the refusal to assassinate), but they did reveal the unresolved moral dilemmas, which most adherents of positive social action militantly avoided.

In Trilling's view the American novel had been deficient in attaining such a dialectic between social and individual knowledge. 'American writers of genius have not turned their minds to society', he wrote in another famous passage. 'Poe and Melville were quite apart from it; the reality they sought was only tangential to society. Hawthorne was acute when he insisted that he did not write novels but romances' (*The Liberal Imagination*, p. 200). If Henry James was the only nineteenth-century American writer capable of complicating the subjective lives of his characters by immersing them in a dense, highly textured class society, nonetheless a writer of the romance such as Hawthorne was to be preferred to the modern American social novelists – to Dreiser, Anderson, Lewis, Steinbeck, Dos Passos, or Wolfe – whose passivity before aspects of material reality attenuated the subjective lives they depicted. Hawthorne, 'forever dealing with shadows', was nonetheless dealing with 'substantial things' *by virtue* of his aloofness from '"Yankee reality"'. It was his very distance from society that allowed him to raise 'those brilliant and serious doubts about the nature and possibility of moral perfection' (*The Liberal Imagination*, p. 8).

These judgements, of course, have been extremely influential: they have provided part of the conceptual framework for the prevailing literary histories from the 1950s to the 1970s, among them Richard Chase's *The American Novel and Its Tradition* (1957), Leslie Fiedler's *Love and Death in the American Novel* (1960), and Leo Marx's *The Machine in the Garden* (1964). For his part, Trilling modified these views in the later essay 'Hawthorne in Our Time' (1964), arguing with James and himself that Hawthorne's 'hidden, dark, and dangerous' world of internal moral conflict 'interpenetrates the world of material circumstance' (*Beyond Culture*, p. 174). If 'romance' implied a material world that was but 'thinly composed', it was nonetheless a world 'of iron hardness', which proved entirely 'intractable' to those wishing for personal or social transfiguration. Hawthorne was therefore not a writer to be embraced by the 1960s, Trilling claimed, a period in which he believed the inner life had been commercially and publicly appropriated, in the name, paradoxically, of noncontingency and spontaneity.

For some progressive critics, the essays of *The Opposing Self* (1955) and *Beyond Culture* (1965) have represented something of a retreat for Trilling. It has appeared to them as though his interest in broad cultural and political tendencies was replaced by a new concern for individual, relatively private experience, and this has been thought to reflect, and contribute toward, the Cold War consensus. There is some basis for this view, surely, when we consider how much more ideologically efficacious Trilling's anti-Communism became in this period, and how relatively narrow, though certainly not shallow, was the 'critical non-conformism' that he advocated in the famous *Partisan Review* symposium of 1952, 'Our Country and Our Culture' (*A Gathering of Fugitives*, p. 83). Indeed few of the abuses of American global power, the threats to democracy posed by McCarthyism or examples of the continuing effects of racial oppression, diverted Trilling from his increasingly prominent role as critic of the liberal-radical culture. Throughout his career Trilling paid little heed to conservative opinion, believing that because it had won virtually no assent among intellectuals it was not dangerous or worth refuting. Instead, during the 1950s and 1960s it was becoming increasingly clear to Trilling that the great danger for American culture arose from the left, and although he himself never renounced liberalism, by the 1970s it was nearly impossible in a polarised society for many progressives to consider him an ally.

But Trilling's failure to criticise the abuses of postwar American capitalism does not in itself invalidate his insights into certain of liberalism's deficiencies. As we have seen, Trilling identified as chief among these a profound and historic uncertainty with regard to irrational, intuitive, or otherwise unsociable experience that did not lend itself to organised forms of social cooperation. In the 1940s and early 1950s Trilling sought to correct this problem through complicating liberalism's notion of experience by assimilating to it the insights of romanticism and modernism. The key figure here was Freud, who despite the inadequacies of his own theory of artistic production and the function of art, nonetheless rightly conceived of mind as something to which poetry was indigenous – in Trilling's words the mind was to Freud 'a poetry-making faculty' (*Beyond Culture*, p. 79). The mind was, moreover, a thoroughfare of biology, culture, and creativity. But rarely did the traffic flow smoothly. In 'Freud: Within and Beyond Culture', Trilling argued for the necessary, and tragic, conjunction of all three, claiming at once that Freud 'made it apparent how entirely implicated in culture we all are'; that this principle of culture is 'terrible' for the self set against it; and that biology, for all its asociality, may after all provide 'a residue of human quality beyond the reach of cultural control' (*Beyond Culture*, pp. 91, 93, 98). Then, identifying a social phenomenon central to Antonio Gramsci's idea of hegemony, he observed, 'In a society like ours, which, despite some appearances to the contrary, tends to be seductive rather than coercive, the individual's old defenses against the domination of the culture become weaker' (*Beyond Culture*, p. 98). In order to bolster these defences, Trilling spoke on behalf of difficult, even inadmissible experience. In what many consider to be his finest essay, 'Keats: The Poet As Hero', he credited the poet for delighting in 'the infantile wish' despite his culture's fear and repression of 'the passive self-reference of infancy'. Keats's 'geniality toward himself, his bold acceptance of his primitive appetite', extended to his abiding capacity for indolence, which Trilling, following Keats himself, distinguished from what we would call laziness, apathy, or self-indulgence. Keats referred to 'diligent indolence', marking the power of passivity as a source for what Trilling called 'conception, incubation, gestation' (*The Opposing Self*, p. 16), all of which were constitutive of the active life. Similarly, in 'Wordsworth and the Rabbis' Trilling counterposed Wordsworth's quietism, 'which is not in the least a negation of life but, on the contrary an affirmation of life so complete that it needed no saying', to 'the predilection for the powerful, the fierce, the assertive, the personally militant, [which] is very strong in our culture' (*The Opposing Self*, pp. 115, 117).

In *Sincerity and Authenticity* (1971) and the major essays of the 1960s and 1970s – 'On the Teaching of Modern Literature' (1961), 'The Fate of Pleasure' (1963), 'Mind in the Modern World' (1972), 'Art, Will, and Necessity' (1973) – Trilling's position hardened against what he considered the ubiquitous systems of mass and middlebrow culture, systems that in his view had devoured the adversary culture of modernism and discharged the ersatz avant-garde of the Beats and then the counter-culture. Confronted by the counter-culture and the student movement at Columbia, where he taught for some thirty-five years, Trilling sounded notes of increasing despair, even questioning whether the 'adversary culture' was not in part responsible for the uses to which it was being put. Only time will tell the extent to which his enemies and their successors, now extensively reevaluating the period, will find it prudent to acknowledge the wisdom of portions of Trilling's attack, especially where he assailed the movement for its anti-intellectualism, its sectarianism, its hedonism, and its irrationalism. As things now stand, reasons other than simple ideological differences conspire to make Trilling's criticism underappreciated today. His work presents a direct challenge to the long-standing separation in the United States between politics and intelligence, to the academicisation of post-war American criticism and the ensuing pressure to distance criticism from immediate cultural and social problems, and to the resulting tendency for even historical, ideological, and politicised critics to remain aloof from nonacademic cultural and political movements. Trilling's criticism serves to remind us that this distance has helped cause these critics at times to express their militancy by exaggerating or simplifying the efficacy of material factors on authors, texts, and readers, instead of finding ways to encourage wilful acts of 'critical non-conformism' on the part of a wider public audience.

To these reasons we must add the particular limitations of Trilling's criticism. These centre on his relative neglect of power. Not the power of culture and the word – of these he was an exemplary critic – but power that descends upon middle-class intellectuals and the university from corporate, state, and military sources, and the power of the innumerable small acts of circumvention and dissent in the daily routines of those who do not live in certain Manhattan neighbourhoods. Trilling, for all his social perspective and for all his understanding of the conditioned nature of life, was perhaps a bit possessive of the intellectual life and the authority it generously bestowed upon him. One senses that he lacked, as did most intellectuals 'withdraw[n] from the ordinary life of the tribe', as Trilling himself put it, the worldliness for which he praised Orwell so profusely, a worldliness rooted in the 'passion for the literal actuality of life' (*The Opposing Self*, p. 141). Had Trilling been such a man 'whose hands and eyes and whole body were part of his thinking apparatus' (*The Opposing Self*, p. 144), he might have understood just how fine is the line between the 'populist sentimentality' he deplored and the perspicacious generosity Orwell exhibited toward the culture of ordinary people in an essay such as 'The Art of Donald McGill'. He might also have acknowledged that in certain important respects the progressive politics and postmodern culture of the 1950s and 1960s challenged dangerous values coupled with great power, and were thus worthy of the name 'critical non-conformism'.

But for all the claims that have been made for the conservatism of Trilling's cold war liberalism and his adamant anti-utopianism, on the question of the need for and the possibility of radically transforming American liberal-radical culture, he was a visionary. He wished to make thoroughgoing self-criticism the prevailing mode within the liberal-radical culture, and he implored those sharing this culture to consider private, politically passive acts as not only sustaining, but, as Whitman believed, the very criterion of democracy. It is, finally, as close to religion as we might expect a secular cultural critic to come. Trilling placed a very heavy burden on liberalism indeed, a burden that as yet it has refused to bear.

19

Poet-critics

Lawrence Lipking

The early modern period is an age of poet-critics. At the turn of the twentieth century, as new schools and movements of poetry sprang up throughout Europe, the poets who created them also spread the word of a critical revolution. 'Ladies and Gentlemen', Stéphane Mallarmé told his Oxford and Cambridge audiences in 1894, 'I am truly bringing news. Astonishing news. And never seen before. – We have been meddling with verse.'[1] Many later poets brought similar news. A flood of essays and lectures and position papers and manifestos accompanied each innovation in style. Indeed, in some cases, such as Marinetti's 'Manifesto of Futurism' (1909) or Breton's first *Manifesto of Surrealism* (1924), the manifesto may have been more influential than the verse it recommended. Nor were these documents merely the public relations or by-products of changes in poetry. Often they served as 'gunsights' (Ezra Pound's word), forerunners of new composition. Thus Mikhail Kuzmin's Russian manifesto 'On Beautiful Clarity' (1910) is important less for what it explains or defends than for pointing out critical directions to poets of the future: Gumilev, Akh-matova, Mandelstam. At such times the critic unites with the artist. This interpenetration of criticism and poetry, their mutual influence and vitality, helps to define the early modern period. The leading figures tend not to be poets only, or critics only, but genuine poet-critics.

What accounts for this alliance? Part of the answer may be that it was already long overdue. Poets had been among the best critics since ancient times, so ready to discuss their art that a history of criticism might be composed entirely from their statements. As practical critics, Horace and Dante and Keats have more to say about poems than do Plato, Aquinas, and Hegel. Yet such a history would falter in the mid-nineteenth century, when many poets fervently scorned to be critics. This defection was especially prevalent in England. Great poets like Tennyson and Browning abstain on principle from criticism, as if too great a dose of theory might contaminate their creative powers. It was just this separation of creative activity from disinterested inquiry, in fact, that Matthew Arnold set

---

[1] 'J'apporte en effet des nouvelles. Les plus surprenantes. Même cas ne se vit encore. On a touché au vers' (Stéphane Mallarmé, 'La Musique et les Lettres', *Œuvres complètes*, ed. Henri Mondor and G. Jean-Aubry (Paris, 1945), p. 643).

himself against in 'The Function of Criticism at the Present Time' (1864), which calls for a literature nourished by 'a current of fresh and true ideas' (p. 28). Arnold upholds the ideal of the poet-critic. Yet his own example seems ambiguous; he views the ideal with nostalgia and regret. When he criticised his own work, in the 'Preface' to *Poems* (1853), rather than trying to defend himself or point out new directions he explained why even his masterpiece, *Empedocles on Etna*, simply would not do.[2] In practice, Arnold's criticism often functions as the enemy of his poems. The quarrel with himself suggests the dangers of self-consciousness and doubt that shadow the poet-critic. And although other Victorian poets – Swinburne, for instance – produced a good deal of criticism, they usually held their poetry apart from it. At the end of the century, when Oscar Wilde declared that good critics were necessarily artists and William Butler Yeats avowed that artists needed to be inspired by 'some philosophy, some criticism of their art' ('The Symbolism of Poetry', p. 154), they did so with an air of paradox. The poet-critic had long been out of style.

Styles were changing, however. At first in France, then elsewhere in Europe, and eventually through the Western world, some of the best poets insisted on redefining every aspect of their art, from prosodic conventions to the aims and ends of poetry. Nothing was to be taken for granted. The aesthetic movement and the symbolist movement are the best publicised but by no means the only instruments of this redefinition; after Mallarmé, almost everyone began to meddle with verse. New rhythms and languages of poetry, new forms, new understandings of how and what a poem ought to mean, aroused a fever of experimentation. Hence poets were forced to be critics, whether to conceive the terms on which poetry could be written or to explain them to the public. New codes require decoders. Nor can a historian ignore the cultural capital produced by this surplus of artistic inventions. To some extent, the rise of the modern poet-critic might be viewed as an effect of the marketplace, in which the suppliers of a little-known luxury item create a demand for it.[3] Why should anyone take an interest in 'The Afternoon of a Faun'? Readers may need to be persuaded that their investment of money, time, and attention will bring rewards of delight and sophistication. Wordsworth had addressed this concern, in the Preface to the second edition of *Lyrical Ballads* (1800), by promising his audience abundant recompense for learning how to read

---

[2] Arnold's reason for omitting *Empedocles on Etna* – its painful, not tragic, representation of a prolonged state of mental distress that can find no vent in action (p. 592) – suggests that the work has allegorised his own painful efforts to inform a poetic action with a continuous stream of critical ideas.

[3] In *The Rules of Art: Genesis and Structure of the Literary Field*, Pierre Bourdieu argues that Mallarmé was quite conscious of the methods of mystification that he and other poets used to manipulate the 'field of cultural production' (tr. Susan Emanuel (Cambridge, 1996), pp. 274–7).

him. A century later an increasing number of poet-critics offered a similar lesson: poetry was changing; old habits of reading had to be unlearned; new principles had to be mastered; the initiate would discover extraordinary pleasures, the satisfaction of desires as yet unknown; all the best people were already experiencing this; the future belonged to them.

There are two particular reasons, moreover, why early modern poems so often come escorted by a convoy of criticism. The first is the notorious obscurity of many modern classics. Uninitiated readers can hardly hope to fathom Mallarmé or Eliot without assistance. The reasons for this difficulty are still disputed by critics. But the practical consequence of such obscurity is to make poems seem incomplete until interpreted by some expert – preferably the poet himself. At one academic extreme, typified by Eliot's notes to *The Waste Land*, the gloss creeps gradually like ivy over the text. The poet-critic may dislike this situation and respond to it with irony and resentment.[4] But it also aggrandises his authority. For better or worse, obscurity tempts readers to hope for a key, and no one seems more qualified than the poet to provide it. When Socrates asked poets what their writings meant, according to Plato's *Apology*, he found that 'any of the bystanders could have explained those poems better than their actual authors'. Wimsatt and Beardsley quoted this anecdote in their influential essay, 'The Intentional Fallacy' (1946), to warn against giving the poet's interpretations too much credit: 'Critical inquiries are not settled by consulting the oracle' (p. 18). But the need to issue such warnings coincided with an era of dominant poet-critics who ruled the critical roost. Consulted again and again, many authors learned to talk like oracles. Hard poems attract the commentary of sanctioned authorities.

A second reason for the close relations between modern poetry and criticism may be the value placed on *purity* in verse. The idea that poetry should aspire to the condition of music, an art of sound and form independent of subject matter and meaning, was best articulated by the French symbolists, but it runs through many other schools as well. By twentieth-century convention, 'A poem should not mean / But be' (MacLeish, 'Ars Poetica', p. 311). Thus poems cannot speak for themselves. One effect of this silence may be to confer a special mystery on the poetic act, which inhabits a realm outside ordinary discourse or the possibility of explanation. But another result may be to enhance the role of the interpreter. In

---

[4] In 1956 Eliot famously described the notes to *The Waste Land* as a 'remarkable exposition of bogus scholarship that is still on view to-day. I have sometimes thought of getting rid of these notes; but now they can never be unstuck. They have had almost greater popularity than the poem itself' ('The Frontiers of Criticism', *On Poetry and Poets* (New York, 1957), p. 121). As A. Walton Litz has pointed out, however, this comment cannot be taken at face value; it reflects a tension between Eliot's critical theory (which regards each work of art as self-sufficient) and his poetic practice (which relies on allusions) ('*The Waste Land* Fifty Years After', *Eliot in His Time* (Princeton, 1973), pp. 9–13).

itself, *la poésie pure* defines a theory, or a theoretical goal, rather than a specific body of verse. And even if such verse existed, at least approximately, it would be inarticulate, unable to tell the reader its secrets. Hence critics must lend it a voice. Right from the beginning, in Poe's essays 'The Philosophy of Composition' (1846) and 'The Poetic Principle' (1849), the dream of pure poetry required a critic to shield it from the adulterations and frailties of the ordinary world and ordinary language. French poets – Baudelaire, Mallarmé, Valéry – took up the burden, translating Poe himself into a pure poet and protecting him from being corrupted by his mere earthly existence.[5] But to do so they had to turn critic. The advocate of pure poetry resorts to prose in order to explain whatever the verse has left out. A similar function is served by the champions of surrealism, who provide logical reasons for the necessity of irrationalism. There is nothing illegitimate about this division of responsibilities; to defend purity, one need not be pure. But in practice the growing ideal of pure poetry resulted in a corresponding growth of poet-critics – those who could interpret mute poems for the talking world.

To restrict the function of a poet-critic to explicating specific poems, however, reduces the network of relations between poetry and criticism to a single thread. In practice their interconnections are far more complex. A poet can act as a critic in a variety of ways. First of all, authors revise. If 'every true poet is necessarily a first-rate critic', in Valéry's words,[6] that is because a poet's work only begins at the moment when the poem first takes form. Afterward comes the labour of getting it right. Once a poet finishes struggling with the Muse, according to W. H. Auden, he 'submits his work in progress' to another part of the self, the Censor, who ruthlessly picks all its faults to pieces ('Writing', p. 16). Manuscripts are routinely covered with blots. Even the exception provides the rule: Shakespeare 'never blotted out line', his fellow players said, but the bit of *Sir Thomas More* that most scholars believe to be in Shakespeare's hand blots several lines and alters many words.[7] Modern poets have often been heroes of revision. 'It is myself that I remake' (*Variorum Edition*, p. 778), wrote Yeats, defending his irresistible urge to repair or tinker with his songs long after publication. Other poets have tried to kill the Censor. Allen Ginsberg's 'On Improvised Poetics' (*Independence Day*, 1973) consists of four

[5] According to Eliot, the tradition of purity begun by Poe and culminated by Valéry 'represents the most interesting development of poetic consciousness anywhere' in the last hundred years ('From Poe to Valéry' (1948), *To Criticize the Critic* (New York, 1965), p. 42).
[6] 'Mais tout véritable poète est nécessairement un critique de premier ordre'; 'Poésie et pensée abstraite' (1939) (Paul Valéry, *Œuvres*, ed. Jean Hytier, 2 vols. (Paris, 1957), 1:1335, *Collected Works*, ed. Jackson Mathews, 15 vols. (New York and Princeton, 1956–75), 7:76).
[7] A. F. Scott provides a photograph and transcription of the page, along with holograph manuscripts and revisions by other poets (*The Poet's Craft* (Cambridge, 1957), pp. 2–3).

words: 'First thought best thought.' But even there the critic reigns, not only in the didactic content and edifying title but in the implied rebuttal to a famous graffito, 'Allen Ginsberg revises.' He did, in fact. In that respect he became, like every other poet, a critic.

Poets practise criticism on a larger scale as well. They can help revise another writer's work, for instance, as Ezra Pound played midwife to *The Waste Land*. They can send advisory letters to younger poets; publish reviews; or issue manifestos. They can write guidebooks, arts of poetry, in verse or prose. They can comb the past for evidence of what has already been done. They can try to predict what styles will serve best in the future. They can deal with the theory of poetry, its relation to other arts, to philosophy, to rival uses of language, to the sciences, or to human life as a whole. At a final extreme, they can even aim at a discourse where poetry and criticism might unite in a single activity, the search for an all-encompassing *poetics*. A full history of poet-critics would have to take all these modes into account.

Yet critics who are not poets can use the same modes. A study of what is distinctive about the modern poet-critic needs to ask two further questions: how do poet-critics differ from critics at large? And how does the modern poet-critic differ from poet-critics in earlier ages?

The first question has often been answered with conventional, cynical wisdom: whatever poet-critics seem to be writing about, they are really always writing about their own work. Like many other commonplaces about the prevalence of self-interest, this answer makes a good deal of sense. When Dryden debates whether plays ought to be written in rhyme or blank verse, when Lorca describes the mysterious power of the *duende*, each is clearly thinking about his previous work and the work he has yet to do. But counter-examples might also be cited. Samuel Johnson, for instance, took a dim view of verse imitations, the one kind of poetry in which he had achieved success: 'what is easy is seldom excellent: such imitations cannot give pleasure to common readers' (*Lives*, 3: 246–7). Similarly, Coleridge the critic usually writes as if Coleridge the poet had never existed. To be sure, a sceptic might always detect a secret self-reference in the midst of such denials. Perhaps when poet-critics appear to forget their own poems, they are privately hatching some plan to even the score in the future. This suspicion cannot be dismissed out of hand. Yet neither can it be proved. The argument is circular at best: when we bring a critic's poems to his or her criticism, we always discover them already there. Moreover, as poets like to point out, critics who are *not* poets are by no means free from self-interest; they may even be thinking about the poems they wish they could write. Poet-critics have no monopoly on egocentricity. Their tendency to use criticism to advance their own work should always be kept in mind, but it does not define them.

A more rigorous definition might be grounded on the doubleness intrinsic to the term, the powerful hyphen that draws poet and critic together: a poet-critic is someone whose work incorporates and reflects the shifting relations between poetry and criticism, the practice and the theory of an art. Some poets, like Housman and Larkin, write poems sometimes and criticism sometimes, but take care never to connect one activity with the other. They are not poet-critics. Neither are critics like I. A. Richards, Edmund Wilson, and Kenneth Burke, who write poems as recreation from the serious business of their lives (although occasionally this distinction becomes problematic, as with William Empson, Yvor Winters, and R. P. Blackmur, all eminent critics who harboured ambitions as poets). Strictly speaking, the term poet-critic should be reserved for writers who do not compartmentalise their devotion to poetry and criticism, but bring them into balance or conflict with one another. Poet-critics test practice by theory and theory by practice. That marks the difference between their work and the work of other poets and critics.

It does not follow, however, that the poet and critic necessarily get on well together, even when they are the same person. The marriage between them tends to be uneasy, characterised by tensions, ambiguities, or unresolved contradictions. During a poet's most productive period, his or her critical faculties often lie fallow; while a critic's thinking and writing is at its best, he or she may feel incapable of a poem. Most poet-critics live through at least one stage of 'dejection', like the emptiness described by Coleridge's ode, or through a time of suspension, like Valéry's famous 'silence' of almost two decades, when 'abstruse research' seems to dominate the imagination. The opposite – a stage of 'joy', in Coleridge's terms – can also occur, especially early in a career, when critical ideas and poems burst out together. But such moments tend to be fleeting. More typically, poetry and criticism cohabit in a strained alliance, each indicating the other's faults and limitations. Even when fixed ideas about the nature of poetry and criticism change, the difference between the two still helps to define them. That is, we can usually identify what poetry is thought to be, at some specific period, by noting how it is distinguished from criticism; and vice versa. Logically, then, modern poet-critics will be set apart from poet-critics of earlier ages by the way they perceive the tension between poetry and criticism in their own work.

No genre reveals this process more clearly than the *ars poetica*, the verse treatise on the art of verse. Here if anywhere the poet and critic join, in a poem that also claims to be a piece of criticism. Two talents of the writer test each other: the poet may be judged by how well he exemplifies his own critical principles, and the critic by how well his precepts stand up to verse. Yet right from the start, in Horace's *Ars Poetica* (or *Epistle to the*

Pisos), the genre depends less on decorum than on internal oppositions. Antagonistic visions of the poet quarrel within it: the inspired madman (or *vates*) who violates nature by dreaming up centaurs and mermaids struggles against the wise craftsman (*poeta*) who knows how to follow the Greeks and the rules. Horace sides with the craftsman, of course. Self-conscious and ironic about his own conversational style (*sermones*) – he may have been versifying a treatise by Neoptolemus of Parium – he claims to be incapable of poetry even while he writes it. Only a superficial reader will believe him.[8] Yet the divisions and paradoxes in the work are not superficial. Much of its energy derives from the madman it satirises, and its poetic quality subtly argues against the didactic common sense conveyed by the usual prose translations. The *Ars Poetica* presents a dialogue between two voices, one matter-of-fact and one inspired. Horace gives each of them weight and makes his poem from their cross-purposes.

Later versions of the *ars poetica* exploit similar sorts of tension. Pope's *Essay on Criticism*, for instance, preserves the antagonism of poet and critic while cleverly reversing their roles. Here judgement undergoes a trial by wit, and critics bow to the superior authority of poets: 'Let such teach others who themselves excell, / And *censure freely* who have *written well*' (ll. 15–16). Pope translates Horace's crazed leech of a poet into a mad abandoned critic, fool enough to rush in where angels (and poets) fear to tread. The *Essay* suggests, by example as well as by precept, that in a better world, such as Eden, ancient Greece, or a fully realised poem, the poet and critic might be one. But the real world is different. There wit and judgement are at strife, the dunces rule, and poet-critics feel the shock of discord in their vitals.

By the late nineteenth century, the divorce between the poet's and the critic's ways of seeing had become so absolute that the very possibility of an *ars poetica* came to be mocked. Verlaine's notorious 'Art Poétique' (1882), first among dozens of its breed, commences its air of parody and scandal with its title; in fact there is no such 'art'. Instead the verses celebrate an outlaw poetics (not just by chance, they were written in prison). Verlaine wittily warns against wit, eloquently wrings the neck of eloquence, and rhymes against rhyme. Above all he cultivates a taste for the disreputable. Even in the fugitive beauty at the end, a whiff of gypsy leaves its pungent traces.

> Make your verse a lucky favor
> Strewn on the crisp morning wind
> That passes scenting thyme and mint...
> And all the rest is literature.[9]

[8] C. O. Brink argues at length that Horace engages in 'consummate irony' (*Horace on Poetry: The 'Ars Poetica'* (Cambridge, 1971), p. x) by calling his poetry 'prose'; pp. 443–523 describe the poetic quality of Horace's *sermones*.

The pleasures of poetry flit through the air, hints and nuances – 'rien que la nuance!' – reminiscent of vagabond spirits. And the fixities of literature, that rest home for superannuated bourgeois classics, condemn it to everlasting boredom.

Most modern poems on poetry repeat the same defiance of literary rules. Thus Max Jacob's *Art Poétique* (1922), for all its spontaneity, strictly follows the line of Verlaine: poetry is a game, its only principle is not to be boring, ideas should be turned into feelings or be avoided like the plague. By twentieth-century convention, the title 'ars poetica' always signals an ironic twist. Yet that convention itself represents a paradox, since the attack on programmatic rules supplies a programme for writing. Verlaine does not hesitate to use the imperative mode ('Take eloquence and wring its neck!') and MacLeish's poem insists with unequivocal meaning that a poem should not mean. Such formulas are not lapses in the modern *ars poetica* but its logical consequence, the result of defining poetry as the diametrical opposite of criticism.

The supposed hostility that pits criticism against poetry provides the modern poet-critic with a constant theme. Some writers, like Valéry, probe the opposition in order to deconstruct it; others, like Stefan George, consider it a basic principle of life. But both parties use the eternal warfare between creation and abstract thought as the received doctrine that sets the basic conditions of their art. The symbolist fascination with mystery and the surrealist investment in irrationalism were instigated by poet-critics who thought their way to the abandonment of thought. Their methods are not just poetic experiments but critical provocations, deliberate raids on the inarticulate by very articulate theorists. To read through a series of essays by the founders of modern poetry is to be told in a hundred different ways that poetry escapes the exercise of defining it. 'Inseparable from each other, poetry and prose are two opposite poles' (Pasternak, 'Some Statements', p. 84). Hence the point of criticism is often to demonstrate its own failure, clearing a space for the poem to continue serenely on its way. The inability of poet-critics to apprehend the nature of poetry proves that poetry belongs to a separate sphere, inviolate and infinitely precious. That sphere might be called the creative unconscious. In this respect the function of the conscious or critical mind is to reveal, through its own blindness and frequent slips, the presence of a hidden, unquenchable power. Poet-critics discovered this before the heyday of Freud.

The opposition between poetry and criticism in the early modern period, an opposition that serves to validate the worth of poetry in an age more likely to recognise its image in prose, employs a great variety of

---

9 'Que ton vers soit la bonne aventure / Éparse au vent crispé du matin / Qui va fleurant la menthe et le thym . . . / Et tout le reste est littérature.' Although unpublished until 1882, 'Art Poétique' was composed in prison in 1874.

terms. Depending on the school, the contraries might be identified with the symbolic order and the everyday world, the irrational and rationality, action and contemplation, formal perfection and the formless, feeling and detachment, concreteness and abstraction, or vision and science. Often such oppositions contest the spirit of modernity itself. Some poets considered their art the last refuge of human values in a century driven by soulless technology; others embraced the machine and the accelerating pace of change. Thus criticism might set out to attack either the modern world or else writers who desperately clung to the past. Modern poet-critics quarrel with themselves as well as others; their energy is sparked by discord, not by agreement.

In practice, however, the issue that probably divided modern poet-critics most, and had the most lasting consequences for their work, was not the incompatibility of poetry and criticism but a historical tension. Did a poem represent the spirit of a particular nation, or did it belong to the world? The national and international ideals of poetry proved difficult to reconcile. As wars broke out over aggressive nationalistic claims, in the late nineteenth and early twentieth centuries, many poets were forced to declare their allegiance. Broad-minded critics leaned toward internationalism. Even in the mid-nineteenth century, when Matthew Arnold called on criticism to come to the aid of English literature, he made it clear that 'the criticism I am really concerned with, – the criticism which alone can much help us for the future, the criticism which, throughout Europe, is at the present day meant, when so much stress is laid on the importance of criticism and the critical spirit, – is a criticism which regards Europe as being, for intellectual and spiritual purposes, one great confederation, bound to a joint action and working to a common result' ('The Function of Criticism', p. 29). What English poets needed was an infusion of Greek and French and German: a cosmopolitan, international overview. If poetry is what gets left out in translation, then criticism might be a reminder of what translations let in, the sense of another culture with other ideas. Arnold preached the virtue of such translations.

Later poet-critics had their doubts. But the clash between two views, the view that identifies poetry with exploring the resources of a given language and the view that recommends infusing the poems of one language with the spirit of another, causes trouble from the beginning of the modern movement. Consider the implications of Mallarmé's endlessly quoted praise for Poe as an angel who gave 'a purer sense to the words of the tribe'.[10] What words, what tribe are being referred to? Presumably the

---

[10] 'Donner un sens plus pur aux mots de la tribu' (Mallarmé, 'Le Tombeau d'Edgar Poe', Œuvres complètes, p. 189). Lawrence Lipking's *The Life of the Poet: Beginning and Ending Poetic Careers* (Chicago, 1981) analyses this poem as an instance of the *tombeau*, a genre in which a poet-critic incorporates the legacy of a precursor (pp. 164–9).

English of Americans; Mallarmé was enthralled by the sounds of English words. Yet his poetic tribute translated Poe into a foreign idiom, the 'eternity' of French. One might equally equate 'the words of the tribe' with some imagined prehistoric language, a barbaric dialect that awaits Poe's civilising touch. In any case, the point is that the poet does not belong to the tribe into which he was born, the savage Americans who hounded him to death because they hated his linguistic purity. Poe is better off in France, where poets appreciate him. To come over, however, he must lose his contact with American English and perhaps with his sense (whether pure or not). Nor does Mallarmé shake off a similar dilemma: to purify French, he needs to import some English sounds and to break his ties with the tribe of common demotic French. The example sends a mixed message. As a poet, Mallarmé remains untranslatable; his effects belong quintessentially to the particular combinations of letters and sounds in one language. As someone who thinks about poetry, however, he seems an internationalist, drawn not only to Poe but to the idea of a poetic language purified of its contamination by any one time, place, or country. If 'everything in the world exists in order to end up in a book' (*Œuvres complètes*, p. 378), in his famous assertion, then that book must be capable of taking in a universal language, the words of the tribe of mankind. Such a book, and the critic who helps prepare it, cannot afford to recognise any borders.

In many other nations as well, poets argued with critics and with themselves about whether to found their art exclusively on native grounds. It was not a new argument. Ever since Dante, European poets had been forced to decide whether they descended from the ancients or represented a new vernacular line, and the issue had become even more acute with the nationalism of the nineteenth century, when Whitman gave up English for American and Dostoevsky rebuked Turgenev for allowing European cosmopolitanism to taint the well of Russian undefiled. But in the twentieth century the argument took a vicious turn. As wars carved out new boundaries and nations, poets were often conscripted for patriotic causes. Such wars were internal as well. In Germany, for instance, such poet-critics as George and Rilke, whose early work had been nourished by powerful foreign influences (especially, though not exclusively, French), eventually became symbols of a regenerate German spirit. While based to some extent on a misunderstanding (it is not accidental that both poets died in Switzerland rather than Germany), these national laurels do respond to aspects of each poet – the militaristic ancestor-worship of Rilke's *Lay of the Love and Death of the Cornet Christoph Rilke* and the prophetic Greco-German cult that George organized around the boy he deified as Maximin.[11] Both poets had returned home, however briefly, to

11 Although the *Cornet* was first drafted in 1899 and revised for publication in 1904 and 1906, its republication in 1912 (and subsequent use for war propaganda) led to Rilke's

an ideal German. To write such poems they had to put aside the internationally minded critic who also lived in them.

English poets and critics were less tempted to belong to other nations, and the modern style of poetry took longer to reach them. But foreigners dwelt in their midst. For William Butler Yeats, the choice between an indigenous Irish verse born of the people, or the intoxicating new rhythms and emanations that wafted from the continent, was resolved in a sort of delirium, as the critic managed to convince the poet that ancient Ireland and modern France could be the same place. Other foreign poet-critics smuggled still more daring innovations past English customs. With Ezra Pound and T. S. Eliot, the international style of poetry takes root. Restlessly searching for ways to make language new and for critical ideas that violate British specifications, they pay no attention to provincial territorial claims. Pound insists that English verse can import qualities from Chinese and Provençal, and Eliot builds the most influential poem of the century from the materials of Babel. Perhaps these were not the critics whom Arnold had called for. Yet they did carry out his programme for grafting world literature onto the stock of English – if English was the language in which they wrote.

They were also, undeniably, poet-critics. If Pound swears, with polemical impatience, that poets are the best and indeed the only true critics, Eliot propagandises more subtly for the identity of poet and critic, under the rubric of 'the perfect critic': 'It is fatuous to say that criticism is for the sake of "creation" or creation for the sake of criticism. It is also fatuous to assume that there are ages of criticism and ages of creativeness, as if by plunging ourselves into intellectual darkness we were in better hopes of finding spiritual light. The two directions of sensibility are complementary; and as sensibility is rare, unpopular, and desirable, it is to be expected that the critic and the creative artist should frequently be the same person' ('The Perfect Critic', p. 16). That proposition may be hubristic as well as elitist. Eliot went through more than one period of creative drought, and the dry misgivings expressed by his criticism sometimes took revenge on his poems. When the voice of the critic enters the verse – 'That was a way of putting it – not very satisfactory' (*East Coker*) – self-parody never seems far away. Eliot's reference to the 'two directions of sensibility' recalls one of his best-known sentences: 'In the seventeenth century a dissociation of sensibility set in, from which we have never recovered' ('The Metaphysical Poets', p. 247); and the congruence of these passages suggests that in each case he may have been thinking about himself, the

renown as a national hero. George's apotheosis of Maximin was announced by *Der Siebente Ring* (1907). Claude David has elucidated the influence of French poetry on George as well as the turn to Dante in the Maximin poems; see *Stefan George: son œuvre poétique* (Lyon, 1952).

schizophrenic 'we' who is struggling to make his divided nature one. But the effort was more than personal. It impelled a generation of poet-critics around the world, diverse as Delmore Schwartz and George Seferis, to follow Eliot's lead. The unified sensibility, the critic and creative artist joined in one person, became an international ideal.

What are the principles of this modern, cosmopolitan poet-critic? No set of maxims and conventions can do justice to so many varied lessons, promulgated all around the world; and much of the energy of poet-critics, one should always remember, goes into arguing with each other. Yet their arguments often share common assumptions and forms. Even the row-diest battles of poet-critics have a certain coherence, often unintelligible to theorists who stand outside the circle. Inside, the issues seem clear; it ought to be possible to sketch them.

The first principle concerns the function of criticism. In the eyes of almost every poet-critic, a criticism worthy of the name must *intervene* in poetry. Critics who are not poets may well regard their function as essentially descriptive and objective. When such critics write essays on poet-critics, for instance, they may do so without taking any stand on whether poets ought to be critics, whether the results have been healthy or unhealthy for the creation of poetry, or whether the practice ought to be continued in the future. This lack of firm recommendations might be regarded as a sign of scholarly impartiality or merely as wishy-washy. At any rate, not many poet-critics remain so aloof. Their criticism tends to offer a programme, to issue directives for what poetry ought to be. The history of verse is no more distant or neutral, in such an analysis, than the raging controversies of the present; both must be put to use. Despite Eliot's support for an 'impersonal theory of poetry', in 'Tradition and the Individual Talent' (1919), he assumes that every real poet actively inter-venes in the progress of verse, changing the whole existing order with each new work of art. Thus 'the historical sense', which makes a writer tradi-tional, also 'makes a writer most acutely conscious of his place in time, of his own contemporaneity' (p. 4). It is that contemporaneity, that deliber-ate effort to modify the ways that poets think about their art, which gives Eliot his view of tradition or what might be called his moral: 'What is to be insisted upon is that the poet must develop or procure the consciousness of the past and that he should continue to develop this consciousness throughout his career.' Some critics have interpreted this statement, and the essay in which it appears, as a theory of tradition. Eliot himself, however, called it a doctrine, or more explicitly 'my programme for the *métier* of poetry' (p. 6). The poet-critic wants to change the poetry he looks at.

This interventionism may be as old as criticism itself, but modern poet-critics have carried it to new heights. Apparently many writers regard the effort to become a poet as identical with the effort to formulate a new programme for poetry. The manifesto offers public evidence for this urge. Perhaps a more lasting, more private sort of evidence, however, occurs in those peculiar works where poems alternate with criticism. There is no good word to describe such works (though 'initiation' may be serviceable)[12] but they have spread through the modern period like leaves of grass. Dante's *Vita Nuova* provides a model: the writer gathers a group of his poems together, explains the circumstances of their composition, demonstrates how each should be interpreted, works out the secret significance of his career to that point, and predicts the future course of his new life. No later author has used exactly the same form. Nevertheless, Dante's method of self-reading has influenced a great many other works, sometimes explicitly (as in Yeats's *Per Amica Silentia Lunae*, 1918), sometimes more indirectly (as in Joyce's *Portrait of the Artist as a Young Man*, 1914). The clear division between creation and criticism vanishes in such writings. They initiate the writer himself, as well as his interpreters, into new modes of reading, in which an early work may suddenly turn into the prefiguration of work yet to come, while the problems of the age are converted into facsimiles of the writer's own fresh self-understanding. The poet-critic teaches us how to read by teaching himself. And the principles that are discovered issue forth not only in critical readings but in a sense of poems still forming and yet to be written.

These works are protean in form. Quite frequently they draw on diaries or journals, where the sequence of entries can provide a context for emerging poems, while the poems and commentaries together compose an artistic autobiography. Such journals have been especially popular in Spanish. Juan Ramón Jiménez' important *Diary of a Newly Married Poet* (1916), for instance, mixes verse with short prose poems that suggest a decisive turn toward a new poetics; its influence is reflected in García Lorca's *Poet in New York*. The last part of Joyce's *Portrait*, with its narrative of the birth of a villanelle, its intense aesthetic discussions, and its concluding journal entries, records a fictional initiation. So does Rilke's *Notebooks of Malte Laurids Brigge* (1910), which has always been recognised as less a novel than a visionary antechamber where memories are stored and future poems are begotten. If prose like Rilke's verges on poetry, verse like Pound's 'Hugh Selwyn Mauberley' (1921) sometimes plays deliberately with prose, as in its famous opening: 'For three years, out of key with his time, / He strove to resuscitate the dead art / Of poetry; to maintain 'the sublime' / In the old sense. Wrong from the start –' (p. 187). Pound both mocks and shares in the search for a better poetics.

[12] 'Initiation' is the term used for this genre by Lipking in *The Life of the Poet* (pp. 13–64), which focuses on Dante, Blake, and Yeats.

Presiding over the end of Aestheticism and the Vortex, he makes way for the style of the *Cantos* and works his critical umbrage into the texture of the verse. 'Mauberley' surpasses Pound's overt manifestos; it performs the initiation for which it calls.

More typically, however, such works remain in process, and the quarrel between the poet and the critic goes on forever. No peace is made between them, for example, in that remarkably mixed-up sally by William Carlos Williams, *Spring and All* (1923). Juggling his chapters freely, suddenly interrupting prose with verse and verse with prose, improvising both form and content, Williams invites the reader to share his problems. The main problem is the relation between prose and poetry, which the little book exemplifies and tirelessly debates. All sorts of ideas pass in review, including the idea that 'no discoverable difference between prose and verse' exists (p. 144). But most of the work insists that 'the cleavage is complete' and that a shift from prose to poetry would usher in a new world of freedom: 'prose: statement of facts concerning emotions, intellectual states, data of all sorts – technical expositions, jargon, of all sorts – fictional and other – // poetry: new form dealt with as a reality in itself' (p. 133). *Spring and All* strains to accomplish that reality. Beginning in hostility and violence, with a reader who hates modern books like the one he finds himself reading and writing, it sprouts a group of poems against the grain and tells us they are SPRING. 'One by one objects are defined –': bushes by the road to the contagious hospital, or a red wheelbarrow. The creation of such poems might certainly be viewed as a triumph, especially in the dark and murderous age that Williams imagines. But the tone of the book is very far from triumphant. Though full of humour, it also seems harried, querulous, impatient – an experiment whose results have burst out of control. Nor do the verse and prose fit smoothly with each other. More often they collide.

Spring and All wants to be jarring. An edgy polemic keeps breaking in, so urgent that Williams frequently does not bother to finish one sentence before skipping to the next. The objects of this polemic are many: prosodic conventions, the greedy ruling class, deracinated intellectuals, all enemies of the imagination. More specifically, however, the book takes aim at an author and work it refuses to mention: Eliot's *Waste Land*. Even the title of *Spring and All* rebels against the Europeanised aridity of Eliot's cruel April of the spirit, as 'the reddish / purplish, forked, upstanding, twiggy / stuff' of 'By the road to the contagious hospital' (p. 95) awakens from the grip of the past. The idea of tradition outrages Williams, who views it as a euphemism for plagiarism. Nor can he abide the notions of the 'symbol' or 'pure poetry'. 'Writing is likened to music. The object would be it seems to make poetry a pure art, like music . . . I do not believe that writing is music. I do not believe writing would gain in quality or force by seeking to attain to the conditions of music... The writer of imagination would attain closest to the conditions of music not when his words are disassociated from natural objects and specified meanings but when they are liberated from the usual quality of that meaning by transposition into another medium, the imagination' (p. 150). Concrete reality, a reality not opposed to imagination but affirming and affirmed by it, must replace the abstraction and elitism of the modern tradition that Eliot had helped to define.[13] Williams does not pretend to know exactly what sort of art he is *for*; that must be discovered through the act of writing poems. Yet he knows quite well what he is *against*. The fury of opposition inspires his book.

Many poet-critics unleash a similar fury. To intervene in poetry calls for a power of destruction as well as creation. Williams does not waste time arguing with tradition and *The Waste Land*; he wants to wipe them off the face of the earth, or at least to clear a space they cannot enter. A more benign critic, such as Northrop Frye, might reasonably maintain that the total order of literature has plenty of room for Eliot as well as Williams, and that the works of both fit comfortably into the archetype of Spring. Poet-critics seldom feel so accepting. The need to seize the initiative, to define the exclusive path that poetry must follow, motivates much of their criticism and closes off alternatives that do not seem productive (as Eliot himself notoriously judged Milton to be a bad influence, 'an influence against which we still have to struggle').[14] History itself must march to their tune. When a very ambitious poet like Ezra Pound writes criticism, it may come to pass that the issues of civilisation, of war and peace and economics and race and the state of the world, collapse into the issue of what ideas can best explain and generate the poems he wants to write. This is a chilling and extreme example, but far from unique. Again and again, during their periods of initiation, poet-critics discover that the course of their development as poets perfectly coincides with the universal history of their times. Eliot's and Williams' rival versions of Spring inscribe not only two different poetic autobiographies but two different interpretations of where the world is going; Spengler battles head to head with Henry Ford. Each version wins what it most wants: the ground on which to write more poems.

If the first principle of many modern poet-critics is not so much to describe poetry as to change it, however, their second principle insists that every significant change must be confirmed by a specific revolution in technique.

---

[13] Williams's antipathy to *The Waste Land* is stated most fully and forcefully in 'An Essay on *Leaves of Grass*' (1955). See also 'The Poem as a Field of Action'.

[14] T. S. Eliot, 'Milton I' (1936), *On Poetry and Poets*, p. 157. Eliot retracted this opinion in 'Milton II' (1947), pp. 181–3.

'Indeed, if technique is of no interest to a writer', Marianne Moore observes, 'I doubt that the writer is an artist'; and the statement would hold with 'critic' and 'poet' inserted for 'writer' and 'artist'. Every poet-critic is concerned with technique, and some are obsessed by it. It distinguishes them from critics who cannot practise the art they talk about; it serves as a point of pride. Moreover, in the early modern period many poets were convinced that they had to invent a technique of their own. Like Eliot's tradition, technique could not be inherited or repeated but must be obtained by great labour. Earlier poet-critics had sometimes written arts of poetry or handbooks to instruct the young. Modern poet-critics tend to be uneasy with such primers. When Rilke writes *Letters to a Young Poet*, for instance, he offers abundant inspiration but almost no practical advice. Technique, the young poet might conclude, is all-important but at the same time personal and untransmittable as sex. Rilke himself compares sex and technique in praising Richard Dehmel: 'his poetic power is great, strong as a primitive instinct; it has its own unyielding rhythms in itself and breaks out of him as out of mountains'. How does one learn such rhythms? Presumably it cannot be done; each true poet must become a mountain (a valley, a constellation) by himself. Yet the mystification of technique does not reduce its importance. Quite the opposite. Achieving it becomes a sign of grace, the inner light that marks one as a poet.

No modern poet-critic wears that sign more openly than Ezra Pound. Technique possesses him. It is the source not only of his self-esteem but of his vision of humanity: 'every man who does his own job really well has a latent respect for every other man who does *his* own job really well; this is our lasting bond; ... the man who really does the thing well, if he be pleased afterwards to talk about it, gets always his auditors' attention; he gets his audience the moment he says something so intimate that it proves him the expert; he does not, as a rule, sling generalities; he gives the particular case for what it is worth; the truth is the individual' ('On Technique', p. 19). This poet-critic exults in his expertise. Yet he also wants to share it, in a Ruskinian guild of craftsmen, each an artist in his or her own sphere, that might eventually take in all the world. A certain contempt for those who are *merely* critics crops up often in Pound. 'If you wanted to know something about an automobile, would you go to a man who had made one and driven it, or to a man who had merely heard about it?' (*ABC*, p. 30). The honest mechanic excels the armchair theoretician. Perhaps some defensiveness colours this view; Pound had good reason to be afraid of professors. But he did go out of his way to impart his mastery of technique. In addition to Eliot, the star pupil, a generation of the best American poets went to his school. When Eliot said that no other poet-critic had been 'so consistently concerned with teaching others how to write', when he contended that 'Pound's critical writings, scattered and occasional as they have been, form the *least indispensable* body of critical writing in our time',[15] he was expressing the gratitude of many poets beside himself.

What Pound passed on, however, seems less a teaching of technique than a technique of teaching. The point may be clarified by looking at his favourite anecdote, Agassiz and the fish, which begins the *ABC of Reading* (1934). The great zoologist hands a postgraduate student a small fish and tells him to describe it. The student returns with some textbook definitions. Again Agassiz tells him to describe the fish. The student produces a four-page essay, and is told once more to look at the fish. 'At the end of three weeks the fish was in an advanced state of decomposition, but the student knew something about it' (p. 18). That, for Pound, exemplifies the method of modern science and ought to be the basis of all teaching. But what exactly has been taught? Nothing, apparently, except the necessity of looking. The last section of the *ABC*, its 'Treatise on Meter', preaches a similar moral: 'The answer is: LISTEN to the sound that it makes' (p. 201). One should not underestimate the value of this technique, in the hands of a respected master who convinces disciples that they too will be ruthlessly looked at and listened to. Yet the method is also very coercive, laying claims to objectivity while actually forcing the student to guess what sort of answer will satisfy the teacher. For teachers do want a specific something (not how the fish *smells*, for instance), and students find what they go looking for. To pass the course, Pound's disciples had to discover modern poetics. They learned how to do this less by grasping principles than by imitating Pound.

A similar point might be made about much of the technical instruction so favoured by many modern poet-critics. From one perspective, self-consciousness about poetic technique may look like the major advance of twentieth-century criticism. Not many critics of the past seem capable of the acts of sustained attention – not so much to the meanings of poems as to their structures, patterns of sound and language – that we take for granted in the best modern critics. Poet-critics led the way to these advances, for instance in the feats of structural analysis by Russian and Czech formalists or in the methods of close reading associated with the New Criticism in America. From another perspective, however, this emphasis on technique looks deceptive. In practice its seeming objectivity endorsed some styles over others and ignored techniques that fell outside its circle. Thus some New Critics taught students to read every literary genre as if it were a short metaphysical lyric like those of Donne or Ransom, and formalists have been accused of reducing Tolstoy to a few

[15] These remarks appear in the introduction to Pound's *Literary Essays*, ed. T. S. Eliot (New York, 1954), p. xiii.

mannerisms. These charges may not be fair, but they do expose a real problem: the potential of the study of technique for latent partiality and bias. It is exactly in discussing technique that poet-critics tend to reveal their strongest personal and ideological commitments. 'Technique', according to Pound, 'is the only gauge and test of a man's lasting sincerity' ('On Technique', p. 20). That may be why Pound and other poet-critics so frequently equivocate on how one acquires technique, as if it had to be experienced to be understood. Discussing the way that poems are made, they are also nakedly telling us who they are.

Some poet-critics even identify technique with their own bodies and spirits. Free verse, according to D. H. Lawrence, should be 'direct utterance from the instant, whole man. It is the soul and the mind and body surging together, nothing left out' (*Selected Literary Criticism*, p. 87). And formal verse too is driven by biology, the quasi-sexual coupling of Love and Law: 'The very adherence to rhyme and regular rhythm is a concession to the Law, a concession to the body, to the being and requirements of the body. They are an admission of the living, positive inertia which is the other half of life, other than the pure will to motion. In this consummation, they are the resistance and response of the Bride in the arms of the Bridegroom' (p. 187). Lawrence's analyses of technique search for 'the hidden *emotional* pattern' that makes the form (p. 80). Similarly, Williams spent much of his life trying to derive poetry from 'the peculiar, actual conformations in which its life is hid', as a physician tries to detect the nature of a disease by charting its physical symptoms. Hence his approval of 'projective verse', which Charles Olson based partly on Williams's own formulations. 'Verse now, 1950, if it is to go ahead, if it is to be of *essential* use, must, I take it, catch up and put into itself certain laws and possibilities of the breath, of the breathing of the man who writes as well as of his listenings' (Olson, 'Projective Verse', p. 147). Williams and his disciples work to vitalise the line, a rhythmical unit organically tied to the pulsing of breath and blood. Technique, conceived in such terms, is a part of living. But it also lays claim to a larger relation to nature, as if it touched or caressed what Ransom calls 'the world's body'. Poetry, such poets contend, is all that modern people have to remind them of the reality of things in their individual, unabstracted, untechnological being. 'We are lucky when that underground current can be tapped and the secret spring of all our lives will send up its pure water', according to Williams. Technique is the force that opens that spring to the surface.

If technique can do so much, it promises a kind of salvation. Not all poet-critics endorse that view; and Eliot frequently warned against the danger of confusing poetry with religion. Nevertheless, many modern poet-critics do mount a fervent defence of their art, a case for its usefulness or even necessity in times when the majority of people remain indifferent to it. Poetry must be saved; perhaps it can save us. That is a third principle that modern poet-critics tend to share. They do not take the survival of their art for granted. As critics, therefore, they come to its rescue with arguments not only for particular poems but for poetry as a way of life. To be sure, poetry had been imperilled in earlier times as well. The apology for poetry is a venerable form, perhaps as old as criticism itself. When Socrates considered barring poets from his republic, Athens did not lack passionate lovers of poetry to oppose him. Indeed, if Western philosophy consists of footnotes to Plato, as some philosophers still maintain, a critic might equally argue that Western literary criticism consists of rebuttals to Plato. Nor have all attacks on poetry been restricted to theory. Throughout history, not only philosophers but clergymen and autocrats have waged war on the poet. If an age lacks an apology for poetry, it is less likely to be an age when poets are safe from attack than one in which they have been completely suppressed. Many poets, like Thomas Gray, identify with the Welsh bards – chieftains and outlaws – slaughtered by Edward the First. Hence poet-critics are often engaged in fighting for their lives. In this respect, at least, the modern poet-critic follows tradition.

The line of defence went through a subtle change, however, in modern times. One way of describing the change would be to stress the antagonism of modern poets to any notion of utility or public service. In the past, apologists for poetry used to claim that it performed a vital social function, instructing as well as delighting the literate citizen, refining behaviour, and imagining perfect worlds toward which humanity might aspire. Thus the enemies of poetry could always be viewed as foes to the true interests of society. The Welsh bards might be rebels against Edward, but that was because they served as souls of the people, reminding them of what their nation ought to be. Good kings should cherish poets. Insofar as poetry failed to live up to this ideal (as Sidney and others conceded), the fault lay in decadent artists, not in the holy art. But modern poets seldom apologise for what they do. Instead their defences aggressively seize the high ground, celebrating art and the artist for their lack of social utility and their resistance to authority. The modern poet-critic prefers not to make friends with people in power. At one extreme, as in the first *Manifesto of Surrealism*, not only authority but existence itself turns into the *bête noire*. 'Surrealism, such as I conceive of it, asserts our complete *nonconformism* clearly enough so that there can be no question of translating it, at the trial of the real world, as evidence for the defense. It could, on the contrary, only serve to justify the complete state of distraction which we hope to achieve here below' (Breton, *Manifestoes*, p. 47). Never apologise, never explain; the real world, not the poet, is the accused that must go on trial.

The pressure not to conform weighs heavily on modern poet-critics. Even someone as hostile to dissent as T. S. Eliot takes pride in resisting the orthodoxies of British poetic practice in his time; and when he describes his own work he leans, however reluctantly, to some analogy with being mystically possessed, 'this disturbance of our quotidian character which results in an incantation, an outburst of words which we hardly recognise as our own' (*Use of Poetry*, p. 138). Other poet-critics feel less diffident about acknowledging their disdain for the everyday world. When Rilke observes the visible things of this world, they press and beseech him to translate them into the realm of the invisible; to shoulder that burden is to become a poet. In this sense poetry does preserve reality, but only by rendering it intangible, eternal, and ideal. Such poets compete to be more unworldy than others – lighter than air. Thus the wonderful letters exchanged by Rilke, Pasternak, and Marina Tsvetayeva offer both detailed practical criticism and a mutual alliance against the inertia of being, the vegetable existence that drags spirit down. A modern poet labours to escape. Immediately after Rilke's death, Tsvetayeva wrote Pasternak that if she had met the late great poet, 'I would have balked and kicked and struggled free, Boris, because, after all, it is still *this world*. Oh, Boris, Boris! How well I know the other one! From dreams, from the ambient air of dreams, from the density, the essentiality of dreams. And how little I know of this one, how much I dislike it, and how hurt I have been by it! But the other one – just fancy! – light, radiance, things illuminated quite *differently*, with your light and mine!' (*Letters*, p. 209). Exile becomes such poets. Their art reproaches the society that tortures them and it requires no defence. Indeed, the virtue of poetry, from this point of view, consists exactly of its indifference to everything the world values: happiness, morals, power. According to Tsvetayeva, a true poet listens only to what is important, and she prays constantly to be deaf to the lures of comfort and material success. 'In this realm the poet can have only one prayer: not to understand the unacceptable – let me not understand, so that I may not be seduced. The sole prayer of the poet is not to hear the voices: let me not hear, so that I may not answer' (*Art*, p. 174).

The prayer of modern poet-critics to be deaf to the world has been granted many times over. Earlier poets had also rejected matter-of-factness; some Romantics especially valued poetry for its otherworldly visions or its elevation of desire over reason. Yet most Romantics share the hope that their visions might inspire or help to construct a better society. Wordsworth fancied that his poems would 'excite profitable sympathies in many kind and good hearts' and thus bring rich people to the relief of the poor; and Shelley, who thought that the spirit of the poet creates the spirit of the age, proclaimed that 'poets are the unacknowledged legislators of the world'. Modern poet-critics seldom harbour such optimistic

political aspirations. With rare exceptions, such as D'Annunzio and Sen-
ghor, they shrink from legislation; when they vote, they almost always
vote No. This scorn for politics-as-usual did not inoculate writers against
infection by the extremism and fanaticism of twentieth-century political
conflicts.[16] Contemptuous of modern democracies and technological advances, such poet-critics as Yeats, George, Claudel, Pound, Eliot, and the
Southern Agrarians sought refuge in dreams of the past, and others, such
as Mayakovsky, Aragon, Neruda, and Césaire, in the utopias of a Communist future. Nor did encounters with reality necessarily break the spell
of their ambitions. Despite their frustrations with politics and parties, the
symbolists and surrealists believed at times that they were discovering
nothing less than an alternative universe and a new human race. Mallarmé's absolute book aimed to capture the world, and Breton planted his
flag in the universal unconscious. No legislator could wish for a more total
control of the future. But the world never noticed that it had been
captured by a book, and insofar as the surrealists succeeded in expressing
the unconscious, they brought it dangerously close to consciousness. In
any case, such defences of poetry gain their ground by tacitly conceding
that they will not interfere in matters that do not concern them – not even
the matter of what most people want to read. This strategy avoids the risk
of retaliation. In many Western countries, poetry has no apparent enemies, if only because those in power have never recognised poetry as
something that might threaten their interests. Who would question Rilke's
right to consort with angels? Unworldly poets need not fear the censor.

    This strategy worked out less well in other countries, however, where
poetry did have enemies and censors were strong. Notoriously, in the old
Soviet Union poetry mattered so much that people died for it. This casts a
different light on poetic defences. Writing just after the Revolution, Mandelstam could experience both the danger and the exhilaration of the
struggle in which, as a poet, he had to be caught. 'Social differences and
class antagonisms pale before the new division of people into friends and
enemies of the word: literally, sheep and goats. I sense an almost physical-
ly unclean goat-breath emanating from the enemies of the word' ('The
Word and Culture', p. 113). That smell continued to grow until it choked
him. In such times of trouble (not only in the Soviet Union) the poet-critic
must fight too hard for existence to indulge in the luxury of dismissing it.
Yet Mandelstam did use the modern weapons: a sense of poetry as the
most revolutionary of all activities, and an infinite disdain for the state and
its henchmen. Identifying totally with the word, he thinks of the poet as
the ultimate conscience of humanity, invincible even when martyred. 'The

---

[16] The contradictions and self-deceptions involved in the efforts of writers to aestheticise
    political issues have preoccupied many late twentieth-century literary scholars (Terry
    Eagleton, for example).

life of the word has entered a heroic era. The word is flesh and bread. It shares the fate of bread and flesh: suffering. People are hungry. The State is even hungrier. But there is something still hungrier: Time. Time wants to devour the State' (p. 115). And only the poet has an appetite as ravenous as time's.

Such extreme situations help to reveal what is at stake in modern defences of poetry. The value of poetry, for most of its champions, might be defined almost entirely in negative terms. The poet stands for everything that resists domination – the domination of the state, of reason, science, consciousness, abstraction – of parties and tyrannies of every kind – or even of existence. This elemental resistance takes many forms: conservative or radical, nonsensical or profound, principled or instinctive. A modern poet-critic hardly needs to pause for reflection, as Tsvetayeva notes: 'When, at the age of thirteen, I asked an old revolutionary: "Is it possible to be a poet and also be in the Party?", he replied, without a moment's thought: "No."' . . . So I too shall reply: no' (*Art*, p. 174). To be a poet, such a writer may have to sacrifice everything else. Yet the act of renunciation also implies a positive value. In the words of Wallace Stevens, 'Resistance to the pressure of ominous and destructive circumstance consists of its conversion, so far as possible, into a different, an explicable, an amenable circumstance' ('Irrational Element', p. 789).

What is that better circumstance? Stevens calls it 'freedom'. The special value of modern poetry, from this point of view, depends on its irrepressible spirit, its declaration of universal independence. Nor is such freedom a limited, negative virtue, meaningful only when in the presence of some restraint to oppose – mere freedom *from*. Instead, Stevens argues, the search for artistic freedom goes hand in hand with the rage for order, the intense and specific demands of art itself. 'It is not that nobody cares. It matters immensely. The slightest sound matters. The most momentary rhythm matters. You can do as you please, yet everything matters. You are free, but your freedom must be consonant with the freedom of others' (*ibid*). Conceived in such terms, poetry represents at once the utmost range of freedom and the most severe test of freedom as a way of life.

These had not been the terms of defence in earlier ages. Although Kant may have laid the groundwork, in defining the 'disinterestedness' of aesthetic judgement and the autonomy or 'purposiveness without purpose' of the work of art, he and his followers gave little weight to the revolutionary potential of art, its power to change the world. Modern poet-critics claim more for freedom. Sometimes they envision a gradual encroachment of the invisible on the visible, as if poetic passion could make all things transparent; sometimes they insist that this liberation has already taken place, unknown to property owners, and that all the earth need only be looked at through the eyes of art in order to *be* art. More modestly, many poets think of themselves as explorers. To quote Stevens once more: 'If we say that we desire freedom when we are already free, it seems clear that we have in mind a freedom not previously experienced. Yet is not this an attitude toward life resembling the poet's attitude toward reality? In spite of the cynicisms that occur to us as we hear of such things, a freedom not previously experienced, a poetry not previously conceived of, may occur with the suddenness inherent in poetic metamorphosis. For poets, that possibility is the ultimate obsession' (p. 790).

The defence of poetry as at once the freest of all activities and the unfolding of the secret laws that govern freedom has been repeated often in the modern era. To some extent this double purpose represents the poet-critic's own divided nature. The artist recognises no constraints; the critic sees them everywhere, even in the gestures where freedom is asserted. Internal arguments such as these have proved to be fruitful. The fact that so many of the best poets and critics of the early modern period are poet-critics lends plausibility to Valéry's dictum that 'every poet will *finally* be worth what he has been worth as a critic (of himself)'.[17] Anyone born a poet, this implies, should set to work at fashioning a critic. But Valéry does not regard criticism as merely an aid to creation. When he mounts a defence, it is not for the sake of poetry itself. 'I couldn't care less about poetry', he once told Gide. 'It only interests me by a fluke!' (quoted in Hytier, *Poetics of Paul Valéry*, p. 12). Instead, what interests him essentially is poetics – not simply the theory of poetry but an adventure of thought in which the act of making the poem and the activity of thinking about it play equal parts. In this respect Valéry is the model of a modern poet-critic – not exactly a poet, not exactly a critic, but primarily both at once. He aspires to a condition in which the mind contemplates its own works even as they take form. This is not without risk; a shadow of self-consciousness looms over his project, threatening to paralyse any creative impulse. 'Achilles cannot outrun the tortoise if he thinks of space and time', and the poet cannot perform his acts while analysing them. Yet the poet-critic hopes to be rewarded by something even more valuable than a poem: an insight into the poetic state of mind. 'One may take so keen an interest in this curiosity and attach so high an importance to pursuing it that in the end, perhaps, one will look with greater pleasure and even passion upon *the act of making* than upon *the thing made*' (13:92–3). A fascination with that act of making is what Valéry calls poetics.

Many of the problems that interest him most, therefore, address the poem less as product than as process. At times Valéry seems quite indiffer-

---

[17] 'Tout poète vaudra *enfin* ce qu'il aura valu comme critique (de soi)' (Valéry, *Œuvres* 2:483). *Collected Works* is the source of page references in the text unless they are otherwise identified.

ent to the mere thing made. Its spurious tangibility represents an illusion to him, the fallacy committed by readers but not by writers that a work can be finished. 'The decision that writes *finis* to a work can only be extraneous, alien to the work itself ... In fact the completion of a work is no more than a surrender, a halt that may always be regarded as fortuitous, in a development that might have continued indefinitely' (13:126). Even language reflects this perpetual artistic postponement of closure; it is anything but a coincidence, from the workman's point of view, that Latin *opus*, French *œuvre*, and English *work* should all refuse to distinguish the product that art has made from the labour that went into its making. What counts is the *work*, not the fixed image congealing on a canvas or sheet. Similarly, Valéry prizes the notion that art and thought alike are *exercise*, ways of putting the faculties into play without straining after some definite result. The poet-critic ignores the vulgar teleology of the single-minded poet whose labour is forced to culminate in a realised poem, or of the single-minded critic whose self-definition demands consummate judgements and valid interpretations. On the contrary, a poet-critic's destination must lie in the journey itself. He is thus more free than either a poet or critic, and more empowered to defend the freedom of art.

It follows that Valéry's heroes are heroes of thought. Despite his own reputation as a masterly poet and critic, he does not idolise poets and critics. Even those poets closest to his heart, like Poe and Mallarmé, seem valued less for their accomplishments than for their experimental methods. Typically, when Valéry translates Poe he chooses fragments from the *Marginalia* and decks them with his own marginal gloss to adumbrate a theory of the mind as an incessant, self-reflexive compiler of notes.[18] 'The essential object of the mind is the mind. What it pursues in its analyses and its construction of worlds, what it tracks down in heaven and on earth, can only be itself' (8:182). Poe's theoretical project, the effort to chart the laws of aesthetics with mathematical precision, interests Valéry far more than Poe's works of art. Other heroes of thought loom even larger: at first Leonardo, and later Descartes. Each of them represents a magnificent, doomed effort to carry the most rigorous principles of science and logic into the realms of art and the soul, where men of less mind might think that science did not belong. Valéry does not often use the phrase 'a great poet', but he uses it for Descartes. The philosopher had dared to confront the most difficult problem of language, its reference to mental phenomena that cannot be defined except through the mind that recreates them, and had turned it into an inexhaustible resource. '*Thought, mind* itself, *reason, intelligence, understanding, intuition*, or *inspiration*? ... Each of these terms is both a means and an end in turn, a

[18] Relations between Valéry's theories of glossing and mind are analysed by Lawrence Lipking, 'The Marginal Gloss', *Critical Inquiry*, 3 (1977), pp. 609–55.

problem and a solution, a state and an idea; and each of them, in each of us, is adequate or inadequate according to the function which circumstances impose on it. You are aware that at this point the philosopher becomes a poet, and often a great poet: he borrows metaphor from us and, by means of splendid images which we might well envy, he draws on all nature for the expression of his profoundest thought' (9:19). Poets as well as poet-critics ought to envy this achievement. Converting all the world into a metaphor for mind, Descartes had made, if not a poem, at least the most far-reaching of poetics.

Valéry's defence of poetics aims similarly at transfiguring the world. Unlike Romantic, symbolist, or surrealist defences, which characteristically opposed the methods of poetry to those of science, his ideal of art envisions a rapprochement of consciousness and sensibility – Monsieur and Madame Teste at home with each other. A true poetics, like a true poet-critic, will appreciate both the immediacy of sensuous experience and the adventure of pure thought. Only the human being capable of criticism as well as poetry can attain that state of absolute freedom where existence itself becomes an object of curiosity and pleasure, grist for the mill of the mind. Once again Descartes offers a model. 'The properly organised consciousness turns everything to account. Everything contributes to its detachment; everything serves to engage it; it stops at nothing. The more relationships it absorbs, or endures, the more closely integrated it is and the freer and more flexible it becomes. A mind completely *connected* would certainly be, at this extreme, a mind infinitely *free*, because in the last resort freedom is simply the use of the *possible*, and the essence of the mind is a desire to be at one with its whole potential' (9:11). The sense of that potential is what Valéry loves; and he loves poetry only for its sake. But since poetry exemplifies the desire and struggle of the mind to realise its potential, the poet-critic cannot resist its lure. The mind needs a world of things and feelings to tame – the world as a poem might conceive it. Thus a science of science would prove far less instructive than a science of art, since ultimately the slippery realm of art can never be fixed in words. Valéry's consciousness goes on forever, reflecting whatever it likes and stopping at nothing. Quite comfortable with obscurity and infinity, it is capable of regarding anything, even its own reality or being, as merely provisional. Hence poetry finds its best defence or refuge in the mind of the poet-critic, where even the poet's need to create and the critic's to judge may be disarmed for the moment. Only the process itself abides. That is where Valéry finds his delight and his freedom.

The elevation of poetics above the arts of poetry and criticism from which it rose represents an extreme position. Not many poet-critics agree with such high-mindedness, and Valéry's influence has lately been quite restricted. Yet the prominence and authority of modern poet-critics do seem to have challenged the old divisions between those who practise an art and those who explain it. Traditionally, even the best of critics acknowledged the priority of poets. Though the critical powers of Samuel Johnson surely surpassed the power of much of the verse he judged, nonetheless he believed that criticism 'is only to be ranked among the subordinate and instrumental arts'.[19] Most poets still insist on this distinction: the poem comes first, the critic trails in its wake. But Valéry is not the only modern critic or poet-critic or critic-poet to condemn such discrimination. The critic, Wilde said in artistic prose, should strive to be an artist, or more than an artist; and the host of early twentieth-century poets who write bravura criticism furnish the proof. Nor is it always clear that they are better poets in their verse than in their prose. Sometimes the critic appears more original and inventive than the poet; sometimes the two merge.

Consider Yeats's example. No one (I think) would consider his criticism equal to his verse; and some might argue that his critical writing, like the automatic writing of his mystical instructors in *A Vision*, came only to give him metaphors for poetry. But Yeats himself often proselytised for the cause of the poet-critic or poet-philosopher, who alone could prepare the way for great art: 'It has often been this philosophy, or this criticism, that has evoked their most startling inspiration' ('Symbolism of Poetry', p. 154). Early in his career he seems to have thought that a theory derived from symbolism could bring about a poetic revolution: 'With this change of substance, this return to imagination, this understanding that the laws of art, which are the hidden laws of the world, can alone bind the imagination, would come a change of style' (p. 163). Yeats wants laws to *bind* the imagination, laws passed from critics to poets. And even after this early hope had faded, he never gave up looking for such laws. Yeats refuses on principle to segregate poetry from prose. He writes the prose of a poet, often in a language far more gorgeous than the style of his verse, nor is he ashamed to pick out choice bits and embed them in poems. But his most notorious conflation of criticism and poetry was his selection of a piece of criticism, arranged as *vers libre*, to open *The Oxford Book of Modern Verse*. Pater's description of Mona Lisa foreshadowed, Yeats argued, 'a poetry, a philosophy, where the individual is nothing, the flux of *The Cantos* of Ezra Pound' ('Introduction', p. xxx); it had led the revolt against Victorianism and gained the 'entire uncritical admiration' of a new generation (p. viii). The word 'uncritical' is interesting here. Yeats

---

[19] Samuel Johnson, *The Rambler* 208. Randall Jarrell's well-known essay, 'The Age of Criticism', complains that modern critics have reversed the priorities. 'Once, talking to a young critic, I said as a self-evident thing, "Of course, criticism's necessarily secondary to the works of art it's about." He looked at me as if I had kicked him, and said: "Oh, that's not so!"' (*Poetry and the Age* (New York, 1953), p. 84).

means no disrespect to criticism; it was exactly the critical attitude taught by Pater, putting not only moral pieties but life itself to the question, that captivated the young. The older Yeats keeps a certain critical distance, however. Perhaps he vibrates more to Pater's rhythms than to his philosophy; perhaps he regards the 'pure gem-like flame' as a little passé. But Yeats never gave up his search for a sage, or a medium, whose wisdom could inform his verse and turn it into something more: a poetry to criticise the modern world, a poem on fire with intellect and vision. The greatest poet, in his view, must be a poet-critic.

What happened to this quest? It did not die as the dreams of the modern age faded. Some poets continued to write fine criticism, and in the 1960s Octavio Paz (himself a major poet-critic) went so far as to maintain that 'in our time criticism is the cornerstone of literature. As literature comes to be a criticism of words and the world, a self-questioning, criticism comes to look upon literature as a world of words, as a verbal universe. Creation is criticism and criticism creation.'[20] Critics tended to find that view congenial. As 'beautiful theories' proliferated, during the second half of the twentieth century, the line between theory and art was increasingly smudged. A set of critical commonplaces – at least among critics – assumed that poetry had yielded the initiative to criticism, that each could be equally 'literary', and that the supposed priority of poetic over critical acts survived as nothing but an outworn hierarchical myth. The strength of imagination and intellect is manifested, in this view, by the writing itself, not the form that it happens to take. Far from being subordinate to poets, in an age when theory ascended, many theorists scarcely noticed poems. Nor had they any cause to bow before 'creative writing' – 'creation is criticism and criticism creation'. If poet-critics seem less prominent in the postmodern era than in 'classic modern' times, therefore, perhaps the reason is simply that the hyphen broke down, so that the distinction between poets and critics no longer needed to be bridged. That would be one explanation.

A more plausible explanation might begin from the premise that the gap between poets and critics has widened. Through the 1950s a preponderance of the most influential critics of poetry were themselves poets – critic-poets if not poet-critics. Even in academia, the literary criticism of a poet such as Eliot carried far more weight than that of any academic, and the cutting edge of criticism, especially but not uniquely in the United States, was wielded by such poets as Ransom, Tate, Richards, Winters,

---

[20] Octavio Paz, 'On Criticism', *Alternating Current*, tr. Helen Lane, p. 39. Sometimes Paz regards the relation between criticism and creation as 'symbiosis', sometimes as 'contradiction' (see *Children of the Mire: Modern Poetry from Romanticism to the Avant-Garde*, tr. Rachel Phillips (Cambridge, Mass., 1974)).

Jarrell, and Blackmur. By 1960 that had begun to change. The acclaim for Northrop Frye's *Anatomy of Criticism*, published in 1957, marks a decisive watershed, which systematically severs the poet and critic. 'The axiom of criticism must be, not that the poet does not know what he is talking about, but that he cannot talk about what he knows. To defend the right of criticism to exist at all, therefore, is to assume that criticism is a structure of thought and knowledge existing in its own right, with some measure of independence from the art it deals with' (p. 5). Here Frye extends the notion of the intentional fallacy from the poet's (mis)interpretation of particular poems to the poet's (mis)understanding of poetry as a whole. A poet-critic, on this view, would be a contradiction in terms – sometimes a poet, sometimes a critic, but never both at once.[21] Criticism stakes its claim as an autonomous art and science. Frye's book works out the schematic implications of this autonomy and posits a theory divorced from the experiences of any individual artist. Many later theorists take that divorce for granted. Moreover, the theoretical divide between poet and critic has been accompanied by practical divisions. Though more and more poets teach in universities, they usually teach 'creative writing', and fewer and fewer make a stir as critics. Poets and critics often occupy separate departments. Hence poet-critics, though far from extinct, may be an endangered species.

One result of this division has been a rewriting of the history of literary criticism. Not long ago, any survey of early modern criticism would routinely have included a host of poet-critics. When Wimsatt and Brooks published their short history of *Literary Criticism* in 1957, the year of Frye's *Anatomy*, poet-critics dominated the volume, in spite of Wimsatt's well-known opposition to crediting the authority of poets. More recently, the rising emphasis on theory has tended to wipe poets out. In volume eight of *The Cambridge History of Literary Criticism* (1995), for example, poet-critics are virtually invisible. Similarly, in current anthologies of earlier criticism Saussure replaces Valéry as a precursor and Rilke's thoughts on poetry count less than Heidegger's.[22] Whatever the justice of

---

[21] 'The union of poet and critic is not necessarily good for either poetry or criticism', according to Wellek. The 'few shining examples of great poet-critics' did not unify poetry and criticism; 'rather they managed somehow to alternate' them and 'were poets at one moment and critics at another' ('The Poet as Critic, the Critic as Poet, the Poet-Critic', *The Poet as Critic*, ed. Frederick McDowell (Evanston, Ill., 1967), p. 107).

[22] Two anthologies published in 1972, *20th Century Literary Criticism*, ed. David Lodge (London, 1972), and *Modern Literary Criticism 1900–1970*, ed. Lawrence Lipking and A. Walton Litz (New York, 1972), put a heavy emphasis on poet-critics, particularly in the early twentieth century; Lipking and Litz begin with extensive selections from Pound and Eliot and end with a section devoted to fourteen poet-critics. By comparison, two weighty anthologies published in 1998, *Contemporary Literary Criticism*, fourth edition, ed. Robert Con Davis and Ronald Schleifer (New York, 1998), and *Literary Theory: An Anthology*, ed. Julie Rivkin and Michael Ryan (Oxford, 1998), include no poet-critics except for Eliot (the first selection in Davis and Schleifer) and a few women grouped under

such verdicts, they subtly modify the reader's sense of the past, translating early modern criticism into a by-product of developments in linguistics and philosophy. That was not what writers and readers thought was happening at the time. The revolution in poetics that inspired so many twentieth-century critics was sparked by poets thinking about their art. This self-reflection has been neglected in recent years, but it still offers an alternative way of writing the history of criticism. Moreover, it is likely to be revived whenever a new revolution in poetics comes along to inspire a new group of poet-critics. Those critics will discover ancestors.

The legacy of modern poet-critics is hardly uniform, however. Collectively they manifest not only the interconnections of poetry and criticism but also the friction between them. Indeed, the usefulness of such internal strife may be the most valuable lesson a poet-critic can teach. Many of the best modern poets feel uncomfortable practising criticism, and many of the best modern critics feel unsure about the place of poetry in the contemporary world; they cannot resolve these strains. Nevertheless, they can put them to work. If the greatest poets are often critics in spite of themselves, their criticism still helps make their poems what they are. Such explorers test, as no one else can, the validity of theories about poetry – what they account for when they succeed, and also what they leave out when they fail. The perspectives of poet-critics helped form the consciousness of modern times. No history of criticism can be complete without them.

'Feminism' (in Rivkin and Ryan, who also include some women novelists in a section on 'Ethnic Studies, Post-Coloniality, and International Studies').

20

Criticism of fiction

Michael Levenson

It would be tempting to cast a chapter on the 'Criticism of Fiction' in the form of its own continuous narrative, and as will shortly appear, the history between 1900 and 1960 does have a plausible beginning and a recognisable middle. But it has no coherent end. In the early years of this century serious reflection on the novel was largely the province of novelist-critics who developed a working theory of fiction based on the exigencies of creative activity, and the first phase of the exposition to follow will trace the unsteady development of critical principles as they emerged not only out of literary practice but also out of heated polemical exchange. Indeed a notable feature of the modern consideration of narrative art is that when it passed from the hands of the novelists into the hands of the professors, it continued to bear the imprint of the local controversies that originally set the terms of discussion. The struggle to free a conception of the novel from narrow partisanship makes a large part of the later history of the problem, but instead of providing a denouement for the conceptual drama, it prepares for the radical transformations of the last decades of the century.

The extraordinary range and wearying quantity of criticism of the novel means that several regions of fruitful thought must be neglected or tautly paraphrased. My hope is that a focus on a particular web of figures and concepts will let us see the inner design of the Anglo-American critical bearing during a period when it remained strikingly impervious to outside influences. A last preliminary word: no weight will be placed upon the distinction between 'fiction' and 'novel', or the distinction between 'criticism' and 'theory'. Useful discriminations could be made, but the terms are so loosely employed by the writers under discussion that it would make for endless complication to try to preserve terminological hygiene.

At the beginning of his essay on 'The Art of Fiction' (1884, 1888), Henry James remarked that until very recently the English novel had 'no air of having a theory, a conviction, a consciousness of itself behind it', and fifteen years later he would note that the novel has arrived 'late at self-consciousness; but it has done its utmost ever since to make up for lost opportunities' ('The Future of the Novel'). It gradually becomes clear that when James speaks of the new self-consciousness, he chiefly has in mind his own self-consciousness. This is pardonable pride given the role he played in the emerging line of critical inquiry. Through the eighties and nineties he criticised as he created, but it was not until the first decade of the twentieth century, when he undertook the series of prefaces for the New York edition of his work, that he established the concerns and styles that would dominate so much subsequent consideration of the novel and that earns him a place at the beginnings of this history.

What distinguishes James's bearing in the prefaces is not simply the unprecedented concentration on the finer anatomy of storytelling but also a heightened awareness of the act of criticism itself. 'There is the story of one's hero', he writes, and then there is 'the story of one's story itself'. In telling these second-level narratives, he weaves three major emphases. The first is what he calls 'the general adventure of one's intelligence', namely the author's quest for a subject and pursuit of a form. But for James the memory of his creative experience is not the memory of visionary recognitions; there are no opium dreams here. There is only the lucidity of the craftsman relishing the difficulty of the task. Certainly what James offered most immediately to his Anglo-American successors was a Flaubertian respect for the workshop of fiction, a delight in the tools of trade, and a pride in the stresses of labour.

The conviction that no detail is too homely for critical attention accompanies an interest in the *effects* on the reader, where these effects are understood not as gross movements of the sensibility, laughter or tears, but as fine adjustments of readerly intelligence. This forms a second thread of concern through the prefaces. The attention to the responsiveness of his audience led James to insights that would not be elaborated for over half a century, in particular the perception that the reader must become a collaborator in the art of fiction. The canny novelist must study the subtlety of effects, recognising that such success depends on 'the spectator's, the critic's, the reader's experience'. It is this line of thought that led James toward the idea of the *ficelle* character, who appears in a novel to contribute not to the workings of the plot but rather to its apprehension. Maria Gostrey in *The Ambassadors*, we learn, is not so much 'Strether's friend' as the 'reader's friend' – 'in consequence of dispositions that make him so eminently require one'.

Between the fastidious author and the susceptible reader stands the text itself, and the third and most prominent theme in James's criticism concerns the inner workings of the fictional artifact. This is no doubt the area that has been most closely tracked by James's admirers, but as soon as one demarcates this broad interest, it too divides into two patterns of emphases. On the one hand, James's idea of novelistic realism – an idea based not only on the 'illusion of reality' but also, as Wayne Booth has insisted, on the 'intensity' of that illusion – led him to some celebrated views on the privileges of a witnessing consciousness within a fictional world. Left to themselves, he argued, narrative events are speechless, lifeless, tasteless; only the presence of a registering intelligence, a 'reflecting and colouring medium', can drape naked events in the folds of moral significance. Thus, in discussing *The Princess Casamassima*, he wrote that he could 'never see the *leading* interest of any human hazard but in a consciousness (on the part of the moved and moving creature) subject to fine intensification and wide enlargement'. In place of the artifice of omniscience, Jamesian realism offers the 'ordeal' of consciousness as it is played out in a 'bewildered, anxious, restless, fallible' individual character struggling toward intelligence.

One needs to recognise, however, that the Jamesian central consciousness is important not only because it is conscious but because it is central – important, that is, not only because it lends moral meaning but also because it anchors aesthetic form. This leads to another preoccupation that runs just as insistently through the prefaces. As a 'form-lover' who delights in 'the refinements and ecstasies of method' James finds the destiny of forms as beguiling as human destinies. He relishes the 'superior roundness' of *The Ambassadors*, and he summarises his intentions for *The Awkward Age* in 'the neat figure of a circle consisting of a number of small rounds disposed at equal distance about a central object'. Geometry becomes a virtue in its own right, and all through his mature criticism the value of human consciousness and the value of formal roundness sit side by side. As if in recognition of this dichotomy he writes of Maggie Verver in *The Golden Bowl* that 'in addition to feeling everything she has to, and to playing her part just in that proportion, [she] duplicates, as it were, her value and becomes a compositional resource, and of the finest order, as well as a value intrinsic'.

For James these strains of emphasis create no instability in the theory or practice of fiction. The contributions of the author and the reader, the text's central consciousness and its geometric form, all exist in tight solidarity, and to give value to one is to give value to all. The later history of narrative theory will bring tension into this community of ideas, but James locates the strength of the novel in its capaciousness and flexibility which make it 'the most independent, most elastic, most prodigious of literary forms'. Fiction, in James's mature view, is as inexhaustible as life itself, but unlike life which can miss its greatest opportunities, the novel creates forms in which life's values can realise themselves.

This last point, the novel as the privileged site of human value, became the basis for a famous quarrel between James and H. G. Wells. In a 1914 essay on 'The Younger Generation', James admits the attraction of Wells's fiction but also regrets that the compelling 'presence of material' is not accompanied by 'an interest in the use of it'. James traces Wells's descent from Tolstoy, who will become a frequent touchstone in critical debate and who for James serves 'execrably, pestilentially, as a model' of the willingness to separate 'method from matter'. From this point of view Wells, like Arnold Bennett and D. H. Lawrence, shows a Tolstoyan indifference to the aesthetic transformation of raw experience. Wells, for his part, happily accepted this criticism, insisting that he had too many ideas to concern himself with nicety of form. In his satire *Boon* he wrote that 'if the novel is to follow life it must be various and discursive. Life is diversity and entertainment, not completeness and satisfaction.' The trouble with James, he goes on, is that he 'set himself to pick the straws out of the hair of Life before he paints her'; in pursuit of formal refinement he creates 'eviscerated people' who 'never make a lusty love, never go to angry war, never shout at an election or perspire at poker'. After enduring this portrait of himself, James wrote to Wells restating his belief that life does not simply yield up its values, that the value of experience must be 'exquisitely made and created, and that if we don't make it ... nobody and nothing will make it for us'. Wells responded by saying that whereas James regarded the novel as an end, he saw it as a means and that he would rather be known as a journalist than an artist. This brought James to his rousing last word in the dispute: 'It is art that *makes* life, makes interest, makes importance ... and I know of no substitute whatever for the force and beauty of its process.'

The critical position of Joseph Conrad takes on an interesting aspect in light of this dispute between Wells and James. It might, after all, seem that Conrad, with his taste for physical adventure, exotic setting, and conditions of bodily stress, would stand close to Wells's side of this question. Indeed he dedicated *The Secret Agent* to Wells. But though Conrad was not inclined to theory and though he played only a small part in the growing debate, his few considered critical judgements align him in important respects with James or, more exactly, with a particular aspect of Jamesian criticism which had immediate historical importance.

Conrad's most notable act of criticism was the short preface to *The Nigger of the 'Narcissus'* in which he, like James, defended a flaubertian view of the novelist as an indefatigable labourer, a 'worker in prose', who must display 'an unremitting never-discouraged care for the shape and ring of sentences'. For Conrad the immediate expression of this labour is the novelist's devotion to the physical world, with art itself being defined 'as a single-minded attempt to render the highest kind of justice to the visible universe'. He goes on to write in his most celebrated critical utterance that his task is 'to make you hear, to make you feel – it is, before all, to make you *see*'. This formulation anticipates James's remark in the preface to *The Ambassadors* that 'Art deals with what we see', but it is well worth remarking that in both James and Conrad there appears a

subtle shift from the visible universe to the viewing eye, from what we see
to the activity of seeing.

Fiction, writes Conrad, 'appeals to temperament' because it is human
temperament 'whose subtle and resistless power endows passing events
with their true meaning'. Not the visible universe in itself, but the universe
as apprehended by our subjectivity gives art its significant datum; here
Conrad confirms the Jamesian proposition that it is only the workings of
mind that can animate events with meaning. But if Conrad shares this
commitment with James, and if this character / narrator Marlow epitomises the principle of a witnessing consciousness who mediates between the
reader and the plot, he does not display a similar devotion to geometric
formalism, to the delights of exquisite symmetry. When James characterises the essence of Conrad's novelistic method, he describes it as 'a definite
responsible intervening first person singular' – namely Marlow – whose
contribution is 'a prolonged hovering flight of the subjective over the
outstretched ground of the case exposed'. This image might serve equally
well to evoke James's own use of the reflecting consciousness, and the
convergence of James and Conrad on this point, a convergence in both
theory and practice, had weighty consequences for early modernist criticism of the novel.

Ford Madox Ford was the figure best situated and most willing to
exploit a developing consensus. Having collaborated with Conrad, having
written a book on James, and having formed ties with those in a younger
generation (such as Ezra Pound and Wyndham Lewis), Ford was keen to
turn aperçus into insights. Over time, he devised a sketch of the history of
the English novel that consigned Fielding, Scott, Thackeray, and Dickens
to insignificance, while interpreting the important line of development
as a European not an English accomplishment. The novel began with
Richardson, but then passed over the Channel to Diderot, and matured in
the hands of Flaubert, Maupassant, and Turgenev. Only through the
efforts of James and Conrad did the serious novel return to England, just
in time to coincide with the beginnings of Ford's own career.

The fiction of James, Conrad, and Ford had been called 'Impressionist'
on analogy with Impressionist painting, and Ford accepted the term as a
description for the new literary movement. In a series of essays between
1910 and 1914, he set out to articulate the distinguishing features of
Impressionist fiction, beginning with a commitment to an austere form of
literary realism. The interventions of authorial commentary, which James
had deprecated, Ford deprecated even more vigorously. Fielding, Trol-
lope, and Thackeray had committed the unpardonable sin of shattering
novelistic illusion by coming forward to speak in their own persons; the
Impressionist author, on the contrary, 'is sedulous to avoid letting his
personality appear in the course of his book'; or as Ford put it elsewhere,

'You must not as an author utter any views.' From this it follows that 'the greatest literary crime ever committed was Thackeray's sudden apologetic incursion of himself into his matchless account of the manoeuvres of Becky Sharp on Waterloo day in Brussels'. Ford here is only consolidating a principle derived from his chosen predecessors – Flaubert, Maupassant, James, Conrad – but he put the point so energetically that he became the recognised bearer of this standard. Thus Allen Tate wrote that it was through Ford 'more than any other man writing in English in our time that the great traditions of the novel came down to us'. James may have perfected the distinction between 'showing' and 'telling', between novels that allow the reader to judge events and novels that rudely intervene to tell the reader what to feel, but Ford was the one who nursed the distinction into critical prominence.

Behind Ford's attack on intrusive moral commentary lay a particular conception of the realist aim. For Ford, it was not enough for the novel to *represent* life; it was necessary for it to *mimic* the processes of life: 'the general effect of a novel must be the general effect that life makes on mankind'. Furthermore, once one recognised that 'Life did not narrate but made impressions on our brains', the novelistic goal became the rendering of impressions set free from the artificiality of narrative coherence. The reliance on chronological sequence, on long discursive speeches, on panoramic views, on moral summary – according to Ford all these traditional features of the novel violate a strict realism. In our daily experience, we must be content with hints and glimpses which gradually accumulate into a picture of the world; so too a properly realist fiction must move from the 'rounded annotated record of a set of circumstances' toward 'the impression of the moment', creating 'the sort of odd vibration that scenes in real life have'. It is in this insistence on the shimmering haze of perception that Fordian Impressionism comes closest to its precedents in painting.

A prevailing ambiguity in Ford's theory is whether his Impressionism is to be justified in terms of its 'objectivity' or its 'subjectivity'. Ford invokes each in order to defend his method, but the confusion is chiefly a matter of his shifting focus. Considered from the perspective of the author, Impressionism aspires to the objectivity of detachment, in the spirit of Stephen Dedalus's famous dictum in Joyce's *A Portrait of the Artist as a Young Man*: 'The artist, like the God of the creation, remains within or behind or beyond or above his handiwork, invisible, refined out of existence, indifferent, paring his fingernails.' Considered, on the other hand, from the standpoint of the character, Impressionism is resolutely subjective, attending to the startled movement of the mind at the instant of perception. More eagerly than his predecessors, Ford presides over the steep devaluation of authorial consciousness and the sharp ascendancy of the consciousness of fictive characters – a double adjustment that reorders traditional privileges and initiates a line of debate which has not yet exhausted itself.

One implication of Ford's realist severity is that prose fiction becomes the preeminent literary form. All through early modernism a recurrent critical motif is a defence of the novel against the claims of rival genres; in Ford this becomes a pervasive theme which often takes the shape of a commitment to prose at the expense of poetry. Ezra Pound praised Ford as 'the defender of the prose tradition', but he might just as well have described him as an assailant upon the poetic tradition. The problem with poetry – and Ford is characteristically sweeping in his critique – is that it pursues beauty by sacrificing precision and clarity. The artifices of poetic structure and poetic diction are essentially inimical to the realist programme. This is particularly true in the twentieth century when complex social issues overwhelm the capacities of verse; it is only a supple prose which can capture the subtlety of modern life. The novel, as the supreme manifestation of the prose temperament, thus receives historical warrant for its privilege.

Because Ford formulated his critical position in the years just before the First World War, his conception of poetry tended to remain pre-modernist; Tennyson and Browning, not Pound or Eliot, were his examples. Virginia Woolf, on the other hand, who shared many of Ford's assumptions, entered the debate at a slightly later stage when the successes of modern poetry were becoming clear, and although she too sought to make a case for the special eminence of the novel, she was not prepared to do so by discrediting the poets. Like Ford, Woolf held that prose was the special instrument of the modern sensibility; prose, as she once put it, is so humble that it can go anywhere.

In her essay 'The Narrow Bridge of Art' (1927), Woolf offers a diagram of literary history that resembles T. S. Eliot's picture of a 'dissociation of sensibility'. The Elizabethan drama, she writes, succeeded as an encompassing form which could assimilate an extraordinary range of experience, but with its disappearance a broad division of imaginative labour ensued, in which the poets claimed beauty while the workaday task of representing common life fell to prose. Woolf suggests that Byron had gestured toward a flexible poetry that could digest a variety of emotions, but his example had not been followed. Now in the twentieth century, however, the novel may now engender a new form – a form that will be written in prose but that will share many of the characteristics of poetry. It 'will stand further back from life' than the traditional novel; it will neglect the 'fact-recording power' and give 'the outline rather than the detail'. Whereas Ford sought a clean, exact prose which might overcome poetic stylisation, Woolf imagined (and composed) a prose straining the boundary separating it from poetry.

In writing of James's ghost stories, Woolf observed that the 'visionary imagination was by no means his. His genius was dramatic, not lyric.' This brief comment contains two important suggestions. First, it reminds us of the modern novel's uneasy proximity to other genres. That James can take the drama as a paradigm for his fiction and that Woolf can absorb the lessons of the lyric makes clear just how readily the novel avails itself of techniques and tones developed in neighbouring forms. The novel, as Woolf put it, is the great cannibal among the genres, devouring other forms in order to feed its own development.

A second implication in Woolf's remark lies in the specific opposition she draws between the dramatic and lyric temperaments. Her own lyricism, together with her hope for a reconciliation between poetry and prose, suggests a shift away from the Jamesian conception of the novel. It is true that Woolf continues to pursue many of the critical aims associated with the James–Conrad–Ford lineage. Her demand that the novelist 'record the atoms as they fall upon the mind in the order in which they fall' links her to the Impressionist programme, and in her two influential essays 'Modern Fiction' (1919) and 'Mr. Bennett and Mrs. Brown' (1924), she carries out an energetic attack on the 'materialism' of Wells (along with that of Arnold Bennett and John Galsworthy) while calling for a 'spiritual' novel attentive to the movements of consciousness. But for James the ephemera of consciousness are tightly bound to the complexity of personal relations: consciousness is essentially consciousness of social life; this is what establishes the dramatic field of the novel. Woolf, on the other hand, intermittently contemplates an escape from the novel's ancient entanglement with social life. She imagines a novel that would only incidentally describe the drama of social relations and that would emphasise instead the lyricism of 'soliloquy in solitude'.

Although it cannot be the task of the present chapter to describe social changes, the reader must bear in mind that historial urgencies continually intersect with the course of novelistic criticism. T. S. Eliot once remarked that only within a settled society is it possible to give attention to the finer details of literary form, and it seems clear that the turn from, say, James to Woolf cannot be separated from the radical unsettling of social norms. The technical concerns introduced by James persist up to the present day, but since the First World War, they have stood in unstable relation to the press of history. The desire to exclude extra-literary preoccupations in order to achieve formal precision struggles against the desire to open the forms until they can include social issues of great moment.

This latter ambition shows itself in another significant concern separating Woolf from the modernist contemporaries with whom she otherwise shares so much, and it appears most clearly in her attitude toward Joyce. Frequently, in finding an example for progressive tendencies in modern fiction, Woolf invokes Joyce; but just as frequently she marks her distance. In 'An Essay in Criticism' (1927) she writes that Joyce (and also Lawrence, Douglas, and Hemingway) 'spoil their books for women readers by their display of self-conscious virility'; at one point in her diary she describes Joyce as a 'he-goat'. Woolf, that is, insists on the pertinence of the sexual issue, an issue that had flickered briefly in Wells's critique of the passion-less James, but that Woolf develops into a revaluation of the novelistic tradition. The 'effect of sex upon the novelist' is how she bluntly states it in *A Room of One's Own* (1929), and the great manifestation of that effect, according to Woolf, has been the distortion of women's creativity within a culture dominated by masculine values. From the form of the sentence to the form of the epic, women have confronted structures unsuited to them. The novel is the most promising literary form, partly because it is new, and partly because centuries spent in the drawing-room have trained women to observe character and to analyse emotion; but among women novelists only Jane Austen and Emily Brontë have sur-passed the distortions of patriarchy and the powerful temptations of rage and indignation.

Following Coleridge, Woolf suggests that the mind of the complete artist is androgynous, 'woman-manly' or 'man-womanly'. Historically, she argues, the condition of women has kept them from this creative ideal, but now in an age of acute self-consciousness in sexual attitudes, both sexes must struggle to overcome the polarities of gender. The specific task for the woman novelist is not to deny the effect of sex – 'It would be a thousand pities if women wrote like men' – but rather to write 'as a woman who has forgotten that she is a woman'. *A Room of One's Own* thus anticipates a feminist theory of fiction that will become prominent forty years later, but it also belongs to its contemporary critical environ-ment in which gender and sexuality became important and troubling issues.

D. H. Lawrence is another figure deeply interested in the 'effect of sex on the novelist', and, like Woolf, he does not take sexuality to be an independent concern. Lawrence is intent to reveal the power of the buried sexual life within the history of the novel, and his 'Study of Thomas Hardy' and his 'Studies in Classic American Literature' (1923) go in pursuit of the erotic energies that underlie and control the fictional sur-face. But although Lawrence's criticism, like his fiction, sometimes re-solves into an insistence on the primacy of the sexual narrative, his more characteristic line of argument regards eros as only part of an encompass-ing metaphysic. That metaphysic leads him to a view of the novel that breaks sharply with the emerging modernist consensus. Setting himself against a concentration on the workings of private consciousness – whether this takes the form of James's 'lucidity', Conrad's 'temperament',

Ford's 'frank egoism', or Woolf's 'spirituality' – Lawrence posed the claims of the body. Rupert Birkin remarks in *Women in Love* that 'It's the fact you want to emphasize, not the subjective impression to record', and the following passage from the Hardy study indicates how far Lawrence stands from the Jamesian delight in lucid consciousness:

the bringing of life into human consciousness is not an aim in itself, it is only a necessary condition of the progress of life itself. Man is himself the vivid body of life, rolling glimmering against the void. In his fullest living he does not know what he does, his mind, his consciousness, unacquaint, hovers behind, full of extraneous gleams and glances, and altogether devoid of knowledge.

In 'Surgery for the Novel – or a Bomb' (1923), he identifies the decay of serious fiction with the work of Joyce, Proust, and Dorothy Richardson, describing their accomplishment as 'the dismal, long-drawn-out comedy of the death-bed of the serious novel. It is self-consciousness picked into such fine bits that the bits are most of them invisible, and you have to go by the smell.' Lawrence demands 'wholeness' of character, not bits of mind, and he seeks that wholeness not in what characters think or feel but in what they *are*. As he puts it in a well-known letter, he wants the carbon in personality not the diamond, the non-human in humanity, the unthought beneath self-knowledge. He similarly disdains that other early modernist value, the perfection of form; for Lawrence *le mot juste* is just *un mot*; and he mocks 'the critical twiddle-twaddle about style and form'. In his striking phrase, the novel 'is the one bright book of life', and 'Nothing is important but life.' Finally, to the modernist reluctance to offer general philosophic commentary within fiction Lawrence responds by mourning the day when philosophy and fiction grew apart.

Although Lawrence's critical principles are even more variable than those of his asystematic contemporaries, it is clear enough that he produces a roaring counter-current in the modernist critical programme. The celebration of life recalls Wells's attack on James, but life for Wells was essentially the object of a kind of scientific journalism, whereas for Lawrence it is precisely what resists the canons of knowledge. In his more visionary moods the task he sets for the novel is to uncover the Real that is incommensurable with the Known. Unlike Wells, then, Lawrence attributes high value to the art of fiction, because in the novel life plays itself out before us: 'only in the novel are *all* things given full play . . . [and] out of the full play of all things emerges the only thing that is anything, the wholeness of a man, the wholeness of a woman, man alive, and live woman'.

The special merit of E. M. Forster's *Aspects of the Novel* (1927) is that at a moment of increasing polemical severity, it displays a relaxing of the normative fist. Forster prefers to regard the novel as a 'spongy tract' which resists 'elaborate apparatus': 'Principles and systems may suit other forms of art, but they cannot be applicable here.' He is equally indifferent to the movements of literary history, with no interest in arguing for the novel's ascent to subtlety or its decline into barbarism. His working metaphor is an image of all the English novelists sitting in a room 'writing their novels simultaneously'. Cast as a motto: 'History develops, Art stands still.' This disdain for theory and this indifference to history are part of Forster's attempt to rise above partisanship and to restore a more inclusive appreciation. Some of his sturdiest insights – the distinction between flat characters (those who evince a single unchanging idea or quality) and round characters (those capable of surprising the reader), or the contrast between story (events narrated in time sequence) and plot (events linked by causality as well as sequence) – are offered as universal aspects of fiction, independent of the winds of fashion. Yet beneath the studied detachment can be found some strong commitments that bind Forster to the local struggles he would rather transcend.

Early in *Aspects of the Novel* Forster draws a contrast between 'life in time' and 'life by values', proposing this as a division in daily life that becomes still more fundamental in the novel. Life in time drives the novel toward plot, while life by value creates the interest in character: the drama of Forster's argument turns on 'the battle that plot fights with character'. What makes plot such a formidable adversary is that it submits time to the pressures of form, to the structural constraints of beginning, middle, and end. Forster thus writes that plot 'is the novel in its logical intellectual aspect'. A sustaining ambition of his book is to preserve a humanist fiction against the encroachments of the formalist plot, and it becomes evident by the end of the work that for all Forster's avowed disengagement from literary history, his opponent resolves into a recognisable historical personage. Henry James appears in the final chapter as the connoisseur of narrative pattern whose 'premise' is that 'most of human life has to disappear before he can do us a novel'. For James, a 'pattern must emerge, and anything that emerged from the pattern must be pruned off as wanton distraction. Who so wanton as human beings?' Forster refers to the James/Wells contention and frankly confesses that his sentiments are with Wells. This last phase of argument in *Aspects of the Novel* situates the work within the controversies that dominated early twentieth-century discussion of fiction, and the rendering of the Jamesian provocation raises a concrete historical problem of the sort Forster claimed he would ignore.

For it is clear that James held no such premise as the one Forster imputes to him. Far from asserting that human life is a distraction and an excrescence, James insists that his deepest imaginative habit, even his imaginative weakness, is his attraction to 'the stray figure, the unattached character' as the source of a novel. He recalls that the origin of *The Portrait of a*

Lady lay 'not at all in any conceit of a "plot" . . . but altogether in the sense of a single character'. In 'The Art of Fiction' he had established a balance and then had tipped it decisively: 'What is character but the determination of incident? What is incident but the illustration of character? What is either a picture or a novel that is *not* of character? What else do we seek in it and find in it?' It is not that Forster has somehow misunderstood the Jamesian position; it seems rather that he senses the unsteadiness of the balance between human value and the 'value of composition'. Forster's reading of James as an uncompromising formalist is in part a response to the fiction of the late phase where pattern becomes such a lofty virtue; but it is perhaps more significantly a response to what had happened to James in the hands of the Jamesians.

Percy Lubbock, who stands for Forster as the representative of a critical position precisely opposed to his own, appears at the argumentative centre of *Aspects of the Novel*, where Forster invokes Lubbock's claim in *The Craft of Fiction* (1921) that 'The whole intricate question of method . . . [is] governed by the question of point of view – the question of the relation in which the narrator stands to the story.' Even as Forster concedes his utter lack of interest in the formulae of method, he happily admits that those who follow Lubbock 'will lay a sure foundation for the aesthetics of fiction'. This is an apt characterisation of Lubbock's aim, and it points to a sharpening divergence in critical approaches to the novel.

Until now, the writers who have concerned us have been novelists first and critics second, and although many of their insights have been highly influential for later critics, they developed for the most part as the working maxims of creative artists. Accordingly, these writers tended toward a relative informality. They made no attempt to develop an encompassing architectonic; and even one as eager for lucidity as James found the impulse to system corrected by the local concerns of his own unrepeatable achievement. At one point in *The Craft of Fiction* Lubbock distinguishes between the late novels of James, which 'are so odd and so personal and so peculiar in all their aspects', and the question of method raised by those novels, 'which is a general question, discussible apart'. This distinction suggests the broader historical movement within which Lubbock's work found its place, a movement toward abstract principles, general criteria, and formal systems. At the same time it suggests an event in the social history of criticism, namely the establishment of an academic standpoint which aimed to separate itself from the interested perspective of creative partisans. Although *The Craft of Fiction* is written in an informal conversational style, and although it situates itself in no academic context, its influence was felt most forcefully in the academy, where for decades it remained the most prominent entry in any bibliography of modern criticism of fiction.

'How [novels] are made is the only question I shall ask', writes Lubbock, who then interprets this as a question about 'the various forms of narrative, the forms in which a story may be told'. Lubbock confesses that he is, as it were, a typologist without a nomenclature, a scientist of narrative structure who has no established labels on which to rely. And in attempting to justify the terms he chooses for his central distinction, he remarks that 'Henry James used them in discussing his own novels.' It is surely notable that in the absence of a received terminology, James's prefaces became the source for a founding work of narrative formalism, and in ways that will become evident this connection blurs the distinction between polemic and science.

The Craft of Fiction begins with a reading of Tolstoy's *War and Peace*, in which Lubbock acknowledges the epic force of the novel but then goes on to discuss its formal ambiguities. Forster is doubtless correct when he writes that, great as Lubbock finds Tolstoy's novel, 'he would find it greater' if it had had a consistent point of view. The root problem for Lubbock is that Tolstoy avails himself of two different narrative designs, two rival principles of structure: one is the product of the characters' points of view, and the other is Tolstoy's perspective. The inconsistent movement between them deprives the novel of any coherent centre. The result is that the book is 'wasteful of its subject'; it achieves the effects of grandeur but its lines are uncertain and confused.

The instability in Tolstoy's work opens a way for Lubbock to formulate the Jamesian opposition which he extends and refines, the opposition between novel as picture and novel as drama. In the course of *The Craft of Fiction* this dualism is variously characterised, but the most definitive statement is based on the reader's relation to a narrator: 'in one case the reader faces towards the storyteller and listens to him, in the other he turns towards the story and watches it'. The former situation is said to be 'pictorial' because when our attention turns to the teller, we apprehend events as they are 'pictured' by an individual temperament. On the other hand, when the reader looks directly at events, unobstructed by a mediating presence, the novel approaches the condition of drama, where characters speak and act without the interventions of a narrator. As Lubbock summarises the distinction which Plato had described long before him, 'so much of a novel therefore, as is not dramatic enactment, not *scenic*, inclines always to picture, to the reflection of somebody's mind'. Such a characterisation, however, should not imply that drama and picture are two equally valuable narrative forms. Lubbock follows James in attaching the highest importance to the scene and in regarding picture as 'subordinate, preliminary, and preparatory'. The realist illusion finds its full realisation in the direct dramatic encounter, and this fact establishes an unambiguous hierarchy of forms.

It is worth noting that on this central point Lubbock and Ford disagree in their interpretation of Jamesian doctrine. In developing the Impressionist position, Ford had named 'the great scene' as the 'curse of the novel' because it tempted the novelist into the artifice of dramatic peaks, convenient scenic bundles never found in ordinary life. In place of passionate declamation in a grand dramatic encounter, Ford wants 'a quiet voice', 'just quietly saying things'. Furthermore, in abandoning long speeches (because no bystander could really remember them), and in preventing characters from answering one another directly (because in life this rarely happens), Ford guided attention away from incidents themselves and toward the 'pictures' of the narrator. The privilege that James had granted to the observing mind impressed Ford just to the extent that James's praise of drama impressed Lubbock, and the split in emphasis here – more narrator, more incident – points to an important tension within this critical lineage.

And yet to recognise the strain as relatively superficial is to see the degree to which Lubbock has enlarged the Jamesian inheritance. The central argument of *The Craft of Fiction* depends on extending the concept of drama to include not only the direct exchange between characters but *any* aspect of a narrative that is presented directly to the reader's view. What this means to Lubbock is that picture and drama are not unalterably opposed, that picture can be dramatised – or to express it another way, the observer can be implicated in the realm of incident. Thackeray, as usual, serves as a convenient negative instance: in *Vanity Fair* he permits the authorial eye to remain wholly detached, picturing events without entering the landscape of the story, observing without being himself observed. This epitomises the extreme dissociation of picture and drama that Lubbock regrets. Fortunately, according to Lubbock, Thackeray discovered a way to prevent such formal 'wastefulness' by developing in *The History of Henry Esmond* a device for bringing the teller into the tale: 'the characterized "I" is substituted for the loose and general "I" of the author'. This is precisely what Ford had demanded, and it becomes clear how in the extended concept of drama, it is possible to place great weight on the narrator's subjectivity and still achieve dramatic impersonality. The author can (and must) remain supremely detached even as the narrator/observer becomes entangled in the dramatic struggle. For Lubbock, however, although the characterised 'I' is a long 'first step in the dramatization of picture', it is not the last.

The difficulty with characterised first-person narrative is that while it brings the narrating eye into the fictional world, it gives us no reliable way to see the seeing eye itself. How can we have a dramatically objective view of the mind which observes events? The solution, Lubbock argues, is for the novel to return to the third person – but the third person with a difference. If the consciousness that pictures the world does not tell its own story, if it is represented from an impersonal third-person standpoint, and if its perceptions are seen as well as seeing, then the mind will at last be fully dramatised. Lubbock described this grand achievement by way of describing James's *The Ambassadors*. In effect, *The Craft of Fiction* becomes a Whig history of recent English fiction, according to which the 'dramatization of picture' passes through a series of stages culminating in James's development of strictly limited third-person narrative. Not only is this further indication of the preeminence of the Jamesian paradigm, but it is also a mark of the normative aspect of Lubbock's critical project. The typology of literary forms organises itself into a frank hierarchy of values, with the consequence that the Jamesian narrative method is not only the latest development in the novel; it is, other things being equal, the highest development. Other things, as Lubbock concedes, are not always equal; genius can work its way in spite of the logic of forms; but it is clear that from the standpoint of *The Craft of Fiction* the way of genius would be more triumphant if it obeyed the just governance of the laws of drama.

When Forster separates his own views from Lubbock's, he does so by insisting that a strict narrative formalism is not a just governor but a narrow tyrant. Rigid pattern, as he puts it, 'shuts the doors on life and leaves the novelist doing exercises'. To Lubbock's demand for consistency in perspective, Forster responds that a novelist's only task is 'to bounce the reader into accepting what he says': 'A novelist can shift his view-point if it comes off, and it came off with Dickens and Tolstoy.' Forster is not engaging in a philistine's anti-formalism; the serious purpose behind the informality of *Aspects of the Novel* is to liberate criticism of the genre from the fetishism of plot and to restore attention to fictional modes which cannot be understood in terms of the logic of structure. Forster calls these modes fantasy and prophecy, and while he traces a long history for each, it is telling that he can name only one living representative of the higher prophetic mode, D. H. Lawrence.

In the opening chapter of *The Great Tradition* (1948), F. R. Leavis names Lawrence as 'the great genius of our time', the figure who has carried on the tradition created by Jane Austen, George Eliot, Henry James, and Joseph Conrad. Like Forster, Leavis celebrates the prophetic Lawrence, who writes 'from the depth of his religious experience', and it is evident that he sees Lawrence not only as the most recent heir to the great tradition but also as a model for the critic struggling to preserve high standards in a time of cultural decadence. 'One must speak for life and growth, amid all this mass of destruction and disintegration' – Leavis quotes these words of Lawrence, which might well have stood as an epigraph to *The Great Tradition*. What James was to Lubbock, Lawrence is to Leavis; and allowing for the imprecision of the analogy, we can say with confidence that the opposition between James and Lawrence captured a broad distinction in critical attitude. Lawrence, as it were, replaced Wells as the antithetical term to James; and it is plain that he represented a more weighty point of contrast. Lawrentian criticism, by the very nature of its assumptions, is bound to be less well defined than Jamesian criticism, but clearly for Leavis the first lesson to be drawn from Lawrence's example is the necessity of moral passion in the critic's encounter with the fate of the novel.

Certainly a leading feature of neo-Jamesian criticism has been the distaste for overt moral judgement. James himself, in a much-quoted phrase, wrote of the 'perfect dependence of the "moral" sense of a work of art on the amount of felt life concerned in producing it'. Carefully embedded inside quotation marks, morality loses the specificity of doctrine and becomes, like art itself, a measure of the intensity of experience. One may debate the extent to which morality is aestheticised in James, but it cannot be doubted that he prefers to describe moral value in aesthetic terms. In 'The Art of Fiction', he holds that 'the essence of moral energy is to survey the whole field', and then in responding to demands for a moral purpose in art, he adds that the artist's fundamental purpose is 'the purpose of making a perfect work'. Ford, who thought that 'Profound Moral Purpose' had been the bane of English fiction, praised James for having no sympathies, for advocating no cause, for remaining 'passionless and pitiless'. Lubbock simply rules the moral question out of order by announcing his intention of studying narrative forms independent of all other questions.

Leavis denies that this can be done – denies, that is, that one can account for the worthy formal achievements in the great tradition by disentangling technique from the moral matter. He writes, for instance, that 'when we examine the formal perfection of *Emma*, we find that it can be appreciated only in terms of the moral preoccupations that characterize the novelist's peculiar interest in life'. Lawrence had argued that 'every work of art adheres to some system of morality', adding that the work must also offer 'the essential criticism of the morality to which it adheres'. Leavis denies the intelligibility of a merely formal account of the novel, and in Lawrentian tones and terminology he affirms that all the great English novelists share 'a vital capacity for experience, a kind of reverent openness before life, and a marked moral intensity'. At the beginning of his discussion of George Eliot, he consolidates this line of argument by repudiating James's view that George Eliot's fiction attained no high formal value: 'Is there any great novelist whose preoccupation with "form" is not a matter of his responsibility towards a rich human interest, or complexity of interests, profoundly realized? – a responsibility involving, of its very nature, imaginative sympathy, moral discrimination and judgment of relative human value.'

Although one would never confuse Lawrence with Forster, they approach one another on several important matters, and there is rough justice in seeing Lawrence, Forster, and Leavis as constituting a rival line to that of James, Ford, and Lubbock. For the former group, critical terminology is organised around such terms as 'life', 'humanity', and 'moral value', while for the latter the recurrent terms tend to be 'narrative', 'technique', and 'illusion'. It is true, of course, that James himself stands squarely in the middle of Leavis's great tradition. Notably, however, it is not the James of the late formal experiments, but the author of such works as *The Europeans*, *The Bostonians*, and especially *The Portrait of a Lady*. Central to the argument of *The Great Tradition* is a distinction between the 'classical' accomplishment of James's early and middle phases and the precipitous decline in the last works; within the critical climate of the forties Leavis's work can be seen as an attempt to challenge the neo-Jamesians by reinterpreting the achievement of the master. Alluding to Lubbock's work on *The Ambassadors*, Leavis deplores the emphasis on a novel which does not belong in the first rank. The vaunted craftsmanship is no point in James's favour, because the self-conscious professionalism meant that James 'did not live enough', with the result that in *The Ambassadors* the 'subtleties and elaborations' of technique 'are not sufficiently controlled by a feeling for value and significance in living'. One can hear the echoes of Wells and Forster, but what distinguishes Leavis's treatment is that it stands as part of a thoroughgoing reconstruction of James's career which is at the same time a reconstruction of the novelistic tradition.

Although Leavis insists upon the formal character of moral vision, he betrays little interest in the technical concerns which held such pride of place among English modernists of the first and second generation. When he writes of Conrad, he disparages the formal effects generated by the figure of Marlow, relegating downward the works most closely associated with Impression – 'Heart of Darkness', *Lord Jim*, and *Chance* – and praising most highly the novels that give a moral impersonal rendering of moral crisis, *Nostromo* and *The Secret Agent*. What Leavis values in Conrad are the 'present particulars' and the pattern of 'moral significances'. Similarly, in his embrace of early and middle James, he pays no heed to 'drama', to 'witnessing consciousness', to the geometry of form. Placed in critical context, the insistent argument of *The Great Tradition* can be seen as an attempt to construct a literary genealogy that might recover James and Conrad for a Lawrentian perspective. In order to challenge the ascendancy of narrative formalism, it became necessary to cut sharply into the unity of individual careers and also into the unity of international modernism. By naming George Eliot as the figure behind James and Conrad, Leavis ensures that his great tradition will be a tradition of the *English* novel; he takes pains to loosen the ties between his modern instances and the Continental precedents they acknowledged. Instead of Flaubert, Maupassant, and Turgenev, the relevant precursors are Bunyan, Fielding, and Austen, and Leavis argues for the essentially 'un-Flaubertian quality of the line of English classical fiction'.

This commitment to a national tradition has bearing not only on the question of literary history, but also on the question of contemporary critical perspective. Here the relevant opposition is not between England and the Continent but between England and America. Both Woolf and Forster amuse themselves with Clayton Hamilton's *Materials and Methods of Fiction*, which (in Forster's paraphrase) 'classified novels by their dates, their length, their locality, their sex, their point of view', and 'the weather', and which, according to Woolf, 'teaches us a great deal about the Americans'. Q. D. Leavis has a singular importance to be noted below, but here it can be said that, like her husband F. R. Leavis, she rarely hesitates to point out the inanities of American scholarship, once describing the American critical tradition as 'brutally cold'. The pertinence of this minor bickering is that it exposes a tension between two critical perspectives which have begun to resolve into a tension between two national temperaments. For although the ascendancy of the Jamesian aesthetic occurred first through the efforts of English critics, by the mid-thirties the leading neo-Jamesians were American. Moreover, by the forties the Jamesian current had met the New Criticism, and this convergence helped to consolidate a strong formalist tendency in American approaches to the novel.

Cleanth Brooks Jr and Robert Penn Warren, having elaborated New Critical poetic principles in *Understanding Poetry* (1938), published a companion volume called *Understanding Fiction* (1943), a critical anthology of short fiction which stands at the confluence of the neo-Jamesian inquiry into point of view and the New Critical concern with poetic irony. The glossary at the end of the book is itself an historical document of some note, certifying as it does the marriage of two terminologies into a single conception of aesthetic value; indeed throughout the text, the Jamesian lexicon offers Brooks and Warren a way to extend the concern with organic form from lyric poetry to prose fiction. In *The House of Fiction* (1950), a similar anthology prepared by Caroline Gordon and Allen Tate, the connection between story and poem is explicitly avowed and cele-brated – not, however, as a sign of the visionary lyricism that Woolf had sought for the novel. What guides Gordon and Tate is the perception that, since Flaubert, the school of Impressionist fiction 'has achieved something of the self-contained objectivity of certain forms of poetry', or as Tate himself put it in the essay 'Techniques of Fiction' (1944), 'it has been through Flaubert that the novel has at last caught up with poetry'. It is not then surprising that 'fiction' in these collections tends to resolve into 'the short story', nor that form is conceived in terms of 'unity' and 'resolution'. ('A story', in the definition of Brooks and Warren, 'is a movement through complexity to unity, through complication to simplicity, through confusion to order.') The critical commentary in both books restricts itself almost entirely to those issues that came to dominate the formal study of fiction at mid-century: tone, pace, focus, scale, distance, denouement.

In anticipating the objection that their approach neglects 'idea' – the ethical, metaphysical, or religious proposition – in favour of 'form', Brooks and Warren retort that it does no such thing, that a proper appreciation of fictional ideas locates them as elements of the total form and recognises that there are no good ideas in literature apart from the structural wholes to which they contribute. One might see the claim that fictional ideas have no independent literary existence as a reverse image of Leavis's claim that in great fiction the forms cannot live without morality. Much as Leavis's emphasis falls heavily on the morality within 'moral form', so Brooks and Warren, having made ideas into constituents of form, can safely ignore them.

Working within the same theoretical perspective, Mark Schorer makes a strenuous attempt to enlarge the concept of form until it fully assimilates content. In his essay 'Technique as Discovery' (1948), Schorer follows Brooks and Warren in holding that the novel must at last yield to the formal methods developed in the analysis of poetry, but he gives this insight a more radical turn. For Schorer the task is not to assimilate the idea to the form; it is to overcome the fundamental distinction of form and content – or in the essay's preferred terminology, the antithesis of technique and subject-matter. 'When we speak of technique', he writes, 'we speak of nearly everything', because 'everything is technique which is not the lump of experience itself'. It follows that the novel does not begin with a subject and then press it into shape. Technique is not supplementary but primary: it creates and defines the materials of fiction. There is no content prior to form. Armed with this thought, Schorer reviews the modern critical contention, concluding that Wells was 'totally wrong' in his dispute with James and that Lawrence's failure to achieve 'technical scrutiny of his material' mars his entire career. James and Conrad learned the lessons of technique that Lawrence suppressed or never knew, and if Joyce has written the most satisfying novel of the century, this is due to the austerity of his technical ambitions. The arrangement of these names suggests that while Schorer means to overcome certain crippling dualisms in the theory of fiction, he leaves intact the opposing traditions. All fiction is technique, but some novels are more technical than others.

The dualism of form and content was submitted to the scrutiny of Aristotle through the offices of the 'Chicago Critics', who saw the recovery of an Aristotelian perspective as a way to introduce rigour into the contemporary polemic. Specifically, the notion of plot as developed in the Poetics became an instrument for reshaping various difficult oppositions. In an essay called 'The Concept of Plot and the Plot of Tom Jones' (1952), R. S. Crane argued that plot had become an unjustifiably narrow notion, typically restricted to those 'plots of action' that concentrate on a change in the situation of a protagonist. Because this has indeed been the dominant mode in traditional narrative, critics have rashly regarded it as the only one, with the result that a writer such as Forster comes to devalue plot and to place it in rivalry with character. In fact, argues Crane, the plot of action constitutes only one aspect of the concept of plot; a more exact account must acknowledge 'plots of character' and 'plots of thought'. The former renders a change in the protagonist's moral character (as in James's The Portrait of a Lady), and the latter a change in the protagonist's thought and therefore feelings (as in Pater's Marius the Epicurean). Although one or other of these forms is likely to dominate any given narrative, the central claim in Crane's essay is that all three concerns must enter into the successful plot, 'the positive excellence of which depends upon the power of its peculiar synthesis of character, action, and thought'. Conceived in this broad sense, a plot is not a means but the 'final end' toward which all else in the work must tend. The good plot depends on the happiest synthesis, and by implication the good critic is the one who performs corresponding synthetic acts, bringing together considerations of abstract form and moral considerations, metaphysical concerns and the concerns of language.

If R. P. Blackmur appears in Leavis's The Great Tradition as a prime mover behind 'the cult of Henry James', this is due almost entirely to his introduction to James's prefaces collected in The Art of the Novel (1934), an introduction that indeed celebrated and circulated fundamental Jamesian tenets. And yet if Blackmur began as an unrestrained admirer of James's critical work – calling the prefaces 'the most sustained', 'the most eloquent and original piece of literary criticism in existence' – he kept returning to that work in order to test his nervous perceptions, and although he never lost his admiration, he edged away from perfect congruity with the Jamesian aesthetic. Specifically, he came to question the supremacy granted to what he called 'technical or executive form', arguing that the 'fetishes' made of Jamesian technique distort their proper function, which is not to offer independent satisfaction but to 'bring into being – to bring into performance, for the writer and for the reader – an instance of the feeling of what life is about'. This line of thought begins as a critique of the neo-Jamesians, but it melts into a critical view of James himself. The quoted remarks are drawn from an essay called 'The Loose and Baggy Monsters of Henry James' (1951), in which Blackmur cites James's famous description of Tolstoy, Thackeray, and Dumas as creating 'large loose baggy monsters' at odds with 'a deep-breathing economy and an organic form'. Blackmur rejects this opposition and proposes a view of form which acknowledges Tolstoy's economy and James's own large looseness. That he turns increasingly toward the European novel is itself a fact of note. In the crowning essay of *Eleven Essays in the European Novel* (1964), the celebratory reading of *The Brothers Karamazov*, Blackmur opposes Dostoevsky to James and writes that 'What we nowadays call "form" in the novel might economize [Dostoevsky's] achievements, but it could not have produced them.'

The opposition between 'life' and 'form' might suggest an affinity with Leavis, but in fact Blackmur is as stern with the moralists as he is with the formalists. He insists on an angle of vision broad enough to include both late James and late Dostoevsky and generous enough to accommodate not only the play of forms but the play of such themes as money and murder, beauty and love. As opposed to the crisp Aristotelianism in Crane's adjustments of 'plot' and 'character', Blackmur's movements between 'life' and 'form' are speculative, figural, provisional, and idiosyncratic. But for all their idiosyncrasy, his essays might stand for (while also standing above) many other works of criticism that worked free of partisan dispute, that cannot be sorted according to school or doctrine, and that tend to be left out of a general historical account such as this one.

One other element of Blackmur's criticism has bearing on our history. To this point, the emphasis in most of the critical positions we have encountered has fallen on fiction as an independent cultural activity, and while there has been bitter partisan dispute, it has taken place on the site of the independent artifact, the self-enclosed text as a repository of formal possibilities and moral powers. It is not difficult to imagine a further development in this line of inquiry, in which the negotiations suggested in work such as Blackmur's would be adjusted ever more finely in pursuit of some ideal equilibrium between moralists and formalists, professionals and prophets, plots and characters, minds and desires. In fact, however, a far more complicated development ensued, one greatly enlarging the terms of discussion and expanding the field of research. What begins to occur, for instance, in Blackmur's essays – and this is the other sense in which his highly personal work becomes historically representative – is that the reinterpretation of 'form' and 'life' leads steadily toward an opening of the fictional text until it stands as a register of psychological pressures and social urgencies. Such a change became conspicuous in the work of many critics of the fifties, but it had been prepared through various earlier efforts.

In the first paragraph of *Fiction and the Reading Public* (1932), Q. D. Leavis distinguishes two dominant approaches to the novel, the method of the critic and the method of the scholar. The former she associates with James and Lubbock, and although she acknowledges its seriousness, she considers it unsuitable for dealing with the broader range of texts produced within a culture. The latter, the scholarly method, she identifies with the writing of textbooks, whose task is to offer paraphrases of literary plots arranged in chronological sequence and whose limitations are evident. Leavis considers that the problem which she has posed for herself – 'What has happened to fiction and the reading public since the eighteenth century?' – requires a third method, which she names 'anthropological'. Because a 'novel pulled up as a unit of inspection clings with its tentacles round so many non-technical matters that it cannot always be safely severed from them', *Fiction and the Reading Public* finds its 'unit of inspection' not in a novel or a series of novels but in nothing less than the anthropological unity of a culture.

The controlling argument of her book rests on a historical account familiar in its broad outlines but original and influential in its details. Leavis sees the folk-history inherited by the Elizabethans, the Puritan bourgeois code, and the journalism developed by Addison and Steele as aspects of a shared popular sensibility which substituted for formal education and which gradually produced 'an idiom for common standards of taste and conduct'. That idiom made possible the eighteenth-century novel, but it is part of the pathos of Leavis's account that no sooner does the novel enter the culture than the symptoms of decline begin to appear. By the latter stages of the eighteenth century, writers and readers discovered that the novel could be used as a compensation for life, a source of vicarious satisfaction instead of a means to extend, deepen, and refine experience. The process is not described as a change internal to the workings of fiction; it is a complex reaction to the growth of the reading public, the transformation of the periodical, and the new relations between author and publisher.

A salient feature of early twentieth-century criticism had been an optimistic, even visionary, interpretation of the historical development of the novel. Ford's notion that serious fiction had just returned to England, Lubbock's sense that James had at last uncovered the full range of the novel's possibilities, Woolf's speculation that the marriage of prose and poetry was now imminent, Lawrence's demand that philosophy and fiction meet again in a new revolutionary form – all suggest that the modern period will be a time of extraordinary, even unprecedented, novelistic accomplishment. *Fiction and the Reading Public*, on the other hand, sets fictional achievement within the context of a long and accelerating decline. From the middle to the end of the eighteenth century there is a dulling of the sensibility which becomes in the next century a perceptible coarsening of taste: 'The loss in maturity and poise noticeable between Pope and Shelley is paralleled by the same disparity between Sterne and Thackeray, Jane Austen and Charlotte Brontë, Smollett and Dickens. The nineteenth-century writers appeal at a different level, they require far less from the reader and they repay him abundantly in inferior coin.' Leavis does not mean to deny great individual success, only to show how such success increasingly occurs at the price of cultural disintegration. Serious fiction comes to require the separation between a small 'cultivation' public and a sensation-seeking 'popular' audience.

In the twentieth century, according to Leavis, the fissure has widened and a crisis has ensued. Having discovered that fiction can now be used as consolation for moral failure, a tribe of popular novelists has thoroughly vulgarised the general reader. In the age of the cinema, the circulating library, the dance-hall, and the loudspeaker, the public no longer has the strength to resist the lure of immediate pleasure. Given the 'disintegration of the reading public', the serious novelist can cherish no hope of a wide audience but must sacrifice the common reader in order to write for the uncommon intelligence. As against the various Whig histories of the novel, *Fiction and the Reading Public* offers a view that would become familiar, a view of the loss of a common culture and a broad decline of aesthetic and moral standards, leaving the only hope in 'resistance by an armed and conscious minority'.

'Minority', of course, is a term that separates Leavis from her Marxist contemporaries, who in other respects share her sense of cultural crisis. Alick West in *Crisis and Criticism* (1937) and Granville Hicks in *The Great Tradition* (1933) pursued the double activity characteristic of the prevailing Marxist aesthetic: they demonstrated the failure of bourgeois fiction to confront the realities of mass struggle, and they celebrated the engaged fiction of the revolutionary left. In both respects, they coincided with the most sustained Marxist analysis of the novel in the thirties, Ralph Fox's *The Novel and the People* (1937) which elaborated a theory closely resembling the views Georg Lukács was formulating in his essays of the period. For Fox the novel is at once the great artistic accomplishment of the bourgeoisie and its most cruelly suffering victim. A confident individualism had produced the triumph of eighteenth-century fiction in which 'the best, most imaginative representatives of the bourgeoisie examined the new man and woman and the society in which they lived', but by the middle of the Victorian period the expanding pressures of capitalism had overwhelmed the bourgeois individual. The English novel underwent a period of evasion and retreat, and in the twentieth century retreat has become the 'panic rout' of a cowardly modernism unable to engage with the present historical crisis. The broad downward curve which Q. D. Leavis had traced through the last three centuries also gives the shape of Fox's cultural history, but Fox is confident that the revolutionary turn toward socialism will give the English novel a renewed sense of historical purpose and literary grandeur.

George Orwell vigorously opposed the Marxist austerity exemplified by Fox, suggesting for example in 'The Prevention of Literature' (1946) that 'if the liberal culture that we have lived in since the Renaissance actually comes to an end, the literary art will perish with it'. But Orwell made his criticisms of Marxism from the standpoint of the left, and through the forties he kept alive the possibility of a left-wing political criticism uncompromised by Stalinist orthodoxy. Orwell's essay on Dickens might serve as an epitome of his approach to the novel. There he sets himself the task of freeing Dickens from his Marxist champions, but at the same time he carries out his own resolutely political reading. Dickens, argues Orwell, does not adopt the perspective of the working-class; he fails to anticipate a revolutionary change in the social structure; he never escapes the pretensions of gentility. Yet what gives radical force to his fiction is that it engages with shared political ideals more fundamental than official ideologies. 'The common man', writes Orwell, 'is still living in the mental world of Dickens, but nearly every modern intellectual has gone over to some or other form of totalitarianism.' In Orwell's work the opposition between proletarian and bourgeois frequently transforms into the contrast between common man and intellectual, but for Orwell the reformation means an engagement, not a withdrawal, from politics. Seen from this point of view, one of the charged political acts in Orwell's criticism is its extension of interest to works that produce common delight but not canonical awe. Insisting that 'art is not the same thing as cerebration', he writes with seriousness and sympathy about the 'good bad books' that constitute no great tradition but that satisfy the imaginative cravings of a mass public. In an essay such as 'Boys' Weeklies' (1940), Orwell follows Q. D. Leavis in taking commercial fiction as a worthy subject of inquiry, if only on the assumption that 'the worst books are often the most important'; and in this and other essays he anticipates the study of popular narrative which has become prominent in contemporary criticism.

Orwell offered nothing so systematic as a methodology for political criticism but simply a robust interest in the politics of fiction, informed by the belief that 'All art is propaganda' (though 'not all propaganda is art'). Due partly to a general anti-Stalinism and partly to Orwell's particular precedent, the conjunction of political engagement and methodological flexibility becomes common in critical studies of fiction during the fifties. Irving Howe's *Politics and the Novel* (1957), which studies a line of fiction from Stendhal to Orwell, is guided by an interest in 'what happens to the novel when it is subjected to the pressures of politics and political ideology', but the book is notably unconcerned to formulate analytic principles of inquiry. The first volume of Arnold Kettle's *An Introduction to the English Novel* (1951), which appeared just three years after Leavis's *The Great Tradition*, might be read as a reinterpretation of the Leavisite project from the point of view of the asystematic left. The name of Karl Marx does not appear in the book's index, but Kettle goes about the Leavis-inspired task of constructing an English novelistic tradition while assuming throughout that the development of the novel can only be understood in relation to the history of capitalism. In *Culture and Society* (1958) Raymond Williams, who was clearly though ambiguously affected by Orwell's example, restored serious attention to the 'propaganda' of the mid-Victorian industrial novel, which he read in Marxist terms as a symptom of bourgeois society but also in Orwellian terms as a symptom which is 'significant and continuing'.

Ian Watt's *The Rise of the Novel* (1957) looks back to Q. D. Leavis's *Fiction and the Reading Public* as its 'great stimulus', and to juxtapose the two works is to draw another strand of the historical web. One might see the 'anthropological' perspective of Leavis's book as itself the product of two methodological currents which would increasingly diverge, one leading toward political and social engagement, especially on the left, and the other toward academic sociology. The problem which led Leavis to broad cultural speculations – the emergence of the novel and the expansion of the reading community – becomes for Watt the occasion for concentrated historical research. *The Rise of the Novel* is unconcerned to determine the fate of English culture; it is deeply concerned to give concrete specificity to a relatively precise historical moment. In effect, the literary and social problem which is broached in one short chapter of Leavis's book expands into a subject for sustained scholarly treatment. Perhaps the most influential contribution of Watt's book was his characterisation of the novel in terms of what he called 'formal realism': that is, 'the premise, or primary convention, that the novel is a full and authentic report of human experience, and is therefore under an obligation to satisfy its reader with such details of the story as the individuality of the actors concerned, the particulars of the times and places of their actions, details which are presented through a more largely referential use of language than is common in other literary forms'. This is the preliminary 'formal' definition of the genre, but the real activity of the study is to lend historical pith to a critical abstraction. Notably, Watt relies on developments in extra-literary domains, specifically philosophy and sociology. The working assumption of *The Rise of the Novel* is that in accounting for such a striking fact as the emergence of a new literary form, we have no choice but to rely on insights gathered in other fields of inquiry. The novel's formal realism is embedded in other cultural strata; as Watt put it, 'just as there is a basic congruity between the non-realist nature of the literary forms of the Greeks, their intensely social, or civic, moral outlook, and their philosophical preference for the universal, so the modern novel is closely allied on the one hand to the realist epistemology of the modern period, and on the other to the individualism of its social structure'. The rise of the novel must then be understood in relation to post-Cartesian philosophy and to the sociology of early capitalism. Whereas *Fiction and the Reading Public* had relied on impressionist renderings of the social background, Watt offers a more precise, often statistical, characterisation of such events as the growth of urbanisation, the development of the publishing industry, and the changing patterns of marriage, situating all of these in relation to the new literary form.

The reliance on other academic disciplines, the belief that the best understanding of the novelistic text requires an understanding of its context – these aspects of *The Rise of the Novel* were highly characteristic of criticism of fiction in the fifties. But this fact should not suggest any emerging consensus. Everything depended on how one answered certain fundamental methodological questions, such as, which other disciplines? Which contexts for the novel? Lionel Trilling, whose critical viewpoint emerged out of the radical political setting of the American thirties, always retained a conception of the novel as a social document, writing in the widely anthologised essay 'Manners, Morals, and the Novel' (1948) that fiction 'is a perpetual quest for reality, the field of its research being always the social world, the material of its analysis being always manners as the indication of the direction of man's soul'. It is the appearance of 'soul' at the end of this sentence that is most immediately pertinent, signalling as it does another direction in Trilling's thought, which is also another direction in the larger community of critics.

For the soul whose fate manifests itself in social manners is in Trilling's work preeminently the domain of psychoanalysis, and it is among the most salient aspects of his development that a perspective so resolutely social and political should come to accommodate a psychoanalytic approach to the novel. Trilling is unimpressed by the widely presumed antagonism between public and private methodological orientations, between the legacy of Marx and the legacy of Freud. In the essay on James's *The Princess Casamassima* (1948) Trilling begins by defending the 'solid accuracy of James's political detail' and praising the novel as 'a brilliantly precise representation of social actuality'. But then he turns sharply in order to suggest how a 'personal fantasy' of family life is concealed behind the pattern of narrative events, and he sees no tension between these two perspectives. Even more striking is the movement in the later essay on

Little Dorrit (1953) where Trilling first suggests that even within a body of fiction as socially concerned as that of Dickens, *Little Dorrit* is '*more* about society than any of the others, that it is about society in its very essence'. Just a few pages later he writes that the novel anticipates Freud's 'essential theory of the neurosis', and describes the congruity between the Dickensian and the Freudian conceptions of the mind. This startling juxtaposition of society and psyche is not intended as a relaxed eclecticism; Trilling wants to situate the novel at the point of intersection of apparently distinct realms, and accordingly he describes his subject as 'the psychological aspects of the representation of society'. This last is a characteristic locution. Trilling seeks a picture of the novel large enough to assimilate contrasting methodologies, a picture in which Marx and Freud, politics and the psyche, can be seen to meet and marry.

Trilling's Freud exists as part of a fragile web of interpretative positions, but for other critics of the novel, a commitment to psychoanalysis – encouraged in part by Trilling's own example – implied a radical critique of other approaches. Among the many post-war applications of psychoanalysis to fiction, Simon O. Lesser's *Fiction and the Unconscious* (1957) has the virtue of explicitly announcing its principles. Whereas Trilling's goal is to sustain the commerce between moral and psychological categories, according to Lesser, 'The claim that moral issues constitute the basic subject matter of fiction is, I believe, seriously inflated.' *Fiction and the Unconscious* is not interested in how fiction edifies the moral sense but rather in how it compels the instinctual sense: the answer it derives from Freud is that the novel emanates from the same deep psychic sources that regulate play, fantasy, and wit. Lesser follows Hanns Sachs in defining the basic novelistic subject as 'the struggle between impulse and inhibition', contending that the novelist 'provides us with images of our emotional problems expressed in an idiom of characters and events'. Just as he sees moral concerns as largely superficial, so Lesser repudiates the autonomy of form. Form, he hypothesises, 'has but a single objective: the communication of the expressive content in a way which provides a maximum amount of pleasure and minimizes guilt and anxiety'. These are extreme propositions, and it is the psychoanalytic radicalism of Lesser's book that makes it historically interesting. *Fiction and the Unconscious*, just to the extent that it is more uncompromising than other works of psychoanalytic criticism, indicates how fundamental were the implications of such a reinterpretation of the critical debate. It was one thing for critics to choose Freudian concepts according to taste, and it was another to carry through the logic of the psychoanalytic view of the novel, a logic that challenged prevailing approaches as thoroughly as did the logic of Marxism.

The other significant, though less radical, manifestation of psychoanalytic influence appeared in 'myth criticism', that loose rubric draped around an ill-defined perspective. Here the important figure was frequently Jung, though Freud's *Totem and Taboo* played a part, and the attractive Jungian hypothesis was that of a collective unconscious, a form of racial memory that might explain the striking recurrence of certain fictional motifs and narrative structures. At the same time, the maturing of anthropology offered more systematic characterisations of myth and ritual, formulations largely derived from the study of non-European communities, which might then be applied to the grand ceremony that is Western literature. In his introduction to a collection of essays called *Myth and Literature* (1966), John B. Vickery wrote that 'myth forms the matrix out of which literature emerges both historically and psychologically. As a result, literary plots, characters, themes, and images are basically complications and displacements of similar elements in myths and folktales.' Beginning in the late forties, a rash of mythic readings of the novel appeared, in which such paradigms as the hanged man, the sacrificial scapegoat, and the rite of passage were seen as determinants of the fiction and bases for interpretative activity.

In his *Anatomy of Criticism* (1957) Northrop Frye writes that 'the structural principles of literature are as closely related to mythology and comparative religion as those of painting are to geometry', and while Frye's ambitious work cannot be contained by the category 'myth criticism' it defends and illustrates the view that we must 'stand back' from the particular text if we are to recognise 'its archetypal organization' and its 'mythopoeic designs'. In line with the programme of 'standing back' in order to let pattern emerge, Frye insists on the distinction between 'fiction' and 'novel' so little respected in the writings we have encountered. According to Frye, the tendency to identify the former term with the latter has led to a loss of crucial distinctions and an impoverishment of a literary tradition.

By fiction Frye means nothing less than 'the genre of the written word, in which prose tends to become the predominating rhythm'. He then reserves 'novel' to name just one form of fiction, epitomised by the work of Defoe, Fielding, Austen, and James. Once we grant this point, then it becomes possible to make more of James's claim, offered in the preface to *The American* (1907), that romance is an independent strain in the fictional tradition – a strain, adds Frye, that essentially differs from the novel by aiming toward psychological archetypes rather than 'real people'. Similarly Frye argues for the *confession* as a distinct prose form, one that merges into the novel but that has its own independent lineage and its own modal integrity. In his most original proposal he suggests that we recognise a fourth tradition identified with such names as Rabelais, Swift, Voltaire, Peacock, and Huxley. Menippean satire is what once served as the classifying rubric, but Frye suggests that we call this form the 'anatomy' and he characterises it in terms of 'variety of subject-matter and a strong interest in ideas'. Fortified with this battery of distinctions – novel, romance, confession, anatomy – Frye goes on to suggest that these strains have entered into every possible combination, with Joyce's *Ulysses* attaining the dignity of 'a complete prose epic with all four forms employed in it, all of practically equal importance, and all essential to one another'. There is no great novelistic tradition, according to Frye, but diverse traditions of fiction; there is no progress in technique, only a variety of technical conventions.

Wayne Booth's *The Rhetoric of Fiction* (1961) will mark the final boundary of this chapter, not because it represents any conclusion to an increasingly complex history, but because with Frye's *Anatomy* it effectively challenged a dominant structure of critical ideas and in so doing prepared for the radical transformations of these last twenty-five years. Booth kept his attention on the Jamesian concern with technical matters that had been consistently ignored by the Marxists, the Freudians, and the myth-critics, but he invoked the Jamesian tradition only to place himself in opposition to its orthodoxy. Indeed, it is part of Booth's task to establish the coherence of an orthodoxy that had rarely acknowledged its dogmas.

The value-laden distinction between telling and showing, so prominent in the Jamesian view of the novel, is the thread Booth tugs until the web of assumptions begins to loosen. The pursuit of the perfect realist illusion, the prohibitions against authorial commentary, the demand for direct presentation of scene – Booth contests the hold of these familiar propositions by reminding us that verisimilitude 'always operates within a larger artifice', and that the presence of an author is a convention like another. He goes further by arguing that the 'telling' function cannot be restricted to explicit authorial intervention and that even without overt commentary 'hundreds of devices remain for revealing judgment and molding responses'. The notion that the author can withdraw to the perfect objectivity of pure *showing* is utopian: 'Everything he *shows* will serve to *tell*; the line between showing and telling is always to some degree an arbitrary one.' The author of a novel can never disappear, can never avoid implying values, can never eradicate the image of an 'implied author' who is responsible for the moral and emotional tone of the work.

Both the pursuit of an austere realism and the pursuit of an uncompromising formalism, the two ambitions that controlled so much thinking about fiction, betrayed unmistakable hostility to the 'impurity' of the author's presence. Both repudiated what Booth means by 'rhetoric', the writer's appeal to the reader, the author's attempt to guide the responses of the audience. *The Rhetoric of Fiction* seeks to show that 'the most admired literature is in fact radically contaminated with rhetoric'. What follows is that the techniques of modernist fiction have none of the historical preminence that Lubbock, for instance, had granted them. James's use of the 'third-person reflector' is not a culmination of fictional progress; it is just 'one mode among many'. Indeed the desire to establish general principles of fictional success is the book's largest target, a target large enough to encompass such distinct figures as Lubbock and F. R. Leavis. Booth criticises the schematising of technical alternatives in *The Rhetoric of Fiction*, just as he sees *The Great Tradition* as 'seriously marred by the desire to elevate one kind of fiction above all others'. The need to respect the plurality of novelistic kinds is an abiding motif of the argument, ratified by the perception that all authors are at some point disloyal to their general standards: 'in place of abstract rules about consistency and objectivity in the use of point of view, we need more painstaking accounts of how great tales are told'.

What Booth calls his 'antidogmatism' comes very close to being 'antimodern'. He is keen to demonstrate the dangers of an authorial silence that leaves unclear how distant we should be from a character such as Joyce's Stephen Dedalus. He points to the danger of the 'inside views' so prevalent in modern fictional technique and, from Booth's standpoint, so likely to paralyse our moral judgement. A stated aim of the book is to free us from arbitrary distinctions which limit the satisfactions the novel can provide, but it is evident that in order to achieve that freedom, we are obliged to emancipate ourselves from major presuppositions of the modernist critical programme. The image of multiple interests and satisfactions leads to what Booth describes as a 'critical pluralism'. Although he regrets that Frye's categories in the *Anatomy of Criticism* are so broad, Booth shares Frye's enthusiasm for multiplying distinctions as a way of liberating the critical intelligence. Frye's call for a 'total acceptance' of the imaginative fields harmonises with Booth's acknowledgment of many modes, many traditions, and many techniques; and no doubt a reason for the immediate influence of their two books is that they seemed to offer academic criticism the prospect of at last eradicating the normative generalities that had shadowed the emergence of modernist theories of fiction.

And yet there is a telling paradox which attends this moment of apparent liberation. Having demonstrated the undesirability of a 'general rhetoric' of the novel, Booth suggests that it is now time to divert attention from abstract principles to particular studies of given novels. On the other hand, Frye makes particular distinctions on his way to archetypes of high generality, inspired by the thought that there are 'narrative categories of literature broader than, or logically prior to, the ordinary literary genres'. These arguments are sharply contrasting, but they have one similarly powerful consequence for the history we have been following: if we fully accept the logic of either argument, the novel begins to dissolve as a coherent object of study. If we are as particular as Booth asks us to be, if we abandon the search for a 'general rhetoric', then we must wonder why that generality 'the novel' should set the terms of any inquiry. On the other side, if we grant Frye's premises, then we are led to the opinion that a 'novel-centred' view of fiction must be abandoned and further that the novel, like any other genre, is derivative from broader 'narrative categories'. In an important respect the generalising habits of a critic such as Frye fed upon the particularising habits of a critic such as Booth. Deprived of an essence of its own, the novel is more likely to be assimilated by the essences of the narratologists, the mythographers, the Marxists, the linguists, the psychoanalysts.

The paradox, then, is that in the effort to free novelistic criticism from the constraints of narrow definition and valuation, the form loses force as a locus of critical activity. Under the stress of these two commitments, to the irreducible particularity of individual works and to the generality of archetypes, the domain marked out by the name 'novel' loses some of its clarity, with the result that the boundaries of novelistic criticism become increasingly unsure. It is of course true that many critics were able to ignore the methodological confusion and to compose distinguished studies of novels and novelists, but it is also true that radical challenges were soon posed by highly technical, cross-disciplinary methods which employed a new body of concepts in reinterpreting the 'criticism of fiction' in terms of the 'theory of narrative'. Consideration of this latter development belongs to another essay, while this chapter ends by emphasising how an unsteady critical tradition, in the act of broadening its concerns, perfected its vulnerability.

Bibliography

Introduction

Bledstein, Burton J., *The Culture of Professionalism: The Middle Class and the Development of Higher Education in America* (New York, 1976).

Bürger, Peter, *The Institution of the Avant-Garde*, tr. Michael Shaw (Minneapolis, 1984).

Eliot, T. S., *To Criticize the Critic: Eight Essays on Literature and Education* (New York, 1965).

The Use of Poetry and the Use of Criticism: Studies in the Relation of Criticism to Poetry in England (London, 1933).

Flint, R. W. (ed.), *Let's Murder the Moonshine: Selected Writings of F. T. Marinetti* (1971; rpt. Los Angeles, 1993).

Graff, Gerald, *Professing Literature: An Institutional History* (Chicago, 1987).

Habermas, Jürgen, 'A Review of Gadamar's *Truth and Method*', in Fred R. Dallmayr and Thomas A. McCarthy (eds.), *Understanding and Social Inquiry* (Notre Dame, 1977), pp. 335–63.

Huyssen, Andreas, *After the Great Divide: Modernism, Mass Culture, Postmodernism* (Bloomington, 1986).

Kimball, Bruce A., *The 'True Professional Ideal' in America: A History* (Cambridge, Mass., 1992).

Larson, Magali Sarfatti, *The Rise of Professionalism: A Sociological Analysis* (Berkeley, 1977).

Newman, Charles, *The Post-Modern Aura* (Evanston, Ill., 1985).

Rainey, Lawrence, 'The Creation of the Avant-Garde: F. T. Marinetti and Ezra Pound', *Modernism/Modernity*, 1 (September 1994), pp. 195–219.

'The Price of Modernism: Publishing *The Waste Land*', in Ronald Bush (ed.), *T. S. Eliot: The Modernist in History* (Cambridge, 1990), pp. 90–133.

Saintsbury, George, *The History of Criticism and Literary Taste in Europe, from the Earliest Texts to the Present* (3 vols., Edinburgh, 1900–4).

Veeser, H. Aram (ed.), *The New Historicism* (New York, 1989).

Veysey, Laurence, *The Emergence of the American University* (Chicago, 1965).

THE MODERNISTS
1 T. S. Eliot

Works by Eliot:

'The *Action Française*, M. Maurras, and Mr. Ward', *Criterion*, 7 (1928),

pp. 195–203.

After Strange Gods: A Primer of Modern Heresy (London, 1934).

'A Commentary', *Criterion*, 7 (1928), pp. 97–9.

'Critical Note', *The Collected Poems of Harold Monro* (London, 1933), pp. xiii–xvi.

Dante (London, 1929).

Elizabethan Essays (London, 1934).

Essays Ancient and Modern (London, 1936).

'Experiment in Criticism', *Bookman*, 70 (1929), pp. 225–33.

Ezra Pound: His Metric and Poetry (New York, 1917).

For Lancelot Andrewes (London, 1928).

Homage to John Dryden: Three Essays on the Poetry of the Seventeenth Century (London, 1924).

'Homage à Charles Maurras', *Aspects de la France et du monde*, 25 April (1948), p. 6.

The Idea of a Christian Society (London, 1939).

'The Idea of a Literary Review', *Criterion*, 4 (1926), pp. 1–6.

'In Memory of Henry James', *Egoist*, 5 (1918), pp. 1–2.

Knowledge and Experience in the Philosophy of F. H. Bradley (London, 1964).

'Last Words', *Criterion*, 18 (1939), pp. 269–75.

'Leibniz' Monads and Bradley's Finite Centres', *Monist*, 26 (1916), pp. 566–76.

The Letters of T. S. Eliot, Volume 1: 1898–1922, ed. Valerie Eliot (London, 1988).

'Lettre d'Angleterre', *Nouvelle Revue Française*, 21 (1923), pp. 619–25.

'The Literature of Fascism', *Criterion*, 8 (1928), pp. 280–90.

'Literature, Science, and Dogma', *Dial*, 82 (1927), pp. 239–43.

'London Letter', *Dial*, 70 (1921), pp. 448–53.

'Mr. Read and Mr. Fernandez', *Criterion*, 4 (1926), pp. 751–7.

'Modern Tendencies in Poetry', *Shama'a*, 1 (1920), pp. 9–18.

'A Note on Poetry and Belief', *Enemy*, 1 (1927), pp. 15–17.

'Notes on the Way', *Time and Tide*, 16 (1935), pp. 6–7.

Notes towards the Definition of Culture (London, 1948).

'Observations', *Egoist*, 5 (1918), pp. 69–70.

On Poetry and Poets (London, 1957).

'The Post-Georgians', *Athenaeum*, 11 April (1919), pp. 171–2.

'Reflections on Contemporary Poetry', *Egoist*, 4 (1917), p. 151.

The Sacred Wood: Essays on Poetry and Criticism (London, 1920; 2nd edn., 1928).

'A Sceptical Patrician', *Athenaeum*, 23 May (1919), pp. 361–2.

Selected Essays, new edn. (New York, 1950).

A Sermon Preached in Magdalene College Chapel (Cambridge, 1948).

'Shakespeare and Montaigne', *Times Literary Supplement*, 24 December (1925), p. 895.

Syllabus of a Course of Six Lectures on Modern French Literature (Oxford, 1916).

To Criticize the Critic and Other Writings (London, 1965).

The Varieties of Metaphysical Poetry: The Clark Lectures at Trinity College, Cambridge, 1926, and the Turnbull Lectures at the Johns Hopkins University, 1933, ed. Ronald Schuchard (London, 1993).

The Use of Poetry and the Use of Criticism: Studies in the Relation of Criticism to Poetry in England (London, 1933).

'Verse Pleasant and Unpleasant', *Egoist*, 5 (1918), pp. 43–4.

'The Voice of His Time', *Listener*, 27 (1942), pp. 211–12.

Secondary sources:

Ackroyd, Peter, *T. S. Eliot: A Life* (New York, 1984).

Asher, Kenneth George, *T. S. Eliot and Ideology* (Cambridge, 1995).

Babbitt, Irving, *Democracy and Leadership* (Boston, 1925).

    Literature and the American College: Essays in Defense of the Humanities (Boston, 1908).

    Masters of Modern French Criticism (Boston, 1912).

    Rousseau and Romanticism (Boston, 1919).

Bell, Clive, *Art* (London, 1913).

Benda, Julian, *Belphégor: Essai sur l'esthetique de la présente société française* (Paris, 1918); tr. S. J. I. Lawson (New York, 1929).

    La trahison des clercs (Paris, 1927); tr. Richard Aldington, *The Treason of the Intellectuals* (New York, 1928).

Bergonzi, Bernard, *T. S. Eliot* (New York, 1972).

Bergson, Henri, *Essai sur les données immédiates de la conscience* (Paris, 1889); tr. F. L. Pogson, *Time and Free Will: An Essay on the Immediate Data of Consciousness* (London, 1913).

    Introduction à la metaphysique', *Revue de metaphysique et de morale*, 11 (1903), pp. 1–36; tr. T. E. Hulme, *An Introduction to Metaphysics* (London, 1913).

    L'Évolution créatrice (Paris, 1907); tr. Arthur Mitchell, *Creative Evolution* (New York, 1911).

    Matière et memoire (Pris, 1896); tr. Nancy Margaret Paul and W. Scott Palmer [pseud.], *Matter and Memory* (New York, 1911).

Blackmur, Richard P., *The Lion and the Honeycombe: Essays in Solicitude and Critique* (New York, 1955).

    'T. S. Eliot', *Hound and Horn*, 1 (1928), pp. 187–213, 291–319.

Bradley, Andrew Cecil, *A Miscellany* (London, 1929).

Bradley, Francis Herbert, *Appearance and Reality: A Metaphysical Essay*, 2nd edn. (Oxford, 1897).

    Essays on Truth and Reality (Oxford, 1914).

Brooke, Rupert, 'John Donne, the Elizabethan', *Nation*, 12 (1913), pp. 825–6.

Burne, Glenn S., *Remy de Gourmont: His Ideas and Influence in England and America* (Carbondale, Ill., 1963).

Bush, Ronald, *T. S. Eliot: A Study in Character and Style* (New York, 1983).

Chace, William, *The Political Identities of Ezra Pound and T. S. Eliot* (Stanford, 1973).

Donoghue, Denis, *The Old Moderns: Essays on Literature and Theory* (New York, 1994).

Douglass, Paul, *Bergson, Eliot, and American Literature* (Lexington, Ky., 1986).

Ford, Ford Madox, 'From China to Peru', *Outlook*, 35 (1915), p. 900.

Gallup, Donald C., *T. S. Eliot: A Bibliography*, rev. edn. (New York, 1969).

Gordon, Lyndall, *Eliot's Early Years* (New York, 1977).

Gourmont, Remy de, *Lettres à l'Amazone* (Paris, 1914); tr. Richard Aldington, *Letters to the Amazon* (London, 1931).

  Le Livre des masques (Paris, 1896).

  Le Problème du style (Paris, 1902).

  Promenades littéraires, 7 vols. (Paris, 1904–27).

  Selected Writings, tr. Glenn S. Burne (Ann Arbor, 1966).

Gray, Piers, *T. S. Eliot's Intellectual and Poetic Development, 1909–1922* (Sussex, 1982).

Harwood, John, *Eliot to Derrida: The Poverty of Interpretation* (London, 1995).

Howarth, Herbert, *Notes on Some Figures Behind T. S. Eliot* (Boston, 1964).

Hulme, Thomas Ernest, *Speculations: Essays on Humanism and the Philosophy of Art*, ed. Herbert Read (New York, 1924).

  Further Speculations, ed. Sam Hynes (Minneapolis, 1955).

Jain, Manju, *T. S. Eliot and American Philosophy* (Cambridge, 1992).

Jay, Gregory, *T. S. Eliot and the Poetics of Literary History* (Baton Rouge, 1983).

Jones, Alun R., *Life and Opinions of T. E. Hulme* (London, 1960).

Julius, Anthony, *T. S. Eliot, Antisemitism, and Literary Form* (Cambridge, 1996).

Kermode, Frank, *Romantic Image* (London, 1957).

Kojecky, Roger, *T. S. Eliot's Social Criticism* (London, 1971).

Lasserre, Pierre, 'La philosophie de M. Bergson', *L'Action Française*, 27 (1911), pp. 168–80.

  Le Romantisme français (Paris, 1907).

Leavis, Frank Raymond, 'T. S. Eliot – A Reply to the Condescending', *The Cambridge Review*, 8 (1929), pp. 254–6.

Levenson, Michael, *A Genealogy of Modernism: A Study of English Literary Doctrine, 1908–1922* (Cambridge, 1984).

Lobb, Edward, *T. S. Eliot and the Romantic Critical Tradition* (London, 1981).

Margolis, John D., *T. S. Eliot's Intellectual Development* (Chicago, 1972).

Maritain, Jacques, *Art et scholastique* (Paris, 1920; rev. edn. 1927); tr. John O'Connor, *The Philosophy of Art* (Ditchling, 1923), J. F. Scanlan, *Art and Scholasticism, with Other Essays* (New York, 1952).

  Une Opinion sur Charles Maurras et le devoir des catholiques (Paris, 1926).

  Réflexions sur l'intelligence et sur sa vie propre (Paris, 1924).

  Three Reformers: Luther, Descartes, Rousseau (Paris, 1925).

Martin, Graham, *Eliot in Perspective: A Symposium* (New York, 1970).

Matthiessen, Francis Otto, *The Achievement of T. S. Eliot: An Essay on the Nature of Poetry* (Boston, 1935).

Maurras, Charles, *L'Avenir de l'intelligence* (Paris, 1905).

Menand, Louis, *Discovering Modernism: T. S. Eliot and His Context* (New York, 1987).

'Eliot and the Jews', *The New York Review of Books*, 43 (6 June 1996), pp. 34–41.

Michaels, Walter Benn, 'Philosophy in Kinkanja: Eliot's Pragmatism', *Glyph*, 8 (1981), pp. 170–202.

Moody, A. D., *Thomas Sterns Eliot, Poet* (Cambridge, 1979).

Tracing T. S. Eliot's Spirit: Essays on His Poetry and Thought (Cambridge, 1996).

More, Paul Elmer, *Aristocracy and Justice* (Boston, 1915).

Murry, John Middleton, 'Milton or Shakespeare?', *Nation and the Athenaeum*, 28 (1921), pp. 916–17.

Newton-De Molina, David (ed.), *The Literary Criticism of T. S. Eliot: New Essays* (London, 1977).

North, Michael, *The Political Aesthetic of Yeats, Eliot, and Pound* (Cambridge, 1991).

Pound, Ezra, 'This Hulme Business', *Townsman*, 2 (1939), p. 15.

Richards, Ivor Armstrong, *Science and Poetry* (London, 1926).

Ricks, Christopher, *T. S. Eliot and Prejudice* (London, 1988).

Robertson, John M., *The Problem of 'Hamlet'* (London, 1919).

Montaigne and Shakespeare (London, 1897; rev. edn. 1909).

Ross, Robert H., *The Georgian Revolt: The Rise and Fall of a Poetic Ideal* (Carbondale, Ill., 1965).

Schwartz, Delmore, 'T. S. Eliot as the International Hero', *Partisan Review*, 12 (1945), pp. 199–206.

Sorel, Georges, *Réflexions sur la violence* (Paris, 1907); tr. T. E. Hulme, *Reflections on Violence* (London, 1916).

Spender, Stephen, *T. S. Eliot* (New York, 1975).

Stead, C. K., *The New Poetic* (London, 1964).

Sternhell, Zeev, *Neither Right Nor Left: Fascist Ideology in France* (Berkeley, 1986).

Stoll, Elmer Edgar, *'Hamlet': A Historical and Comparative Study* (Minneapolis, 1919).

Symons, Arthur, *The Symbolist Movement in Literature* (London, 1899; rev. edn. 1908).

Thibaudet, Albert, 'L'esthetique des trois traditions', *La Nouvelle Revue Française*, 9 (1913), pp. 5–42, 355–93.

Waugh, Arthur, *Tradition and Change: Studies in Contemporary Literature* (London, 1919).

Weber, Eugen, *Action Française: Royalism and Reaction in Twentieth-Century France* (Stanford, 1962).

Wellek, René, 'T. S. Eliot', in *A History of Modern Criticism, 1750–1950, Volume 5: English Criticism, 1900–1950* (New Haven, 1986), pp. 176–220.

Worringer, Wilhelm, *Abstraktion und Einfühlung* (Munich, 1908); tr. Michael Bullock, *Abstraction and Empathy* (New York, 1953).

2 Ezra Pound

Works by Pound:

ABC of Reading (1934; rpt. New York, 1960).
Ezra Pound's Poetry and Prose Contributions to Periodicals, ed. Lea Baechler, A. Walton Litz, and James Longenbach (New York and London, 1991).
Guide to Kulchur (1938; rpt. New York, 1970).
The Letters of Ezra Pound, ed. D. D. Paige (New York, 1950).
Literary Essays of Ezra Pound, ed. T. S. Eliot (New York, 1968).
Machine Art and Other Writings: The Lost Thought of the Italian Years, ed. Maria Luisa Ardizzione (Durham, 1996).
Selected Letters of Ezra Pound, 1907–1941, ed. D. D. Paige (1950; rpt. New York, 1971).
The Selected Letters of Ezra Pound to John Quinn, 1915–1924, ed. Timothy Materer (Durham, 1991).
Selected Prose, 1909–1965, ed. William Cookson (New York, 1973).
The Spirit of Romance (1910; rpt. New York, 1968).

Secondary sources:

Albright, Daniel, *Quantum Poetics: Yeats, Pound, Eliot, and the Science of Modernism* (New York, 1997).
Beach, Christopher, *ABC of Influence: Ezra Pound and the Remaking of American Poetic Tradition* (Berkeley, 1992).
Bell, Ian F. A., *Critic as Scientist: The Modernist Poetics of Ezra Pound* (London, 1981).
Coyle, Michael, *Ezra Pound, Popular Genres, and the Discourse of Culture* (University Park, Penn., 1995).
Gallup, Donald, *Ezra Pound: A Bibliography* (Charlottesville, Va., 1983).
Lentricchia, Frank, *Modernist Quartet* (Cambridge, 1994).
North, Michael, *The Political Aesthetic of Yeats, Eliot, and Pound* (Cambridge, 1991).
Rainey, Lawrence, *Institutions of Modernism: Literary Elites and Public Culture* (New Haven, 1998).
Ruthven, K. K., *Ezra Pound as Literary Critic* (London, 1990).
Seiburth, Richard, *Instigations: Ezra Pound and Remy de Gourmont* (Cambridge, Mass., 1978).
Sherry, Vincent, *Ezra Pound, Wyndham Lewis, and Radical Modernism* (New York, 1993).
Wellek, René, 'Ezra Pound', in *A History of Modern Criticism, 1750–1950, Volume 5: English Criticism, 1900–1950* (New Haven, 1986), pp. 152–69.

3 Gertrude Stein

Works by Stein:

As Fine As Melanctha (New Haven, 1954).

The Autobiography of Alice B. Toklas (1933; rpt. New York, 1990).
Everybody's Autobiography (1937; rpt. London, 1985).
The Geographical History of America or The Relation of Human Nature to the Human Mind (1936; rpt. Baltimore, 1995).
Geography and Plays (1922; rpt. Madison, Wis., 1993).
Gertrude Stein and the Making of Literature, ed. Shirley Neuman and Ira B. Nadel (Boston, 1988).
How to Write (1931; rpt. Los Angeles, 1995).
How Writing Is Written, ed. Robert Bartlett Haas (Los Angeles, 1974).
Lectures in America (1935; rpt. Boston, 1985).
The Letters of Gertrude Stein and Carl Van Vechten, ed. Edward Burns (New York, 1986).
The Making of Americans (1925; rpt. Normal, Ill., 1995).
Narration (Chicago, 1935).
Portraits and Prayers (New York, 1934).
A Primer for the Gradual Understanding of Gertrude Stein, ed. Robert Bartlett Haas (Los Angeles, 1971).
Reflections on the Atomic Bomb, ed. Robert Bartlett Haas (Los Angeles, 1973).
Selected Writings of Gertrude Stein, ed. Carl Van Vechten (1946; rpt. New York, 1962).
Sherwood Anderson/Gertrude Stein: Correspondence and Personal Essays, ed. Ray Lewis White (Chapel Hill, 1972).
A Stein Reader, ed. Ulla E. Dydo (Evanston, Ill., 1993).
Wars I Have Seen (New York, 1945).
What Are Master-pieces (Los Angeles, 1940).

Secondary sources:

Berry, Ellen E., *Curved Thought and Textual Writing: Gertrude Stein's Postmodernism* (Ann Arbor, 1992).
Bloom, Harold (ed.), *Modern Critical Views on Gertrude Stein* (New York, 1986).
Bowers, Jane Palatini, *Gertrude Stein* (New York, 1993).
Bridgman, Richard, *Gertrude Stein in Pieces* (New York, 1970).
Bush, Clive, *Halfway to Revolution: Investigation and Crisis in the Work of Henry Adams, William James, and Gertrude Stein* (New Haven, 1991).
Caramello, Charles, 'Gertrude Stein as Exemplary Theorist', in Shirley Neuman and Ira B. Nadal (eds.), *Gertrude Stein and the Making of Literature* (Boston, 1988), pp. 1–7.
Cavell, Stanley, *This New Yet Unapproachable America* (Albuquerque, 1989).
Chessman, Harriet Scott, *The Public is Invited to Dance: Representation, the Body, and Dialogue in Gertrude Stein* (Stanford, 1989).
Copeland, Carolyn Faunce, *Language and Time and Gertrude Stein* (Iowa City, 1975).
Dearborn, Mary V., *Pocahontas's Daughters: Gender and Ethnicity in American Culture* (New York, 1986).

DeKoven, Marianne, *A Different Language: Gertrude Stein's Experimental Writing* (Madison, Wis., 1983).

Dubnick, Randa, *The Structure of Obscurity: Gertrude Stein, Language, and Cubism* (Urbana, 1984).

Eliot, T. S., *Homage to John Dryden* (London, 1924).

Emerson, Ralph Waldo, *Essays and Lectures* (New York, 1983).

Gallup, Donald (ed.), *The Flowers of Friendship: Letters Written to Gertrude Stein* (New York, 1979).

Hoffman, Michael J., *Gertrude Stein* (New York, 1976).

James, William, *The Principles of Psychology*, 2 vols. (1890; rpt. Cambridge, Mass., 1983).

Knapp, Bettina, L., *Gertrude Stein* (New York, 1990).

Luhan, Mabel Dodge, *Movers and Shakers* (New York, 1936).

Matthews, T. S., 'Gertrude Stein Comes Home', *The New Republic*, 81 (5 December 1934), pp. 100–1.

Mellow, James, *Charmed Circle: Gertrude Stein & Company* (New York, 1974).

Miller, Rosalind S., *Gertrude Stein: Form and Intelligibility* (New York, 1949).

Newman, Shirley C., *Gertrude Stein: Autobiography and the Problem of Narration* (Victoria, Canada, 1979).

Perloff, Marjorie, *The Poetics of Indeterminacy: Rimbaud to Cage* (Princeton, 1981).

Pound, Ezra, *Literary Essays*, ed. T. S. Eliot (New York, 1954).

Rogers, W. G., *When This You See Remember Me: Gertrude Stein in Person* (New York, 1948).

Ruddick, Lisa, *Reading Gertrude Stein: Body, Text, Gnosis* (Ithaca, 1990).

Steiner, Wendy, *Exact Resemblance to Exact Resemblance: The Literary Portraiture of Gertrude Stein* (New Haven, 1978).

Weinstein, Norman, *Gertrude Stein and the Literature of Modern Consciousness* (New York, 1970).

White, Ray Lewis, *Gertrude Stein and Alice B. Toklas: A Reference Guide* (Boston, 1984).

4 Virginia Woolf

Works by Woolf:

'"Anon" and "The Reader": Virginia Woolf's Last Essays', ed. Brenda Silver, *Twentieth-Century Literature*, 25 (1979), pp. 356–441.

The Captain's Deathbed and Other Essays (London, 1950).

Collected Essays, 4 vols. (London, 1967).

The Common Reader: First Series (London, 1925).

The Common Reader: Second Series (London, 1932).

Contemporary Writers (London, 1965).

The Death of the Moth and Other Essays (London, 1942).

The Diary of Virginia Woolf, ed. Anne Olivier Bell, 5 vols. (London, 1977–84).

The Essays of Virginia Woolf, ed. Andrew McNeillie, 3 vols. (London, 1986–9).

Granite and Rainbow (London, 1958).
The Letters of Virginia Woolf, ed. Nigel Nicolson and Joanne Trautmann, 6 vols. (London, 1975–80).
The Moment and Other Essays (London, 1947).
Moments of Being: Unpublished Autobiographical Writings, ed. Jeanne Schulkind (London, 1976).
A Room of One's Own (London, 1929).
Three Guineas (London, 1938).
Virginia Woolf's Reading Notebooks, ed. Brenda Silver (Princeton, 1983).
A Writer's Diary (London, 1954).

Secondary sources:

Batchelor, J. B., 'Feminism in Virginia Woolf', in Claire Sprague (ed.), *Virginia Woolf: A Collection of Critical Essays* (Englewood Cliffs, N.J., 1971), pp. 169–79.
Beer, Gillian, 'The Body of the People in Virginia Woolf', in Sue Roe (ed.), *Women Reading Women's Writing* (Brighton, 1987), pp. 83–114.
Benjamin, Walter, *Illuminations*, ed. Hannah Arendt (New York, 1968).
Daugherty, Beth Rigel, 'The Whole Contention Between Mr. Bennett and Mrs. Woolf, Revisited', in Elaine K. Ginsberg and Laura Moss Gottlieb (eds.), *Virginia Woolf: Centennial Essays* (New York, 1983), pp. 269–94.
Davenport, Tony, 'The Life of Monday or Tuesday', in Patricia Clements and Isobel Grundy (eds.), *Virginia Woolf: New Critical Essays* (London, 1983), pp. 157–75.
Ezel, Margaret, J. M., 'The Myth of Judith Shakespeare: Creating the Canon of Women's Literature', *New Literary History*, 21 (1990), pp. 579–92.
Fernald, Anne, 'A Room of One's Own: Personal Criticism and the Essay', *TCL*, 40 (1994), pp. 165–89.
Friedman, Susan Stanford, 'Virginia Woolf's Pedagogical Scenes of Reading: *The Voyage Out, The Common Reader*, and her "Common Readers"', *Modern Fiction Studies*, 38 (1992), pp. 101–25.
Goldman, Mark, *The Reader's Art: Virginia Woolf as Literary Critic* (The Hague, 1963).
Hyman, Virginia R., 'Late Victorian and Early Modern: Continuities in the Criticism of Leslie Stephen and Virginia Woolf', *English Literature in Transition*, 23 (1980), pp. 144–54.
Hynes, Samuel, 'The Whole Contention Between Mr. Bennett and Mrs. Woolf', *Novel: A Forum on Fiction*, 1 (1967), pp. 34–44.
Jones, Ellen Carol, 'Androgynous Vision and Artistic Process in Virginia Woolf's *A Room of One's Own*', in Morris Beja (ed.), *Critical Essays on Virginia Woolf*, (Boston, 1985), pp. 227–39.
Kamuf, Peggy, 'Penelope At Work: Interruptions in *A Room of One's Own*', *Novel: A Forum on Fiction*, 16 (1982), pp. 5–18.
Kirkpatrick, B. J., *A Bibliography of Virginia Woolf* (3rd edn., Oxford, 1980).
Klein, Kathleen Gregory, 'A Common Sitting Room: Virginia Woolf's Critique

of Women Writers', in Elaine K. Ginsberg and Laura Moss Gottlieb (eds.), *Virginia Woolf: Centennial Essays* (New York, 1983), pp. 231–48.

Marcus, Jane, *Art and Anger: Reading Like a Woman* (Columbus, Ohio, 1988).

'Liberty, Sorority, Misogyny', in Carolyn Heilbrun and Margaret R. Higgonet (eds.), *The Representation of Women in Fiction* (Baltimore, 1983), pp. 60–97.

'Taking the Bull by the Udders: Sexual Difference in Virginia Woolf: A Conspiracy Theory', in Jane Marcus (ed.), *Virginia Woolf and Bloomsbury: A Centenary Celebration* (Bloomington, Ind., 1987), pp. 146–69.

Marder, Herbert, *Feminism and Art: A Study of Virginia Woolf* (Chicago, 1968).

Meisel, Perry, *The Absent Father: Virginia Woolf and Walter Pater* (New Haven, 1980).

Moi, Toril, *Sexual/Textual Politics: Feminist Literary Theory* (London, 1985).

Richter, Harvena, *Virginia Woolf: The Inward Voyage* (Princeton, 1970).

Rigney, Barbara Hill, '"A Wreath Upon the Grave": The Influence of Virginia Woolf on Feminist Critical Theory', in Jeremy Hawthorn (ed.), *Criticism and Critical Theory*, (London, 1984), pp. 72–81.

Schwartz, Beth C., 'Thinking Back Through Our Mothers: Virginia Woolf Reads Shakespeare', *English Literary History*, 58 (1991), pp. 721–67.

Showalter, Elaine, *A Literature of Their Own: British Women Novelists from Bronte to Lessing* (Princeton, 1977).

Spender, Stephen, *World within World* (New York, 1951).

Steele, Elizabeth, *Virginia Woolf's Literary Sources and Allusions: A Guide to the Essays* (New York, 1983).

Wellek, René, 'Virginia Woolf', in *A History of Modern Criticism, 1750–1950, Volume 5: English Criticism, 1900–1950* (New Haven, 1986), pp. 65–84.

Zwerdling, Alex, *Virginia Woolf and the Real World* (Berkeley, 1986).

5 Wyndham Lewis

Works by Lewis:

The Art of Being Ruled (London, 1926).

Blasting and Bombardiering (1937; rpt. London, 1967).

The Demon of Progress in the Arts (London, 1954).

The Diabolical Principle and the Dithyrambic Spectator (London, 1931).

The Doom of Youth (London, 1932).

The Lion and the Fox: The Role of the Hero in the Plays of Shakespeare (London, 1927).

Men Without Art (London, 1934).

Paleface: The Philosophy of the 'Melting Pot' (London, 1929).

Rude Assignment: A Narrative of My Career Up-to-date (London, 1950).

Satire & Fiction (London, 1930).

Time and Western Man (London, 1927; rpt. Boston, 1957).

Wyndham Lewis on Art: Collected Writings, 1913–1956, ed. Walter Michel and C. J. Fox (London, 1969).

Secondary sources:

Baker, Keith Michael, 'Closing the French Revolution: Saint-Simon and Comte', in François Furet and Mona Ozouf (eds.), *The French Revolution and the Creation of Modern Political Culture, 1789–1848* (Oxford, 1989), pp. 325–31.

Benda, Julian, *Belphégor: Essai sur l'esthétique de la présente société française* (Paris, 1918); tr. S. J. I. Lawson (New York, 1929).

Bridson, D. G., *The Filibuster: A Study of the Political Ideas of Wyndham Lewis* (London, 1972).

Burns, Edward (ed.), *Gertrude Stein on Picasso* (New York, 1970).

Campbell, Sue Ellen, *The Enemy Opposite: The Outlaw Criticism of Wyndham Lewis* (Athens, Ohio, 1988).

Chapman, Robert, *Wyndham Lewis: Fictions and Satires* (London, 1972).

Gourmont, Remy de, *Esthétique de la langue française* (Paris, 1905).
Le Problème du style (Paris, 1902).

Grigson, Geoffrey, *A Master of Our Time: A Study of Wyndham Lewis* (1951; rpt. New York, 1972).

Jameson, Fredric, *Wyndham Lewis: The Modernist as Fascist.*

Kennedy, Emmet, *A Philosophe in the Age of Revolution: Destutt de Tracy and the Origins of Ideology* (Philadelphia, 1978).

Kenner, Hugh, *Wyndham Lewis* (Norfolk, Conn., 1954).

Norris, Christopher, and Nigel Mapp (eds.), *Wyndham Lewis: The Critical Achievement* (Cambridge, 1993).

Robinson, Alan, *Symbol to Vortex: Poetry, Painting, and Ideas, 1885–1914* (New York, 1985).

Schenker, Daniel, *Wyndham Lewis: Religion and Modernism* (Tuscaloosa, Ala., 1992).

Sherry, Vincent, *Ezra Pound, Wyndham Lewis, and Radical Modernism* (New York, 1993).

Wellek, René, 'Wyndham Lewis', *A History of Modern Criticism, 1750–1950, Volume 5: English Criticism, 1900–1950* (New Haven, 1986), pp. 169–75.

6 W. B. Yeats

Works by Yeats:

Autobiographies (New York, 1955).
Essays and Introductions (New York, 1961).
Explorations (New York, 1962).
Letters (New York, 1955).
Senate Speeches (New York, 1960).
Uncollected Prose, 2 vols. (New York, 1970–6).
The Variorum Edition of the Poems of W. B. Yeats (New York, 1966).

Secondary sources:

Brater, Enoch, 'W. B. Yeats: The Poet as Critic', *JML*, 4 (1975), pp. 651–76.

Christ, Carol T., *Victorian and Modern Poetics* (Chicago, 1984).

Cullingsford, Elizabeth Butler, *Gender and History in Yeats's Love Poetry* (Cambridge, 1993).

Eliot, T. S., 'Yeats', *On Poetry and Poets* (New York, 1957), pp. 295–308.

Foster, R. F., *W. B. Yeats: A Life. 1. The Apprentice Mage* (Oxford, 1997).

Frazier, Adrian, *Behind the Scenes: Yeats, Horniman, and the Struggle for the Abbey Theatre* (Berkeley, 1990).

Heaney, Seamus, 'Yeats as an Example?', *Preoccupations: Selected Prose, 1968–1978* (New York, 1980).

Howes, Marjorie, *Yeats's Nations: Gender, Class, and Irishness* (Cambridge, 1966).

Jain, Virendra Vijai, *W. B. Yeats as Literary Critic* (Dehli,1980).

Kearney, Richard, 'Between Politics and Literature: The Irish Cultural Journal', in *Transitions: Narratives in Modern Irish Culture* (Oxford, 1988), pp. 250–68.

The Irish Mind: Exploring Intellectual Traditions (Dublin, 1985).

Komesu, Okifumi, *The Double Perspective of Yeats's Aesthetic* (Totowa, N.J., 1984).

Leerssen, Joep, *Remembrance and Imagination: Patterns in the Historical and Literary Representation of Ireland in the Nineteenth Century* (Cork, 1996).

Lipking, Lawrence I., *The Life of the Poet: Beginning and Ending Poetic Careers* (Chicago, 1981).

Orr, Leonard, 'Yeats's Theories of Fiction', *Eire*, 21 (1986), pp. 152–8.

Prasad, Baidya Nath, *The Literary Criticism of W. B. Yeats* (New Dehli, 1985).

Said, Edward, *The World, the Text, and the Critic* (Cambridge, Mass., 1983).

Sena, Vinod, *W. B. Yeats: The Poet as Critic* (London, 1981).

Stallworthy, Jon, 'Yeats as Anthologist', in A. Norman Jeffares and K. G. W. Cross (eds.), *In Excited Reverie: A Centenary Tribute to William Butler Yeats* (New York, 1965).

Stanford, Derek (ed.), *Critics of the 'Nineties* (London, 1970).

Stuart, Francis, 'Irish Novelist Replies to Mr. Shaw', *The Irish Press*, 13 February 1937, p. 8.

Wellek, René, 'W. B. Yeats', in *A History of Modern Criticism, 1759–1950, Volume 5: English Criticism, 1900–1950* (New Haven, 1986), pp. 1–13.

7 The Harlem Renaissance

Primary sources:

Du Bois, W. E. B., *Book Reviews*, ed. Herbert Aptheker (New York, 1977).

W. E. B. Du Bois: A Reader, ed. Meyer Weinberg (New York, 1970).

Writings in Non-Periodical Literature Edited by Others, ed. Herbert Aptheker (New York, 1982).

Writings in Periodicals Edited by Others 1910–1934, ed. Herbert Aptheker, 4 vols. (New York, 1982).

Hurston, Zora Neale, *The Sanctified Church: The Folklore Writings of Zora Neale Hurston* (Berkeley, 1981).

Johnson, James Weldon, *Along This Way* (New York, 1933).
  The Autobiography of an Ex-Colored Man (Boston, 1912).
  Black Manhattan (New York, 1930).
  (ed.), *The Book of American Negro Poetry* (New York, 1922).
  (ed.), *The Book of American Negro Spirituals* (New York, 1925).
  'The Dilemma of the Negro Author', *American Mercury*, 15 (1928), pp. 477–81.
  'Negro Authors and White Publishers', *The Crisis*, 36 (1929), pp. 228–9.
  'Race Prejudice and the Negro Artist', *Harper's*, 157 (1928), pp. 769–76.
  (ed.), *The Second Book of American Negro Spirituals* (New York, 1926).
Locke, Alain, *The Critical Temper of Alain Locke: A Selection of His Essays on Art and Culture*, ed. Jeffrey C. Stewart (New York, 1983).
  (ed.), *The New Negro* (New York, 1925).
McKay, Claude, *The Passion of Claude McKay*, ed. Wayne F. Cooper (New York, 1973).
Schuyler, George S., 'At the Coffeehouse', *The Messenger*, 7 (1925), pp. 236–7.
  'The Negro-Art Hokum', *The Nation*, 122 (1926), pp. 662–3.
  'Our Greatest Gift to America', in Charles S. Johnson (ed.), *Ebony and Topaz: A Collectanea* (New York, 1927).
  'Our White Folks', *The American Mercury*, 12 (1927), pp. 385–92.

Secondary sources:

Andrews, William L. (ed.), *Critical Essays on W. E. B. Du Bois* (Boston, 1985).
Baker, Houston, A., Jr, *Modernism and the Harlem Renaissance* (Chicago, 1987).
Bassett, John E., *Harlem in Review: Critical Reactions to Black American Writers, 1917–1939* (London, 1992).
Bontemps, Arna (ed.), *The Harlem Renaissance Remembered* (New York, 1972).
Cooper, Wayne F., *Claude McKay: Rebel Sojourner in the Harlem Renaissance* (Baton Rouge, 1987).
Davis, Arthur P., and Michael W. Peplow (eds.), *The New Negro Renaissance: An Anthology* (New York, 1975).
Fleming, Robert E., *James Weldon Johnson* (Boston, 1987).
Gates, Henry Louis, Jr (ed.), *'Race', Writing, and Difference* (Chicago, 1986).
  The Signifying Monkey: A Theory of African-American Literary Criticism (New York, 1988).
  'The Trope of the New Negro and the Reconstruction of the Image of the Black', *Representations*, 24 (1988), pp. 129–55.
Harris, Leonard (ed.), *The Philosophy of Alain Locke: Harlem Renaissance and Beyond* (Philadelphia, 1989).
Huggins, Nathan Irvin, *Harlem Renaissance* (New York, 1971).
Hutchinson, George, *Harlem Renaissance in Black and White* (Cambridge, Mass., 1995).
Ikonné, Chidi, *From Du Bois to Van Vechten: The Early New Negro Literature,*

1903–1926 (Westport, Conn., 1981).

Johnson, Abby Arthur, and Ronald Maberry Johnson, *Propaganda and Aesthetics: The Literary Politics of Afro-American Magazines in the Twentieth Century* (Amherst, 1979).

Kellner, Bruce (ed.), *The Harlem Renaissance: A Historical Dictionary for the Era* (New York, 1984).

Kramer, Victor A. (ed.), *The Harlem Renaissance Re-examined* (New York, 1987).

Levy, Eugene, *James Weldon Johnson: Black Leader, Black Voice* (Chicago, 1973).

Lewis, David Levering, *W. E. B. Du Bois: Biography of a Race, 1868–1919* (New York, 1993).

    When Harlem Was in Vogue (New York, 1981).

Linnemann, Russell J. (ed.), *Alain Locke: Reflections on a Modern Renaissance Man* (Baton Rouge, 1982).

Martin, Tony, *Literary Garveyism: Garvey, Black Arts and the Harlem Renaissance* (Dover, Mass., 1983).

Peplow, Michael W., *George S. Schuyler* (Boston, 1980).

Perry, Margaret, *The Harlem Renaissance: An Annotated Bibliography and Commentary* (New York, 1982).

Rampersad, Arnold, *The Art and Imagination of W. E. B. Du Bois* (Cambridge, 1976).

Singh, Amrijit, William S. Shriver, and Stanley Brodwin, *The Harlem Renaissance: Revaluations* (New York, 1989).

Wall, Cheryl, *Women of the Harlem Renaissance* (Bloomington, 1995).

Washington, Johnny, *Alain Locke and Philosophy: A Quest for Cultural Pluralism* (New York, 1986).

Wintz, Carg D. (ed.), *Black Culture and the Harlem Renaissance* (Houston, 1988).

    The Critics and the Harlem Renaissance (New York, 1996).

    (ed.), *The Harlem Renaissance: Analysis and Assessment, 1940–1979* (New York, 1996).

    (ed.), *The Harlem Renaissance: Analysis and Assessment, 1980–1994* (New York, 1996).

THE NEW CRITICS

8 I. A. Richards

Works by Richards:

Basic English and Its Uses (New York, 1943).

Basic Rules of Reason (London, 1933).

Beyond (New York, 1973).

Coleridge on Imagination (1934; rpt. Bloomington, 1969).

Complementarities: Uncollected Essays, ed. John Paul Russo (Cambridge, 1976).

Correspondence: Selections, ed. John Constable (Oxford, 1990).

Design for Escape: World Education Through Modern Media (New York, 1968).

'Donne: "A Valediction: Forbidding Mourning"', in Oscar Williams (ed.), *Master Poems of the English Language* (New York, 1966), pp. 111–13.

(with C. K. Ogden and James Wood) *The Foundations of Aesthetics* (1922; rpt. New York, 1925).

How to Read a Page: A Course in Effective Reading with an Introduction to a Hundred Great Words (New York, 1942).

Internal Colloquies: Poems and Plays of I. A. Richards (New York, 1971).

Interpretation in Teaching (New York, 1938).

(with C. K. Ogden) *The Meaning of Meaning: A Study of the Influences of Language Upon Thought and of the Science of Symbolism* (1923; rpt. New York, 1956).

Mencius on the Mind: Experiments in Multiple Definition (London, 1932).

'On TSE: Notes for a Talk at the Institute of Contemporary Arts, London, June 29, 1965', in Allen Tate (ed.), *T. S. Eliot: The Man and His Work* (New York, 1966), pp. 1–10.

The Philosophy of Rhetoric (New York, 1936).

'Poetic Process and Literary Analysis', in Thomas A. Sebeok (ed.), *Style in Language* (Cambridge, 1960), pp. 9–24.

Poetries: A Collection of Essays by I. A. Richards Published to Celebrate his 80th Birthday, ed. Trevor Eaton (The Hague, 1974).

Poetries and Sciences: A Reissue of Science and Poetry (1926, 1935) with Commentary (New York, 1970).

Practical Criticism: A Study of Literary Judgment (1929; rpt. New York, 1966).

Principles of Literary Criticism (1925; rpt. New York, 1964).

The Republic of Plato, trans. (New York, 1942).

So Much Nearer: Essays Toward a World English (New York, 1968).

Speculative Instruments (London, 1955).

'Verse v. Prose', The English Association (London, 1978).

Why So Socrates? A Dramatic Version of Plato's Dialogues Euthyphro Apology Crito Phaedo (Cambridge, 1964).

Wyndham Lewis and I. A. Richards: A Friendship Document, 1928–57, ed. John Constable and S. J. M. Watson (Cambridge, 1989).

'Yale – Bergen Lecture', *Furioso*, 1 (1941), pp. 83–90.

Secondary sources:

Berthoff, Ann E., 'I. A. Richards and the Audit of Meaning', *New Literary History*, 14 (1982), 63–79.

Bethell, S. L. 'Suggestions Toward a Theory of Value', *Criterion*, 14 (1934), pp. 239–50.

Black, Max, 'Some Objections to Ogden and Richards' Theory of Interpretation', *Journal of Philosophy*, 39 (1942), pp. 281–90.

'Some Questions About Emotive Meaning', *Philosophical Review*, 57 (1948),

pp. 111–26.

Bové, Paul A., *Intellectuals in Power: A Genealogy of Critical Humanism* (New York, 1986).

Brooks, Cleanth, 'I. A. Richards and Practical Criticism', *Sewanee Review*, 89 (1981), pp. 586–95.

Brower, Reuben, Helen Vendler, and John Hollander (eds.), *I. A. Richards: Essays in His Honor* (New York, 1973).

Crane, R. S., 'I. A. Richards on the Art of Interpretation', *Ethics*, 59 (1948–9), pp. 112–26.

Cruttwell, Patrick, 'Second Thoughts, IV: I. A. Richards's *Practical Criticism*', *Essays in Criticism*, 8 (1958), pp. 1–15.

Dickie, George, 'I. A. Richards's Phantom Double', *British Journal of Aesthetics*, 8 (1968), pp. 54–9.

Eastman, Max, *The Literary Mind: Its Place in an Age of Science* (New York, 1932).

Eliot, T. S., 'Literature, Science, and Dogma', *Dial*, 82 (1927), pp. 239–43.
   Selected Essays, new edn. (London, 1950).
   The Use of Poetry and the Use of Criticism: Studies in the Relation of Criticism to Poetry in England (London, 1933).

Empson, William, *Argufying: Essays on Literature and Culture*, ed. John Haffenden (Iowa City, 1987).
   The Structure of Complex Words (1951; rpt. Ann Arbor, 1967).

Graff, Gerald E., 'The Later Richards and the New Criticism', *Criticism*, 9 (1967), pp. 229–42.
   Poetic Statement and Critical Dogma (Evanston, Ill., 1970; 2nd edn. 1980).

Hamlin, Cyrus, 'I. A. Richards (1893–1979): Grand Master of Interpretations', *University of Toronto Quarterly*, 49 (1980), pp. 189–204.

Harding, D. W., 'Evaluations (1): I. A. Richards', *Scrutiny*, 1 (1933), pp. 327–38.

Hotopf, W. H. N., *Language, Thought, and Comprehension: A Case Study of the Writings of I. A. Richards* (London, 1965).

Hyman, Stanley Edgar, 'I. A. Richards and the Criticism of Interpretation', in *The Armed Vision: A Study in the Methods of Modern Literary Criticism* (1948; rev. edn. New York, 1955), pp. 278–326.

James, D. G., *Scepticism and Poetry: An Essay on the Poetic Imagination* (London, 1937).

Krieger, Murray, 'The Critical Legacy of Matthew Arnold; Or, The Strange Brotherhood of T. S. Eliot, I. A. Richards, and Northrop Frye', *Southern Review*, 5 (1969), 457–74.
   The New Apologists for Poetry (Minneapolis, 1956).

Leavis, F. R., 'Dr. Richards, Bentham and Coleridge', *Scrutiny*, 3 (1935), pp. 382–402.

MacCabe, Colin, 'The Cambridge Heritage: Richards, Empson and Leavis', *Southern Review*, 19 (1986), pp. 242–9.

McCallum, Pamela, *Literature and Method: Towards a Critique of I. A. Richards, T. S. Eliot, and F. R. Leavis* (Dublin, 1983).

McLuhan, H. M., 'Poetic vs. Rhetorical Exegesis: The Case For Leavis Against Richards and Empson', *Sewanee Review*, 53 (1944), pp. 266–76.

Martin, Janet, and Rom Harre, 'Metaphor in Science', in David S. Miall (ed.), *Metaphor: Problems and Perspectives* (Sussex, 1982), pp. 89–105.

Needham, John, *The Completest Mode: I. A. Richards and the Continuity of English Literary Criticism* (Edinburgh, 1982).

Pottle, Frederick A., *The Idiom of Poetry* (Ithaca, 1946).

Ransom, John Crowe, *The New Criticism* (New York, 1941).

 'The Psychologist Looks at Poetry', *Virginia Quarterly Review*, 11 (1935), pp. 575–92.

Robbins, Derek, 'Culture and Criticism: Willey, Richards, and the Present', in A. P. Foulkes (ed.), *The Uses of Criticism* (Berne, 1976).

Russell, Bertrand, 'The Meaning of Meaning', *Dial*, 81 (1926), pp. 114–21.

Russo, John Paul, *I. A. Richards: His Life and Work* (Baltimore, 1989).

 'I. A. Richards in Retrospect', *Critical Inquiry*, 8 (1982), pp. 743–60.

 "The Mysterious Mountains: I. A. Richards and High Mountaineering', *Shenandoah*, 30 (1979), pp. 69–91.

 'The Recent Career of I. A. Richards', *Papers on Language and Literature*, 8 (1972), pp. 102–9.

 'Richards and the Search for Critical Instruments', in Reuben Brower (ed.), *Twentieth-Century Literature in Retrospect* (Cambridge, 1971).

Schiller, Jerome P., *I. A. Richards' Theory of Literature* (New Haven, 1969).

Spanos, William V., 'The Apollonian Investment of Modern Humanist Education: The Examples of Matthew Arnold, Irving Babbitt, and I. A. Richards (I)', *Cultural Critique*, 1 (1982), pp. 67–74.

Staten, Henry, 'Language and Consciousness in Richards and Wittgenstein', *Western Humanities Review*, 36 (1982), pp. 67–74.

Tate, Allen, *Collected Essays* (Denver, 1959).

Vivas, Eliseo, 'Four Notes on I. A. Richards' Aesthetic Theory', *Philosophical Review*, 44 (1935), pp. 354–67.

Wellek, René, 'I. A. Richards', in *A History of Modern Criticism, 1750–1950, Volume 5: English Criticism, 1900–1950* (New Haven, 1986), pp. 221–38.

West, Alick, *Crisis and Criticism* (London, 1937).

Wimsatt, W. K., *The Verbal Icon: Studies in the Meaning of Poetry* (1954; rpt. New York, 1964).

 and Cleanth Brooks, *Literary Criticism: A Short History*, 2 vols., (1957; rpt. Chicago, 1978).

9 The Southern New Critics

Co-authored works:

Brooks, Cleanth and Robert Penn Warren, *Understanding Fiction* (New York, 1943).

 Understanding Poetry (1938; rpt. New York 1960).

 eds., *Understanding Poetry: An Anthology for College Students* (1938; rev. edn. New York, 1950).

Brooks, Cleanth and William K. Wimsatt, *Literary Criticism: A Short History*, 2
  vols. (New York, 1957).
Twelve Southerners, *I'll Take My Stand: The South and the Agrarian Tradition*
  (Baton Rouge, 1980).

Works by Ransom:

Beating the Bushes: Selected Essays, 1941–1970 (Norfolk, Conn., 1972).
'Criticism as Pure Speculation', in Morton D. Zabel (ed.), *Literary Opinion in
  America* (New York, 1951), pp. 639–54.
'Editorial Note: The Arts and the Philosopher', *Kenyon Review*, 1 (1939),
  p. 198.
God Without Thunder: An Unorthodox Defense of Orthodoxy (London, 1931).
The New Criticism (Norfolk, Conn., 1941).
'A Poem Nearly Anonymous II: The Poet and His Formal Tradition', *American
  Review*, 1 (1933), p. 446.
Poems and Essays (New York, 1955).
'Poetry I: The Formal Analysis', *Kenyon Review*, 9 (1947), pp. 436–56.
'Poetry II: The Final Cause', *Kenyon Review*, 9 (1947), pp. 640–58.
'Poetry: A Note on Ontology', *American Review*, 3 (1937), p. 784.
Selected Essays, ed. Thomas Daniel Young and John Hindle (Baton Rouge,
  1984).
The Selected Letters of John Crowe Ransom, ed. Thomas Daniel Young and
  John Hindle (Baton Rouge, 1985).
'The South – Old and New', *Sewanee Review*, 36 (1928), pp. 139–47.
'The State and the Land,' *New Republic*, 66 (1932), pp. 8–10.
'The Teaching of Poetry', *Kenyon Review*, 1 (1939), pp. 81–3.
'Waste Lands', *Evening Post's Literary Review*, 3 (1923), pp. 825–6.
The World's Body (New York, 1938; rpt. Baton Rouge, 1968).

Works by Brooks:

The Hidden God: Studies in Hemingway, Faulkner, Yeats, Eliot, and Warren
  (New Haven, 1963).
'I. A. Richards and *Practical Criticism*', *Sewanee Review*, 89 (1981), pp. 586–95.
'Implications of an Organic Theory of Poetry', in M. H. Abrams (ed.), *Literature
  and Belief* (New York, 1958), pp. 53–79.
'Irony as a Principle of Structure', in Morton D. Zabel (ed.), *Literary Opinion in
  America* (New York, 1951), pp. 729–41.
The Language of the American South (Athens, Ga., 1985).
Modern Poetry and the Tradition (1939; rpt. Chapel Hill, N.C., 1970).
(with David Nichol Smith, eds.), *The Percy Letters*, 6 vols. (Baton Rouge, 1944–
  61).
'The Poem as Organism', in Rudolf Kirk (ed.), *English Institute Annual, 1940*
  (New York, 1941), pp. 20–41.
The Relation of the Alabama–Georgia Dialect to the Provincial Dialects of

Great Britain (Baton Rouge, 1935).
A Shaping Joy: Studies in the Writer's Craft (New York, 1972).
The Well Wrought Urn: Studies in the Structure of Poetry (New York, 1947).
William Faulkner: First Encounters (New Haven, 1983).
William Faulkner: The Yoknapatawpha Country (New Haven, 1963).
William Faulkner: Toward Yoknapatawpha and Beyond (New Haven, 1978).

Works by Warren:

All the King's Men (New York, 1946).
At Heaven's Gate (New York, 1943).
Democracy and Poetry (Cambridge, Mass., 1980).
John Brown: The Making of a Martyr (New York, 1929).
New and Selected Essays (New York, 1989).
Night Rider (New York, 1939).
The Republic of Letters in America: The Correspondence of John Peale Bishop and Allen Tate, ed. Thomas Daniel Young and John Hindle (Lexington, Ky., 1981).
Selected Essays (New York, 1958).
'Twelve Poets', *American Review*, 3 (1934), pp. 212–27.
World Enough and Time (New York, 1950).

Works by Tate:

Essays of Four Decades (Chicago, 1968).
The Forlorn Demon: Didactic and Critical Essays (Chicago, 1953).
'The Function of the Critical Review', *Southern Review*, 1 (1936), pp. 586–602.
The Hovering Fly and Other Essays (Cummington, 1949).
The Literary Correspondence of Donald Davidson and Allen Tate, ed. Thomas Daniel Young and John Tyree Fain (Athens, Ga., 1974).
The Man of Letters in the Modern World: Selected Essays, 1928–1955 (New York, 1955).
Memoirs and Opinions, 1926–1974 (Chicago, 1975).
'Narcissus as Narcissus', *Virginia Quarterly Review*, 14 (1938), p. 110.
On the Limits of Poetry: Selected Essays, 1928–1948 (New York, 1948).
The Poetry Reviews of Allen Tate, ed. Ashley Brown and Frances Neel Cheney (Baton Rouge, 1983).
Reactionary Essays on Poetry and Ideas (New York, 1936).
Reason in Madness: Critical Essays (New York, 1941).
The Republic of Letters in America: The Correspondence of John Peale Bishop and Allen Tate, ed. Thomas Daniel Young and John J. Hindle (Lexington, Ky., 1981).
'A Traditionalist Looks at Liberalism', *Southern Review*, 1 (1936), p. 740.
'Waste Lands', *Evening Post's Literary Review*, 3 (1923), 902.

Secondary sources:

Aaron, Daniel, *Writers on the Left* (New York, 1979).

Arac, Jonathan, 'Repetition and Exclusion: Coleridge and the New Criticism Reconsidered', *Boundary 2*, 8 (1979), pp. 261–73.

Berman, Art, *From the New Criticism to Deconstruction: The Reception of Structuralism and Post-Structuralism* (Urbana, Ill., 1988).

Bishop, Ferman, *Allen Tate* (New York, 1967).

New Criticism in the United States (1959; rpt. Folcroft, 1971).

Blackmur, R. P., 'San Giovanni in Venere: Allen Tate as Man of Letters', *Sewanee Review*, 47 (1959), pp. 614–31.

Bové, Paul A., 'Cleanth Brooks and Modern Irony: A Kierkegaardian Critique', *Boundary 2*, 4 (1975–6), pp. 727–59.

Bradbury, John M., *The Fugitives: A Critical Account* (Chapel Hill, N.C., 1958).

Renaissance in the South (Chapel Hill, N.C., 1963).

Burt, John, *Robert Penn Warren and American Idealism* (New Haven, 1988).

Clark, William Bedford (ed.), *Critical Essays on Robert Penn Warren* (Boston, 1981).

Conkin, Paul K., *The Southern Agrarians* (Knoxville, 1988).

Core, George, 'Southern Letters and the New Criticism', *Georgia Review*, 24 (1970), pp. 413–31.

Cowan, Louise, *The Fugitive Group: A Literary History* (Baton Rouge, 1959).

Crane, R. S., 'The Critical Monism of Cleanth Brooks', in *Critics and Criticism* (Chicago, 1952), pp. 83–107.

Cutrer, Thomas W., *Parnassus on the Mississippi: The Southern Review and the Baton Rouge Literary Community, 1935–1942* (Baton Rouge, 1984).

de Man, Paul, 'Form and Intent in the American New Criticism', in *Blindness and Insight* (New York, 1971; rev. edn. Minneapolis, 1983), pp. 20–35.

Elton, William, *A Glossary of the New Criticism* (Chicago, 1949).

Fallwell, Marshall, *Allen Tate: A Bibliography* (New York, 1969).

Fekete, John, *The Critical Twilight: Explorations in the Ideology of Anglo-American Literary Theory from Eliot to McLuhan* (London, 1978).

Forster, Richard, *The New Romantics: A Reappraisal of the New Criticism* (Bloomington, 1962).

Graff, Gerald, *Poetic Statement and Critical Dogma* (Evanston, 1970).

Gray, Richard (ed.), *Robert Penn Warren: A Collection of Critical Essays* (Englewood Cliffs, 1980).

Grimshaw, James A., Jr, *Robert Penn Warren: A Descriptive Bibliography, 1922–1979* (Charlottesville, 1982).

Guillory, John, 'The Ideology of Canon-Formation: T. S. Eliot and Cleanth Brooks', *Critical Inquiry*, 10 (1983–4), pp. 173–98.

Heilman, Robert, 'Cleanth Brooks and *The Well Wrought Urn*', *Sewanee Review*, 91 (1983), pp. 322–34.

Holman, C. Hugh, 'The Defense of Art: Criticism Since 1930', in Floyd Stovall (ed.), *The Development of American Literary Criticism* (Chapel Hill, 1955), pp. 199–245.

Hough, Graham, 'John Crowe Ransom: The Poet and the Critic', *Southern Review*, 1 (1965), pp. 1–21.

Howarth, William C., 'The Politics of *I'll Take My Stand*', *Sewanee Review*, 16

(1980), pp. 757–75.

and Walter Sullivan (eds.), *A Band of Prophets: The Vanderbilt Agrarians After Fifty Years* (Baton Rouge, 1982).

Hyman, Stanley Edgar, *The Armed Vision: A Study in the Methods of Modern Literary Criticism* (1948; rev. edn. New York, 1955).

Janssen, Marian, *The Kenyon Review, 1939–1970: A Critical History* (Baton Rouge, 1990).

Justus, James H., *The Achievement of Robert Penn Warren* (Baton Rouge, 1981).

Karanikas, Alex, *The Tillers of Myth: Southern Agrarians as Social and Literary Critics* (Madison, 1966).

King, Richard H., *A Southern Renaissance: The Cultural Awakening of the American South, 1930–1955* (New York, 1980).

Krieger, Murray, *The Classic Vision: The Retreat from Extremity in Modern Literature* (Baltimore, 1971).

The New Apologists for Poetry (Minneapolis, 1956).

Leitch, Vincent B., *American Literary Criticism from the Thirties to the Eighties* (New York, 1988).

Lentricchia, Frank, 'The Place of Cleanth Brooks', *Journal of Aesthetics and Art Criticism*, 29 (1970–71), pp. 235–51.

Longley, John L., *Robert Penn Warren: A Collection of Literary Essays* (New York, 1965).

McDowell, Frederick P. W., 'Robert Penn Warren's Criticism', *Accent*, 15 (1955), pp. 173–96.

Meiners, R. R., *The Last Alternatives: A Study of the Works of Allen Tate* (Denver, 1963).

Nakadate, Neil (ed.), *Robert Penn Warren: Critical Perspectives* (Lexington, 1981).

O'Brien, Michael, *The Idea of the American South, 1920–1941* (Baltimore, 1979).

Ohmann, Richard, *English in America: A Radical View of the Profession* (New York, 1976).

Olson, Elder, 'A Symbolic Reading of the *Ancient Mariner*', *Modern Philology*, 45 (1948), pp. 275–9.

Pritchard, John Paul, *Criticism in America* (Norman, Okla., 1956).

Rubin, Louis D., 'Robert Penn Warren: Critic', in Walter B. Edgar (ed.), *A Southern Renaissance Man: Views of Robert Penn Warren* (Baton Rouge, 1984), pp. 19–37.

Rubin, Louis D., Jr, *The Wary Fugitives: Four Poets and the South* (Baton Rouge, 1978).

Russo, John Paul, 'The Tranquilized Poem: The Crisis of the New Criticism in the 1950s', *Texas Studies in Literature and Language*, 30 (1988), pp. 198–229.

Simpson, Lewis (ed.), *The Possibilities of Order: Cleanth Brooks and His Work* (Baton Rouge, 1976).

Singal, Daniel Joseph, *The War Within: From Victorian to Modernist Thought in the South, 1919–1945* (Chapel Hill, 1982).

Spears, Monroe K., 'The Criticism of Allen Tate', *Sewanee Review*, 57 (1949), pp. 317–34.

Squires, Radcliffe, *Allen Tate: A Literary Biography* (New York, 1971).

Stallman, R. W., 'The New Criticism and the Southern Critics', in Allen Tate (ed.), *A Southern Vanguard* (New York, 1947), pp. 28–51.

Stewart, John L., *The Burden of Time: The Fugitives and Agrarians* (Princeton, 1965).

Strier, Richard, 'The Poetics of Surrender: An Exposition and Critique of New Critical Poetics', *Critical Inquiry*, 2 (1975–6), pp. 171–89.

Sutton, Walter, *Modern American Criticism* (Englewood Cliffs, 1963).

Thompson, Ewa M., *Russian Formalism and Anglo-American New Criticism: A Comparative Study* (The Hague, 1971).

Walker, Marshall, *Robert Penn Warren: A Vision Earned* (Edinburgh, 1979).

Walsh, John, *Cleanth Brooks: An Annotated Bibliography* (New York, 1990).

Watkins, Floyd C., *et al.* (eds.), *Talking with Robert Penn Warren* (Athens, Ga., 1990).

Webster, Grant, *The Republic of Letters: A History of Postwar American Literary Opinion* (Baltimore, 1979).

Wellek, René, 'Allen Tate', in *A History of Modern Criticism, 1750–1950, Volume 6: American Criticism, 1900–1950* (New Haven, 1986), pp. 174–87.

'Cleanth Brooks', in *A History of Modern Criticism, 1750–1950, Volume 6: American Criticism, 1900–1950* (New Haven, 1986), pp. 188–213.

'John Crowe Ransom', in *A History of Modern Criticism, 1750–1950, Volume 6: American Criticism, 1900–1950* (New Haven, 1986), pp. 159–73.

'The New Criticism', in *A History of Modern Criticism, 1750–1950, Volume 6: American Criticism, 1900–1950* (New Haven, 1986), pp. 144–58.

'Robert Penn Warren', in *A History of Modern Criticism, 1750–1950, Volume 6: American Criticism, 1900–1950* (New Haven, 1986), pp. 214–17.

and Warren, Austin, *Theory of Literature* (New York, 1949).

Willingham, John R., 'The New Criticism: Then and Now', in G. Douglas Atkins and Laura Morrow (eds.), *Contemporary Literary Theory* (Amherst, 1989), pp. 24–41.

Winchell, Mark Royden, 'Cleanth Brooks and Robert Penn Warren', in Ray Willbanks (ed.), *Literature of Tennessee* (Macon, 1984), pp. 8–114.

Winters, Yvor, 'John Crowe Ransom; Or Thunder Without God', in *In Defense of Reason* (New York, 1947), pp. 502–55.

Young, Thomas Daniel, *Gentleman in a Dustcoat: A Biography of John Crowe Ransom* (Baton Rouge, 1976).

John Crowe Ransom: An Annotated Bibliography (New York, 1982).

(ed.), *John Crowe Ransom: Critical Essays* (Baton Rouge, 1968).

(ed.), *The New Criticism and After* (Charlottesville, 1976).

Waking Their Neighbors Up: The Nashville Agrarians Rediscovered (Athens, 1982).

10 William Empson

Works by Empson:

Argufying: Essays on Literature and Culture, ed. John Haffenden (London, 1987).

The Book, Film, and Theatre Reviews of William Empson: Originally Printed in the Cambridge Magazine 'Granta', 1927–1929, and Now Collected for the Foundling Press (Turnbridge Wells, 1993).

Collected Poems (1949; rpt. London, 1955).

'Empson on Tennyson', *Tennyson Research Bulletin*, 4 (1984), pp. 107–9.

Essays on Renaissance Literature (Cambridge, 1993).

Essays on Shakespeare (Cambridge, 1986).

Faustus and the Censor (Oxford, 1987).

The Gathering Storm (London, 1940).

Milton's God (1961; rpt. Cambridge, 1981).

Poems (London, 1935).

The Royal Beasts (London, 1986).

Seven Types of Ambiguity (1930; rpt. New York, 1966).

Some Versions of Pastoral (1935; rpt. Norfolk, Conn., 1960).

The Strength of Shakespeare's Shrew: Essays, Memories, Reviews (Sheffield, 1996).

The Structure of Complex Words (1951; rpt. Ann Arbor, 1967).

Using Biography (Cambridge, 1984).

'Yeats and Byzantium', *Grand Street*, 1 (1982), pp. 67–95.

Secondary Sources:

Bradbrook, M. C., 'Sir William Empson (1906–1984): A Memoir', *Kenyon Review*, 7 (1985), pp. 106–15.

Constable, John (ed.), *Critical Essays on William Empson* (Brookfield, 1993).

Culler, Jonathan, 'The Future of Criticism', in Clayton Koelb and Virgin Lokke (eds.), *The Current in Criticism: Essays on the Present and Future in Literary Theory* (West Lafayette, 1987), pp. 27–41.

Day, Frank, *Sir William Empson: An Annotated Bibliography* (New York, 1984).

de Man, Paul, 'The Dead-End of Formalist Criticism', in *Blindness and Insight* (New York, 1971; rev. edn. Minneapolis, 1983), pp. 229–45.

Eagleton, Terry, 'The Critic as Clown', in *Against the Grain* (London, 1986), pp. 149–65.

Fry, Paul H., *William Empson: Prophet against Sacrifice* (London, 1991).

Gardner, A. and P. Gardner, *The God Approached* (Totowa, 1978).

Gardner, Helen, Mark Justin, and William Empson, '"There Is No Penance Due To Innocence": An Exchange', *New York Review of Books*, 29 (1982), p. 43.

Gill, Roma (ed.), *William Empson: The Man and His Work* (London, 1974).

Haffenden, John, *The Royal Beasts and Other Works* (Iowa City, 1988).

Hardy, Barbara, 'William Empson and *Seven Types of Ambiguity*', *Sewanee Review*, 90 (1982), pp. 430–9.

Hyman, Stanley Edgar, 'William Empson and Categorical Criticism', in *The Armed Vision: A Study in the Methods of Modern Literary Criticism* (1948; rev. edn. New York, 1955), pp. 237–77.

Kenner, Hugh, 'Alice in Empsonland', in *Gnomon: Essays on Contemporary Literature* (New York, 1958), pp. 249–62.

Lerner, Laurence, 'On Ambiguity, Modernism, and Sacred Texts', in Vereen Bell and Laurence Lerner (eds.), *On Modern Poetry: Essays Presented to Donald Davie* (Nashville, 1988), pp. 133–44.

McCabe, Colin, 'The Cambridge Heritage: Richards, Empson and Leavis', *Southern Review*, 19 (1986), pp. 242–9.

Norris, Christopher, 'The Importance of Empson (II): The Criticism', *Essays in Criticism*, 35 (1985), pp. 25–44.

'Some Versions of Rhetoric: Empson and de Man', in Robert Con Davis and Ronald Schleifer (eds.), *Rhetoric and Form: Deconstruction at Yale* (Norman, Okla., 1985), pp. 191–214.

William Empson and the Philosophy of Literary Criticism (London, 1978).

'Reason, Rhetoric, Theory: Empson and de Man', *Raritan*, 5 (1985), pp. 89–106.

Prichard, R. E., 'Milton's Satan and Empson's Old Lady', *Notes and Queries*, 34 (1987), pp. 59–60.

Ransom, John Crowe, *The New Criticism* (New York, 1941).

Sale, R., 'The Achievement of William Empson', in *Modern Heroism: Essays on D. H. Lawrence, William Empson, and J. R. R. Tolkien* (Berkeley, 1973), pp. 107–92.

Wellek, René, 'William Empson', in *A History of Modern Criticism, 1750–1950, Volume 5: English Criticism, 1900–1950* (New Haven, 1986), pp. 275–92.

Wihl, Gary, 'Empson's Generalized Ambiguities; Essays Presented to A. E. Malloch', in Gary Wihl and David Williams (eds.), *Literature and Ethics* (Kingston, 1988), pp. 3–17.

'"Resistance" and "Pregnancy" in Empsonian Metaphor', *British Journal of Aesthetics*, 26 (1986), pp. 48–56.

11 R. P. Blackmur

Works by Blackmur:

The Double Agent (1935; rpt. Gloucester, 1962).
Eleven Essays in the European Novel (New York, 1964).
The Expense of Greatness (1940; rpt. Gloucester, 1958).
Form and Value in Modern Poetry (Garden City, 1957).
From Jordan's Delight (New York, 1937).
The Good European (Cummington, 1947).
Henry Adams (New York, 1980).
Language as Gesture (1952; rpt. New York, 1981).
The Lion and the Honeycomb: Essays in Solicitude and Critique (New York,

1955).
New Criticism in the United States (1959; rpt. Folcroft, 1971).
Outsider at the Heart of Things, ed. James T. Jones (Urbana, Ill., 1989).
Poems of R. P. Blackmur (Princeton, 1977).
A Primer of Ignorance (New York, 1967).
The Second World (Cummington, 1942).
Selected Essays (New York, 1986).
Studies in Henry James (New York, 1983).

Secondary sources:

Boyers, Robert, *R. P. Blackmur: Poet-Critic: Towards a View of Poetic Objects* (Columbia, Mo., 1980).
Cone, Edward T., Joseph Frank, and Edmund Keeley (eds.), *The Legacy of R. P. Blackmur* (New York, 1987).
Davie, Donald, 'Poetry or Poems?', in *The Poet in the Imaginary Museum* (Princeton, 1977).
Donoghue, Denis, 'Introduction: The Sublime Blackmur', in *Selected Essays of R. P. Blackmur* (New York, 1985), pp. 3–16.
  'R. P. Blackmur and *The Double Agent*', *Sewanee Review*, 91 (1983), pp. 634–43.
  'R. P. Blackmur's Poetry: An Introduction', in *Poems of R. P. Blackmur* (1977), pp. ix–xxix.
Frank, Joseph, 'R. P. Blackmur: The Later Phase', in *The Widening Gyre: Crisis and Mastery in Modern Literature* (New Brunswick, 1963), pp. 229–51.
Fraser, Russell, *A Mingled Yarn: The Life of R. P. Blackmur* (New York, 1981).
  'My Two Masters', *Sewanee Review*, 91 (1983), pp. 614–33.
  'R. P. Blackmur: America's Best Critic', *Virginia Quarterly Review*, 57 (1981), pp. 569–93.
  'R. P. Blackmur and Henry Adams', *Southern Review*, 17 (1981), pp. 69–96.
Edel, Leon, 'Criticism's Double Agent', *Grand Street*, 1 (1982), pp. 143–50.
Hyman, Stanley Edgar, 'R. P. Blackmur and the Expense of Criticism', in *The Armed Vision: A Study in the Methods of Modern Literary Criticism* (1948; rev. edn. New York, 1955), pp. 197–236.
Jones, James T., *Wayward Skeptic: The Theories of R. P. Blackmur* (Urbana, Ill., 1986).
Kenner, Hugh, 'Inside the Featherbed', in *Gnomon: Essays on Contemporary Literature* (New York, 1958), pp. 242–7.
Lewis, R. W. B., 'Casella as Critic: Notes on R. P. Blackmur', *Kenyon Review*, 13 (1955), pp. 458–74.
Merwin, W. S. 'Affable Irregular: Recollections of R. P. Blackmur', *Grand Street*, 1 (1982), pp. 151–64.
Pannick, G. J., *Richard Palmer Blackmur* (Boston, 1981).
Parker, Hershel, 'Deconstructing *The Art of the Novel* and Liberating James's "Prefaces"', *Henry James Review*, 14 (1994), pp. 284–307.
Ransom, John Crowe, *The New Criticism* (New York, 1941).

Schwartz, Delmore, 'The Critical Method of R. P. Blackmur', in *Selected Essays of Delmore Schwartz*, ed. Donald A. Dike and David H. Zucker (Chicago, 1970), pp. 351–9.

Wellek, René, 'R. P. Blackmur', in *A History of Modern Criticism, 1750–1950, Volume 5: English Criticism, 1900–1950* (New Haven, 1986), pp. 218–34.

Wood, Michael, 'No Success Like Failure', *New York Review of Books* (7 May 1987), pp. 28–30.

12 Kenneth Burke

Works by Burke:

Attitudes Toward History (1937; 3rd edn. Berkeley, 1984).

Collected Poems, 1915–1967 (Berkeley, 1968).

The Complete White Oxen: Collected Short Fiction (Berkeley, 1968).

Counter-Statement (Los Altos, 1953).

A Grammar of Motives (1945; rpt. Berkeley, 1969).

Language as Symbolic Action: Essays on Life, Literature, and Method (Berkeley, 1966).

Permanence and Change (Berkeley, 1984).

The Philosophy of Literary Form (1941; rpt. Berkeley, 1974).

A Rhetoric of Motives (1950; rpt. Berkeley, 1969).

The Rhetoric of Religion: Studies in Logology (Boston, 1961).

The Selected Correspondence of Kenneth Burke and Malcolm Cowley, 1915–1981, ed. Paul Jay (New York, 1988).

Toward a Better Life: Being a Series of Epistles, or Declamations (Berkeley, 1966).

Secondary sources:

Brown, Merle Elliott, *Kenneth Burke* (Minneapolis, 1969).

Bygrave, Stephen, *Kenneth Burke: Rhetoric and Ideology* (London, 1993).

Frank, Armin Paul, *Kenneth Burke* (New York, 1969).

Gunn, Giles, *Criticism of Culture and Cultural Criticism* (New York, 1987).

Harris, Wendell, 'The Critics Who Made Us: Kenneth Burke', *Sewanee Review*, 96 (1988), pp. 452–63.

Henderson, Greig, *Kenneth Burke: Literature and Language as Symbolic Action* (Georgia, 1988).

Hyman, Stanley Edgar, 'Kenneth Burke and the Criticism of Symbolic Action', in *The Armed Vision: A Study in the Methods of Modern Literary Criticism* (1948; rev. edn. New York, 1955), pp. 327–85.

Irmscher, William, 'Kenneth Burke', in John C. Brereton (ed.), *Traditions of Inquiry* (New York, 1985), pp. 105–35.

Jameson, Fredric R., 'The Symbolic Inference; or, Kenneth Burke and Ideological Analysis', *Critical Inquiry*, 4 (1978), pp. 507–23.

Jay, Paul, 'Kenneth Burke and the Motives of Rhetoric', *American Literary History*, 1 (1989), pp. 535–53.

Kimberling, C. Ronald, *Kenneth Burke's Dramatism and Popular Arts* (Bowling Green, 1982).

Lentricchia, Frank, *Criticism and Social Change* (Chicago, 1983).

Rueckert, William Howe, *Critical Responses to Kenneth Burke, 1924–1966* (Minneapolis, 1969).

Encounters with Kenneth Burke (Urbana, Ill., 1994).

Kenneth Burke and the Drama of Human Relations (Minneapolis, 1969).

Simons, Herbert, and Travor Melia (eds.), *The Legacy of Kenneth Burke* (Madison, Wis., 1989).

Wellek, René, 'Kenneth Burke', in *A History of Modern Criticism, 1750–1950, Volume 5: English Criticism, 1900–1950* (New Haven, 1986), pp. 235–56.

Wess, Robert, *Kenneth Burke: Rhetoric, Subjectivity, Postmodernism* (Cambridge, 1996).

White, Hayden, and Margaret Brose (eds.), *Representing Kenneth Burke: Selected Papers from the English Institute* (Cambridge, Mass., 1982).

13 Yvor Winters

Works by Winters:

The Anatomy of Nonsense (Norfolk, Conn., 1943).

The Bare Hills: A Book of Poems (Boston, 1927).

Before Disaster (Tryon, 1934).

The Collected Poems of Yvor Winters (Manchester, 1978).

The Early Poems of Yvor Winters, 1920–1928 (Denver, 1960).

Edwin Arlington Robinson (1949; rev. edn. New York, 1971).

Forms of Discovery: Critical and Historical Essays on the Forms of the Short Poem in English (Chicago, 1967).

The Function of Criticism: Problems and Exercises (1957; rpt. London, 1962).

The Giant Weapon (Norfolk, Conn., 1943).

In Defense of Reason (New York, 1947).

Maule's Curse: Seven Studies in the History of American Obscurantism (Norfolk, Conn., 1938).

On Modern Poets (New York, 1957).

Quest for Reality: An Anthology of Short Poems in English, selected by Yvor Winters and Kenneth Fields (Chicago, 1969).

Yvor Winters: Uncollected Essays and Reviews, ed. Francis Murphy (Chicago, 1973).

Secondary sources:

Comito, Terry, *In Defense of Winters: The Poetry and Prose of Yvor Winters* (Madison, Wis., 1986).

Davis, Dick, *Wisdom and Wilderness: The Achievement of Yvor Winters* (Athens, Ga., 1983).

Holloway, John, 'The Critical Theory of Yvor Winters', *Critical Quarterly*, 7 (1965), pp. 54–68.

Hyman, Stanley Edgar, 'Yvor Winters and Evaluation in Criticism', in *The Armed Vision: A Study in the Methods of Modern Literary Criticism* (1948; rev. edn. New York, 1955), pp. 23–53.

Isaacs, Elizabeth, *An Introduction to the Poetry of Yvor Winters* (Ohio, 1981).

Mazzaro, Jerome, 'Yvor Winters and *In Defense of Reason*', *Sewanee Review*, 95 (1987), pp. 625–32.

Powell, Grosvenor, *Yvor Winters, An Annotated Bibliography, 1919–1982* (Metuchen, 1983).

Ray, Mohit, 'Yvor Winter's Theory of Form', in Anna Balakian, *et al.* (eds.), *Proceedings of the Xth Congress of the International Comparative Literature Association*, vol. 2: *Comparative Poetics* (New York, 1985), pp. 199–205.

Ransom, John Crowe, *The New Criticism* (Norfolk, Conn., 1941).

Sexton, Richard J., *The Complex of Yvor Winter's Criticism* (The Hague, 1973).

Special issue, *Southern Review* 17 (1981), pp. 711–982.

Stanford, Donald, *Revolution and Convention in Modern Poetry: Studies in Ezra Pound, T. S. Eliot, Wallace Stevens, Edwin Arlington Robinson, and Yvor Winters* (Newark, N.J., 1983).

Trimpi, Wesley, 'Mimesis as Appropriate Representation', *Renascence*, 37 (1985), pp. 203–8.

Wellek, René, 'Yvor Winters', in *A History of Modern Criticism, 1750–1950, Volume 5: English Criticism, 1900–1950* (New Haven, 1986), pp. 257–80.

THE CRITIC AND THE INSTITUTIONS OF CULTURE

14 Criticism and the academy

Primary sources:

'The Aims of Literary Study', *PMLA*, 53 (1938), pp. 1367–71.

Arnold, Matthew, *Schools and Universities on the Continent*, ed. R. H. Super (Ann Arbor, 1964).

Babbitt, Irving, *Literature and the American College: Essays in Defense of the Humanities* (Boston, 1908).

'The Basic Issues in the Teaching of English', *PMLA*, 74 (1959), pp. 1–19.

Bateson, F. W., *Essays in Critical Dissent* (London, 1972).

'The Function of Criticism at the Present Time', *Essays in Criticism*, 3 (1953), pp. 1–27.

Bennett, Arnold, *Books and Persons* (London, 1917).

Brooks, Cleanth, 'I. A. Richards and Practical Criticism', *Sewanee Review*, 89 (1981), pp. 586–95.

'The New Criticism', *Sewanee Review*, 87 (1979), pp. 592–607.

Campbell, Oscar (ed.), *The Teaching of College English* (New York, 1934).

Canby, Henry Seidel, 'The American Scholar – Ninety Years Later', *Saturday Review of Literature*, 4 (1928), pp. 981–3.

Cardinal Principles of Secondary Education (Washington, 1918).

Clapp, June (ed.), *College Textbooks* (New York, 1960).

Conant, J. B., 'Free Thinking or Dogma?', *Atlantic Monthly*, 155 (1935),

pp. 436–42.

Cook, Albert, *The Higher Study of English* (Boston, 1906).

Cooper, Lane, *Methods and Aims in the Study of Literature* (Boston, 1915).

Craig, Hardin, *Literary Study and the Scholarly Profession* (Seattle, 1944).

Crane, R. S., 'History vs. Criticism in the Study of Literature', *English Journal*, 24 (1935), pp. 645–67.

de Man, Paul, 'The Return to Philology', in *The Resistance to Theory* (Minneapolis, 1986), pp. 21–6.

Essays on the Teaching of English in Honour of Charles Swain Thomas (Cambridge, Mass., 1940).

Foerster, Norman, *The American Scholar: A Study in Litterae Inhumaniores* (Chapel Hill, 1929).

—— (ed.), *Humanism and America: Essays on the Outlook of Modern Civilisation* (New York, 1930).

—— 'Literary Scholarship and Criticism', *English Journal*, 25 (1936), pp. 224–32.

—— *Towards Standards: A Study of the Present Critical Movement in American Letters* (New York, 1930).

Frye, Northrop, *Anatomy of Criticism* (Princeton, 1957).

—— 'Literary Criticism', in *The Aims and Methods of Scholarship in Modern Languages and Literatures* (New York, 1963), pp. 47–69.

Gardner, Helen, *The Business of Criticism* (Oxford, 1959).

Gerber, John C. (ed.), *The College Teaching of English* (New York, 1965).

Graff, Gerald, and Michael Warner, *The Origins of Literary Studies in America: A Documentary Anthology* (New York, 1989).

Grattan, C. Hartley (ed.), *The Critique of Humanism: A Symposium* (New York, 1930).

Greenlaw, Edwin, *The Province of Literary History* (Baltimore, 1931).

Harrison, G. B., *Profession of English* (New York, 1962).

Hough, Graham, *The Dream and the Task: Literature and Morals in the Culture of Today* (London, 1963).

Hughes, Merritt Y., 'Our Social Contract', *College English*, 1 (1940), pp. 495–504.

James, William, 'The Ph.D. Octopus', in *Essays, Comments and Reviews* (Cambridge, Mass., 1987).

Knight, G. Wilson, 'The New Interpretation', *Essays in Criticism*, 3 (1953), pp. 382–95.

Leavis, F. R., *Education and the University: A Sketch for an 'English School'* (London, 1943).

—— 'Literary Criticism and Philosophy: A Reply', *Scrutiny*, 6 (1937), pp. 59–70.

Lewis, C. S., *An Experiment in Criticism* (Cambridge, 1961).

Lowes, John Livingston, 'The Modern Language Association and Humane Scholarship', *PMLA*, 48 (1933), pp. 1399–408.

Lyman, R. L., 'English in Relation to Three Major Curriculum Trends', *English Journal*, 25 (1936), pp. 190–9.

Nitze, Albert, 'Horizons', *PMLA*, 44 (1930), iii–xi.

Perry, Bliss, 'College Professors and the Public', in *The Amateur Spirit* (Boston,

1904), pp. 95–115.

Quiller-Couch, Arthur, 'Inaugural', in *On the Art of Writing* (Cambridge, 1916), pp. 1–25.

Raleigh, Walter, *On Writing and Writers*, ed. George Gordon (London, 1926).

Ransom, John Crowe, *The World's Body* (New York, 1938; rpt. Baton Rouge, 1968).

Richards, I. A., *Practical Criticism* (New York, 1969).

Principles of Literary Criticism (London, 1952).

Saintsbury, George, *A History of Criticism and Literary Taste in Europe*, 3 vols. (Edinburgh, 1900–4).

Skeat, W. W., *Questions for Examination in English Literature* (3rd edn. London, 1890).

Spingarn, J. E., *The New Criticism* (New York, 1911).

Stoll, E. E. 'Certain Fallacies and Irrelevancies in the Literary Scholarship of the Day', *Studies in Philology*, 24 (1927), pp. 485–508.

'Training for the New Social Order', *English Journal*, 23 (1934), pp. 681–3.

Wellek, René, 'Academic Criticism', in *A History of Modern Criticism, 1750–1950, Volume 6: American Criticism, 1900–1950* (New Haven, 1986), pp. 59–88.

'Literary Criticism and Philosophy', *Scrutiny*, 5 (1937), pp. 375–83.

and Warren, Austin, *Theory of Literature* (New York, 1949).

Wimsatt, William K., and Cleanth Brooks, *Literary Criticism: A Short History*, 2 vols. (New York, 1957).

Woodberry, G. E., 'Two Phases of Criticism: Historical and Esthetic', in *Criticism in America*, ed. J. E. Spingarn (New York, 1924), pp. 46–87.

Secondary sources:

Applebee, Arthur N., *Tradition and Reform in the Teaching of English: A History* (Urbana, 1974).

Arac, Jonathan, *Critical Genealogies* (New York, 1987).

Axelrod, Joseph (ed.), *Graduate Study for Future College Teachers* (Washington, 1959).

Baldick, Chris, *The Social Mission of English Criticism, 1848–1932* (Oxford, 1983).

Bush, Douglas, 'Memories of Harvard's English Department 1920–1932', *Sewanee Review*, 89 (1981), 595–603.

Culler, Jonathan, *Framing the Sign* (Norman, Okla., 1988).

Davidson, H. Carter, 'Our College Curriculum in English', *English Journal*, 20 (1931), pp. 407–19.

Douglas, Wallace, 'Accidental Institution: On the Origin of Modern Language Study', in Gerald Graff and Reginald Gibbons (eds.), *Criticism in the University* (Evanston, Ill., 1985), pp. 35–61.

Elton, Oliver, *Essays and Addresses* (London, 1939).

French, J. Milton, 'The Introductory Course in Literature', *College English*, 3 (1941), pp. 53–63.

Graff, Gerald, *Professing Literature: An Institutional History* (Chicago, 1987).

and Reginald Gibbons (eds.), *Criticism in the University* (Evanston, Ill., 1985).

Gross, John, *The Rise and Fall of the Man of Letters: A Study of the Idiosyncratic and the Humane in Modern Literature* (New York, 1969).

Haber, Tom Burns, Review of *Understanding Poetry*, *English Journal*, 27 (1938), 870–1.

Hawkins, Eric W., *Modern Languages in the Curriculum* (Cambridge, 1981).

Hays, Edna, *College Entrance Requirements in English: Their Effects on the High Schools* (New York, 1936).

Historical Statistics of the U.S., 2 vols. (Washington, 1975).

Hoeveler, J. David, Jr, *The New Humanism: A Critique of Modern America 1900–1940* (Charlottesville, 1977).

Holloway, John, *The Charted Mirror: Literary and Critical Essays* (London, 1960).

The Colours of Clarity: Essays on Contemporary Literature and Education (London, 1972).

Hook, J. H., *A Long Way Together: A Personal View of the NCTE's First Sixty-Seven Years* (Urbana, 1979).

Hosiac, James F., *Reorganisation of English in Secondary Schools* (Washington, 1917).

Hyman, Stanley Edgar, *The Armed Vision: A Study in the Methods of Modern Literary Criticism* (1948; rev. edn. New York, 1955).

Knapp, Robert H., *The Origins of American Humanistic Scholars* (Englewood Cliffs, 1964).

Knights, L. C., 'Scrutiny of Examinations', *Scrutiny*, 2 (1933), pp. 137–63.

Ladd, Everett Carl, Jr, and Seymour Martin Lipset, *The Divided Academy: Professors and Politics* (New York, 1975).

Leary, Lewis (ed.), *Contemporary Literary Scholarship: A Critical Review* (New York, 1958).

Lovett, Robert Morse, *All Our Years* (New York, 1948).

Mathiesen, Margaret, *The Preachers of Culture: A Study of English and Its Teachers* (London, 1975).

McMurtry, Jo, *English Language, English Literature: The Creation of an Academic Discipline* (Hamden, 1985).

Menand, Louis, 'The Demise of Disciplinary Authority', in *What's Happened to the Humanities?*, ed. Alvin Kernan (Princeton, 1997), pp. 201–19.

Palmer, D. J., *The Rise of English Studies: An Account of the Study of English Language and Literature from Its Origins to the Making of the Oxford English School* (London, 1965).

Pattee, Fred Lewis, *Tradition and Jazz* (New York, 1925).

Potter, Stephen, *The Muse in Chains: A Study in Education* (London, 1937).

Ruland, Richard, *The Rediscovery of American Literature: Premises of Critical Taste, 1900–1940* (Cambridge, Mass., 1967).

Sherman, Stuart, *Shaping Men and Women*, ed. Jacob Zeitlin (Garden City, N.J., 1928).

Smith, Nowell, *The Origin and History of the [English] Association* (London,

1942).

Tillyard, E. M. W., *The Muse Unchained: An Intimate Account of the Revolution in English Studies at Cambridge* (London, 1958).

Van Deusen, Marshall, *J. E. Spingarn* (New York, 1971).

Vanderbilt, Kermit, *American Literature and the Academy: The Roots, Growth, and Maturity of a Profession* (Philadelphia, 1987).

Vaughn, W. E., *Articulation in English Between the High School and College* (New York, 1929).

Warner, Michael, 'Professionalisation and the Rewards of Literature: 1875–1900', *Criticism*, 27 (1985), pp. 1–28.

Wilcox, Thomas W., *The Anatomy of College English* (San Francisco, 1973).

Williams, Raymond, *Writing in Society* (London, 1983).

Wray, Edith A., 'A Modern Odyssey', *College English*, 16 (1955), pp. 507–12.

15 The critic and society, 1900–1950

Primary sources:

Bourne, Randolph, *History of a Literary Radical*, ed. Van Wyck Brooks (New York, 1920).
  The Radical Will: Selected Writings, 1911–1918, ed. Olaf Hansen (New York, 1977).

Brooks, Van Wyck, *An Autobiography* (New York, 1965).
  The Confident Years, 1885–1915 (New York, 1952).
  The Flowering of New England (New York, 1936).
  New England: Indian Summer, 1865–1915 (New York, 1940).
  Opinions of Oliver Allston (New York, 1941).
  The Ordeal of Mark Twain (New York, 1920).
  Sketches in Criticism (New York, 1932).
  Three Essays on America (1934; rpt. New York, 1970).
  The Times of Melville and Whitman (New York, 1947).
  Van Wyck Brooks: The Early Years, A Selection from His Works, 1908–1925, ed. Claire Sprague (New York, 1968).
  The World of Washington Irving (New York, 1944).
  The Writer in America (1953; rev. edn. Boston, 1993).

Chapman, John Jay, *Selected Writings*, ed. Jacques Barzun (Garden City, 1957).
  Unbought Spirit: A John Jay Chapman Reader, ed. Richard Stone (Urbana, Ill., 1998).

Chase, Richard, *The American Novel and Its Tradition* (Garden City, 1957).
  The Democratic Vista (Garden City, 1958).

Cowley, Malcolm (ed.), *After the Genteel Tradition* (1937; rev. edn. Carbondale, 1965).
  – *And I Worked at the Writer's Trade: Chapters of Literary History, 1918–1978* (New York, 1978).
  The Dream of the Golden Mountains: Remembering the 1930s (New York, 1980).
  Exile's Return (1934; rev. edn. 1951; rpt. New York, 1956).

The Flower and the Leaf: A Contemporary Record of American Writing Since 1941, ed. Donald W. Faulkner (New York, 1985).

The Literary Situation (New York, 1954).

The Portable Malcolm Cowley (New York, 1990).

'*Think Back on Us...*': *A Contemporary Chronicle of the 1930s*, ed. Henry Dan Piper (Carbondale, Ill., 1967).

Dupee, F. W., *Henry James: His Life and Writings* (Garden City, New York, 1956).

'*The King of the Cats' and Other Remarks on Writers and Writing* (1965; rev. edn. Chicago, 1984).

Hicks, Granville, *The Great Tradition: An Interpretation of American Literature Since the Civil War* (New York, 1933).

Howe, Irving, *A Critic's Notebook* (New York, 1994).

Decline of the New (New York, 1970).

Politics and the Novel (New York, 1957).

Selected Writings, 1950–1990 (San Diego, 1992).

A World More Attractive: A View of Modern Literature and Politics (New York, 1963).

World of Our Fathers (New York, 1976).

James, Henry, *The Art of the Novel*, ed. R. P. Blackmur (New York, 1934).

Literary Criticism, 2 vols. (New York, 1984).

Jay, Paul (ed.), *The Selected Correspondence of Kenneth Burke and Malcolm Cowley* (New York, 1988).

Kazin, Alfred, *An American Procession* (New York, 1984).

Contemporaries (Boston, 1962).

God and the American Writer (New York, 1997).

The Inmost Leaf (New York, 1955).

A Lifetime Burning in Every Moment: From the Journals of Alfred Kazin (New York, 1996).

New York Jew (New York, 1978).

On Native Grounds: An Interpretation of Modern American Prose Literature (New York, 1942).

Our New York (New York, 1989).

Starting Out in The Thirties (Boston, 1965).

A Walker in the City (New York, 1951).

A Writer's America (New York, 1988).

Writing Was Everything (Cambridge, Mass., 1995).

Knights, L. C., *Drama and Society in the Age of Jonson* (1937; rpt. London, 1951).

Leavis, F. R., *The Common Pursuit* (London, 1952).

The Great Tradition: George Eliot, Henry James, Joseph Conrad (London, 1952).

Lewis, R. W. B., *The American Adam* (Chicago, 1955).

Macdonald, Dwight, *Discriminations: Essays and Afterthoughts, 1938–1974* (New York, 1974).

Memoirs of a Revolutionist: Essays in Political Criticism (New York, 1957).

Marx, Leo, *The Machine in the Garden: Technology and the Pastoral Idea in America* (New York, 1964).

Matthiessen, F. O., *American Renaissance: Art and Expression in the Age of Emerson and Whitman* (New York, 1941).

The Responsibilities of the Critic: Essays and Reviews, ed. John Rackiffe (New York, 1952).

Mencken, H. L., *A Book of Prefaces* (New York, 1917).

The Diary of H. L. Mencken, ed. Charles Fecher (New York, 1990).

Prejudices, 6 vols. (New York, 1919–27).

Prejudices: A Selection, ed. James T. Farrell (New York, 1958).

Thirty-Five Years of Newspaper Work, ed. Fred Hobson, Vincent Fitzpatrick, and Bradford Jacobs (Baltimore, 1994).

The Vintage Mencken, ed. Alistair Cooke (New York, 1955).

Mumford, Lewis, *The Brown Decades* (New York, 1932).

The Golden Day (1926; rpt. Westport, 1983).

Orwell, George, *Collected Essays* (London, 1961).

The Collected Essays, Journalism and Letters of George Orwell, ed. Sonia Orwell and Ian Angus (London, 1968).

Homage to Catalonia (1938; rpt. New York, 1952).

The Rode to Wigan Pier (1937; rpt. New York, 1956).

Parrington, Vernon Louis, *Main Currents in American Thought: An Interpretation of American Literature from the Beginning to 1920*, 3 vols. (New York, 1927–30).

Rahv, Phillip, *Essays on Literature and Politics, 1932–1972*, ed. Arabel J. Porter and Andrew J. Dvosin (Boston, 1978).

Image and Idea (1949; rev. edn. Norfolk, 1957).

Literature and the Sixth Sense (Boston, 1969).

The Myth and the Powerhouse: Essays on Literature and Ideas (New York, 1965).

Rosenberg, Harold, *Discovering the Present: Three Decades in Art, Culture and Politics* (Chicago, 1973).

The Tradition of the New (New York, 1959).

Rourke, Constance, *American Humor: A Study of the National Character* (New York, 1931).

The Roots of American Culture, ed. Van Wyck Brooks (New York, 1942).

Santayana, George, *Essays in Literary Criticism*, ed. Irving Singer (New York, 1956).

Interpretations of Poetry and Religion, ed. William Holzberger and Herman Saatkamp (Cambridge, 1989).

The Last Puritan: A Memoir in the Form of a Novel (Cambridge, Mass., 1994).

Selected Critical Writings, ed. Norman Henfrey, 2 vols. (London, 1968).

The Sense of Beauty: Being the Outlines of Aesthetic Theory, ed. William Holzberger and Herman Saatkamp (Cambridge, 1988).

Schorer, Mark, *The World We Imagine: Selected Essays* (New York, 1968).

Smith, Henry Nash, *Virgin Land: The American West as Symbol and Myth*

(1950; rpt. Cambridge, Mass., 1968).

Spingarn, Joel, *Creative Criticism and Other Essays* (New York, 1931).

Trilling, Lionel, *Beyond Culture: Essays on Literature and Learning* (1965; rpt. New York, 1968).

E. M. Forster (1944; rev. edn. New York, 1964).

'From the Notebooks of Lionel Trilling', ed. Christopher Zinn, *Partisan Review*, 4 (1984–5), pp. 496–515.

A Gathering of Fugitives (Boston, 1956).

The Last Decade: Essays and Reviews, 1965–1975, ed. Diana Trilling (New York, 1979).

The Liberal Imagination: Essays on Literature and Society (New York, 1950).

Matthew Arnold (New York, 1939).

The Opposing Self: Nine Essays in Criticism (New York, 1955).

Sincerity and Authenticity (Cambridge, Mass., 1972).

Speaking of Literature and Society, ed. Diana Trilling (New York, 1980).

Warshow, Robert, *The Immediate Experience* (Garden City, N.Y., 1962).

Wilson, Edmund, *The American Earthquake: A Documentary of the Twenties and Thirties* (Garden City, N.Y., 1958).

Apologies to the Iroquois (1958; rpt. New York, 1978).

Axel's Castle: A Study in the Imaginative Literature of 1870–1930 (New York, 1931).

The Bit Between My Teeth: A Literary Chronicle of 1950–1965 (New York, 1965).

Classics and Commercials: A Literary Chronicle of the Forties (New York, 1950).

The Devils and Canon Barham: Ten Essays on Poets, Novelists, and Monsters (New York, 1973).

Europe Without Baedecker (New York, 1947).

From the Uncollected Edmund Wilson, ed. Janet Groth and David Castronovo (Athens, Ga., 1995).

I Thought of Daisy (1929; rpt. Baltimore, 1963).

The Journals, 'from Notebooks and Diaries of the Period': A Prelude, The Twenties, The Thirties, The Forties, The Fifties, and *The Sixties* (New York, 1967–91).

Letters on Literature and Politics: 1912–1972, ed. Elena Wilson (New York, 1977).

Memoirs of Hecate County (1946; rev. edn. New York, 1961).

O Canada: An American's Notes on Canadian Culture (New York, 1965).

Patriotic Gore: Studies in the Literature of the American Civil War (New York, 1962).

A Piece of My Mind: Reflections at Sixty (New York, 1956).

The Portable Edmund Wilson, ed. Lewis M. Dabney (New York, 1983).

Red, Black, Blond and Olive: Studies in Four Civilizations (London, 1956).

Scrolls from the Dead Sea (New York, 1955).

The Shores of Light: A Literary Chronicle of the Twenties and Thirties (Garden City, N.Y., 1952).

To The Finland Station: A Study in the Writing and Acting of History (1940; rev. edn. New York, 1972).
The Triple Thinkers: Ten Essays in Literature (1938; rev. edn. New York, 1948).
Upstate: Records and Recollections of Northern New York (New York, 1971).
A Window on Russia: For the Use of Foreign Readers (New York, 1972).
The Wound and the Bow: Seven Studies in Literature (Boston, 1941).

Secondary sources:

Aaron, Daniel, *Writers on the Left* (1961; rpt. New York, 1992).
Bak, Hans, *Malcolm Cowley: The Formative Years* (Athens, Ga., 1993).
Bercovitch, Sacvan and Myra Jehlen (eds.), *Ideology and Classic American Literature* (Cambridge, Mass., 1986).
Bloom, Alexander, *Prodigal Sons: The New York Intellectuals and Their World* (New York, 1986).
Castronovo, David, *Edmund Wilson* (New York, 1984).
Commager, Henry Steele, *The American Mind: An Interpretation of American Thought and Character Since the 1880s* (New Haven, 1950).
Crick, Bernard, *George Orwell: A Life* (1980; rpt. New York, 1982).
Dabney, Lewis (ed.), *Edmund Wilson: Centennial Reflections* (Princeton, 1997).
Dickstein, Morris, *Double Agent: The Critic and Society* (New York, 1992).
Douglas, George, *Edmund Wilson's America* (Lexington, 1983).
Dupee, F. W., 'The Americanism of Van Wyck Brooks', *Partisan Review*, 6 (1939), pp. 69–85.
French, Philip, *Three Honest Men* (Manchester, 1980).
Graff, Gerald, and Reginald Gibbons (eds.), *Criticism in the University* (Evanston, 1985).
Gross, John, *The Rise and Fall of the Man of Letters: A Study of the Idiosyncratic and the Humane in Modern Literature* (New York, 1969).
Groth, Janet, *Edmund Wilson: A Critic for Our Time* (Athens, Oh., 1989).
Hobson, Fred, *Mencken: A Life* (Baltimore, 1994).
Hoopes, James, *Van Wyck Brooks* (Amherst, 1977).
Hyman, Stanley Edgar, *The Armed Vision: A Study in the Methods of Modern Literary Criticism* (New York, 1948).
Kazin, Alfred, 'Edmund Wilson: The Critic and the Age', in *The Inmost Leaf: A Selection of Essays* (New York, 1955).
Krupnick, Mark, *Lionel Trilling and the Fate of Cultural Criticism* (Evanston, 1986).
Lasch, Christopher, *The New Radicalism in America: 1889–1963: The Intellectual as a Social Type* (New York, 1965).
Michaels, Walter Benn and Donald Pease (eds.), *The American Renaissance Reconsidered: Selected Papers from the English Institute* (Baltimore, 1985).
O'Connor, William Van, *The Age of Criticism, 1900–1950* (Chicago, 1952).
Paul, Sherman, *Edmund Wilson: A Study of Literary Vocation in Our Time* (Ur-

bana, 1965).

Pritchard, John Paul, *Criticism in America* (Norman, 1956).

Ramsey, Richard David, *Edmund Wilson: A Bibliography* (New York, 1971).

Rodden, John, *The Politics of Literary Reputation: The Making and Claiming 'St. George' Orwell* (New York, 1989).

(ed.), *Lionel Trilling and the Critics: Opposing Selves* (Lincoln, Neb., 1999).

Rosenfeld, Paul, *Port of New York* (1924; rpt. Urbana, 1966).

Ruland, Richard, *The Rediscovery of American Literature: Premises of Critical Taste, 1900–1940* (Cambridge, Mass., 1967).

Shelden, Michael, *George Orwell: The Authorised Biography* (London, 1991).

Smith, Bernard, *Forces in American Criticism: A Study in the History of American Literary Thought* (New York, 1939).

'Van Wyck Brooks' in Malcolm Cowley (ed.), *After the Genteel Tradition* (Carbondale, 1964), pp. 64–78.

Stallman, R. W. (ed.), *Critiques and Essays in Criticism, 1920–1948* (New York, 1949).

Stovall, Floyd (ed.), *The Development of American Literary Criticism* (Chapel Hill, N.C., 1955).

Sutton, Walter, *Modern American Literary Criticism* (Englewood Cliffs, 1963).

Trilling, Lionel, 'Edmund Wilson: A Background Glance', *A Gathering of Fugitives* (Boston, 1956), pp. 45–55.

Vitelli, James, *Van Wyck Brooks* (New York, 1969).

Wain, John, (ed.), *Edmund Wilson: The Man and His Work* (New York, 1978).

Wellek, René, *A History of Modern Criticism, 1750–1950*, vols. 5 and 6. (New Haven, 1986).

Wimsatt, William K., Jr, and Cleanth Brooks, *Literary Criticism: A Short History* (New York, 1957).

Wreszin, Michael, *A Rebel in Defense of Tradition: The Life and Politics of Dwight Macdonald* (New York, 1994).

16 The British 'man of letters' and the rise of the professional

Works by John Middleton Murry:

Aspects of Literature (New York, 1920).

Countries of the Mind: Essays in Literary Criticism, First Series (Freeport, N.Y., 1968).

Countries of the Mind: Essays in Literary Criticism, Second Series (1922; rpt. Oxford, 1931).

D. H. Lawrence: Son of Woman (Milwood, N.Y., 1980).

Discoveries: Essays in Literary Criticism (London, 1924).

Fyodor Dostoevsky: A Critical Study (New York, 1966).

Heroes of Thought (New York, 1938).

John Clare and Other Studies (New York, 1950).

Jonathan Swift: A Critical Biography (New York, 1955).

Katherine Mansfield and Other Literary Studies (London, 1949).

Keats (New York, 1962).

Keats and Shakespeare: A Study of Keats's Poetic Life from 1816 to 1820 (London, 1925).
The Mystery of Keats (New York, 1949).
Novels and Novelists (New York, 1930).
Pencillings: Little Essay on Literature (Freeport, N.Y., 1969).
Poets, Critics, and Mystics: A Selection of Criticisms Written Between 1919–1955 (Carbondale, Ill., 1970).
Problems of Style (New York, 1922).
Reminiscences of D. H. Lawrence (Freeport, NY., 1971).
Selected Criticism: 1916–1957 (New York, 1960).
Shakespeare (New York, 1936).
Studies in Keats (New York, 1972).
Swift (London, 1970).
Things to Come: Essays (Freeport, NY., 1969).
Unprofessional Essays (Westport, Conn., 1975).
William Blake (New York, 1971).

Works by A. R. Orage:

The Art of Reading (New York, 1930).
Readers and Writers (London, 1922).
Selected Essays and Critical Writings (Freeport, NY., 1967).

Secondary sources:

Abbott, Andrew, 'Status and Strain in the Professions', *American Journal of Sociology*, 86 (1981), pp. 819–35.
Court, Franklin E., *Institutionalizing English Literature: The Culture and Politics of Literary Study, 1750–1900* (Stanford, 1992).
Goldstein, Doris, 'The Professionalization of History in the Late Nineteenth and Early Twentieth Centuries', *Storia della Storiografia*, 1 (1983), pp. 3–23.
Gross, John, *The Rise and Fall of the Man of Letters: A Study of the Idiosyncratic and the Humane in Modern Literature* (New York, 1969).
Guy, Josephine M., and Ian Small, *Politics and Value in English Studies* (Cambridge, 1993).
Halsey, A. H., and M. A. Trow. *The British Academics* (London, 1971).
Heyck, T. W., *The Transformation of Intellectual Life in Victorian England* (London, 1982).
Jackson, J. A. (ed.), *Professions and Professionalization* (London, 1970).
Kearney, Anthony, *John Churton Collins: The Louse on the Locks of Literature* (Edinburgh, 1985).
Larson, Magali Sarfatti, *The Rise of Professionalism: A Sociological Analysis* (London, 1970).
Martin, Wallace, *Orage as Critic* (London, 1974).
Mill, John Stuart, 'Some Thoughts on Poetry and its Varieties', in John M. Robson and Jack Stillinger (eds.), *The Collected Works of John Stuart Mill:*

Autobiography and Literary Essays (London, 1981), pp. 343–65.
Proceedings of the English Association Bulletin, 22 (February 1914).
Reader, W. J., *Professional Men: The Rise of the Professional Classes in Nine-teenth-Century England* (London, 1966).
Robertson, Eric S., *Life of Henry Wadsworth Longfellow* (London, 1887).
Rothblatt, Sheldon, *The Revolution of the Dons* (London, 1968).
  Tradition and Change in English Liberal Education (London, 1967).

17 F. R. Leavis

Works by Leavis:

'Anna Karenina' and Other Essays (London, 1967).
The Common Pursuit (London, 1952).
The Critic as Anti-Philosopher: Essays and Papers, ed. G. Singh (London, 1982).
(with Denys Thompson), *Culture and Environment: Training in Critical Aware-ness* (London, 1933).
D. H. Lawrence (Cambridge, 1930).
D. H. Lawrence: Novelist (London, 1955).
Determinations (London, 1934).
(with Q. D. Leavis), *Dickens the Novelist* (London, 1970).
Education and the University: A Sketch for an English School (London, 1943).
English Literature in Our Time and the University: The Clark Lectures (London, 1969).
Essays and Documents, ed. Ian MacKillop and Richard Storer (Sheffield, 1995).
The Great Tradition (London, 1948).
How to Teach Reading: A Primer for Ezra Pound (Cambridge, 1932).
(with Q. D. Leavis), *Lectures in America* (London, 1969).
Letters in Criticism, ed. John Tasker (London, 1974).
The Living Principle: 'English' as a Discipline of Thought (London, 1975).
Mass Civilization and Minority Culture (Cambridge, 1930).
(ed.), *Mill on Bentham and Coleridge* (London, 1950).
New Bearings in English Poetry (London, 1932).
Nor Shall My Sword: Discourses on Pluralism, Compassion and Social Hope (London, 1972).
Revaluation: Tradition and Development in English Poetry (London, 1936).
Thoughts, Words and Creativity: Art and Thought in Lawrence (London, 1976).
Toward Standards of Criticism (London, 1933).
Two Cultures? The Significance of C. P. Snow, with an essay by Michael Yudkin on Snow's Rede Lecture (London, 1962).
'Valuation in Criticism' and Other Essays, ed. G. Singh (London, 1986).

Secondary sources:

Anderson, Perry, 'Components of the National Culture', *New Left Review*, 50 (1968), pp. 3–57.
Annan, Noel, 'Bloomsbury and the Leavises', in Jane Marcus (ed.), *Virginia*

Woolf and Bloomsbury: A Centenary Celebration (Bloomington, 1987), pp. 23–38.

Bakhtin, Mikhail, *Problems of Dostoevsky's Poetics*, tr. R. W. Rotsel (Ann Arbor, 1973).

Baldick, Chris, *The Social Meaning of English Criticism, 1848–1932* (Oxford, 1983).

Barry, Peter, 'The Enactive Fallacy', *Essays in Criticism*, 30 (1980), pp. 95–104.

Bateson, F. W., *Essays in Critical Dissent* (London, 1972).

Bell, Michael, *F. R. Leavis* (London, 1988).

(ed.), *Context of English Literature 1900–1930* (London, 1980).

Bergonzi, Bernard, 'Leavis and Eliot: The Long Road to Rejection', in *The Myth of Modernism and Twentieth Century Literature* (Brighton, 1986), pp. 21–43.

Bewley, Marius, *The Complex Fate* (London, 1952).

Bilan, R. O. *The Literary Criticism of F. R. Leavis* (Cambridge, 1979).

Boyers, Robert, *F. R. Leavis, Judgement and the Discipline of Thought* (Columbia, Mo., 1978).

Bradley, A. C., *Shakespearean Tragedy* (London, 1904).

Buckley, Vincent, *Poetry and Morality: Studies in the Criticism of Matthew Arnold, T. S. Eliot and F. R. Leavis* (London, 1959).

Casey, John, *The Language of Criticism* (London, 1966).

Collini, Stefan, *Public Moralists: Political and Intellectual Life in Britain 1850–1930* (Oxford, 1991).

Cornelius, D. K., and E. St. Vincent, *Cultures in Conflict: Reflections on the Leavis–Snow Controversy* (Chicago, 1964).

Day, Gary, *Re-Reading Leavis: Culture and Literary Criticism* (London and New York, 1996).

Edel, Leon, *Henry James, Volume 2: The Conquest of London, 1870–1881* (Philadelphia, 1962).

Eliot, T. S., 'In Memory of Henry James', *Egoist*, 5 (1918), pp. 1–2.

The Sacred Wood (London, 1920).

Selected Essays (London, 1932).

Empson, William, *Milton's God* (London, 1951).

Seven Types of Ambiguity (London, 1935).

Some Versions of Pastoral (London, 1935).

The Structure of Complex Words (London, 1951).

Greenwood, Edward, *F. R. Leavis* (London, 1978).

Gregor, Ian, 'F. R. Leavis and *The Great Tradition*', *Sewanee Review*, 93 (1985), pp. 434–46.

Hayman, Ronald, *F. R. Leavis* (London, 1976).

Heidegger, Martin, *On the Way to Language*, tr. Peter D. Herz (New York, 1971).

Poetry, Language, and Thought, tr. Albert Hofstadter (New York, 1971).

The Question Concerning Technology and Other Essays, tr. William Lovitt (New York, 1977).

What Is Called Thinking, tr. F. P. Wieck and J. Glenn Gray (New York,

1968).

Holloway, John, *The Estabishment of English* (London, 1972).

Hopkins, Gerard Manley, *A Selection of His Poems and Prose*, ed. Helen Gardner (Harmondsworth, 1953).

Inglis, Fred, *Radical Earnestness: English Social Theory 1880–1980* (Oxford, 1982).

James, Henry, *The Art of the Novel*, ed. R. P. Blackmur (New York, 1934).

Kermode, Frank, *Romantic Image* (London, 1957).

Kinch, M. B., W. Baker, and J. Kimber, *F. R. Leavis and Q. D. Leavis: An Annotated Bibliography* (London, 1989).

Knight, G. Wilson, *The Crown of Life* (London, 1947).
  The Imperial Theme (London, 1951).
  Principles of Shakespearean Production (London, 1936).
  The Shakespearean Tempest (London, 1932).
  The Wheel of Fire (London, 1949).

Knights, L. C., *Explorations* (London, 1946).
  Drama and Society in the Age of Jonson (London, 1937).
  How Many Children Had Lady Macbeth?: An Essay in the Theory and Practice of Shakespearean Criticism (Cambridge, 1933).

Lawrence, D. H., *Studies in Classic American Literature* (London, 1924).

Lewes, George Henry, *The Principles of Success in Literature* (London, 1869).

MacCabe, Colin, 'The Cambridge Heritage: Richards, Empson and Leavis', *Southern Review*, 19 (1986), pp. 242–9.

McCallum, Pamela, *Literature and Method: Towards a Critique of I. A. Richards, T. S. Eliot and F. R. Leavis* (Dublin, 1983).

MacKillop, Ian, *F. R. Leavis: A Life in Criticism* (London, 1995).

McLuhan, H. M., 'Poetic and Rhetorical Analysis: The Case For Leavis Against Richards and Empson', *Sewanee Review*, 52 (1944), pp. 266–76.

Martin, Graham, 'F. R. Leavis and the Function of Criticism', *Essays in Criticism*, 46 (1996), pp. 1–15.

Martz, Louis, *The Paradise Within* (New York, 1964).

Mulhern, Francis, *The Moment of 'Scrutiny'* (London, 1979).

Nietzsche, Friedrich, *The Portable Nietzsche*, ed. Walter Kaufmann (New York, 1954).

Palmer, D. J., *The Rise of English Studies* (London, 1965).

Richards, I. A., *Coleridge on Imagination* (London, 1934).
  Interpretation in Teaching (London, 1937).
  The Philosophy of Rhetoric (London, 1936).
  Practical Criticism: A Study of Literary Judgement (London, 1929).
  Principles of Literary Criticism (London, 1924).
  Science and Poetry (London, 1926).

Ricks, Christopher, *Milton's Grand Style* (London, 1963).

Ricoeur, Paul, *The Rule of Metaphor*, tr. Robert Czerny, *et al.* (London, 1978).

Robertson, P. J. M., *The Leavises on Fiction: An Historic Partnership* (London, 1981).

Robinson, Ian, *The Survival of English* (Cambridge, 1973).

Samson, Anne, *F. R. Leavis: Social and Literary Critic 1895–1978* (London and
    New York, 1992).
Schorer, Mark, 'Technique as Discovery', in *The World We Imagine* (London,
    1969), pp. 3–23.
Singh, G., *F. R. Leavis: A Literary Biography* (London, 1995).
Sontag, Susan, *Against Interpretation* (New York, 1966).
Stein, Arnold, *Answerable Style* (Minneapolis, 1953).
Steiner, George, 'F. R. Leavis', in *Language and Silence* (London, 1967),
    pp. 229–47.
Strickland, Geoffrey, *Structuralism or Criticism* (Cambridge, 1981).
Symposium on Leavis, *Critical Quarterly*, 1, no. 3 (1959).
Symposium on Leavis, *New Universities Quarterly*, 30 (1975).
Thompson, Denys (ed.), *The Leavises: Recollections and Impressions* (Cam-
    bridge, 1984).
Tillyard, E. M. W., *The Muse Unchained: An Intimate Account of the Revol-
    ution in English Studies at Cambridge* (London, 1958).
Trilling, Lionel, *Sincerity and Authenticity* (Cambridge, Mass., 1972).
Vaihinger, Hans, *The Philosophy of 'As If'*, tr. C. K. Ogden (London, 1924).
Walsh, William, *F. R. Leavis* (London, 1980).
Watson, Garry, *The Leavises, the 'Social' and the Left* (Swansea, 1977).
Wellek, René, 'F. R. Leavis and the *Scrutiny* Group', in *A History of Modern
    Criticism, 1750–1950, Volume 5: English Criticism, 1900–1950* (New Ha-
    ven, 1986), pp. 239–64.
Williams, Raymond, *The Country and the City* (London, 1973).
    Culture and Society (London, 1958).
Wittgenstein, Ludwig, *Philosophical Investigations*, tr. G. E. Anscombe (rpt. Ox-
    ford, 1968).

18 Lionel Trilling

Works by Trilling:

Beyond Culture: Essays on Literature and Learning (1965; rpt. New York,
    1968).
E. M. Forster (1944; rev. edn. New York, 1964).
A Gathering of Fugitives (1956; Oxford, 1980).
The Last Decade: Essays and Reviews, 1965–1975, ed. Diana Trilling (New
    York, 1979).
The Liberal Imagination: Essays on Literature and Society (New York, 1950).
'Literature and Power', *Kenyon Review*, 11 (1989), pp. 119–25.
Matthew Arnold (New York, 1939).
The Opposing Self: Nine Essays in Criticism (New York, 1955).
Prefaces to the Experience of Literature (New York, 1979).
Sincerity and Authenticity (Cambridge, Mass., 1972).
Speaking of Literature and Society, ed. Diana Trilling (New York, 1980).

Secondary sources:

Barzun, Jacques, 'Remembering Lionel Trilling', *Encounter*, 47 (1976), pp. 82–8.

Bender, T., 'Lionel Trilling and American Culture', *American Quarterly*, 42 (1990), pp. 324–47.

Blackmur, R. P., 'The Politics of Human Power', in *The Lion and the Honeycomb: Essays in Solicitude and Critique* (New York, 1955).

Boyers, Robert, *Lionel Trilling: Negative Capability and the Wisdom of Avoidance* (Columbia, 1977).

(ed.), Special Issue on Lionel Trilling, *Salmagundi*, 41 (1978).

Brustein, Robert, 'Lionel Trilling: Memories of a Mentor', *Yale Review*, 76 (1987), pp. 162–8.

Chace, William, *Lionel Trilling: Criticism and Politics* (Stanford, 1980).

Dickstein, Morris, 'The Critics Who Made Us: Lionel Trilling and *The Liberal Imagination*', *Sewanee Review*, 94 (1986), pp. 323–34.

Donoghue, Denis, 'Trilling, Mind, and Society', in *Reading America: Essays on American Literature* (New York, 1987), pp. 175–96.

Frank, Joseph, 'Lionel Trilling and the Conservative Imagination', in *The Widening Gyre: Crisis and Mastery in Modern Literature* (New Brunswick, 1963), pp. 253–72.

Greenfield, Robert M., 'The Politics of *The Liberal Imagination*', *Perspectives on Contemporary Literature*, 11 (1985), pp. 1–9.

Gunn, Giles, 'The Moral Imagination in Modern American Criticism', in *The Culture of Criticism and the Criticism of Culture* (New York, 1987), pp. 19–40.

Hartman, Geoffrey, 'Lionel Trilling as Man in the Middle', in *The Fate of Reading* (Chicago, 1975), pp. 294–302.

Hirsch, David, 'Reality, Manners, and Mr. Trilling', *Sewanee Review*, 72 (1964), pp. 420–32.

Krupnick, Mark, *Lionel Trilling and the Fate of Cultural Criticism* (Evanston, 1986).

'Lionel Trilling and the Politics of Style', in F. A. Bell and D. K. Adams (eds.), *American Literary Landscapes: The Fiction and the Fact* (New York, 1988), pp. 152–70.

Leitch, Thomas M., *Lionel Trilling: An Annotated Bibliography* (New York, 1993).

Lopate, Philip, 'Remembering Lionel Trilling', in *Bachelorhood: Tales of the Metropolis* (Boston, 1981).

Marcus, Steven, 'Lionel Trilling, 1905–1975', *New York Times Book Review*, 8 February 1976, p. 1.

Nowlin, Michael E., 'Lionel Trilling and the Institutionalization of Humanism', *Journal of American Studies*, 25 (1991), pp. 23–38.

O'Hara, Daniel T., *Lionel Trilling: The Work of Liberation* (Madison, 1988).

Reising, Russell, '"Nothing That Is Not There And The Nothing That Is": Cultural Theories of American literature', in *The Unusable Past: Theory and the Study of American Literature* (New York, 1986), pp. 92–196.

Robinson, Jeffrey Cane, 'Lionel Trilling and the Romantic Tradition', *Mass-achusetts Review*, 20 (1979). pp. 211–36.

Sale, Roger, 'Lionel Trilling', *Hudson Review*, 26 (1973), pp. 241–7.

Schwartz, Delmore, 'The Duchess's Red Shoes', in *Selected Essays of Delmore Schwartz*, ed. Donald A. Dike and David H. Zucker (Chicago, 1970), pp. 203–22.

Scott, Nathan A., *Three American Moralists: Mailer, Bellow, and Trilling* (Notre Dame, Ind., 1973).

Shoben, Edward Joseph, *Lionel Trilling* (New York, 1981).

Slade, G., 'Trilling and *Ulysses*', *Partisan Review*, 59 (1992), pp. 275–81.

Tanner, Stephen L., *Lionel Trilling* (Boston, 1988).

Trilling, Diana, *The Beginning of the Journey: The Marriage of Diana and Lionel Trilling* (New York, 1993).

Vendler, Helen, 'Lionel Trilling and Wordsworth's Ode', in *The Music of What Happens* (Cambridge, Mass., 1988), pp. 93–114.

Wellek, René, 'Lionel Trilling', in *A History of Modern Criticism, 1750–1950, Volume 6: American Criticism, 1900–1950* (New Haven, 1986), pp. 123–43.

West, Cornel, 'Lionel Trilling: The Pragmatist as Arnoldian Literary Critic', in *The American Evasion of Philosophy: A Genealogy of Pragmatism* (Madison, Wis., 1989), pp. 164–81.

19 Poet-critics

Primary sources and texts:

Arnold, Matthew, 'The Function of Criticism at the Present Time', *Essays in Criticism, First Series*, ed. Sister Thomas Marion Hoctor (Chicago, 1968), pp. 8–30.

'Preface to the First Edition of *Poems*', *Poems*, ed. Kenneth Allott (London, 1965), pp. 589–607.

Auden, W. H., 'Writing', *The Dyer's Hand and Other Essays* (New York, 1962), pp. 13–27.

Breton, André, *Manifestoes of Surrealism*, tr. Richard Seaver and Helen Lane (Ann Arbor, 1969).

Eliot, T. S., *Four Quartets* (New York, 1943).

'From Poe to Valéry' (1948), *To Criticize the Critic* (New York, 1965), pp. 27–42.

'The Frontiers of Criticism' (1956), *On Poetry and Poets* (New York, 1961), pp. 113–31.

'The Metaphysical Poets' (1921), *Selected Essays* (New York, 1960), pp. 241–50.

'The Perfect Critic', *The Sacred Wood* (London, 1920), pp. 1–16.

The Use of Poetry and the Use of Criticism (Cambridge, Mass., 1933).

Jacob, Max, *Art Poétique* (Paris, 1922).

Jarrell, Randall, 'The Age of Criticism', *Poetry and the Age* (New York, 1953), pp. 63–86.

Jiménez, Juan Ramón, *Diario de un poeta reciencasado* (1916), ed. Michael Predmore (Madrid, 1998).

Johnson, Samuel, *The Lives of the English Poets*, ed. G. B. Hill, 3 vols. (Oxford, 1905).

The Rambler, ed. W. J. Bate and A. B. Strauss, 3 vols. (London, 1969).

Kuzmin, Mikhail, *Selected Prose and Poetry*, ed. and tr. Michael Green (Ann Arbor, 1980).

Lawrence, D. H., *Selected Literary Criticism*, ed. Anthony Beal (New York, 1966).

Lorca, Federico García, 'The Duende: Theory and Divertissement' (1934), *Poet in New York*, tr. Ben Belitt (New York, 1955), pp. 154–66.

MacLeish, Archibald, 'Ars Poetica' (1926), in *Poems on Poetry: The Mirror's Garland*, ed. Robert Wallace and James Taaffe (New York, 1965), p. 311.

Mallarmé, Stéphane, *Œuvres complètes*, ed. Henri Mondor and G. Jean-Aubry (Paris, 1945).

Mandelstam, Osip, 'The Word and Culture' (1921), *The Complete Critical Prose and Letters*, tr. Jane Gary Harris and Constance Link (Ann Arbor. 1979), pp. 112–16.

Marinetti, Filippo Tommaso, 'The Founding and Manifesto of Futurism' (1909), *Selected Writings*, tr. R. W. Flint and Arthur Coppotelli (New York, 1972), pp. 39–44.

Moore, Marianne, 'Idiosyncrasy and Technique', in *The Poet's Work*, ed. Reginald Gibbons (Boston, 1979), pp. 215–29.

Olson, Charles, 'Projective Verse', in *The Poetics of the New American Poetry*, ed. Donald M. Allen and Warren Tallman (New York, 1973), pp. 147–58.

Pasternak, Boris, 'Some Statements', tr. Angela Livingstone, in *Modern Russian Poets on Poetry*, ed. Carl Proffer (Ann Arbor, 1976), pp. 81–5.

Paz, Octavio, 'On Criticism', *Alternating Current*, tr. Helen Lane (New York, 1973), pp. 35–9.

Children of the Mire: Modern Poetry from Romanticism to the Avant-Garde, tr. Rachel Phillips (Cambridge, Mass., 1974).

Poe, Edgar Allan, *Literary Criticism*, ed. Robert L. Hough (Lincoln, Nebr., 1965).

Pope, Alexander, *Pastoral Poetry and An Essay on Criticism*, ed. E. Audra and Aubrey Williams (London, 1961).

Pound, Ezra, *ABC of Reading* (New York, 1960).

'Hugh Selwyn Mauberley' (1921), *Personæ* (New York, 1926), pp. 185–204.

Literary Essays, ed. T. S. Eliot (New York, 1954).

'On Technique' (1912), in *Modern Literary Criticism 1900–1970*, ed. Lawrence Lipking and A. Walton Litz (New York, 1972), pp. 18–21.

Ransom, John Crowe, *The World's Body* (New York, 1938).

Rilke, Rainer Maria, *Letters to a Young Poet*, tr. M. D. Herter Norton (New York, 1954).

The Notebooks of Malte Laurids Brigge (1910), tr. M. D. Herter Norton (New York, 1949).

Seferis, George, *On the Greek Style: Selected Essays in Poetry and Hellenism*, tr.

Rex Warner and Th. D. Frangopoulos (Boston, 1966).

Shelley, Percy Bysshe, *A Defence of Poetry*, and Thomas Love Peacock, *The Four Ages of Poetry*, ed. John E. Jordan (Indianapolis, 1965).

Stevens, Wallace, 'The Irrational Element in Poetry' (1936), in *Collected Poetry and Prose* (New York, 1997), pp. 781–92.

Tsvetayeva, Marina, *Art in the Light of Conscience: Eight Essays on Poetry*, tr. Angela Livingstone (Cambridge, Mass., 1992).

Letters Summer 1926, by Boris Pasternak, Marina Tsvetayeva, and Rainer Maria Rilke, tr. Margaret Wettling and Walter Arndt, ed. Yevgeny Pasternak, Yelena Pasternak, and Konstantin M. Azadovsky (New York, 1985).

Valéry, Paul, *Collected Works*, ed. Jackson Matthew, 15 vols. (New York and Princeton, 1956–75).

Œuvres, ed. Jean Hytier, 2 vols. (Paris, 1957).

Verlaine, Paul, *Œuvres poétiques*, ed. Jacques Robichez (Paris, 1969).

Wilde, Oscar, *The Artist as Critic: Critical Writings*, ed. Richard Ellmann (New York, 1969).

Williams, William Carlos, 'An Essay on *Leaves of Grass*', in *Leaves of Grass One Hundred Years After*, ed. Milton Hindus (Stanford, 1955), pp. 22–31.

'The Poem as a Field of Action' (1948), *Selected Essays* (New York, 1969), pp. 280–91,

Spring and All (1923), in *Imaginations* (New York, 1970), pp. 83–151.

Wordsworth, William, *Literary Criticism*, ed. Paul M. Zall (Lincoln, Nebr., 1966).

Yeats, W. B., 'Introduction', *The Oxford Book of Modern Verse 1892–1935* (Oxford, 1936).

'The Symbolism of Poetry' (1900), *Essays and Introductions* (New York, 1968), pp. 153–64.

The Variorum Edition of the Poems, ed. Peter Allt and Russell Alspach (New York, 1957).

Secondary sources:

Bourdieu, Pierre, *The Rules of Art: Genesis and Structure of the Literary Field*, tr. Susan Emanuel (Cambridge, 1996).

Brink, C. O., *Horace on Poetry: The 'Ars Poetica'* (Cambridge, 1971).

David, Claude, *Stefan George: son œuvre poétique* (Lyon, 1952).

Eagleton, Terry, *The Ideology of the Aesthetic* (Oxford, 1990).

Frye, Northrop, *Anatomy of Criticism: Four Essays* (Princeton, 1957).

Hytier, Jean, *The Poetics of Paul Valéry*, tr. Richard Howard (New York, 1966).

Lipking, Lawrence, *The Life of the Poet: Beginning and Ending Poetic Careers* (Chicago, 1981).

'The Marginal Gloss,' *Critical Inquiry*, 3 (1977), pp. 609–55.

Litz, A. Walton, '*The Waste Land* Fifty Years After', *Eliot in His Time* (Princeton, 1973), pp. 3–22.

Schwartz, Delmore, 'T. S. Eliot as the International Hero', *Partisan Review*, 12 (1945), pp. 199–206.

Scott, A. F., *The Poet's Craft* (Cambridge, 1957).

Selden, Raman, ed., *The Cambridge History of Literary Criticism*, vol. 8, *From Formalism to Poststructuralism* (Cambridge, 1995).

Wellek, René, 'The Poet as Critic, the Critic as Poet, the Poet-Critic', in *The Poet as Critic*, ed. Frederick McDowell (Evanston, Ill., 1967), pp. 92–107.

Wimsatt, W. K., and Cleanth Brooks, *Literary Criticism: A Short History* (New York, 1957).

    and Monroe Beardsley, 'The Intentional Fallacy', in *The Verbal Icon* (Lexington, Ky., 1954), pp. 3–18.

20 Criticism of fiction

Blackmur, R. P., *Eleven Essays in the European Novel* (New York, 1964).

Booth, Wayne, *The Rhetoric of Fiction* (1961; rpt. Chicago, 1983).

Brooks, Cleanth, and Robert Penn Warren (eds.), *Understanding Fiction* (New York, 1946).

Conrad, Joseph, *Collected Essays*, ed. C. K. Moncrieff (Folcroft, 1973).

Crane, R. S. (ed.), *Critics and Criticism, Ancient and Modern* (Chicago, 1952).

Ford, Ford Madox, *The English Novel: From the Earliest Days to the Death of Joseph Conrad* (1930; rpt. Manchester, 1983).

    Henry James: A Critical Study (New York, 1916).

    Joseph Conrad, A Personal Remembrance (1924; rpt. New York, 1989).

    The March of Literature: From Confucius to Modern Times (London, 1939).

Forster, E. M., *Aspects of the Novel* (1927).

    Selected Letters, ed. Mary Lago and P. N. Furbank (Cambridge, 1985).

Fox, Ralph, *The Novel and the People* (New York, 1937).

Frye, Northrop, *Anatomy of Criticism* (Princeton, 1957).

Gordon, Caroline and Allen Tate (eds.), *The House of Fiction* (New York, 1950).

Hamilton, Clayton, *Materials and Methods of Fiction* (New York, 1908).

Hicks, Granville, *The Great Tradition: An Interpretation of American Literature Since the Civil War* (New York, 1933).

Howe, Irving, *Politics and the Novel* (New York, 1957).

James, Henry, *The Art of Criticism*, ed. William Veeder and Susan Griffin (Chicago, 1986).

    The Art of the Novel, ed. R. P. Blackmur (New York, 1934).

    Literary Criticism, 2 vols. (New York, 1984).

Kettle, Arnold, *An Introduction to the English Novel* (London, 1951).

Lawrence, D. H., *Studies in Classic American Literature* (New York, 1986).

    Study of Thomas Hardy and Other Essays, ed. Bruce Steele (New York, 1985).

Leavis, F. R., *The Great Tradition: George Eliot, Henry James, Joseph Conrad* (1948; rpt. London, 1952).

Leavis, Q. D., *Fiction and the Reading Public* (1932; rpt. London, 1990).

Lubbock, Percy, *The Craft of Fiction* (1921; rpt. London, 1932).

Orwell, George, *A Collection of Essays* (New York, 1953).

    The Lion and the Unicorn: Socialism and the English Genius (New York,

1976).

Schorer, Mark, *The World We Imagine: Selected Essays* (New York, 1968).

Tate, Allen, *Memories and Essays Old and New, 1926–1974* (Manchester, 1976).

Trilling, Lionel, *The Liberal Imagination: Essays on Literature and Society* (New York, 1950).

Vickery, John B. (ed.), *Myth and Literature: Contemporary Theory and Practice* (Lincoln, 1969).

Watt, Ian, *The Rise of the Novel* (London, 1957).

Williams, Raymond, *Culture and Society* (New York, 1958).

The English Novel from Dickens to Lawrence (London, 1970).

Woolf, Virginia, *The Essays of Virginia Woolf*, ed. Andrew McNeillie, 6 vols. (San Diego, 1986–).

A Room of One's Own (1929; rpt. London, 1931).

Index

NOTE: this index is arranged in word by word order. Works are listed under authors' names. Page numbers in bold refer to main sections on the subject.

Abbey Theatre, Dublin 151, 152–3, 159, 160–1, 166
Abercrombie, Lascelles 289
Abrams, M. H. 291, 314
Action Française 45, 52, 291
Adams, Henry 243–4, 264
Adler, Mortimer 190
aesthetics, critique of pure 214–18
Aesthetics and Language (collected essays 1954) 313
African-American writers **167–78**
Agrarian movement 203, 294, 346
Aldington, Richard 26, 76, 261
Alger, Horatio 339
Allston, Washington 28
American Modern Language Association 293
American New Critics 181, 485–7
see also Southern New Critics
American Studies 346–52, 358–9, 374–6
Anderson, Margaret 83, 84
Anderson, Sherwood 99, 100–1
antihumanism 49
antimodernism 48–9
antisemitism
    Eliot's 35, 44, 45, 49–50, 51–2
    Pound's 57, 150
Arac, Jonathan 315
Ardizzone, Patrizia 70n
Aristotle 37, 193
Arnold, Matthew 31, 35, 54, 184, 275, 277
    and poet-critics 440

Trilling on 353, 430, 431
ars poetica 444–5
Asquith, Herbert 68
Athenaeum 19
Auden, W. H. 372
Augustine of Hippo, Saint 254
Austen, Jane 134
authority, concept of intellectual 379–83

Babbitt, Irving 47, 49, 279, 290–1
Bain, Alexander 380
Baker, Houston 167
Bakhtin, M. M. 258
Baldick, Chris 283
Barbusse, Henri 252
Barrès, Maurice 48
Barthes, Roland 253
Barzun, Jacques 320
Basic English 181
Bateson, F. W. 301–2
Baudelaire, Charles 38, 62, 263
Baugh, Albert 314
Beach, Sylvia 101n
Bel Esprit project to aid T. S. Eliot 87
Bell, Clive 26, 36
Bella-Villada, Gene H. 62n
Benda, Julien 47, 49, 143–4
    Belphégor 49–50, 144
    Trahison des Clercs, La (1928) 145–6
Benjamin, Walter 134
Benn, Gottfried 36
Bennett, Arnold 289–90

Bennett, Gwendolyn 175
Bentham, Jeremy 193
Bentley, G. E. 314
Bergson, Henri 28–9, 44–5, 63
  Eliot and 46, 48
  *Essai sur les données immédiates de
    la conscience* (1889) 44
  L'Evolution créatrice (1907) 44
  and Wyndham Lewis 140, 142
Bewley, Marius 248–9, 257, 395
Bird, William 83
Black, Max 257
Blackmur, R. P. 181, 219, 235–47,
    294
  background 235–6
  cult of spontaneity 236–7
  and Eliot 237, 240
  on European novel 246–7
  on form 235, 236–7, 247
  and Henry James 242–4, 487–8
  on idiom 238–40
  'industrialization of intellect' 245
  motions of the words 238–40
  order 237–8
  and Richards 240
  schools of insight 244–7
  'techniques of trouble' 246
  theory of failure 241–4
  Works
    'Anni Mirabiles' (lectures
      1921–25) 245
    early books 235
    Lion and the Honeycomb (1955)
      239, 244
Blake, William 38, 403, 404–5
Blast magazine 26, 80, 81–2, 148
Bohemianism 341
Bookman 155, 157
Booth, Wayne 469, 496–8
Bourdieu, Pierre 214–16
Bourne, Randolph 288, 325–6
Bradley, A. C. 273
  'Reaction against Tennyson' 38
Bradley, F. H. 25
  Appearance and Reality 21–2
  'On Our Knowledge of Immediate

Experience' 22
Breton, André 439, 457
Bridges, Robert 153, 261, 263
Briffault, Robert 428
British Journal of Aesthetics 313
British Modern Languages Association
    275
Brontë, Charlotte 136
Brooks, Cleanth 209, 297–8
  An Approach to Literature 300
  Literary Criticism: A Short History
    (1957) 313, 466
  Modern Poetry and the Tradition 20
  Understanding Fiction 485
  Understanding Poetry 213, 298,
    300, 301, 485
Brooks, Van Wyck 288, 326–30, 346,
    360, 363
Brower, Reuben 298
Brown, Edmund 99, 100*n*
Browne, Sir Thomas 134
Browning, Robert 40
Burke, Kenneth 181, 248–59, 294
  contradiction and incongruity in
    258
  as critic of modernist debunking
    251–2
  and defamiliarisation 257
  definition of man 250
  disciplinary boundaries 249–50
  dramatism 255–8
  and Keats 256
  and the pentad 256–8
  rhetoric and demystification 252,
    253
  scepticism 250–1
  theology and logology 254–5
  see also Cunningham; Moore;
    Robinson; Synge; Valéry; Yeats
  Works
    Attitude Toward History 248–9
    Counter-Statement 248, 250–1
    Grammar of Motives, A 249
    Language as Symbolic Form 254
    Permanence and Change 250
    Rhetoric of Religion 248, 249, 254

Burney, Fanny 136
Burrow, Trigant 193
Bush, Douglas 298
Butler, Samuel 63, 132
Byron, George Gordon, Lord 38

Canby, Henry Seidel 287, 293
Carlyle, Thomas 253
Carpenter, Humphrey 81n
Casement, Roger 154
Catholicism 48, 51
Cavalcanti, Guido 64, 67
Cavendish, Margaret 124
Chapman, John Jay 328–9
Chase, Richard 359
Chekov, Anton 364
Child, Frances 274
Chiswick Press 60, 68
Christian News-Letter 19
Churchill, Charles 265
Churchill, Winston 73
Classical Association 278
classicism 45, 47, 48, 49, 54
classroom teaching
    Leavis and 392, 418–19
    Richards and 181, 185
Claudel, Paul 48
close reading 190, 200, 219–20
cognition and feeling 96–7
Cohen, Elliott 426–7
Coleridge, Samuel Taylor 36, 38, 429
    I. A. Richards on 198
    Virginia Woolf on 122, 137
Coliseum theatre, London 79–81
Collingwood, R. G. 313
Collins, John Churton 275, 279, 380
Comito, Terry 264
Communism 368, 369, 427–8
Conant, James Bryant 292
Conrad, Joseph 83, 470–3, 484–5
Contemporary Jewish Record 427
Contemporary Literary Scholarship
    (collected essays 1958) 313
Cook, Albert 285–6
Cowley, Malcolm 340–6
    And I Worked at the Writer's Trade

    (1978) 340
    Dream of the Golden Mountains,
        The (1980) 340
    Exile's Return 340, 342
Craig, Hardin 307, 314
Crane, Hart 238, 239, 241, 261, 264,
    341–2
Crane, R. S. 197, 308–10, 487
Cravens, Margaret 59, 72
Crisis, The 171, 172
Criterion magazine 19, 33, 40, 47, 92
criticism
    concept of intellectual authority
        379–83
    function of 450–3
    opposition between poetry and
        446–8
    rise of academic professionalism
        377–88
    since World War II 312–21
    and social change 388–8
    specialisation 382–5
    see also English studies; fiction
        criticism; poet-critics
critics and professors 269–71, 286–8
critics and society 322–76
    attack on the Gilded Age 326–33
    critic as man of letters 333–46
    England and America 374–6
    generation of 1910 critics 324–6
    Kazin, Rahv, and Partisan Review
        359–68
    New York intellectuals 424
    Orwell: politics, criticism, and
        popular culture 368–74
    public sphere and modern criticism
        423–4, 457
    rise of American Studies 346–52
    Trilling as cultural critic 352–9
    see also poet-critics
Critique of Humanism 293, 294
Cruikshank, Dan 68n
Cubism 140, 147
Cullen, Countee 175
Culler, Jonathan 277
cultural studies 150

culture, popular 217
Cunningham, J. V. 260

Dadaism 341
Daiches, David 312
Daily Mail 76
Daniel, Arnaut 63, 64, 65, 67, 68–9
Dante Alighieri 41–2, 53, 240, 241,
    451
Daryush, Elizabeth 261
Davies, Sir John 38
decadence, cultural 44
Defoe, Daniel 134
Depression (1930s) 338–9, 342, 343–4
Descartes, René 462, 463
DeVane, William C. 301
Dial, The 261, 280
Dickens, Charles 338, 370–1, 391,
    397–8, 414–15, 491
Dilthey, Wilhelm 32
dissociation of sensibility 20, 46,
    53–4, 96–7, 103, 143, 408, 449
doctrinal adhesion and response to
    poetry 186
Donne, John 30, 38, 40, 41, 134
Donoghue, Denis 237
Dos Passos, John 339
Dostoevsky, Feodor 246–7, 338,
    366–7
Dowden, Professor Ernest 155, 158
Dreiser, Theodore 331–2, 361–2, 433
Dreyfus affair 45, 52
Du Bois, W. E. B. 167, 170–3
Dublin societies and institutions
    158–60
Duffy, Sir Charles Gavan 156, 157,
    158
Duncan, Robert 120
durée réele see Bergson, Henri
Dynamists 72

Eagle, Solomon (John Collings Squire)
    81*n*
Eagleton, Terry 200, 423
Early English Text Society 287
Eastman, Max 194*n*, 327

Ebony and Topaz anthology 177
Egoist magazine 19, 26, 30, 77, 79
Einstein, Albert 140
Elgar, Edward 80
Eliot, George 483, 485
Eliot, T. S. 17–56
    aesthetic theory 20–1, 41
    antimodern movement 48–9
    antisemitism 35, 44, 50, 51
    Bel Esprit project 87
    and Blackmur 237
    Catholicism 43, 48, 51
    classicism 47, 49, 51, 54
    on compromises of W. B. Yeats 158
    as controversialist 19
    on Dante 41–2, 53
    deplorable aspects of modern
        culture 17–18
    dissociation of sensibility 20, 46,
        53–4, 96–7, 103*n*, 408, 449
    and Empson 220
    and European culture 51
    fascism 51
    Georgian poets 26, 33
    his thought as sum of three kinds of
        writing 43–4
    Imagism 26, 28, 44, 45
    immediate experience 22–4
    impersonality 20, 30–2, 142, 450
    integrity and autonomy of self 31
    interest in other poets 36–43
    Leavis and 407–8
    liberalism 25–6
    on Milton 53, 408–9
    objective correlative 20, 27–8, 29,
        55
    own poetry 24–5
    paradox of success 19–20
    philosophy 21–4
    as poet-critic 449–50
    poetry and belief 37, 43, 410, 456
    principal books of literary criticism
        18
    as reactionary 17
    relation between new and existing
        art 32

relativism 24
on Renaissance writers 38
and Richards 186, 192, 194
romanticism 17, 34, 48
royalism 17
scepticism 19, 25
secularism 38
sensationalism 28, 40, 46
on Shakespeare 27-8, 30, 41-2
on social function of literature 54
on Tennyson 38-9, 40
tradition 20, 31-2, 34-5
on women 50-1
    see also Dante; Milton;
    Shakespeare
Works
    After Strange Gods (1934) 18, 20,
        34-5, 37, 44, 51
    'Borderline of Prose' (1917) 26
    Dante (1929) 18
    Elizabethan Essays (1934) 18
    Enemy, The 40
    Essays Ancient and Modern
        (1936) 18
    essays on nineteenth-century
        writers 38
    essays on Renaissance writers 38,
        46
    'Experience and the Objects of
        Knowledge in the Philosophy of
        F. H. Bradley' (1916) 21-2
    'Experiment in Criticism' (1929)
        55
    Ezra Pound: His Metric and
        Poetry (1917) 26, 28
    For Lancelot Andrewes (1928)
        18, 37, 48
    Four Quartets 53, 240
    'Frontiers of Criticism' (1956) 55
    'Function of Criticism' (1923) 20,
        33-4
    'Hamlet and His Problems'
        (1919) 27, 29
    Homage to John Dryden (1924) 18
    Idea of a Christian Society, The
        (1939) 18, 19, 51, 429

'Idea of a Literary Review' (1926)
    47
'Literature of Fascism' (1928) 51
'Literature, Science and Dogma'
    194
'Love Song of J. Alfred Prufrock',
    'The' 46, 50
'Metaphysical Poets', 'The' 30,
    40, 46, 449
'Modern Education and the
    Classics'(1932) 43
'Modern Tendencies in Poetry' 30
Norton lectures (1933) 42
'Note on Poetry and Belief'
    (1927) 40
Notes towards the Definition of
    Culture (1948) 18, 19, 51
On Poetry and Poets (1957) 18
'Perfect Critic', 'The' 30, 46, 449
'Preludes' 46
'Reflections on Contemporary
    Poetry' (1917-19) 26
'Reflections on vers libre' (1917)
    26
'Religion and Literature' (1935) 37
Sacred Wood (1920) 18, 30, 37,
    41
Science and Poetry (1926) 40
'Second Thoughts about
    Humanism' (1928) 41, 42
Selected Essays 18, 314
'Shakespeare and Montaigne'
    (1925) 41
'Shakespeare and the Stoicism of
    Seneca' (1927) 41
'Studies in Contemporary
    Criticism' (1918) 26
'Syllabus of a Course of Six
    Lectures on Modern French
    Literature' (1916) 47-8
'Three Voices of Poetry' (1953) 36
To Criticize the Critic (1965) 18,
    27
'Tradition and the Individual
    Talent' (1919) 20, 30, 31-4,
    35-6, 54, 450

Eliot, T. S. (*cont.*)
　Use of Poetry and the Use of Criticism (1933) 18, 36, 41, 54, 186
　Waste Land, The 83, 201, 241, 441, 453
Eliot, Vivien (née Haigh-Wood) 21
Elton, Oliver 292
Empson, William 97, 120, 181, 190, 219–34, 310
　ambiguity 221–3, 224
　double plots 225, 226
　and Eliot 220
　'equations' 228–9
　irony 223–7, 230–1
　on *King Lear* 230
　and Leavis 417–18
　on *Macbeth* 24, 221–2
　on Marlowe 232–4
　meanings of words 229–30
　metaphor 222–3
　method 220–1
　on Milton 225, 229, 231–2
　pastoral 225–8
　on *Tom Jones* 230–1
　Works
　　Faustus and the Censor 232–4
　　Milton's God 231–2, 233
　　Seven Types of Ambiguity 219, 221–3, 224, 240, 417
　　Some Versions of Pastoral 225–8, 231
　　Structure of Complex Words 228–9
Encyclopedists of Unified Science 181
engineering and poetic precision 63–5
English Association 280
English Journal 304, 310
English Review, The 59
English School at Cambridge 390–1
English studies
　absorption of practical criticism into curriculum 306–7
　academic audience 287–8
　aesthetic criticism 272–3
　'Aims of Literary Study' 304–5

　in America 209–11, 274–5, 276, 278, 280–2, 298–306
　assault by new humanists 290–4
　in Britain 275–6, 277–80
　changes in character after World War II 312
　criticism and scholarship (1950s) 312–21
　critics and professors 269–71, 286–90, 294–5
　differences between British and American universities 271, 276
　dissatisfaction with teaching of 288
　examinations 275–6, 282–4, 296, 302
　explication de texte 299
　founding of 271–9
　fragmentation of curriculum 317
　history and philology 279–86, 293
　introduction of practical criticism 286–312
　literary histories (post-1948) 314–15, 319
　literature 288, 302–4, 316, 318
　meaning of term 'criticism' 318–20
　modernist fiction 303–4
　and other languages 280, 282, 284
　and politics of critics 317
　redefinitions of criticism before World War II 306–10
　and Richards 296, 298, 307–9, 320
　rise of 270–3, 284–5
　scholarly activity and rise of 286–94
　and social issues 304–5, 317
　Teaching of College English 299, 301
　Teaching of English in England (1911) 280
　three types of criticism 289
　unintelligibility of modernism 316–17
epistemology, empiricist 44
Epstein, Jacob 82, 83
Erasmus, Desiderius 230
Ernest, Thomas 29*n*
Evans, B. Ifor 289

explication de texte 299

Fabian Society 61
failure, theory of (Blackmur) 241–4
fascism 49, 87, 150
Fausset, Hugh l'Anson 39
Feidelson, Charles 315
Fenollosa, Ernest 77, 78, 85
Fernandez, Ramon 261
Fianna Éireann (Irish Boy Scouts) 159
fiction criticism **468–98**
    Conrad 471–3
    dualism of form and content 487
    Ford Madox Ford 472–4
    Forster 477–9
    historical development of the novel
        489–90
    James (Henry) 468–72
    Lawrence 476–7
    Leavis 411–15, 482–5
    Lubbock 479–81
    Orwell 491–2
    Trilling 493–4
    Watt (Ian) 492–3
    Woolf (Virginia) 474–6
Fiedler, Leslie 359
Field Day Anthology of Irish Writing
    (1991) 151
Fielding, Henry 231
Fish, Stanley 196, 318
Fisher, John H. 301
Flint, F. S. 70, 72
Foerster, Norman 290, 293, 307
Forbes, Mansfield 182
Ford, Ford Madox 28, 29, 59, 472,
    481
Ford, John 38
Forster, E. M. 26, 134, 432
    Aspects of the Novel 477–9, 482
Foster, William Z. 339
Four Seas Company of Boston 99
Fox, Ralph 490–1
Frayne, John 153, 157, 158
Frazier, Adrian 161
Freeman's Journal 155
Freud, Sigmund 220, 436, 494, 495

Fry, Roger 71
Frye, Northrop 466, 495–6, 497
Fugitive, The (poetry magazine) 201
Fugitive group 201
Fugitives 62, 263
Futurism 69–70, 72, 75, 147
Futurist Poets, The (Marinetti) 75

Gadamer, Hans-Georg 32, 198
Gaelic League 158
Galway Library Committee 166
Gardner, Helen 307, 311, 312
Garvey, Marcus 170, 175
Gates, Henry Louis 169, 178
Gaudier-Brzeska, Henri 83
Gautier, Théophile 62
Gazette de France 52
General Semanticists 181
Georgian Poetry 72, 75
Georgian poets, Eliot and 26, 33
Ghan Shyam Sing 57n
Gide, André 251
Glenconner, Lord and Lady 67–8, 80
Goethe, Johann Wolfgang von 38, 41
Gold, Michael 344
Gordon, Caroline 485–6
Gordon, Lyndall 24n
Gourmont, Rémy de 37, 46, 143–4
    Le problème du style 46, 145
    Lettres à l'Amazone (1914) 46
Graff, Gerald 209–10, 316
Gramsci, Antonio 259, 436
Graves, Robert 120, 220
Great War *see* World War I
Greenberg, Clement 370
Greenlaw, Edwin 293, 307
Gregory, Lady 160
Grene, Marjorie 397
Greville, Fulke 261
Grierson, H. J. 273
Guild Socialism 61
Gunn, Giles 257
Gyroscope 261

Habermas, Jürgen 423
Haigh-Wood (later Eliot), Vivien 21

Hall, G. Stanley 325
Hamlet, Eliot on 27–8
Harding, D. W. 417
Hardy, Thomas 35, 265
Harlem Renaissance 167–78
  African-Americans and Africa 174
  literary art and politics 167–8
  propaganda and art 170–1, 174,
    178
  slavery 168–9
  white racism 168
Harrison, G. B. 307
Hartman, Geoffrey 187
Havelock, Eric 190
Hawthorne, Nathaniel 435
Hazlitt, William 125–6
Heaney, Seamus 153
Heidegger, Martin 399–401, 402, 404
Hemingway, Ernest 101, 428
Henry, Hubert 52
Herbert, George 223
Heywood, Thomas 38
Hick, Granville 347, 490
Hine, Daryl 75
history
  intellectual 306–7, 314–15, 320
  literary 314–15, 319–20
  and literary criticism 269–70, 324–5
  and philology 279–86, 322
Hitler, Adolf 343
Holloway, John 311, 316
Homer 91, 190
Hook, Sidney 251–2
Hopkins, Gerard Manley 409
Horace 444–5
Horniman, Annie 161, 162, 166
Hotopf, W. H. N. 192*n*
Hough, Graham 307, 311, 312, 320
Hound and Horn, The 262
Howe, Irving 368, 369, 491–2
Howells, William Dean 361, 362
Hughes, Langston 176, 177
Hughes, Merritt 305–6
Hulme, T. E. 29, 44, 45, 63, 291, 313
  'Humanism and the Religious
    Attitude' 45, 46

poems appended to Pound's
  Ripostes 71
'Romanticism and Classicism' 45,
  46
Speculations (1924) 47
'Tory Philosophy', 'A' (1912) 45, 49
humanism 49
Humanism and America 293
humanists, new 290–4
Hurston, Zora Neale 177–8
Hyde, Douglas 158
Hyman, Stanley Edgar 219, 312, 323

ideograms 58, 77–8
ideology, use of the term 143–4
idiom 238–40
I'll Take My Stand symposium on the
  South (USA) 34, 203, 346
Illustrated London News 69
Imagism 26, 28, 44, 45, 62, 70–5,
  79–80
immediate experience, T. S. Eliot on
  22–4
impersonality doctrine 20, 30–2, 142,
  450
Impressionists 71
Independent, The 175
inhibition and literature 185
investment in art 84–5
Irish Academy of Letters 154
Irish arts business (1890s) 154–8
Irish Intelligentsia 154–5, 157, 161
Irish Literary Society, London 155
Irish Literary Theatre 159
Irish National Dramatic Company
  159
Irish National Theatre Society 159
Irish Times 159
irony 223–5
irrelevant association and poetry 185
Iser, Wolfgang 196

Jacob, Max 446
Jaeger, Werner 190
Jakobson, Roman 186
James, Henry 40, 134, 224, 242–4,

322, 334
'Art of Fiction', 'The' 468–72, 487
  Blackmur on 487–8
  Forster on 478–9
  Leavis and 413–14, 484
  Lubbock on 480–1
  Rahv and 364–5
  Trilling on 434
James, William 24, 49, 93–7, 106, 291
Jameson, Frederic 150
Jammes, Francis 48
Jarrell, Randall (quotation) 235
Jiménez, Juan Ramón 451
Johnson, James Weldon 168–71, 176
Johnson, Samuel 55
Journal of Aesthetics and Art Criticism
  313
Jowett, Benjamin 275
Joyce, James 35, 83, 87, 141, 451, 473

Kafka, Franz 367
Kant, Immanuel 460
Kazin, Alfred 348, **359–63**
  as reader 361–2
  as writer 360
Keats, John 33, 256, 401–2, 436
Kenyon Review 213, 355
Ker, W. P. 273
Kermode, Frank 315
Kettle, Arnold 492
Knight, G. Wilson 315
Knights, L. C. 281, 310, 418
knowledge, William James on 94–7,
  106
Krieger, Murray 313, 321
Kuzmin, Mikhail 439
Kyle, Galloway 60

Lacerba (Marinetti's magazine) 80
Ladies' Education Association 277
Laforgue, Jules 41, 263
Lalou, René 261
Lane, John 99
Langbaum, Robert 315
Langer, Susanne 313
languages in teaching of English

studies 280, 282, 284
Lasch, Christopher 326
Lasserre, Pierre 44–5, 48
Lawrence, D. H. 35, 134, 395–6, 415,
  456
  criticism of fiction 476–7, 482–3
Leary, Lewis 314, 320
Leavis, F. R. 20, 186, 197, 296–7,
  301, 310, 312, **389–422**
  attitude to philosophy 397, 405
  and C. P. Snow 395–6
  career and themes 389–9, 389–97
  and collective creative process 401
  on Conrad 484–5
  criticism and collaboration 415–20
  on Dickens 338, 414–15
  and Eliot 407–8, 410
  and Heidegger 399–401, 402
  on Henry James 413–14, 484
  his apparent exclusiveness 402–3
  impersonality and 404–5
  on Keats 401–2
  on Lawrence 415, 482–3
  literature and language 398–405
  and the novel 411–15, 482–5
  poetry and literary tradition 407–11
  on Pound 391–2
  prophet and the word 420–2
  and Richards 416–17
  school teaching of literature 392,
    418–19
  on Shakespeare 394
  and 'sincerity' 403
  social tradition and 'organic
    community' 405–7
  and Trilling 357–8
  Works
    *'Anna Karenina' and Other
      Essays* 396
    Common Pursuit, The 357, 393,
      394
    D. H. Lawrence 391, 395, 413
    Determinations 392
    Dickens the Novelist 396, 413,
      414
    Education and the University 392

Leavis, F. R. (*cont.*)
  *English Literature in Our Time
    and the University* 396
  For Continuity 392
  Great Tradition, The 393, 413
  How to Teach Reading 391
  Lectures in America (with Q. D.
    Leavis) 396
  Living Principle 397, 421
  *Mass Civilization and Minority
    Culture* (1930) 390, 391
  Mill on Bentham and Coleridge
    (ed.) 393
  New Bearings in English Poetry
    391
  Nor Shall My Sword 397
  Revaluation 392
  Thought, Words and Creativity
    397
Leavis, Q. D. 357, 370, 390, 397, 485
  Fiction and the Reading Public
    489–90, 491, 492
Leibniz, G. W. 22
Lentricchia, Frank 257
Lesser, Simon O. 494
Levenson, Michael 44*n*
Lewes, G. H. 403, 404
Lewis, C. S. 311, 312, 314
Lewis, R. W. B. 315
Lewis, Sinclair 360
Lewis, Wyndham 26, 29, 76, 79, 82*n*,
  139–50
  authority and independence of the
    critic 138–9
  cartoons 147
  critique of modern politics 145–6
  fascism 150
  and Gertrude Stein 141–2, 144
  and Gourmont 145
  and 'impersonality principle' 143
  influence of Machiavellian thought
    139–40
  influence of World War I 146–7
  on Joyce's *Ulysses* 141–2
  modern experience of time 140–2,
    147

  on 'pseudo-belief' 143
  on race-consciousness in literature
    138
  rewriting of history 149–50
  visual discrimination 144–5
  Works
    Apes of God, The (1930) 145
    Art of Being Ruled, The (1926)
      149
    Childermass, The (1928) 145
    Doom of Youth, The 146
    Lion and the Fox, The 139–40,
      142
    Man of the World, The 139
    Men Without Art (1934) 149
    *Paleface: The Philosophy of the
      Melting Pot* 138
    Plan of War (cartoon) 147
    Satire and Fiction (1930) 145
    Slow Attack (cartoon) 147
    Tarr 83
    Time and Western Man 140
Lewisohn, Ludwig 287
Lippmann, Walter 327
literary histories (post-1948) 314–15
literary studies in America 210–14
litotes 72
Little Review 83, 84
Lloyd, Marie 81
Locke, Alain 167, 170–1, 172–4, 175,
  176
London, Jack 288
Lorca, Federico García 451
Lowell, Amy 82, 85
Lowell, Robert 57
Lowes, John Livingston 307
Lubbock, Percy 479–81
Lukács, Georg 201, 367

Macaulay, T. B. 275
MacCallum, Pamela 195
MacDonagh, Thomas 157
MacDonald, Dwight 217, 370
Machiavelli, Niccolò 41, 139
McKay, Claude 167, 171, 175, 177
MacLeish, Archibald 206, 441, 446

McLuhan, Marshall 196
McMurtry, Jo 283, 284
McTaggart, J. M. E. 182
Macy, John 288
Mallarmé, Stéphane 439, 447–8
Man, Paul de 259, 298
Manchester Guardian 288
Mandelstam, Osip 459–60
Manly, J. M. 280
Mann, Thomas 247, 251
Marinetti, Filippo Tommaso 69–70,
    72, 75–6, 79–81, 439
Maritain, Jacques 47
    Art et scholastique (1920) 54
Markievicz, Constance 159
Marlowe, Christopher 38
Marsden, Dora 77
Marsh, Edward 72
Marston, John 38
Marvell, Andrew 38, 225–6
Marwick, Arthur 61*n*
Marxism 342–4, 347, 353, 356, 359
    and criticism of fiction 490–2
    Orwell and 368, 370
    Rahv and 363–4
Massinger, Philip 38, 46
Masson, David 273, 274
Mathiesen, Margaret 283
Matthews, Brander 289
Matthews, Elkin 60, 61
Matthews, T. S. 107
Matthiessen, F. O. 20, 314, 322, 323,
    347, **349–52**, 359
Maurras, Charles 45, 47, 48–9, 50, 52
media, I. A. Richards and use of the
    190–1
Meinecke, Friedrich 32
melopoeia (musical aspect of
    language) 89–90
Mencken, H. L. 323, 325, 330–3, 360
Menorah Journal 352, 426–7
Messenger 176
metaphor 189, 194–5, 199
Middleton, Thomas 38
Mill, John Stuart 429
Miller, Henry 372–3

Miller, Perry 330, 348
Milton, John 53, 91, 225, 226, 231,
    303, 408–9
Modern Language Association 213,
    275, 301
monarchism 48–9
Monist, The 21
Monk, Samuel 314
Monro, Harold 36, 60–1, 72–3, 75–6
Monroe, Harriet 62, 70
Montaigne, Michel de 25, 41, 134
Moore, G. E. 182
Moore, Marianne 261, 454
Moore, T. Sturge 261, 262
More, Paul Elmer 48, 287, 290, 322
Morley, Henry 273, 274
Multiple Definition 183
Mumford, Lewis 334
Murphy, Francis 261
Murry, John Middleton 19, 34, 53,
    382, 383
music and criticism 89–90
music-hall as culture of modernity
    79–82
Mussolini, Benito 51, 57, 87

Napier, A. S. 277–8
Nation, The 352
National Council of Teachers of
    English 299
National Gallery of Ireland 160
National Literary Society, Dublin 155
National Theatre Society Ltd. (Abbey
    Company, Dublin) 159
National University of Ireland 159
naturalism 48
Negro World 175
New Age, The 29, 45, 61, 86, 382
New American Caravan, The 263
New Criticism *see* Southern New
    Critics
New English Weekly 19
New Freewoman, The 77
New Historicists 150
New Irish Library 155, 156
New Negro, The 171, 173, 174, 175

New Republic, The 107, 333, 340, 342, 352
New Statesman 19, 26, 48
New York Little Renaissance 173
New Yorker, The 333
newspaper references to Futurism exhibition 69–70, 70n
newspapers and poetry 76
Nicolson, Harold, on Tennyson 39
Nietzsche, F. 399–400, 412
Nitze, William A. 293
Noh drama, Japanese 79
Norris, Christopher 225
Norris, Frank 288
Northcliffe, Lord 76
Nouvelle revue française 48
novel
  Leavis and the 411–15, 482–5
  see also fiction criticism

objective correlative 20, 27–8, 29, 55, 78
O'Connor, William Van 312
O'Faolain, Sean 166
Ogden, C. K. 183, 184, 187
O'Grady, Standish 157, 158
Olson, Charles 456
Opportunity (house organ of Urban League) 168, 175
Orage, Alfred Richard 61, 382–3
organic community, idea of 405–7
original sin 46, 48, 49
Orwell, George 337
  on Dickens 491
  fascination with popular culture 370–1, 437
  on McGill postcards 373–4, 437
  politics, criticism and popular culture 368–74, 491–2
  on Swift 371–2
  Works
    Animal Farm 369
    Homage to Catalonia 369
    Inside the Whale (1940) 370, 372–3
    Nineteen Eighty-Four 369

Road to Wigan Pier 373

Pall Mall Gazette 69
Palmer, D. J. 296
Paris, Gertrude Stein on 116–18
Parrington, V. L. 347–8, 349, 432–3
Partisan Review 346, 352, 363, 427, 428
  see also Kazin; Rahv
Paston family 124, 133–4
pastoral 225–8
Pater, Walter 28, 30, 31, 37, 192
Patmore, Coventry 126
Pavlov, I. P. 183, 187
Paz, Octavio 465
Pearse, Patrick 157, 159
Péguy, Charles 48
Pepper, Stephen 313
Perry, Bliss 287, 289, 292
personae technique in poetry 92
Phelps, William Lyon 289, 325
philology 210–12, 279–86, 293, 454
Pierce, C. S. 183
Pilley, Dorothy (wife of I. A. Richards) 182
Plato 189, 190, 193, 441, 457
Poe, Edgar Allen 447–8, 462
poet-critics **439–67**
  changing styles 440–1
  defence of poetry 457–65
  difference from critics at large 443–4
  function of criticism 450–3
  obscurity of modern classics 441
  opposition between poetry and criticism 446–8, 465–7
  pressure of non-conformity 458–61
  principles of the modern 450–6
  revolution in technique 453–6
  value placed on purity in verse 441–2
  see also Valéry
Poetical Gazette, The (formerly *The Poetical*) 60
Poetry 61–2, 261
Poetry: A Magazine of Verse 70

poetry and belief, Eliot on 37
Poetry Bookshop 36, 60, 76
poetry and criticism
    interventionism 450–1
    modern **441–67**
    nationalism 448–9
    opposition between 446–8
Poetry and Drama 60, 75
Poetry Recital Society 60
Poetry Review 60, 61, 70
Poetry Society 68
Polanyi, Michael 397
Pope, Alexander 445
Popular Front 349, 354, 430
Post-Impressionist Exhibition
        (December 1910) 67
Post-Impressionists 71–2
Potter, Stephen 283
Pound, Ezra 21, 26, 29, **57–92**
    aims of criticism 87–8
    antisemitism 57
    on Arnaut Daniel 63, 64, 65
    background and education 59
    change in pace of critical writings
        86–7
    Chinese poetry 88, 91
    and contemporary movements 66–7
    on craftsmanship and experts 66
    criticism
        by discussion 88
        by exercise in style of given period
            89
        by translation 88–9
        in new composition 90–2
        via music 89
    engineering as epitome of efficiency
        63–5
    on 'exactness'/'fineness' 65–6, 69
    on the ideogram 58, 77–8
    Imagism 58, 62, 70–5, 82, 85
    on 'investment' in art 84–5
    Italian fascism 87
    Leavis and 391–2
    lectures 67–70
    on life and art 63
    major figures in his tradition 91

    as poet-critic 449
    politics 57
    style of writing 58–9
    and technique 454–5, 456
    two phases of criticism 58
    on *vers libre* 85
    Vorticism 58, 78–9
    Winters on 262
    see also Cavalcanti; Cravens;
        Daniel; Fenollosa; Marinetti;
        Quinn
    Works
        (1917–26) 87
        ABC of Reading (1934) 77, 92,
            455
        Cantos 77–8
        Canzoni (1910) 60
        Cathay 28
        'Chinese Written Character as a
            Medium for Poetry' 85
        Des Imagistes (1914) 79
        'Early Translations of Homer' 85
        'Elizabethan Classicists' 85
        Exultations (1909) 60
        Guide to Kulchur (1938) 77–8, 92
        'How I Began' (1913) 78
        How to Read (1929–31) 92
        Hugh Selwyn Mauberley 85, 89,
            391, 451–2
        'I Gather the Limbs of Osiris'
            (1911–12) 58, 62, 63, 64, 66
        'In a Station of the Metro' 78
        'On Criticism in General' (1923)
            92
        output (1917–26) 85–6
        Personae (1909) 60
        'Prolegomena' 63, 66, 67
        'Provincialism the Enemy' (1917)
            85
        Ripostes 70–1, 72–3
        Spirit of Romance, The (1910) 58
        'Status Rerum' 73, 74
        'Status Rerum – The Second'
            (1917) 85
        'Studies in Contemporary
            Mentality' 85

Pound, Ezra (*cont.*)
    translations 62, 85, 86, 88–9
Pound, Omar 59*n*
Pritchett, V. S. 371
professionalisation of literary criticism
    377–88
Prothero, G. W. 81
Proust, Marcel 25, 134
Purser, Jack 300
Pynchon, Thomas 198

Quarterly Review 81
Quiller-Couch, Arthur 183, 289, 292
Quinn, John 82–4, 87

racism, white 168, 175
Raftery (blind Gaelic poet) 162
Rahv, Philip 35, 337–8, 363–8, 432,
        433
    on the novel 365–6
    Orwell and 369
Raleigh, Walter 273, 288–9
Ransom, John Crowe 181, 200–2,
        204–6, 209, 256
    and practical criticism 309–10, 323
    Winters and 264
Read, Herbert 40, 47, 188
realism 201
Reed, John 327
Reid, B. L. 83*n*
relativism, Eliot on 24
Revue de l'Action Française 45
Revue universelle 47
Reynolds, Horace 153
Richards, I. A. 40, 181–99
    affectiveness 196
    background 182–3
    in China 186–7
    close reading 190, 219
    compared with Coleridge, Ricoeur
        and Pynchon 198–9
    and Eliot 192, 194
    ethics of equilibrium 194–5
    first lectures on practical criticism
        296
    influence on English studies 296,

        298, 307–9
    and Leavis 416–17
    on metaphor 189, 196–7, 199
    multiple definition 183, 188, 190
    Orientalism 195
    and Plato 189, 198
    'pseudo-statement' 142
    rhetoric, grammar and logic 188–9
    suspension of disbelief 185
    synaesthesis 183, 192–3
    ten reading malfunctions in
        response to poetry 185–6
    theory of translation 187
    'triad' or meaning situation 183–4
    use of the media 190–1
    on value 192–3
    see also Crane, R. S.; English
        studies
    Works
        Basic Rules of Reason 187
        Beyond 190
        Coleridge on Imagination 187–8,
            196
        Complementarities 191
        Design for Escape 191, 195
        Foundations of Aesthetics (1922)
            183
        How to Read a Page (1942) 181,
            190, 193, 198
        Interpretation in Teaching (1938)
            181, 189, 195, 196
        Meaning of Meaning (1923) 183,
            189
        Mencius on the Mind 186–7, 188,
            193, 195
        Philosophy of Rhetoric (1936)
            181, 184, 189
        Poetries 191
        Poetries and Sciences 182, 184–5,
            197
        Practical Criticism 125, 181, 182,
            185, 189, 193, 296
        Principles of Literary Criticism
            184, 307–8
        Science and Poetry 54, 184, 188
        So Much Nearer 191, 195

Speculative Instruments 187, 191, 197
'Toward a Theory of Comprehending' 191–2
Wrath of Achilles, The 190
Ricks, Christopher 35*n*
Ricoeur, Paul 198
Riding, Laura 97, 120, 220
Rilke, Rainer Maria 448–9, 451, 454
Roberts, Elizabeth Madox 262
Robertson, J. M. 27
Robinson, Edwin Arlington 260, 262
Robinson, Ian 403
romanticism 17, 44–5, 48, 49, 291
Rourke, Constance 347, 348–9
Rousseau, Jean-Jacques 44
Royce, Josiah 21
Rueckert, William 254
Ruland, Richard 291
Russell, Bertrand 21, 96, 183, 395
Russo, John Paul 183*n*
Ruthven, K. K. 57*n*, 86

Said, Edward 152, 195
Saintsbury, George 269, 273, 274, 287, 288, 292
Sandburg, Carl 262, 346
Santayana, George 327–8
Saussure, Ferdinand de 229, 239
Schiller, Jerome P. 194*n*
School of Images *see* Imagism
Schorer, Mark 337–8, 486
Schuyler, George 167, 176
science and poetry 188
Scopes trial (1925) 202
Scrutiny 391, 392, 394–5, 416–20
sensationalism 28, 40, 46
sentimentalism 48, 185
Severini, Gino 75
Shakespear, Olivia 59, 61
Shakespeare, Judith 127
Shakespeare, William
    Blackmur on 241
    Eliot on 27–8, 30, 41–2
    Empson on 221–2, 224–5, 230
    omitted from Pound's tradition 91

Orwell on 371
Virginia Woolf on 137
Shama'a Indian journal 30
Shaw, George Bernard 63, 154, 325, 330–1
Shelley, Percy Bysshe 33
Sherman, Stuart 287, 288, 290
Sidgwick, Henry 182
sincerity in response to poetry 186
Skeat, W. W. 274, 284
Smith, Bernard 347
Snow, C. P. 395–6
society and the critic (1900–1950) 322–76, 386–8
Socrates 441, 457
Sorel, Georges 47, 48
Southern New Critics 200–18, 455–6
    Agrarian movement 203–4
    and capitalism 203–4
    focus on textuality 212–13
    heresy of paraphrase 206
    literature and social criticism 204–8
    meaning and form 204–8
    New Criticism
        and the academy 208–14
        and critique of pure aesthetics 214–18
    social origin 200–4
    teaching of English in America 209–13
    see also Bourdieu; Mencken; Ransom; Tate; Warren
Southern Review 213, 260, 355
Spanos, William V. 195*n*
specialisation in literary criticism 382–5
Spencer, Theodore 314
Spender, Stephen 26
Spiller, Robert E. 314
Spingarn, J. E. 292, 324, 326
Spoo, Robert 59*n*
Spurgeon 314
Squire, J. C. 19
Stanford, Donald E. 260, 262

Stein, Gertrude 93–121
  'beginning again and again' 102,
    141–2
  composition of World War I 147
  distinctive formal qualities of her
    criticism 94–5
  'feeling in print' 95–7
  four modes of composition 97–8
  history and romance 116–17
  Lewis and 141–2, 144
  the literary idea 94, 97–8
  method and aims 100
  spoken and written language
    117–21
  temporality and writing 120–1
  'the continuous present' 102–3
  and Virginia Woolf 128, 128–9, 130
  William James's influence 94–6
  Works
    'An American and France' 116–18
    As Fine as Melanctha 93, 95
    Autobiography of Alice B. Toklas,
      The 93*n*, 98, 101*n*, 104, 107
    'Composition as Explanation'
      (1926) 95, 96, 97, 100–4, 120
    Everybody's Autobiography
      (1936) 98
    Four in America (1932–3) 98
    Four Saints in Three Acts (1934)
      105
    Geographical History of America
      (1935) 98, 116, 119
    Geography and Plays 99, 101,
      102, 119
    Lectures in America (1935) 93,
      98, 104–10
    Making of Americans, The 101,
      116
    Narration 98, 110–15
    Tender Buttons (1912) 102
    'What are Master-pieces' 116,
      118–19
    'What is English Literature' 128,
      130
Steinbeck, John 360
Stendhal (Henri Beyle) 241

Stephen, Leslie 128
Stevens, Wallace 264, 460, 461
stock response to poetry 185
Stoll, E. E. 27, 293
Stoll, Oswald 80
Strachey, Lytton 26
stream of consciousness 44
Stuart, Francis 154–5
Stubbs, William 380
Sturt, George 406
suspension of disbelief 185
Swift and Company (Publishers) 72
Swift, Jonathan 371–2
Symbolism 46
Symons, Arthur 30, 46
synaesthesis 183, 192–3
Synge, J. M. 151, 160, 161, 262

Tagore, Rabindranath 62
Taine, Hippolyte 335, 343, 346
Tate, Allen 200–2, 203, 204–5, 209,
  211, 261, 485–6
Tennyson, Alfred, Lord 38, 40, 409
textuality, focus on 212
Thackeray, W. M. 481
Thibaudet, Albert 48
Thomism 49
Thoreau, H. D. 350
Tillotson, Geoffrey 289
Tillyard, J. M. W. 279, 296, 311
time, modern attitude to *see* Bergson
Time and Tide 19, 25
Times, the 80
Times Literary Supplement 19, 318
Tolstoy, Leo 371, 480
Toomer, Jean 171
Tourneur, Cyril 38
tradition, Eliot and 20, 31–2, 34–5
Transatlantic Review 101
Transition 261
Trilling, Lionel 336–7, 362–3, 365,
  368, **423–38**
  on American realism 358–9
  as cultural critic **352–9**
  on Eliot 428–9
  on Forster 432

on Hawthorne 435
on Hemingway 428
on Henry James and the American
    novel 434–5, 493
on Keats 436
Liberal Imagination, The (1950)
    353–5
and liberal-radical culture 425–6
on the novel 356–7, 493–4
on Orwell 369
and politics 435–6, 438
and popular culture 430, 436–8
uniqueness of 424–5
on Wordsworth 436
Works
    Beyond Culture 429–30, 431,
        432, 435, 436
    E. M. Forster 431–2
    Gathering of Fugitives, A 435
    Liberal Imagination, The 426,
        429, 432–5
    Matthew Arnold 430, 431
    Opposing Self, The 435, 436, 437
    Speaking of Literature and
        Society 428, 428–9, 429
truth of literature 384
Tsvetayeva, Marina 460
Tuckerman, Frederick Goddard 261
Tyler, M. C. 274
Tyro magazine 19, 26

United Ireland 155
United World Federalists 181

Valéry, Paul 260–1, 461–4
Van Doren, Carl 170, 287
Van Vechten, Carl 167
Vanity Fair 333
verbal analysis see close reading
Verlaine, Paul 445–6
vers libre 85
Vickery, John 495
Virgil 51
visual discrimination 144–5
Vivas, Eliseo 194
Vorticism 29, 147–8

Warner, Michael 273n
Warren, Austin 309, 323
Warren, Robert Penn 200, 202,
    204–6, 209, 297–8
    An Approach to Literature 300
    Understanding Fiction 485
    Understanding Poetry 213, 298,
        300, 301, 485
Warshow, Robert 371
Washington, Booker T. 167
Watson, J. B. 183, 187
Watt, Ian, Rise of the Novel 492
Waugh, Arthur, Tradition and Change
    33
Weber, Eugen 45n, 54n
Weber, Max 328
Wellek, René 309, 313, 323, 393–4
Wells, H. G. 470–1
West, Alick 490
Wharton, Edith 102
Whitman, Walt 330, 348–9, 364
Wiener, Norbert 24
Wilcox, Ella Wheeler 195
Wilde, Oscar 28, 32, 62–3, 148, 440
Willey, Basil 314
Williams, Raymond 306, 321, 406–7,
    492
Williams, William Carlos 97, 99, 264,
    456
    Spring and All 452–3
Wilson, Edmund 294, 329, 333–40,
    342–6, 360, 367
    Works
    American Jitters, The 342
    Axel's Castle 334, 335, 338
    Bit Between my Teeth, The
        (1965) 335
    I Thought of Daisy (1929) 336
    Memoirs of Hecate County 336
    Patriotic Gore (1962) 345–6
    Piece of My Mind, A (1956) 345
    To the Finland Station 342–3
    Triple Thinkers, The 344
    Upstate (1971) 345
    Wound and the Bow, The 344
Wimsatt, W. K. 212, 313, 466

Winters, Yvor **260–5**, 294
  on Eliot 262
  on metre 264–5
  on romanticism 263, 265
  Works
    Anatomy of Nonsense, The 264
    'Audible Reading of Poetry', 'The'
      265
    'Brink of Darkness', 'The' 263
    Forms of Discovery 265
    Function of Criticism, The 265
    Maule's Curse 261, 265
    Quest for Reality 265
Wittgenstein, Ludwig 143, 182, 221,
    241, 398, 405
women
  Eliot on 50–1
  Pound on 67
Wood, Clement 170
Wood, James 183
Woodberry, George 289
Woolf, Leonard 127
Woolf, Virginia 26, 29, 67, 122–37
  and 'Anon.' 128
  on bad writing 130
  on character 132–3
  and Coleridge 122, 137
  on the common reader 122–3, 127
  critical legacy 126
  criticism of fiction 474–6
  desire of the mind for change 125
  'Essay in Criticism', 'An' 476
  and Gertrude Stein 128–9, 130
  on integrity of the novel 129–30
  on Jane Austen 134
  as literary outsider 127–8
  literary revivalism 127–8
  on Montaigne 134
  reading at a window 128–9
  sex-consciousness in literature
    135–7
  on Shakespeare 137
  on Sir Thomas Browne 134
  on women writers 126–7, 135–6
  Works
    Common Reader 124, 131, 133–4

    'How it Strikes a
      Contemporary' 124, 126, 135n
    'How Should One Read a
      Book?' 125, 132
    'Lives of the Obscure' 124
    'Pastons and Chaucer' 124, 133
    'Leaning Tower', 'The' 135n
    'Modern Fiction' (1919) 29,
      135n, 475
    'Mr Bennett and Mrs Brown'
      (1924) 29, 135n, 475
    Mrs Dalloway 134
    'Narrow Bridge of Art', 'The'
      135n
    'On Not Knowing Greek' 131
    Orlando 135
    'Phases of Fiction' 125
    Reading 123
    Reading at Random 124
    Reviewing (1939) 127
    Room of One's Own, A 123,
      128, 131–2, 476
    Three Guineas 135n
    Women Novelists 135–6
Wordsworth, William 31, 33, 38, 239,
    241, 436, 440–1
World War I 146–8
Worringer, Wilhelm 29

Yeats, W. B. 38, 59, 79, 82, 151–66,
    241
  and Annie Horniman 161, 162,
    166
  arts in Dublin (early twentieth
    century) 158–63
  books for the Irish people 156–7,
    163
  classroom as cultural site (1920s)
    163–4
  dissemination of culture 155–8
  dramatic criticism 162–3
  Great McCoy persona (1920s and
    1930s) 164–6
  Irish arts business (1890s) 154–8
  Irish Intelligentsia 154–5, 157, 161
  Leavis and 410–11

literary criticism and national
   identity 151–4, 158–9, 449
patronage of culture 159–61, 164
and *Playboy of the Western World*
   riots 161
on the poet-critic 464–5
politics and 153–4
Winters on 262
Works
   Arrow, The 160
   Beltaine 160
   'Child and the State', 'The' 164
   Essays and Introductions 151
   Explorations 151, 160–1
   'Fisherman', 'The' (1913) 162–3

'List of the Best Irish Books'
   (1895) 157
'Literature and the Living Voice'
   162
non-fiction prose 152–3
Samhain 160, 161
Senate Speeches 164
Uncollected Prose 151, 153
Young Ireland League 156
Yellow Book, The 148
Young, Karl 299
Young Ireland League 156

Zabel, M. D. 302
Zukofsky, Louis 97